Indian
Philosophy and Religion

Indian Philosophy and Religion

A Reader's Guide

Bibhu Padhi
Minakshi Padhi

D.K.Printworld (P) Ltd.
New Delhi

Cataloging in Publication Data — DK
[Courtesy: D.K. Agencies (P) Ltd. <docinfo@dkagencies.com>]

Padhi, Bibhu, 1951–

Indian philosophy and religion: a reader's guide.
Includes bibliographical references (p.)
Includes Index.
ISBN 812460116X

1. India — Religion. 2. Philosophy, Indic.
I. Padhi, Minakshi, 1953– II. Title.

ISBN 81-246-0116-X
First Published in USA in 1990
Indian Edition, 1998
Second impression in 2005

Published and printed by:
D.K. Printworld (P) Ltd.
Regd. office : *'Sri Kunj'*, F-52, Bali Nagar
New Delhi - 110 015
Phones : (011) 2545-3975; 2546-6019; *Fax* : (011) 2546-5926
E-mail: dkprintworld@vsnl.net
Web: www.dkprintworld.com

To
our sons
Buddhāditya and Silāditya
with profoundest love

The Authors acknowledge to the following publishers for material quoted within:

Surendranath Dasgupta, *History of Indian Philosophy* (5 volumes), reprinted by permission of the Cambridge University Press.

S. Radhakrishnan and S.A. Moore, *A Source Book in Indian Philosophy*, copyright ©1988 by Princeton Unitersity Press, reprinted with permission of Princeton University Press.

Chandradhar Sharma, *A Critical Survey of Indian Philosophy*, copyright ©1976 by Motilal Banarsidass, reprinted with permission of Motilal Banarsidass.

S. Radhakrishnan, *Indian Philosophy* (2 volumes), copyright ©1966 by George Allen & Unwin.

Contents

Preface

This is not a textbook on Indian philosophy and religion inasmuch as it is intended to raise as many questions as it seeks to answer. A typical textbook, on the other hand, almost always remains satisfied with the noncontroversial and the minimal. It is not a highly specialized treatise on its subject, for we never meant it to be one. We feel that that need has been more than amply fulfilled by S. Radhakrishnan's two-volume *Indian Philosophy* and Surendra Nath Dasgupta's monumental five-volume *History of Indian Philosophy* (besides of course the ongoing multivolume project on Indian philosophy under the editorship of Karl H. Potter, called *Encyclopedia of Indian Philosophies*). The present book, as its subtitle indicates, is a comprehensive reference guide to its subject for the uninitiated, but inquisitive, reader of Indian philosophy and religion.

Most of the critical studies of Indian philosophy have been written with some bias or other. If the Indian interpreters have been overly idealistic (even eulogistic), their Western counterparts, barring a very few, have been overly critical (at times even damaging). We have tried to be objective and clear without neglecting to show the limitations and weaknesses that are, or so we feel, peculiar to matters Indian. We feel that the book could be profitably used by advance undergraduates and graduate students, as well as by the general reader interested in the subject. It is particularly intended for those institutions who are introducing an Indian content into a required core curriculum and do not possess a faculty trained in Indian thought and culture. We sincerely believe that the chapters on religion (Buddhism, Jainism, and Hindu gods and goddesses) will prove especially useful to students taking courses in comparative religion or working toward a degree in religious studies.

We are of course aware of our great debt to the excellent writings of Theos Bernard, Surendra Nath Dasgupta, Erich Frauwallner, Mysore Hiriyanna, Karl H. Potter, S. Radhakrishnan, and Chandradhar Sharma. We must also confess that on certain occasions we have tended to depend on particular books—as, for instance, on Alfonso Verdu's well-researched *Early Buddhist Philosophy* for our chapter on Buddhism, and on Haridas Bhattacharyya's excellent but now out-of-print *Foundations of Living Faiths* for our chapter on the Hindu gods and goddesses. We have three reasons for this: first, because of the consistently high quality of these books; second, because of their inaccessibility, especially for the non-Indian reader; and third, because they spontaneously catered to our very human temptation to exploit things we loved and admired.

We take this opportunity to thank our friend Paki, and our children (and dedicatees of this book) Buddhāditya and Silāditya, without whose emotional support this book could never have been written.

Bibhu Padhi & Minakshi Padhi
Ravenshaw College

1

Introduction
The Vedas, the Upanishads, the Bhagavad-Gitā

The earliest Indian speculation concerned itself with the innermost unity and the ultimate cause of the world, and it originated in close association with religion and has unfolded itself out of its connection with the Absolute. In a sense, every philosophy owes its origin to religion, but Indian philosophy shows a characteristic difference. Leo Gabriel, in his Introduction to Erich Frauwallner's celebrated *History of Indian Philosophy,* attempts to distinguish the nature of Indian speculation from that of the ancient Greeks:

> The Greek Philosophy is related to religion dialectically and develops itself out of contrast to it, in the form of that other religion of thought, purified through reason, formed in the form of the concept which has brought forth the philosophical God-idea, independent of religion in the idea of the good (Plato) and of the unmoved mover (Aristotle). Such is not the case with Indian thought. The Indian speculation has never departed from the soil or field of religion; it rather nourishes itself continually and directly out of the forces of this soil (of religion) from which it never uprooted itself. The speculation has, however, from its side reformed and developed the structure of religion from the inside. And thus the process was introduced which led from polytheism, the doctrine of many godheads and henotheism, through the favouring of one god, to Pantheism so characteristic of Indians—the unity of God and the world [Frauwallner, xiii].

Thus, any study of Indian philosophy is necessarily related to the Indian religion, which is basically that of the Hindus as distinct from that of several other communities which have had their place in India. The orthodox, or (as it is sometimes referred to) "classical," Indian philosophy is the philosophy of the Hindus. It is not surprising, therefore, that Indian philosophy as we know it has not developed much after A.D. 1000, when "the fortunes of the Hindus became more and more linked with those of the non-Hindus" (Radhakrishnan, *Indian Philosophy,* 56).

The history of Indian philosophy can be broadly divided into four periods: (1) the Vedic Period (1500 B.C. to 600 B.C.); (2) the Epic Period (600 B.C. to A.D. 200); (3) the *Sutra* Period (A.D. 200 to A.D. 1700); and (4) the Scholastic Period (which more or less coincides with the *Sutra* period). The Vedic Period covers the entire phase of the Aryan culture and civilization and shows the beginnings of "the sublime idealism of India" (Radhakrishnan, *Indian Philosophy,* 57). It was the period of the four Vedas and the Upanishads. However, as Radhakrishnan and Moore point out, this period "can hardly be called a philosophical age." "It is to be thought of as an age of groping, in which religion, philosophy, superstition, and thought were inextricably interrelated and yet in perpetual conflict" (Radhakrishnan and Moore, xvi). They concede, however, that it was an age of philosophical development, whose "culminating doctrines, those expounded in the major Upanishads, have determined the tone if not the precise pattern of the Indian philosophical development ever since." In the oldest philosophical texts of the Vedas, we find the simplest of philosophical notions—questions relating to the bearer of life, fate after death, and the processes in sleep—which, in the Upanishads, were to be explored in a much bolder fashion. The literature of the Vedic period consists of the four Vedas, namely, *Rig-Veda, Yajur-Veda, Sāma-Veda,* and *Atharva-Veda*. Each of these is divided into four parts—the *Mantras,* the *Brāhmanas,* the *Āranyakas,* and the *Upanishads* (some scholars have reduced this division into three—the *Mantras* or *Samhitās,* the *Brāhmanas,* and the *Upanishads*).

The second period of Indian philosophy—the Epic Period—refers to the period of development between the early Upanishads and the systems of philosophy or *darsanas.* It is "characterized by the indirect presentation of philosophical doctrines through the medium of nonsystematic and nontechnical literature," particularly the two great epics of the *Ramāyana* and the *Mahābhārata,* besides the several treatises on ethical and social philosophy, called the *Dharma-sāstras.* The *Ramāyana,* the *Mahābhārata,* and the *Dharma-sāstras* are classed as *smrtis* or "traditional texts," as against the Vedas and the Upanishads, which are classed as *sruti* or "revealed scriptures or authoritative texts." In addition to the composition of these texts, the Epic period includes the rise and early development of Saivism and Vaishnavism as well as the two heterodox religious philosophies of Jainism and Buddhism. The *Bhagavad-Gitā,* which forms a part of the *Mahābhārata* and is considered to be one of the three most authoritative texts in Indian philosophical literature, also belongs to this period. It is also during this period that most of the Indian philosophical systems—both orthodox and unorthodox—had their beginnings, although the first systematic texts of these systems were written at a later period.

The third period of Indian philosophy—the *Sutra* period—refers to a phase of systematization of a mass of material which "grew so unwieldly that it was found necessary to devise a shorthand scheme of philosophy." This reduction and summarizing took the form of *Sutras*—a kind of highly aphoristic verse-form, embodying the basic principles of a system for the purpose of preservation and transmission. These brief, sometimes enigmatic, sets of aphorisms have been viewed by some as "reminders for the initiated to enable them to recall the details of philosophical systems to which they belonged and whose fuller doctrines were known only to those within the fold of the system." These *Sutras* do not merely represent the basic tenets of the relevant systems, but an obviously polemical defense of these systems against opposing ones; and whereas the literature of the Epic Period exemplified philosophical speculation at a precritical level and with some amount of imaginative spontaneity, the *Sutras* epitomize "self-conscious thought and reflection" (Radhakrishnan and Moore, xvii, xviii). These *Sutras,* highly cryptic as they are, are difficult to understand without commentaries *(bhāsyas);* these commentaries, which have become "more important than the *Sutras* themselves" represent the development of "the critical attitude" in Indian philosophy. Radhakrishnan writes:

> In the preceding periods we have philosophical discussions, no doubt, where the mind did not passively receive whatever it was told, but played round the subject, raising objections and answering them. By happy intuition the thinkers pitch upon some general principles which seem to them to explain all aspects of the universe. The philosophical syntheses, however profound and acute they may be, suffered throughout from the defect of being pre-critical, in the Kantian sense of the term.... [These] efforts to understand and interpret the world were not strictly philosophical attempts, since they were not troubled by any scruples about the competence of the human mind or the efficiency of the instruments and the criteria employed.... So when we come to the *Sutras* we have thought and reflection become self-conscious, and not merely constructive imagination and religious freedom. Among the systems themselves, we cannot say definitely which are earlier and which later. There are cross-references throughout [Radhakrishnan, *Indian Philosophy,* 58].

The six Hindu orthodox systems based on the *Sutras* are *Vaiseshika* or "realistic pluralism"; Nyaya or "logical realism"; *Sāmkhya* or "evolutionary dualism"; *Yoga* or "disciplined meditation"; *Purva Mimāmsa* or "earlier interpretative investigations of the Vedas," relating mainly to conduct; and *Uttara Mimāmsa* or *Vedānta,* or "later investigations of the Vedas, relating to knowledge."

The fourth period of Indian philosophy—the Scholastic Period—includes the now-famous "commentaries" *(bhāsyas)* on the *Sutras,* which were almost always difficult to the point of being unintelligible. It is nearly impossible to provide a chronological place to this period, for the original commentaries were followed by commentaries upon themselves, which again were commented upon, until we reach our own time. Radhakrishnan and Moore, however, would place it between the *Sutra* Period and the 17th century. It is with this period that such famous names like Kumarila, Samkara, Sridhara, Rāmānuja, Madhva, Vāchaspati, Udayana, Bhāskara, Vijñānabhikshu and Raghunatha are associated. As Radhakrishnan and Moore point out, the literature of this period is basically "exploratory, but is also strongly and sometimes grossly polemical." Although these commentaries were meant to explore and explain the original *Sutras,* many of these consisted of "quibbling and unphilosophical debates" and are therefore "relatively worthless":

> There is a brood of "Schoolmen," noisy controversialists, indulging in oversubtle theories and finespun arguments . . . Sometimes the commentaries are more confusing than enlightening. Instead of clear explanation and thought, one often finds mere words; instead of philosophy, logic-chopping. Obscurity of thought, subtlety of logic, and intolerance of opposition are marks of the worst types of commentators. The better types, however, are invaluable and are respected almost as much as the creators of the systems themselves [Radhakrishnan and Moore, xviii].

Samkara, for instance, who wrote a commentary on Bādarāyana's *Vedānta/ Brahma-Sutra* called *Samkara Bhāsya,* restates original *Sutras* and his "restatement is just as valuable as a spiritual discovery" (Radhakrishnan, *Indian Philosophy,* 59); not surprisingly, therefore, Samkara is often regarded more highly as a philosopher than Bādarāyana. The same can be said of Rāmānuja and Madhva who, together with Samkara, were responsible for the creation of different "schools" of Vedānta, although all the three took their cue from Bādarāyana's text. Their commentaries are not merely explanations but "new expositions," so that Radhakrishnan and Moore would argue: "This type of development is indicative of the unique way in which Indian philosophers have maintained their traditional respect for the past and their recognition of the value of authority in philosophy, but, without seeming to break this tradition, have also carried along the free development of thought as their insight and reason directed" (Radhakrishnan and Moore, xix).

Although Indian philosophical thought has had a varied and complex history and is in itself extremely complex, it has survived over a long stretch of time. There *are* features that are archaic, but there are also those which are "the products of an impressively penetrating insight," such as the Sanskrit phonology, nonsequential logic, the theory of constant change and perpetual motion, and the concept of cyclical time (Lannoy, 271). Richard Lannoy, in his fine study of Indian culture and society, *The Speaking Tree,* identifies three elements of continuity in the long history of Indian thought, which (as we have already indicated) originated in "remote antiquity, when the society was still organized on a relatively primitive basis" and was thus a product of "non-literate unified sensibility." The most significant characteristic of primitive society is "its sense of the unity of all life, the sense of solidarity and emotional sympathy with the various levels of nature"—something which enabled the primitive man to conceive the idea of "*co-operation* with nature and its sacred powers by means of propitiatory sacrifice." The Vedic Aryans, although barbarian so far as their "frontier" attitudes were concerned (see Kosambi, 76–88), were sensitive and intelligent enough to organize such a society and evolve a relevant sacrificial religion. At this stage, the Vedic Aryan culture, totally oral, was one in which sacrificial lore, myth and language were inseparably linked, one with the others; so that the Vedic Aryan believed that "a deity could be compelled by utterance of the correct verbal formula to do exactly what the worshipper desired": "Here we have our first example of a primitive trait—the magical power of the word—which has at no stage in the cultural evolution of India been wholly abandoned. . . . From this belief in the magical efficacy of a formula is derived an extremely widespread and persistent Indian conviction in the mechanical *efficiency* of spirituality, rites, or mystical exercises" (Lannoy, 271.) For Lannoy, it is this belief in the absolute authority of "the Word as a universal metaphysical principle" which is the most basic characteristic in the continuity and survival value of Indian thought.

The second element of continuity, according to Lannoy, is to be found in the concept of the flux of all things—a concept which India shares with the sixth century Greek philosopher Heraclitus. In order to explain this, Lannoy quotes from Jane Harrison's *Prolegomena to the Study of Greek Religion,* substituting his own word "Hindu" for Harrison's "Olympian":

> [O]ur minds are imbued with classical Hindu mythology, our imagination peopled with the vivid personalities, the clear-cut outlines of Hindu gods; it is only be a severe mental effort that v e realise that *there were no gods at all,* but only conceptions of the human mind, shifting and changing colour with every human mind that conceived them. Art which makes the image, literature which crystallises attributes and functions, arrest and fix this shifting kaleidoscope; but until the coming of art and literature and to some extent after, the formulatory of theology is "all things are in flux" [Harrison, quoted in Lannoy, 272].

The all-important difference between the evolution of Hindu and Greek religions is in the *continuous* presence of the idea of flux in Hindu mythology: "The goal of knowledge is to pierce the veil of appearances and perceive the flux of *continuous creation* and dissolution wherein the plurality of gods, all variety of name and form participate. . . . The magic power of the Word and the idea of flux . . . conform to the archaic pattern of retrospective faith in the potency of things as they were 'in the beginning'" (Lannoy, 272).

The third basic element that Lannoy identifies is "the primitive tendency to draw no clear distinction between matter, life, and mind." This hylozoistic-monistic conception is a common feature of thought at the tribal stage of social development and is to be found in several major philosophical systems, but nowhere more so than in the Sāmkhya theories of the three *gunas—sattva, rajas,* and *tamas*—of which both mind and matter are composed and of *prakrti* and *purusha.* Both pre-Socratic thought and Indian thought started from the premise "that without an identity between the knowing subject and the reality known, the fact of knowledge would be unaccountable"—that subject and object, thesis and antithesis only constitute two aspects of the same thing. Lannoy offers a note of warning, though, for those who are ready to ascribe hylozoistic thought to some form of prelogical irrationalism:

> Under primitive, pre-technological conditions man is in an especially favourable position in relation to nature; as a microcosmic organism he sees himself as an exact counterpart of the macrocosm—Nature.

> For this reason he obtains knowledge of the latter in a direct way: by immediate sensory awareness.... A logic of symbols such as India's proceeds not only on assumptions but on modes of perception which happen to have been suppressed in Western thinking for many centuries through specialization in a certain kind of consciousness. There is nothing "mystical" or "uncanny" in this kind of thought if one uses the word "mystical" in the sense which Santayana gives it: the most *natural* mode of thinking [Lannoy, 273].

Although both ancient Greek and Indian philosophers saw the identity of being and thought in a strictly material sense, the Indian philosophers proceeded to "appropriate the external world to the mind-brain." The ancient Hindu "enhanced, expanded, intensified, and deepened his sensory awareness of colours, sounds, and textures until they were transformed into vibrations continuous with his own consciousness." In this enhanced state of consciousness—produced by meditation and concentration—the apparently separate entities of the subject and the object, the self and the world, fused in a single process. In this connection Lannoy refers to the philosopher-mystic Alan Watts' analysis of descriptions of perpetual modification and alteration of the nervous system by *yoga* and his conclusion that the closest analogy to hylozoistic thought is the scientist's description of ecological relationship, according to which the behavior of the environment and the behavior of the organism are seen as a single unified field.

Lannoy's three basic concepts—the magic power of the Word, the flux of all things, and the total identity between the knowing subject and the reality known—urge us towards a definition of what might be called the spirit of Indian philosophy. It is difficult to separate Indian philosophy from Indian religion, but while the principal aim of the former is to *understand* the nature of reality , the chief aim of the latter is to induce *devotion* in one's heart for the Supreme. The final objective of both is the same, however, which is to make one realize his only end—that is, a release from the samsāric cycle of birth and death. As T.M.P. Mahadevan writes: "The purpose of religion is not only to refine man's emotions, but also to sublimate them and transform his entire life. Similarly, the task of philosophy is to bring light to the understanding and thereby help man realize his true nature" (Mahadevan, 165).

It is not therefore surprising that, in India, philosophy has been essentially a quest for values in terms of speculations about the nature of existence and theories of spiritual liberation *(moksha)*. Thus, the most significant feature of Indian philosophy is its concentration upon the spiritual. Except for the materialistic school of the Chārvāka, no other Indian school regards man and the universe as essentially physical or looks upon material welfare as the prime goal of human life. Radhakrishnan and Moore have tried to explain the close link between Indian philosophy and religion:

> Philosophy and religion are intimately related because philosophy itself is regarded as a spiritual adventure, and also because the motivation both in philosophy and in religion concerns the spiritual way of life

> in the here-and-now and the eventual spiritual salvation of man in relation to the universe. Practically all of Indian philosophy .. has striven to bring about a socio-spiritual reform in the country, and philosophical literature has taken many forms, mythological, popular, or technical, as the circumstances required, in order to promote such spiritual life. The problems of religion have always given depth and power and purpose to the Indian philosophical mind and spirit [Radhakrishnan and Moore, xxi].

Closely related to this is the Indian belief in the "intimate relationship of philosophy and life," in the necessity of the practical application of philosophy to life:

> While natural abundance and material prosperity paved the way for the rise of philosophical speculation, philosophy has never been considered as a mere intellectual exercise. Every Indian system seeks the truth, not as academic "knowledge for its own sake," but to learn the truth which shall make men free. This is not, as it has been called, the modern pragmatic attitude. . . . It is not the view that truth is measured in terms of the practical, but rather . . . that truth alone has efficacy as a guide for man in his search for salvation. . . . It is not enough to *know* the truth; the truth must be *lived.* The goal of the Indian is not to know the ultimate truth but to *realize* it, to become one with it [Radhakrishnan and Moore, xxi–xxii].

The intimate relationship of theory and practice in Indian philosophy is also reflected in the "universally prevalent demand for moral purification as an imperative preliminary" for the student of philosophy as well as for the common man in search of truth.

The moral character of Indian philosophy is inseparably related to the Indian's "introspective attitude and the introspective approach to reality." Philosophy, for the ancient Indian, was "the knowledge of the self" or *ātmavidyā;* and although a study of philosophy could start with the external world, more often than not it started with "the internal world of man's inner nature, the self of man." "This introspective interest," write Radhakrishnan and Moore, "is highly conducive to idealism, of course, and consequently most Indian philosophy is idealistic in one form or another." The general tendency has been in the direction of monistic idealism—that reality is "*ultimately* one and *ultimately* spiritual." Radhakrishnan and Moore attribute this "rather unusual attitude" to the "nonrigidity of the Indian mind and to the fact that the attitude of monistic idealism is so plastic and dynamic that it takes many forms and expresses itself even in seemingly conflicting doctrines" which are in fact "merely different expressions of an underlying conviction which provides basic unity to Indian philosophy as a whole." True, at one time materialism did enjoy widespread acceptance, but its influence has not been quite as great as that of idealism. However, Indian philosophy has not totally ignored materialism; rather, "it has known it, has overcome it, and has accepted idealism as the only tenable view, whatever specific form that idealism might take" (Radhakrishnan and Moore, xxiii).

Further, though Indian philosophy does not neglect reason and, in fact, makes extensive use of it, it considers reason alone as insufficient for the *realization* of truth; and hence, accepts direct intuitive apprehension of the object as the only means of realizing the ultimate, a fact which is well described by the word *darsana,* which is derived from the verbal root *drs,* meaning "to see." "To see" is to realize an object or situation "in the sense of becoming one with it" (an experience which is so powerfully evoked by Wordsworth in his "Tintern Abbey"—"And I have felt/ A presence that disturbs me with the joy/ Of elevated thoughts..." and the earlier lines: "While with an eye made quiet by the power/ Of harmony, and the deep power of joy/ We *see into the life of things.*"); it is, ultimately, a mystical experience. Radhakrishnan and Moore write:

> No complete knowledge is possible as long as there is the relationship of the subject on the one hand and the object on the other. Later developments in Indian philosophy, from the time of the beginning of the systems, have all depended in large part upon reason for the systematic formulation of doctrines and systems, for rational demonstration or justification, and in polemical conflicts of system against system. Nevertheless, all the systems, except the Charvaka, agree that there is a higher way of knowing reality, beyond the reach of reason, namely, the direct perception or experience of the ultimate reality, which cannot be known by reason in any of its forms. Reason can demonstrate the truth, but reason cannot discover or reach the truth. While reason may be the method of philosophy in its more intellectual sense, intuition is the only method of comprehending the ultimate. Indian philosophy is thus characterized by an ultimate dependence upon intuition, along with the recognition of the efficacy of reason and intellect when applied in their limited capacity and with their proper function [Radhakrishnan and Moore, xxiv].

Perhaps it is in this emphasis on intuition that Indian philosophy differs from the philosophies of the West; it is also the reason why historians of the West have shrunk from including Indian philosophy in their "Histories of Philosophy." (The credit of recognizing, for the first time, the existence of philosophies other than the "Western" goes to Bertrand Russell, who called his book *History of Western Philosophy.*)

Another important feature of Indian philosophy—and closely related to its emphasis on intuitive perception—is its acceptance of authority. Apart from their acceptance of the authority of the Vedas (they are believed to be authorless by the Mimāmsa school), all the schools of Indian philosophy, with the exception of the Chārvāka, accept the intuitive insights of the ancient seers, "whether it be the Hindu seers of the Upanishads, the intuitive experience of the Buddha, or the similarly intuitive wisdom of Mahāvira." Indian philosophers have always been respectful about tradition while the commentators—"the great system-builders of later periods"—have only explained and interpreted the traditional wisdom of the past without, at the same time, interfering with the general spirit and basic concepts of the past. "Reverence for authority does not militate against progress, but it does lend a unity of spirit by providing a continuity of thought which has rendered philosophy especially significant in Indian life and solidly unified against any philosophical attitude contradicting its basic characteristics of spirituality, inwardness, and the strong belief that the truth is to be lived, not merely known" (Radhakrishnan and Moore, xxiv).

It must however be pointed out, that despite this respect for authority and the wisdom of the past, Indian philosophical systems show a variety which is not generally associated with a dogmatic religious creed. This freedom from traditional bias is plainly evident in the attitude toward God, which differs from system to system. For instance, the original Sāmkhya system is completely silent about the possible existence of God, although it speaks of the "theoretical undemonstrability of his existence." The Vaiseshika and the Yoga systems admit the existence of God, but deny him the creation of the universe. The Mimāmsa system speaks of God but denies his importance and efficacy in the moral ordering of the world. The Chārvākas deny God without qualification, while the early Buddhist systems reject him. But, even with these and such other differences, it is difficult to differentiate precisely one system from another, for there exists among them an intimately mutual influence. As Lannoy writes: "Not even the famous Six Schools of philosophy are *schools* in the usual sense of the word; they are more like *styles* of thought expressed in the language of metaphor" (Lannoy, 280–281).

This brings us to one of the most important aspects of Indian philosophy – its "over-all synthetic tradition."

> The Hindu is prone to believe even that all the six systems, as well as their varieties of subsystems, are in harmony with one another, in fact, that they complement one another in the total vision, which is one. As contrasted with Western philosophy, with its analytic approach to reality and experience Indian philosophy is fundamentally synthetic. The basic texts of Indian philosophy treat not only one phase of experience and reality, but of the full content of the philosophic sphere. Metaphysics, epistemology, ethics, religion, psychology, facts, and value are not cut off from the other but are treated in their natural unity as aspects of one life and experience or of a single comprehensive reality" [Radhakrishnan and Moore, xxv–xxvi].

The synthetic nature of Indian philosophy is apparent in what Richard Lannoy calls "the aesthetic orientation of Indian thought" – a point of view which was earlier cogently put forward by F.S.C. Northrop in his book *The Meeting of East and West: An Inquiry Concerning World Understanding* (New York: Macmillan, 1946). Northrop writes: "Western science has been concerned with the indirectly verified, unseen, theoretic component in things upon which the philosophy and culture of the West are based [as against the] Oriental conception of the nature of things and of the nature of the divine as essentially immediate, passionate and aesthetic in character. . . . [in the East] they insist that no reality exists except that which is immediately apprehended" (Northrop, quoted in Lannoy, 281). It is indeed this formulation of a philosophy in terms of "the *aesthetic component* of things, and the development of religions and other cultural forms in terms of such a philosophy" which have been instrumental in bringing about the attitude of tolerance in Indian thought and in the Indian mind throughout history.

Radhakrishnan and Moore have identified certain other characteristics which have been responsible in providing a fundamental unity of perspective to Indian philosophy. These characteristics refer to "the practical realm . . to a practical motivation, stemming from man's practical problems of life, his limitations and suffering, and culminating in every case except the Chārvāka in a consideration of his ultimate liberation" (Radhakrishnan and Moore, xxvi). Liberation or emancipation (*moksha* in Hinduism and Jainism, *nirvāna* in Buddhism) remains the ultimate goal of life, although its precise meaning has remained the same for all the schools, which is liberation from the samsāric cycle of birth, suffering, death and rebirth. In certain schools, the goal appears to be "negative, consisting essentially of freedom from pain and freedom from rebirth, but in reality it is the positive achievement of a richer and fuller life and the attainment of infinite bliss."

The individual spirit is restored to its original condition of purity, sometimes by becoming identical with the Absolute or the larger Reality by bringing itself into harmonious relation with It, sometimes by a life of communion with God in a state of enhanced consciousness, and sometimes simply by existing in its state of pure, undefiled individuality by a process of gradual isolation and withdrawal. However, the end remains the same: freedom from limitations and tradition-dominated conditions of life. As Lannoy writes, "the antinomian transcendence of subject-object relationships, the reconciliation of opposites, finally brings immediate experience of solidarity with all things and *a stance of benign tranquillity* is attained amidst the contradictions of everyday life. Whatever the course, spiritual realization is invariably believed to permit the emergence of other than normal forms of consciousness, aesthetic, visionary, or mystical" (Lannoy, 283; emphasis added).

While liberation remains the goal in all the systems of Indian philosophy, the basis of that goal is the same for all these systems, which is good and virtuous life. With the exception of the Chārvākas, the essential spirit of Indian philosophical schools consists in nonattachment, which is defined as "an attitude of mind with which the individual fulfills his part in life and lives a 'normal' everyday existence in company with his fellow men, without being entangled in or emotionally disturbed by the *results* of his actions" (Radhakrishnan and Moore, xxvii). It must be emphasized, however, that this does not refer to any negativism or escapism, for the individual does partake in worldly activities, but he maintains his "spiritual superiority to worldly *values*."

Related to the concept of nonattachment or spiritual withdrawal, are two doctrines of *karma* (action) and rebirth. All the schools of Indian philosophy presuppose the necessity of individual moral and spiritual perfection for the purpose of salvation; they also believe that "justice is the law of moral life exactly as cause-and-effect is the law of the natural world" and that, since "justice and moral and spiritual perfection are not achievable n one life," rebirth is a necessity—to provide the opportunity for moral progress and eventual release. As Lannoy remarks, in its original sense, *karma* did not have any ethical connotation, but was simply "a biological law of causality linked with that of *samsāra,* rebirth" (Lannoy, 284). "*Karma* and rebirth are the instrumentalities by which the moral order of the universe is worked out in the life of man" (Radhakrishnan and Moore, xxvii). It is not surprising therefore to find even the Supreme Deity—whether Shiva or Vishnu—along with all the mythological deities subject to the law of *karma,* to the immensely impersonal drama of cyclical change: "The only constant phenomenon of empirical reality is the fact of dynamic change. The corollary of this idea is that an unchanging reality subsists beneath all apparent change, and therefore that change itself is without ultimate significance" (Lannoy, 284).

Notwithstanding certain metaphysical and epistemological differences, all schools of Hinduism (except the three heterodox schools of Chārvāka, Jainism and Buddhism) accept a common way of life, which includes the fourfold division of society, the four stages of life, and the four basic values an ideal person seeks. The fourfold division of society—or the caste system—seems to have developed out of the multiracial nature of Indian society. K.M. Sen writes about the initial stages of the development of the caste system:

> Within the boundaries of the country almost all the racial features of the world can be seen, and the majority of the people seems to be racially very mixed indeed. Before the Sanskrit-speaking Aryans arrived, India already contained various racial elements, of which the Dravidians were perhaps the most prominent. The Aryans who conquered most of India do not seem to have had much respect, at least initially, for the dark-skinned natives. This was not so much because they felt culturally superior, since the urban Indus Valley Civilization, with its scripts, arts, sculpture, town-planning knowledge, and other crafts, represented a more developed, though less vigorous, culture than that of the illiterate, sharp-shooting, nomadic Aryans. As conquerors, however, they must have felt more powerful, and as strong believers in the Vedic religion, with its elaborate pantheon, they may have thought themselves right-minded. Whatever the truth, the resultant plural society with different communities, different religious beliefs, different attitudes to life, and different occupations (the conquerors formed most of the new upper classes), produced a rigid class-structure. In all probability some sort of caste divisions existed when the Aryans arrived, and the Aryans made most of it [Sen, 27–28].

The four groups or castes (*varna* = literally "color") into which Hindu society is divided are: *Brāhmana* or *Brāhmin,* the priests and religious teachers; *Kshatriya,* the kings, warriors, and aristocrats; *Vaisya,* the merchants and traders, and people engaged in similar professional activities or careers; and *Sudra,* the class of laborers. The theory of the racial origin of the caste system is grounded in the association of caste with "color." K.M. Sen quotes an interesting piece of conversation between the two sages, Bhrigu and Bharadvāja, in the first-century B.C. epic *Mahābhārata,* in which the association between caste and color is discussed in an argumentative, doubting fashion.

Bhrigu explains the nature of castes to Bharadvāja: "*Brāhmins* are fair, *Kshatriyas* are reddish, *Vaisyas* are yellowish, and the *Sudras* are black." However, as Sen observes, "even in those early days the races do not seem to have been by any means pure," and hence, Bharadvāja's reply: "If different colours indicate different castes, then all castes are mixed castes" (*Mahābhārata,* "Santi Parva"). Obviously, Bharadvāja was not quite convinced by caste divisions. The division of the society into four castes has "in all probability always been theoretical" and (as Bharadvāja asserts) "mixed complexions seem to have been represented in every caste" (Sen, 28, 29). The caste differences were generally determined according to occupational ability and not the color of the skin. In fact, several ancient Hindu texts question the idea of a hereditary class/caste structure and suggest class/caste-determination "by conduct and not by birth." Although, theoretically, caste system has been viewed as an integral part of Hinduism, a large part of the religious literature of the Hindus testifies against a rigidly hereditary caste division.

The first three of the four castes, namely, the *Brāhmins,* the *Kshatriyas* and the *Vaisyas* are called "the twice-born, that is, they are religiously initiated Hindus, whereas the *sudras* are not so accepted" (Radhakrishnan and Moore, xxvii). According to Hindu scriptures, the ideal life of the "twice-born" consist of four stages or *āsramas.* These are: *brahmacharya,* the period of discipline and education or the stage of studentship; *gārhasthya,* the stage of the householder; *vānaprasthya,* the stage of the forest dweller or the period of withdrawal from the worldly bonds; and *sannyāsa,* the stage of the wondering monk or the period of hermitage. In the Hindu scheme of values, knowledge *(jñāna)* and modes of physical and mental discipline *(yoga)* have always had the highest place and hence, discipline through education was considered "the prime religious duty of youth." "It must not be assumed," warns Sen, "that according to this view of life education should consist of only metaphysics and religious instruction." A significant part of the early Indian contribution to logic, grammar, phonetics, medicine (the sage Charaka wrote a book on medicine), surgery (the sage Susruta successfully conducted surgical operations and wrote a treatise on surgery), literature, arithmetic, trigonometry and algebra came from "religious people." "While Hindu philosophers have tried to go *beyond* the material world, the realities of the material world were not neglected. In fact a sound knowledge of the physical world was always considered to be a part of Hindu education" (Sen, 22; for a somewhat extreme view of the Hindu's worldly orientation, see Nirad Chaudhuri, *Hinduism* [London: Chatto & Windus, 1979]). K.M. Sen quotes the 20th century neo–Vedantin Sri Aurobindo:

> It is necessary, therefore, that advancing Knowledge should base herself on a clear, pure, and disciplined intellect. It is necessary, too, that she should correct her errors sometimes by a return to the restraint of sensible fact, the concrete realities of the physical world. The touch

> of Earth is always reinvigorating to the son of Earth, even when he seeks a supraphysical knowledge. It may even be said that the supraphysical can only be really mastered in its fullness . . . when we keep our feet firmly on the physical. "Earth is His footing," says the *Upanishad* whenever it images the Self that manifests in the Universe [Sri Aurobindo, *The Life Divine,* quoted in Sen, 22].

These words should be sufficient to dispel any doubt in the Western mind as to the world-affirming character of Indian philosophy.

Although renunciation is an important Hindu value, *gārhyasthya* (the phase of the householder) "is not looked upon as a less important period of life than the later ones"; in fact, it is considered to be "the mainstay of the four *āsramas,* for it gives unity and cohesion to the entire social structure, and the other *āsramas* depend on it for their sustenance" (Sen, 22). Several scriptural passages refute the view—widely held in the West—that the Hindu ideal is inactivity. In the *Bhagavad-gitā,* for instance, we find the following passage: "Do you perform prescribed action, for action is better than inaction, and the body too cannot be supported without action." As Radhakrishnan and Moore write, "one does not enter the life of asceticism until after he has fulfilled his obligations to his fellow man as a student and as a householder" (Radhakrishnan and Moore, xxviii). The mere fulfillment of the ideals of social living and familial success are not sufficient, however. The celebrated poet and grammarian Bhartrihari writes: "What if you have secured the fountain-head of all desires; what if you have put your foot on the neck of your enemy, or by your good fortune gathered friends around you? What, even, if you have succeeded in keeping mortal bodies alive for ages—*tatah kim,* what then?" (quoted in Sen, 23). Bhartrihari's question presupposes the Hindu ideal of *moksha/mukti/nirvāna* (liberation or freedom), which refers to a state of completeness, of "fullness of being, free from bondage of *karma* and, thus, from rebirth"—something which requires a loosening of familial and social associations, a gradual retreat from mortal life. This is the third stage or *āsrama* of *vānaprasthya,* which is spontaneously and inevitably followed by *sannyāsa,* which is the ideal individual's period of life as a hermit or monk.

K.M. Sen summarizes the complex system of Hindu values: "It includes knowledge, it embraces active work, it emphasizes sacrifice and service to others, and it culminates in renunciation" (Sen, 24). With the four *āsramas* or stages of life go the four goals of life and which are accepted by all Hindus: these are obedience to the moral law *(dharma),* material wealth *(artha),* physical pleasure *(kāma),* and freedom or emancipation *(moksha).*

The Vedas

The Vedas stand "in the beginning of Indian Literature in general as well as in the beginning of Indian Philosophy" (Frauwallner, 27). Generally referred to as "The Sacred Books of India," they are believed to be "the earliest record of the Indo-European race" (Dasgupta, I, 10), "the earliest source of our information regarding Indian thought" (Hiriyanna, *Essentials,*

9), "the oldest extant literary monument of the Aryan mind" (Sharma, 13). In their *A Sourcebook in Indian Philosophy* Radhakrishnan and Moore write: "Whatever may be the truth of the theory of the racial affinities of the Indian and the European peoples, there is no doubt that Indo-European languages derive from a common source and illustrate a relationship of the mind. The oldest Indo-European literary and philosophical monument is the *Rg-Veda*" (Radhakrishnan and Moore, 3). In his own pioneering study of *Indian Philosophy*—a book written several decades earlier—Radhakrishnan goes a step further when he writes: "The Vedas are the earliest documents of the human mind that we possess." He then goes on to quote from a paper by Wilson (?) published in the *Journal of the Royal Asiatic Society:* "When the texts of the *Rg* and *Yajur* Vedas are completed, we shall be in the possession of materials sufficient for the safe appreciation of . . . the actual condition of the Hindus, both political and religious, at a date coeval with that of the yet earliest known records social organisation—long anterior to the dawn of Grecian civilisation—prior to the oldest vestiges of the Assyrian Empire yet discovered—contemporary probably with the oldest Hebrew writings, and posterior only to the Egyptian dynasties, of which, however, we yet know little except barren names; the Vedas give us abundant information respecting all that is most interesting in the contemplation of antiquity" (Radhakrishnan, *Indian Philosophy,* 63–64).

Whatever be the antiquity value of the Vedas—a subject which still remains the researcher's paradise—the Hindus trace the original source of their cultural life to the ancient Aryan religion of the Veda, and the Vedic age has had "a decisive influence on the trend of Indian culture" (Sen, 45). The orthodox Hindus consider the Vedas to be divine truths revealed from time to time to the great seers *(rishis)* in their "supra-normal consciousness." Although their religious practices, philosophical leanings, civic conduct, and familial and social relations are governed by a set of codes known as *Smrtis,* these have the "sacred sanction of Vedic authority"; and whenever there is any conflict between the *Smrtis* and the Vedas (which are known as *Sruti*), it is the authority of the latter which is finally accepted: "It is a recognized rule of procedure that whenever there seems to be a difference between the *Sruti* (the Vedas) and the *Smrti,* the *Sruti* has to be upheld as the supreme authority and the *Smrti* has to be interpreted in consonance with it. No school of philosophy will be recognized as orthodox, if it is not supported by the authority of the Vedas" (Swami Sharvananda, 182).

Manu, who is believed to be India's greatest lawgiver, has asserted that even history and myth *(Itihāsas and Purānas)* should be considered as "an elaboration of the Vedas" and are to be read as "commentaries on the sacred Vedas." It is easy to see, in the light of the facts we have enumerated above, the nature and extent of the influence of the Vedas not only on the autonomous system of Indian philosophy—which, as we said earlier, has developed almost wholly unaffected by outside influences—but also on the overall growth of the Indian mind.

Although the word "Veda" literally means "knowledge," to the orthodox, it means "knowledge par excellence, the sacred or revealed knowledge" as concretely embodied in a vast body of literature comprising (as we said earlier) *Samhitās, Brāhmanas, Āranyakas* and *Upanishads.* The ancient Indians, as Erich Frauwallner notes, had already developed an elaborate sacrificial cult, and "every great sacrifice consisted of not only ceremonial sacrificial rites distributed over a long period but also required the co-operation of a great number of priests" (Frauwallner, 27). There were at least three kinds of priests who participated in or conducted such a sacrifice: the *Adhvaryu,* who conducted the proper sacrificial ritual and gave offerings to the gods; the *Hotā,* who recited the holy hymns or *mantras* in praise of the gods so that the latter would participate in such sacrificial process; and the *Udgātā,* who sang the hymns "in sweet musical tones to entertain and please the gods" (Sharma, 14). Apart from these three kinds of priests, there was also the fourth priest Brahmā, who invisibly supervised the entire ritual drama. The Veda contains "in its oldest and most important parts the handbooks or manuals for these different priests" (Frauwallner, 27).

The four *Samhitās* or collections of hymns *(mantras)* addressed to gods and goddesses are believed to fulfill the needs of these four main priests—*Rg-samhitā* for the *Hotā, Sāma-samhitā* for the *Udgātā, Yajursamhitā* for the *Adhvaryu,* and *Atharva-samhitā* for *Brahmā.* The *samhitās* therefore form the *mantra*-portion of the Veda and express the loftiest sentiments of the ancient Indian for his deity; consequently, they are all in the form of metred verse. Several of these hymns, however, are obscure enough to defy any satisfactory interpretation, although it is generally believed that "these early *mantras* inculcate a form of nature worship, and that this religion of nature was, in its essence, transplanted from their original home when the ancestors of the future Aryans immigrated into India" (Hiriyanna, *Essentials,* 10).

The Vedic religion, as represented in the earlier hymns *(mantras),* is nature-oriented: the various forces of nature, like fire *(agni),* wind *(vāyu)* and the sun *(surya),* which influenced every single activity of the Vedic Aryan, are deified, having undergone a process of personification on the basis of the belief that "the order which is observed in the world, such as the regular succession of seasons or of day and night, is due to the agency of these powers" (Hiriyanna, *Essentials,* 10). And, since the Aryans were basically a people whose "prosperity was a mere gamble in rain," the rain-god or Indra naturally became their leading deity, although several other deities in the Vedic pantheon did play a role conducive to the agrarian culture. The world, according to these early hymns, is not only governed by the gods but owes its existence to them, who are its creators. The hymns represent the relation of man to the gods as one of complete dependence and submission, although "it is of quite an intimate kind." The nature of this intimacy is primarily *human:* if the Vedic Aryan addressed his gods as "father," the gods were also "fond of the worshipper." E.W. Hopkins writes: "The *bhakti* or loving devotion, which some scholars imagine to be only a late development of Hindu religion, is already evident in the Rigveda" (*Ethics of India,* quoted in Hiriyanna, *Essentials,* 203).

The Vedic hymns or *mantras* are in verse; the *Brāhmanas* are mostly in prose. The *Brāhmanas* are a set of precepts and religious duties; they contain detailed descriptions of the sacrificial rites and the modes of their performance. According to the famous Vedic commentator Sayanāchārya, they include eight broad subjects: history, ancient legends, esoteric knowledge about the meditative activity, supreme knowledge, verses, aphorisms, explanations and elaborations. The word *Brāhmana,* which is derived from the word *brahman* (not to be confused with *Brahman* or the immanent Power) meaning "devotion" or "prayer," refers to "an authoritative utterance of a priest, relating particularly to sacrifice" and are so called because they are "the repositories of such utterances" (Hiriyanna, *Essentials,* 14). Each of the four Vedas contains one or more *Brāhmanas:* the *Rig-Veda* has two, viz. the *Aitereya* and the *Kausitaki* or *Sankhyayana;* the *Sāma-Veda* has two, viz. the *Tandya* or *Panchavimsa* and the *Shadvimsa;* the *Yajur-Veda* has two, viz. the *Taittiriya* (a continuation of the *Taittiriya Samhitā*), and the *Satapatha* in two revised forms, viz. the *Kanva* and *Madhyandina;* and, finally, the *Atharva-Veda* has the *Gopatha Brāhmana.*

As it should be apparent by now, the *Brāhmanas* originated much later than the collection of *mantras* or the *Samhitās,* the intermediate period between the two showing a gradual change in the Vedic Aryan's understanding with regard to the character of the sacrifices. The complex nature of the sacrifice during the later Vedic period can be explained in terms of the importance the Aryan attached to every word or movement in even the most modest ritual exercise. Erich Frauwallner has found the reason for this: "The sacrifices were no more considered as a means of winning the favour of the gods and of impelling them to fulfil the proffered request; they no more served as a way of thanking the gods for the fulfilment of the request; the sacrifices, on the other hand, were considered to hold good as magic rites, the exact execution of which could enforce the wished-for result, independent of the will of the gods" (Frauwallner, 28). The *Brāhmana* texts describe not only the different sacrifices but also the "secret significance of different sacrificial implements and rites," thus indirectly offering us a knowledge of the world-view of the ancient Indian.

The third part of the Vedas, the *Āranyakas* (literally "forest-books"), as their name implies, were meant for the hermits—those who "had withdrawn to the forest towards the end of the their life in order to live there a life of pious practices and reflection" (Frauwallner, 29) and could not, for obvious reasons, perform large-scale sacrifices. Although the *Āranyakas* are sometimes considered as part of the *Brāhmanas,* they are indeed independent texts, except perhaps the *Taittiriya Āranyaka* which forms the latter part of the *Taittiriya Brāhmana.* There is little philosophy in the *Brāhmanas,* though "some philosophical ideas flash here and there in the course of some speculative digressions" (Sharma, 14). Since the *Brāhmanas* were concerned mainly with the "sacred significance" of the different rituals and "the distribution of the different sacrificial functions among several distinct classes of priests," there was in them little scope for free speculative thinking, which was thus "subordinated to the service of sacrifice" (Dasgupta, I, 13).

The *Āranyakas* represent the transition from ritualistic thought to philosophic thought and mystic interpretation, from active participation in sacrificial activities to extended meditation on certain sacrifice-related symbols. For instance, instead of the actual performance of the horse sacrifice *(asvamedha),* we find elaborate directions for meditating upon the dawn *(Ushas)* as the "head of the horse, the sun as the eye of the horse, the air as its life." "This is indeed," writes Dasgupta, "a distinct advancement of the claims of speculation or meditation over the actual performance of the complicated ceremonials of sacrifice. The growth of the subjective speculation, as being capable of bringing the highest god, gradually resulted in the supercession of Vedic ritualism and the establishment of the claims of philosophic meditation and self-knowledge as the highest goal of life" (Dasgupta, I, 14). Thus the *Āranyakas,* with their emphasis on speculation, on the sacrificial significance of the different processes of daily life, on the secrecies involved in the course of ordinary existence, paved the way for the *Upanishads.*

The doctrine of self-knowledge of the *Āranyakas* become the center of philosophical interest and was responsible in highlighting the lean speculative content of the *Brāhmanas.* Erich Frauwallner writes: "There arose entire sections of preponderatingly philosophical contents which continually gained greater esteem and importance . . . and the most important of these sections were separated from their original contextual connection and were handed down as independent texts . . . which are known and have become famous under the name of the *Upanishads* and which represent the venerable monuments of Indian Philosophy" (Frauwallner, 30).

The *Upanishads*—the concluding portions of the *Āranyakas*—are only the "philosophically valuable parts of the liturgical *Brāhmana* texts, separated from them and independently handed down." The separation of these sections from their original context was sometimes "superficial and arbitrary," however, so that there are several important philosophically-relevant sections in the *Brāhmanas* which have not been included in the *Upanishads* even as the latter contain a lot of material dealing with "crude sacrificial symbolism and priestly speculation" (Frauwallner, 30). It is therefore necessary for the serious scholar to "separate the chaff from the grain" in order that he may consider things in their proper perspective and order. Though there are as many as 250 *Upanishads* claiming Vedic connection, Samkara, the earliest known commentator of the *Upanishads* and chief propounder of the Vedanta school, has recognized only 16 of these to be "authentic and authoritative" (Swami Sharvananda, 184). We shall have more to say on these major *Upanishads* later in this chapter.

The *Mantras* and the *Brāhmanas* are called the "Karma-Kānda" or the portion of the Vedas dealing with the sacrificial rituals; the *Āranyakas* and the *Upanishads* are called the "Jñāna-Kānda" or the portion of the Vedas dealing with knowledge. According to some scholars, however, the *Āranyakas* represent the transition from the "Karma-Kānda" (*Karma* = "action") to the "Jñāna-Kānda" (*Jñāna* = "knowledge"), while the *Upanishads* represent what is called *Vedānta* (*Veda* + *anta* = "Veda + end" or "the end of the Vedas"), since they form the concluding part of the Vedas as well as the "essence, the cream, the height, of the Vedic philosophy" (Sharma, 15).

As for the development of the *Mantras,* the *Brāhmanas,* and the *Upanishads,* Radhakrishnan writes: "While the hymns [i.e. the *Mantras*] are the creation of the poets, the *Brāhmanas* and the religion of spirit of the *Upanishads,* correspond in a very close way to the three great divisions in the Hegelian conception of the development of religion. Though at a later stage the three have existed side by side, there is no doubt that they were originally developed in successive periods. The *Upanishads,* while in one sense a continuation of the Vedic worship, are in another a protest against the religion of the *Brāhmanas*" (Radhakrishnan, *Indian Philosophy,* 65–66; emphasis added). As for the *Āranyakas,* the *Brāhmanas* and the *Upanishads,* "these three literatures gradually grew up in one process of development and they were probably regarded as parts of one literature" (Dasgupta, I, 28–29).

In the pre-Upanishadic philosophy, we notice a transition from "the naturalistic and anthropomorphic polytheism through transcendent monotheism to immanent monism" (Sharma, 15). The several forces of nature, personified by the awe-struck Vedic poets, turn into real gods who, in course of time, became "mere forms of one personal and transcendental God," and who finally became the immanent *Purusha.* Thus the chief motivation of Vedic philosophy, beginning with the earliest of the hymns, has been "the search for a basic unity underlying the manifold of the universe" (Zimmer, 338). The earliest Vedic deities, as represented in the hymns of the *Rg-Veda,* are not independent of each other. As Hiriyanna writes: "[O]wing to the incomplete individualization of deities and the innate connection or mutual resemblance of one natural phenomenon with another . . . there is in Vedic mythology . . . an overlapping of divinities" (*Outline,* 38). Indeed we find a certain overall similarity in the description of these many deities: all of them are luminous, maintain physical order, and are friendly to the virtuous. Each of these deities becomes important to the exclusion of others at any one time, only to be followed by yet another enjoying the same importance. This was a period of what Max Mueller calls "henotheism"—a belief in single gods, each in turn standing out as the most powerful, as distinguished from pure monotheism or belief in only one God. This henotheism or "opportunist monotheism" was only a passing phase, but it certainly represents a definite stage in the movement from polytheistic to monotheistic belief; it was conducive to the formulation of a belief in a single and supreme God who took the place of the multiple deities of an earlier time.

R.C. Zaehner, in his Introduction to *Hindu Scriptures,* writes about this phase of transition: "The religion of the *Rig-Veda* is related and comparable to the religion of the other Indo-European peoples . . . It starts by being polytheistic, but it does not develop into the modified monotheism that we find in Greece and Rome, with only one god—Zeus or Jupiter—emerging as the undisputed ruler of the rest; it takes a very different turning and develops into something wholly Indian . . . None of the gods . . . ever reaches the supreme distinction of being the undisputed king of gods and men. Rather they tend to coalesce the one into the other, and in so doing they lose their identity and indeed their relevance" (Zaehner, vi). This tendency of the Vedic Indian to let the gods overlap does not, however, result in a "fully crystallized conception of a supreme God"; it rather gives way to a tendency to discover and realize the "common power" behind all the gods, "the principle immanent in all of them." Thus, the conception of the supreme God in the later Vedic period is "more philosophic than religious" (Hiriyanna, *Essentials,* 14).

At the end of the Rg-Vedic period, new "functional" deities appear, their names representing the creative functions they were supposed to perform, but once again, through a process of intuitive and speculative personification. For instance, omnipotence, a feature of all the gods, is personified into *Visva-karmā* ("maker of all"/"all-doer"), who becomes the great architect of the universe—"who knows all, who assigns the gods their names and to whom all go for instruction."

The Vedic Indian, remarkably speculative and imaginative as he was, strove to derive "a general, and virtually impersonal, conception of the supreme God from the common characteristics of deities" (Hiriyanna, *Essentials,* 15); a number of such conceptual deities succeeded one another during this period. Thus we have *Prajāpati* or "Lord of the creatures"/ "Father-god," who became in the course of time the "receiver" of all sacrifices, the highest conceptualized form of unitary godhead. However, in the *Upanishads,* even *Prajāpati* is reduced to "a clearly secondary rank" and appears as *Brahmā* (in the *Aitareya Upanishad, Brahmā* is referred to as the "head of all living beings").

Behind all the polytheistic leanings and monotheistic exaggeration, however, there was yet another tendency, which (as we have said already) was clearly philosophic in nature. Although the conception of *Brahman* (the Ultimate Principle/the Universal Spirit) "which has been the highest glory for the Vedanta philosophy of later days had hardly emerged in the *Rg-Veda* from the associations of the sacrificial mind" (Dasgupta, I, 20), the Vedic Indian, in his attempt to go beyond his ordinary religion in order to understand the source of the mystery of the Universe, traced the world "not to a creator but to a single primordial cause which unfolds itself as the universe in all its diversity" (Hiriyanna, *Essentials,* 15), the fundamental reality in which all duality ceases, the highest being who is both immanent in the world and transcendent. It is important to know at this point that several passages in the Rg-Vedic hymns show a mixture of monotheistic and monistic conceptions. The monistic tendency which becomes the basis of the *Upanishads,* is foreshadowed and anticipated in the Vedic hymns.

Paul Deussen writes of the monistic theory of the *Rg-Veda:*

> The Hindus arrive at this monism by a method essentially different from that of the other countries. Monotheism was attained in Egypt by a mechanical identification of the various local gods, in Palestine by proscription of other gods and violent prosecution of their worshippers

> for the benefit of their natural god Jehovah. In India they reached monism, though not monotheism on a more philosophical path, seeing through the veil of the manifold the unity which underlies it [Deussen, *Outlines of Indian Philosophy,* quoted in Radhakrishnan, *Indian Philosophy,* 96].

The Vedic Indian attained a firmly rooted monistic position "where the dynamism of the phenomenal spectacle and the permanence of the animating principle could be experienced simultaneously as one and the same great mystery—the mystery of that absolutely transcendent, serene being which is immanent, and made partially manifest, in the phenomenal becoming of the world" (Zimmer, 355). We have one of the hymns saying: "In the beginning, there was neither being nor non-being. *That one* breathed calmly, self-sustained" (emphasis added). We have here a clear instance of the self-creating, self-evolving, dynamic principle which was to become the *Brahman* of the *Upanishads.*

According to Hiriyanna, Vedic literature shows "at least two distinct shades of such monistic thought." First, there is the view, somewhat pantheistic, which identifies God with nature, and its most noteworthy expression is located in a passage of the *Rg-Veda* in which the goddess Aditi ("the Boundless") is identified with all gods and all men, with the sky and the air, with "all that was and all that shall be." This doctrine denies something which is the basis of monotheistic thinking—it is the denial of the difference between God and nature. It conceives God as immanent in nature, as the world as itself God, thus implicitly rejecting the notions of God transcending nature and the world issuing from God. Hiriyanna, however, thinks: "Although the object of this view is to postulate unity, it retains, somewhat inconsistently as it seems, both the notions of God and nature and so far fails to satisfy the mind in its search after true unity."

A consideration of this problem appears to have been responsible for another conception of unity, a conception which is finely rendered in the famous "Song of Creation" of the *Rg-Veda.* Here, the Vedic poet recognizes the principle of causality, traces the entire creation to a First Cause which subsumes all opposites and unfolds in a spontaneous fashion:

> Then there was neither Aught nor Nought, no air nor sky beyond.
> What covered it all? Where rested all? In watery gulf profound?
> Nor death was then, nor deathlessness, nor change of night and day.
> That One breathed calmly, self-sustained; nought else beyond it lay.
> Gloom hid in gloom existed first—one sea, eluding view.
> That One, a void in chaos wrapt, by inward fervour grew.
> Within it first arose desire, the primal germ of mind,
> Which nothing with existence links, as sages searching find.
> The kindling ray that shot across the dark and drear abyss—
> Was it beneath? or high aloft? What bard can answer this?
> There fecunding powers were found, and mighty forces strove—
> A self-supporting mass beneath, and energy above.
> Who knows, who ever told, from whence this vast creation rose?
> No gods had then been born—who then can e'er the truth disclose?
> Whence sprang this world, and whence framed by hand divine or no—

> Its Lord in heaven alone can tell, if even he can show [J. Muir, *Original Sanskrit Texts,* quoted in Hiriyanna, *Outlines,* 42].

The cosmological conception here is wholly impersonal, without a theistic coloring of any kind, free from mythological elements; it suggests "nothing beyond the positive and unitary character of the ultimate principle." "We are here on the threshold of Upanishadic monism" (Hiriyanna, *Outlines,* 43). The second shade of monistic thought discernible in the Vedic literature, which manifests itself as doubt and disbelief and shows itself as the opposite of the orthodox teaching of the Veda, is evident in the many interrogations in the Creation hymn. There is in fact a whole hymn in the *Rg-Veda* addressed to Faith which concludes with the wish-prayer: "O Faith, make us faithful." There are several other hymns in the *Rg-Veda* where we have direct and indirect instances of unbelief. The invocation to Faith "would be unintelligible if we did not assume a certain lack of faith as prevalent in the age in which the hymn was composed" (Hiriyanna, *Outlines,* 44). It was this trait of disbelief that gave rise to the heterodox schools in later times. Radhakrishnan describes these times of unbelief: "We reach the 'twilight of the gods,' in which they are slowly passing away. In the Upanishads the twilight changed into night and the very gods disappeared but for the dreamers of the past" (Radhakrishnan, 93).

As for eschatology, there are several hymns in the Vedas expressing the Vedic Indian's belief in the possibility of the soul's separation from the body and its postmortem existence, in the existence of another world, although they do not offer a doctrine of transmigration in a developed form. In the *Satapatha Brāhmana* there is a mention of those who do not perform the rites in the proper manner and thus are born again only to suffer yet another death. In many other hymns there are references to another world, where the highest material joys are attained as a result of sacrifices properly conducted, as well as to "the deep abyss of eternal darkness" into which the souls of the wicked and the evil are cast away. In the *Satapatha Brāhmana* we find that the dead pass between two "fires" which burn the wicked and the evil, but let the good go by unscathed; that everyone is born after death, is weighed in a balance, and receives punishment or reward according as his works are bad or good.

There is also a passage in the *Rg-Veda* which reads: "After he has completed what he has to do and has become old he departs hence; departing hence he is once more born; this is the third birth." As Radhakrishnan points out, this has reference to the Vedic theory that every individual human being has three births—the first as a child, the second by moral and spiritual education, and the third after physical death—and is related to the belief in the related theory of the soul as a moving life principle (Radhakrishnan, *Indian Philosophy,* 115–116). "These ideas of the possibilities of a necessary connection of the enjoyments and sorrows of a man with his good and bad works when combined with the notion of an inviolable law or order *[Rta]* ... and the unalterable law which produces the effects of sacrificial works, led to the Law of Karma and the doctrine of transmigration" (Dasgupta, I, 26). The Rg-Vedic hymns "form the foundation of subsequent Indian thought. While the *Brāhmanas* emphasize the sacrificial ritual shadowed forth in the hymns, the *Upanishads* carry out their philosophical suggestions" (Radhakrishnan, *Indian Philosophy,* 116).

The Upanishads

As we have already seen, the *Upanishads* are the concluding portion of the *Vedas* and therefore are called "Vedānta" (*Veda + Anta* = Veda + End); they also form the essence of the *Veda.* Notwithstanding the orthodox classification, which shows the *Upanishads* as "appendices" to the Vedic *Āranyakas* which again are linked with the Vedic *Brāhmanas,* they have been treated as separate and independent treatises by the scholars and historians. If the *Vedas* indicate and extoll the path of deeds or works *(karma-mārga),* the *Upanishads* show the path of knowledge *(jñāna-mārga).* The *Upanishads,* which (unlike the *Brāhmanas* that were intended for the householders who were active and strong enough to conduct the Vedic rites and perform the related sacrificial duties) were meant for those who renounced the world to attain the ultimate salvation through meditative activities, do not require the performance of any action. This fact is underlined by the literal meaning of the term *upanishad* (derived from *upa* = near, *ni* = down, *sad* = sit), which refers to sitting down near the teacher to receive instruction, and which, in course of time, came to refer to a sort of "secret teaching" *(rahasya)*—"the teaching which was jealously guarded from the unworthy and was imparted, in private, only to pupils of tried character" (Hiriyanna, *Essentials,* 18). Thus, according to the *Kathā Upanishad,* when Nachiketas wants to know about the postmortem condition of the soul, Yama refuses to reply until he tests the sincerity and strength of mind of the young inquirer (see Hiriyanna, *Outlines,* 50, for other instances of this reluctance to impart the knowledge of the highest truth indiscriminately).

The *Upanishads,* therefore, may be regarded as a reaction against that of the Vedic *Brāhmanas* which supported an elaborate system of ritual. The *Brihadāranyaka Upanishad,* for instance, declares that "it is not pleasing to the gods that man should know the ultimate truth, for that, by revealing to him their true place in the universe which is by no means supreme, will result in their losing the sacrificial offerings they would otherwise receive from him." According to this view, the gods are very much human and hence, worshipping them or offering them sacrifices does not bring any lasting result, "as devotion to philosophic truth does."

Commenting on this initial antagonism between *Brāhmanic* sacrificial-ritual duties and the Upanishadic emphasis on self-realization, and their later reconciliation, Hiriyanna writes: ". . . [I]t has to be added that, within the Vedic period itself, the spirit of antagonism to ritual is modified and ceremonial life comes to be recognized as necessary, either directly or indirectly, for attaining the true and final goal of life. The *Upanishads* thus came finally to represent the teaching of Veda in its entirety, and not of its final portions only. Here we see illustrated a characteristic feature of all advance in Indian culture, viz. that when a new stage of progress is reached, the old is not discarded but is, sooner or later, incorporated in it" (*Essentials,* 18-19). The fact remains, however, that the monistic absolutism of the *Upanishads* differs as much from the monotheism of the Vedic hymns as the Copernican from the Ptolemaic system in astronomy (Dasgupta, I, 31-33).

The *Upanishads* do not, however, offer a systematic philosophy, and they were not written by one person or during a particular period; in fact, they contain several things that are "inconsistent and unscientific." But, "there is a unity of purpose, a vivid sense of spiritual reality in them all" (Radhakrishnan, *Indian Philosophy,* 138, 139). The Upanishadic philosophers, transcending the traditional priestly view of the cosmos, "advanced now one thing and now another as an image of the primary material out of which the whole world is made" and were always aware of the "underlying unity of all being" (Hume, 1). This intuitive awareness and interpretation of the world of the early Indian thinkers has been used by later commentators to suit their own special beliefs and doctrines. The heterodox schools of the *Chārvākas* and Buddhism and, among the orthodox schools, the logical *Nyāya* and the ritualistic *Purva-Mimāmsā* appealed to the *Upanishads* in support of their varying theories. Even the dualistic school of *Sāmkhya* claims to find scriptural authority in the *Upanishads.* The *Upanishads* thus have a great historical value. They have a great comparative value too, for they have had a considerable influence on mystics and philosophers outside India.

As R.E. Hume points out in his celebrated *The Thirteen Principal Upanishads,* in the case of Schopenhauer, "the chief of modern pantheists of the West," his philosophy is "unmistakably transfused with the doctrines expounded in the *Upanishads*"—a fact indicated by his eulogistic remark on a Latin translation of a Persian rendering of the *Upanishads:* "It is the most rewarding and the most elevating reading which (with the exception of the original text) there can possibly be in the world. It has been the solace of my life and will be of my death" (Arthur Schopenhauer, *Parerga,* quoted in Hume, 3-4).

The *Upanishads* are believed to be 108 in number, although only 13 of them are accorded the status of "major" or "principal" *Upanishads.* They are *Brihadāranyaka, Chāndogya, Taittiriya, Aitereya, Kaushitaki, Kena, Kathā, Isā, Mundaka, Prasna, Māndukya, Svetāsvatara,* and *Maitri.* The earliest of the *Upanishads* are supposed to have been written between 1000 B.C. and 300 B.C.; in other words, a majority of them are pre-Buddhistic. The oldest *Upanishads* are written in prose and are nonsectarian in nature; these include the *Aitereya,* the *Kaushitaki,* the *Taittirya,* the *Chāndogya,* the *Brihadāranyaka,* and parts of the *Kena.* Although we find at least two later *Upanishads* which are written in prose, viz. the *Prasna* and the *Maitrāyani,* the middle sections of the *Kena* and the *Brihadāranyaka Upanishads* represent the transition to the metrical, sectarian, later *Upanishads.* If the early prose *Upanishads* contain more of pure speculation, the later metrical ones emphasize religious worship and devotion and lay stress upon the practice of Yoga, asceticism, the cult of Siva, of Vishnu and the philosophy of the body ("body" = *sarira*). Sri Aurobindo, the great 20th century Indian philosopher and mystic, comments on the diverse and profound character of this large body of spiritual revelation:

> The Upanishads are at once profound religious scriptures . . . documents of revelatory and intuitive philosophy of an inexhaustible light, power and largeness and, whether written in verse or cadenced prose, spiritual poems of an absolute, an unfailing inspiration inevitable in phrase, wonderful in rhythm and expression. It is the expression of a mind in which philosophy and religion and poetry are made one . . . Here the intuitive mind and intimate psychological experience of the Vedic seers passes into a supreme culmination in which the Spirit, as is said in a phrase of the Kathā Upanishad, discloses its own body, reveals the very word of its self-expression and discovers to the mind the vibration of rhythms which repeating themselves within in the spiritual hearing seem to build up the soul and set it satisfied and complete on the heights of self-knowledge [Sri Aurobindo, *The Upanishads,* 1].

According to Sri Aurobindo, this more-than-intellectual character of the *Upanishads* is something which is largely ignored by their foreign readers and translators, "who seek to bring out the intellectual sense without feeling the life of thought-vision and the ecstasy of spiritual experience which made the ancient verses . . . a revelation not to the intellect alone, but to the soul and the whole being, make of them in the old expressive word not intellectual thought and phrase, but *sruti,* spiritual audience, an inspired Scripture" (Sri Aurobindo, *The Upanishads,* 2). Although there are patches of philosophical discussion in the *Upanishads,* the latter, to say the least, do not rely on pedantry or gymnastics of logic.

The basic idea which runs through the early *Upanishads* is that of the ultimate reality—unseen, but pervasive—underlying the exterior world of change and identical with that which underlies the essence of man. Thus we find the following in the *Chāndogya Upanishad:* "It is *Brahman* [ultimate, supreme reality] that is below and is above, that is to the west and to the east, that is to the south and to the north. *Brahman,* indeed, is this whole universe." If the idea is monistic and absolutistic, it is also idealistic, for this single reality is conceived of as spiritual in nature and thus exists in and through everything. Referring to this the *Aitereya Upanishad* says: "All this is based upon spirit; spirit is the foundation of the universe, spirit is *Brahman.*"

There was already a reference to this ultimate reality in an indirect form in the Vedic *Samhitās,* in which we have the idea of a single creator and controller of the universe, variously called (as we have said earlier) *Prajāpati, Visvakarmā, Purusha* and *Brahman.* The difference between the Vedic and the Upanishadic conception is that, in the *Vedas,* the divine controller is only a *deity,* while in the *Upanishads* it is identified with an unseen and indefinable *principle,* which is all-inclusive and yet is glorious in its objectivity. The Vedic sacrifice and worship is replaced by the Upanishadic meditation on the nature of *Brahman*, although, in the early Upanishadic period, the *Brahman* was still being "worshipped" almost as if It were a deity. As Dasgupta writes: "The minds of the Vedic poets so long accustomed to worship deities of visible manifestation could not easily dispense with the idea of seeking after a positive and definite content of *Brahman*" (Dasgupta, I, 44). Thus, the philosopher, unable to find a positive definition of *Brahman*, attempted to describe it indirectly: "He is *asat*, non-being, for the being which *Brahman* is, is not to be understood as such being as is known to us by experience; yet he is being, for he alone is supremely real, for the universe subsists by him. We ourselves are but he, and yet we know not what he is" (Dasgupta, I, 45).

The Upanishadic philosopher tried to indicate *Brahman* in terms of elimination: It is not this, not this *(neti neti)*. We might here point out the origin of the word *brahman* and relate it to its Upanishadic meaning. *Brahman* is derived from the root *brh*, which means "to grow or expand" and refers to "the power which of itself burst into utterance as prayer." Philosophically speaking, therefore, *Brahman* is "the power or primary principle which spontaneously manifests itself as the universe" (Hiriyanna, *Essentials*, 20). The second Upanishadic term for the ultimate reality is *Ātman*, which originally meant "life-breath" but subsequently came to be applied to "whatever constitutes the essential part of anything, more particularly of man" (Hiriyanna, *Outlines*, 54–55). The Vedic philosophers and, later, the Upanishadic sages, tried to discover not merely a cosmic principle or the source of the universe as a whole, but the psychic principle or the inner essence of man. Like the *Brahman*, the *Ātman* is also described negatively, by denying that it is breath *(prāna)* or the senses *(indriya)*, for both breath and the senses are the not-self *(anātman)*; but there are also passages where it is described as the "true subject which knows but can never be known," "the unseen seer, the unheard hearer and the unthought thinker." Its uniquely unknowable character is stated in terms of a paradox: It is known only to those who do not *know* it. Which of course means that it is not, nor can be made, the *object* of thought; it is only intuitively realizable.

Before we proceed further, it needs to be said how the meaning of *Ātman* changes through history. In the hymns of the *Rg-Veda*, *Ātman* referred both to the ultimate essence of the universe and the vital breath in man. In the *Upanishads* (as we have just discussed) the word *Brahman* is used in the former sense, while the word *Ātman* denotes the inmost essence in man. The basic doctrine of the *Upanishads* involves the identification of *Brahman* with *Ātman*: *Brahman* = *Ātman*. The Supreme manifests Itself in every Soul/Self. This explicit identification of *Brahman* with *Ātman* is the supreme truth that the philosophers were after and is peculiarly Upanishadic. The meaning of *Ātman* is apparently quite ambiguous, for it might refer to one of several things, but it is not difficult to differentiate the Self from other selves.

Thus, insofar as man consists of the essence of food, he is *annamaya ātman* (*anna* = food/that which sustains the physical body). But behind the cover of the physical body there is the other self consisting of the vital breath and is called *prānamaya ātman* (*prāna* = breath). Behind the self as vital breath is the other self consisting of "will" and is called *manomaya ātman* (*manas* = will), which contains within it the self consisting of "consciousnesses" and is called *vijñānamaya ātman* (*vijñāna* = consciousness). But behind and within it all is the final essence of the self as pure bliss, which is *ānandamaya ātman* (*ānanda* = pure bliss). It is this "self as pure bliss" which is in continuous correspondence with the unconditioned *Brahman,* the impersonal God.

Their superficial difference but essential unity is admirably illustrated in the famous metaphor of the two birds on one tree in the *Mundaka Upanishad:* "Two birds of beautiful plumage (the soul and God), close friends and companions, reside in intimate fellowship on the selfsame tree (the body). One of them (the soul) eats sweet (and bitter) fruits (experiences the consequences of its past work), while the other looks on without eating. Buried in the selfsame tree (wholly identified with the body), the infinite Being (the soul or *Purusha*) is deluded and overwhelmed by his impotence and suffers. But when he beholds on the same tree the other, the Lord in whom the pious take delight, the adorable One, and the glory (the world) as His, he is free from grief."

The tree with the two birds *(dvā suparnā)*—the tree of life or of the human personality—has in fact become a well-known motif in Indian tapestries and points to the way this philosophical identification has become a part of an ordinary Indian's daily existence. We may cite yet another instance, occurring in the *Chāndogya Upanishad,* of the identity of the *Brahman* and the *Ātman;* it involves a conversation between the sage Uddālaka and his son Svetaketu:

"Bring hither a fig from there."
"Here is one, Sir."
"Divide it."
"It is divided, Sir."
"What do you see there?"
"These seeds, almost infinitesimal."
"Divide one of them."
"It is divided, Sir."
"What do you see there?"
"Nothing at all, Sir."

The father said: "Verily, my dear, that subtile essence which you do not perceive there, of that very essence this great nyagrodha (sacred fig) tree exists. Believe it, my son. That which is the subtile essence, in it all that exists has its self. That is Reality. That is *Ātman,* and thou, O Svetaketu, art it."

"Good sir, will you kindly instruct me further?"

"I will, my dear child," the father said. "Put this piece of salt in the water and come to me tomorrow morning."

The son did as he was commanded. Then the father said to him: "Bring me the salt which you placed in the water yesterday."

The son having groped for it, found it not, for, of course, it had dissolved.

> The father said: "Would you please sip it at this end? What is it like?"
> "It is salt."
> "Sip it in the middle. What is it like?"
> "It is salt."
> "Sip it at the far end. What is it like?"
> "It is salt."
> "Throw it away, and then come to me."
> He did as he was told; but [that did not stop the salt from] remaining ever the same.
> Then the father said: "Here also, in this body, forsooth, you do not perceive the Being; but there indeed it is. That which is the subtile essence,—this whole world has that as its self. That is Reality. That is *Ātman,* and thou, O Svetaketu, art it."

Though derived from the religion of the *Vedas,* this doctrine is far removed from it. According to the Upanishads, the realization of the one *Brahman* pervading everything amounts to the realization of the Self, and the fullness of this realization transcends the desire for heavenly comfort—a view which is further developed in the *Bhagavad-Gitā.* This state of supreme realization is described in *Brihadāranyaka Upanishad:*

> This, verily, is that form of his which is beyond desires, free from evil, free from fear. Just as a man, when in the embrace of his loving wife, knows nothing within or without, so this person, when in the embrace of the all-knowing, supremely intelligent Self, knows nothing within or without. Verily, that is his true form in which his desire is satisfied, in which the Self is his desire, in which he is without desire and without sorrow. In that state a father is no longer a father, a mother no longer a mother; states of being no longer states of being, gods are no longer gods, the Vedas no longer Vedas, a thief no longer a thief, the destroyer of an embryo no longer the destroyer of an embryo, outcastes no longer outcastes, a mendicant no longer a mendicant, an ascetic no longer an ascetic. Unattended by virtuous works, unattended by evil works, he has passed beyond all sorrows of the heart.

Monism is the ruling conception of the *Upanishads,* though, as R.C. Zaehner points out, the *Brahman-Ātman* identification is not always complete, and "it would be quite false to ascribe to the *Upanishads* as a whole the later *absolute* monism of Sankara and his school according to which *Brahman-Ātman* alone exists and the phenomenal world and empirical lives as ordinarily lived by men and women are, from the absolute point of view, illusory" (Zaehner, viii). In fact, the word *māyā* (illusion, occurs very rarely in the *Upanishads* and, when it does occur, it refers to God's "creative power." In one verse in the *Svetāsvatara Upanishad* the word *māyā* (illusion) is identified with Nature *(prakrti),* which is "real enough, though eternally changing, as against *Brahman* which, being absolutely real, is changeless Being" (Zaehner, viii).

Thus, the *Upanishads* contain the seeds of the nondualistic philosophy of Samkara, but they also contain enough hint within them to produce a dualistic philosophy like *Sāmkhya.* Zaehner sums up the principal preoccupations of the *Upanishads:*

> [They] investigate the nature of reality and their main conclusion is that in both the universe at large and in the individual human being there is a ground of pure Being which is impervious to change. To realize this Being in oneself means salvation. Once this is done, re-birth and re-death are done away with, and man realizes himself as at least participating in eternal Being. Even when he comes to a knowledge of God as being transcendent as well as immanent, he does not interpret this realization as union with God. The immanent God is everything, the transcendent largely irrelevant [Zaehner, xiv–xv].

It is from here that the *Bhagavad-Gitā* carries on.

The Bhagavad-Gitā

The *Bhagavad-Gitā,* which is believed to form a part of the great Indian epic *The Mahābhārata* (scholars are of the view that it was composed in the third century A.D. and inserted into the *Mahābhārata*), is the most popular religious text of the Hindus and, along with the *Upanishads* and the *Brahma-Sutra* (of Bādarāyana), is regarded as one of the three essential texts ("*Prasthāna-traya*" or "Basic Trio") that have shaped and guided the Indian consciousness over the centuries. It thus belongs to the "Epic Period" in Indian philosophy. The epic *Mahābhārata* is an account of the origins, the actual course and the consequences of a great war between two royal families, between the five sons of Pāndu (called Pāndavas) and their cousins, the hundred sons of Dhritarāshtra (called Kauravas). The kingdom of the Pāndavas has been usurped by the Kauravas, but the Pāndavas are good enough to be satisfied with only five villages as a token payment for their lost kingdom—an offer which is turned down by the Kauravas, in spite of the intervention of Krishna, the god Vishnu in human form. The great battle is about to begin, with Krishna as the charioteer of Arjuna (the third of the five Pāndava brothers).

The *Bhagavad-Gitā* opens dramatically at the battlefield of Kurukshetra, just before the battle begins, with Arjuna deciding to lay down his arms, having felt revulsion at the thought of war and the large-scale slaughter that it would obviously involve. With a conscience which is troubled, a heart torn with anguish, and with a state of mind which is similar to a little kingdom suffering from a vast insurrection, Arjuna "typifies the struggling individual who feels the burden and the mystery of the world": "He has not yet built within himself a strong centre of spirit from which he can know not only the unreality of his own desires and passions, but also the true status of the world opposing him. The despondency of Arjuna is not the passing mood of a disappointed man, but is the feeling of a void, a sort of deadness felt in the heart, exciting a sense of the unreality of things" (Radhakrishnan, *Indian Philosophy,* 520). Arjuna expresses his agitation and distress before Krishna:

> When I see my own people arrayed and eager for fight, O Krishna, my limbs quail, my mouth goes dry, my body shakes and my hair stands

> on end. The bow Gandiva slips from my hand, and my skin too is burning all over. I am not able to stand steady. My mind is reeling. . . . I do not long for victory, O Krishna, nor kingdom nor pleasures. Of what use is kingdom for us, O Krishna, or enjoyment or even life? Those for whose sake we desire kingdom, enjoyments and pleasures—they stand here in battle, renouncing their lives and riches: teachers, fathers, sons, and also grandfathers; uncles and fathers-in-law, grandsons and brothers-in-law, and other kinsmen. These I would not consent to kill, though killed myself, O Madhusudana (Krishna), even for the kingdom of the three worlds; how much less for the sake of the earth? What pleasure can be ours, O Krishna, after we have slain the sons of Dhritarashtra? Only sin will accrue to us if we kill these criminals. . . . Alas, what a great sin have we resolved to commit by striving to slay our own people through our greed for the pleasures of the kingdom! Far better would it be for me if the sons of Dhritarashtra, with weapons in hand, should slay me in the battle, while I remain unresisting and unarmed.
>
> Having spoken thus on the field of battle, Arjuna sank down on the seat of his chariot, casting away his bow and arrow, his spirit overwhelmed by sorrow [Radhakrishnan and Moore, 104–105].

Krishna is greatly disappointed by his friend's sudden decision and proceeds to tell him why he should and must fight. Thus begins the debate between the two, the dialogue which is *Bhagavad-Gitā*. The entire thing is reported to the blind and kind-hearted Dhritarāshtra by his minister Sanjaya, who "overhears the dialogue by miraculous means" (Zaehner, xv).

Krishna's advice takes into account the problems of action and non-action, of violence and nonviolence, of sin and right action, of being and reality, of the meaninglessness of the body and the untouched immortality of the soul. The *Gitā* is thus a dialogue between the "initiator and the initiate," between the "genius of initiation" (Krishna, who is an Incarnation of the Creator, Preserver, and Destroyer of the universe) and his "archetypal disciple, an Indian Everyman caught on the horns of an ethical dilemma" (Lannoy, 306). Krishna's advice assumes the form of "an exclusive, an aristocratic, doctrine," for "this divine particle of the holy supramundane essence who had descended to earth for the salvation of mankind, was himself a slayer of demons, himself an epic hero," while the noble youth, impotent in despair—he does not know, at this critical hour, what for him would be *dharma* or right conduct—was "the fairest flower of the epic period of Hindu chivalry" (Zimmer, 381).

Krishna here plays a dual role: he is the spiritual adviser to his friend in the allegorical role of a charioteer; he is also the proclaimer to the world and to all mankind of his doctrine of salvation *in* the world through dispassionate, selfless action *(karma-yoga)* and the way of self-surrender and complete devotion *(bhakti)* to the Lord who is identical with the Self *(Ātman)* within all. To his discourses on the pure life, nonviolence, self-surrender and the absence of greed, Arjuna throws the disguised challenge: "Why, then, do you urge me into the battle?" The god "neatly glides away" to the next step in his discourse, leaving the direct question unanswered: "At a critical moment the divine character reveals his true self, shows that he is the creator of all beings and their destroyer as well. He fills the whole universe, heaven, earth, and several underworlds; as destroyer, he has already devoured all members of the mighty hosts about to fight. Arjuna would commit no sin in killing a kinsman dispassionately. So long as one has absolute faith in the absolute god, the ultimate gain of union with that god in life not of this world is assured to him. If Arjuna won the purely formal and symbolic battle, he would have the further joys of universal sovereignty in this world as a bonus" (Kosambi, 207).

D.D. Kosambi writes ironically of Krishna's argument: "This divine but rather scrambled message with its command of expository Sanskrit is characteristically Indian in attempting to reconcile the irreconcilable, in its power of gulping down sharp contradictions painlessly." Many scholars have found Krishna's argument unjust and immoral. It must however be pointed out that Krishna's injunction is not without a context, for the belief that every act must be performed dispassionately and without any anticipation of its fruits forms the basis of Hindu ethics. In the *Gitā* itself we find the lines: "He who resigns his activities to the Universal Self by forsaking attachment to them and their results, remains unstained by evil—just as the lotus leaf remains unstained by water."*

As C.D. Sharma remarks, the *Gitā* attempts to build up a philosophy of action *(karma)* based on knowledge *(Jñāna)* and supported by devotion *(bhakti)* to the Universal One *(Brahman)*. Heinrich Zimmer calls the ultimate message of Gita "applied *bhakti*": "The *bhakta*, the devotee, brings into realization in space and time, as the merely apparent cause, what for the time-and-space-transcending God is beyond the categories of the uneventuated and eventuated, the 'not yet' and the 'already done.' The imperishable Self, the Owner of the perishable bodies, is the supreme director of the harrowing spectacle of Time" (Zimmer, 384). Thus Krishna, the divine proclaimer of the doctrine of the *Bhagavad-Gitā*, offers himself not only as a teacher but also as an essential example, representing as he does the voluntary participation of the Supreme Self in the "mysterious joy and agony of the forms of the manifested world," which, ultimately, are only His own reflection. It is in this that we must find the reason for the popularity of the ethical message of the *Gitā* "in spite of utterly unorganized media of its propagation"—in this "amazingly construed blending between determinism and activism" (Sinari, 218).

It is interesting to note that, at the end of his long discourse, Krishna tells Arjuna: "Do as you please." Those words make the message all the more ambiguous; in fact, ambiguity remains the basic technique of the *Gitā*. The *Gitā* has been called "a religious classic rather than a philosophical treatise" (Radhakrishnan and Moore, 101), but it is also a literary masterpiece. It represents a meditative pause in the sweeping horizontal flow of the narrative of *The Mahābhārata*, a temporary withdrawal from dramatic action into a reflective annotation on the nature of such action.

Before proceeding to discuss the modes of spiritual life as envisaged in

**For a fine critique of* Gitā's *formulation of this ethical doctrine, see Lannoy, 307–308.*

the *Gitā,* we shall linger a while over the concept of *avatāra* or divine Incarnation, for it is the basis of the Hindu faith and the prime reason behind the Indian's acceptance of the ethics of the *Gitā.* Radhakrishnan writes: "The metaphysical idealism of the *Upanishads* is transformed in the *Gitā* into a theistic religion.... The *Gitā,* anxious to adapt the Upanishadic idealism to the daily life of mankind, supports a divine activity and participation in nature. It tries to give us a God who satisfies the whole being of man, a real which exceeds the mere infinite and the mere finite" (Radhakrishnan, *Indian Philosophy,* 539). The *Gitā* reconciles the metaphysical aspect of the supreme soul as the origin and cause of the universe and as all-pervading, indivisible energy with the moral aspect of the divine incarnation as the translation of our "truth of intuition into terms of thought." The exact nature of this transformation of the Supreme/Absolute as impersonal nonactive spirit into the active and personal Lord is intellectually inexplicable, however, although it is intuitively tenable. It must be remembered, however, that both creation and incarnation belong to the world of manifestation and change and *not* to the Absolute. "If the Infinite God is manifested in finite existence throughout time, then Its special manifestation at one given moment and through the assumption of one single human nature is but the free fulfilment of that same movement by which the Divine plenitude freely fulfils itself and inclines towards the finite" (Radhakrishnan, *Bhugavadgitā,* 33).

In the *Gitā* itself Krishna reveals the quality of the divine transformation:

> Though I am unborn, though my Self is changeless, though I am the Divine Lord of all perishable things, nevertheless, residing in my own material nature *(prakrti),* I become a transitory being *(sambhavāmi)* through the magic divine power of playful illusive transformation which produces all phenomena and belongs to my own Self. Whenever there occurs a relaxation or weakening of the principle of duty and a rise of unrighteousness, then I pour Myself forth. For the protection of the just and the destruction of the workers of evil, for the confirmation of virtue and the divine moral order of the universe, I become a transitory being among the perishable creatures in every age of the world.

The Supreme, according to a passage in *The Mahābhārata,* has four forms: one of these inhabits the earth practicing penance; the second watches over the actions of erring humanity; the third participates in all activity that is human; while the fourth is plunged in a thousand-year slumber. Although in His manifested residence on the earth the God is translating only a portion of His endless glory, His presence is nonetheless essential, self-complete and sufficient. "While dwelling in man and nature the Supreme is greater than both. The boundless universe in an endless space and time rests in Him and *not* He in it. The expression of God may change, but in Him is an element which is self-identical, the permanently fixed background for the phenomenal alterations. The diversified existence does not affect His identity" (Radhakrishnan, *Indian Philosophy,* 541; emphasis added).

Radhakrishnan continues: "We are not, therefore, in a position to institute any comparison between the *Gitā* conception of the *Purushottama,* or the whole ['the personalized Supreme *Purusha* or Soul'], and Bergson's theory of an eternal durée, or of the Gita doctrine of *purusha* and *prakrti* [the intelligent soul and the primal matter] with Bergson's conception of life and matter." In the *Gitā,* the immutable character of the Absolute and the endless activity of the personal God *(Isvara)* are subsumed in the conception of *"Purushottama"* or the Supreme Soul. From the strictly religious point of view, however, the *personal* Purushottama – the impartial governor who is always ready to help individual beings in distress – is "higher than the immutable self-existence untouched by the subjective and the objective appearances of the universe": "The impersonal absolute is envisaged as Purushottama for the purposes of religion. The idea of *Purushottama* [literally 'the finest person'] is not a wilful self-deception accepted by the weak heart of man. While the dry light of reason gives us a featureless reality, spiritual intuition reveals to us a God who is both personal and impersonal" (Radhakrishnan, *Indian Philosophy,* 542).

The *Gitā* synthesizes the imperishable self and the changing experience. The supreme spiritual being with inexhaustible energy is *Purushottama,* whereas the same being in a state of eternal rest is *Brahman. Purushottama* is thus *Brahman* in its manifested state – involved in the work of creation, absorbed in the temporal order; but *Purushottama* reconciles the two states of the "manifested" and the "unmanifested," the twin status of change and immutability. The *Gitā* frequently refers to the "manifested aspect" as a creation of Krishna's own mystic power: "The undiscerning ones, not knowing my transcendental and inexhaustible essence, than which nothing is higher, think me, who am unperceived, to have become perceptible." Thus the Absolute's assumption of the status of *Purushottama,* in the last analysis, becomes less than real (except in a theistic sense). "It is therefore wrong to argue that according to the *Gitā* the impersonal self is lower in reality than the personal *Isvara,* though it is true that the *Gitā* considers the conception of a personal God to be more *useful* for *religious* purposes" (Radhakrishnan, *Indian Philosophy,* 544). The concept of *avatāra* or divine incarnation implies a loving and responsible God who is eager to renew the dignity of man by spontaneous self-creation and successive penetration of earthly existence.

Heinrich Zimmer describes the nature of this "descent" and distinguishes it from the Christian idea of Incarnation:

> According to the Hindu view, the entrance of God into the strife of the universe is not a unique, astounding entrance of the transcendental essence into the welter of mundane affairs (as in Christianity, where the Incarnation is regarded as a singular and supreme sacrifice, never to be repeated), but a rhythmical event, conforming to the beat of the world ages. The savior descends as a counterweight to the forces of evil during the course of every cyclic decline of mundane affairs, and his work is accomplished in a spirit of imperturbable indifference.... The savior, the divine hero..., having set things aright by subduing the

> demon forces . . . withdraws from the phenomenal sphere as calmly, solemnly, and willingly as he descended. He never becomes the seeming temporary victim of the demon powers (as did Christ nailed to the Cross) but triumphant in his passage, from beginning to end. The Godhead, in its very aloofness, does not in the least mind assuming temporarily an active role on the phenomenal plane of ever-active Nature [Zimmer, 389–390].

In the *Gitā,* Krishna is such an *avatāra,* ready to reveal to the world the nature and extent of his transcendent power and to show the way towards individual salvation or *nirvāna.*

The question of salvation is inextricably related to the concept of *Māyā* or the Supreme Being's creative power to produce worldly forms. On the human level, the power of thought that produces temporary forms or appearances as against the Supreme or Eternal Reality is called *avidyā* (ignorance). Thus *avidyā* becomes the power of self-manifestation possessed by the Supreme, for though the latter is "birthless" and "relationless," He manifests Himself by His innate power of *ātmāmāyāya.* It is this creative force of *māyā* which is responsible for man's "partial consciousness which loses sight of the reality and lives in the world of phenomena." The world and its changes constitute God's "self-concealment" or *tirodhāna;* they are a part of the larger process of cosmic deception. It must however be borne in mind that this objectivised descent of a minute part of the infinite supramundane essence of the Godhead, does not affect the latter at all; the creation of the world-objects does not in any way diminish the plenitude and ultimately unmanifested *Brahman* any more than "the putting forth of a dream diminishes the substance of our own Unconscious."

Heinrich Zimmer remarks that "the Hindu view and symbolism of the macrocosmic universal *māyā* is based on millenniums of introspection, as a result of which experience the creative processes of the human psyche have been accepted as man's best clues to the powers, activities, and attitudes of the world-creative supramundane Being" (Zimmer, 390–91). Man's dream-activities as well as activities during the waking state—which involve *not* a diminution but an expansion of a sort through their self-delighting mode of self-realization—are a microcosmic counterpart of the creative principle of the universe. "God's *māyā* shapes the universe by taking shape itself, playing through all the transitory figures and bewildering events, and therein it is not the least diminished, but on the contrary only magnified and expanded" (Zimmer, 391). As we shall see in a later chapter, the field of micro-macrocosmic manifestation is characterized in the *Sāmkhya* school in terms of an interplay of the three constituents or qualities *(gunas)* of the Primal Matter *(prakrti);* the *Gitā* accepts this idea, but it assimilates it into the Vedic Brahmanical conception of the Supreme Self. Thus we find Krishna declaring:

> And whatever states of being there may be, be they harmonious *(sāttvika),* passionate *(rajasa),* slothful *(tamasa)*—know thou that they are all from Me alone. I am not in them, they are in Me. Deluded by these threefold modes of nature *(gunas)* this whole world does not recognize Me who am above them and imperishable. This divine *māyā*

> of Mine, consisting of the modes is hard to overcome. But those who take refuge in Me alone cross beyond it [Radhakrishnan, *Bhagavadgitā,* 217, 218).

The image of the divine ferryman bringing the willing devotees to the other shores of the dangerous river of ignorance, is a recurrent image in Indian philosophical literature.

Radhakrishnan distinguishes the six different senses in which the word "māyā" is employed in the *Gitā* and indicates the bearings of the text on these: (1) If the Supreme Reality is totally unaffected by the world-events, then the latter becomes an inexplicable mystery; and the author of the *Gitā* does not use the term *māyā* in this sense, although such a sense is implied in his views. The author of the *Gitā* does not visualize *avidyā*—the ignorance which is both beginningless and unreal—which causes the world-illusion and urges us to concentrate on the outer world to the total exclusion of the creator of that world who is behind it. (2) The personal *Isvara,* who combines within himself the immutability of the *Brahman* and the mutation of becoming, produces mutable matter by his power of *māyā; māyā* is *Isvara*'s energy *(sakti),* his power of self-becoming *(ātma-vibhuti).* (3) Matter and consciousness *(prakrti* and *purusha)* are said to be God's *māyā,* for it is through these two elements of His being that God produces the entire universe. (4) *Māyā* comes to mean, in the course of the text, the lower *prakrti* or Primal Matter, since *purusha* or the Intelligent Cosmic Spirit is said to be the "seed" which the Lord casts into the womb of *prakrti* for the birth of the universe. (5) The delusive character of the manifested world is due to man's inability to pierce through that world and thus see the real: the Divine *māyā* thereby becomes *avidyāmāyā* (*avidyā* = ignorance). For God, however, it is *vidyāmāyā* (*vidyā* = conscious/clear), for He knows all and controls it and seems to be "enveloped in the immense cloak of *māyā.*" Radhakrishnan relates it to its Vedantic extension: "*Māyā* which does not produce *avidyā* is said to be *sāttviki māyā* [*sāttviki* from *sattva,* which here means "clarity"]. When it is polluted, it breeds ignorance or *avidyā.* *Brahman* reflected in the former is *Isvara,* while that reflected in the latter is *jiva* or the individual self." (6) Since the manifested world is only an "effect" of God, who is the cause, and since the cause is always more real than the effect, the world as "effect" is less real than God the "cause." The relative unreality of the world is confirmed by the self-contradictory nature of the process of becoming. There is a struggle of opposites in the world of experience and change, but the real is above all opposites (see Radhakrishnan, *Indian Philosophy,* 546-7, and *Bhagavadgitā,* 42–43).

It is clear from the six shades of the character of *māyā* that the individual self/soul *(jiva)* is a part *(amsa)* of the Supreme Soul. In the *Gitā* Krishna says: "A part of My very Self, an eternal one, becomes a life-monad *(jiva-bhuta)* in the realm of life-monads (*jiva-loka* or the manifested sphere of creation). This draws to itself mind and the five sense forces, which are rooted, and which abide, in the matter of the universe. When this Divine Lord *(Isvara)* thus obtains a body, and when again he steps out of it and departs, he carries these six forces or functions along with him from their abode and goes his way; just as the wind carries scents along with it from their abode.... People deluded by ignorance fail to behold Him whether He steps out of the body or remains within it united with the *gunas* and experiencing the objects of sense; those do behold Him, however, who possess the eye of wisdom." Elsewhere, emphasizing the Lord's universal aspect, Krishna says: "The Lord *(Isvara)* dwells in the region of the heart of all perishable creatures and causes all beings to revolve by His power of *māyā* as if they were mounted on a machine *(yantraruddha)*." Here we find the fundamental metaphysical teaching of the *Gitā:* The Divine Owner of the Body, inhabiting the bodies of all, is "no non-being" and is indestructible *(avināshi)*, eternal *(nitya)*, unborn *(aja)*, undiminishing *(avyaya)*, all-pervasive *(sarva-gata)*, immovable *(achala)*, ancient *(sanātana)*, unmanifest *(avyakta)*, unthinkable *(achintya)*, and immutable *(avikārya)*.

Krishna speaks of himself: "For him who sees all things in me and me in all things, I am not lost nor is he lost to me." In a most dramatic turn in his long course of advice to Arjuna, Krishna shows the latter his "world-vision" or *visva-rupa*—a shattering revelation of his complex identity to a terrified human being who exclaims: "In a vision I have seen what no man has seen before: I rejoice in exultation, and yet my heart trembles with fear.... Show me again thine own human form.... When I see thy gentle human face, Krishna, I return to my own nature, and my heart is at peace." Lannoy writes: "Faced with Krishna as the Terror of Time ['I am come as Time, the waster of the peoples,/ Ready for the hour that ripens to their ruin.'], Arjuna surrenders, becomes the agent of the divine will" (Lannoy, 309). This is the *Gitā*'s climactic moment of the individual's shattering theophanic encounter with Krishna-as-Vishnu acting out his human role as the wise, all-knowing "charioteer."

Zimmer's remarks are pertinent here: "The Supreme Being, according to the Hindu view, is not avid to draw every human creature into his supramundane sphere immediately, through enlightenment, nor even to broadcast to everyone identical and correct notions concerning the nature and function of his divinity. He is not a jealous God. On the contrary, he permits and takes benign delight in all the differing illusions that beset the beclouded mind of *Homo sapiens*.... Though he is himself perfect love, and inclined to all his devotees, no matter what their plane of understanding, he is also, and at the same time, supremely different, absolutely unconcerned; for he is himself possessed of no ego" (Zimmer, 396). And thus we find the following lines in the *Gitā:* "Whatever form any devotee with faith wishes to worship, I, verily, make that faith of his steady and unwavering. He, united to that form by that faith, keeps it worshipfully in mind and thereby gains his desires which, in reality, are satisfied by Me alone. Finite, however, is the fruit gained by these men of little understanding: the worshippers of the gods go to the gods, but My devotees come to Me."

This brings us to the ethics of the *Gitā*. Radhakrishnan synthesizes several *Gitā* passages when he writes:

> The distinctness of particular persons, their finiteness and individuality, are only accidental, and do not represent the underlying truth....

> True freedom means self-transcendence or union with the highest truth through logic, love or life. The end we seek is becoming *Brahman* or touching the eternal, *brahmasamsparsam.* This is the absolute truth.... Man is a complex of reason, will and emotion, and so he seeks the true delight of his being through all these. He can reach the end by a knowledge of the supreme reality, or by love and adoration of the supreme person, or by the subjection of his will to the divine purpose.... The end is the same whichever standpoint we adopt. It is the harmonious efficiency of the several sides of our life by which truth is attained, beauty created and conduct perfected. The *Gitā* is emphatic that no side of conscious life can be excluded. The several aspects reach their fulfilment in the integral divine life [Radhakrishnan, *Indian Philosophy,* 552–553].

The *Gitā* represents a fine synthesis of action *(karma),* devotion *(bhakti)* and knowledge *(jñāna)*—a synthesis which is known by the term *yoga,* which literally means "union" but ultimately refers to that balanced state of the mind which alone can bring one in touch with the Absolute. Thus we find the following description of *Yoga* in the *Gitā:*

> That in which thought is at rest, restrained by the practice of concentration, that in which he beholds the Self through the self and rejoices in the Self; that in which he finds supreme delight, perceived by the intelligence and beyond the reach of the senses, wherein established, he no longer falls away from the truth; that, on gaining which he thinks that there is no greater gain beyond it, wherein established he is not shaken even by the heaviest sorrow; let that be known by the name of *yoga,* this disconnection from union with pain [tr. Radhakrishnan, *Bhagavadgitā,* 200–201].

The *Gitā* offers a comprehensive and flexible mode of discipline or *yoga-sāstra,* which subsumes three submodes, each of which refers to a unique individual application of one's inherent nature. Thus we have *jñāna-yoga* or the way of knowledge, *bhakti-yoga* or the way of devotion, and *karma-yoga* or the way of action. In the *Gitā,* however, the word *yoga* is not used in the technical sense as in Pātānjali's *Yoga-sutra* (see the chapter on "Sāmkhya-Yoga").

The *Gitā*'s treatment of *yoga* is also different from its treatment in the *Upanishads.* The *Kathā Upanishad,* for instance, refers to *yoga* in the sense of sense-control; in the *Gitā* sense-control is only "a preliminary to *yoga* and not itself *yoga*" (Dasgupta, II, 453). In fact, the *Gitā* speaks of two distinct types of spiritual aspirants: the *sāmkhya,* representing the philosophical type, who believes only in the Absolute and relies mainly on self-effort, abstract intellectual analysis, and meditation; and the *yogin,* representing the devotional type, who accepts the Divine Personality, practices loving devotion to Him, serves Him by doing every piece of work in a spirit of total dedication, and depends on Divine Grace alone. The *Gitā* maintains, however, that their ultimate goal is identical, although it warns the *sāmkhya* aspirants about the greater difficulty to be encountered by those who set their minds on the Unmanifest Absolute. The *Gitā* advocates a harmonious combination of knowledge, concentration, action and devotion.

The initial part of Krishna's advice to Arjuna, as Sri Aurobindo points out, is not that of a friend and lover of man but of a guide and teacher who has to remove from Arjuna "his ignorance of his true self and of the nature of the world and of the springs of his own action": "For it is because he acts ignorantly, with a wrong intelligence and therefore a wrong will in these matters, that man is or seems to be bound by his works; otherwise works are no bondage to the free soul" (Sri Aurobindo, *Essays on the Gitā,* 88). Hence, it is the Yoga of Knowledge *(jñāna* or *buddhi)* that is first enjoined on Arjuna. Knowledge or *jñāna* is used here for both the goal of perfection and the way to it, "for the recognition of reality as well as the scheme of spiritual knowledge" (Radhakrishnan, *Bhagavadgitā,* 54)—a fact which should not, however, lead us to regard it as superior to other pathways to perfection. It is quite different from scientific or discursive knowledge, however; that is, from the intellectual apprehension of the details of environmental existence *(vijñāna). Jñāna* is "the integral knowledge of the common foundation of all existence" (Radhakrishnan, *Indian Philosophy,* 555). Sri Aurobindo, who calls it "unified intelligence," describes it as "concentrated, poised, one, homogeneous, directed singly towards the Truth; unity is its characteristic, concentrated fixity is its very being."

The term *buddhi* (Intelligence) is used in the *Gitā* in a sense which is larger than just "mental power of understanding." It refers to "the whole action of the discriminating and deciding mind which determines both the direction and use of our thoughts and the direction and use of our acts; thought, intelligence, judgment, perceptive choice and aim are all included in its functioning: for the characteristic of the unified intelligence is not only concentration of the mind that knows, but especially concentration of the mind that decides and persists in the decision, *vyavasāya,* while the sign of the dissipated intelligence [Sri Aurobindo nearly equates scientific intelligence with "dissipated intelligence"] is not so much even discursiveness of the ideas and perceptions as discursiveness of the aims and desires, therefore of the will" (Sri Aurobindo, *Gitā,* 88, 89).

Scientific or investigative knowledge has to be supplemented by intuitive knowledge; discursive truth is to be combined with spiritual vision: "Knowledge as a sacrifice is greater than any material sacrifice . . . Learn that by humble reverence, by inquiry and by service" (*Gitā,* Chapter IV). Thus the opposite of knowledge or *jñāna* is *ajñāna,* which is not intellectual error but spiritual blindness. In the *Gitā,* Arjuna's "blindness" is removed by the divine sight granted by Krishna, whose "world-vision"/"world-form" *(visvarupa)* is "a poetic exaggeration of the intuitional experience where the individual possessed by God sees all things in Him" (Radhakrishnan, *Indian Philosophy,* 556).

The *Gitā* rejects the old Brahmanical way of elaborate sacrificial rites and offerings in favor of the purely psychic-spiritual ritualism of the "path of knowledge" *(jñāna-mārga).* Krishna assures:

> Even if thou art the most sinful of sinners, yet by the raft of knowledge alone thou shalt go across all wickedness. Just as a fire, come to a full blaze, reduces the fuel to ashes, so does the fire of knowledge reduce

> all kinds of *karma* (the burden of past deeds) to ashes. For there exists in this world nothing so purifying as knowledge. When, in good time, one attains to perfection in *yoga,* one discovers that knowledge oneself, in one's Self.

What Krishna means by *yoga* here is not external asceticism or the physical renunciation of the objects of sense, but the self-discipline that is attained through a renunciation of desire by a mature, contemplative introversion. The ultimate status of the *yogin* is Brahmic; he *remains* in the *Brahman (brāhmi-sthiti).* Krishna is the lord of *yoga (yogesvara),* the supreme lord of spiritual experience who is ready to help Arjuna—and thus, symbolically, all mankind—to save himself.

Sri Aurobindo's description of the perfect Brahmic status of the *yogin* is worth quoting in this context:

> It is a reversal of the whole view, experience, knowledge, values, seeings of earth-bound creatures. The life of the dualities which is to them their day, their waking, their consciousness, their bright condition of activity and knowledge, is to him a night, a troubled sleep and darkness of the soul; that higher being which is to them a night, a sleep in which all knowledge and will cease, is to the self-mastering sage his waking, his luminous day of true being, knowledge and power. . . . While they are filled with the troubling sense of ego and mind and thine, he is one with the one Self in all and has no "I" or "mine." He acts as others, but he has abandoned all desires and their longings. He attains to the great peace and is not bewildered by the shows of things; he has extinguished his individual ego in the One, lives in that unity and, fixed in that status as his end, can attain to extinction in the *Brahman, Nirvāna,*—not the negative self-annihilation of the Buddhists, but the great immergence of the separate personal self into the vast reality of the one infinite impersonal Existence" [Sri Aurobindo, *Gitā,* 96–97].

The *Gitā* indicates the means for the attainment of *jñāna* or knowledge by emphasizing the qualities of intense faith *(sraddhā)* and sense-control. "It is the knowledge gained through faith that becomes knowledge by experience when *jñāna* dawns on an aspirant" (Swami Tapasyananda, 175). *Sraddhā* here refers to the aspirant's faith in his spiritual teacher and in the scriptures that give him a preliminary idea of what he is after, although, in a larger context, *sraddhā* (faith) is the basis of *bhakti* or devotion, the latter being a relationship of love and trust to a personal God. Thus the *bhakti-mārga* or the "path of devotion" refers to "the law of the right activity of the emotional side of man" and to the "emotional detachment distinct from knowledge or action": "Through it *[bhakti]* we offer our emotional possibilities to the divine" (Radhakrishnan, *Indian Philosophy,* 558).

Bhakti is a mode of dissolution of the individual ego and a means of perceiving the Supreme; it is a compound of intense emotion and intense religious feeling. Although there have been instances of advaitins or non-dualists who have offered the unmanifested Impersonal Reality a sufficiently personal emotional content—by dismissing the Advaitic overemphasis on knowledge as "a damnable heresy or a soul-killing error"—the worship of an abstract Supreme is difficult for ordinary human beings, and therefore, worship of the personal God is recommended for all, "the weak and the lowly, the illiterate and the ignorant." In fact, *bhakti-yoga* is sometimes said to be "greater" than the other two *yogas* (i.e. *jñāna-yoga* and *karma-yoga*), first, because "it is its own fruition, while others are means to some other end," and second, because it is the "dominating factor which effects the unity of these diverse strands of the inner life [i.e. action, concentration, and knowledge]" (Radhakrishnan, *Indian Philosophy,* 559; Swami Tapasyanandra, 177). Swami Tapasyanandra writes: "the special quality of the *Gitā* teachings on the other *yogas* is derived from their blend with its teachings on devotion to the supreme Deity" (177).

Bhakti is derived from the root, *bhaj* or "to serve," and refers to the service of the Lord in terms of a loving attachment to Him. "The distinction between creature and creator is the ontological basis of the religion of *bhakti.* The Eternal One is viewed in the *Bhagavadgitā* not so much as the God of philosophical speculation as the God of grace such as the heart and the soul need and seek, who inspires personal trust and love, reverence and loyal self-surrender" (Radhakrishnan, *Gitā,* 61).

Sri Aurobindo describes the continuity existing between knowledge and *bhakti:*

> In the way proposed by the *Gitā* knowledge is indeed the indispensable foundation, but an integral knowledge. Impersonal integral works are the first indispensable means; but a deep and large love and adoration, to which a relationless Unmanifest, an aloof and immovable *Brahman* can return no answer, since these things ask for a relation and an intimate personal closeness, are the strongest and highest power for release and spiritual perfection and the immortal *Ānanda* [bliss]. The Godhead with whom the soul of man has to enter into this closest oneness, is indeed in his supreme status a transcendent Unthinkable too great for any manifestation . . . but he is at the same time the living supreme Soul of all things. He is the supreme Lord, the Master of works and universal nature. He at once exceeds and inhabits as its self the soul and mind and body of the creature. . . . It is this supreme soul, *Purushottama,* transcendent of the universe, but also its containing spirit, inhabitant and possessor, even as it is mightily figured in the vision of Kurukshetra, into whom the liberated spirit has to enter once it has reached to the vision and knowledge of him in all the principles and powers of his existence, once it is able to grasp and enjoy his multitudinous oneness" [*Gitā,* 383–4].

The liberation envisaged in the *Gitā* is not just a self-oblivious abolition of the soul's personal being in the absorption of the immutable One, but all kinds of union at once. The *Gitā* speaks of a complete unification of the individual soul with the supreme Godhead "in essence of being and intimacy of consciousness and identity of bliss," for the one object of this *yoga* is to *become Brahman (brahmabhuta).* It anticipates an eternal ecstatic dwelling in the highest existence of the Supreme *(sālokya),* an absorption of the liberated soul by its divine Lover *(samipya),* an identity of the soul's liberated nature with the divine nature *(sadrsya mukti),* the perfection of the liberated soul to become even as the Divine *(madbhavam āgatah),* to be one with the Divine in the latter's law of being, its law of work, and its law of nature *(sadharmyam āgatah)*. Thus the forms which *bhakti* takes are contemplation of the Lord's power, wisdom and glorious goodness, constant remembrance of His greatness with a devout heart, "singing His praises with fellow-men"—all of which are converted into the light of knowledge by *nishkāma karma* (desireless action). Thus, to know God is to love Him, and to love God is to know Him. It is God's grace, brought forth by loving self-surrender, that destroys the distinction between *bhakti* and *jñāna* (devotion and knowledge) by bringing both to their common experience of Godhead. "What begins as a quiet prayer, a longing for the sight of the beloved, ends in an irresistible rapture of love and delight" (Radhakrishnan, *Indian Philosophy,* 564).

But, while those who insist on *bhakti* as the ultimate mode of spiritual life speak of a union with the *Purushottama* rather than any immersion in the impersonal *Brahman,* the *Gitā* recognizes devotion to the qualityless and nameless Indefinable *(nirguna bhakti)* as superior to all else, wherein the Absolute becomes the "most ultimate category": "When devotion is perfected, then the individual and his God become suffused into one spiritual ecstasy, and reveal themselves as aspects of one life. Absolute monism is therefore the completion of the dualism with which the devotional consciousness starts" (Radhakrishnan, *Indian Philosophy,* 565).

The third of the three *yogas* that the *Gitā* enunciates is the *karma-yoga* or the *yoga* of action. It relates to the problem with which the *Gitā* began, that is, Arjuna's decision to renounce action, and it remains the basis of Krishna's elaborate advice. Renunciation, however, is meant for those who have succeeded in attaining a certain stage of spiritual progress, and Arjuna has not yet attained it. Further, in refusing to fight, he is also indifferent to his role as warrior *(dharma)* as well as to his duties as expected from those who belong to his caste *(varna)*. But, most important of all, he is going against the law of creation, for the universe itself—the very world process—is dependent on actions, for inertia is death. Throughout the *Gitā* Krishna emphasizes the need for action, the importance of individual and social duties; he speaks of the individual as the divine agent and thus of the nonsignificance of the consequences of particular acts, of the necessity of "acting" in a spirit of absolute detachment. "By thus combining asceticism and activity, the new form of discipline elevates them both. Asceticism thereby becomes much more than self-denial, and activity is freed from all egoistic motives" (Hiriyanna, *Essentials,* 52). Thus the ideal of the *Gitā* (as many Western readers think) is not escapism or asceticism *(naishkarmya),* but positive action carried out in a detached spirit *(nishkāma karma)*.

It must be borne in mind, that when Krishna persuades Arjuna to fight, he is not supporting the validity of warfare as such; war is only the occasion which the teacher-friend exploits to indicate the spirit in which all work (including warfare) will have to be performed. The Mahābhārata war is illustrative rather than normative: "We may be obliged to do painful work but it should be done in a way that does not develop the sense of a separate ego" (Radhakrishnan, *Gitā,* 69). Renunciation refers "not to the act itself but to the frame of mind behind the act" (Radhakrishnan, *Gitā,* 67–68); the *Gitā* teaching stands "not for renunciation *of* action, but renunciation *in* action" (Hiriyanna, *Outlines,* 121). To Arjuna's question, "If you say that the path of understanding is superior to the path of action, why then do you urge me to perform this savage deed?" Krishna replies:

> There is a two-fold way of life, the path of knowledge for men of contemplation and that of works for men of action. Not by abstention from work does a man attain freedom from action; nor by mere renunciation does he attain to his perfection. For none, verily, even for an instant, ever remains doing no work; every one is driven to act by the impulses born of Nature. He who restrains his organs of action but continues to brood over the objects of sense, self-deluded, is said to be a hypocrite, a man of false conduct. But he who controls the senses by the mind and engages, without attachment, the organs of action in the path of work, is superior. Do thou thy allotted deed, for action is superior to inaction, and even the maintenance of the body is not possible without action. Except work done as a sacrifice this world is work-bound. Therefore, O Arjuna, do thy work as a sacrifice, free from attachment.

It is this "work without attachment" or "work as a sacrifice" which furthers the basic principle of the universe, helps it towards completeness and perfection. This, according to Radhakrishnan, is the essential difference between Buddhism and the *Gitā:* "Buddhism no doubt made morality central to the good life, but it did not sufficiently emphasize the relation of moral life to spiritual perfection or the purpose of the universe. In the *Gitā* we are assured that even though we may fail in our efforts, the central divine purpose can never be destroyed" (*Indian Philosophy,* 566–7). Thus, by becoming the instrument of the continuing purpose of God, the individual is only fulfilling his own destiny. The realization of this fulfillment is truly spiritual, for it refers to an inner rebirth, an "upward transference."

The *Gitā*'s solution, writes Sri Aurobindo, is to "rise above our natural being and normal mind, above our intellectual and ethical perplexities into another consciousness with another law of being and therefore another standpoint for our action; where personal desire and personal emotions no longer govern it; where the dualities fall away; where action is no longer our own and where the sense of personal virtue and personal sin is exceeded; where the universal, the impersonal, the divine spirit works out through us its purpose in the world" (*Gitā,* 238–9). This does not involve any inconsistency between the nature of the work and the spirit in which it is to be performed, since the spirit of our action issues from the nature of our being and the inner foundation it has taken while this nature is itself influenced by the trend of our action. "If life and action were entirely illusory . . . if the Spirit had nothing to do with works of life, this would not be so; but the soul in us develops itself by life and works and, not indeed so much the action itself, but the way of our soul's inner force of working determines its relations to the Spirit" (Sri Aurobindo, *Gitā,* 240).

But even though the *Gitā* insists on the performance of one's own duty, it speaks of the necessity of *loka-samgraha* or world-solidarity by repudiating the notion of individual claims and emphasizing the welfare of the world, the maintenance of social order. Krishna warns Arjuna about the meaninglessness of the life of one who does not help to turn the "wheel" of the principle of creation, the "wheel" of righteousness and justice:

> Whatsoever a great man does, the same is done by others as well. Whatsoever standard he sets, the world follows. There is not for me, O Arjuna, any work in the three worlds which has to be done nor anything to be obtained which has not been obtained; yet I am engaged in work. For, if ever I did not engage in work unwearied, men in every way follow my path. If I should cease to work, these worlds would fall in ruin and I should be the creator of disordered life and destroy these people. As the unlearned act from attachment to their work, so should the learned also act, O Arjuna, but without any attachment, with the desire to maintain the world-order [*Gitā,* Ch. III].

The *Gitā* refers to two stages of spiritual growth and to two different disciplines relating to the two stages:

> Work is said to be the means of the sage who wishes to attain to *yoga;* when he has attained to *yoga,* serenity is said to be the means. When one does not get attached to the objects of sense or to works, and has renounced all purposes, then he is said to have attained to *yoga*.... When one has conquered one's lower self and has attained to the calm of self-mastery, his Supreme Self abides ever concentrate, is self-established: he is at peace in cold and heat, in pleasure and pain, in honour and dishonour. The ascetic *(yogi)* whose soul is satisfied with wisdom and knowledge, who is unchanging and master of the senses, to whom a clod, a stone, and a piece of gold are the same, is said to be controlled in *yoga.* He who is equal-minded among friends, companions, and foes, among those who are neutral and impartial, among those who are hateful and related, among saints and sinners, he excels [*Gitā,* Ch. VI, tr. Radhakrishnan].

The advice in favor of selfless activity for the aspirant and serenity for the man of realization, implies that "until the attainment of *yoga,* spiritual progress is positively barred if dedicated action is not practiced, and that pure psychological disciplines are the means to be adopted afterwards for further development" (Swami Tapasyanandra, 178).

The two stages of spiritual growth suggested by the two terms *aruruksha* (wishing to ascend) and *ārudha* (the ascended), along with the respective laws of their development, *karma* (action) and *sama* (serenity), are part of one continuous process. The man of serenity is *not* an idle person enjoying complete worklessness, but one who has immersed himself (like the great sage-king Janaka, whom the *Gitā* cites) in the conservation of the social order *(loka-samgraha).* Krishna counsels: "Thou shouldst do works also with a view to the maintenance of the world." The concept of *loka-samgraha* is in fact raised from its social status to a law of Divine Life itself, transcending all narrow notions of individual spiritual growth, with the example of the ever-active God in his supreme role as the creator, preserver, and annihilator of the universe. As Sri Aurobindo writes, "*Nirvāna* (liberation) is clearly compatible with world-consciousness. For the sages who possess it are conscious of and in intimate relation by works with the Divine in the mutable universe" (*Gitā,* 226).

Since *yoga* is equanimity and indifference to failure and success and thus is attainable only through a freedom from desire for enjoyment and a firm fixing of the mind in the Self, Arjuna is asked to go into the battle in a yogic state and not to identify himself with his actions on the actual-physical plane, for such actions are the creations of the *gunas* (constituent qualities) of Primal Matter *(prakrti)* which must be transcended in order that one may hold oneself aloof as a witness of the doings of *prakrti.* When one acts with this attitude, work loses its binding effect and one sees inaction in action. Such a man, experiencing the eternal calmness of the soul in the very midst of activity, is called a *sthitaprajña* (literally "the uninvolved intellect"). Along with the related concept of *niskāma karma* or desireless action, *sthitaprajña* is believed to be the "most powerful representation of the doctrine of the ethical nonattachment of the enlightened" in the *Gitā.* The *sthitaprajña* is the image of the ontological man "in his most primeval mental condition"—"a recluse in the sanctuary of his own inner domain" (Sinari, 222). In the second chapter of the *Gitā* Krishna describes at length the nature of this integrated man, the perfect sage who has firmly founded wisdom and settled intelligence:

> When a man puts away all the desires of the mind, O Pārtha (Arjuna), and when his spirit is content in itself, then is he called stable in intelligence. He whose mind is untroubled in the midst of sorrows and free from eager desire amid pleasures, he from whom passion, fear, and rage have passed away . . . He who is without affection on any side, who does not rejoice or loathe as he obtains good or evil . . . He who draws away the senses from the objects of sense on every side as a tortoise draws in his limbs into the shell—his intelligence is firmly set in wisdom. The objects of sense turn away from the embodied soul who abstains from feeding on them, but the taste for them remains. Even the taste turns away when the Supreme is seen. Even though a man may ever strive for perfection and be ever so discerning, O Son of Kunti (Arjuna), his impetuous senses will carry off his mind by force. Having brought all the senses under control, he should remain firm in *yoga,* intent on Me; for he, whose senses are under control, his intelligence is firmly set. . . . For the uncontrolled, there is no intelligence; nor for the uncontrolled is there the power of concentration; and for him without concentration, there is no peace; and for the unpeaceful, how can there be happiness? When the mind runs after the roving senses, it carries away the understanding, even as a wind carries away a ship on the waters. Therefore, O Mighty-armed (Arjuna), he whose senses are all withdrawn from their objects—his intelligence is firmly set. What is night for all beings is the time of waking for the disciplined soul; and what is the time of waking for all beings is night for the sage who sees . . . He unto whom all desires enter as waters into the sea, which, though ever being filled, is ever motionless, attains to peace, and not he who hugs his desires. He who abandons all desires and acts free from longing, without any sense of mineness or egotism—he attains to peace. This is the divine state, O Pārtha (Arjuna); having attained

> thereto, one is not again bewildered; fixed in that state at the hour of death, one can attain to the bliss of God [*Gitā,* tr. Radhakrishnan].

As the above passage repeatedly indicates, *sthitaprajña* is one who is unmoved by the pairs of opposites, remaining as he does in a state of perfect translucence and transcendental calmness *(Brāhmi-sthiti),* a state of eternal nonreturn to the world of contingent activities. "In his status of a worldly and social being, a *sthitaprajña* would literally behave as a nonaligned, fully self-controlled and meditative, and active-in-will-but-passive-in-attitude agent" (Sinari, 222). Although his activity is "ordinarily not only unwarranted but also meaningless" in the light of his supreme perfection, he remains active "out of a mysterious anxiety to draw others up to his level": "The goal between what one is and what one should be, or between what one does and what one should do no more prevails in a *sthitaprajña.* Hence he is the most ideal embodiment of free action—action which is not governed even by the unaccomplished goal or desire—the most genuine expression of the supreme self" (Sinari, 223). The *sthitaprajña*'s state of actionlessness should not, however, be confused with "inaction" *(nivrtti);* it is synonymous with a state of desireless action *(niskāma-karma),* a state devoid of phenomenal necessities or volitions. "He must disconnect himself not only from all flexibility of decision, but also from the plausible psychological sense that it is from his choice that his actions issue forth" (Sinari, 225). The *sthitaprajña* has the deeply rooted feeling that he is "fundamentally a mode of the Absolute and that his acts are a means of the self-fulfilment of the Supreme Spirit" (Sinari, 225).

Radhakrishnan (along with many others) is of the view that the *Gitā* is silent about the basis of individuality in the ultimate state; that is, about questions relating to free will and freedom of choice. The several expressions of the final condition (*siddhi* or perfection, *parā-siddhi* or supreme perfection, *param-gatim* or the supreme goal, *padam anāmayam* or the blissful seat, *sāsvatam padam avyayam* or the eternal indestructible abode) are "colourless, and do not tell us whether there is a continuance of individuality in the state of freedom" (Radhakrishnan, *Indian Philosophy,* 576). Radhakrishnan identifies two conflicting views in the *Gitā* about the ultimate state—one which makes the freed soul lose itself in the impersonality of the *Brahman* and thus attain peace, and the other which allows us to possess and enjoy God in a condition beyond suffering, pain and worldly desires. The *Gitā* "insists on the ultimateness of a personal God," which should not, however, lead one to conclude that the *Gitā* view is opposed to the Upanishadic view; the controversy relates only to "a particular application of the general problem whether the absolute *Brahman* or the personal *Purushottama* is the highest reality." According to the *Gitā,* the absolute Brahman reveals itself as the personal Lord. The *Gitā* thus envisages the ultimate reality from a human-subjective point of view.

> Adopting the same standpoint, we may say that the two views of the ultimate state of freedom are the *intuitional* and the intellectual ways of representing the one condition. . . . In the highest reality impersonality, i.e. Brahman as a passive, relationless identity and personality

are combined in a manner that is incomprehensible to us. Even so the freed spirits may have no individuality, and yet have one by self-limitation. It is in this way that the *Gitā* harmonises the ever immobile quietism of the timeless self with the eternal play of the energy of nature [Radhakrishnan, *Indian Philosophy,* 578].

Works Cited

Chaudhuri, Nirad C. *Hinduism: A Religion to Live By*. London: Chatto & Windus, 1979.

Dasgupta, Surendra Nath. *A History of Indian Philosophy*. (5 vols). Vols. I, II. Cambridge, England: Cambridge University Press, 1973.

Frauwallner, Erich. *History of Indian Philosophy*. (2 vols). Vol. I. tr. V.M. Bedekar. New Delhi: Motilal Banarsidass, 1984.

Hiriyanna, M. *The Essentials of Indian Philosophy*. 1949, London: George Allen & Unwin; rpt. Bombay: Blackie & Son, 1978.

________. *Outlines of Indian Philosophy*. 1932, London: George Allen & Unwin; rpt. Bombay: Blackie & Son, 1983.

Hume, Robert Ernest. *The Thirteen Principal Upanishads*. 1921; rpt. New Delhi: Oxford University Press, 1983.

Kosambi, D.D. *The Culture and Civilisation of Ancient India in Historical Outline*. 1970, London: Routledge & Kegan Paul; rpt. New Delhi: Vikas Publishing House, 1981.

Lannoy, Richard. *The Speaking Tree: A Study of Indian Culture and Society*. London and Oxford: Oxford University Press, 1974.

Mahadevan, T.M.P. "The Religio-Philosophic Culture of India," in *The Cultural Heritage of India*. (5 vols). Vol. I. ed. Haridas Bhattacharyya. Calcutta: The Ramakrishna Mission Institute of Culture, 1969.

Radhakrishnan, S. *Indian Philosophy*. (2 vols). Vol. I. Muirhead Library of Philosophy. London: George Allen & Unwin, and New York. Humanities Press, 1966.

________. *The Bhagavadgitā: With an Introductory Essay, Sanskrit Text, English Translation and Notes*. London: George Allen & Unwin, 1948; rpt. Bombay: Blackie & Son, 1977.

Radhakrishnan, S., and Moore, Charles A. eds. *A Sourcebook in Indian Philosophy*. Princeton: Princeton University Press, 1957.

Sen, K.M. *Hinduism*. 1961; rpt. Harmondsworth: Penguin Books, 1982.

Sharma, C.D. *A Critical Survey of Indian Philosophy*. New Delhi: Motilal Banarsidass, 1983.

Sinari, Ramakant A. *The Structure of Indian Thought*. 1970, Springfield, Illinois: Charles C. Thomas; rpt. New Delhi: Oxford University Press, 1984.

Sri Aurobindo. *Essays on the Gitā*. Pondicherry, India: Sri Aurobindo Ashram Press, 1976.

________. *The Upanishads: Texts, Translations and Commentaries*. 1971; rpt. Pondicherry: Sri Aurobindo Ashram Press, 1981.

Swami Sharvananda. "The Vedas and Their Religious Teachings," in *The Cultural Heritage of India*. (5 vols). Vol. I. ed. Haridas Bhattacharyya.

Swami Tapasyananda. "The Religion of the Bhagavad-Gitā," in *The Cultural Heritage of India*. (5 vols). Vol. II. ed. Haridas Bhattacharyya.

Zaehner, R.C. trns. and ed. *Hindu Scriptures*. 1938; rpt. London: J.M. Dent & Sons, 1978.

Zimmer, Heinrich. *Philosophies of India.* ed. Joseph Campbell. London: Routledge & Kegan Paul, 1953.

Suggested Further Reading

Bergaigne, Abel. *Vedic Religion.* tr. V.G. Paranjpe, with an Index by Maurice Bloomfield. New Delhi: Motilal Banarsidass, 1978.

Deutsch, Eliot. tr. *The Bhagavad Gitā.* With interpretive essays. New York: Holt, Rinehart & Winston, 1968.

Edgerton, Franklin. tr. *The Bhagavad Gitā.* With commentary. New York: Harper & Row, 1964.

Keith, A.B. *The Religion and Philosophy of the Veda and Upanishads.* Harvard Oriental Series. Vols. 31 and 32. Cambridge, Mass.: Harvard University Press, 1925.

Parrinder, Geoffrey. *Upanishads, Gitā and Bible: A Comparative Study of Hindu and Christian Scriptures.* New York: Harper & Row, 1972.

———. *Mysticism in the World's Religions.* New York: Oxford University Press, 1976.

Peterson, Peter. tr. *Hymns from the Rigveda.* 1888; rpt. Poona, India: Bhandarkar Oriental Research Institute, 1924.

Ranade, R.D. *A Constructive Survey of Upanishadic Philosophy.* Poona: Oriental Book Agency, 1926.

Swami Nikhilananda. tr. *The Upanishads.* (2 vols). New York: Harper & Row, 1951.

2

Chārvāka and Indian Materialism

There has been a lot of controversy centering around the term, *Chārvāka.* While some historians are of the opinion that there was a person bearing that name, others refer to it as a complex of beliefs which gradually took the form of a philosophical system. We shall not, however, concern ourselves with the controversy. It would be sufficient to say that Chārvāka philosophy originated and later flourished during the period between the Vedas and Upanishads and the time of the Buddha. But even this may not sound sufficient or accurate. Referring to this period, S. Radhakrishnan writes, "It was the era of the Chārvākas as well as of the Buddhists. Sorcery and science, scepticism and faith, license and asceticism were found commingled." It was a period when intuition was being replaced by "inquiry," religion by "philosophy," when "opinion was set against opinion, ideal against ideal." The seeds of this cultural turmoil could be found in the *Rg-Veda,* in which there are references to both free speculation and skepticism.

It was a period when the majority of the people showed their impatience with every kind of formal authority and there was a "wild outbreak of the emotional life long repressed by the discipline of the ceremonial religion." It is also of importance to note that while Upanishadic thought developed spontaneously in the western part of the Gangetic tract, it was much less spontaneous on the eastern side, where it was acquired rather than assimilated, and that, too, not without much debate and discussion. To add to this cultural stress, there was very little stability on the political scene, which was repeatedly inundated by invasions from outside, as well as the greed and lust of the princes ruling at that time. The scene is lucidly presented by S. Radhakrishnan:

> The sense of failure, the failure of state and society, the loss of hope in the world, the diffidence of humanity threw the individual back on his soul and his emotions. . . . The faith of centuries was dissolving like a dream. The hold of authority was loosened and traditional bonds weakened. In the tumult of thought consequent on the disintegration of faith and the declaration of the independence of man, ever so many

> metaphysical fancies and futile speculations were put forward. An age stricken with a growing sense of moral weakness is eager to clutch at any spiritual stay. [Thus] We have the materialists with their insistence on the world of sense, [and] the Buddhists with their valuable psychological teaching and high ethics [Radhakrishnan, *Indian Philosophy,* 272–274].

And so began a period of heterodox schools, beginning with Chārvāka. The Buddhist texts of the period mention several heterodox teachers, like Sanjaya, who repudiated all knowledge of self and confined himself to the problem of the attainment of peace; Ajita, the materialist, who rejected all knowledge received through insight or intuition and described man in terms of the four elements of water, earth, fire and air and which dispersed at death; Purāna Kasyapa, the "indifferentist, who refused to acknowledge moral distinctions" and spoke of "fortuitous origin" *(ahetu-vāda)* and passivity of soul; Gosala, the fatalist, who maintained that man had no power over life or death and believed that all things were living entities *(jivas)* that were going through a process of constant change "determined by their immanent energy till they attained perfection"; and Katyāyana, who spoke of the qualitative distinctness of the six elements of being (earth, water, fire, air, space, and soul), with pleasure and pain as principles of their combination and change.

It may therefore be said that Chārvāka philosophy originated in a social and cultural setting which was far from stable. It was about this time (600–400 B.C.) that the Ionians, the Atomists, and the Sophists flourished in Greece. Although it is doubtful if the Greeks—the Ionians and the Atomists, particularly—exerted any positive and direct influence on the Chārvākas, it is true that the latter shared certain things with these early Greek philosophers. As Dale Riepe writes, "they were both critical of official theology, disposed to treat dogma lightly, presenting uncommonly open minds to speculation concerning epistemology, metaphysics, and ethics. Both were remarkably free from the trammels of the past; both felt it to be a right of the philosopher to look at the universe as a matter of private interest and not as a spokesman for some cherished tradition" (Riepe, 56). Those heretical thinkers who came together to form what we today call Chārvāka school, held that the sacred texts (Vedas, Upanishads, etc.) should be rejected, that there is no supernatural being nor any immortal soul since nothing exists after the body's death, that *Karma* is inoperative and is an illusion, that everything is derived from material elements *(mahābhuta)* which have an inherent force *(svabhāva),* that only direct perception gives true knowledge, and that the aim of life is to get the maximum of pleasure (see Riepe, 56).

Chārvāka was also called *Lokāyata,* which is a combination of the two words, *loka* (the world) and *āyata* (basis or prevalence), and means "that which is prevalent among the common people." As it appears, *lokāyata* has been referred to by historians and philosophers as a technical word also, meaning "the science of disputation, sophistry and casuistry." Similarly, *Chārvāka* can be translated as "sweet-tongued" (from *charv* = to chew or eat, and *vāk* = words). The translated equivalent of the original Sanskrit word points to the general feeling about this philosophy of pleasure and "superficial attractiveness" (Hiriyanna, *Outlines,* 187). The Chārvāka doctrine is well summed up by one of the three characters in the allegorical play by Krsna Misra, called *Prabodha-chandrodaya:* "Lokāyata is always the only sastra; in it only perceptual evidence is authority; the elements are earth, water, fire and air; wealth and enjoyment are the objects of human existence. Matter can think. There is no other world. Death is the end of all" (quoted by Radhakrishnan, *Indian Philosophy,* 278-279).

Chārvāka/Lokāyata Literature

As far as the scholar is concerned, it is quite unfortunate that the original Chārvāka texts, if at all there were any, are no longer extant. What is available today is only the writings of those who sought to refute or ridicule Chārvākas. Thus, Lokāyata or Chārvāka is "preserved for us only in the form of the *purvapaksha,*" that is, as represented by its opponents. The chief among these are Krsna Misra's *Prabodha-chandrodaya* (which we have already quoted from), Mādhavāchārya's *Sarva-darsana-samgraha,* and Samkara's *Sarva-siddhānta-samgraha.* The only exception, as far as an original Chārvāka text is concerned, is perhaps Jayarasi Bhatta's *Tattvopaplava-simgha,* although recent scholars have been disappointed by the actual contents of this text. Its title, which literally means "the lion that throws overboard all categories," was so chosen because the main purpose of the text was "upsetting of all principles" [basically, Vedic and Upanishadic] by showing the impossibility of any valid knowledge or *pramāna* and, consequently, of any view of reality. As Debiprasad Chattopadhyaya says, "it represented the standpoint of extreme scepticism according to which no category—either epistemological or ontological—was possible" (Chattopadhyaya, 186). As a result of this, the view expounded by Jayarasi Bhatta was called *Tattvapaplava-vāda* and *not* materialism. It would therefore be appropriate to say that Jayarasi Bhatta only "carries to its logical end the skeptical tendency of the Chārvāka school" (Sukhlalji Sanghavi and Rasiklal C. Parikh [editors of *Tattvapaplava-simgha*], quoted by Chattopadhyaya, 188).

Apart from these texts, there is one more which is mentioned in connection with Chārvāka or Lokāyata school and is called *Lokāyata-sutra* or *Chārvāka-sutra.* It is generally attributed to one Brihaspati, who is also traditionally regarded as the founder of the school. But, as S.N. Dasgupta writes, "it is difficult to say who this Brhaspati may have been," since there is yet another text, called *Brhaspati-sutra* (a work on political economy), which too is attributed to the same person. Krsna Misra's *Prabodha-chandrodaya,* however, says that the Lokāyata *sutras* were initially formulated by Brihaspati and later handed over to Chārvāka who popularized them through his pupils (see Dasgupta, *History,* III, 531). It would be safe to conclude, though, that Brihaspati, the supposed author of *Lokāyata-*

sāstra, is only a mythical figure who is celebrated in his humanized form by enthusiastic supporters of the system.

Theory of Knowledge

The Chārvākas emphasized that perception was the only source of knowledge, that there was nothing else except what was perceived by the five senses. They rejected the principle of causation, for, according to them, it was not supported by direct sensuous perception. They rejected every other means of valid knowledge, including inference *(anumāna)* and verbal testimony *(sabda),* so that philosophy, which "according to the common Indian view ought to be a discipline of life, ceases here to be even a discipline of the mind" (Hiriyanna, *Outlines,* 189). They maintained that inference was "a mere leap in the dark": "We proceed here from the known to the unknown and there is no certainty in this, though some inferences may turn out to be accidentally true" (Sharma, 42). For the Chārvākas, as long as there is a body untouched by death, there is an entity that can be the enjoyer of experience. Perception is of two kinds, namely, external and internal, the former kind involving the operation of the five senses while the latter involves the operation of the mind. Knowledge results from a contact between an external object and one or more of the five senses, "although further knowledge may be acquired through the processes of the mind operating with the sense knowledge" (Riepe, 60). Ultimately, therefore, all knowledge is derived from the senses. Mādhavāchārya sums up the Chārvākas' end and purpose in life in his *Sarva-darsana-samgraha:*

> The only end of man is enjoyment produced by sensual pleasures. Nor may you say that such cannot be called the end of man as they are always mixed with some kind of pain, because it is our wisdom to enjoy the pure pleasure as far as we can, and to avoid the pain which inevitably accompanies it; just as the man who desires fish takes the fish with their scales and bones, and having taken as many as he wants, desists. . . . It is not therefore for us, through a fear of pain, to reject the pleasure which our nature instinctively recognises as congenial [Radhakrishnan and Moore, *Sourcebook,* 229].

Some 400 years later than the early Chārvākas, the Greek philosopher Lucretius was to say almost the same thing. Lucretius asks: "What must be held to be of greater surety than sense? Will reason . . . avail to speak against the sense, when it is wholly sprung from the senses? For unless they are true, all reason too becomes false." More recently, Charles S. Peirce, the founder of American Pragmatism, once said: "I myself happen, in common with a small but select circle, to be a pragmatist, or 'radical empiricist,' and as such, do not believe in any thing that I do not (as I think) perceive: and I am far from believing the whole of that" (see Riepe, 60). It is thus seen that the Chārvākian pragmatic hedonism, though as old as the Vedas and Upanishads, has had a more or less consistent history.

Inference, according to the Chārvākas, cannot be regarded as a valid means of knowledge, because it must depend upon some universal and necessary relation; it is impossible to attain a knowledge of universals by "a mere multiplication of individual instances obtained by sense perception" (Riepe, 60), for the universal must be shown to exist in instances of unvarying concomitance perceived at all times by the senses. And, since the mind itself depends upon information supplied by the senses, it too cannot offer the required information in order to establish concomitance. In his *Sarvadarsana-samgraha* Mādhavāchārya outlines the Chārvāka argument against inference:

> Those who maintain the authority of inference accept the sign or middle term as the causer of knowledge, which middle term must be found in the minor and be itself invariably connected with the major. Now this invariable connection must be a relation destitute of any condition accepted or disputed; and this connection does not possess its power of causing inference by virtue of its existence, as the eye, &c., are the cause of perception, but by virtue of its being known. What then is the means of this connection's being known?
>
> We will first show that it is not perception. Now perception is held to be of two kinds, external and internal. The former is not the required means; for although it is possible that the actual contact of the senses and the object will produce the knowledge of the particular object thus brought in contact, yet as there can never be such contact in the case of the past or the future, the universal proposition which was to embrace the invariable connection of the middle and major terms in every case becomes impossible to be known. Nor may you maintain that this knowledge of the universal proposition has the general class as its object, because, if so, there might arise a doubt as to the existence of the invariable connection in this particular case [as, for instance, in this particular smoke as implying fire].
>
> Nor is internal perception the means, since you cannot establish that the mind has any power to act independently towards an external object, since all allow that it is dependent on the external senses...
>
> Nor can inference be the means of the knowledge of the universal proposition, since in the case of this inference we should also require another reference to establish it, and so on, and hence would arise the fallacy of an *ad infinitum* retrogression.
>
> Nor can testimony be the means thereof, since we may either allege in reply ... that this is included in the topic of inference; or else we may hold that this fresh proof of testimony is unable to leap over the old barrier that stopped the progress of inference, since it depends itself on the recognition of a sign in the form of the language used in the child's presence by the old man; and, moreover, there is no more reason for our believing on another's word that smoke and fire are invariably connected than for our receiving the *ipse dixit* of Manu, &c. [which, of course, we Chārvākas reject] [Radhakrishnan and Moore, *Sourcebook,* 231–231].

Thus the Chārvākas' reason for refuting inference is that there is insufficient warrant for believing in the truth of the inductive relation *(vyāpti)* or invariable concomitance, which is its basis. The proof of this relation—if at all there was one—depends upon individual observation of facts, and since every kind of observation (including that by direct sensuous perception) is necessarily limited in its scope, it does not warrant any universalization of the conclusion based on it. Although they implicitly agree that observation might be able to include and comprehend all instances under a general norm *in the present,* they speak of still other instances which may lie beyond the present and hence, beyond the possibility of observation and comprehension. Things differ in their power and capacity according to the difference of circumstance, time and place; and thus, since the nature and quality of any particular thing is not constant, it is impossible that "any two entities should be found to agree with each other under all circumstances in all times and in all places."

Further, an identical experience of a large number of cases cannot exhaust the "possibility of a future failure of agreement" (see Dasgupta, 535). S.N. Dasgupta explains the Chārvāka case: "It is not possible to witness all cases of fire and smoke and thus root out all chances of a failure of their agreement, and if that were possible there would be no need of any inference. The Chārvākas do not admit 'universals,' and therefore they do not admit that the concomitance is not between smoke and fire but between smoke-ness *(dhumatva)* and fire-ness *(vahnitva)*" (Dasgupta, 537). As Hiriyanna writes in a quasi-defensive vein:

> "[T]he Indian materialist was aware of the lack of *finality* in reasoned conclusions, because all of them rest implicitly, if not explicitly, on some inductive truth which, though it may be highly probable, is never demonstrably certain.... There is nothing strange about such a view of inferential knowledge. In fact, the Indian materialist is here only upholding a position that is quite familiar to the student of modern logic. To deny inference in any other sense would be absurd, since the denial itself would be a generalized conclusion like those to which he objects on the score of uncertainty" [Hiriyanna, *Essentials,* 57–58].

The Chārvākas brought several other objections against the possibility of a valid inference. They are as follows: (1) impressions made by inferential knowledge are not as vivid *(aspastavat)* as those produced by perception; (2) inference has to depend on other things for the determination of its object; (3) inference has to depend on perceptual statements; (4) inferential cognitions are not directly produced by the objects; (5) inference is not concrete *(avastu-vishayātvat);* (6) inference is often contradicted *(badhyamanatvat);* and (7) there is no proof which may establish that every case of the presence of the reason *(hetu)* should also be a case of the presence of the probandum *(sādhya),* i.e., there is no proof establishing the invariable and unconditional concomitance between the middle and the major terms.

As S.N. Dasgupta points out, from the Jaina point of view, none of the above can be taken as a reason for the invalidity of inference. We may here take up two of the seven reasons mentioned above. In reply to the first objection it may be said that "vividness has never been accepted as a definition of *pramāna* (evidence), and therefore its absence cannot take away the validity of an inference; illusory perceptions of two moons are vivid, but are not on that account regarded as valid." Further, an inference does not always depend on perception, and "even if it did, it utilized its materials only for its own use and nothing more" (Dasgupta, *History,* 537). Although it is true that the Chārvākas admitted perception as the only valid means of knowledge *(pramāna),* "since illusions occurred in perception also, ultimately all *pramānas* were regarded as indeterminate by them" (Dasgupta, *History,* 539).

The Chārvāka epistemology is criticized by various schools and standpoints. The Mādhyamika Buddhists who called themselves Sunyavādins as well as the Advaita Vedāntins also reject the ultimate validity of inference, but there is a gulf of difference between the Chārvāka view and the view of the two later schools. While the Chārvākas accepts perception and rejects all other means of knowledge, the Mādhyamikas (especially, the Sunyavādins) and the Advaitins "reject the ultimate validity of *all means* of knowledge as such including perception, though they insist on the empirical validity of all means of knowledge." This distinction between "ultimate and empirical knowledge is unknown to the Chārvāka." C.D. Sharma therefore concludes: "To accept the validity of perception and, at the same time and from the same standpoint, to reject the validity of inference is a thoughtless self-contradiction" (Sharma, *Survey,* 43). Sharma further criticizes what he calls "the crude Chārvāka position":

> To refuse the validity of inference from the empirical standpoint is to refuse to think and discuss. All thoughts, all discussions, all doctrines, all affirmations and denials, all proofs and disproofs are made possible by inference. The Chārvāka view that perception is valid and inference is invalid is itself a result of inference. The Chārvāka can understand others only through inference and make others understand him only through inference.... Hence the self-refuted Chārvāka position is called sheer nonsense and no system of philosophy. Perception itself ... is often found untrue. We perceive the earth as flat but it is almost round.... Moreover, pure perception in the sense of mere sensation cannot be regarded as a means of knowledge unless conception or thought has arranged into order and has given meaning and significance to the loose threads of sense-data. The Chārvāka cannot support his views without giving reasons which presuppose the validity of inference [Sharma, *Survey,* 43–44].

Hiriyanna had criticized the Chārvākas on the same lines, although he conceded that it was doubtful whether the latter had stated their views so formally as to be refuted in any systematic manner:

> [H]is very attempt to convince others of the correctness of his view would imply a knowledge of their thoughts which, not being directly knowable, could only have been inferred by him. But the probability is that the Chārvāka did neither state his view so formally, nor try to convince others of its rightness, but was content with merely refuting the position of the opponents [Hiriyanna, *Outlines,* 190].

All this criticism is directed at the early Chārvākas, however. Their crude position was later modified by Purandara (? seventh century A.D.), who has been described as "a writer with the Chārvāka views." He is mentioned in the *Panjikā* of Kamalasila the Buddhist philosopher, and in

Pramāna-naya-tattva-loka-lankāra of the Jaina logician, Vadideva Suri (Dasgupta, 536). S.N. Dasgupta sums up Purandara's modified attitude toward the inferential process:

> [He] admits the usefulness of inference in determining the nature of all worldly things where perceptual experience is available; but inference cannot be employed for establishing any dogma regarding the transcendental world, or life after death or the laws of *Karma* which cannot be available to ordinary perceptual experience. The main reason for upholding such a distinction between the validity of inference in our practical life of ordinary experience, and in ascertaining transcending truths beyond experience, lies in this, that an inductive generalization is made by observing a large number of cases of agreement in presence together with agreement in absence, and no cases of agreement in presence can be observed in the transcendent sphere; for even if such spheres existed they could not be perceived by the senses. Thus, since in the supposed supra-sensuous transcendent world no case of a *hetu* [reason] agreeing with the presence of its *sādhya* [probandum] can be observed, no inductive generalization or law of concomitance can be made relating to this sphere.

This certainly was a sensible position, and that this could have been the real position of the Chārvākas is suggested by the Nyāya philosopher Jayanta Bhatta, who in his *Nyāya-manjari* writes of "the more sophisticated ones among the Chārvākas" (he calls them *Susiksita* Chārvākas) who maintained that there were two kinds of inference—one called *utpanna-pratiti* and meant inference about something the knowledge of which already existed, and the other *utpādya-pratiti* and meant inference about something the knowledge of which did not exist [inference concerning God, Soul, After-Life, etc.]. Hiriyanna comments on this: "[I]t is commonly assumed by the critics that the Chārvākas denounced reasoning totally as a *pramāna;* but to judge from the reference to it in one Nyāya treatise [Jayanta Bhatta's *Nyāya-manjari*], they seem to have rejected only such reasoning as was ordinarily thought sufficient by others for establishing the existence of God, of a future life, etc. Such a discrimination in using reason alters the whole complexion of the Chārvāka view." But even while we are beginning to think that the skeptical tendency so fluently attributed to the Chārvākas was unfounded, Hiriyanna hastens to add: "But this is only a stray hint we get about the truth. What we generally have is a caricature" (Hiriyanna, *Outlines,* 188).

Metaphysics

Chārvāka metaphysics, which is a direct consequence of their epistemological position, is "an unqualified materialistic monism" (Riepe, 67). Since sense perception is the only reliable source of knowledge, matter becomes the only reality. The Chārvākas admit the existence of four elements, namely, earth, water, fire, and air; they call these the "ultimate principles." They reject "ether," traditionally accepted by the orthodox systems as the fifth element, on the ground that it cannot be known by perception. These eternal elements, which explain "the development of the world from the protozoon to the philosopher," combine in their atomic state in a certain proportion and according to a certain order to produce an organism.

The Chārvāka regards consciousness as a mere product of matter. It does not "inhere in particles of matter," but when the latter come to be arranged in a specific form, they are fo und to show signs of life. Thus consciousness is inseparable from life; it is always found associated with the body and is destroyed with the body's disintegration. As Mādhavāchārya writes in *Sarva-darsana-samgraha,* from the four original principles or elements alone, "when transformed into the body, intelligence [consciousness] is produced, just as the inebriating power is developed from the mixing of certain ingredients; and when these are destroyed, intelligence at once perishes also.... Therefore the soul is only the body distinguished by the attribute of intelligence, since there is no evidence for any self distinct from the body" (Radhakrishnan and Moore, 229). Consciousness or intelligence is "the result of an emergent and dialectical evolution ... an epi-phenomenon, a by-product of matter" (Sharma, *Survey,* 44). The Chārvāka would say: "Matter secretes mind as liver secretes bile." The soul therefore is nothing other than the conscious living body. Samkara in his *Sarva-siddhānta-samgraha* defines the Chārvāka position with regard to the soul:

> The soul is but the body characterised by the attributes signified in the expressions, "I am stout," "I am youthful," "I am grown up," "I am old," etc. It is not something other than that body.
>
> The consciousness that is found in the modifications of non-intelligent elements [i.e., in organisms formed out of matter] is produced in the manner of the red colour out of the combination of betel, areca-nut and lime.
>
> There is no world other than this; there is no heaven and no hell; the realm of Siva and like regions are invented by stupid imposters of other schools of thought [Radhakrishnan and Moore, 235].

The Chārvāka thus denies soul or *Ātman* as a surviving or transmigrating entity. As Hiriyanna puts it, the Chārvāka "does not deny a conscious or spiritual principle; only he refuses to regard it as ultimate or independent" (Hiriyanna, *Outlines,* 191). It is interesting to note, that although the Vedāntin, Sadānanda, in his *Vedānta-sāstra,* speaks of four different schools of materialism, each identifying the soul with something different from those of the others, all the four schools regard the soul as a product of matter, "a natural phenomenon" (Radhakrishnan, *Indian Philosophy,* 280). One school identifies the soul with the gross body *(sthula sarira),* a second with the senses *(indriya),* a third with the vital breath *(prāna),* and the fourth with the organ of thought *(manas).*

The total and unqualified dependence of consciousness on the physical organism, the Chārvāka argues, is indicated by the former's continuous and uninterrupted association with the latter. Hiriyanna considers the Chārvāka theory "as a rough Indian counterpart of the view that mind is a function of matter." The Chārvāka view, "as it is sometimes set forth, borders upon modern behaviourism" (Hiriyanna, *Outlines,* 191–192). For instance, the Chārvāka regards feeling as directly characterizing the physical body and describes it in terms of bodily expression; but, at the same time, he maintains that what is characteristic of one entity cannot affect another, for then "the cause would be operating where it was not" (Hiriyanna, *Outlines,* 192). D.R. Shastri summarizes the Chārvāka standpoint on body, consciousness (intelligence), sense-organs, mind, and soul:

> The instinctive movements and expressions of new-born babies are as much due to external stimuli "as the opening and closing of the lotus and other flowers at different hours of the day or night, or the movement of iron under the influence of loadstone. In the same way the spontaneous generation of living organisms is frequently observed, as in the case of animalcules which develop in moisture or infusions, or of maggots or other worms which grow in the constituent particles of curds and the like. . . ." It is an indisputable fact that sensations and perceptions can arise only in so far as they are conditioned by a bodily mechanism. But it would not be so, were not the body the receptacle of consciousness. . . . As contraction is the function of muscles, so are thoughts, feelings, etc., the functions of the brain. The mind therefore has no substantial reality of its own; it springs out of the vibrations of the molecules of the brain. When the molecular activity of the brain sinks below a certain level, consciousness disappears and the mind ceases to exist, as for example in sleep. When it rises again above a certain degree, consciousness reappears. The conscious life is not a life of continuity. It is coming out of and sinking again into unconscious elements. The hypothesis of a continuous stream of consciousness is a myth of divines and theologians.

We may here argue that since the body is the supposed agent of all actions, it alone is responsible for their natural consequences; but the Chārvāka is ready to refute this by saying that his system does not accept "the existence of consequences of good and evil actions":

> The particles which form the body are always in a state of flux; and the body which performs an action at one moment does not continue at the next to feel its reaction. . . . [T]he experience of pleasure and pain come by chance.

This is criticized by other schools on the ground that the Chārvāka theory of matter is unable to explain the facts of memory and recognition. They argue that reason demands that memory and the original experience which brings it about, should be "referred to one and the same conscious subject," and that this is possible only when "the subject is fundamentally an unchangeable entity." The Chārvākas put their counter-argument thus:

> The traces left by previous experiences are capable of being transmitted from the material cause to its direct product, an analogous instance being the transference of the odour of musk to the cloth in contact with it [see Shastri, 174–175].

True to their basic theory, the Chārvākas deny past and future births. Except the four ultimate principles or primary elements, there is no reality existing before birth or after death; the mind is only a product of these elements. It cannot therefore be said that, at death, the mind migrates to another body. Minds differ according to the bodies which "hold" them. The Chārvāka rejects the theory that the fetus is endowed with consciousness on the ground that consciousness "presupposes sensation through the sense-organs, all knowledge being posterior to and derived from experience," and the sense-organs do not function in the fetus. Thus, a future existence of an entity that is nonexistent cannot be predicated. Also, as nothing survives death, there is no possibility of any accumulative action *(karma)* being carried over beyond the present, no possibility of any mysterious universal agency (fate or *adrsta*) supervising any sequence of birth, death, and rebirth. As Saṁkara writes in his *Sarva-siddhānta-samgraha,* for the Chārvāka:

> Only the perceived exists; the unperceivable does not exist, by reason of its never having been perceived; even the believers in the invisible never say that the invisible has been perceived.
>
> If the rarely perceived be taken for the unperceived, how can [the Chārvāka asks] they call it the unperceived? How can the ever-unperceived, like things such as the horns of a hare, be an existent?
>
> Others should not here postulate (the existence of) merit and demerit from happiness and misery. A person is happy or miserable through (the laws of) nature; there is no other cause [such as past actions or *karma*].
>
> Who paints the peacocks, or who makes the cuckoos sing? There exists here no cause excepting nature [Radhakrishnan and Moore, 234–235].

Several criticisms have been levelled against the Chārvāka doctrines, especially against their view of consciousness as an inseparable part of the human body. We may begin with C.D. Sharma's refutation of the Chārvāka claim:

> In swoons, fits, epilepsy, dreamless sleep etc. the living body is seen without consciousness. And on the other hand, in dreams, consciousness is seen without the living body. When a dreamer awakes, he disowns the dream-body but owns the dream-consciousness. The dream-objects are sublated in the waking life, but the dream-consciousness is not contradicted even in the waking life.... This proves that consciousness persists through the three stages of waking life, dream life and deep sleep life and is much superior to material body which is its instrument and not the cause.... Moreover, if consciousness is a property of the body, it must be perceived like other material properties, but it is neither smelt nor tasted nor seen nor touched nor heard. Again, if consciousness is a property of the body, then there should be no consciousness of the body, for why should the body, qualified to produce consciousness, itself stand in need of being manifested by consciousness? Further, if it is a property of matter, then like other material properties it should be known by all in the same manner ... But we find that consciousness is intimately private and consciousness of an individual cannot be shared by others. Again, if the existence of the soul surviving death cannot be *demonstrated,* its non-existence too cannot be demonstrated [Sharma, *Survey,* 45].

The next, and more severe, criticism is directed against the Chārvāka's denial of the soul or *Ātman* which, unfortunately for the Chārvāka, occupies an important place in the other Indian systems. The Chārvāka had to contend on the one hand with the Jainas, the Nyāya philosophers, the Sāmkhya philosophers, and the Mimāmsakas, who advocated the theory of a permanent soul, and with the idealistic Mahāyāna Buddhists who believed in a permanent series of conscious states. The school of *Susikshita* Chārvākas, however, acknowledge an entity, "a knowing self," as long as the body is not destroyed, and which remains "as the constant perceiver and enjoyer of all experiences" (Dasgupta, *History,* 540).

The Buddhist argues that there is an *uncreated* but continuous series of states of consciousness which, when placed against a narrower perspective of time (such as 50 years), is called the present, past or future life (It must be pointed out here that the Buddhist too does not believe in any "permanent soul"). Further, if the body was the sole cause of the mind, then deformities of the body (however slight) would have affected the character of the mind; or, minds associated with the large bodies of elephants would be greater than those of human beings. Therefore, if any change in one is not associated with a change in the other, the two cannot be causally related. It can neither be said that the body "with the complete set of senses is the cause of mind," for in that case the loss of any one of those senses would proportionately affect the nature and character of the mind. But this is not true, for when the motor organs are rendered inoperative, the mind may still continue to work with unabated vigor (Dasgupta, 543, citing a line from the Buddhist philosopher Kamalasila's *Panjikā).* Again, if the mind inhered in the body and was of the same stuff as the body, then the mental states should be as perceptible by the visual organ as the body itself.

The mental states, however, can be perceived only by the mind in which they occur, whereas the body can be perceived both by that mind as well as by others; which goes to prove that the two are entirely different from each other. It is the unitary series of conscious states that produces the impression of the identity of the body, which in fact is continually changing. Though the individual consciousnesses are being destroyed every moment, the series remains unitary in its continuity in the past lives, the present life, and the future. Further, if on account of co-existence of body and mind they are claimed to be connected with each other in bonds of causation, then "since body is as much co-existent with mind as mind with body, the mind may as well be said to be the cause of the body": "Co-existence does not prove causation, for co-existence of two things may be due to a third cause. . . . So the co-existence of body and mind does not necessarily mean that the former is the material cause of the latter" (Dasgupta, 543).

The arguments of the Jaina and the Nyāya philosophers are slightly different from those of the Buddhists, for the former (unlike the latter) admit permanent souls. Thus Vidyānandi, in his *Tattvārtha-sloka-vartika,* locates the reason for the soul's not being a product of matter in "the fact of undisputed, unintermittent and universal self-consciousness unlimited by time or space" (Dasgupta, 546). Statements like "I am happy" and "I am sad" which directly refer to the self-perception of the ego do not depend (unlike perceptual statements like "This is red" and "The sky is blue") on any external instruments such as the sense-organs. This self-consciousness is established by itself, for otherwise no doctrine (including the unorthodox doctrine of the Chārvāka) could be asserted; in other words, all assertions are made by the virtue of this self-consciousness. As Dasgupta writes:

> If any consciousness required another consciousness to have itself attested, then that would involve a vicious infinite and the first consciousness would have to be admitted as unconscious. Thus, since the self manifests itself in self-consciousness *(sva-samvedana),* and since the body is perceived through the operation of the senses like all other physical things, the former is entirely different from the latter and cannot be produced by the latter, and because it is eternal it cannot also be manifested by the latter. Again, since consciousness exists even without the senses, and since it may not exist even when there is the body and the senses (as in a dead body), the consciousness cannot be regarded as depending on the body [Dasgupta, 546–547].

As Dasgupta, following Vidyānandi's argument, shows, the self is directly known as different from the body by the testimony of self-consciousness.

Among the Advaita philosophers, Samkara tries to refute the Chārvāka doctrine of soullessness. His argument mainly involves the Chārvāka claim that life-movements, consciousness, memory and the related intellectual functions belong to the body for the simple reason that they are experienced only in the body and not without it. According to Samkara, life-movements and the like do not sometimes exist even when the body exists (as at death), and hence they cannot be products of the body. The fact that the self (or consciousness) is found to reveal itself in terms of a body and thus "uses" the latter as its instrument, does not in any way confirm the view that it is a product of the same. The Chārvākas' complete break with tradition, their unqualified criticism of Hindu orthodoxy, and their appeal to empirical evidence as the basis of their metaphysics, are cogently summed up by Sriharsha in his *Naishadhacharita:*

> The scriptural view that the performance of sacrifices produces wonderful results is directly contradicted by experience, and is as false as the Puranic story of the floating of stones. It is only those who are devoid of wisdom and capacity for work who earn a livelihood by the Vedic sacrifices, or the carrying of three sticks *(tridanda),* or the besmearing of the forehead with ashes. There is no certainty of the purity of castes, for, considering the irrepressible sex-emotions of men and women, it is impossible to say that any particular lineage has been kept pure throughout its history in the many families on its maternal and paternal sides. Men are not particular in keeping themselves pure, and the reason why they are so keen to keep the women in the harem is nothing but jealousy; it is unjustifiable to think that unbridled sex-indulgence brings any sin or that sins bring suffering and virtues happiness in another birth; for who knows what will happen in the other birth when in this life we often see that sinful men prosper and virtuous people suffer? [quoted by Dasgupta, 549].

The passage clearly refers to the Chārvāka's audacious rejection of all the contemporary philosophical and religious beliefs and practices, his passionate defense of those elemental truths which were obscured by ritualistic excesses; but, more importantly, the passage is a testimony to the Chārvāka's acute feeling of desperation and disgust, to his zealous attempt to save man from himself by making him conscious of his worldly rights and privileges. This naturally leads us to a discussion of his basic ethical views.

Ethics

Before proceeding to discuss the Chārvāka ethics, it is important to recall the most significant moment in the *Bhagvadgitā*. On the eve of the great war, when Arjuna suddenly feels depressed and decides not to take up arms against his cousins and elders, Krishna consoles him with words which ultimately imply the utter insignificance of death. But, before delineating the nature of death, Krishna speaks of the things of the present, of material and mundane matters, so that his argument against Arjuna's decision centers on this: "You will attain heaven if you are killed in this battle, and, if you win it, you will enjoy this earth." We might say that Krishna's philosophy is a philosophy of pleasure, for there is the prospect of pleasure in either alternative. The Chārvāka, for whom there is no heaven or hell and for whom paradises could only be on this earth, reduces the two alternatives into one complex and necessary end. Samkara's *Sarva-siddhānta-samgraha* speaks of what has been repeatedly called the Chārvāka's philosophy of hedonism:

> The enjoyment of heaven lies in eating delicious food, keeping company of young women, using fine clothes, perfumes, garlands, sandal paste, etc.
>
> The pain of hell lies in the troubles that arise from enemies, weapons, diseases; while liberation *(moksha)* is death which is the cessation of life-breath.
>
> The wise therefore ought not to take pains on account of that (liberation); it is only the fool who wears himself out by penances, fasts, etc.
>
> Chastity and other such ordinances are laid down by clever weaklings. Gifts of gold and land, the pleasure of invitations to dinner, are devised by indigent people with stomachs lean with hunger.
>
> The construction of temples, houses for water-supply, tanks, wells, resting places, and the like, is praised only by travellers, not by others.
>
> The *Agnihotra* ritual, the three Vedas, the triple staff carried by the priests, the ash-smearing, are the ways of gaining a livelihood for those who are lacking in intellect and energy...
>
> The wise should enjoy the pleasures of this world through the proper visible means of agriculture, keeping cattle, trade, political administration, etc. [Radhakrishnan and Moore, 235].

It is quite obvious that the emphasis is on the individual, rather than any collective, good; consequently, the Chārvāka accepts only two of the four *purushārthas* or traditional human values, namely, attainment of worldly pleasure *(kāma)* and the means of securing it (*artha* = wealth), thus rejecting religious merit *(dharma)* and liberation *(moksha)*. The Chārvāka does not disregard pleasure merely because it is rarely found unmixed with pain. He asks: "Should you cast away the grain because of the husk?" He does not make any qualitative distinction among pleasures, nor does he try to distinguish the pleasures of the body from the pleasures of the mind, but he does seem to (except perhaps, in case of activities relating to trade and agriculture) accept immediately available pleasures rather than any promised ones of the future: "A pigeon today is better than a peacock tomorrow. A certain copper is better than a doubtful gold" (Mallanāga Vatsyāyana's *Kāmasutra,* which is believed to contain some of the highly aphoristic, utility-oriented statements originally contained in the now-lost *Lokāyata-Sutra).*

Dale Riepe writes that the philosophy of the Chārvākas fits "unqualifiedly in the highest level of naturalism," and he supports his thesis by saying that its "epistemological outlook is empirical, its metaphysics materialistic, and its ethics hedonistic." Riepe quotes from the early Greek philosopher, Democritus' *The Canon,* indicating the parallels between the Indian materialists and their Greek counterpart:

> There are two sorts of knowledge, one genuine, one bastard (or "obscure"). To the former belong all the following: sight, hearing, smell, taste, touch.
>
> . . . . .
>
> Pleasure and absence of pleasure are the criteria of what is profitable and what is not.
>
> . . . . .
>
> Men ask in their prayers for health from the gods, but do not know that the power to attain this lies in themselves; and by doing the opposite through lack of control, they themselves become the betrayers of their own health to their desires [Dale Riepe, 77–78].

Like the philosophy of Democritus, the Chārvāka philosophy is "a fanatical effort made to rid the age of the weight of the past that was oppressing it. The removal of dogmatism which it helped to effect was necessary to make room for the great constructive efforts of speculation" (Radhakrishnan, *Indian Philosphy,* 284).

Debiprasad Chattopadhyaya quotes from *History of Indian Literature* by Maurice Winternitz, who observed that "it proved fatal for the development of Indian philosophy that the Upanishads should have been pronounced to be revelations." Chattopadhyaya then offers a defense of Chārvāka-Lokāyata materialism, taking Winternitz's line as the basis of his defense (Chattopadhyaya, 198–199):

> This is true particularly in the sense that it meant a divine sanction for the world-denying idealistic outlook, and as such this became the most serious obstacle to the development of the scientific spirit in Indian philosophy. No less fatal, however, had been the loss of our materialistic texts. This has deprived us of a proper idea of our heritage of scientific thinking and has in consequence given idealism and spiritualism exaggerated importance in Indian philosophy.

The fact, however, remains that the Chārvāka philosophy became increasingly feeble until it lost its independent existence and was absorbed by the rival schools. It remains for the interested scholar to recover its relics and reconstruct the once distorted and now forgotten history of Indian materialism.

Works Cited

Chattopadhyaya, Debiprasad. *Indian Philosophy: A Popular Introduction.* New Delhi: People's Publishing House, 1964.

Dasgupta, S.N. *A History of Indian Philosophy.* Vol. III (5 vols). Cambridge, England: Cambridge University Press, 1973.

Hiriyanna, M. *The Essentials of Indian Philosophy.* 1949, London: George Allen & Unwin; rpt. Bombay: Blackie & Son, 1978.

________. *Outlines of Indian Philosophy.* 1932, London: George Allen & Unwin; rpt. Bombay: Blackie & Son, 1983.

Radhakrishnan, S. *Indian Philosophy.* Vol. I (2 vols). Muirhead Library of Philosophy. London: George Allen & Unwin, and New York: Humanities Press, 1966.

Radhakrishnan, S., and Moore, Charles A. eds. *A Sourcebook in Indian Philosophy.* Princeton, N.J.: Princeton University Press, 1957.

Riepe, Dale. *The Naturalistic Tradition in Indian Thought.* 1961, Seattle: University of Washington Press; rpt. New Delhi: Motilal Banarsidass, 1964.

Sharma, C.D. *A Critical Survey of Indian Philosophy.* New Delhi: Motilal Banarsidass, 1983.

Shastri, D.R. "Materialists, Sceptics, and Agnostics," *The Cultural Heritage of India.* Vol. III (5 vols). ed. Haridas Bhattacharyya. Calcutta: The Ramakrishna Mission Institute of Culture, 1969.

Suggested Further Reading

Barua, B.M. *A History of Pre-Buddhistic Indian Philosophy.* Calcutta: University of Calcutta Press, 1921.

Conger, G.P. "Did India Influence Early Greek Philosophies?" *Philosophy East and West* (East-West Center, University of Hawaii, Honolulu), II (1952).

Mahadevan, R. "The Conception of Personality in Indian Materialism," *The Philosophical Quarterly* (Calcutta), 14 (1938).

Shastri, D.R. *A Short History of Indian Materialism.* Calcutta: Book Company, 1930.

3

Jainism

The word "Jainism" is derived from the root-word "Jina" which, in its literal translation, means "the conqueror" and refers to one who has successfully overcome his passions and desires, a liberated soul who has conquered *karmas* and thereby attained emancipation. The Jainas believe in a line of 24 prophets or *tirthānkaras,* of whom the first was Risabhadeva and the last was Vardhamāna or Mahāvira (who was a contemporary of Buddha and lived in the sixth century B.C.). We find a mention of some of these tirthankaras in some of the earliest scriptures.

The *Yajur-Veda* mentions the names of at least three thirthānkaras—Risabhadeva, Ajitanātha and Arishtanemi; the *Vishnu Purāna* and the *Bhā gavata Purāna* mention the name of Risabhadeva; in the *Mahābhārata* war, the Jaina Neminātha is believed to have led an army on the Pāndava side and is recognized by Jaina tradition as the twenty-second tirthānkara. It is quite likely that Arishtanemi and Neminātha were one, although other Jaina sources mention Arishtanemi as having died 84,000 years before Mahavira's Nirvāna (see Dasgupta, 168).

Pārsvanātha, the twenty-third tirthānkara (i.e., Arishtanemi's successor and Mahāvira's predecessor), is however the only *historical* figure (besides of course Mahāvira), the other tirthānkaras being only mythical or purānic ones. He was born in Vārānasi and died 250 years before Mahāvira's birth, which, according to a Jaina traditional era still current, corresponds to 599 B.C. (Hiralal Jain, 400). According to the orthodox Jaina belief, "the Jaina religion is eternal, and it has been revealed again and again in every one of the endless succeeding periods of the world by innumerable Tirthānkaras" (Dasgupta, 169). We may therefore say that, in the present period, the twenty-fourth and last tirthānkara was Vardhamāna Mahāvira. Thus Mahāvira is *not* the founder of Jainism (as believed by most European scholars and several Indian scholars); he only gave a fresh impetus to and consolidated an already existing philosophy and religion. The list of the tirthānkaras, apart from showing us the mythological nature of the Jains' placing of their prophets in time, has one more interest for the modern scholars in that all of them had had their own totemic emblems (for instance, the elephant, the horse, the bull, the ape). This fact gives us some idea of the nature of the primitive beliefs which form "the subsoil of Jainsim throughout the long history of its survival in the country" (Chattopadhyaya, 132).

Both Jainism and Buddhism were originally "orders of monks outside the pale of Brahmanism," but the two creeds grew independently of each other. It must be admitted, however, that Jainism resembles Buddhism in several aspects, such as in its rejection of the authority of the Vedas and in its refusal to accept any supreme Being, its acceptance of all members of the community, irrespective of their caste, financial status, and religious career; its strict observance of a set of ethical principles; and in its encouragement of a life of renunciation *(pravrajya).* But there are several differences too, the most important of which is the Jaina's recognition of permanent entities like the self and matter; it is by such differences that Jainsim resembles Brāhmanism, justifying E.W. Hopkins' description that it is "a theological mean between Brāhmanism and Buddhism" (quoted by Hiriyanna, *Outlines,* 155).

Jainism has several things in common with Sāmkhya too. Both the philosophies believe in "the eternity of matter and the perpetuity of the world," although while the Sāmkhya ascribes the development of the material world to the two principles of *purusha* and *prakrti* (see discussion under "Sāmkhya-Yoga"), the Jainas trace its origin to primeval nature. Moreover, the Jaina conception of the activity of the soul has more in common with the Vaiseshika-Nyāya theory than with the Sāmkhya view of "the unaffected and inactive nature of the soul" (see Radhakrishnan, *Indian Philosophy,* 292–293). Radhakrishnan tries to view Jainism in the perspective of the Vedas and Upanishads too, and remarks, that since the system is unorthodox (*avaidika* = non-Vedic) and rejects the authority of the Vedas, it is not possible therefore "for it to look upon its own system of thought as a mere revelation by the Jina"; its "claim to acceptance is its accordance with reality." Radhakrishnan further writes:

> In their metaphysics, the Jains accept the Vedic realism, though they do not systematise it in the spirit of the Upanishads. Prakrti is analysed and given an atomic constitution. The purushas cease to be passive spectators, but become active agents. The central features of Jaina philosophy are its realistic classification of being, its theory of knowledge, with its famous doctrines of Syādvāda and Saptabhangi, or seven-fold mode of predication and its ascetic ethics. Here, as in the other systems of Indian thought, practical ethics is wedded to philosophical speculation [Radhakrishnan, 294].

Jainism resembles the system of Purva-Mimāmsa (a *vaidika* or Vedic system, like Sāmkhya and Yoga, Vaiseshika and Nyāya, and Vedānta or Uttara-Mimāmsa: see discussions in the relevant chapters) in emphasizing the potency of *karma* (actions) as the basic principle of *samsāra* (relative or material world), but differs from it in maintaining that there is an omniscient Being or *Sarvajña* who is an ideal for every person to follow, although it does not, as we have said earlier, accept the idea of a supreme God. Jainism also resembles Vedānta in maintaining that every individual being *(Jiva)* is potentially a *Sarvajña* or *Paramātmā* (omniscient, ideal Being).

Hence, although Jainism is a non-Vedic philosophy, it is not for that reason to be considered as an atheistic one, for it believes in a reality which is higher and subtler than the sense-perceived world.

Before we turn to Jaina philosophy and religion, we shall say a few words about its founder, Vardhamāna Mahāvira. He was born in 599 B.C. (some sources however put it at 549 B.C.) in the noble family of Jñata in Kundapura near the ancient city of Vaisāli. He married Yasodā with whom he had a daughter. Soon after the death of his parents, at the age of 32, he decided to leave his family and wander as a naked ascetic. His wandering life lasted for 12 years at the end of which he became a *Jina* (conqueror or victor). This was followed by several years of preaching, first at Rājagriha, and then at Srāvasti and Kausāmbi. When he attained *nirvāna* at Pāva in 527 B.C. (477 B.C., according to some sources), he had left behind him "a not too large but firmly bound community" (Frauwallner, 198)—something which is confirmed by the fact that his creed is still a *living* creed in India. One is always tempted to compare the life of Mahāvira with that of Buddha, and although asceticism and Enlightenment remain their common features, there were large differences too. While Buddha (as we shall see in the next chapter) is generally mild, kind, and affable, Mahāvira is reserved and severe; while Buddha is adjusting and liberal, Mahāvira is sternly ascetic; while Buddha "rejects the self-torture of asceticism as objectionable extravagance" and teaches "the middle way," Mahāvira "affirms the penance and practises it to its extreme severity" (Frauwallner, 198).

While Jainism is "one and undivided as far as its philosophy is concerned"—something which owes much to the well-developed thought-edifice provided by Mahāvira—it split into two sects when it came to redefine the rules and regulations for the monks. Although some sources indicate that the schism occurred sometime in the first century A.D., there are reasons to believe that even during the lifetime of Mahāvira, followers of two different creeds had joined the Order. The two sects are called *Digambaras* ("sky-clad"), who went naked, and *Svetāmbaras* ("white-clad"), who wore white clothes. The Digambaras are of the view that perfect saints such as the Tirthānkaras, live without food and property (including clothes), that a monk who owns property and wears clothes cannot reach *moksha* or *nirvāna* (liberation), and that no woman can reach *moksha*. Further, they disown the canonical works of the Svetāmbaras and assert that these had been lost immediately following Mahāvira's "nirvāna" (death). During the centuries that followed the first schism, further splits occurred among both the main sects, the chief among these being one that renounced idol worship and lay all its emphasis on the scriptural texts. These are called Terapanthis (belonging to the Svetāmbara sect) and Samaiyas (belonging to the Digambara sect). As S.D. Dasgupta points out, there developed in later times as many as 84 different schools of Jainism differing from one another "only in minute details of conduct" (Dasgupta, 170). The fact remains, however, that all these sects are distinguished "not so much by their philosophical views as by their ethical tenets" (Radhakrishnan, 288); as such they have very little interest for the scholar.

The Jains have played a significant role in the cultural history of India. By utilizing the languages of different times prevailing at different places for their religious teaching, the Jains not only consolidated their faith but helped in the development of the Prakrit languages. The *stupas* which they erected in honor of their saints, with their carved pillars, elaborately decorated gateways, and majestic statues, have become an important part of the traditional Indian art and architecture. The statues of Bahubalin, known as Gomatesvara, at Shravanabelagolā and Karkalā in the state of Karnātaka, the huge rock-cut reliefs near Gwālior in the state of Madhya Pradesh, the Hātigumpha cave temples in the state of Orissa, and the marble temples at Mount Ābu in the state of Rājasthan, are some of the finest examples of Jaina architecture.

Literature

According to the Jains there were originally two broad kinds of sacred texts: the 14 *Purvas* and the 11 *Angas*. The Purvas are no longer extant, but the Angas continue to be read and used and as such are the "oldest parts of the existing Jaina canon" (Dasgupta, 171). In addition to these *Angas* ("limbs"), there are 12 *Upāngas* ("auxiliary limbs"), 10 *Prakirnas* (a series of scattered texts), six *Chedasutras* ("punitive texts"), *Nandi* and *Anuyogadvāra,* and four *Mulasutras* (basic texts). Together these 45 texts constitute what is called *siddhāntas* or *āgamas,* all of which were written in the Ardha-Magadhi or Prakrta language. All these texts may be said to belong to the Svetāmbaras. The Digambaras however assert that these original texts are now lost, and that the present works which pass by the old names are spurious (Dasgupta, 171).

A large literature of glosses and commentaries has grown up round the basic canonical texts; and, besides these, there are other texts containing systematic expositions of the Jaina faith in Prakrit and Sanskrit, the oldest of which is Umasvati's *Tattvārthādhigama-Sutra* (first century A.D.). Some of the most important extra-canonical works of the Jainas are: *Viseshāvasyakabhāshya,* the *Tarkavārttika* with the commentary of Sāntyāchāryya, Nemichandra's *Dravya-samgraha,* Siddhasena's *Nyāyāvatāra,* Mallishena's *Syādvāda-manjari,* Haribhadra's *Shaddarsana-samucchaya,* Merutunga's *Shaddarsana-vichāra,* Vidyānanda's *Jainasloka-vārttika,* Gunabhadra's *Ātmānusāsana,* Amitachandra's *Tattvārthasāra,* Anantaviryya's *Parikshā mu-khasutralaghuvritti,* Prabhāchandra's *Prameyakamalamārtanda,* Hemachandra's *Yogasāstra,* and Devasuri's *Pramānanayatattvālokālamkāra.* Several of these works are available in English translation in the series *Sacred Books of the Jains* [the beginning scholar will find Radhakrishnan and Moore's *A Sourcebook in Indian Philosophy* an invaluable guide, which contains excerpts from some of the main texts].

The Jains also possess secular literature of their own, both in Sanskrit and Prakrit languages. There are also several "moral tales" and Jaina plays. The Jaina authors have significantly contributed to the scientific literature of India in its various branches, such as logic, grammar, poetics, and metrics.

Theory of Knowledge

Knowledge, according to the Jains, are of two broad kinds: immediate knowledge *(aporaksha jñāna),* and mediate knowledge *(paroksha jñāna).* These two broad kinds are further divided as follows: Immediate knowledge are of three kinds, namely, *Avadhi, Manahparyāya,* and *Kevala,* while mediate knowledge is of two kinds, namely, *Mati* and *Shruta* (or *Shruti*).

Mati is ordinary cognition and is based on the usual means of sense-perception. It includes remembrance *(smrti)* and recognition *(samjñā* or *pratyabhijñā),* induction based on observation *(tarka),* and deductive reasoning *(anumāna* or *abhinibodha).* Thus *Mati-jñāna* may be of three kinds: perception *(upalabdhi),* memory *(bhāvanā),* and understanding *(upayoga). Shruta* (testimony) refers to the knowledge which is gained through signs, symbols or words. *Shruta-jñāna* is of four kinds: association *(labdhi),* attention *(bhāvanā),* understanding *(upayoga),* and "aspects of the meaning of things" *(naya).* Thus, while *mati-jñāna* gives us "knowledge by acquaintance," *shruta-jñāna* gives us "only knowledge by description." *Avadhi* (classified under "immediate" or *aporaksha* knowledge) is direct knowledge of things removed in time and space, and hence, refers to knowledge by clairvoyance. *Manahparyāya* is direct knowledge of the thoughts of other persons through psychic or telepathic modes of communication. *Kevala* refers to perfect knowledge of all substances, both primary and secondary. As S. Radhakrishnan writes, "It is omniscience unlimited by space, time or object.... This knowledge, which is independent of the senses, which can only be felt and not described, is possible only for purified souls free from bondage" (Radhakrishnan, 295).

It may be pertinent here to point to a unique feature of Jaina epistemology: it is the Jains' belief that even before our senses perceive an object or situation, we already have the knowledge of such object or situation in our souls. "Perception is merely the necessary condition to remove the veil from the knowledge we already innately possess" (Riepe, 83). The removal of the "veil" depends not only on the sense-object contact, but also upon the past ethical decisions or actions *(karma)* of the individual; so that, even if the senses are a necessary condition to some cognitions of the soul, they are not a sufficient condition, "except as one has attained to perfect knowledge *(kevala-jñāna)* in the state of *moksha* [liberation]" (Riepe, 83). Thus, the finite self *(jiva),* having got rid of all karmic particles and free from the bondage of physical existence, attains to the omniscience it potentially has. Dale Riepe compares the Jaina doctrine of omniscience to the Pythagorean-Platonic doctrine of reminiscence, and supports it with a passage from Plato's "Meno," in which Socrates speaks of the omniscience through reminiscence:

> The soul then, as being immortal, and having been born again many times, and having seen all things that there are, whether in this world

> or in the world below, has knowledge of them all . . . for all nature is akin, and the soul has learned all things; there is no difficulty in her eliciting . . . all out of a single recollection. . . (*The Dialogues of Plato,* trans. Benjamin Jowett [New York: Random House, 1937], Vol. I, secn. 81, p. 360, quoted by Riepe, 84–85).

To return to the Jaina classification of knowledge, *mati, shruta,* and *avadhi* are liable to error, but *manahparyāya* and *kevala* are not. The Jains also speak of erroneous knowledge, which can be identified by (1) doubt or *samsaya* (which affects *mati* and *shruta*); (2) mistake or *viparyaya* (which affects *avadhi*); and (3) indifference or *anadhyavasāya* (which might affect *mati, shruta,* and *avadhi*). Thus there are in all, eight kinds of knowledge, of which five are right and three are wrong or erroneous.

According to the Jains, the validity of knowledge consists in the fact that "it is the most direct, immediate, and indispensable means for serving our purposes"; so that, as long as any knowledge "is uncontradicted it should be held as true." False knowledge is "that which represents things in relations in which they do not exist" and consists in "the misrepresentation of objective facts in experience." It therefore follows that true knowledge is that which gives us a faithful representation of its object "as is never afterwards found to be contradicted" (see Dasgupta, 181–183). Thus knowledge, when disclosed directly in association with sense organs, is clear, vivid, and distinct, and is called perceptual or "perceptional" *(pratyaksha);* but when knowledge is acquired through means other than the sense-organs, it is not so clear, vivid, or distinct, and is called nonperceptual or "non-perceptional" *(paroksha).*

S.N. Dasgupta distinguishes the Jaina theory of perception from that of the Buddhists. According to the Jaina theory, perception (the noun-form is also called *pratyaksha*) reveals to us the external objects *as they are* with most of their varied characteristics of color, texture, form, and so on, and that knowledge arises in the soul from within it "as if by removing a veil which had been covering it before." Further, objects are not (as some Buddhists think) mere forms of knowledge but actually existent. The Jains also distinguish (as we have already indicated earlier) the exterior physical sense from its corresponding faculty or power in the soul, which alone deserves to be called "the sense." Thus there are five such cognitive senses. The process of external-internal interaction is explained and illustrated by Dasgupta:

> The process of external perception does not thus involve the exercise of any separate and distinct sense, though the rise of the sense-knowledge in the soul takes place in association with the particular sense-organ such as eye, etc. . . . I look before me and see a rose. . . . The act of looking at the rose means that such a fitness has come into the rose and into myself that the rose is made visible, and the veil over my knowledge of rose is removed. When visual knowledge arises, this happens in association with the eye; I say that I see through the visual sense, whereas in reality experience shows that I have only a knowledge of the visual type (associated with eye). As experience does not reveal the separate senses, it is unwarrantable to assert that they have an

> existence apart from the self. Proceeding in a similar way the Jains discard the separate existence of *manas* (mind-organ) also, for *manas* also is not given in experience, and the hypothesis of its existence is unnecessary, as self alone can serve its purpose [Dasgupta, 184].

The Jaina denial of separate senses is with reference to "admitting them as entities or capacities having a distinct and separate category of existence from the soul." The sense-organs are like "windows for the soul to look out" (Dasgupta, 185). Unlike the Buddhists, for instance, the Jains denied the existence of any indeterminate stage that preceded the final determinate stage of perception; for them, indeterminate sense-materials were not necessary for the development of determinate perceptions, since there was a direct and immediate revelation of objects from within.

From the standpoint of understanding, knowledge may again be divided into two kinds, namely, *pramāna,* or the knowledge of "the thing as it is in itself," and *naya,* or knowledge of a thing in its relation. It may be mentioned here that not every piece of information *(jñāna)* can be said to be *pramāna;* only that piece of information *(jñāna)* is *pramāna* which is arrived at on the evidence of some or the other *pramānas* (instruments or means of knowledge, such perception and inference). *Pramāna* in this sense is a piece of information or any proposition which is either confirmed or confirmable, although the Jaina thinkers have used that term both as a confirmed piece of knowledge and as a method of knowing. Thus, all the five kinds of knowledge mentioned earlier (*mati, shruta,* etc.) would come under *pramāna,* although this view is debatable in the context of extra-sensory and extra-ordinary perceptions.

Umāsvati's *Tattvārthādhigama-Sutra* describes *naya* as "partial knowledge," but partial knowledge here refers to one of the innumerable aspects of a thing. All truth is relative to our specific and individual standpoints, and *naya* refers to any of these standpoints from which we make a statement about a thing; by extension, therefore, *naya* includes any judgment based on this partial knowledge.

Since *naya* relates to the knowledge of an object in one of its aspects at any given moment of cognizing, it is neither *pramāna* (which is knowledge of an object in its entirety) nor a mode of false knowledge. *Naya* must also be distinguished from *nikshepa,* with which it is sometimes confused. Umāsvati's *Sutra* says: "*Nikshepa* is an aspect of the thing itself. *Naya* is a point of view from which we make some statement about the thing.... If we consider the statement merely as such, its point of view is *naya;* if we consider the fact which justifies the point of view it is *nikshepa*" (Radhakrishnan and Moore, 253).

Naya is of seven kinds *(saptabhangi),* of which the first four relate to the objects and meanings and are therefore called *artha-naya* ("meaning/object standpoint"), whereas the last three relate to the word or words by which the object is expressed and are therefore called *shabda-naya* ("word standpoint"). We give below the seven *nayas* in their traditionally accepted order:

1. *Artha-naya:*

i) *Naigama-naya* (figurative-*naya*): It refers to "taking something for granted," to "speaking of a past or future event as a present one," and to "speaking of a thing in hand as a completed fact." From this standpoint, we consider a thing as possessing both universal and particular qualities without attempting to distinguish between those qualities. Hence, it becomes fallacious when the two sets of qualities—the universal and the particular—are regarded as separately real and absolute (as in Vaiseshika-Nyāya). According to Pujyapāda, *naigama-naya* relates to "the purpose or end of a course of activity which is present throughout" and thus tells us of "the general purpose which controls the series of acts and emphasises the teleological character of life" (Radhakrishnan, 299).

ii) *Samgraha-naya* (general- or common-*naya*): This refers to "a class as a whole," to "a class of things denoted by the same word." From this standpoint, we emphasize the universal qualities and ignore the particulars where they are manifested. It becomes fallacious when we take the abstract absolutist position, that is, when we treat the universals alone as absolutely real and reject the particulars as unreal (as in Sāmkhya and Advaita Vedānta, which accept *sāmānya* [universal] and deny *viseshas* [particulars]).

iii) *Vyavahāra-naya* (distributive-*naya*): It refers to dividing or separating "a general term into its classes, orders, kinds and species." It is thus the ordinary or conventional standpoint based on empirical knowledge, when things are considered as concrete particulars with emphasis on their specific features. It becomes fallacious when particulars alone are accepted as real to the total exclusion of universals on the ground that they are unreal (as in Chārvāka materialism).

iv) *Rjusutra-naya* (actual-*naya*): This refers to "the actual condition at a particular instant, and for a long time." This standpoint "overlooks all continuity and identity" (Radhakrishnan, 300) and identifies the real with the momentary. From this standpoint all particulars are "reduced to a series of moments and any given moment is regarded as real" (Sharma, 50). It becomes fallacious when the partial truth residing in any given moment of particularity is mistaken as the whole truth (as in certain schools of Buddhism). S. Radhakrishnan points out its limited nature: "While this *naya* is useful to expose the hollowness of an abstract philosophy of 'being,' it is useless as an ultimate account of truth" (Radhakrishnan, 300; emphasis added).

2. *Shabda-naya:*

v) *Shabda-naya* (descriptive-*naya*): This includes "grammatical correctness and propriety of expression" and means that a word is necessarily related to the meaning it signifies. This standpoint is based on the fact that "a name has the function of calling up to our mind the particular object referred to or implied by the name, whatever it may be, an individual thing, attribute, relation or action," and that each name has its own meaning, and different words may also refer to the same object. It becomes fallacious when one ignores the *relative* nature of the relation between terms and their meanings.

vi) *Samābhiruddha-naya* (specific-*naya*): It refers to the verbal act of "giving a word one fixed meaning out of several which it has had," and thus consists in "attributing different meanings to synonyms according to their derivations" (Bisht, 32). In other words, it is an application of the *shabda-naya* and it "distinguishes terms according to their roots." Thus, "Pankaja" literally means "that which is born of mud" and therefore signifies any of the several things born of mud, but its meaning is traditionally associated with and restricted to "lotus." The standpoint becomes fallacious when one maintains the difference in objects in accordance with the difference in synonyms (e.g. maintaining that "Pankaja" and "lotus" refer to different objects).

vii) *Evambhuta-naya* (active-*naya*): It refers to "restricting a name to the very activity which is connoted by the name." Thus, "Indra" ("one who rains") is so called because he *rains;* "Sakra" ("one who is potent") is so called because he *wields* power. This standpoint becomes fallacious when one refuses to give the object or person its/his usual name when it/he is not active, that is, when it/he is not functioning. The fallacy occurs, for instance, when we refuse to call the thing called "pitcher" by that name when it is not functioning as one, i.e., when it is inactive as far as its legitimate functional meaning is concerned.

The *nayas* are also divided into two broad categories: (1) *dravyārthika,* or from the point of view of substance *(dravya),* and (2) *paryāyārthika,* or from the point of view of modification or condition *(paryāya).* The *dravyārthika-nayas* (also called *dravyanayas*) relate to the permanent nature of things, while *paryāyārthika-nayas* (also called *paryāyanayas*) relate to their conditional and unstable aspects. Thus, we may notice "the manifold qualities and characteristics of anything but view them as unified in the thing" (Dasgupta, 176). Thus when we say "This is a book" we do not consider its specific qualities as being different from it, but rather perceive these qualities as having no separate existence from the "book" itself *(dravyārthika-naya* or *dravyanaya).* But there is also a second way of framing judgments about things, as when we consider "the qualities separately and regard the thing as a mere non-existent fiction" (Dasgupta, 177). Thus we may speak of the various and different qualities of a "book" separately and maintain that these separate qualities alone are perceptible and there is nothing called "a book" apart from these qualities *(paryāyārthika-naya* or *paryāyanaya).*

As the foregoing discussion of *nayas* shows, every standpoint represents only one of the many points of view from which a thing may be looked at and comprehended; consequently, an affirmation from any one point of view is true or right in a limited sense and under limited conditions. It follows from this that "infinite numbers of affirmations may be made of things from infinite points of view" (Dasgupta, 178), and that the "contributions which each standpoint makes are always partial views reached by processes of abstraction" (Radhakrishnan, 302); which is to say that affirmations or judgments according to any standpoint *(naya)* cannot be absolute. Since the truth of every affirmation is relative and conditional, each affirmation, in order that it may not be misunderstood as absolute, should be qualified by the term *syat* ("perhaps"/"may be"); the resulting doctrine is called *Syādvāda* or the *Saptabhangi.* The doctrine is called *Syādvāda,* since it considers all knowledge as only probable and thus emphasizes the indefinite and infinitely complex nature of reality; it is called *Saptabhangi* (*Sapta* = seven, *bhangi* = kinds or ways) because it involves "the use of seven different ways of judgments which affirm and negate, severally and jointly, without self-contradiction, thus discriminating the several qualities of a thing" (Radhakrishnan, 302). It should be pointed out that the Jains are of the view that subject and predicate are "identical from the point of view of substance and different from the point of view of modification" (Radhakrishnan, 302).

Syādvāda, which has been called "the most conspicuous doctrine of Jainism" (Hiriyanna, *Outlines,* 163), is not skepticism (as might be implied by the translation of *Syāt* as "may be," "perhaps," or "probable"), nor agnosticism (as might be implied by the translation of *Syāt* as "somehow," as some scholars have done), but a kind of relativism (where *Syāt* is the Sanskrit equivalent of "relatively speaking"). It views every judgment as relative and rules out categorical or absolute predication as erroneous. Hence, every standpoint *(naya)* in order to become a valid judgment *(pramāna)* must be qualified by "relatively speaking" *(syāt);* to ignore *syāt* is to expose oneself to unwarranted absolutism, which is directly contradicted by experience.

To support their theory of Relativity of Knowledge, the Jainas quote the old story of the six blind men and the elephant. Each of the six blind men describes the whole animal in terms of the part touched by him. Thus the man who touches the ear describes the elephant in terms of a palm-leaf fan; the man feeling the leg describes it in terms of a pillar; the man feeling the trunk describes it in terms of a python; the man who touches the tail describes the animal in terms of a rope; the man feeling its sides describes it as a wall; and the man touching its forehead describes it in terms of a breast. Each of these men is blind to the animal in its entirety and mistakes the part for the whole. The story illustrates the Jaina "anxiety to avoid all dogma in defining the nature of reality" (Hiriyanna, *Outlines,* 163). C.D. Sharms states the Jaina position:

> All judgments are double-edged. Affirmation presupposes negation as much as negation presupposes affirmation. The infinitely complex reality *(ananta-dharmakam vastu)* admits of all opposite predicates from different standpoints. It is real as well as unreal *(sadasadātmakam).* It is universal as well as particular *(vyāvrtyanugamātmakam).* It is permanent as well as momentary *(nityānityasvarupam).* It is one as well as many *(anekamekātmakam).* Viewed

from the point of view of substance, it is real, universal, permanent and one; viewed from the point of view of modes, it is unreal, particular, momentary and many [Sharma, 52].

In order to understand and appreciate the exact significance of *Syād-vāda,* it is necessary, as M. Hiriyanna suggests, to know the conditions under which it was formulated. It should be discussed in the context of two opposite views, both of which are found in the Upanishads: first, that Being alone is true, and second, that non-Being is the ultimate truth *(Chhāndogya Upanishad).* Both these views, according to Jainism, are only partially true and "each becomes a dogma as soon as it is understood to represent the *whole* truth about reality" (Hiriyanna, *Outlines,* 164). There are two other views occasionally endorsed by the Upanishads which Jainism thought to be equally dogmatic: i) that, because neither Being nor non-Being is the whole truth, reality must be characterized by both or neither *(Mundaka Upanishad, Svetāsvatara Upanishad);* and ii) that reality is both "is" and "is not," and neither "is" nor "is not" (thus adding, with a characteristic subtlety, two more alternatives to the well-known ones of "is" and "is not"). The Jains think that reality is so complex *and* precise that any attempt to describe it directly would amount to falsification, although "it is not impossible to make it known through a series of partially true statements without committing ourselves to any one among them exclusively" (Hiriyanna, *Outlines,* 164). Accordingly, the Jains visualize the nature of reality by a seven-fold judgment *(sapta-bhangi),* and since each judgment (also called "steps" or "ways" or "propositions") is relative, they qualify each by the word *syāt.* The seven steps of *Syādvāda*—which may also be called "the seven possible forms of a statement" (Radhakrishnan and Moore, 261)—are as follows:

1. *Syāt asti* (Relatively, a thing is).
2. *Syāt nāsti* (Relatively, it is not).
3. *Syāt asti nāsti* (Relatively, it both is and is not).
4. *Syāt avaktavyah* (Relatively, it is indescribable/inexpressible).
5. *Syāt asti cha avaktavyah* (Relatively, it is and is indescribable/inexpressible).
6. *Syāt nāsti cha avaktavyah* (Relatively, it is not and is indescribable/inexpressible).
7. *Syāt asti cha nāsti cha avaktavyah* (Relatively, it is, is not, and is indescribable/inexpressible).

Of these seven possible forms of a statement, which show seven possible ways of describing a thing or its attributes, the first two are the most important—the statement of simple affirmation about a thing with regard to its own form *(svarupa),* own matter *(svadravya),* own place *(svakshetra),* and own time *(svakāla),* and the statement of simple negation about a thing with regard to other form *(pararupa),* other matter *(paradravya),* other place *(parakshetra),* and other time *(parakāla).* All things are existent as well as non-existent, because a thing is a positive entity in relation to itself, but a negative entity in relation to another. When we combine both these statements of affirmation and negation—affirm the two different standpoints *successively*—we get the third statement or judgment, that a thing in one sense *is* and in another sense *is not* (i.e., in two different senses, a thing is both real and unreal). But if we affirm or deny both existence and nonexistence of a thing *simultaneously*—assert or negate the aspects of being and nonbeing together—we make a statement about its indescribable or inexpressible nature (i.e., either both real and unreal at the same time or neither real nor unreal): this is the fourth statement or judgment. The first three formal points of view combine, together or separately, with the fourth possibility (that of indescribability or unspeakability) to give us the remaining three standpoints. "Thus understood, no absolute affirmation or negation is possible about anything, for the nature of things is too complex to be exhausted in any single definite predication.... [A]ll predications are predications only from a certain point of view" (Radhakrishnan and Moore, 262).

Several non-Jaina schools have criticized *Syādvada* on the ground that it makes contradictory statements about a thing possible. The most severe criticism came from the Buddhists and the Vedāntins. Dharmakirti, the Buddhist philosopher says: "These shameless and naked Jainas make contradictory statements like a mad man" *(Pramāna-vārttika).* Another Buddhist philosopher, Shāntarakshita, compares the Jaina theory to "a mad man's cry" *(Tattva-samgraha).* Among the Vedāntins, Samkara calls *Syādvāda* "the words of a lunatic" *(Sāriraka-Bhāshya),* while Ramanuja writes: "Contradictory attributes such as existence and non-existence cannot at the same time belong to one thing, any more than light and darkness" (Ramanuja's *Bhāshya* on *Vedānta-Sutras).* These criticisms, however, are untenable, for Jainism never says that contradictory attributes belong to the same thing at the same time and in the same sense. All that Jainism implies is that attributes which are "contradictory in the abstract coexist in life and experience," and that it is necessary for us to know a thing clearly and distinctly, "in its self-existence as well as in its relations to other objects" (Radhakrishnan, 304).

Syādvāda is a logical extension of the Jaina metaphysical theory of *Anekāntavāda,* which maintains the manyness of reality [discussed later in this chapter]. Radhakrishnan offers a passionate defense of *Syādvāda:* "Since reality is multiform and ever changing, nothing can be considered to be existing everywhere and at all times and in all ways and places, and it is impossible to pledge ourselves to an inflexible creed" (Radhakrishnan, 304). Thus, Radhakrishnan's defense is, implicitly, also a mild criticism of the absolutist position of the Vedāntins.

The other Vedāntin charge against *Syādvāda* is that no theory can be sustained by mere probability. If all our knowledge concerning reality is relative, the Vedāntin argues, then *Syādvāda* itself is also relative. "To deny this conclusion," writes Hiriyanna, "would be to admit, at least, one absolute truth; and to admit it [i.e., the said conclusion] would leave the doctrine with no settled view of reality, and thus turn it into a variety of scepticism" (Hiriyanna, *Essentials,* 69). Once again, the Vedāntin's criticism is levelled from the standpoint of the Absolute: the fact that all our judgments are relative requires us to presuppose an Absolute which subsumes all the relatives and through which they are manifested. In this connection, we may briefly discuss C.D. Sharma's comments. While he admits that Jainism is right in pointing out the necessarily relative character of all our knowledge and finds its parallels in the Buddhist and the Vedāntic views regarding empirical knowledge, he also offers the following criticism:

> While they [the Buddhists and the Advaita Vedāntins] have made a distinction between the empirical and the absolute ... Jainism has bluntly refused to make any such distinction. It refuses to rise higher than the relative. It has a bias against absolutism and in favour of common sense realistic pluralism. Being wedded to common sense realism and having pinned its faith to seeming pluralism, Jainism has conveniently forgotten the implications of its own logic and has refused to rise above the relative [Sharma, 56].

Sharma further writes:

> The conception of *Kevala-jñāna* or absolute knowledge is a half-hearted confession of Absolutism made by Jainism in spite of its Syādvāda. ... *Kevala-jñāna* ... constitutes the essence of the soul in its pure and undefiled condition. As it is held to be perfect and intuitive omniscience, it is supra-empirical, absolute and transcendental. This is certainly an admission of Absolutism.... The fundamental fallacy of Jainism that the whole truth means only a mathematical sum total of relative truths vitiates their *Kevala-jñāna* also [Sharma, 59–60].

Radhakrishnan's comments are in a similar vein: "In our opinion the Jaina logic leads us to a monistic idealism, and so far as the Jainas shrink from it they are untrue to their own logic.... The theory of relativity cannot be logically sustained without the hypothesis of an absolute.... The Jainas cannot logically support a theory of pluralism" (see Radhakrishnan, 305–308). Hiriyanna, while criticizing on similar lines, does not hesitate to locate the reason for the Jainas' exclusive emphasis on the relative and the conditional:

> The half-hearted character of the Jaina inquiry is reflected in the sevenfold mode of predication *(sapta-bhangi),* which stops at giving us the several partial views together, without attempting to overcome the opposition in them by a proper synthesis. It is all right so far as it cautions us against one-sided conclusions; but it leaves us in the end ... with little more than such one-sided solutions. The reason for it, if it is not prejudice against Absolutism, is the desire to keep close to common beliefs.... The truth is that the primary aim of Jainism is the perfection of the soul, rather than the interpretation of the universe.... As a result we fail to find in it an ultimate solution of the *metaphysical* problem [Hiriyanna, *Outlines,* 173].

The Jaina reply is summed up thus: "The charge of contradiction lies, if at all, at the door of the absolutist, who affirms or denies a statement about a thing from no point of view, as it were, which ... is impossible" (Radhakrishnan and Moore, 262). No theory, epistemological or otherwise, is ultimate and foolproof; and we shall have opportunity to find, while discussing Buddhism and Vedānta, how even their epistemological positions have failed to remain infallible.

Jaina Logic

In the foregoing pages we have already discussed the salient features of Jaina logic. In this section we propose to summarize the views of some of the important Jaina logicians. Needless to say, the reader will find repetition of certain things that have already been discussed, but it is difficult to present a complete picture without repeating ourselves.

It was sometime during the fifth century A.D. that Jaina teachings were for the first time codified in writing. Thereafter, several Jainas of both sects (Svetāmbara and Digambara) seriously devoted themselves to the study of logic and wrote treatises on logic whose rules clashed neither with the religious dogmas of the Brāhmanas nor with those of the Buddhists and Jains. These works, together with those of the Buddhists, contributed to the formation of what S.C. Vidyabhusana calls the Medieval School of Indian Logic. The chief among the Jaina logicians of this period were Siddhasena Divākara, Sāmantabhadra, Mānikya Nandi, Deva Suri, and Gunaratna.

Siddhasena Divākara (hereafter called "Siddhasena") wrote two important treatises on logic: *Nyāyāvatāra* and *Sammatitarka-Sutra.* We shall concentrate on his *Nyāyāvatāra,* which is written in verse-form in Sanskrit and offers an exposition of the doctrines of *Pramāna* (sources of valid knowledge) and *Naya* (the method of comprehending things from particular standpoints). *Pramāna,* which Siddhasena described as "right knowledge which illumines itself as well as other things without any obstruction," is of two kinds: (1) direct right/valid knowledge *(Pratyaksha),* and (2) indirect right/valid knowledge *(Paroksha).* Again, direct valid knowledge is of two kinds: practical *(Vyāvahārika),* or the knowledge acquired by the soul through the five sense-organs *(indriyas)* and the mind *(manas);* and transcendental *(Pāramārthika),* or the infinite knowledge resulting from the soul's enlightenment, also called *Kevala-jñāna* or absolute knowledge. Likewise, indirect valid knowledge is of two kinds: inference *(Anumāna),* and verbal testimony *(Sabda).*

Verbal testimony or *Sabda* is the knowledge imbibed from the statements of "reliable persons" or sources, and as such, includes knowledge derived from the scriptures. When verbal testimony comes from an individual, it is called personal testimony *(Laukika Sabda),* and when it is related to scriptural sources, it is called scriptural testimony *(Sāstraja Sabda).* Siddhasena defines scripture as "that which was first cognised or composed by a competent person, which is not such as to be passed over by others, which is not incompatible with the truths derived from perception, which imparts true instruction and which is profitable to all men and is preventive of the evil path" (Tr. Vidyabhusana, 175).

Inference or *Anumāna* is the correct knowledge of the major term *(Sādhya)* derived through the middle term (*Hetu* = reason, or *Linga* = sign) which is inseparably connected with it. Inference is of two kinds: (1) inference for one's own sake *(Svārtha-anumāna),* and (2) inference for the sake of others *(Parārtha-anumāna).* The first kind of inference is the result of connecting two things after repeated observations of their inseparable character. Thus, a man concludes that fire is always the antecedent of smoke by repeated observations in the kitchen and allied locales, so that when he sees smoke on a hill, he concludes that there must be fire on the hill too. When the same inference is communicated to others in verbal terms, it would be as follows:

1. The *hill* (minor term or *Paksha*) is full of *fire* (major term or *Sādhya*).
2. Because it is full of *smoke* (middle term or *Hetu*).
3. Whatever is full of smoke is full of fire, e.g., a kitchen (example or *Drshtānta*).
4. So is this hill full of smoke (application or *Upanaya*).
5. Therefore this hill is full of fire (conclusion or *Nigamana*).

Here the example *(Drshtānta)* is a familiar case which establishes the connection between the major term (fire) and the middle term (smoke). It is of two kinds: (1) homogeneous or affirmative *(Sādharmya),* as in the argument above, and (2) heterogeneous or negative *(Vaidharmya),* as in "Where there is no fire there is no smoke, as in a *lake,*" where it establishes the connection between the middle term and the major term by contrariety (i.e., by showing that the absence of the major term is attended by the absence of the middle term).

In an inference for the sake of others *(Parārtha-anumāna),* the minor term *(Paksha)* must be explicitly set forth in order that the reasoning may not be misunderstood by the opponent or listener. The fallacy of the minor term *(Pakshābhāsa)* occurs when one attributes to it as a proved fact that which is yet to be proved, or which is incapable of being proved, or when it is opposed to perception and inference, or is inconsistent with public opinion or one's own statement. We give below an example of each of these fallacies (see Vidyabhusana, 177):

1. The jar is corporeal (a conclusion which is yet to be proved to the opponent).
2. Every thing is momentary (a conclusion which, according to the Jainas, is incapable of being proved).
3. The general particular *(sāmānya visesha)* things are without parts, are distinct from each other, and are like themselves alone (a conclusion that is opposed to perception).
4. There is no omniscient being (this, according to the Jainas, is opposed to inference).
5. The sister is to be taken as wife (this is inconsistent with public opinion/scriptural sanction).
6. All things are nonexistent (this is incongruous with one's own statement).

The fallacy of the middle term *(Hetvābhāsa)* arises from doubt, misconception or nonconception about it. It is of three kinds: (1) the Unproved *(Asiddha):* Example: "This is fragrant, because it is a sky-lotus" (here the reason or middle term, sky-lotus, is unreal/nonexistent); (2) the Contradictory *(Viruddha):* Example: "This is fiery, because it is a body of water" (here the reason is opposed to what is to be established); and (3) the Uncertain *(Anaikāntika):* Example: "Sound is eternal, because it is always audible" (here the reason or middle term is uncertain, for the quality of being audible may or may not be a proof of eternality).

The fallacy of example *(Drshtāntābhāsa)* may occur in the homogeneous or heterogeneous form, from a defect in the middle term or reason *(Hetu)* or major term *(Sādhya),* or both, or from some doubt involving them. Fallacies of the homogeneous example *(Sādharmya-drshtāntābhāsa)* are as follows:

> 1. Inference is *invalid* (major term), because it is a *source of knowledge* (middle term), like *perception* (homogeneous example). (Here the example involves a defect in the major term, for perception is not invalid.)
> 2. Perception is *invalid* (major term), because it is a *source of valid knowledge* (middle term), like a *dream* (homogeneous example). (Here the example involves a defect in the middle term, for dream is not a source of valid knowledge.)
> 3. The omniscient being is *not existent* (major term), because he is not *apprehended by the senses* (middle term), like a *jar* (homogeneous example). (Here the example involves a defect in both the major and middle terms, for a jar is both existent and apprehended by the senses.)
> 4. This person is *devoid of passions* (major term), because he is *mortal* (middle term), like the *man in the street* (homogeneous example). (Here the example involves doubt as to the validity of the major term, for it is doubtful whether the "man in the street" is devoid of passions.)
> 5. This person is *mortal* (major term), because he is *full of passions* (middle term), like the *man in the street* (homogeneous example). (Here the example involves doubt as to the validity of the middle term, for it is doubtful whether the man in the street is full of passions.)
> 6. This person is *nonomniscient* (major term), because he is *full of passions* (middle term), like the *man in the street* (homogeneous example). (Here the example involves doubt as to the validity of both the major as well as middle terms, for it is doubtful whether the man in the street is full of passions and nonomniscient.)

Fallacies of the heterogeneous example *(Vaidharmya-drshtāntābhāsa)* are of the following six kinds, and they too involve some defect or doubt involving the major and middle terms:

> 1. Inference is *invalid* (major term), because it is a *source of knowledge* (middle term); whatever is not invalid is not a source of knowledge, as a *dream* (heterogeneous example). (Here the example involves in a heterogeneous form a defect in the major term, for a dream is invalid whereas it has been cited as not so.)
> 2. Perception is *nonreflective* or *nirvikalpa* (major term), because it is a *source of knowledge* (middle term); whatever is reflective or *savikalpa,* is not a source of knowledge, as *inference* (heterogeneous example). (Here the example involves in the heterogeneous form a defect in the middle term, for inference is really a source of knowledge whereas it has been cited as not so.)
> 3. Sound is eternal and *noneternal* (major term), because it is an *existence* (middle term); whatever is not eternal and noneternal is not an existence, as a *jar* (heterogeneous example). (Here the example involves in the heterogeneous form a defect in both the major and middle terms,

for the jar is both [from different standpoints: see *Syādvāda*] eternal and noneternal and an existence.)

4. Kapila is not *omniscient* (major term), because he is not a *propounder of the four noble truths* (middle term); whoever is omniscient is propounder of the four noble truths, as *Buddha* (heterogeneous example). (Here the example involves in the heterogeneous form a doubt as to the validity of the major term, for it is doubtful whether Buddha was omniscient.)

5. This person is *untrustworthy* (major term), because he is *full of passions* (middle term); whoever is trustworthy is not full of passions, as *Buddha* (heterogeneous example). (Here the example involves a doubt as to the validity of the middle term, for it is doubtful whether Buddha was not full of passions.)

6. Kapila is not devoid of *passions* (major term), because he did *not offer his own flesh to the hungry* (middle term); whoever is devoid of passions offers his own flesh to the hungry, as *Buddha* (heterogeneous example). (Here the example involves doubt as to the validity of both the major and middle terms, for it is doubtful whether Buddha was devoid of passions and offered his own flesh to the hungry.)

According to Siddhasena, the immediate purpose of *Pramāna* (valid knowledge) is the removal of ignorance and doubt. Again, while the consequence of transcendental perception *(Pāramārthika Pratyaksha Pramāna)* is bliss and perfect equanimity consisting in salvation or emancipation *(Moksha,* which is the Jaina equivalent of Buddhist *Nirvāna),* that of the other kinds of *Pramāna* is the opportunity they give us to distinguish the desirable from the undesirable.

Parikshā-mukha-sāstra or *Parikshā-mukha-sutra* of Mānikya Nandi, a Digambara author, is another standard work on Jaina logic. There are several things common to Siddhasena's *Nyāyāvatāra* and Mānikya Nandi's *Parikshā-mukha-sāstra* (notwithstanding the fact that the former was a Svetāmbara author), and we shall therefore discuss only those points in Nandi's work which supplemented and extended Siddhasena's views. According to Nandi, *Pramāna* is of two kinds: (1) direct knowledge *(Pratyaksha Pramāna),* which arises through the senses, and (2) indirect knowledge *(Paroksha Pramāna),* which comes through recollection *(Smriti),* recognition *(Pratyabhijñāna),* argumentation *(Tarka* or *Uha),* inference *(Anumāna),* and the scripture *(Āgama).* Further, Mānikya Nandi divides the middle term or reason *(Hetu)* into perceptible *(upalabdhi)* and imperceptible *(anupalabdhi),* each of which may occur in the form of an affirmation *(vidhi)* or a negation *(pratishedha).* The *perceptible* reason in its *affirmative* form admits of six subdivisions according as it is:

i) the pervaded (*vyāpya* [*Note:* When the middle term and the major term exist simultaneously, the former is called *vyāpya* or pervaded/contained, and the latter *vyāpaka* or pervader/container; but if the middle term follows the major term, the former is called *kārya* or effect, and the latter *kārana* or cause]). Example: "Sound is mutable, because it is factitious."

ii) an effect *(kārya):* Example: "This person has got intellect, because there are intellectual functions in him."

iii) a cause *(kārana):* Example: "There is a shadow here, because there is a tree full of leaves."

iv) prior *(purva):* Example: "The Rohini stars will rise because the Krttikās have risen."

v) posterior *(uttara):* Example: "The Bharani stars certainly rose, for the Krittikās have risen."

vi) simultaneous *(sahachara):* Example: "This mango has a particular colour, because it has a particular flavour."

Similarly, the *perceptible* reason in the *negative* form admits of six subdivisions according as it is:

i) the pervaded *(vyāpya):* Example: "There is no cold sensation, because of heat."

ii) an effect *(kārya):* Example: "There is no cold sensation, because of smoke."

iii) a cause *(kārana):* Example: "There is no happiness in this man, because of the betrayal his heart has been subjected to."

iv) prior *(purva):* Example: "The Rohini stars will not rise shortly, for the Revati [only] has risen."

v) posterior *(uttara):* Example: "The Bharani [star] did not rise a moment ago, for the Pushyā has risen."

vi) simultaneous *(sahachara):* Example: "There is no doubt about the existence of the other side of this wall, for this side of it is clearly perceived."

The *imperceptible* reason in the *negative* form admits of seven subdivisions according as it is:

i) identity *(svabhāva):* Example: "There is no jar here, because it is imperceptible."

ii) the pervaded *(vyāpya):* Example: "There is no Simsapa [tree] here, because here there is no tree at all."

iii) an effect *(kārya):* Example: "There is no smouldering fire here, because there is no smoke."

iv) a cause *(kārana):* Example: "There is no smoke here, because there is no fire."

v) prior *(purva):* Example: "The Rohini stars will not rise in a moment, for the Krttikās are not perceptible."

vi) posterior *(uttara):* Example: "The Bharani [star] did not rise a moment ago, for the Krttikās are not perceptible."

vii) simultaneous *(sahachara):* Example: "In this even balance there is no bending upwards, because it is not perceptible."

The *imperceptible* reason in the *affirmative* form, however, may appear in the following three ways only:

i) as an effect *(kārya):* Example: "In this man there is some disease, because there is no healthy movement about him."

ii) as a cause *(kārana):* Example: "This man is sorrowful, because he has no union with his loved ones."

iii) as an identity *(svabhāva):* Example: "There is uncertainty here, because certainty is not discernible."

Unlike Siddhasena, who seems to have accepted "example" *(drshtānta)* as an important part of a syllogistic argument, Mānikya Nandi, like the Svetāmbara logician Deva Suri, finds the example of a superfluous part of an inference, although (again, like Deva Suri) he admits that it is required for the sake of explaining matters to "men of small intellect." According to him, objects of valid knowledge are either general *(sāmānya)* or particular *(visesha)*. The general is of two kinds: (1) homogeneous *(tiryak-sāmānya)*, which includes several individuals of like nature (e.g., the "cow" is a general notion which signifies many individual cows); and (2) heterogeneous *(urddhvatā-sāmānya)*, which includes several individuals or objects of dissimilar nature (e.g., as "gold" is a general notion which might signify an earring, a necklace, a bracelet and so on). The particular is also of two kinds: (1) relating to things *(vyatireka-visesha)*, such as cow, buffalo, horse, elephant, which are four particular things distinguished from one another; and (2) relating to action, such as pleasure or pain, experienced by the soul.

Deva Suri (12th century A.D.), a logician belonging to the Svetāmbara sect, whose *Pramāna-naya-tattvālokālankāra* is also regarded as a representative text on Jaina logic, deals with his subject on the same lines as those of Siddhasena and Mānikya Nandi. His two most important contributions to the subject are the fallacies of *Naya* (which we have already discussed under "Theory of Knowledge") and the method of debate. Discussion *(Vāda)*, according to Suri, consists in assertion and counter-assertion for the sake of establishing a certain proposition by rejecting its opposite. There are four constituents of a council of discussion: they are (1) the disputant or the person who opens the discussion *(Vādi)*; (2) the opponent or respondent *(Prativādi)*; (3) the members *(Sabhya)*; (4) the President *(Sabhā-pati)*.

The duty of the disputant and his opponent consists in supporting their respective sides and opposing the other side by means of proof. The members must be acceptable to both parties in respect of the competence in grasping their respective dogmas; in addition, they should possess a good memory, be sufficiently learned so as to be impartial in their views, and should possess genius and patience. Their duties consist in "stating the assertions and replies of the disputant and his opponent with reference to the particular subject of discussion, in estimating the merits and demerits of their arguments and counterarguments, in occasionally interrupting them for setting forth some established conclusions, and in, as far as possible, declaring the result of the discussion" (Vidyabhusana, 204). The President must be endowed with wisdom, authority, forbearance and impartiality, and should be able to judge the speeches of the parties and the members and to prevent any possible quarrel that may result from an extended and vigorous debate. Deva Suri writes: "In the event of the parties being desirous of victory alone, they may continue the discussion with vigour as long as the *members* wish; but if they are eager to ascertain the truth alone, they may continue the discussion as long as the truth is not ascertained and so long as they retain their vigour" (Vidyabhusana, 205).

As we said at the beginning of this section, the basics of Jaina logic did not clash with those of the Brāhmanas and the Buddhists. In their social practices, the Brāhmanas did not differ very much from the Jainas, and therefore their attack on the Jaina logic was much less hostile than their attack on the Buddhist logic. In fact, we find several parallels in the terms used by the Jainas and the Brāhmanas. Several Jaina logicians quoted from Brāhmanic texts in a more or less academic spirit; and, although the Jaina doctrines of *Naya* and *Syādvāda/Sapta-bhangi* were occasionally criticized by the Brāhmanas, these criticisms were academic rather than dogmatic. As far as the Buddhists were concerned, Jaina logic did not differ much from Buddhist logic. In fact, as Vidyabhusana writes, there was some kind of intersupplementation between the Jaina and the Buddhist texts: in his *Tattva-samgraha,* the Buddhist author Sāntarakshita makes an extended inquiry into the Jaina doctrine of soul; and in his *Saddarsana-samucchaya,* the Jaina author Haribhadra Suri attempts a complete summary of the Buddhist philosophy. Further, Jaina logic has never been the sole property of the monks, for Mahāvira created his Order in a way which distributed authority equally between the monks and nuns on the one hand, and the lay people on the other. These are some of the reasons why Jaina logic is still active and relevant, while Buddhist logic has almost been absorbed into the Brāhmanic.

Metaphysics

The Jains divide all things into two uncreated, everlasting, and independent categories, namely *jiva* and *ajiva. Jiva* is variously translated and referred to as "spirit," "the conscious," "the animate," and "the living," while *ajiva,* similarly, is taken to mean "matter," "the nonspirit," "the unconscious," "the inanimate," and "the nonliving." The distinction clearly indicates the realistic-relativistic character of Jaina metaphysics. According to Jainism, "the subject that knows" exists to the same extent as "the object that is known." It must be pointed out, however, that by "spirit" Jainism means only the individual self and not, as in the Upanishads, the supreme soul. For, even though Jainism speaks of even material entities having their own souls, it does not believe in any universal spirit or God "in the common acceptation of that term" (Hiriyanna, *Essentials,* 61). Hiralal Jain, a Jaina himself, tries to describe the Jaina philosophy in one sentence:

> The living and the non-living [*jiva* and *ajiva*], by coming into contact with each other, forge certain energies which bring about birth, death, and various experiences of life; this process could be stopped, and the energies already forged destroyed, by a course of discipline leading to salvation [Hiralal Jain, 403].

On a close examination, we come to know the seven propositions that Hiralal Jain's brief description involves: (1) there is something called the living; (2) there is something called the nonliving; (3) the two come into contact with each other; (4) the contact leads to the production of certain energies; (5) the process of contact could be stopped; (6) the existing energies could also be exhausted; and (7) salvation could be achieved. These seven propositions are called the seven *tattvas* or realities, of which the first two – that there is a *jiva* or soul, and that there is an *ajiva* or nonsoul – "exhaust between them all that exists in the universe" (Jain, 403).

As Hiriyanna writes, the Jaina notion of *jiva* "in general corresponds to that of *ātman* or *purusha* of the other schools of Indian thought," but as the etymology of the word implies ["what lives or is animate"], "the concept seems to have been arrived at first by observing the characteristics of life and not through the search after a metaphysical principle underlying individual existence." In its original significance, therefore, the word stands for "the vital breath than for the soul" (Hiriyanna, *Outlines,* 157). It is described as "an eternal substance *(dravya)* of limited, but variable, magnitude," and thus is capable of "adjusting its size to the dimensions of the physical body in which it happens to be housed for the time being" (Hiriyanna, *Essentials,* 61).

Every *jiva* is "a composite of body and soul, of which the soul is the active partner, while the body is the inactive passive one" (Radhakrishnan, 309). Thus, by implication, the soul, by itself, is imperceptible, and manifests itself in terms of its distinctive qualities in a material body. Its chief characteristic is consciousness, which is accompanied by sense-activity, respiration, and a certain period of residence in a particular body. In its pure state, the soul is possessed of infinite perception *(ananta-darsana),* infinite knowledge *(ananta-jñāna),* infinite bliss *(ananta-sukha),* and infinite power *(ananta-virya).* [Note: The Jainas distinguish between *darsana* and *jñāna,* and refer to the former as "the knowledge of things without their details" ("This is a shirt") and to the latter as "the knowledge of details" ("This is a shirt made from cotton, and handwoven, and belongs to . . ."). Thus *darsana* always precedes *jñāna,* but the pure souls possess both—the infinite general perception of things as well as infinite knowledge of all things in all their details.] Generally however, with the exception of a few liberated pure souls *(mukta-jiva),* all the other souls *(jivas)* have their quality of the infinite covered with a thin shroud of kārmic matter accumulated from "beginningless time."

These *jivas* (souls) are infinite in number, eternal, and occupy innumerable space-points in our finite, mundane world *(lokākāsa).* They are limited in size, and are neither all-pervasive nor atomic, although they are believed to have an ability to expand and contract according as they occupy an elephant-body or an ant-body. In their material, empirical form, the *jivas* are classified according to the number of sense-organs they possess—a classification which implies a graduated level of their development (i.e., the more the number of senses, the higher the level of the soul's development). Thus the lowest class consists of plants, which possess only the sense of touch; in contrast, the vertebrates possess all the five senses and are therefore placed at the top of the conventional Jaina ladder of development. But some animals, like men, denizens of hell, and the gods, possess (in addition to the usual five sense-organs) an inner sense-organ called *manas* (which in other schools of Indian philosophy refers to the mind) by virtue of which they are called rational *(samjñin);* the lower animals are devoid of *manas* and hence, of reason, and are therefore called nonrational *(asamjñin).*

The whole universe, the Jainas say, is filled with minute, invisible beings called *nigodas,* which are group-souls—infinite number of souls forming small clusters—possessing the characteristics of respiration and nutrition and experiencing extreme pains. They inhabit the entire world, including the bodies of men and animals. They are slowly evolving clusters and serve as a source for a regular furnishing of souls to replace those that pass out of the cycle of birth and death by attaining *moksha.* As Dasgupta writes, "an infinitesimally small fraction of a single *nigoda*" is sufficient to fill in the vacancy caused in the world by "the Nirvana of all the souls that have been liberated from beginningless past to the present," which implies that the world *(samsāra)* will never be empty of living beings. Those of the soul-clusters/group-souls who "long for development come out and continue their course of progress through successive stages" (Dasgupta, 190).

We have already said that the cause of the soul's material embodiment is the kārmic matter which the soul accumulates over a period of time and which obscures the soul's natural state of perfection. The kārmic matter is of different kinds and they obscure different aspects of the soul's purity: (1) those which obscure right knowledge of details *(jñāna)* are called *jñāna-varaniya;* (2) those which obscure right perception *(darshana)* are called *darshana-varaniya;* (3) those which obscure the beatitude of the soul and thus produce pleasure and pain, are called *vedaniya;* and (4) those which obscure the soul's inherently right attitude toward faith and moral conduct are called *mohaniya.* In addition to these four chief kinds of *karma*—a result of the presence of four different kinds of karmic matter in the soul—there are four other kinds of karma. These determine and regulate four aspects of the soul's material existence: they are (1) the length of life in any particular birth *(āyushka-karma);* (2) the particular body with its general and special/peculiar qualities and faculties *(nāma-karma);* (3) the individual body's nationality, social position, family, caste, etc. *(gotra-karma);* and (4) the inherent energy of the soul whose obstruction prevents the doing of a good action when there is a desire to do it *(antarāya-karma).*

According to Jainism, we are continually producing—by our physical, verbal and mental actions—a kind of subtle *karma*-matter (Dasgupta, 192: "infra-atomic particles of matter") called *bhāva-karma,* which soon turns into gross *karma*-matter *(dravya-karma)* and "pours itself into the soul and sticks there by coming into contact with the passions of the soul" (Dasgupta, 191) whenever the soul is in a state of iniquity. This leads to the formation of the *kārmana-sarira* (body of subtle *karma*-matter), which accompanies the soul throughout life as well as in its migrations from one body to another. That this *kārmana-sarira* is made of kārmic particles is obvious from the fact that it has both weight and color.

Ignorance of truth *(avidyā),* together with the four primary passions—anger *(krodha),* greed *(lobha),* pride *(māna),* and delusion *(māyā)*—attract the flow of *karma*-matter towards the soul. These are called *kashāyas* or viscous and gluey substances having the power to retain the inpouring subtle *karma*-matter *(bhāva-karma).* The kārmic particles also impart to the soul certain colors or complexions *(lesyās)* according as they represent good *karma*-matter or bad *karma*-matter. The feelings generated by the accumulation of *karma*-matter are called *bhāva-lesyā* (subtle-color feelings), while the actual coloration of the soul by such *karma*-matter is called *dravya-lesyā* (gross-color feelings) and are perhaps mimetically represented by the color of our various expressions. According as any *karma*-matter has been generated by good, bad, or indifferent actions, it gives us feelings corresponding with these. This is also true in case of knowledge, or obscurity of knowledge, good *karma* removing the veil of obscurity and bad *karma* thickening it. As Dasgupta writes: "All knowledge, feeling, etc. are thus in one sense generated from within, the external objects which are ordinarily said to be generating them all being but mere coexistent external conditions" (Dasgupta, 191).

Once the effect of a particular *karma*-matter is complete, it is purged off the soul. This process of purgation or "wearing out" of *karma*-matter is called *nirjara*. In the event of nonaccumulation of *karma*-matter, following their purgation, the soul is gradually freed of *karma*-matter, although, as experience shows, even while the earlier *karma*-matter is being cleaned out, new *karma*-matter is continually pouring in; and, thus "the purging and binding processes continuing simultaneously force the soul to continue its mundane cycle of existence, transmigration, and rebirth" (Dasgupta, 192). After the death of each individual, his soul, together with its kārmic body *(kārmana-sarira)*, immediately assumes a new body, expanding or contracting in accordance with the size of that new body. "Bondage, therefore, means union of the soul with matter and consequently liberation means separation of matter from the soul" (Sharma, 65). Since its aim is the perfection of the soul through an annihilation of *karma*-matter, Jainism is basically an ethical teaching.

The flow of the kārmic particles into the soul is called *asrava*. Though *asravas* refer to the channels or modes through which the kārmic particles move into the soul, the Jainas distinguish between these channels or modes and the *karma*-matter which actually enters into the soul through these channels and thus speak of two kinds of *asravas*, namely, *bhāvasrava* and *karmāsrava*. Nemichandra, in his commentary on *Dravya-samgraha*, refers to *bhāvasrava* as that kind of change in the purity of the soul on account of which the *karmas* enter it. *Bhāvasravas* are of several kinds, each referring to one of the soul's several inclinations: *ekānta* (a false belief unknowingly accepted and uncritically followed), *viparita* (uncertainty as to the exact nature of truth), *vinaya* (retention, due to old habit, of a belief even when one knows it to be false), *samsaya* (doubt as to right or wrong), *ajñāna* (absence of any belief due to the want of application of the power of reasoning), *himsā* (injury), *anrta* (falsehood), *chauryya* (stealing), *abrahma* (incontinence), *parigrahākānshā* (the desire to possess things one does not already possess), *vikathā* (harmful or base conversation), *kashāya* (passions), *indriya* (unhealthy use of the five senses), *nidrā* (sleep), and *rāga* (attachment).

Dravyāsrava, which refers to the actual inflow of *karma*-matter, affects the soul in eight different manners and, accordingly, these *karmas* are classed into eight different kinds *(jñāna-varaniya, darsana-varaniya,* etc., discussed earlier in this section). The states of thought which condition the influx of the *karmas* are called *bhāva-bandha* (*bandha* = bondage), while the actual bondage of the soul by the active karmas themselves is called *dravya-*

bandha. That is to say, *bhāva-bandha* inevitably leads to *dravya-bandha.* The bondage is believed to be of four kinds—according to the nature of *karma (prakrti),* the duration of such bondage *(sthiti),* intensity of the *karmas (anubhāga),* and their extension in the different parts of the soul *(pradesa).*

If there are two modes of the flow of *karmas* into the soul *(bhāvāsrava* and *dravyāsrava),* there are also two corresponding ways of opposing or controlling this inflow. They are called *bhāvasamvara* (which is the force opposite to *bhāvāsrava* and refers to "actual thought modification of a contrary nature"), and *dravyasamvara* (which is the mode opposite to *dravyāsrava* and refers to "the actual stoppage of the inrush of *karma* particles"). The *bhāvasamvaras,* which also form the ethical basis of Jaina metaphysics, include the following: i) vows of noninjury to others and to oneself, truthfulness, abstinence from stealing, controlling one's sexual urges, and nonacceptance of objects of desire; (2) the use of trodden or traditionally used tracks in order to avoid any possible injury to insects and other beings belonging to the lower orders, gentle and holy talk, and receiving proper alms; (3) restraints of body, speech, and mind; (4) sharpening the habits of forgiveness, humility, straightforwardness, truth, restraint, cleanliness in dress and manners, penance, indifference to any kind of material loss and gain; (5) meditation about the changing and impermanent character of the world, about man's total helplessness in the face of his failure to grasp the truth, about cycles of world-existence, about our own responsibilities for our good, bad, or indifferent actions, about the difference between the soul and the nonsoul, about the impure and corrupt nature of the body and all that is associated with it, about the inrush of *karma*-matter and its stoppage as well as the destruction of those *karmas* which have already entered the soul, about soul and matter and the substance of the universe, about the difficulty of attaining true knowledge, faith, and conduct, and about the essential principles of the world; (6) the ways of overcoming all physical discomforts; and (7) right conduct (see Dasgupta, 195).

At this point we may go back to the beginning of this section—to the distinction we made between *jiva* (soul) and *ajiva* (nonsoul)—and start our discussion of *ajiva* or nonsoul. As is evident from our foregoing discussion, *ajiva* is nonliving, lifeless substance, and, unlike *jiva* or soul, is characterized by its lack of consciousness. It is divided into seven types (some scholars believe in a five-fold division): *pudgala, dharma, adharma, ākāsa, kāla, punnya,* and *pāpa* (Dasgupta, 195). Except the last three *ajivas,* all the other four *ajivas* are called *astikāyas,* that is, occupying different places simultaneously, or, to put it differently, occupying space, although original Jaina texts and the Jaina scholars have not been quite consistent in explaining this characteristic of the relevant *ajivas.*

Pudgala, the first type of matter, includes all that is perceptible by the senses and is made up of atoms which are without size and eternal. It may exist in two states—gross (such as the things we see around us), and subtle (such as the *karma*-matter which contaminates the essentially pure *jiva* or soul). The formation of different substances is due to the different geometrical modes of the combination of atoms, the diverse modes of their arrangement, and different degrees of interatomic space. Some of these atomic combinations may be traced to simple mutual contacts at two points, but others may be due to active points of atomic force which attract each other. Two atoms form a compound, and compounds combine with other compounds to produce the gross matter. As Dasgupta points out, the perception of grossness is not "an error which is imposed upon the perception of the atoms by our mind" (as the Buddhists think), nor due to "the perception of atoms scattered spatially" (as supposed by Sāmkhya-Yoga), but due to "the accession of a similar property of grossness, blueness or hardness in the combined atoms, so that such knowledge is generated in us." For instance, when a thing appears as blue, it simply means that its atoms have all acquired the property of blueness and that our soul, the "veils" of *karma* having been removed, perceives *and* knows that "blue thing." This sameness *(samāna-rupatā)* of a particular quality in an aggregate of atoms by virtue of which it appears as one object is called *tiryak-sāmānya*. "When we think of a thing to be permanent," writes Dasgupta, "we do so by referring to this sameness in the developing tendencies of an aggregate of atoms resulting in the relative permanence of similar qualities in them" (see Dasgupta, 196–197).

Unlike the Buddhists, the Jains believe that things are not momentary and, notwithstanding the loss of some of their old qualities and acquisition of new ones, the thing as a whole may continue to remain the same for some time. This sameness of qualities through time is called *urdhva-sāmānya*. In other words, if the atoms are regarded from the standpoint of change and acquisition of new qualities, they appear as liable to destruction, but if they are regarded from the standpoint of substance *(dravya),* they are eternal. Matter constitutes the *physical* basis of the universe even as the *jivas* constitute the *psychical*. Even the four elements—earth, water, air, and fire—are gross manifestations of matter.

The Jainas go further than this: for them qualities like heat, light, sound, and darkness are only forms of fine matter, whose atoms are constantly in motion, thus leading to "a perpetual succession of integration and disintegration, with a variety of forms and appearances as the result" (Jain, 405). As we have already indicated, the Jaina view of matter differs from the atomic theory of the Vaiseshika-Nyāya system, which speaks of as many kinds of atoms as there are elements (see under "Vaiseshika-Nyāya").

Dharma and *adharma* are used by the Jainas not in their usual sense of "merit" and "demerit," but in the special sense of conditions of movement or motion *(dharma)* and rest *(adharma)*. Although *dharma* is imperceptible—is devoid of taste, touch, smell, sound and color—it pervades every part of the mundane universe *(lokākāsa)*. It is the principle of motion, "the accompanying circumstance or cause which makes motion possible" (Dasgupta, 197) and thus helps movement, as water does a moving fish: "Just as water helps the fish to move about, even so *dharma* makes the movement of soul and matter possible."

Hence, beyond the limits of this universe of life and matter, in the region of the liberated souls, where *dharma* is absent, the liberated souls attain perfect rest. *Adharma* is the necessary counterpart of *dharma* and serves as the principle or "medium" of rest, "like the shade of a tree helping the wayfarer to stop for rest." Like *dharma,* it is passive and without form. As *dharma* cannot generate motion, so *adharma* cannot arrest it; water cannot force the fish to move nor the shade of the tree force a person to rest under it. Thus, *dharma* and *adharma* are two nonphysical, inactive conditions of movement and rest, which are conceived as real substances. Dasgupta attempts to explain the necessity on the part of the Jaina metaphysicians in admitting these two categories into the larger category of *ajivas:*

> [It is] on account of their notion that the inner activity of the *jiva* or the atoms required for its exterior realization the help of some other extraneous entity, without which this could not have been transformed into actual exterior motion. Moreover since the *jivas* were regarded as having activity inherent in them they would be found to be moving even at the time of liberation *(moksha),* which was undesirable; thus it was conceived that actual motion required for its fulfillment the help of an extraneous entity which was absent in the region of the liberated souls" (Dasgupta, 198).

The fourth *ajiva* substance, *ākāsa* (space), is that subtle entity which spreads over both the mundane universe *(lokākāsa) and* that transcendent region of liberated souls *(alokākāsa)* which allows space for all other substances such as *dharma, adharma, jiva, pudgala, pāpa,* and *punnya.* Unlike the other substances, *ākāsa* is infinite and is "inferred as the condition of extension": "All substances except time *[kāla]* have extension and extension is afforded only by space. [But] Space itself is not extension; it is the locus of extension" (Sharma, 64).

The fifth (and according to most scholars, last) *ajiva* substance is *kāla* (time), which also pervades the entire world of life and movement *(lokākāsa)* in the form of single, independent, innumerable minute particles which never mix together to form a composite entity, but which helps bring about changes and modifications in all the other substances and affords them extension in time, although, by itself, it is eternal and infinite. Just as *ākāsa* (space) "helps interpenetration and *dharma* motion, so also *kāla* helps the action of the transformation of new qualities in things" (Dasgupta, 198). For practical purposes, however, *kāla* is divided into limited periods such as seconds, minutes, hours, days, months, and so on; in this aspect, *kāla* is "time perceived as moments" and is called *samaya.*

Jaina writers have, accordingly, distinguished between real or absolute *(pāramārthika)* and empirical or relative *(vyavāhārika)* time, the former referring to its infinite and indivisible aspect, which makes continuity possible, and the latter referring to its *samaya*-aspect, which makes changes other than duration possible. "*Kāla* thus not only aids the modifications of other things, but also allows its own modifications [in terms of moments, hours, etc.]" (Dasgupta, 198).

Radhakrishnan quotes from the Jaina text, *Panchāstikāyāsamayasāra:* "Relative time is determined by changes or motions in things. These changes themselves are the effects of absolute time" (Radhakrishnan, 317). Time is viewed as a wheel *(kāla-chakra)* because of its eternality, and, since all things are liable to dissolution in course of time, it is also called the destroyer (in the implied sense that it is time alone that *is*). Dasgupta includes two other substances—*pāpa* (sin or "fruits of bad actions") and *punnya* (bliss or "fruits of good actions")—under the category of *ajivas,* although canonical sources and later Jaina texts do not seem to indicate any such inclusion.

According to the Jainas, there is "but one world *(loka)* and beside it but one nonworld *(aloka),*" the latter surmounting the former on all sides like a hollow sphere and is out of reach, since beyond the boundaries of the world *(loka)* the medium of motion is absent. The world in its vertical cross-section is visualized as narrowing from below to the center and then widening again "in nearly the same degree to above"; both the summit and the base are built up in a convex shape. Canonically, the three sections—the lower, the center, and the upper world—are compared with a bed to rest on, a so-called thunderbolt, and an upright-standing drum (see Schubring, 204–205). The canonical sources also refer to the seven regions of the lower world, each separated from its neighboring region by a space of "unmeasured extension" (Schubring, 210). As mentioned already, the world is composed of three parts: the upper world or *urdhva-loka,* where the gods reside; the center-world or *madhya-loka,* which is the ordinary world of men; and the lower world or *adho-loka,* where the hell-beings reside. The perfected soul moves to the top of the world *(urdhva-loka),* where it takes its perfect rest.

The Jaina system regards (like the Sāmkhya-Yoga, and the Mimāmsakas) the universe as without a beginning or an end; it does not believe (like the Purānic and the Vaiseshika systems) in the periodic dissolution and recreation of the universe. Thus, there is no place in the Jaina system for an independent, all-powerful being like God, or Creator, or Destroyer. Every individual self, according to Jainism, is alone responsible for its own "creation," which is to say, the "creation of its own *karma* and its results, such as the body and the like"; it follows therefore that there is Godhood in every individual, which becomes manifest in the state of deliverance or emancipation. The soul which has manifested its Godhood becomes "the object of worship of the common people."

Pandit Sukhalal Sanghvi compares this principle of worship in Jainism with that in the Yoga school: "The God of the Yoga school is also only an object of worship and not the Creator or Destroyer. But there is [a] basic difference between the conceptions of the Jaina and the Yoga schools. The God of the Yoga school is eternally free and was never in bondage, and thus belongs to a separate category from that of the ordinary souls. Jainism believes that every component spiritual aspirant can attain to Godhood, inasmuch as it is capable of being achieved by proper spiritual exertion, and that all the emancipated souls are equally the objects of worship as Gods" (Sanghvi, 440–441). Or, as Radhakrishnan writes, for the Jaina, "God is only the highest, noblest and fullest manifestation of the powers which lie latent in the soul of man" (Radhakrishnan, 331).

Although Jainism appears to offer every Tirthānkara the stature of a god, "there is no room for devotion or *bhakti* in the Jaina system," according to which every form of personal love and attachment "is to be burnt up in the glow of asceticism" (Radhakrishnan, 331). But, as Jainism began to spread beyond the place of its origin, the necessity to satisfy the religious urges of its lay members – who looked for "a creed and a cult suited to their moral and religious condition" – became increasingly urgent, and as an inevitable consequence of this, several Hindu gods (the most prominent among whom was Krishna) were admitted into the Jaina system. Radhakrishnan explains the reason for this theological invasion:

> The liberated souls according to orthodox Jainism are above the gods.... They have no longer any connexion with the world and exert no influence on it.... When prayers are addressed to the famous Jinas who have reached perfection and passed out of the world of change and woe, they cannot and do not return answers to the prayers, since they are utterly indifferent to all that happens in the world and are entirely free from all emotion. But there are the gods who ... hear the prayers and bestow favours.... Since the severely simple religion of the Jainas did not admit grace or forgiveness, it could not appeal to the masses, and so halting compromises were made [Radhakrishnan, 331–332].

Thus we find divisions of Jainas into the *Vaishnavas* (those who follow the Krishna/Vishnu cult) and the non-*Vaishnavas* (those who belong to the conservative Jaina order).

Jaina Ethics

Jaina ethics is inseparably linked with Deliverance or *moksha,* which can occur only when the soul is freed from *karma* which binds it. Therefore the "instreaming" of new *karma* must be prevented and the *karma* which has already penetrated the soul must be destroyed. In order to achieve this, it is above all necessary to observe a strict moral conduct, for it is through such conduct that the instreaming of new *karma* "suffers an enormous diminution" (Frauwallner, 200). It is also necessary to keep a strict watch over the sense-organs and to avert "the external pernicious impressions transmitted through them," for it is through the guarding of sense-organs that passions are enfeebled, resulting in a corresponding enfeeblement of the unintermittent inflow of *karma*. Further, one must go through a process of penance, for it is through "voluntarily imposed self-mortification" that the *karma* already present in the soul is "artificially brought to ripeness and is prematurely extinguished" (Frauwallner, 200). As Hiriyanna writes, the goal of life for the Jaina, is "to restore the soul to its pristine purity so that it may attain omniscience *(kevala-jñāna)*" – "a discarnate state" in which the soul has not merely infinite knowledge, but also infinite peace and infinite power (Hiriyanna, *Essentials,* 69). The discipline that Jainism recommends for bringing about this spiritual consummation is threefold: right faith in the teaching *(samyagdarsana),* right knowledge *(samyagjñāna),* and right conduct *(samyak-charitra)*. Radhakrishnan quotes the relevant lines from *Panchāstikāyāsamayasāra:* "Belief in real existence or *tattvas* is right faith; knowledge of real nature without doubt or aversion towards the objects of the external world is right conduct: (Radhakrishnan, 325; emphasis added). These three, which must be pursued simultaneously, have been called the "three jewels" or *tri-ratna*.

Thus, Jaina *Yoga* (which literally means "bringing together," but really refers to "discipline") consists of *jñāna* (knowledge of reality as it is), *sraddhā* (a loving faith in the teachings of the *Jinas*), and *charitra* (cessation from doing all that is evil). *Charitra,* which refers to the rules of right conduct, includes the famous "five vows." While Jainism is extremely strict and rigid about the observance of the five vows by the monks, it is much less so in the case of lay people. Accordingly, the five vows for the monks and nuns—the clergy—are called the "Great Vows" or *mahā-vrata,* while the same for the lay people are called the "Small Vows" or *anu-vrata*. The five vows are: (1) *Ahimsā* or noninjury in thought, word, and deed, including "negative abstention from inflicting positive injury to any thing, as well as positive help to any suffering creature" (Sharma,66); (2) *Satya* or truth in thought, word and deed; (3) *Asteya* or not taking anything which has not been given or to which one is not entitled; (4) *Brahmacharyya* or leading a celibate life, i.e., abandoning lust for all kinds of objects in mind, speech and body; and (5) *Aparigraha* or renunciation by thought, word and deed, i.e., abandoning attachment for all things. Right conduct *(samyak-charitra)* must, however, be preceded by right faith *(samyak-darsana)* and right knowledge *(samyak-jñāna)*.

The five Small Vows *(anu-vratas)* are meant to give the spiritual aspirant practice in self-denial, self-control, and renunciation. This becomes more manifest in the next three vows called *guna-vratas*. They are: (1) *dig-vrata* or the laying down of limits in all the four directions beyond which one must not go; (2) *desa-vrata* or laying down further limits of one's movements for a specified period of time; and (3) *anartha-danda-vrata* or setting limits of one's belongings and occupations for particular period of time and eschewing all evil meditations, and avoiding the misuse of one's influence in connection with anything evil.

The next four vows, which are called *sikshā-vratas* or instructive vows (since they initiate one directly in the ascetic practices), take one yet another step forward. These are: (1) *sāmayika* or contemplation at a quiet place and for a period whose duration increases gradually; (2) *poshādhopavāsa* or complete abstention from food for at least one whole day in a week; (3) *bhogāpabhoga-parimāna* or fixing for oneself a restrictive program of food and comforts both in terms of quantity and quality and adhering strictly to it; and (4) *atithi-samvibhāga* or feeding, each day, out of what is cooked for oneself, "such righteous and holy persons as may turn up at [one's] residence at the proper time." These four *sikshā-vratas,* along with the five *anu-vratas* and the three *guna-vratas,* constitute the chief vows of a householder, and a proper observance of these amounts to right conduct *(samyak-charitra),* which together with right faith *(samyak-darsana)* and right knowledge *(samyak-jñāna)* constitute the way to salvation or deliverance *(moksha)*.

As Appaswami Chakravarti writes, the five *anu-vratas* (small vows) are but the "probation" for the five *mahā-vratas*. The householder, who goes through the discipline that would liberate him from the domestic and worldly ties, is expected to enter into a wider realm of spiritual activity as an ascetic. His love and sympathy, "liberated from the sphere of domestic environment, will thereafter become available for the whole living creation" (Chakravarti, 432). The ascetic *(yogin)* further disciplines his body and mind by practicing 22 endurances *(parishaha)*, namely, hunger, thirst, cold, heat, the bite of insects, nudity (although the Svetāmbara sect of the Jainas allows the wearing of white clothes), disgust, the feeling of sex, movement, sitting, lying, anger, beating, begging, nonacquisition, disease, straw-prick, dirt, honor, wisdom, ignorance, and lack of insight. He must train himself as not to be affected by the objects of the senses. "A beautiful or an ugly sight, a charming note or a jarring sound, a fragrant or foul smell, a flavoury or a tasteless dish, and a tender or a rough touch should arouse in him no feelings of joy or hatred, attraction or repulsion" (Jain, 412). All these come under the 28 fundamental qualities *(mula-guna)*, by cultivating which the ascetic prevents any fresh inflow of *karmas* into his soul. He exhausts the existing *karmas* by withdrawing his senses from all objects, concentrating on the Self, and reflecting upon the nature of reality as propounded under the seven principles or *tattvas* (*jiva* or soul, *ajiva* or nonsoul, *āsrava* or the movement of *karma*, *bandha* or bondage, *samvara* or karma-check, *nirjara* or its falling off, and *moksha* or liberation).

There are 14 stages of spiritual development *(guna-sthānas)*, which, in ascending order, are as follows: (1) the stage when the aspirant is steeped in falsehood *(mithyātva)*; (2) when he is lacking in the right belief *(sāsādana)*; (3) when there is a mixture of rightness and falsehood in his mental attitude *(misra)*; (4) right belief *(samyak-darsana)*; (5) partial modification of conduct according to the right faith *(desa-virata)*; (6) partial neglect of conduct and thought *(pramatta-virata)*; (7) regathering and consolidation of conduct and thought *(apramatta)*; (8) attainment of extraordinary spiritual powers following a mastery over the passions *(aspurva-karana)*; (9) the achieving of a unique purity of mind which allows no swerving *(anivrtti-karana)*; (10) getting rid of self-interest *(sukshma-sāmparāya)*; (11) subsiding of all delusion *(upasānta-moha)*; (12) total ceasing of delusion *(kshina-moha)*; (13) the shining forth in perfect knowledge with all the damaging kārmic influences destroyed, when the aspirant is a *sayogi-devalin*, an *arhat*, or a *tirthānkara*; (14) the mortal coils lose their hold altogether and the aspirant is an *ayogi-kevalin*, a *siddha* (one who is free from *samsāra* for all times).

It is the spiritual journey of one aspirant *only* and does not affect the journey of other such aspirants: Jainism, like Buddhism, does not speak of a collective deliverance, although it does not deny the possibility of attaining such a state in *this* life and in *this* world. It is not without reason that Jainism has been seen as a form of "individualistic egoism" (Riepe, 113), with its sole emphasis on the individual, the separate, and the single (rather than the societal, the many, and the collective, as in Confucianism, which lays stress on the moral interdependence of the individual and the society).

To conclude this chapter, we have seen how Jainism offers an empirical classification of things and accordingly argues for a plurality of spirits, and how, in logic, it emphasizes the relativity of knowledge. These two theories (as we indicated earlier) have come for severe criticism from several quarters. We shall here summarize the views of two contemporary scholars—those of C.D. Sharma and S. Radhakrishnan—which of course supplement one another. Radhakrishnan, for instance, writes that "the pluralistic universe in Jainism is only a relative point of view, and not an ultimate truth" (Radhakrishnan, 334). For Sharma, "the doctrine of relativism cannot be logically sustained without Absolutism and . . . Absolutism remains implied in Jainism as the necessary implication of its logic in spite of its superficial protests" (Sharma, 67). Radhakrishnan goes on to explain his position:

> When reflection by imperfect abstraction reduces the subject to a finite mind conditioned by an organism, with a particular location in space and time, we get the idea of the independence of the jivas. . . . If we follow the implications of thought and disentangle the subject from embodiment in sensation and feeling, free it from all contact with the object, we shall see that there is only one subject in reality. Jainism did not choose to realise this height or look towards this ideal . . . There is no need to deny the plurality at the psychological or the empirical level, where only the question of the enjoyment of the fruits of karma arises. When the mind is bound by organic conditions the doctrine of plurality has meaning, but our question is, can we consider this limited jiva to be the ultimate truth? If this limitation be an essential condition of the soul which it can never shake off, then the plurality of jivas is real, but the Jainas believe that the limitations are accidental in the sense that they do not pertain to the essence of the soul, and in the state of freedom the soul is utterly freed from them. In that case we shall be illogical if we consider the accidental plurality of souls to be the final expression of truth [Radhakrishnan, 337–338].

The Jaina "bias" against Absolutism, which is at the basis of the theory of pluralism of souls, cannot, for the same reason, make its related theory of liberation *(moksha)* a convincing one, for liberation is "inconsistent with a separate personality that is throughout hampered by what is external and contingent and is bound up with the bodily organism and nature itself" (Radhakrishnan, 338). If, on the other hand, we emphasize the Jaina theory of the essential nature of the soul which is always in a state of potential manifestation, we are led to "a monism absolute and unlimited, which would require us to look upon the striving world, where all things roam about midway between reality and nothingness, as unreal" (Radhakrishnan, 340). C.D. Sharma continues Radhakrishnan's criticism by asking the essentialistic question: "How can the soul which is pure consciousness and power be really tinged with ignorance, passions and karma?" He argues, "If ignorance and karma are inseparable from the soul, liberation is impossible; if ignorance and karma are external to the soul, bondage is impossible."

According to Jainism, spirit and matter can never be found as separate entities; they are always found together and such union is "beginningless." Which naturally leads us to believe that in such a case liberation is impossible, for that which is "beginningless and real" can never be removed. C.D. Sharma asserts: "If kevala-jnana is a reality, if the inherent nature of the spirit is pure consciousness and pure bliss, if ignorance is the root-cause of bondage, if the union of the soul with matter is beginningless, if relativity and plurality are the necessities of empirical life, then Jainism has necessarily to accept the Absolute in order to avoid the contradictions which its bias in favour of commonsense realism and relativistic pluralism has made it subject to" (Sharma, 68). As we shall see, these contradictions were to be absorbed and transcended only in the Sāmkhya-Yoga system, which "unites the doctrine of permanence of the Upanishads with the doctrine of momentariness of the Buddhists and the doctrine of relativism of the Jains" (Dasgupta, 212).

Works Cited

Bisht, Umrao Singh. *Jaina Theories of Reality and Knowledge*. Delhi: Eastern Book Linkers, 1984.

Chakravarti, Appaswami. "Jainism: Its Philosophy and Ethics." *The Cultural Heritage of India*. (5 vols). Vol. I. ed. Haridas Bhattacharyya. Calcutta: The Ramakrishna Mission Institute of Culture, 1969.

Chattopadhyaya, Debiprasad. *Indian Philosophy: A Popular Introduction*. New Delhi: People's Publishing House, 1964.

Dasgupta, S.N. *A History of Indian Philosophy*. (5 vols.) Vol I. Cambridge, England: Cambridge University Press, 1973.

Frauwallner, Erich. *History of Indian Philosophy*. (2 vols). Vol. I. tr. V.M. Bedekar. New Delhi: Motilal Banarsidass, 1984.

Hiriyanna, M. *The Essentials of Indian Philosophy*. 1949, London: George Allen & Unwin; rpt. Bombay: Blackie & Son, 1978.

________. *Outlines of Indian Philosophy*. 1932, London: George Allen & Unwin; rpt. Bombay: Blackie & Son, 1983.

Jain, Hiralal. "Jainism: Its History, Principles, and Precepts." *The Cultural Heritage of India*. (5 vols). Vol. I. ed. Haridas Bhattacharyya. Calcutta: The Ramakrishna Mission Institute of Culture, 1969.

Radhakrishnan, S. *Indian Philosophy*. (2 vols). Vol. I. Muirhead Library of Philosophy. London: George Allen & Unwin, and New York: Humanities Press, 1966.

________, and Moore, Charles A. eds. *A Sourcebook in Indian Philosophy*. Princeton, N.J.: Princeton University Press, 1957.

Riepe, Dale. *The Naturalistic Tradition in Indian Thought*. 1961, Seattle: University of Washington Press; rpt. New Delhi: Motilal Banarsidass, 1964.

Sanghvi, Pandit Sukhalal. "Some Fundamental Principles of Jainism." *The Cultural Heritage of India*. (5 vols). Vol. I. ed. Haridas Bhattacharyya. Calcutta: The Ramakrishna Mission Institute of Culture, 1969.

Schubring, Walther. *The Doctrine of the Jainas*. tr. Wolfgang Beurlen. New Delhi: Motilal Banarsidass, 1978.

Sharma, C.D. *A Critical Survey of Indian Philosophy*. New Delhi: Motilal Banarsidass, 1983.

Vidyabhusana, Satish Chandra. *A History of Indian Logic*. New Delhi: Motilal Banarsidass, 1978.

Suggested Further Reading

Ghoshal, Sarat Chandra. ed. *The Sacred Books of the Jainas*. (11 vols). Arrah and Lucknow (India): The Central Jaina Publishing House, 1917–1937.

Jacobi, Hermann. tr. *The Jaina Sutras*. Sacred Books of the East. London: Oxford University Press, 1884.

Mehta, Mohan Lal. *Outlines of Jaina Philosophy*. Bangalore (India): Jaina Mission Society, 1954.

Mookerji, Satkari. *The Jaina Philosophy of Non-Absolutism: A Critical Study of Anekāntavāda*. Calcutta: Bharati Mahavidyalaya, 1944.

Stevenson, S. *The Heart of Jainism*. London: Oxford University Press, 1915.

Vidyabhusana, Satish Chandra. tr. *Nyāyāvatāra: The Earliest Jaina Work on Pure Logic* (by Siddhasena Divakara). Calcutta: Indian Research Society, 1909.

4

Buddhism

Like Jainism, Buddhism is a hetrodox system which flourished in India in the sixth century B.C. The basic teachings of this system were offered by Gautama Buddha, who is also accepted as the founder of the system. Later on, however, the original teachings of Buddha found several interpretations, and thus several schools appeared because of the followers' agreement or disagreement with the founder's teachings.

The philosophical atmosphere in which Buddhism was born, was characterized by three things. The sacrifices and rituals of the Vedas dominated the atmosphere, but at the same time, a belief in the Upanishadic Absolute *(Ātman* or *Brahman)* was at its peak. There also prevailed the revoutionary philosophy of materialism, which considered mimetic substances as the only truth, although it manifested itself in at least three major forms. We have the view that all the objects come forth of their own accord and by their own nature *(svabhāva);* second, that everything is left to destiny *(ajivikas);* third, that every perceptible object, including consciousness, is a result of matter-combinations *(chārvaka).*

Such was the state of philosophy when Gautama Buddha was born. It was a time when diversities and contradictions were being encouraged, and such encouragement gladly found its basis in a belief in the permanent Upanishadic Absolute on one hand and in "changing, temporary phases" on the other. It is true, Jainism brought a partial solution to the problem, by propounding the metaphysical doctrine called *anekāntavāda* (philosophy of the several), taking into account all the different aspects of Reality. According to it, both the permanent substance and the temporary phases are equally real—a doctrine which was self-contradictory and was soon to be replaced by what we have known as Buddha's dynamic philosophy, according to which Reality is neither being, nor nonbeing, but "becoming." *Becoming is the only truth.* The world order, or the process which determines the universe, is a neverending process in which there lurks, within every little thing, an intense urge to "become." It was a philosophy of flux, of change, and it was the first systematic philosophy of its kind in India and could well be compared with Bergson's in the west.

Buddha came from a royal family near Kapilavastu, at the foot of the Himalayas. Known as Prince Gautama, he was the son of a Sakya king whose kingdom was a neighbor to the district in which Mahavira, the twenty-fourth and most important tirthankara of the Jainas, grew up. It is quite likely that Mahavira's ideas – anti-Vedic, caste-rejecting, aiming to help the follower escape the evil cycle of births – had had a profound influence on his younger, though equally sensitive, contemporary. But while Buddha rejected "unrestrained individualistic self-indulgence" of the school of materialism, he was also against Mahavira's "equally individualistic but preposterous ascetic punishment of the body" (Kosambi, *Culture,* 105). It is this basically social character of Buddha's philosophy which differentiates it from Jainism and has afforded it a much deeper and wider significance than the latter.

Although young Gautama started with a pessimistic outlook of the world, he soon overcame it. While an adolescent, he was moved by the sight of things which underlined his latent belief that the world was full of misery and suffering: each of these sights became a primary symbol for disease, old age, and death. But the sight of an ascetic, presumably as ignorant or indifferent to the *cause* of suffering as to its *result,* brought within him a faint ray of hope and urged him to take upon himself a life of ascetic renunciation. At the age of 29, Gautama renounced every material thing, including wife, child, and kingship, and went into rigorous meditation, which continued for six years at the end of which he became the *Buddha* or the Enlightened One. He was, first and foremost, a great lover of mankind and hence, after the attainment of divine wisdom, spent the rest of his life by spreading among the suffering many the message of "truth" with a view to removing the wall of ignorance which darkened human existence. Even during his six-year meditation, he had come to learn that a mode of living that was based on self-torture was useless to the same extent that a mode of living that was based on passions. He therefore spoke of the Middle Way *(majhima-māga),* "which gives sight and knowledge, and tends to calm, to insight, enlightenment, *nirvāna*" (Radhakrishnan and Moore, *Sourcebook,* 274). The now famous Eightfold Path and Four Noble Truths are supposed to have formed the most important two parts of Buddha's "first sermon."

In this typical catechistic fashion of most philosophers and prophets, Buddha asks: "What, O monks, is the Middle Way. . . ?" He then provides the answer himself: "It is the noble Eightfold Path, namely, right views, right intention, right speech, right action, right livelihood, right effort, right mindfulness, right concentration." He thus provided an ethical-psychological framework to *life in time;* he also provided an "ethical alternative" to "world-negation" (Lannoy, *Speaking Tree,* 329). Disregarding every kind of caste and creed, ignoring polytheism, and rejecting the prevalent Brahmanic image-worship, Buddha was "far more interested in human psychology than in religion" and attracted followers "as a spiritual physician more than a religious reformer" (Lannoy, 329).

Apart from the noble Eightfold Path, he also spoke of the Four Noble Truths and in the same catechistic vein. They are: (1) the noble truth of pain, i.e., the world is full of suffering *(dukha);* (2) the noble truth of the cause of such suffering or pain *(dukha-samudaya);* (3) the noble truth of the cessation of suffering *(dukha-nirodha);* and (4) the noble truth of the way that leads to the cessation of suffering *(dukha-nirodha-gamini-pratipat).* All the later Buddhist thought originates from these Four Noble Truths *(ārya-satya).*

Buddha was able to command a large following during his lifetime and, after his death at the age of 82(?) at a place called Kusinara, the appeal of his radical humanist philosophy was substantial enough to help it spread to other lands, like China, Japan, Korea, Mongolia, Burma, and Ceylon. In return, Buddhism became richer by incorporating several philosophical ideas which were native to those countries. Although Buddha's own teaching was "too pessimistic and austere to be acceptable without some special leaven" in the country of his birth, its basically antipolitical stance (it was not concerned with changing the social order, but rather emphasized "a moral principle of conduct for the individual," thus disengaging itself from "the hierarchical interdependence of the caste system" [Lannoy, 331]) was greatly appreciated throughout the noncaste societies of the Far East.

Under the great Mauryan king Asoka (whose intense feeling of remorse at the bloody violence his army had inflicted on the people of Kalinga at a battle which was eventually won by Asoka and which moved him to embrace the "religion of non-violence and compassion"), Buddhism became the state religion. Asoka was responsible in building several centers of Buddhist learning within his kingdom; he was also the first public figure to send Buddhist missionaries abroad. His famous rock-edicts have remained a significant part of the Buddhist canon. His work was carried further with similar zeal by the Kusana king Kaniska. As Romila Thapar writes, "Buddhism hovers in the background of most activities in this period, and it enjoined the support of the rich and powerful elements" (Thapar, *History of India,* 129). The Buddhist absorption of new ideas, however, "led to re-interpretations of the original doctrine, until finally there were major differences of opinion and the religion was split into two main sects. This schism, as well as the growing tendency of the Buddhist clergy to live off the affluent section of society, bred the seeds of decay in Buddhism" (Thapar, 129).

Literature

As has been said already, Buddha was basically an ethical teacher. True, philosophical problems attracted his attention, but he preferred tc remain silent on issues like soul and God. His teachings were mainly oral and have been collected by his followers into the Pali Canon (so named because they were written in Pali), popularly known as *Tipitaka* (Three Baskets). The canonical literature consists of (1) *Sutta-pitaka* (relating to the doctrines and forming the best source for an understanding of the religion), (2) *Vinaya-pitaka* (relating to the rules and regulations for the Buddhist monks and, roughly translated, means "the basket of discipline"), and (3) *Abhidhamma-pitaka* (relating to the technicalities and complexities within the doctrine and can be roughly called "the basket of higher religion").

After Buddha's death in (?)483 B.C., the first stirrings of the conflict between his followers could be discerned. Several attempts were made, in the form of Councils, to establish the true canonical literature. The first such Council was held at Rajgrha, the second at Vaisali, and the third at Pataliputra during the reign of Asoka in 241 B.C. In all these Councils the disciples attempted to complete the Pali Canon, comprising the teachings of the elders, and it came to be known as *sthaviravāda* (doctrine of the elders).

The *Sutta-pitaka* contains five sections or collections, known as *Nikāyas*. They are: (i) *Digha-Nikāya* (section of the greater length), (ii) *Majjhima-Nikāya* (section containing the middle portion of the *sutta*), (iii) *Samyutta-Nikāya* (section containing an account of different meetings), (iv) *Anguttara-Nikāya* (section depending on the increase of the topic by one), and (v) *Khuddaka-Nikāya* (section containing further extension in the form of several "sub-sections," such as *Khuddakapātha, Dhammapada, Jātaka Niddesa, Buddhavamsa,* and *Charyāpitaka*). The second major text or "basket" is called *Vinaya-pitaka* and prescribes rules and regulations for monks and nuns. It is divided into three main parts, which are (i) *Suttavibhanga,* further divided into *Pārājika* and *Pāchittiya,* (ii) *Khandaka,* further divided into *Mahāvagga* and *Chullavagga,* and (iii) *Parivāra.* The third main text, *Abhidhammas,* which deals with Buddhist ethics, psychology, and metaphysics, has the following seven sections: (i) *Patthāna,* (ii) *Dhammasangani,* (iii) *Dhātukathā,* (iv) *Puggalapaññatti,* (v) *Vibhanga,* (vi) *Yamaka,* and (vii) *Kathāvatthu.*

Apart from these three major texts, together constituting *Tipitaka,* there are quite a few noncanonical texts, like *Milinda-panha* (questions and arguments of King Milinda in the company of the monk Nagasena), *Dipavamsa, Mahāvamsa, Visuddhi-māgga* (relating to the doctrine of the *theras* or purists), the last written by the well-known scholar of Asokan times, Buddhaghosa, who also wrote several commentaries on the principal texts.

Early Buddhism: A Glance

Although, as historians have pointed out, Buddhism came as a reaction to Brāhmanism, the relation between the two is not one of complete disagreement. In fact, as Hiriyanna sums up, Buddhism was to a large extent influenced by Brāhmanism: "Buddhism represents a new expansion, not against, but within Brāhmanism. The canonical literature, no doubt, now and again criticizes Brāhmanism, but mostly on its ritualistic side" (Hiriyanna, *Essentials,* 72). Buddhism thus attacks the ritualistic aspect of Brāhmanism and, by considering it as less significant, emphasizes the moral character of specific, individual beings. For Buddha, rituals did not have any significant role to play in the moral and psychological development of human character. But he did not deviate from the Upanishadic doctrine that eternal peace and freedom from unhappiness and misery was the final goal of every individual being. Unlike Brāhmanism, however, which had kept the doctrine beyond the reach of the ordinary human being by assigning to it exotic interpretations with the elitist language of Sanskrit, Buddha made his teaching as simple and convincing as possible, so that it satisfied the demands of those who most needed it. His fine parables were used to this end. He encouraged his disciples and followers not to believe in or rely on secondhand instruction; he urged them to have complete faith in self-effort. Authority was rejected, personal experience was glorified. Individual effort alone can lead one towards the "end"; and, by experience and not through rigorous self-mortification that Buddha himself had been able to know his past "lives" as well as the origin of his present life vis-a-vis the past ones. His own realization, achieved through his long experience as a thinker and a teacher, made him conscious that others as well might know themselves and their past through their own effort and experience.

He was one with the Upanishadic belief that the essence of man is divine in character and therefore persuaded others to locate that essential divinity in the very midst of the dark ignorance and terrible suffering of their separate lives. The spirit of his philosophy was the same as that of the Upanishads, which is to know the "in-thing"—the innermost man—from the out-wrappings, like passion, hatred, jealousy, anger and the like.

His Four Noble Truths and the related Eightfold Path are a quiet but persuasive means of initiation into the process leading to individual salvation. We quote the relevant portions from *Samyutta-Nikāya* where they occur:

> Now this, O monks, is the noble truth of pain: birth is painful, old age is painful, sickness is painful, death is painful, sorrow, lamentation, dejection, and despair are painful. Contact with unpleasant things is painful, not getting what one wishes is painful. In short the five *khandhas* [which are form, feeling (or sensation), perception (volitional disposition), predispositions (or impressions), and consciousness] of grasping are painful.
>
> Now this, O monks, is the noble truth of the cause of pain: that craving which leads to rebirth, combined with pleasure and lust, finding pleasure here and there, namely, the craving for passion, the craving for existence, the craving for non-existence.
>
> Now this, O monks, is the noble truth of the cessation of pain: the cessation without a reminder of that craving, abandonment, forsaking, release, non-attachment.
>
> Now this, O monks, is the noble truth of the way that leads to the cessation of pain: this is the noble Eightfold Path... [Radhakrishnan and Moore, 274–275].

It is through a realization of the four noble truths that the individual attains "highest complete enlightenment," the following being the fruits of his realization: "Thus I knew. Knowledge arose in me; insight arose that the release of my mind is unshakable; this is my last existence; now there is no rebirth" (Radhakrishnan and Moore, 275). While Brāhmanism made "virtuous conduct the means to achieve status in the sequence of rebirths of the individual soul," Buddha made his "ethical disposition the means to achieve salvation, *nirvāna,* or liberation" (Lannoy, 330). Buddha rejected the Brahmanic ideal of the soul's *(Ātma's)* absorption in the universal soul *(Brahman),* replacing it with the idea of a pure mind, a compassionate heart, an inward detachment from the material world with a simultaneous outward expression of right conduct. As Richard Lannoy rightly finds, this was why he rejected "hereditary priesthood": no person is born holy and perfect, but every person can become so by right conduct.

It would not be out of place here to refer to Richard Lannoy's insightful, comparatist observation on the place of "world redemption" in Buddhism. Although Buddha spoke of the righteous monk who is compassionate and merciful and "strives with friendly feeling for the good of all living things," he does not by this imply "active love, for active love feeds attachment to earthly cares, and though Buddhism is an ethic of inner perfection like the teaching of Christ, it does not promote *active* compassion" (Lannoy, 330). The Christian idea of a possible transformation of evil into good is absent in Buddhism, for whose founder the perfect man was a man beyond good and evil, "who cares not for others, who has no relations, who controls himself, who is firmly fixed in the hearth of truth, in whom the fundamental evils are extinguished."

The Theory of Dependent Origination (Pratitya-Samutpāda)

The theory of dependent origination is derived from the second of the four noble truths. It has its basis in the assumption that if there is a cause of suffering, there must be a cause of everything. Something being there, something else arises out of or issues from it; reversely, nothing arises out of nothing. The second noble truth aims at, implicitly though, proving the dependent existence of things and phenomena. A thing originates from another thing by way of the dependence of the former on the latter. Both the existence and the origination of a thing are subject to a certain condition and thus, a thing has only a conditional existence. According to Buddhism, permanent or absolute existence is an illusion. Substance and self, which elsewhere in Indian philosophy are taken as permanent entities, have received scanty attention of the Buddhist for the purpose of philosophy. Buddha's doctrine of dependent origination is only yet another version of the "middle path"—this time between absolutism and nihilism or annihilationism. Buddha believed that both extremes are equally unreal. What is real is the "becoming," the process which disallows either an end or a beginning.

If Jainism is concerned with the relative character of judgments, Buddhism is concerned with the relative character of the existence of things. Relativity, according to the Buddhist, is in the very nature of phenomenal existence. The existence of a thing is relative, since it hangs between the real and the unreal. It is relative in the sense that a thing comes into being "in dependence on the accidental existence" of another, and it continues to exist till that time when it allows yet another thing take its place. To explain this, Buddhists offer their familiar example of the flame and the river. It appears to one that the flame of a lamp is constant, when in fact there is a series of flames, each appearing immediately after another; every time it is a new flame which is different—though not separate—from the preceding one. Similarly, in a river, the same water does not flow all the time. One is therefore unable to take a bath twice in the same stream of water. The nature of all phenomenal objects is analogous to that of the flame of a lamp and the water in a river. Change is the essence of the phenomenal world, the governing principle behind its objects.

Change being the essence of Buddhist philosophy, the Buddhist interprets human life in terms of a cyclic process involving birth, death, and rebirth. The process of continuous and ceaseless and it is called *Dharma-Chakra* or *Samsāra-Chakra* (the wheel of life or the wheel of existence). One who knows and appreciates the mystery of the "wheel of life" is able to know the truth and avoid ignorance.

The "wheel" consists of 12 links or *nidānas.* There is suffering because there is birth; there is birth because there is the will to be born; the will to be born follows from the desire to cling to the objects around one; the desire to cling to the objects is because of the desire to enjoy; the desire to enjoy is due to sense-experience; the sense-experience is due to the sense-object-contact, which again is due to the presence of the *six* sense organs. The six sense organs (according to the Buddhist, mind is the sixth sense organ) are due to the psycho-physical organism, which in turn has its antecedent in the embryonic consciousness; the embryonic consciousness appears because of the past impressions of *karma* or action; finally, these kārmic impressions are a result of ignorance, which is the first cause of the entire process. The whole process, consisting of the 12 links, can be systematically arranged in the following order:

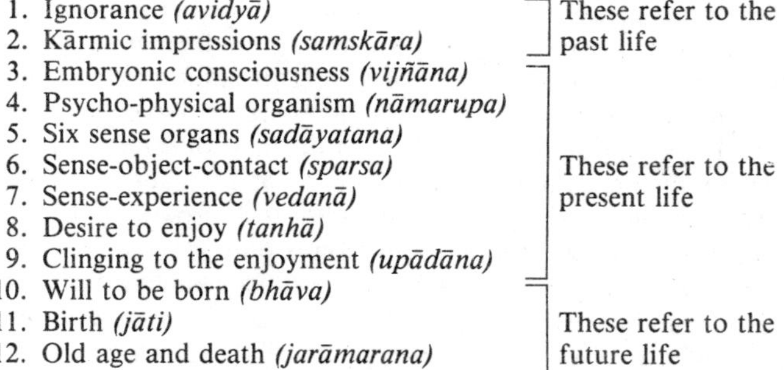

Links	
1. Ignorance *(avidyā)* 2. Kārmic impressions *(samskāra)*	These refer to the past life
3. Embryonic consciousness *(vijñāna)* 4. Psycho-physical organism *(nāmarupa)* 5. Six sense organs *(sadāyatana)* 6. Sense-object-contact *(sparsa)* 7. Sense-experience *(vedanā)* 8. Desire to enjoy *(tanhā)* 9. Clinging to the enjoyment *(upādāna)*	These refer to the present life
10. Will to be born *(bhāva)* 11. Birth *(jāti)* 12. Old age and death *(jarāmarana)*	These refer to the future life

Although for the sake of convenience, we have presented the 12 links *(nidānas)* in a manner that suggests a linear movement, with ignorance as the initial point and death as the final point, it is actually a circular process. As Junjiro Takakusu writes in *The Essentials of Buddhist Philosophy:*

> The death of a living being is not the end; at once another life begins to go through a similar process of birth and death, and thus repeats the round of life over and over again. In this way a living being, when con-

> sidered in relation to time, forms an endless continuum.... The whole series of stages must be taken in their entirety as representing the one individual being. Thus, a living being, when regarded in relation to space, forms a complex of five elements. The Wheel of Life is a clever representation of the Buddhist conception of a living being in relation to both space and time [Takakusu, 24-25].

The whole thing is understood clearly by observing Takakusu's figural representation of the "wheel of life" and the corresponding process of continuity and change:

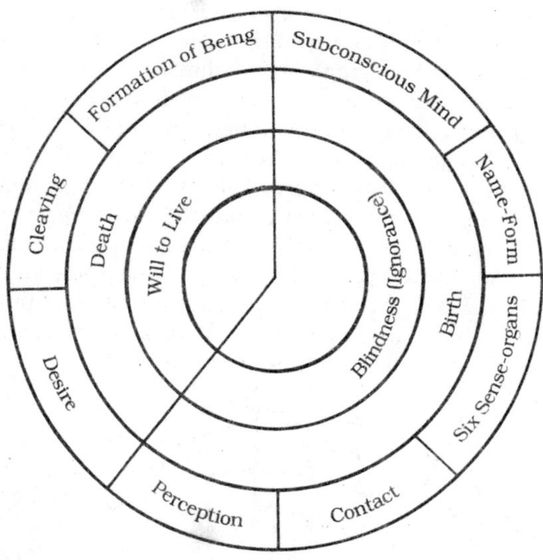

Although, as the figure suggests, the "wheel of life" is a continuous and unbroken circle without a beginning or an end, it is customary to begin any explanation at Ignorance (or, as Takakusu calls, Blindness), for Ignorance is synonymous with Death or only a continuation of it. Although the body is abandoned at death, "Blindness remains as the crystallization of the effects of the actions performed during life" (Takakusu, 25). Ignorance or Blindness as to the nature of truth naturally produces within one the "I-sense," which is the basis of individuality and the bearer of kārmic impressions. These two, namely, Ignorance and the resulting I-sense, and the kārmic impressions, refer to the past life, which in itself is whole and complete and is very much like the present one; and yet, in the context of the present, they belong to the past life.

The present life begins with the subconscious mind or the embryonic consciousness, which refers to the initial moment of the conception of a child and contains within itself the blind will to live. The succeeding stage involves the formation of mind-body or psycho-physical organism *(nāmarupa)*

[*Nāma* = Mind/*Rupa* = Body]. Once the mind-body combination is formed, it is in need of sense organs and therefore there occurs the combination of sense organs: the formation of all this takes place in the mother's womb.

After the child is born, the sense organs become fully active within a year and the next stage is that of sense-object as the growing child comes into increasing contact with the surrounding world. The child's consciousness allows the child to respond to the outside world through contact and begins to accumulate sense-experience. This happens within five years after birth. Following this, the particular individual being, complete with all the faculties, overtakes the child. The individual being, capable of perceiving similarities and differences, spontaneously craves to enjoy, such craving arouses within him the all-powerful desire to cling to the object of enjoyment. The urge for the clinging, the attachment, is so intense that the will to be born in the future is seeded in the present life; one life-phase is complete, the next life follows, and the "wheel" moves on. The last two stages in the wheel—old age and death—refer to the future life.

Taking into account the several "effects of the past appearing in the present," "the causes in the present," and the two "effects of the future," Takakusu reconstructs the Wheel of Life, in which Birth and Death are regarded as merely "an abbreviated description of a whole life," while Blindness and Will to Live are regarded as "an ideological description of a round of life," and in which Past, Present and Future are purely relative terms. Takakusu represents it in the following inclusive chart:

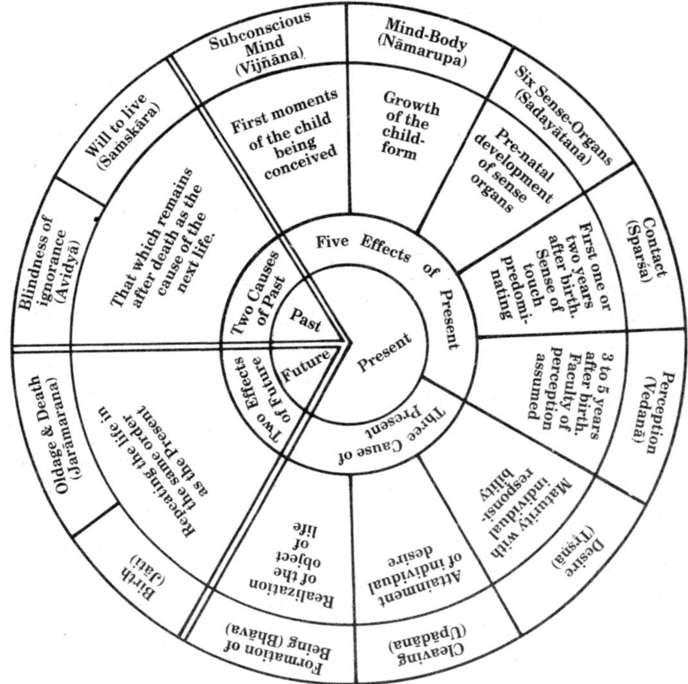

The Buddhist theory of causation is different from the theory of causality of physical science in that, in Buddhism "every stage is a cause when viewed from its effect; when viewed from the antecedent cause, it is an effect" (Takakusu, 28). In other words, unlike in case of physical science, there is nothing fixed in the Buddhist theory. Thus blindness, which survives the physical death of a living being is the "crystallization of the actions *(karma)* which the living being performed during its life, or, in other words, the 'energy' or influence of the actions that remain. One's action *(karma)* is the dynamic manifestation of mental and physical energy" (Takakusu, 29). Such latent energy has been called "action-influence or potential energy," which remains long after the action has ceased and is the cause behind the movement of the wheel of life. It can therefore be said that every living being is, in a sense, self-created and goes through the cycle of 12-divisioned causes and "becomings" over and over again.

Following the nature and quality of the present actions, the next wheel of life may be of a higher or lower order, opening up formal possibilities for every living being; accordingly, a living being may assume human form, animal form, or the form of a heavenly being *(deva)*. Such repetition of the change from one form of life to another is called *samsāra* (constant and continuous reorganization of life). Thus, Buddhism denies the existence of the soul and, by implication, its probable transmigration. It also denies the existence of any superior authroity (e.g., God), for "self-creation is regulated by the action of the individual being" (Takakusu, 29–30). However, it speaks of two kinds of action-influence: individual action-influence or "individual effect," which creates the individual being, and common action-influence or "common effect," which creates and sustains the universe itself.

Theory of Causation (Arthakriyākāritva)

The principal Buddhist doctrine of Dependent Origination relates to how one thing gives rise to another, how one event follows another; that is, the existence of every object or event is conditional and is determined by a cause without, at the same time, ceasing to be one. The antecedent existence lasts only for a moment and disappears with the emergence of that "which follows." The essence of the cause or the antecedent existence lies in its causal efficiency: the theory which supports this statement is called *Arthakriyākārika* or the Theory of Causation. *Artha* means "purpose," while *kriyā* means "action," and hence *Arthakriyākārika* can be translated as "the capacity for the purpose of producing." It follows, therefore, that that which is incapable of producing anything is unreal and non-existent.

The capacity to produce implies *change,* which usually means the change of something, which something must be a permanent substance or thing. But, in Buddhism, the concept of "change of . . ." has been totally and exclusively denied. It rejects the concept of "something changes into something else" and accepts the idea of *change* itself as the only reality. To change or to be changed is, according to Buddhism, the basic principle accounting for any explanation of the phenomenal world. We cite here the well-known analogy of the chain for a clearer understanding of the theory. As the links of a chain imply its continuity, so similar existences account for the continuity of the wheel of life. No two existences are identical, but they can be similar; and, *similarity* instead of *identity* is a strong evidence in support of a continuous process.

A comparison with the two major schools of *Nyāya* and *Sāmkhya* would not be out of place at this point. As we shall see in the relevant chapters, *Nyāya* and *Sāmkhya* advocate what are called *asatkāryavāda* and *satkāryavāda* respectively. Effect, in *Nyāya,* is unreal prior to its creation, for it does not preexist in the cause. While the *Nyāya* theory is one of emergence, the *Sāmkhya* theory of causal relation is one of transformation. *Sāmkhya* justifies the preexistence of the effect in the cause. Cause (i.e., material cause) or *prakrti* gets transformed in order to produce the world of mimetic objects. It may be said that Buddhism looks forward to the *Nyāya* theory of *asatkāryavāda.* The effect, in Buddhism, as in *Nyāya,* is a fresh creation. The only difference between the two systems lies in their different ideas about the cause, which, in Buddhism, is unreal. Thus the Buddhists advocate the theory of *asatkāranavāda* (*kārana* = cause) rather than *asatkāryavāda* (*kārya* = effect).

Dale Riepe suitably applies the concept of the healer or physician to Buddha, who shows the way to remove misery and suffering in the fashion in which the physician attempts to remove the illness of a suffering man. The healer knows the cause of the ailment, so that the cure no more remains a difficult task; and since the cause of misery is ignorance, its removal never seems to be an impossibility (Riepe, 145). Buddha's doctrine of causality has significance in cosmic morality. Although he did not employ the doctrine as a means to explain his particular cosmology, his doctrine has got an instrumental value in its orientation toward the cessation of cosmic, world-pervading suffering. This clearly indicates the utility-based, pragmatic aspect of the doctrine. Buddha's idea of enlightenment, attained through knowledge, is a sure way of removing ignorance; more importantly, it is individual enlightenment alone which removes individual ignorance. Buddha successfully introduces into his doctrine the concept of free will (and hence differs from the deterministic theory of the *Ajivikas,* who were his contemporaries), although he does not exclude determinism in the plane of empirical existence. Buddhist *nirvāna* is thus "described negatively as freedom from ignorance, selfishness, and suffering, and positively as the attainment of wisdom *(prajñā)* and compassion *(karunā)*" (*Sourcebook,* 272), but as far as each is concerned, it presupposes a strong *individual* will.

Doctrine of No-Self (Anattā)

All the orthodox systems of Indian philosophy speak of a permanent spiritual substance or self. It is because of their Upanishadic origin that all these schools continue the tradition of the Upanishads by maintaining such a belief. Indian philosophy shows its spiritual excellence by its emphasis on spiritual calmness and tranquility, which is possibly experienced in the state of self-realization. Consequently, the individual's search has been for something permanent and unchanging within the depths of his being, while its external manifestation takes the form of his withdrawal from the world of objects and consequences. The Self is the only reality, which cannot be perceived in the same fashion in which the external objects are perceived; it cannot be known through the means by which objects other than the Self are known or cognized. Its transcendent character defies the use of ordinary language or empirical symbols. If at all any attempt is made towards its description, such an act of describing must be made in a negative way: Self is not this, nor that, not sensation of this kind, not perception of that kind, not cognition and so on. We have what may be called a relatively negative concept; we may arrive at a definition by way of negation.

To Buddha, such a definition appeared to be highly unsatisfactory. He does not "affirm a positive reality underlying the world of change, a self underlying the empirical series of mental happenings, and the positive character of *nirvāna*" (*Sourcebook*, 272). He points out that we require to make an inquiry not into the nature of the "I" or the self *(attā)* but into the nature of the "not-self" *(anattā)*. The Buddhist theory of *anattā*, like the theories of impermanence and momentariness, is a logical corollary of dependent origination or natural/relational causation *(pratitya-samutpāda)*.

Buddha did not explicitly deny the existence of a self or soul. As Radhakrishnan and Moore write, "As he is deeply interested in the ethical remaking of man, as he feels that metaphysical disputations would take us away from the task of individual change, he keeps silent on the nature of the absolute reality, the self, and *nirvāna*. But his silence is not a cloak for ignorance or skepticism. Whereof we cannot speak we must keep silent. This is the great tradition of the mysticism of the Upanishads" (*Sourcebook*, 272). Although Buddha arrived at the theory of no-self through the employment of his theory of causality, this should not lead one to think that he denied the soul's existence. Only he did not believe in the knowability of the self-as-a-transempirical-substance through any human, objective agency. In fact he makes an indirect mention of the self (or soul) in *Samyutta-nikāya*, in which there are references to the three indications of existence, namely, impermanence *(anicca)*, suffering *(dukkha)*, and non-self *(anattā)*. He further speaks of the five aggregates which constitute a being—aggregates of material and mental forces which are changing all the time—and are the prime cause of suffering. They are:

1. *Rupa* (form)
2. *Vedanā* (feeling or sensation)
3. *Samjñā* (perception or notion)
4. *Samskāra* (volitive/kārmic formations)
5. *Vijñāna* (consciousness or the faculty which discerns and discriminates)

Each of these forms a division or *skandha* (Pali: *khandha*) and together form what can be called "the five divisions of attachment." Buddha sums up their nature in *Majjhima-Nikāya:*

> All corporeal phenomena, whether past, present or future, one's own or external, gross or subtle, lofty or low, far or near, all belong to the group of corporeality; all feelings belong to the group of feeling; all perceptions belong to the group of perception; all mental formations belong to the group of formations; all consciousness belongs to the group of consciousness.

According to Buddha, none of the five aggregates alone is the self or soul *(attā);* and, apart from these there remains nothing to be called the soul. Thus, Buddha goes a step further than the Upanishads, beyond all modes of positivity, cognition, perception and so on, so that he is able to make us implicitly conscious of the kārmic fetters from which one must free oneself in order that one may elevate oneself to a level of awareness which is equivalent to *nirvāna.* Against this background, let us describe and analyze each of the five aggregates or divisions *(skandhas).*

1. ***Rupa-Skandha: Rupa*** refers to all that is material, that is, the body, the senses, and the objects of the surrounding world. The canonical texts refer to *rupa-skandha* as made up of four "primary elements" *(bhuta)* and 11 secondary elements, also called "derived elements" *(bhautika).* The *Abhidharmakosa* speaks of the four great or primary elements *(chatvārimahābhutāni)* as the "very origin of all the constituents of material manifestation." They are earth *(prithivi),* water *(up),* fire *(tejas),* and air *(marut).* Their specific characteristics provide the basis for the four primary states of all material things—solid, liquid, heat, and motion. Hence, the four great elements are to be taken as "simple primordial *dharmas* or materiality [in other words, *not* in their literal sense], each one carrying its own specific kind of activity or energy and thus establishing the basis for each one of the fundamental states which can characterize or affect any of the appearing things in the material world" (Verdu, 22). These activities and the specific physical states they produce are as follows:

1. Repulsion *(khara),* creating the state of "solidity"—earth *(prithivi);*
2. Cohesion *(sneha),* creating the state of "fluidity"—water *(up);*
3. Heat *(usmatā),* causing the degree of "temperature"—fire *(tejas);*
4. Motion *(iranakarman),* producing the state of "lightness" and "mobility," which are qualities peculiar to all moving bodies as well as organisms that are expanding in terms of growth and development—air *(marut).*

The 11 secondary or derived elements are the result of different combinations of these four "primary elements" *(bhutas).* It therefore naturally follows that no single primary element *(bhuta)* has an independent or exclusive existence and that there can be no "secondary element" *(bhautika)* without the *bhutas* and, reversely, no *bhutas* without *bhautikas.* Accordingly, the first five "secondary elements" or *rupas* constitute a subtle, translucent matter, which is light and fine enough not to offer any resistance *(pratighāta)* to the subjective consciousness *(vijñāna).* It is called *prasāda* and refers to a state of perfect tranquility or equilibrium among the four primary elements. As Alfonso Verdu says:

> Its *prasāda*-translucidity *(acchatva)* would allow the permeation of these *prasāda-indriyāni* (sense-organs) by the subject-awareness seated

> in the *vijñāna-dharma* (fifth of the *skandhas*). Their being "not resistant" *(apratigha)* to the *dharma* of the subjective awareness *(vijñāna)* would make them suprasensitive to the "grosser" resistance *(pratighāta)* offered to them by the other five derivative matters, i.e., the gross-matters or objects of sensation.... The absence of "tranquility" or "equilibrium" *(aprasāda)* among the four elements—always entering into the composition of these coarse and external *(bāhya)* matters—would bring about the different physical determinations which these latter exhibit, either as "colors and shapes" or as "sounds," or as "smells"... These five derivative *rupas* are called the *visayas* ... [or] coarse matters which pose "resistance" *(pratighāta)* and thus "objection" (i.e., objectivity) to the five "subjective" *indriyas* or sense-organs, these latter being innerly constituted by the subtle and translucid *rupaprasāda*" [Verdu, 24].

Thus ten of the eleven derivative elements or matters are as follows (reference: Verdu, 25):

Inner and subjective *(ādhyātmika)*	Five sense-organs *(indriyas)* constituted by the subtle and "translucent" *rupa-prasāda* (i.e., the four primary elements in the state of perfect equilibrium)	1. sight organ *(chaksur-indriya)* 2. auditory organ *(srotra-indriya)* 3. olfactory organ *(ghrāna-indriya)* 4. taste organ *(jihvā-indriya)* 5. touch organ *(kāya-indriya)*
Outer and Objective *(bāhya)*	Five coarse and "opaque" sense matters or elements *(visayah)* derived from the four elements in the state of unbalance	1. visual matter *(rupa-visaya)* 2. sound-matter *(subda-visaya)* 3. smell-matter *(gandha-visaya)* 4. taste-matter *(rasa-visaya)* 5. tangible matter *(sprastavya-visaya)*

The aforementioned ten derivative matters play a crucial and direct role in the production of sensorial experience. The eleventh *rupa-prasāda,* which is imperceptible, forms the very essence of the sense organs and, through its contact with consciousness, helps one perceive the *visaya* which is gross in nature. It is the unmanifested residual will which finds expression in physical movement and speech and is carried over to the future life. It is called *avijñapti-rupa* or "non-conscious, non-manifest" material element. Alfonso Verdu defines it as "subtle, 'non-manifest' residues released by the act of physical *karma* as enacted through the two *vijñaptis,* the 'verbal' and the 'corporeal.' Such residues, which probably are thought to accumulate in the 'heart-basis' *(hrdaya-vastu),* become the physical carriers of potentials ('seeds' or *bijas*) for future retribution, and thus they have to be transmitted from the 'dying' individual to the conceptional matrix of its subsequent rebirth" (Verdu, 37).

2. ***Vedanā-Skandha:*** *Vedanā* refers to the raw sensations and feelings that arise out of the contact (*sparsa,* which has a very wide connotation in Buddhism) between the five sense-organs and their corresponding sense-objects *(visayas).* The aforesaid "contact" or *sparsa* implies much more than mere tactile proximity; in fact, it is the very foundation for the "manifestation of all feelings and sensations." It is much more subtle and much finer than mere touch, since it involves the meeting or "resistance-encounter" *(pratigha)* of the "conglomerates of gross atoms with the subtle, inner *prasāda*-element of the five organs" (Verdu, 38). This is the reason why the five sense-organs are also called the "bases of contact" *(sparsāyatanāni).* According to *Abhidharmakosa,* such "contact" *(sparsa)* is the "encounter of the triad of consciousness *(vijñāna),* sense-organ *(prasādendriya)* and material object *(visayalambana);* by virtue of this contact there is sensation *(vedanā)* and perception *(samjñā).*"

There are, broadly, nine different raw sensations, which can be either pleasant *(sukhavedanā),* unpleasant *(dukkhavedanā),* or indifferent *(asukhadukkhavedanā,* i.e., sensations which are neither pleasant nor unpleasant). The *Abhidharmakosa* uses the term *vedanā* to "such specific 'sense-data' as the experience of color, sound, etc., only as these 'present' themselves in association with the primary feelings" of pleasant, unpleasant, and neutral. In other words, *sparsa* is primarily responsible in producing the feelings of pleasantness, unpleasantness and indifference, but it only presents the specific sense-data such as colors, sounds or smells. However, as Verdu writes, "the feelings of pleasantness or unpleasantness, agreeability or disagreeability, pleasure or pain are 'new' in that they do not pre-exist in regard to their experience and thus are totally original sensations that *come to be* through the function of 'contact' [which], therefore, is not merely a condition for their manifestation, but is their immediate and generative cause *(kārana)*" (Verdu, 39–40). As S. Radhakrishnan says, "Vedanā is affectional reaction. It is mental experience, awareness and enjoyment" (Radhakrishnan, *Indian Philosophy,* I, 401).

The three primary feelings are "primitive and pre-reflexive in themselves" and as such "have nothing to do with the subsequent experience of reflexive attraction or repulsion that lays the basis for the acts of will." In this sense the three "raw" *vedanās* are "totally generic, unthematic and pre-reflexive, and as such they associate with the original presence of the specific raw sense-data previous to the formal discernment of full-fledged objects. It is obvious that these original feelings might persist in the further development of specific sense-data into perfected object-experience and grow into proper acts of will" (Verdu, 40). Further, *sparsa* (contact) also produces the same set of primary feelings in the purely mental and nonsensuous form appropriate to the mind ("mental organ" or *manas*). Thus the total number of sensations is given as nine: the three primary sensations of pain, pleasure and indifference as these accompany the manifestation of five specific sense-data through "contact" with the five sense-organs; and, as they accompany the manifestation of nonsensuous matter *(ālambana)* to the mind. We quote a pertinent passage from the *Abhidharmakosa,* whose words echo similar things in *Samyutta-nikāya:*

> The *vedanāskandha* is the triple modality of sensing *(anubhoga),* namely, the sensations of pain, pleasure and indifference. Six further classes of sensations have to be distinguished; those which arise from the contact *(sparsa)* of the five material organs ... with their own respective, material objects; and those feelings of "pleasure-displeasure-indifference" which originates from the contact of the mental organ *(manas)* with its non-sensuous, immaterial objects.

Finally, it is *vedanā* which is responsible in producing desire or craving *(tanhā)* thereby committing the individual to his long and arduous course of suffering.

3. ***Samjñā-Skandha:*** *Samjñā* refers to the cognitive apprehension *(udgrahana)* of distinct external objects, like a black umbrella or a juicy yellow fruit. As S. Radhakrishnan says, it is "the recognition of the general relations as well as the perception of all kinds, sensuous and mental" (*Indian Philosophy,* 401). Thus we do not merely experience certain colors, smells, or tastes; we have the ability to know and recognize a sweet-smelling flower or a juicy pineapple. *Samjñā* therefore is the result of a "synthesis of the raw sensations *(vedanā)* as these are integrated into an organic and sense-making 'whole'" (Verdu, 41). To put it differently, ideas *(samjñā)* are operations of abstract thought or that which "abstracts" and comprehends *(udgrahana)* a common characteristic sign *(nimitta)* from the individual objects *(Abhidharmakosa),* including, for instance, the definite representation *(parichitti)* of a particular color or smell. As Theodore Stcherbatsky finds, it is "exactly what in later Indian philosophy, Buddhist as well as Brāhmanical, was understood by 'definite' *(savikalpa)* cognition" (*Central Conception,* 18). In fact, as Stcherbatsky points out, every construction (*kalpanā,* which literally means "imagination"), abstraction *(udgrahana),* and definite representation *(parichinna),* such as red or green, thick or thin, male or female, friend or enemy, happy and miserable, can be brought under the category of "ideas" *(samjñā)* as distinguished from *vijñāna,* which is "pure sensation." The whole thing nearly corresponds to the part taken in Kant's system by "productive imagination." Thus, the series of cognitions *(chittasamtāna)* goes on uninterruptedly through the successive existences.

We may note here that the two functions of "abstraction" or "apprehension" *(udgrahana)* and "comprehension" *(samgrahana)* whereby the *dharma* of *samjñā* (as content of perception) is defined, refer to the higher mental faculty (*manas* or mind) and hence, *samjñā* can originate only on the basis of a triple contact, that is, the contact among the two *rupas* of *prasāda* and *visaya* (sense-organs and sense-matters) and the *dharma* of discriminative consciousness and subjective, pure sensation which is called *vijñāna* (Verdu, 42).

4. ***Samskāra-Skandha:*** *Samskāra* comprises a number of tendencies—

intellectual, affectional and volitional—and refers to their synthesis. Some of these tendencies are related to the cognitive acts like *vedanā* and *samjñā* (as explained earlier), while others represent "either instinctive or subconscious proclivities which operate on the basis of various sources of 'karmic' causation" and thus, "the most significant of the *samskāras*" is restricted to the conscious acts of the will—those which are associated with such "cognitive acts as are performed by the senses and the mind *(manas)*" (Verdu, 42–43). Such an act of "willing intention" is called *chetanā* (volition).

Volition or *chatanā* has been described as "the mental effort that precedes action" and hence, is a force which plays a crucial role in the composition of a personal life *(santāna)*. It is the force or element which arranges the other elements in "streams" and is synonymous with the law of moral causation *(karma)* as well as with the "vital force" *(bhāvanā/vāsanā)*, which in the Buddhist system is the equivalent of any "conscious agent, whether soul or God or even a conscious human being. A moment of this kind of will accompanies every conscious moment *(chitta)*" (Stcherbatsky, *Central Conception,* 19–20).

There are, broadly, ten mental elements which accompany every conscious moment and are called general mental elements *(chitta-mahābhumikā)*, ten others which are especially favorable for progress towards the final sublimation of life (like faith, equanimity, courage, and so on), ten others which have the "unfavorable" or "oppressive" *(klista)* character, and still others which possess no definite moral character. Thus the 46 mental elements *(chaitta-dharma)* or faculties which are intimately associated with the principal element of consciousness *(chitta-samprayukta-samskāra)* are divided and subdivided as follows (refer Stcherbatsky, *Central Conception,* pp. 100–104):

1. Ten General Mental Faculties present in every moment of Consciousness *(chitta-mahābhumikā):*
    - i) *vedanā* (faculty of feeling—pleasant, unpleasant, indifferent).
    - ii) *samjñā* (faculty of concepts—capable of "coalescing" with a word).
    - iii) *chetanā* (faculty of will, intentional effort).
    - iv) *sparsa* (faculty of sensation).
    - v) *chanda* (faculty of desire).
    - vi) *prajñā* (faculty of understanding and discriminating).
    - vii) *smrti* (faculty of memory).
    - viii) *manasikara* (faculty of attention).
    - ix) *adhimoksa* (faculty of inclination).
    - x) *samādhi* (faculty of concentration).
2. Ten Universally "good" Moral Forces, present in every favorable moment of Consciousness *(kushala-mahābhumikā):*
    - i) *shraddhā* (faculty of belief in retribution, the purity of mind).
    - ii) *virya* (faculty of courage in good actions).
    - iii) *upeksā* (faculty of equanimity/indifference).

iv) *hri* (faculty of humility and modesty).
v) *apatrapa* (faculty of aversion to things objectionable).
vi) *alobha* (faculty of absence of love).
vii) *advesa* (faculty of absence of hatred).
viii) *ahimsā* (faculty of causing no injury).
ix) *prassrabdhi* (faculty of mental dexterity).
x) *apramāda* (faculty of acquiring and preserving good qualities).

3. Six Universally "Obscured" Elements present in every unfavorable moment of Consciousness *(klesha-māhābhumikā):*

i) *moha* or *avidyā* (faculty of ignorance, the opposite of *prajñā,* and therefore the primordial cause of the commotion *[dukkha]* of the world-process).
ii) *pramāda* (the faculty of carelessness, the opposite of *apramāda*).
iii) *kausidya* (faculty of mental clumsiness, the reverse of *prassrabdhi*).
iv) *ashraddhā* (faculty of disturbed mind, the reverse of *shraddhā*).
v) *styana* (faculty of indolence or inaction).
vi) *auddhatya* (faculty of being addicted to pleasure and sports).

The above-mentioned six faculties may not always be absolutely bad, although they are always "hidden" or "obscured" *(nivrta* or *āchhādita)* by "promoting the belief in an existing personality." The two faculties that are always and absolutely bad are the following:

4. Two Universally bad Elements present in every unfavorable moment of Consciousness *(akushala-mahābhumikā-dharma):*

i) *ahrikya* (faculty of irreverence and arrogance, the reverse of *hri*).
ii) *anapatrapya* (faculty of ignoring the offenses done by others or objectionable things, the reverse of *apatrapa*).

5. Ten Vicious Elements of limited occurrence *(upaklesha-bhumika-dharma):*

i) *krodha* (faculty of anger or violence).
ii) *mraksa* (faculty of hypocrisy and deceit).
iii) *matsarya* (faculty of envy).
iv) *irsyā* (faculty of jealousy).
v) *pradasa* (faculty of approving objectionable acts or things).
vi) *vihimsā* (faculty of causing positive harm).
vii) *upanaha* (faculty of dissolving relationships).
viii) *māyā* (faculty of deceit).
ix) *shatya* (faculty of perfidy and trickery).
x) *mada* (faculty of complacency and self-admiration).

These ten elements are taken as purely mental and are never associated with any of the five varieties of sense-consciousness. They must, therefore, be subordinated by knowledge *(drsti-heya)* and not by concentration *bhāvanā-heya);* accordingly, they have been classified as "vices of a limited scope."

6. Eight Elements not having any definite place in the aforementioned system, but capable of entering into various combinations *(aniyata-bhumi-dharma):*

i) *kaukrtya* (faculty of repenting).
ii) *middha* or *nidrā* (faculty of absent-mindedness).
iii) *vitarka* (faculty of a searching of mind).
iv) *vichāra* (faculty of a fixing state of mind).
v) *rāga* (faculty of passion).
vi) *dvesa* (faculty of hatred).
vii) *māna* (faculty of pride).
viii) *vichikitsa* (faculty of a doubting turn of mind).

It should be noted here that at any one moment or in any one mental state, there is always one predominant element in the same way as in material substances we have earth, water, fire, and air, following the predominance of one of the *mahābhutas* (primary elements).

To return to our main line of discussion, the definitions of the will *(chetanā)* and of the force *(samskāra),* as we find them in *Samyutta-Nikāya* and *Abhidharmakosa,* are almost the same: "...that which produces the manifestations of combining elements." As Stcherbatsky has found out, it is quite likely that in the beginning there was only one *samskāra* in the Buddhist system—the will—and that gradually several others were developed and, at times, forcibly, incorporated into the system. Broadly, all elements may be divided into substances *(dravya)* and forces *(samskāra);* the latter are further divided into mental faculties with the will as the mental faculty par excellence, and nonmental forces, among which the forces of origination and decay are the most typical. It is quite interesting to note that even these "non-mental forces are assigned a certain amount of substantiality" *(Abhidharmakosa).* In fact, in Buddhist terminology, there is a large amount of intechangeability between a force *(samskāra)* and a substance influenced by a force *(samskrta).* The Buddhist *samskāra* is as follows: "A force ... should not be regarded as a real influence of something extending beyond its own existence in order to penetrate into another ... but simply as a condition, a fact, upon which another fact arises or becomes prominent *(utkarsa)* by itself" (Stcherbatsky, *Central Conception,* 21–22). We shall discuss the ways in which the different and several forces or elements influence the human deeds or induce particular kārmic formations, later in this chapter.

5. ***Vijñāna-Skandha:*** *Vijñāna* is the most important and the subtlest of the five *skandhas.* It is the basis of all sensations, perceptions, conceptions, and voluntary actions, and hence, is fundamental to what we might call the Buddhist psychology. It therefore refers to the subjective element in an individual being. It is "intelligence which comprehends abstract contents. It is not conditioned by sense contact, while feelings, perceptions and dispositions are" (Radhakrishnan, *Indian Philosophy,* I, 401). It plays a significant role in Buddhist soteriology, "since it is on its 'purification' *(visuddha)* that

the whole and strenuous road to deliverance is built" (Verdu, 49). As Radhakrishnan, following the observation made as early as 1902 by M. Poussin (*Journal Asiatique,* 1902), writes, though there is "no transcendental Atman soul" in Buddhism, its place is taken by *vijñāna* or "consciousness." "That which passes from life to life is vijñana" (Warren, cited in Radhakrishnan, *Indian Philosophy,* I, 406). Thus we have what is called *vijñāna santāna* or "continuum." Radhakrishnan explains: "This is not a permanent, unchanging, transmigrating entity, but a series of individual and momentary consciousnesses, a regular procession of states. The vijnana series is distinct from vedana, or feelings, and is autonomous and independent of physical processes" (*Indian Philosophy,* 406).

Alfonso Verdu explains the nature of *vijñāna* or consciousness, relating it to the Kantian conception of the "transcendental unity of apperception" and the Husserlian idea of "pure subjectivity," and concentrating on the etymological basis and implications of the word. Verdu writes

> The prefix *vi-* plays the role of the Latin *dis-,* the German *ent-,* or the Greek *dia-,* such as in the verb *dis-cernere,* or in such Latin-rooted English nouns as *dis*-tinction, or *dis*-cernment, etc. As the prefix *dis-* entails some sort of separation (whether this be real or purely notional), the prefix *vi-* in the term *vi-jñāna* seems to connote the *dis*tinct sense of subjective awareness that accompanies and thus *dis*-tinguishes itself *from* every objectively appearing object of consciousness.... Thus *vi-jñāna* is the *dharma* of pure *dis*criminative awareness whereby the empirical subject not only discerns objects *from objects,* but *dis*cerns any given objects *from itself*.... Hence *vi-jñāna* (the pure act of *dis*-cerning) *dis*tinguishes itself from its ever flowing companions, the *dis*-cerned *(vi-jñeya)* [Verdu, 50–51].

Accordingly, Verdu provides the following chart, once again incorporating the Husserlian correlation of *noesis-noema* (discerning-discerned) into the Buddhist traffic between *vijñāna* and *vijñeya:*

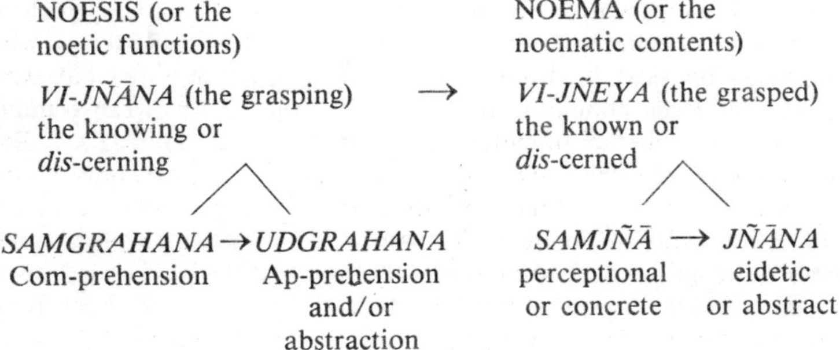

The phenomenological distinction is confirmed by what is said in *Abhidharmakosa,* which defines *vijñāna* as "the *vijñapti* (conscious intimation) which is *relative* to every object" and as "the *upalabdhi* (pure apprehension) which accompanies every manifestation of the *visayas* or objective matters." Since the term *upalabdhi* is made up of the prefix *upa-,* which means "immediately next to" or "on this side of" and the feminine suffix *labdhi* (from root *labh* or "taking hold of"), which means "acquisition," it may be said that *vijñāna* is always "next to" and "on this side of" every "consciously present object" *(Abhidharmakosa).* It is important here to point out that the difference between consciousness as a "receptive faculty" and the same consciousness as an "accompanist to an abstract object" is only a difference of *time.* As Stcherbatsky writes, "Consciousness in the role corresponding to the place occupied in the system by the senses is the consciousness of the preceding moment" (*Central Conception,* 17). Consequently, consciousness and mental phenomena *(chitta-chaitta),* although external in regard to one another, have been seen as being in "a closer, more intimate, connexion than other combining elements" (Steherbatsky, *Central Conception,* 18).

Early Buddhism supported the reality of the "knowing activity" to the exclusion of any permanent, substantial Ego as the transcendent basis of such an activity. As such, while both mind and body are in a continuous state of change and becoming, "impermanence is more marked and the flow more rapid in mind than in body" (Radhakrishnan, *Indian Philosophy,* 383). According to the famous Hinayāna (Early Buddhist school) text *Abhidhramakosa,* "a day of twenty-four hours contains six thousand four hundred millions ninety-nine thousand nine hundred and eighty *ksanas* or moments, and the five *skandhas* are repeatedly produced and destroyed in every *ksana.*" Thus the awareness of continuing subjectivity is "serial" *(samtānaka)* and, therefore, is still a part of the flux or process of "momentary emergences" *(ksanikotsarga)* or "flashes" which make up conscious experience (see Verdu, 52).

The Doctrine of Action (Karma)

In a universe where nothing is permanent, in which every observable fact is a continuously changing combination of the five aggregates *(skandhas),* all change is governed by *karma* (Pali: *kamma*). *Karma,* which means all action, good and bad, refers to every mode of intentional action, whether mental or physical, intellectual or volitional, verbal or nonverbal; which is to say, all deeds, thoughts, and words. It is the "order of cause and effect in action," "a mental intention issuing in an effect" (Thittila, 85; Radhakrishnan, *Indian Philosophy,* 419); and yet, it is not "determinism, nor it is an excuse for fatalism." As U. Thittila writes: "The past influences the present, but does not dominate it. The past is the background against which life goes on from moment to moment; the past and the present influence the future. Only the present moment exists, and the responsibility for using the present moment for good or ill lies with each individual" (Thittila, 85). *Karma* is thus fundamentally related to the Buddhist idea of suffering and, by implication, to the idea of *nirvāna* or the cessation of suffering through individual/universal liberation. Thus we find the following in the *Majjhima-Nikāya:*

> Whatever kind of feeling *(vedanā)* one experiences—pleasant, unpleasant or indifferent—one approves of and cherishes the feeling and

> clings to it. And while doing so, lust originates; but lust of feelings means clinging to existence *(upādāna);* and on clinging to existence depends the *karma*-process *(kamma-bhāva);* on the *karma*-process rebirth depends; and depending on rebirth are decay and death, sorrow, lamentation, pain, grief and despair. Thus arises the whole mass of suffering.

Karma, therefore, has to "offer a comprehensive account of the whole fact of universal organization of worldly existence, in both its amazing disparity in individual allotments and in the aspects of shared and commonly experienced universality" (Verdu, 67–68). In this sense *karma* is primordially objective and does not distinguish between the rich and the poor, the beautiful and the ugly, or the healthy and the sick. As the Buddhist scholar-monk, Maha Thera U Thittilla so lucidly illustrates this point, "*Kamma* knows nothing about us. It does not know us any more than fire knows us when it burns us. . .. It is the nature of fire to burn and it is our responsibility to use it the right way. It is foolish to grow angry and blame fire when it burns us because we made a mistake. In this respect, *kamma* is like fire" (Thittila, 87).

This brings us to the Buddhist's answer to the question, "What or who is the cause of the inequalities which exist in the world?" The Buddhist does not believe that this is the result of blind choice, since he knows that the world goes on according to the laws of cause and effect; he does not believe that it is created by any superhuman agency. Buddha comments on fatalism in the following way:

> So, then, owing to the creation of a Supreme Deity men will become murderers thieves, unchaste, liars, slanderers, abusive, babblers, covetous, malicious, and perverse in views. Thus for those who fall back on the creation of a God as the essential reason, there is neither the desire to do, nor the effort to do, nor necessity to do this deed or abstain from that deed *[Anguttara-Nikāya].*

According to the Buddhist, the disparities exist due to—but only to a certain extent—the environment, which is itself governed by the laws of cause and effect; but, to a greater extent, they are due to "actions" or *karma,* which are in the present, in the immediate past, and in the remote past. The elements which constitute our present life are "conditioned, in addition to the natural course of events, by the mysterious efficiency of past elements or deeds, if the latter have possessed a moral character of some force or prominence" (Stcherbatsky, *Central Conception,* 31). The usual activities of everyday existence have very little or nothing of that efficiency, but a prominent deed, whether good or bad, affects the entire stream of our present life and may show its result either at an early or a very remote date. The resulting event is always indifferent *(avyakrta)* in the moral sense, because it is a natural outflow of a previous cause and hence, is "supposed not to be produced voluntarily." This moral law is also called *karma.*

We must pause here to point out something without which there may arise some confusion. Although, as Stcherbatsky has pointed out, the influence of *karma* in Buddhism is not so very overwhelming as to control the

the whole universe (as it is in other, non-Buddhistic systems, or as it turns out to be, under the term *vāsanā* in later, idealistic schools of Buddhism, where it is one of the forces controlling the world-process and the chief force so far as it controls its gradual progress toward "Final Deliverance"), a distinction has to be made between individual *karma* as the causative action which results in such obvious disparity in individual allotments *(visesa-bhāgya),* and the comprehensive, all-inclusive causative action which brings about the common sharing of the sameness in nature and the cosmos *(samānabhāgya),* like sharing the light of the moon or the heat of the sun.

As far as the individual action is concerned, *karma* is synonymous with mental action *(manokarma)* since any deliberate action issues from and is often confined to plainly mental intention. But the mental intention is externally set forth for others in terms of verbal intimation *(vākvijñāpti* or *vāchika-vijñapti),* so that the willing intention develops into an act of verbal action *(vāchika-karma);* and when such intention is actually executed through the use of the motive organs *(kāyika-vijñapti-indriyāni),* the original intention takes material shape and thus results in an act of tangible or corporeal *karma (kāyika-karma),* which "crowns the process whereby a morally imputable action is posited" (Verdu, 69). As individual action, *karma* carries within itself "the genetic mechanism whereby it will yield its own retribution, either as punishment or as reward." Thus *karma,* which involves more than the time-consciousness of the present, constitutes the causal links between residues *(upadhi)* from conscious states or the past and expectant conscious states of the future.

This cycle of re-embodiment should not be confused with reincarnation or transmigration of the soul, for Buddhism does not believe in such a phenomenon; it rather refers to the transference of kārmic accumulations or residues from "the disintegrative moment of death to a new womb of conception." The kārmic accumulations therefore fix the potential seeds *(bija)* of fructification in a future life. These seeds, which are accumulated by acts of the present and preserved from acts of the past, furnish the basis for the causation of expectant individual existence as based on the law of retribution which keeps us entrenched in the eternal cycle of birth, death, and re-embodiment. Thus the series of existences—in the form of past, present, and future life—revolves round these "potential seeds" or causal factors, otherwise called *karma.*

According to Buddhism, there are six forms of "proximate, principal, or generative causation" *(sadhetahvah)* and four kinds of "remote, secondary, or concomitant causation" *(chatvarah-pratyayah).* The former are also called the root-condition and accordingly divided into the six different forms through which the "root-condition" *(hetu)* was believed to operate. The canonical analogy to explain and illustrate the difference between a "principal or root cause" *(hetu)* and the remote causes *(pratyayas)* is that of a plant, which issues from its seed as its generative condition/cause *(hetu)* and flourishes due to a good soil, proper water, and sun as its concomitant conditions/causes *(pratyayas).*

The Root-Conditions or Generative Causes (Sadhetavah)

1. **Efficient Causality** ***(Kārana-hetu):*** Alfonso Verdu calls this the *"hetu par excellence"* and compares it to the Aristotelian concept of efficient or generative cause. This wide-ranging cause includes the microcosmic activities of the *dhārmic* elements as well as the macrocosmic causation of the universe itself. It refers to the collective sharing of earthly objects, the common participation in the horizontals such as the rivers, the sun, and the moon. Thus, the all-ruling, Universal *Karma (adhipati-bala)* provides us our "intrinsic" nature *(ādhyātmika-bhāva),* the fundamental principle of our "biological similarities" *(ādhyātmika-sabhāgatā);* it also provides us with the external world, the stage of life that we occupy and exploit to our advantage. The external world, which is created directly through the "entitative projection which ensues from the universal KARMIC WILL" (Verdu, 113), is also a kind of "supreme fruition" *(adhipati-phala)* effected by the universal *karma* as supreme force exerting the form of causality which is manifestly efficient and creative and called *kārana.* Thus, by implication, the "creative cause/condition" *(kārana-hetu)* exerted by the "supreme force" *(adhipati-bala)* also becomes a principal condition *(adhipati-pratyaya)* for the common fruition by all sentient beings of "supreme" or "all-ruling" effects *(adhipati-phala),* effects which are "outer and extrinsical to our shared natures as living beings" (see Verdu, 113). In the *Abhidharmakosa* we find the following relevant passage:

> The *kārana-hetu* is the first of all forms of causality. . . . Its fruit (or effect) is called *adhipaja* (as generated by the supreme *karma*) or also *adhipata* (as belonging to the level of the supreme *karma*). Thus . . . the *kārana-hetu* adopts the form of a *supreme* or *all-ruling (adhipati)* force. . . . It is regarded as a *sovereign* cause because it possesses command, and because it is exerted as productive and predominant activity.

Further, the *Abhidharmakosa* ascribes *kārana-hetu* to the function of "nonhindrance" *(avighna-bhāvāvasthāna)* by virtue of which "certain *dharmas* allow or even offer the medium for the manifestation or generation of their dharmas" (Verdu, 73). "Space" may thus be taken as the "non-hindrance-cause" *(avighna-kārana-hetu)* for the manifestation and deployment of all conditioned *dharmas.*

2. **Mutual Co-causality** ***(Sahabhu-hetu):*** This is the causality whereby some elements appear in combination with one another in order to exist and operate efficiently. Thus, in the case of the *dharma*-elements the co-existence causality affects all the four "primary elements" *(mahābhutas)* which cannot exist without the support of one another; hence, these primary elements are "co-existence causality" or *sahabhu-hetu* of one another. As Alfonso Verdu says, even their specific functions as "efficient causes" *(kārana-hetus)* are contingent upon their co-existence or their causing one another to exist by their equal support for one another. Similarly, the volitional forces *(samskāras)* combine with sensation and perception *(vedanā* and *samjñā)* and sustain one another in order to co-exist, and hence, they are *sahabhu-hetu* of

one another. The specific efficient cause *(karana)* which is peculiar to each of the *dharma*-elements is subsequent to their mutual co-existence-causality *(sahabhu)*.

3. **Homogeneous Causality (Sabhāga-hetu):** This is the causality which brings about uniformity and homogeneity between a cause and its immediate effect, and manifests itself as an aspect of the efficient cause *(kārana-hetu)* to the extent to which any effect is formally similar in nature to its generative cause. It therefore covers the whole range of immediate causality which helps in the successive transmission of similarity and continuity in nature and thereby produces the uniformity that is proper to generational chronology or course. Thus a horse causes a horse and a cat causes a cat. Homogeneous causality *(sabhāga-hetu),* to this extent, is related to the "theory of momentariness" *(ksanika-vāda),* according to which a specific *dharma* is causally followed by another *dharma* of the same nature down the "momentary stream of 'dhārmic' co-emergences" (Verdu, 74)—a momentary flash of *chetanā* is followed by another *chetanā,* a flash of *samjñā* by another *samjñā* and so on. In this sense homogeneous causality plays a significant role in effecting sameness or uniformity "within the discrete succession of *dharma*-aggregates that we are," in creating "the illusion of a permanently abiding and substantial ego" and maintaining a "life-continuum" *(naisyandika-samtāna)* which provides for "a true, though relative, basis for what is called 'empirical personality'" (Verdu, 108-109). Thus *sabhāga-hetu* is responsible for the universality of the "down-flow fruition" *(nisyanda-phala)* of specific and essential sameness *(samāna)* which assigns continuity to the vertical succession of human and animal life (see Verdu, 109).

It is important here to clear a certain controversy regarding the range of *sabhāga-hetu.* As we have said, *sabhāga-hetu* is the form of causation which is proper to life-by-generation and vital to the uniformity underlying the "community of nature" *(sabhāgatā).* In the *Abhidharmakosa* we find the relevant explanation:

> *Sabhāgatā* is the principle which causes resemblance among the sentient beings.... There are two kinds of *sabhāgatā* (community of nature), one is *abhinna* (generic) and the other is *bhinna* (particular or specific). The first accounts for a common similitude among all the sentient beings *(sattva-sabhāgatā),* the second accounts for the plurality and diversity of specific divisions.

According to Stcherbatsky, however, the Buddhists distinguish between what he calls "causation among *elements of dead matter,* where the law of homogeneity between cause and effect reigns" and "causation in the *organic world,* where we have the phenomenon of growth" (*Central Conception,* 31; emphasis added). While he ascribes *sabhāga-hetu* to homogeneity in the inorganic world alone, he has an altogether different term for homogeneity in the organic world *(upachaya),* where the phenomenon of *growth* is predominant. Stcherbatsky goes on to elaborate his point:

> In dead, inorganic matter one moment follows the other, obeying solely the law of uniformity or homogeneous production *(sabhāgaja).*

> The next moment follows automatically *(nisyanda)* on the former one. There is neither growth nor decay. This uniform course would represent the Buddhist counterpart of what we might call eternity of matter. Although the same matter is also present in the organic body, nevertheless the term "uniform course" *(sabhāga-hetu)* cannot be applied to it in that condition. It is reserved for those cases where there are no other causes in addition to the uniform sequence of moments constituting inorganic matter.... The pure "uniformity-relation" between consecutive moments—the *sabhāga-nisyanda*-relation—obtains only in the realm of inorganic, dead matter [*Central Conception*, 33].

According to Stcherbatsky, when atoms of organic matter come together, when the principle of growth becomes the controlling principle of development, the atoms increase in number and the very process of growth is supported by favorable circumstances, like good food *(anna-vishesa)*, physical tidiness *(samskāra-vishesa)*, quiet sleep *(swapna-vishesa)*, and good behavior *(samādhi-vishesa)*, although such growth is just *one* of the factors controlling the development of living beings.

Alfonso Verdu, while he rejects Stcherbatsky's partial interpretation and application of *sabhāga-hetu*, does not offer any reason for such rejection. It would be pertinent here to quote his opinion:

> As far as it *[sabhāga-hetu]* produces the human species it is called *purusa-sabhāgatā* (personal, rational nature). Other kinds of *sabhāgatā* produce similitude among other sentient beings, not only inferior to humans, like animals, but also superior, such as *devas* and the conscious beings of the higher realm of "form" and "non-form" *(rupa-* and *arupa-lokas)*. Its effect, the *adhipati-phala* (all-ruling effect), is a fruit which ... is shared by the sentient beings in common "on account of the collective share of the acts which concur to their creation" *[Abhidharmakosa]*. These acts, however, as collectively shared by the beings of each species, proceed from the maturing of such "seeds" as the *nikāya-sabhāga-bijas* ("community of nature" seeds) which in themselves are not individual seeds *(an-ādhārana-bijas)* but common and universal seeds *(sa-ādhārana-bijas)*. Although these universal or "common seeds" are remotely assigned to us by individual *karma*, however they are proximately produced, set and planted by the Universal Force *(adhipati-karma* or *adhipati-bala)* which, as a universally shared *élan vital*, pervades, impregnates and underlies the actions of all individual sentient beings [Verdu, 110–111].

It would seem that while Stcherbatsky ignores certain dimensions of *sabhāga-hetu*, or employs the word inorganic for lack of a better or more proper word, Alfonso Verdu moves to the furthest extremes of idealistic connotation. We might, therefore, take a middle standpoint and say that, while *sabhāga-hetu* is active until a particular time in the generational process, there might be a phase when it coexists with other *hetus*—such as *vipāka*—which takes over the responsibility of maintaining the principle of uniformity even as *sabhāga-hetu* necessarily recedes to the background. We might also say that what Stcherbatsky might have had in mind is not inorganic, dead matter and the compound atoms which appear—and affect the process of growth—in flashes, but *potential-life-seeds* or *potential-life-*

atoms which may not be either inorganic- or organic-oriented, but *neutral.* To take our argument a little further, at a specific, imagined point in time, when an object—inorganic or organic—begins to acquire its peculiar identity (as when a horse is born), *sabhāga-hetu* gives way to other, perhaps subtler, modes of causality.

It is in the idealistic sense that the *sabhāga-hetu* is said to be the "all-ruling" or "supreme" condition *(adhipati-pratyaya)* for the emergence of "universally shared communities of nature in the generative succession of living beings" (Verdu, 111); and thus, the *sabhāga-hetu,* itself a form of proximate causality *(hetu),* becomes also a subordinate "condition" *(pratyaya).* It becomes "the instrumental 'condition' whereby universal KARMA provides universally shared 'channels' (specific natures) for the fruition of the individual karmic retribution" (Verdu, 111). In the *Abhidharmakosa* we come across a clear reference to the relation between the *sabhāga-hetu* (homogeneous causation) and *adhipati-pratyaya* (all-ruling condition): "As said by the *Mahāsāstra,* the great elements *(mahābhutāni)* which are about to pass (within the serial flux) constitute the *hetu* (proximate cause) and the *adhipati* (the "rulers" or "regulators") of the great elements which are about to come. By *adhipati* one has to understand the *adhipati-pratyaya* (the "supreme" condition that presets the form of each element as specifically identical to the preceding one) and as *hetu* one has to understand the *sabhāga-hetu* (i.e., the mode of causality by which a *dharma* begets a subsequent *dharma* or the same form)" (quoted in Verdu, 192).

4. **Conjunction Causality** ***(Samprayuktaka-hetu):*** This is the causality of "association-by-reliance" and is close to "mutual co-causality" *(sahabhu-hetu)* in that both exert their effects in the horizontal manner of simultaneous coordination and not, as in the case of *sabhāga-hetu,* in the vertical manner of successive generation (Verdu, 74). In conjunction causality *(samprayuktaka-hetu),* some elements appear in conjunction with one another by reason of their common reliance of all of them upon another. Thus an act of visual awareness *(chaksurvijñāna)* appears in conjunction with certain sensations *(vedanā)* of pleasure or otherwise, with a certain object of perception *(samjñā),* and with certain acts of volition *(chetanā),* like deciding to use it or not. The conjunction or association of all these elements occurs on the basis of their common "reliance" *(samāsraya)* on the organ of sight *(chaksu-indriya).* As Alfonso Verdu says, "conjunction causality" or *samprayuktaka-hetu* is also the causality which associates an act of mental awareness *(mano-vijñāna)* with an intellectual sensation of pleasure or displeasure with certain abstractions, and with any volitions which might accompany such acts of mental awareness (Verdu, 74–75).

5. **All-pervading Causality** ***(Sarvatraga-hetu):*** It has also been called the general cause and it refers to "ignorance" or *avidyā* as a primordial condition of causation. We have known how the elements of "moral defilement" *(klesha)* are always present in a life *(samtāna)* in a latent condition and how, in their latent form, they are residual and stick to the other elements, polluting them and thus bringing them into commotion and preventing their coming to rest. This influence of the disturbing elements in life is called the

all-pervading or general cause, for it affects an entire stream of life *(samtāna)*. The primordial cause of this unhappy condition is ignorance or illusion *(avidyā)*, which is also the fundamental member in the wheel of life. It continues to exist and wield its influence as long as the wheel is in operation and is gradually neutralized and finally rejected by the "transcending wisdom" *(prajñā-amala)*. This process of the gradual extinction of the elements of moral pollution *(kleshas)* and the consequent purification of life is the ultimate aim of every Buddhist. In the *Abhidharmakosa*, the "general cause" *(sarvatraga-hetu)* is often found in association with the "homogenous cause" *(sabhāga-hetu)*, mainly because our state of illusion or ignorance is the reason by which we are destined, through the kārmic associations that such illusion brings about, for rebirth within a specific order *(sabhāgatā)* of sentient beings in different planes of existence *(bhumi-lokas)*.

6. **Maturation or Heterogeneous Causality** ***(Vipāka-hetu):*** It refers to the causation that takes "a normally imputable act *(karma)* to produce a fruit in a future life as its retribution"; it is the causation which is "proper to the individual positing of *karma* as morally determined and imputable volitive action" (Verdu, 75, 79). The fruit of *karma* as produced by the *vipāka-hetu* is different or dissimilar from the actions *(karma)* which planted its seed. It should be pointed out that "homogeneous causation" *(sabhāga-hetu)* is related to the doings of "heterogeneous causation" *(vipāka-hetu)* in that, regardless of how different the effects might be from their original kārmic causes, there is still the "homogeneous extension of the quality as good or evil throughout the whole causative process" (Verdu, 79). It would be pertinent here to refer to the fine distinction between *sabhāga-* and *vipāka-hetus* that Stcherbatsky makes and thus to the controversy relating to the two causations.

As Stcherbatsky says, when a new life is produced, its constituting elements (which are 18 in number and called *dhātus* or component elements) are present in an undeveloped form. Among these components of the new life, ten represent matter. They are atomic and the atoms are compound atoms, and the matter is dead or inorganic which experience neither growth nor decay. According to Stcherbatsky, as we have said already, "homogeneous causality" or *sabhāga-hetu* relates to the uniform sequence of moments constituting this inorganic matter alone. It is only when the process of growth *(upachaya)* and the influence of intellectual and moral causes *(vipāka)* are superimposed upon the uniform course of the existence of matter—when it becomes organic and living—that the "consecution of its moments receives other names." However, as Stcherbatsky further says, growth is not the only factor which determines the development of organic bodies. Stcherbatsky is of the opinion that, at this point, the influence of heredity is "superimposed upon the natural process of growth." This is the influence of *karma*, the maturing *(vipāka)* influence of moral antecedents and it conditions the constitution of the final bodily form. While natural development constitutes "a rampart, under the protection of which . . . the *vipāka* [which here, according to Stcherbatsky means "heredity"] may safely operate," *vipāka* ("heredity" or maturation) suggests "a more subtle, spiritual, or semi-spiritual character" than mere natural development. Unlike in Jainism, in Buddhism *karma* is not "quite physical . . . since it interferes in the disposition of atoms along with the principle of growth that accumulates them" (Stcherbatsky, *Central Conceptions*, 33, 34). Stcherbatsky's explanation of *vipāka-hetu* is thus an extension of his inorganic/organic differentiation. Alfonso Verdu's explanation is more *inclusive* in nature, according to whom, "as the *sabhāga-hetu* determines that all proximate effects be of the same nature as their immediate causes, the *vipāka-hetu* projects the effects of individual *karma* upon the distant future and determines that these effects be of a totally disparate nature than the remote cause which produced them" (Verdu, 76). If, for Verdu, the two *hetus* (causes) might work simultaneously, for Stcherbatsky one can only follow the other.

The "maturation-cycle" *(vipāka-parināma),* as determined by "maturation causality" *(vipāka-hetu),* involves a whole process of cause-and-effect relationships involving three crucial phases. They are: i) Active *karma (chetayitvā-karanam),* ii) Passive *karma (karmavāsanās* or *karmabijas),* and iii) Re-active *karma (karma-phala).* "Active *karma*" comprises acts characterized as *chetanā*—acts that are mental *(manokarma),* such as mental or intellectual volitions without any external manifestation, as well as acts that are physical, whether they are verbal action *(vāchika-karma)* or corporeal execution *(kāyika-karma).* "Active *karma*" is thus *karma* in itself, and includes all those acts which "determine by way of the *tendency* of will, conditioned or partly conditioned or strengthened by it, the grasping of one of our future rebirths and thus contribute towards our transference into the corresponding external circumstances" (George Grimm, 194). It refers to the act consciously effected by the will, to the acts which may be morally defined either as "good or wholesome" *(kusala)* or as "evil or unwholesome" *(akusala).* Alfonso Verdu argues, however, that since "mental act" *(mano-karma)* is the formal constituent of *chetanā* as pure mental decision and alone carries "the moral quality proper to *karma* as a law of retribution," it is the "*conditio sine qua non* of the extended morality of *vāchika-* and *kāyika-karma* (verbal and corporeal action)" (Verdu, 81).

"Passive *karma*" involves the operation of the most "mysterious and hidden mechanism" of the maturation-causation *(vipāka-hetu)* and has also been referred through the two terms, *karma-vāsanās* (the lingering, perfume-like passion to produce empirical existence) and *karma-bijas* (the expectant *kārmic* seeds). Both *vāsanā* ("moral perfumes") and *bijas* (*kārmic* seeds) must involve carriers: there can be no suffusion of *vāsanā* without a substance to be impregnated, there can be no storage of *bijas* in a state of "suspended activation for future germination" without a depository. But while the *Sarvāstivāda* school speaks of two distinct kinds of carriers for *vāsanās* and *bijas,* the *Sautāntrikas* accept only one kind—the one carrying only *vāsanās.* In any case, both *karmavāsanās* and *karma-bijas* contain, in an implicit form, all the tendencies or traits awaiting effectuation in the forthcoming life. The mental faculty *(chitta)* passively suffuses itself with the moral perfumes of its own moral intentions; it also offers itself as the depository for the mental seeds as these form the mental basis for the maturation-cycle effected by the maturation cause *(vipāka-hetu)* in regard to future retribution. Such maturation or germination (relating to the "seeds" or *bijas*), or re-exhalation (relating to "moral perfumes" or *vāsanās*), takes place not only within the present life but also and more emphatically (Verdu, 83) in future lives. According to the *Anguttara-Nikāya,* there are at least three kinds of *karma*-maturations: i) that which takes place during the present life; ii) that which takes place in the next birth; and, finally iii) that which takes place in successive births.

Re-active *karma* refers to the act of maturation itself whereby passive *karma* reacts and delivers its fruits. Even until today, scholars have not been quite successful in explaining the mysterious gap between the maturation causes *(vipāka-hetu)* and their final effects *(vipāka-phala)*. This process of the transformation of the seeds into their heterogeneous fruits (for instance, an act of lust may result for one individual in bodily deformity, while for another it might result in being born into total emotional and/or material poverty) is called "metamorphosis of the streamlike seeds" *(bijasamtati-parināma-visesa)*. However, all the scholars agree on one point: re-active *karma* as maturation-fruition involves two different levels or kinds of fruition – one which is subjective or inner *(ādhyātmika-phala)* and refers to the inherited passions *(anusaya),* the other objective or outer *(bāhya-phala),* referring to the individual allotments *(bhāgya)* of worldly conditions. The inner maturation is predisposing but not determinative, thus allowing the will to neutralize the inclinations which past *karma* imposes upon our psychological nature, whereas the outer maturation is totally predetermined, making the will accommodate to it but do nothing else about changing it (see Verdu, 88-90).

As Alfonso Verdu represents them in the following chart, the three "moments" in the kārmic cycle of retribution – "active" or the ripening, "passive" or the accumulation in the seeds, and "re-active" or the germination of the seeded tendencies – are shown as a three-spoked wheel turning around the maturation cause *(vipāka-hetu)*:

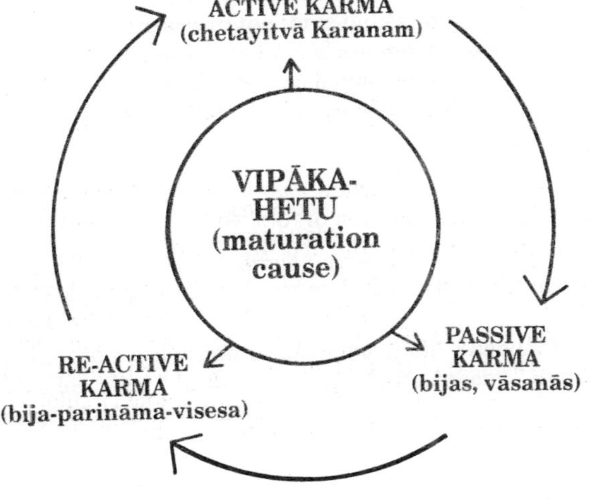

As the chart shows, no single state in the three-state cycle can be taken as a "starting point," since each presupposes the other two as well as is dependent on them. The three links in the maturation process are bridged by two ever-evolving events that take place in invariable sequence, namely, death and rebirth. While death comes in between the links of active *karma* and passive *karma,* rebirth comes in between the links of passive *karma* and reactive *karma.* Passive *karma* comprises two complementary stages – the stage in which it is in the process of being formed or accumulated immediately following the active *karma,* and the stage in which it is already formed – which are separated by death, at which point the seeding or forming of passive *karma* ceases, thereby releasing the accumulated seeds *(bijas)* from the dying body which then become the basis for the chain of reaction beginning with rebirth. Similarly, reactive *karma* involves two stages – the maturation process stage when the seeds are metamorphosed into full-fledged fruition and the stage of the full-fledged fruition itself *(vipāka-phala)* – which are bridged by rebirth. The resulting cycle of kārmic retribution, which now includes seven links, each dependent on the others, is represented in the following chart (see Verdu, 91–93):

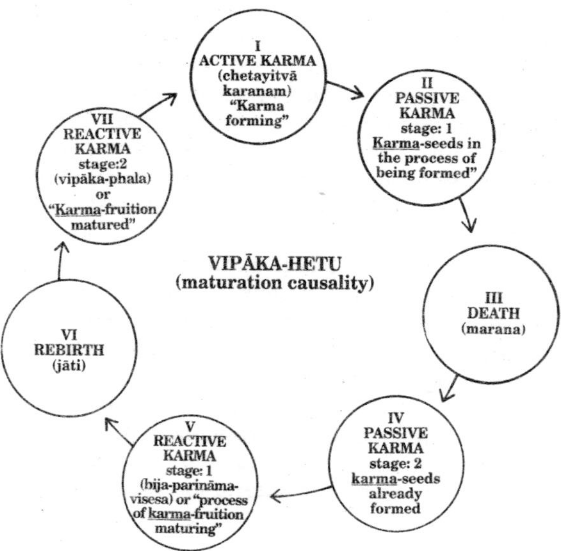

The principle of interdependency *(samutpāda),* which coordinates the causal cycle, "establishes a motion of total co-origination of existence-links as these are originated and coordinated" by maturation causality or *vipāka-hetu.* Alfonso Verdu writes: "In spite of the temporal flux in which the links succeed one another, the closed circularity of the process establishes a simultaneous co-presence of all the links in each one and of each one in all. This is due to the perpetual and underlying act of causal conditioning whereby each one of the links depends on the whole circular series *at the same time*" (Verdu, 93). Which takes us back to the "theory of dependent origination" *(pratitya-samutpāda),* discussed earlier in this chapter: it refers to this principle of "interdependent co-arisal" of all the "successive, temporally flowing links of the chain of individual existence" and it ultimately points to "ignorance" *(avidyā),* which is the basis of *karma.* By implication, therefore, when ignorance is rooted out, empirical existence ceases to *be,* thus leading to liberation or *nirvāna.*

We have explained the six root-conditions or proximate causes. We shall now briefly discuss the four concomitant conditions or subordinate conditions of the kārmic process.

Concomitant Conditions or Subordinate Causes (Chatvārah pratyayah)

1. **Causal Conditions** ***(Hetu-pratyaya):*** All the *hetus* or principal causes can play the role of *pratyaya* or conditions in ways that are different from those following which they are *hetus.* Alfonso Verdu offers the example of the four "primary elements" or *mahābhutas,* whose specific *kārana*-activities are conditioned by "mutual co-causality" *(sahabhu-hetu),* resulting in their co-existence. Thus mutual co-causality operates as *hetu* so far as it brings about the co-existence of the four "primary elements" or *mahābhutas*—which operate only in a group—whereas it acts as a *pratyaya* inasmuch as it conditions the *kārana*-activities of each one of them separately.

2. **Immediate-sameness Condition** ***(Samanāntara-pratyaya):*** To explain this, we have to repeat the nature of "homogeneous causality" or *sabhāga-hetu* by virtue of which the *dharmas* of one species are always followed by *dharmas* of the same specific resemblance in the vertical flow of the personal stream. However, after generating the subsequent *dharma,* the antecedent *dharma* disappears; which is to say, homogeneous causality operates in the context of the impermanence *(anityatā)* of a *dharma* at a given moment. Thus, by implication, the force of origination of the subsequent *dharma* is the condition *(pratyaya)* for the antecedent *dharma* to exert its homogeneous causality on the subsequent *dharma.* Thus, the *sabhāga-hetu* or homogeneous causality is exerted from an antecedent into a subsequent *dharma* while the *samanāntara-pratyaya* (immediate-sameness condition) is exerted by a subsequent *dharma* in respect to its immediate antecedent. Verdu gives the example of the resemblance between parent and child: the parent is the proximate cause of his/her resemblance in the child, but at the same time, the child is the condition for such resemblance to be transmitted (Verdu, 77).

3. **Object-as-support Condition** ***(Ālambana-pratyaya):*** It refers to the causality exercised by the sense-matters *(visayas)* upon the four primary elements *(rupa-prasāda)* and the five sense-organs *(indriyas).* As the *vijñāna-dharma* (discriminative awareness) is the "efficient cause" *(kārana-hetu)* for the generation of visual consciousness *(chakshur-vijñāna)* in the organ of sight *(chakshur-indriya),* the sense-matters *(rupa-visayas)* are the "objective

support" *(ālambana-pratyaya)* for the same visual consciousness. In the same way, *vijñāna* as mind or *manas* is the efficient cause of the mental awareness *(mano-vijñāna),* even as any nonsensuous object of cognition (as mental object) is the "objective support" *(ālambana-pratyaya)* of such mental awareness.

4. **Ruling Conditions** *(Adhipati-pratyaya):* As we explained the nature of these conditions during our discussion of "homogeneous causality" *(sabhāga-hetu),* and as referred to in *Abhidharmakosa,* they refer to the *pratyaya*-aspect of the macrocosmic function of the "efficient cause" *(kārana-hetu)* inasmuch as it acts also as the "causal condition" *(pratyaya)* for the coming into effect of a *karma*-fruition which is all-ruling in that it is commonly shared by all sentient beings.

To sum up the Buddhist doctrine of *karma,* it is not fate or irrevocable destiny or blind determinism. Nor is one bound to reap in "just proportion all that one has sown." It presupposes a certain amount of free will, allowing every individual to shape his life or modify his actions. As Maha Thera U Thittila writes,

> [the] real, essential nature of action, that is, of *kamma* [Sanskrit: *karma*], is mental. . . . [E]ach act, whether mental or physical, tends consistently to produce its like and to be in turn produced. . . . [But] in the case of mentally cultured man, even the effect of a greater evil may be minimized, while the lesser evil of an uncultured man may produce its effect to the maximum according to the favorable and unfavorable conditions of existence" [Thittila, 91-92].

It must be pointed out, however, that "uncultured" in the above quotation is to be understood from the Buddhist standpoint and it implies *an absence of effort* on the part of the individual to bring about that awareness—mainly, moral—which is the basis of individual freedom. "There is more in the world," writes S. Radhakrishnan, "than mechanical law, though there is a perfect natural history of the thoughts and desires of the individual. *Karma* asserts this orderliness of natural process as well as spiritual growth. It is not intended to remove responsibility or invalidate effort, for nothing great can be achieved without effort" (*Indian Philosophy,* 442-443).

Buddha's Ethics

The principal contribution of Buddhism to Indian thought and culture is ethical. R.D. Ranade is appropriately sweeping in his remark as to its basic character: "It may be said that just as Logic sprang full blown from the head of Aristotle, Ethics sprang full blown from the head of Buddha" (Ranade, 137). Buddha refrained from all superfluous *philosophical* discussions and concentrated on ethical teaching. He justified his silence on purely philosophical matters by the now well-known example of the *simsapā* leaves. Thus, holding a handful of those leaves, he asks his disciples whether there are more leaves in his hand than on the trees in the forests. The disciples give the usual answer: "There are more leaves on the trees in the forests." Buddha goes on to use the analogy of the leaves in stating that truths he has known can be compared to the leaves in his hand while the innumerable truths that are waiting to be known are like the leaves on the trees. He therefore prefers to show the path towards the ultimate goal, the final liberation; he lays emphasis on modes of ethical conduct that would help one realize the "state free from misery and pain" which, as he sees, is the way of the world.

Liberation, and the path leading to it, are respectively the third and fourth of the Four Noble Truths. Buddha's doctrine of *anattā* ("no-soul" or "no-self") does not become an obstacle on the way of his explanation of the moral development of an individual being. In fact, he believed that a large part of human misery was due to the ill-founded belief in a permanent individuality and the consequent craving after one's own good by means of satisfying the unending distress in life. As we have seen, past life, present life and future life are linked up in a causal succession, in which the present life is the effect of the past life and the cause of the future life. Further, action in the form of cause is necessarily followed by its effect in the form of punishment or reward. One ought to know, Buddha suggests, the conditions of one's existence, so that the desire to break with those helpless and painful conditions is implanted within one and the free will is allowed to persuade one to turn away from this world of impermanence and momentariness.

The annihilation of pain and misery is a truth realized by Buddha himself. The annihilation of all suffering is *nirvāna* [Pali: *nibbāna*.] The Pali word, *Nibbāna,* means the absence of craving; the Sanskrit word, *Nirvāna,* which comes from the root *va* ("to blow") and the prefix *nir* ("off" or "out,"), means "the blowing out." The predominance of the negative explanation of *nirvāna* resulted in the erroneous notion that it is nothingness or annihilation. *Nirvāna* is "freedom, but not freedom from circumstances; it is freedom from the bonds with which we have bound ourselves to circumstances" (Thittila, 112). Although *nirvāna* consists in the annihilation of suffering, it does not necessarily point to the extinction of the body. Buddha continued to exist long after his attainment of *nirvāna* in this world and in the present life. We quote below a passage from a canonical source which clearly indicates the positive nature of *nirvāna:*

> Just as the rock of one solid mass remains unshaken by the wind, even so neither forms, nor sounds, nor odors, nor tastes, nor contacts of any kind, neither the desired nor the undesired, can cause such a one [i.e., "the freed"] to waver. Steadfast in his mind, gained his deliverance. And he who has considered all the contrasts on this earth, and is no more disturbed by anything whatever in the world, the peaceful one, freed from rage, from sorrow and from longing, he has passed beyond birth and decay [quoted by Thittila, 103].

Thus *nirvāna* shows itself to be "eternal rest," "eternal stillness," the "GREAT PEACE," whose realm the freed and the delivered one enters even *during* his present life, which he completely realizes at death, and in which he has taken possession forever of everything "that is true and real" (Buddha's *Majjhima-Nikāya Discourses*). George Grimm goes one step further in its interpretation:

> Like a stone out of place, a hint of this eternal rest, this eternal peace, is also to be found in the Catholic church, when we hear, quite contrary to its doctrine of eternal *life,* its prayers before the open grave: "Lord, give him eternal rest." – Here also it becomes apparent, that the opposite of life is not death. Death belongs to life, just as much as birth. . . . The opposite to life is really *rest* – since life is movement – namely, rest from the unceasing motion of the five groups. But this rest is only definitively reached with holiness, from which the self-deception involved in such expressions as "rest of the grave," "rest of the dead," becomes at once evident [Grimm, 261].

If, for some Buddhists (such as Nāgasena), *nirvāna* is extinction or cessation of all activities *(chittavrttinirodha)* and of all becoming *(bhāva-nirodha),* for some other early Buddhists it meant "completeness of being" and "eternal beatitude exalted high above the joys and sorrows of the world" (Radhakrishnan, 448). The term "extinction" was in fact chosen by Buddha himself in relation to fire wich may also be extinguished, but fire, as George Grimm notes, "*is* in some way or other, even when extinguished; it is nowhere and everywhere. . . . In exactly the same way the totally extinguished delivered one is nowhere and everywhere. For nowhere can he any longer be found, but everywhere, here upon our earth, even in our very midst, or again, in any other place in the infinity of space; he might now, just as well as at any time in the infinitude of the ages, re-enter the world, if only he *wished* . . . But contrary to the greed with which fire ever and always presses into the world, he has lost all desire of this kind for all eternity. Safe and secure he reposes in the boundlessness and infinitude of his own highest essence" (*Majjhima-Nikāya,* cited in George Grimm, 266).

The path leading to such a state of equanimity and peace is the fourth noble truth realized by Buddha. From his own meditational experience Buddha was able to realize that neither too much of self-indulgence nor too much of austerity can be the basis of the right path. Accordingly, he offers a possible middle path between those two extremes. It is eightfold in nature and is commonly known as the "Noble Eightfold Path" *(ārya-astāngika-mārga);* it suggests a combination of perfect character and perfect knowledge. We briefly discuss the eight "limbs" *(angas)* or "steps":

1. **Right views, right understanding, or right knowledge** *(samyagdrsti):* One must have right views of one's existence as well as of the external world. He must understand clearly the four "noble truths" and that the world is transitory and full of suffering: such an understanding alone can take his mind away from the things of this world. Right knowledge can quench one's thirst or desire and is therefore the foremost requisite for one who wishes to take the path to liberation.

2. **Right thought or right resolve** *(samyaksamkalpa):* Right thought has been described as thought which is free from lust, ill will, cruelty, and thus does not contain any amount of evil in it. One must not be misguided by ignorance, prejudices or superstitions, since it is not always true that a person who is considered to be bad or evil is incapable of goodness, especially in the context of the fact that a robber was converted by Buddha into a saint and absorbed in the Buddhist community *(samgha).*

3. **Right speech** ***(samyakvācha):*** One must abstain from telling a lie, must not be engaged in unnecessary talks or meaningless arguments, must be careful as not to use harsh words. He should be gentle, loving, and kind to his fellow beings. He should unite those who are divided and encourage those who are united. His speech should be like a treasure, uttered at the appropriate moment, and accompanied by arguments which are moderate and sensible.

4. **Right action** ***(samyakkarmanta):*** Right action is abstaining from killing, stealing, and from unlawful sexual intercourse; it refers to the total avoidance of violence and passion at all levels of existence.

5. **Right livelihood** ***(samyagajiva):*** Right livelihood is "that by which the disciple of the Noble One supports himself, to the exclusion of wrong modes of livelihood" *(Majjhima-Nikāya).* One must choose for oneself the right way of earning a living and must avoid all dishonest means of doing so.

6. **Right effort or exertion** ***(samyagvyāyāma):*** The fourfold right effort includes the effort to "stop bad and wrong qualities which have not yet arisen from ever arising, to renounce those which have already arisen, to foster good qualities which have not yet arisen, and, finally, to establish, clarify, multiply, enlarge, develop, and perfect those good qualities which are there already" *(Majjhima-Nikāya).*

7. **Right mindfulness** ***(samyaksmrti):*** Right mindfulness is contemplation on the four fundamentals: contemplation on the body, feeling, mind, and mental objects. One must be conscious of all his acts, both physical and mental.

8. **Right concentration** ***(samyaksamādhi):*** It is concentration on a single object which is associated with wholesome consciousness. The four fundamentals of mindfulness are the objects of concentration, and the four great efforts are the prerequisites for concentration. *Majjhima-Nikāya* says: "Right rapture of concentration is when, divested of lusts and divested of wrong dispositions, an almsman [Buddhist *bhiksu*] develops, and dwells in, the first ecstasy with all its zest and satisfaction, a state bred of aloofness and not divorced from observation and reflection. By laying to rest observation and reflection, he develops and dwells in inward serenity, in the focusing of heart, in the zest and satisfaction of the second ecstasy, which is divorced from observation and reflection and is bred of concentration—passing thence to the third and fourth ecstasies" (Radhakrishnan and Moore, 278).

Buddha's ethical path is a training for different aspects of a personality, a process of purification through the bearing of a highly moral conduct. It aims at the steadiness and integrity of the mind brought about through concentration on a single object until that object slowly disappears and the concentrating mind is gradually reduced to a state of nonattachment and extinction, which is the state of *nirvāna.* Of the above-mentioned eight *angas* or "limbs" in the eightfold path, right speech, right action, and right livelihood constitute the aspect of conduct *(sila);* right effort, right mindfulness and right concentration constitute the ultimate disciplining of the mind *(samādhi);* and, finally, right views and right thought or resolution constitute the aspect of wisdom or knowledge *(prajñā).*

Appropriately therefore, conduct, concentration and wisdom have been known as the "three jewels" *(tri-ratna)*. They also refer to three stages in the path to *nirvāna* or liberation. In the beginning, one has to pay all his attention to good conduct or behavior, which involves things like renouncing the world, being modest and humble, desiring and accepting only those things which are given, and avoiding vain talks. Along with these, Buddha prescribes certain other things, such as eating only once during a day, and fasting during the night. All of which, together, form the group of moral commandments *(silaskandha)* which every monk has to observe. Next, he has to be careful in regard to the guarding of the sense-organs and the practice of wakefulness and sharpening of consciousness, and has to remain alert about the performance of his actions. This is followed by the actual practice of meditation.

In the initial stages of the "first meditation" *(prathamam-jñānam)* the mind is concentrated on the object in order to understand its name and its formal quality and comprehend it with its diverse relations. This state of concentration is called "discursive meditation" *(vitarka)*. The next stage of the first meditation consists in the mind being fixed and settled in the object, penetrating it without effort. This state, in which the mind is moving steadily, is called "sustained meditation" *(vichāra)*. These two stages are associated with a feeling of "buoyant exaltation" *(priti)* and a state of "steady inward bliss" *(sukkha)*. Thus, the first *jñāna* or "knowledge" consists of five elements – *vitarka, vichāra, priti, sukkha,* and *ekāgratā* or "singlemindedness" – and its formation roots out the five ties of ignorance, desires, hatred, sloth, and pride and its accompanying restlessness.

When one acquires the first knowledge, he also realizes its inadequacies and soon wants to move into the "second meditation" *(dvitiyam-jñānam)*. The state of the mind when one enters into the second meditation is placid and unruffled, although it is still associated with *priti, sukkha,* and *ekāgratā*. When the second *jñāna* or "knowledge" is mastered, one gradually ceases to enjoy the *priti* or the "feeling of buoyant exultation" and shows his indifference *(upekshā)* to it, although he still continues to enjoy *sukkha* or "inward bliss." At this stage, unless the mind is carefully watched, one may be tempted to turn back to the enjoyment of *priti* again. The two characteristics of this third *jñāna* are *sukkha* and *ekāgratā*. It must, however, be pointed out that though there is the presence of *sukkha,* the mind at this stage is indifferent to it. In the fourth and final *jñāna,* both *sukkha* (happiness) and *dukkha* (misery) are extinguished and annihilated, and "all the roots of attachment and antipathies are destroyed" (Dasgupta, 106). It is a state which is characterized by total and absolute indifference *(upekshā)*. The characteristics of this final *jñāna* or knowledge are indifference *(upekshā)* and singlemindedness *(ekāgratā)*; its mastery is synonymous with *nirvāna*.

Theory of Knowledge

The explanation of the origin of knowledge by the early Buddhist philosophy – which admits the existence of elements or *dharma* as ultimate realities — was true to their ontology. For the early Buddhist, who believed in a theory of a plurality of separate, though interdependent, elements, the act of knowledge was a "compound phenomenon, resolvable into a number of elements simultaneously flashing into existence" (Stcherbatsky, 55). These elements, since they were conceived as merely momentary flashes, could not come into contact into one another and hence could not influence one another; which is the reason why there could be no grasping of the object by the intellect. But, as we have already known while discussing the theory of "dependent origination" *(pratitya-samutpāda)*, the laws of interaction operated between these elements, making some elements appear to the contiguous accompaniment of other elements. Thus, a moment of color *(rupa)*, a moment of "the sense-of-vision-matter" *(chakshu)*, and a moment of pure consciousness *(chitta)*, arising simultaneously in a contiguous fashion, constitute a sensation *(sparsha)* of color.

According to the same laws of interconnexion, the element of consciousness never appears alone; it is always supported by an object *(visaya)* and a faculty of reception *(indriya)*. It is important to note here, that although there is no real contact between elements, no real seizing of the objective element by the intellect, nevertheless the three elements — the elements of color, visual sense, and consciousness — do not appear on terms of absolute equality; and, there is a special relation between the elements of consciousness and object, a relation of "co-ordination" *(sārupya)* which is instrumental in bringing about the complex phenomenon of cognition and reminding us that it is a cognition of color and *not* of the visual sense.

We may digress here a little and mention that the same "relation of co-ordination" *(sārupya)* reappears in the later, transcendental Buddhist system of Dignaga and Dharmakirti. Dharmakirti, for instance, speaks of an absolute reality, the thing in itself, the single moment of pure sensation which is "the transcendental reality underlying every representation with its complex of qualities, constructed by imagination *(kalpanā)*." Stcherbatsky finds it difficult, however, to offer an explanation of "how this quite indefinite moment of pure sensation combines with the definite construction of reason, and *sārupya* ["relation of co-ordination"] steps in to save the situation. Its role is consequently similar to Kant's schematism that was intended to supply a bridge between pure sensation (reine Sinnlichkeit) and reason" (Stcherbatsky, 56).

In any case, even in the case of early Buddhists, the operation of *sāruptya* sounds a bit unconvincing. We must therefore look for a more convincing theory of cognition. It should be pointed out, however, that early Buddhism accepts intuition *(prajñā*/Pali: *pannā*) as the source of highest knowledge; it also associates intuition with illumination, describes it as self-assured and incapable of empirical verification. Further, it also offers a number of "devices that will promote a state of mind empty of empirical hindrances" (Dale Riepe, 124). It would therefore be unwise to reject the idea of *sārupya* altogether.

S. Radhakrishnan attempts to distinguish the Buddhist theory of knowledge from the *Nyāya* theory of knowledge. The Buddhist accepts the validity of inference in addition to perception, analogy, and authority, and maintains that connections could be established between causes and effects; the *Nyāya* philosopher speaks of other forms of invariable concomitance as well. According to the Buddhist, it is possible to move from effects to causes; according to the *Nyāya* theorist, it is possible to argue not only from effects to causes, but also from signs to things signified. The early Buddhist argues: "If A precedes B, and the disappearance of A means the disappearance of B, other things remaining the same, then A is the cause of B." Later Buddhists extend and develop this "doctrine of difference" by emphasizing immediate antecedents of the cause and describe it in five steps *(panchakarani):* i) We perceive neither the cause nor the effect; ii) The cause appears; iii) The effect appears; iv) The cause disappears; v) The effect disappears. In a somewhat different manner, relations of co-existence—such as those of genus and species—can be established. Following Radhakrishnan's example, if we know an object to be a triangle, we may call it a figure: the generic qualities must be present in the specific (i.e., It cannot be a triangle unless it were also, in the first instance, a figure). According to the Buddhists, therefore, "among successions the causal ones, and among co-existences the genus-species ones, warrant generalisations" (Radhakrishnan, 463). Radhakrishnan is quick to add, however, that we are "not sure that Buddha adhered to these canons of truth." Buddha, according to him, refuses to apply his thought to first causes and final causes; he is concerned with actual existence and not ultimate reality. Buddha asserts that his system is "not a *darsana,* or a philosophy, but a *yāna,* or a vehicle, a practical method leading to liberation;" he adopts "an attitude of pragmatic agnosticism about transcendental realities" (Radhakrishnan, 464; emphasis added). Buddha's silence over all metaphysical questions on the ground that they are ethically unwarranted or irrelevant, caused much concern among some of his followers and has created difficulties for the interpreting philosopher. We may at this point return to Stcherbatsky's reading of the early Buddhist texts.

Stcherbatsky begins with an account of the process of cognition as found in *Abhidharmakosa.* We quote below the *kosa*'s explanation regarding the principle of coordination as existing between consciousness and its objective element. It refers to a "conformity between them"; it is the fact according to which

> cognition, although caused (also) by the activity of the senses, is not something homogeneous with them. It is said to cognize the object and not the senses. (It bears the reflection of the objective element which is its corollary.) And, again, the expression "consciousness apprehends" is not adequate, inasmuch as here also a continuity of conscious moments is the cause of every cognition.... The agent here also denotes simply the cause ... consciousness apprehends similarly to the way in which a light moves.... The light of a lamp is a common metaphorical designation for an uninterrupted production of a series of flashing flames. When this production changes its place, we say that the light has moved, (but in reality other flames have appeared in another place). Similarly, consciousness is a conventional name for a chain of conscious moments. When it changes its place (i.e., appears in co-

ordination with another objective element) we say that it apprehends that object. And in the same way we are speaking about the existence of material elements. We say matter "is produced," it exists, but there is no difference between existence of an element and the element itself that *does* exist. The same applies to consciousness, (there is nothing that *does* cognize, apart from the evanescent flashings of consciousness itself).

Stcherbatsky criticizes the system on the ground that it "denies the existence of a personality, splits everything into a plurality of separate elements, and admits of no real distinction between them" and he discards the "possibility of distinguishing between an external and internal world," for such an internal world does not exist, all elements being "quite equally external towards one another." "Nevertheless," Stcherbatsky continues, "the habit of distinguishing between internal and external, subjective and objective, could not be dropped altogether, and we meet with curious situations into which the philosopher is driven by logical deductions; consciousness itself sometimes happens to be considered as an external element with regard to other elements [such as ideas *(samjñā)*, feelings *(vedanā)*, and volitions *(chetanā)*]." The *Abhidharmakosa* has something to say about the "Self"/ "personality":

> Consciousness if metaphorically called a Self, because it yields some support to the (erroneous) idea of a Self. Buddha himself uses such expressions. He sometimes mentions control of the Self, (sometimes control of consciousness) . . . The sense of vision and other sense-organs are the basic elements for the corresponding sensations; consciousness, on the other hand, is the basic element for the perception of a Self. Therefore, as a consequence of this close connexion with consciousness, the sense-organs are brought under the head of internal elements.

Stcherbatsky writes: "If to be internal means merely to be the basic element of consciousness . . . [as the organ of vision is the basic element *(āshraya)* for any visual consciousness] then, since consciousness could not be its own basis, it could neither be an internal element." According to Stcherbatsky, the Buddhist tries to solve the problem by saying that "the preceding moment of consciousness is the basis for the following one;" and since time is irrelevant in this definition, "consciousness must also be called internal" (Stcherbatsky, 57–59).

We must repeat here what we have said already, that, for the early Buddhist, sense-knowledge is bound up with feeling and desire and hence, is of an inferior kind and a "stumbling block to the ultimate aim of Buddha, the elimination of craving, through understanding or illumination." We have spoken of authority as one of the sources of valid knowledge for the early Buddhist, and it was necessary for the followers of Buddha to have faith in Buddha's enlightenment and thus in his words. As Dale Riepe writes, "The truth . . . is what has been laid down by the Buddha." The epistemology of the early Buddhist is essentially nonnaturalistic and intuitionist. Although it does not deny the role of sense perception, it keeps it subordinate to the role of self-illumination. This naturally leads us to the Buddhist idea of no-soul or no-self *(anattā)*, which is lucidly discussed by George Grimm.

Grimm calls the *Anattā*-idea the "one fundamental axiom which is absolutely irrefutable," the one idea which determines the essential relations between ourselves and everything cognizable and is set forth by Buddha in the form of the "Great Syllogism": "What I perceive to pass away within me, and in consequence of this passing away, cause suffering to me cannot be my real essence. Now I perceive *everything* that is cognizable within me to pass away and with the advent of this transiency, bring me suffering; therefore nothing cognizable is my real essence." George Grimm's "imagined being," striving towards deliverance, profoundly introspective, is the philosopher's version of the perfect Buddhist:

> Everything cognizable is *not* my *I,* therefore I can free myself from everything cognizable. To liberate myself from everything not my *I,* I must become *selfless* . . . I may not relate anything at all to myself. . . . With a gaze thus alienated I must learn so to look upon the mechanism of my personality that in the course of this my activity of thought, "the inclinations of pride which thinks the thoughts, 'I' and 'Me' . . . may arise within me no more," but everything meet me simply and solely as *an object:* a method of thinking which finds its classical expression in the *Paticcasamuppāda* [Sanskrit: *Pratitya-samutpāda* = Dependent Origination].
>
> Thus, it is, of course, *I* who thinks in this entirely impersonal form. . . . I must not only dismiss the thought of boundless space and that of my own boundless consciousness, but also and above all else, the thought of myself, and the thought that there can exist anything belonging to me. This one thought only may I think: "Empty is this (whatever I may be able to cognize) of myself and of everything belonging to me" *[Majjhima-Nikāya]*—"This does *not* belong to me; this am I *not;* this is *not* my Self." And this kind of thinking I must practise for the purpose of realizing also that other saying: "What exists, what has become, shall not be, shall not be there present *for me;* shall not become, shall not become *for me;* I let it go [*Majjhima-Nikāya* Discourse]". . .
>
> When I have understood this also . . . deliverance will become easy for me. For then I know that for the Buddha remains true what has always been true, when I even cannot seriously represent to myself in any other way, namely, that *I* am he who acts and works, that *I* am he who sins and struggles, that *I* am he who suffers and delivers himself, that *I* am he who may win timeless, eternal bliss, that, especially, *I* am he who thinks the not-*I* thought, the Anatta-thought. . . [Grimm, 387–388].

Thus George Grimm's "imagined being" passes from *perceptive* activity to *reasoning* activity, thereby "translating his perception into the abstract form of cognition," where the subject presents itself only indirectly to perception. Such *indirect perceptive apprehending* can be expressed in adequate rational form *only* by the thought: "This is *not* my *I.*" Thus by qualifying the "thing perceived" as *not* one's *I,* one only shows that the "I" does not "immediately present itself to our perception; but that it is only the thing perceived, which in its quality as object, reminds us of the subject opposed to this." Since the "imagined being," endowed with perfect perception, apprehends everything that can be perceived, including its own entire personality, as mere *object,* it arrives at the *I*-idea only in its *negative* form. It only grasps the idea of not-I: "Everything is *not* my I, not my true essence, is Anatta." Buddha's theory of knowledge has this as its basis and end, namely, the "perfect method of cognition," this "meditative contemplation combined with a cognition perfectly accordant with 'reality as it is'" (Grimm, 386). Buddha is concerned with that alone which is cognizable, with the "things of the world"; and these alone he has seen correctly and has apprehended them as being mere *objects* for us and hence, as not our true *I.*

As said in *Majjhima-Nikāya,* Buddha's doctrine rests on the kind of thinking "that roots in perception," on the kind of thinking that is done in "knowing and seeing." As Buddha says, the "Road to the Absolute" is to be found in "concentration combined with energetic logical thought and reflection" *(Samyutta-Nikāya).* Consequently, what is "not accessible to perception through our senses . . . cannot, therefore, be made the object of logical thought. *It does not lie within the realm of logical thought*" (Grimm, 389, 390). For this, Buddha uses the word *atakkavachara* (*a* = not, *takka* = logical thought, *avachara* = realm). Many of his followers were led to believe that, when Buddha used the term *attakavachara,* he implied his own doctrine—*dharma* itself—as inaccessible to logical thought. Buddha, however, uses the term in one clearly defined sense and in relation to a specific state—the state of a "Delivered One." In *Majjhima-Nikāya,* for instance, he says: "Then I knew and saw: 'Eternal is my deliverance, this is my final birth, no further Becoming will there be'." He further says: "Attained I now have *this* thing *(ayam dhammo),* the deep, hard to perceive, hard to discover, peaceful, sublime, *not lying within the realm of logical thought (atakkavachara),* subtle, to be experienced only by the judicious."

Buddha repeatedly talks about the ungraspable nature of a "Delivered One," emphasizes that a "Delivered One" cannot be grasped by knowledge at all and that, he therefore does not enter into any conception or logical thought. In *Udana,* yet another early Buddhist text in Pali, he says: "Just as no one knows the way of the spark that blazes up by the hits of the smith's hammer and then comes to rest by and by, just so there is no one that may know the way of the Fully Delivered Ones who have crossed over the flood of sensual pleasures and have reached the unshakeable well-being." Despite the slight confusion created by that metaphorical mixup, it is not difficult to recognize the import of Buddha's words: the total uncognizability of a "Delivered One."

In his reply to Sundarika the Brahmin's question, "Of what family art thou, lord?" Buddha says: "No Brahmin am I, nor a king's son, nor a man of the people, I am not any one at all" *(Suttanipata).* The Delivered or Perfected one is "unsullied by all things" *[sarvesu dharmesu anulipta] (Majjhima-Nikāya).* Since all things or *dharma* are grasped and defined in terms of the five *skandhas* [corporeal form, sensation, perception, activities of the mind, and cognition], it would also include any attempt to define the Perfected One, for this idea too is purely empirical and is drawn entirely from sensational experience and, for that reason, is discouraged: "'A

Perfected One *is* after death,' or 'a Perfected One *is not* after death,' or 'a Perfected One *is* and *is not,*' or 'a Perfected One *neither is nor is not* after death,' all that, Friend, would mean thinking in terms of corporeality" *(Samyutta-Nikāya)*. It is interesting to read the dialogue that ensued between Buddha and his disciple, the monk Anuradha, when the latter went to his master with the problem of definition:

> "What think you, Anuradha, are the five groups of grasping skandhas permanent or impermanent?"
> "Impermanent, lord."
> "What is impermanent, is that weal or woe?"
> "Woe, lord."
> "Now what is impermanent, what is woe, what is subject to change through its very nature—is it proper to regard that thus: 'This is mine, This am I, This is my self'?"
> "Surely not, lord."
> "Therefore, Anuradha, whatsoever body, whatsoever sensation, whatsoever perception, whatsoever activities of the mind, whatsoever cognition, be it past, present or future, be it your own or another's, is, according to reality and in right wisdom, to be regarded thus: 'This is not mine, This am I not, This is not my self'" *[Samyutta-Nikāya]*.

And when Anuradha returns after a long absence, now freed from everything, a Perfected One himself, Buddha asks him:

> "Now what say you Anuradha, do you regard the corporeal form of a Perfected One as the Perfected One?"
> "Surely not, lord."
> "Do you regard the sensation, the perception, the activities of the mind, the cognition of a Perfected One as the Perfected One?"
> "Surely not, lord."
> "Do you regard a Perfected One as *without* corporeal form, sensation, perception, activities of the mind, consciousness?"
> "Surely not, lord."
> "Then, Anuradha, since in just this life a Perfected One is not to be found out in truth, in reality, is it proper for you to pronounce this of him: 'He who is a Perfected One, a superman, one of the best of beings, a winner of the highest gain, may be definied *in other than* these four ways: A Perfected One is after death—he is not after death—he is and is not after death—he neither is nor is not after death'?"
> "Surely not, lord." [*Samyutta-Nikāya;* emphasis added].

The Delivered or Perfected One is therefore beyond the reach of empirical definition; he is *atakkavachara* or "not lying within the realm of logical thought." Buddha's pronouncements regarding the "grounds of knowledge" indicate his "denunciation of the futility of extra-empirical inquiries" (Radhakrishnan, 468). Radhakrishnan writes that Buddha's "cautious and careful attitude developed into negative systems, and his teaching fell a prey to the very dogmatism which he was anxious to avoid" (*Indian Philosophy,* 469); but such are the traps of human history that what is intended might not be realized, and it would include any scholarly and painstaking *reading* of Buddhistic texts too! We shall have more opportunity of reviewing the epistemological controversy while discussing the schools of Buddhism.

Schools of Buddhism

Although the first great schism in the Buddhistic order took place some 150 years after the founder's death, arguments over the "real meaning" of the original teaching of Buddha began soon after his death. These arguments centered primarily around Buddha's "theory of change" and the resulting "theory of impermanence." The new wing of Buddhism, formed by a highly idealistic minority, called itself *Mahāyāna* or "the Greater Vehicle," while the older, more orthodox majority grouped to form *Hinayāna* or "the Lesser Vehicle." For the Hinayānists "the Buddha is a historical figure; but for the Mahayānists he is eternal and absolute" (Lannoy, 334). While the Hinayānists (also called "Theravāda" school) had their center at Kaushambi and collected Buddha's teachings into the "Pali Canon" (so called because it was written in Pali), Mahāyāna Buddhism flourished in Gandhara in the northwest of India and extended Buddhistic teachings in Sanskrit. Eventually, Hinayāna Buddhism "found its stronghold in Ceylon, Burma, and the countries of south-east Asia, whereas Mahayana Buddhism became the dominant sect in India, central Asia, Tibet, China, and Japan" (Thapar, 130).

The Mahāyānists were of the view that the conservative tradition was lesser on at least two accounts. They criticized its monastic life, which they thought was too austere for the common man to offer him any hope for liberation; instead, they offered their "redemption religion" (Lannoy, 335) whose basis was faith and devotion *(bhakti)* and which incorporated "substantial portions of Hindu metaphysics and polytheism" (Lannoy, 335). They were also critical about the Hinayāna way to *nirvāna,* which, they thought, was narrow in its ethical ideals and was not "outward-looking and compassionate, in the way symbolized by the Bodhisattva." The Hinayāna monk, they argued, "seeks to become an *arhat*—a saint who has attained nirvana: the adherent of the Greater Vehicle follows the path of the Bodhisattva sacrificing himself for others" (Ninian Smart, 136). It must be pointed out, however, that the Mahāyāna Buddhism possesses no canon, represents no "homogeneous sect," and, as Ninian Smart writes, "it is doubtful whether the divisions of Buddhism have ever been serious as those dividing Christianity at the time of the Reformation and thereafter" (Smart, 136).

The two initial sects, in the course of time and over several Councils of debating followers, produced four main schools: Hinayāna Buddhism produced the schools of *Vaibhāsikas* and *Sautāntrikas,* whereas the Mahāyāna school split into the *Yogāchāras* and *Mādhyamikas,* the former two believing in the reality of the external world while the latter two clearly indicating their belief in the reality of the mind and mental forms. Realism and idealism, it might be said, are the two logical consequences of Buddha's dynamic philosophy of becoming. We shall briefly enumerate the salient features of these four subschools.

The School of the Vaibhāsikas

This school derives its name from its emphasis on a particular commentary on the *Abhidharma-pitaka,* known as the *Abhidhamma-mahāvaibhāsā.* It considered the language of all other schools as absurd *(viruddha-bhāsā),* contradictory, and vague, and it carried this to an extent as to form a full-fledged philosophy, which might be called pluralistic realism. It came into prominence in the third century A.D.

The Vaibhāsikas hold the view that the external objects are known directly through perceptual experience. Perception, according to them, justifies the existence of external objects. Their system admits two kinds of perception: determinate, and indeterminate. Indeterminate perception *(nirvikalpaka)* is the result of the contact between the senses and the object; it is the immediate awareness of an object involving no discrimination between a substance/object and its quality. The determination of such discrimination, however, is associated with determinate perception. Since the Vaibhā- sikas do not accept the difference between a substance and its attributes, all perceptual judgments, according to them, are erroneous. But although they refuse to accept such difference, any individual or essential characteristic is significant for them. Thus, when we say, "The rose is red," which is a perceptual judgment, we are passing through the stage of determinate perception, when the mind imposes concepts in the form of universal characteristics *(sāmānya-laksana).*

As Radhakrishnan writes, for the Vaibhāsikas, the objects are of two kinds, namely, "the perceived and the inferred, the sensible and the cogitable," and, though the external objects may at times be known to exist by inference, "still as a rule perception points to their existence." Thus they distinguish between "the inner world of ideas and the outer world of objects": "The mind is conscious of objects. Our knowledge or awareness of things not mental is no creation, but only discovery. Things *are* given to us. The substance of things has a permanent existence throughout the three divisions of past, present and future" (Radhakrishnan, 614).

Naively realistic, the Vaibhāsikas are "natural dualists" who maintain the independent existence of nature and mind and recognize "immediate apprehension and influence as the means providing us with valid knowledge" (Guenther, 41). Contrary to the Sautāntrika belief, the Vaibhāsikas maintain that the existence of external objects cannot be explained or justified by inference alone, which, they argue, is of little use unless we have already perceived these objects at some point of time. They give the example of someone inferring the existence of fire from his perception of smoke; for the Vaibhāsikas, such inference must be grounded on one's earlier perception of fire and smoke together. Perception therefore is a necessary and inescapable condition for inference.

The school believes in permanent substances or elements which always underlie particular objects. They are the "ultimate constituents" *(dharmas)* of reality, but they also constitute the world of our empirical existence. The Vaibhāsikas, in other words, reject "any distinction between the world as it appears to us and as it is in itself" (Puligandla, 74). They also further maintain that these ultimate constituents of existence are absolute and independent of our consciousness; they are also distinct and irreducible. Reality, according to the Vaibhāsikas, is "flux made up of point-instants *[ksanas]* constituted of *dharmas,* each point-instant succeeding the other in an unbroken chain . . . [of] causal connections between successive point-instants" (Puligandla, 74). However, the Vaibhāsikas fail to offer any definite account of the relation existing between "the underlying reality and the phenomenal manifestations" (Radhakrishnan, *Indian Philosophy,* 615).

The Vaibhāsika school accepts only four elements: earth (hardness), water (coolness), fire (warmth), and air (mobility). Further, they put all the objects under a two-fold division: (1) *bāhya* or external, and (2) *abhayāntara* or internal. *Bāhya* includes the *bhutas* or "elements," and *bhautikas* or "those belonging to the elements"; *abhayāntara* includes *chitta* or intelligence, and *chaitta* or "those belonging to intelligence." The external objects, according to the Vaibhāsikas, are the result of a concentration of "the ultimate atoms according to their capacity" (Radhakrishnan, 616). The atomic theory is accepted not only by the Vaibhāsika school, but also by its sister Hinayāna school of Sautāntrika. For the Vaibhāsikas, however, an atom is six-sided, indivisible, singly invisible, and unanalyzable. All the compound objects are the result of an aggregate of atoms. Material things which offer resistance *(pratighāta)* to sense-organs are "collections of the fourfold substrata of *rupa* (of which an atom is the smallest particle), namely, colour, smell, taste and touch"; and the unit having all the four qualities is the *paramānu* or "the ultimate atom." These "ultimate atoms" *(paramānus)* combine to form the smallest perceptible atomic unit or *anu.*

Since the Vaibhāsikas believe that only perception determines the existence of an object, they imply that the object ceases to exist the moment perception ceases, when we "see" only the particular object but not the universal. Thus the problem of universals arises when we use general terms like horse, brown, and energy. The general term horse, for instance, refers to common properties like horseness and brown-ness exemplified in particulars. Unlike essentialists, who maintain that these common properties are "entities having reality of their own independently of the particular objects which exemplify them," the Vaibhāsikas are of the view that the universals are not objectively existent but only concepts abstracted from the perception of properties common to objects of the same type. The Vaibhā-sika denial of an independent ontological status to universals has led R. Puligandla to call them nominalists (see Puligandla, 75–76).

The School of the Sautāntrikas

This is the second major school of the Hinayāna sect. It derives its name from the emphasis it lays on the *Sutra-pitaka* (Pali: *Sutta-Pitaka*). They are so called because of their adherence to the *sutras* (the section containing the discourses of Buddha). There are two divisions among them—those who deny every other appeal than that to the word of the founder, and those who admit other proofs. Kumāralabdha, the author of *Drstāntamata-sāstra,* is believed to be the founder of the school; Dharmottara, the logician, and Yasomitra, the author of the commentary on Vāsubandhu's *Abhidharmakosa,* are two of his principal followers.

While the Vaibhāsikas maintain that we perceive external objects directly, the Sautāntrikas maintain that our perception of the external world is in terms of images or representations from which we infer the existence of that world. Or, as H.V. Guenther writes, "the objective constituents of perceptual situations are particular existents of a pecular kind; they are not literally parts of the perceived object, although they resemble physical objects as ordinarily conceived" (Guenther, 73). Mādhava's *Sarvadarsana-samgraha* describes the way the Sautāntrikas infer the existence of an external world: "Cognition must ultimately have some object since it is manifested in duality. . . . If the object proved were only a form of cognition, it should manifest itself as such, and not as an external object." If modern logic, as Radhakrishnan points out, looks upon this as "a confusion between objectivity and externality" and says that the internal element manifests itself *as if* it were something external, the Sautāntrikas would reply: "This is untenable, for if there be no external objects, there being no genesis of such, the comparison 'as if they were external,' is illegitimate. No man in his sense would say Vāsumitra looks like the son of a childless mother." We infer the objective existence from certain peculiar properties, even as we infer "nourishment" from "a thriving look," "nationality from language," and "emotion from expression" (Mādhava, quoted in Radhakrishnan, 620).

The Sautāntrika's representational epistemology does not deny the independent existence of external objects; it only points to our *indirect* perceptual experience of them. The Sautāntrikas present a well-founded argument in support of the existence of the external world: If the external world were not real, then we would not be able to distinguish between the "actually existent" and an "illusion of it." The mirage in a desert and the actually existing water in a lake or pond differ on the point that while the former is an illusion, the latter is existent. If one had never perceived water as such, he would not in the first place entertain the belief that what he perceived (i.e., the mirage) from a distance looked *like* water. Thus our belief in the independent existence of external objects "is warranted by the fact of our experience of perceptual illusions" (Puligandla, 78).

Unlike the Vaibhāsikas, the Sautāntrikas differentiate the phenomenal appearance of a thing from the noumenal thing-in-itself, on the basis of which distinction they reject the Vaibhāsika thesis of the ultimate constituents *(dharmas)* of existence being the same as those which constitute the world of empirical experience. In other words, the Sautāntrika refuses to offer the "ultimate constituents" any "absolute, ultimate, and independent ontological status" (Puligandla, 79), by keeping the noumenal part away from that which is given through phenomena-based experience.

Having accepted the reality of the external world, the Sautāntrikas explain the process of knowledge which, according to them, is based on four primary conditions. They are: data or *ālambana,* suggestion or *samanantara,* medium or *sahakāri,* and dominant organ or *adhipati-rupa.* Mādhava's *Sarvadarsana-samgraha* gives us an example of a particular process of knowing: "From blue data, the form of blue arises in the understanding, which manifestation is styled a cognition *(jñāna).* From suggestion there is a revival of old knowledge. The restriction to the apprehension of this or that object arises from the medium, light, as one condition and the dominant organ as the other" (quoted in Radhakrishnan, 622). Further, Dharmakirti in his *Nyāyabindu* defines perception as a presentation regulated totally and uniquely by the object without interference of the mind. The resulting knowledge, therefore, is indeterminate knowledge *(nirvikalpa),* for determinate knowledge *(savikalpa)* necessarily involves a "conceptual activity of the mind." It is the knowledge of the object-in-itself *(sva-laksanam).* There is very little difference between the Vaibhāsika and the Sautāntrika theories on the origin of cognition, which for both is a complex phenomenon in which several elements participate, interconnected but separate, with the essential presence of the element of consciousness among them (see Stcherbatsky, 63).

As we have seen, for the Vaibhāsikas, past, present and future are all equally real, although the past and the future are embedded in the present. This naturally brings to the forefront of discussion the theory of point-instants and their durational nature. In order to be causally efficient, according to the Vaibhāsikas, a point-instant must have duration; that is, only a point-instant that has duration is causally efficient to bring about its succeeding point-instant. The Sautāntrikas, however, argue that any attempt to assign duration, however small, to point-instants is to go against the basic theory of dependent origination *(pratitya-samutpāda),* for it would amount to regarding the point-instants as permanent entities. According to the Sautāntrikas, "the relation between point-instants is one of replacement in accordance with the principle of conditioned origination; that is, each point-instant is replaced by its succeeding one, the latter being merely dependent upon, but not caused by, the former." For the Sautāntrikas, the arising and passing away of a point-instant refer to one and the same process; which is to say, existence and nonexistence are different names given to "the single reality of becoming" (Puligandla, 80). The Sautāntrikas were so much obsessed with ideas of "becoming" and "impermanence" that they refused to believe that even *nirvāna* could be a state of permanent bliss; instead, they believed it to be a state of mere cessation of sufferings through a cessation of transmigration. The Vaibhāsikas, however, rejected such an idea on the ground that it was negativisitic.

Nirvāna *in the Hinayāna School*

Both Vaibhāsika and Sautāntrika schools are offshoots of the *Sarvāstivāda* (so called because of their affirmation, "All things exist": derived from *sarva* = everything, and *asti* = exists) school. Although they differ in many ways, the two schools resemble in many ways too.

The Vaibhāsikas present a catalogue of 75 elements or *dharmas,* 72 of which are known as *samskrta-dharma* and are responsible for the individual being's attachment for life. An individual seeking *nirvāna* aims at escaping these elements. Ignorance *(avidyā)* is at the basis of such attachment, while knowledge *(jñāna)* helps one toward the removal of such attachment. To support this, the practical teachings laid down by the early Buddhists are scrupulously followed by the Hinayānas. They accept the two "paths" or ways to achieve their elders' ideal of life, which is emancipation by the elimination of the sources of suffering, although they lay more emphasis on *nivrtti* (withdrawal leading to meditation) as against *pravrtti* (the path of action). Withdrawal from the external world, which is momentary, amounts therefore to a withdrawal from a world of change. Accordingly, the Hinayāna emphasis is on *individual* liberation. The Hinayāna follows with great care Buddha's words: "Be a light unto thyself" *(atmadipo-bhava);* for him *arhathood* (from *arhat* = one who has attained liberation and thus become a saint) is the ultimate state. An *arhat* is one who has overcome all passions and has no attachment for a "home" or a family; he is tolerant like the earth and is undisturbed by the cycle of births and deaths; his mind, indifferent to pleasure and pain alike, is tranquil like the "deep-sea water"; and, he finds delight even in the forest, where common and homebound men are unlikely to have any fruitful experience.

The Hinayāna does not believe in any supreme being or God. Yasomitra, a Sautāntrika, argues that living creatures are created neither by God *(Isvara)* nor by any transcendent spirit *(purusha,* of which we shall know more in the chapter on *Sāmkhya-Yoga),* nor by matter *(pradhāna).* If there was such a primordial cause as God, it would have created the world "in its totality at once and at the same time" and the world would have had a "beginning." God is replaced by the law of *karma* and the orthodox Hindu idea of transmigration is replaced by the transference of deeds and tendencies from one life to another.

The new idea of transmigration-through-transfer implies its cessation and the perfection of a being: *nirvāna* is a state beyond cause and effect as it is beyond good and evil. Out of the three *a-samskrta-dharmas* (in the list of 75 elements we have spoken of earlier in this section) of the Vaibhāsika school, the last two—*pratisamkhyā-nirodha* or cessation with the help of knowledge, and *apratisamkhyā-nirodha* or cessation without the help of knowledge—refer to nothing but *nirvāna.* As we have seen, the Hinayānists stick to a negative definition of *nirvāna* (although the Pali canon gives a positive description as well), for, they argue (following the Upanishadic ideal), that anything transcendental or extra-empirical can be best described as "not this" and "not that."

Immediately after Buddha's death, the first Buddhist council was held at Rājagrha to discuss the Buddhist code of conduct and re-emphasize the founder's practical teachings. The council modified and liberalized that code of conduct. In the second such council, it was decided that the original code of conduct be restored. Some members, who were against it, were expelled. They formed a new group called *Mahāsamghikas;* they introduced changes in Buddha's practical teachings and in the original metaphysical speculations. Notwithstanding the fact that Buddha himself was against any tendency among his followers to deify him, the Mahāsamghikas elevated him to the status of a transcendental being *(Lokāttara Buddha);* they also conceived the mind as pure consciousness. Thus they laid the foundation for the idealistic school of *Mahāyana.*

The third post-Buddha council was held during the reign of King Asoka, in which as many as 11 new schools were rejected by the monks on the ground that they showed definite signs of unorthodoxy and rebellion. The members of these schools took shelter in the monastery at Nalandā before settling in Gāndhāra. Later, under the patronage of King Kanishka, several monasteries were built for them and a lot of attention was given to their religious and literary activities. Under the royal patronage, there came into existence two offshoots of *Sarvāstivāda*—the schools of Vaibhāsika and Sautāntrika.

Both Hinayāna and Mahāyāna schools started with Buddha's teachings, but they differed in their views regarding impermanence *(anitya),* not-Self or not-Soul *(anātma* or *anattā),* and liberation *(nirvāna).* The Hinayānists viewed the constituent elements as transitory *(anitya)* and the beings so constituted as without substance and individuality *(anātma).* They admitted substance-less-ness *(pudgala-sunyatā)* but not element-less-ness *(dharma-sunyatā);* on the other hand, the Mahāyanists argued in favor of both *pudgala-sunyatā* and *dharma-sunyatā.* The Hinayānists described *nirvāna* "negatively," whereas the Mahayānists described it "positively," as the Ever-existing Reality *(vijñāpti-mātrata),* and considered it as the ideal state to bring about *collective,* not merely *individual,* liberation. The two principal schools within the Mahāyāna fold are the school of *Yogāchāra* (also called *Vijñānavāda*) and the school of *Mādhyamika.*

The School of Yogāchāra

There are two different, though related, accounts of the term "Yogāchāra." According to one, the school derives its name from its emphasis on critical inquiry *(yoga)* and on exemplary moral behavior or conduct *(āchāra);* according to the other, the school believed that the absolute truth *(bodhi)* is attainable only by those who train themselves in yogic practices. If the term "Yogāchāra" refers to the practical side of the school, the term "Vijñānavāda" refers to its philosophical and speculative aspects. While some philosopher-historians consider Asanga as the founder of the school, others consider Maitreyanāth, the teacher of Asanga, as the real founder. Asanga's younger brother, Vasubandhu, who was originally a Sautāntrika, was later converted into Mahāyāna; in fact, he became the first Yogāchāra to systematize the philosophical doctrines of that school. Asanga wrote *Yogāchāra-bhumi;* Vasubandhu authored *Vijñānpti-mātrata-siddhi-vimshatikā* and *Vijñānpti-mātrata-siddhi-trimshika. Thus Maitreyanā*th, Asanga, and Vasubandhu are the chief exponents of the Yogāchā school.

although there were other figures like the logician Dinnāga, Dharmapāla, Paramārtha, and Jayasena.

The most important doctrine of the Yogāchāra school is that consciousness or mind alone is real. Vasubandhu, for instance, attributed the existence of the world objects to "inner ideation" and held that "nothing but ideation exists." As to ontology, this school stands between the realistic (Vaibhāsika and Sautāntrika) and the nihilistic (Mādhyamika or Sarvasunyavāda) schools, adhering "neither to the doctrine that all things exist, because it takes the view that nothing outside the mind (mental activity) exists, nor to the doctrine that nothing exists, because it asserts that ideations do exist," but "to the doctrine of the mean, neither going to the extreme of the theory of existence (*ens* = being) nor to that of non-existence (non-*ens* = non-being)" (Takakusu, 81). Thus the Middle Path between the two extremes of hedonistic worldly life and pessimistic ascetic life which Buddha envisaged, is promoted to the middle path between two ontological views. Junjiro Takakusu, therefore, calls this school "Ideal-Realism."

As a consequence of its emphasis on the reality of consciousness, the Yogāchāra school regards all external objects as unreal; but, following the doctrine of dependent origination, it views consciousness as "an everchanging stream" rather than a substance. Further, it is impossible to establish the independent existence of external objects, for no object can ever be experienced apart from consciousness; since "consciousness and its object are simultaneous, they are identical" (Puligandla, 80–81). As Stcherbatsky writes: "The object of cognition is the object cognized by introspection and appearing to us as though it were external. The ultimate reality is thus the 'idea' consciousness" (*Buddhist Logic,* Vol. I, 519–20, quoted by Puligandla, 285). It is because of their unqualified emphasis on consciousness *(vijñāna)* as the ultimate reality that the Yogāchāra school is also called *Vijñāna-vāda.* As R. Puligandla notes, the Yogāchāra theory is similar to the subjective idealism of Berkeley.

According to the Yogāchāras, the thinking being becomes conscious of its own existence and identity of the subject only by knowing objects. Thus the permanent storehouse of individual consciousness *(ālaya),* with its internal duality of subject and object, becomes itself a little world, confined to its own circle of modifications. The Yogāchāras, however, are not quite clear about the exact significance of *ālaya,* although there are indications that *ālaya-vijñāna* or "the sum total of our conscious states" is used in the sense of "the absolute self." It is said to be without any origination, existence and extinction; it alone exists, all individual, intellectual products being mere phenomena, phases of the *ālaya. Ālaya-vijñāna* is thus "the absolute totality, originality and creativity, unconditioned itself by time and space, which are modes of existence of the concrete and empirical individuality"; consequently, *ālaya* becomes "the universal subject, and not the empirical self" (see Radhakrishnan, 629–631).

It would be pertinent here to summarize Radhakrishnan's criticism of the Yogāchāra metaphysics. His basic criticism is directed against the Yogāchāra's reduction of "matter opposed to the empirical individual to a mere sensation or collection of sensations." By maintaining that solidity, distance, and resistance are mere ideas of the finite mind, the Yogāchāras only reduce themselves to crude subjectivists. The school cannot, therefore, account for "the world organism which precedes the birth of human consciousness" or "the seeming reality of a common world which renders our ordinary life possible." In their eagerness to refute the naive realism of the Hinayāna school, "they confused psychological and metaphysical points and countenanced a crude mentalism." While admitting that it was not something that the Yogāchāras intended, Radhakrishnan takes exception to their use of the term *vijñāna* to indicate both the changing and the unchanging aspects of the mind. While *skandha-vijñāna* is the "phenomenal effect of karma," *ālaya-vijñāna* is the "ever active, continuous, spiritual energy dwelling in all ... the foundational fact of reality revealing itself in individual minds and things ... the whole containing within itself, the knower and the known." Unfortunately, as Radhakrishnan notes, the Yogāchāras tended to identify the *ālaya-vijñāna* with *skandha-vijñāna,* which is "only a property of the finite mind" (Radhakrishnan, 631-632).

Ālaya, according to the Yogāchāras, is the potential source of all that we perceive and all that we possess, including our thoughts, the latter having a threefold character: the imagined *(parikalpita),* the dependent *(parāntara),* and the absolute *(parinishpanna).* All elements *(dharmas)* are the external manifestations of the potential kārmic seeds stored in the *ālaya,* some of which are "full of defilement" *(sasrava-bija)* and thus cause the world of suffering to continue, while some others are "free from defilement" *(anāsrava-bija)* and thus urge us towards liberation. Thus every individual has in him "the higher principle bound up with a selfish individuality," the latter clinging to the individual as long as he is subject to ignorance or *avidyā.* It is yoga alone, coupled with exemplary conduct, which can enable the individual to realize the difference between the *illusion of the external world* (caused by *sasrava-bija* with the active support of *avidyā*) and the *truth of thusness* or *tathatā* (encouraged by the *anāsrava-bija* and yogic discipline). Accordingly, one who has realized the absolute truth of consciousness—its *thus-ness*—is called *Tathāgata* (from *tathatā);* and such realization is indeed the attainment of *nirvāna.*

The School of Mādhyamika

The word "Mādhyamika" may be translated as "the follower of the middle path." As we have already said, Buddha himself called his ethical teaching the "Middle Way" (middle = *madhyama*) and thus refuted the two extremes of "exaggerated asceticism and an easy secular life"; similarly, in metaphysics, he rejected all extreme positions. The Mādhyamikas, following the founder's footsteps, accept the "middle way" between extreme affirmation and extreme negation, between "eternalism and annihilationism" (Puligandla, 83).

The Mādhyamika system has had an uninterrupted history of development from the time of its formulation by Nāgārjuna (? second century A.D.) to the total disappearance of Buddhism in India (11th century). In Nāgārjuna we find one of the finest thinkers of India. A man who was at once skeptical and mystical, his skepticism is essentially Buddhistic, while his belief in an absolute standard of reality derives from the Upanishads. But the entire period of Mādhyamika history shows a host of thinkers who were equally brilliant, the chief among whom are Nāgārjuna's immediate disciple Āryadeva, Buddhapālita, Bhāvaviveka, Chandrakirti, Shāntideva, Kumārajiva (who translated Nagarjuna's texts into Chinese), Shantarakshita, and Kamalāsila.

Nāgārjuna's *Mādhyamika-kārikā* (sometimes referred to as *Mādhyamika Sāstra* and *Mādhyamika Sutra*) is the basic text of this school. Nāgārjuna's other texts include *Sunyatā Saptati, Yukti Sashtika, Vigraha-Vyavartani, Vaidalya Sutra, Vyavahāra Siddhi,* and *Ratnāvali.* There are, in addition, a large number of small tracts which are attributed to Nāgārjuna, but it is difficult to decide about the real authorship of these works (see Murti, 88–91). *Chatuh-sataka* or simply *Sataka* as it is now called is the most significant work of Ārya Deva. Bhāvaviveka in his *Karatalaratna* attempts to establish the basic Mādhyamika principles by syllogistic arguments; besides, he has written extensive commentaries on some of Nāgārjuna's texts, the most important of which is the one on *Mādhyamika Sāstra,* called *Prajñā-pradipa.* Chandrakirti and Sānti Deva gave to the Mādhyamika system its rigorous, orthodox form. Chandrakirti's *Prasannapada* (a commentary on the *Mādhyamika-khrikās*) and *Madhyamakavatara,* and Santi Deva's *Siksha Samuccaya* and *Bodhicharyavatara* are four of the most popular works in the entire Mahāyana literature. Sāntarakshita's *Tattvasamgraha* and his disciple, Kamalāsila's *Mādhyamikāloka,* along with the aforementioned works, more or less complete the Mādhyamika literature.

According to the Mādhyamika, true philosophy, which is essentially spiritual and emphasizes the wisdom that liberates the individual, is "the dialectical consciousness of the limitations of our constructions of reality out of *nāma* [name] and *rupa* [form]—it is reason discovering its own shortcomings and powerlessness to give us insight into reality as it is" (Puligandla, 88). The Mādhyamika is wary of metaphysics "not because there is no real for him; but because it is inaccessible to Reason" (Murti, 126). He speaks of a higher faculty, Intuition *(prajñā)* with which the Real *(tattva)* is identical. For him thought-distinctions are "purely subjective, and when taken as the texture of the real they are nothing less than a falsification of it" (Murti, 128). For Nāgārjuna, the highest wisdom *(prajñā-pāramitā)* consists in a simultaneous awareness of the limited and relative nature of all metaphysical constructions of reality and purely intuitive insight into reality. Accordingly—and here we must modify our earlier description of the Madhyamika as the "philosophy of the middle view"—the Madhyamika position is beyond concept or speech, transcendental, "a review of all things," a rejection of all views of Being and Non-Being, of Affirmation and Negation, in short, a daring criticism of all the earlier systems.

The Mādhyamika rejects all views by turning every thesis against itself, by showing the self-contradictory character of a particular view through drawing out its implications. His dialectic is a series of *reductio ad absurdum* arguments; his aim is to disprove his opponent's thesis without proving any thesis of his own *(prasanga)*. *Prasanga* is not to be understood in the Kantian sense, however; it is not apagogic proof, in which we establish the falsity of a specific thesis in order to prove indirectly another. *Prasanga* is "disproof simply, without the least intention to prove any thesis"; it is "pure negation" (Murti, 132).

No fact of experience, when analyzed, is a thing in itself; it is what it is in relation to other facts which in turn depend on still others. Philosophical systems, in their eagerness to establish their own views, become victims of the instability and limitations inherent in their contentions. For instance, the relation between cause and effect cannot be one of identity, nor one of difference, nor both identity and difference. As Nāgārjuna writes in *Mādhyamika-kārikās:* "Neither of those things is established (as real) which cannot be conceived either as identical or different from each other." Again, as Nāgārjuna points out, there is no self apart from the states, nor can the states have unity without the self; nor are they anything together. "Things that derive their being and nature by mutual dependence are nothing in themselves; they are not real." The most significant controversy in this regard centers around *relation,* which in its performance of two mutually opposed functions, becomes a victim of circularity. It must connect two terms and make them relevant to each other by identifying one with the other; it must also differentiate the two terms. In other words, *relation* "cannot obtain between entities that are identical with or different from each other." Thus the Mādhyamika concludes that cause and effect, substance and its attributes, whole and its parts, or subject and object, are mutually dependent and are therefore relative; and, for this reason they are *not things-in-themselves* (see Murti, 136–138). Everything relative is subjective and, therefore, unreal: this is the basis of the Mādhyamika dialectic.

The Mādhyamika rejects every kind of categorization, since categories are only conceptual devices by which Reason conveniently tries to apprehend the Real — something which defies categorization and relativity. He therefore condemns Reason as falsifying the Real. As Murti puts it, no "phenomenon, no object of knowledge . . . escapes this universal relativity" (Murti, 139). Dependence implies a lack of the essence, and the Real *(tattva)* is "self-evident and self-existent"; it is "unconditioned" and hence, cannot be conceived either as existence *(bhava)* or as nonexistence *(abhāva)* or both. Applying his dialectic, Nāgārjuna rejects the *satkārya-vāda* theory of causation (i.e., the material effect is identical with or preexistent in the material cause) which is supported by the Sāmkhya and Advaita Vedānta, and the *asatkārya-vāda* theory of causation (i.e., the material effect is different from or does not preexist in the material cause) which the schools of Nyāya and Vaiseshika as well as Sautāntrika and Vaibhāsika supported (see Puligandla, 89–92).

The Mādhyamika Absolute is "not one reality set against another, the empirical." For him, the Absolute viewed through thought-forms *(vikalpa)* is merely phenomenon; and, phenomenon, freed of superimposed thought-forms *(nirvikalpa, nisprapancha)* is the Absolute. As Murti says, the difference is "epistemic (subjective), and not ontological." Nāgārjuna therefore does not find any difference between the world and the absolute reality; the Absolute, which is beyond thought and speculation, is "immanent in experience," which is to say, the world is only "the phenomenalisation of the absolute." True philosophy is self-critical, "self-consciously aware of the assumptions and inadequacies of Reason": this is the awareness of the relativity of phenomena, and hence, of their unreality. The means and end of true philosophy is intellectual intuition or *Prajñā,* in which knowledge (Reason) and its object (the Real) become one and nondual. Nāgārjuna calls this *Sunyatā* (emptiness/void), for the Absolute *(Prajñā)* is devoid of duality. It is important to distinguish here the terms *Sunya* and *Sunyatā* as applied to phenomena from those applied to the absolute: "phenomena are *Sunya* as they are devoid of thinghood *(nihsvabhāva);* for they are dependent on each other *(pratitya-samutpanṇa).* The Absolute is *Sunya* as it is utterly devoid of the conceptual distinctions of 'is' and 'not-is,' free from all subjectivity *(nirvikalpa, nisprapancha)*" (Murti, 142).

The primary cause of pain and suffering is *avidyā* or ignorance, the tendency on the part of the individual to conceptualize the real. Nāgārjuna writes: "Freedom is the cessation of acts *(karma)* and the roots of evil *(klesha);* these are born of false-ascriptions *(vikalpa)* and this of thought-constructions by Reason *(prapancha); prapancha* ceases with the knowledge of *Sunyatā*" *(Madhyamika-kārikās).* The dialectic as nonconceptual intuitional knowledge *(Prajñā)* takes us beyond the possibility of pain and suffering; it is Freedom itself *(Nirvāna).* The dialectic as highest wisdom *(Prajñā-pāramitā)* is also identified with the consciousness of thusness *(tathāgata),* which is attained by spiritual discipline. Religion is this "mystic pull of the Transcendent (the Ideal) on the actual"; the dialectic "consummates the union of all beings with the perfect Being." Thus the Mādhyamika dialectic as culminating in intuition is "not only the fruition of the theoretic consciousness; it is the fruition of the practical and religious consciousness as well" (Murti, 142).

It is interesting to note that Nāgārjuna, who views *prajñā* as the highest wisdom and identifies it with freedom from every kind of attachment and concept, warns against any clinging to the concept of even *Sunyatā,* of *Nirvāna,* of the Buddha himself. He writes in his *Mādhyamika-kārikās:* "The wise men have said that *sunyatā* or the nature of thusness is the relinquishing of all false views. Yet it is said that those who adhere to the idea or concept of *sunyatā* are incorrigible." By saying this, Nāgārjuna reaffirms the reality of *sunyatā* and *nirvāna* through a warning against any tendency to cling only to the *idea* or *concept* of *sunyatā* or *nirvāna.* It is on the basis of this fine distinction between the *concept* of the Real and *the* Real that critics of the Mādhyamika system have raised their voice. We would quote from one of the more recent ones:

> Some of the modern interpreters try to defend the Mādhyamikas by claiming that the *sunya* is not to be understood as the bare void or the

> mathematical zero, but as the technical term for the indescribable ultimate reality. Even admitting this to be true, it is at best only a terminological innovation. The Upanisadic idealists denied the empirical world and gave to the ultimate reality the name *Brahman.* The Mādhyamikas, proceeding on similar lines, called the ultimate reality the *sunya.* But this *sunya* was with the Mādhyamikas just an esoteric or mystical concept and that made it somewhat impossible even to argue seriously against their position. If the ultimate reality was characterised as consciousness, as was done by the Upanisads and the later Advaita Vedānta, then there could at least be the possibility of looking at it as a serious philosophical thesis and, therefore, of defending or refuting it logically. With mysticism, however, this was not possible [Chattopadhyaya, 155–156].

We have enthusiastic defenders of the Mādhyamika system too. S. Radhakrishnan, for instance, writes:

> To the Mādhyamikas reason and language apply only to the finite world. To transfer the finite categories [including logical defence or refutation] to the infinite would be like attempting to measure the heat of the sun by the ordinary thermometer. We call it *sunyam,* since no category used in relation to the conditions of the world is adequate to it. To call it being is wrong, because only concrete things are. To call it non-being is equally wrong. It is best to avoid all descriptions of it [Radhakrishnan, 667–668].

As it might have been evident already, *nirvāna* is viewed differently by the Yogāchāras and the Mādhyamikas. The *Vijñānamātra Sāstra,* an important text of the Yogāchāra or Vijñānavāda school, speaks of four kinds of *nirvāna:* (1) *Nirvāna* in the sense of "the undefiled essence present in all things," including every sentient individual *(dharma-kāya);* (2) *Nirvāna* in the sense of a "state of relative being which, though freed from all affection, all hindrance, is still under the fetters of materiality" *(upādhisesha-nirvāna);* (3) *Nirvāna* in the sense of total liberation from all material fetters *(anupādhisesha-nirvāna);* and (4) *Nirvāna* in the sense of absolute enlightenment and "has for its object the benefitting of others." For the Mādhyamikas, however, *nirvāna* does not involve degrees or hierarchy; it is "equal and universal in all," a state of unconditioned equality *(samatā).* All beings, "irrespective of their status and attainment, are equally heir to Buddhahood—the highest perfection as unconditioned *Nirvāna.* They contain with them the seed of Enlightenment and Perfection *(Tathāgata-garbha)*" (see Radhakrishnan, *Indian Philosophy,* 642–643, and Murti, 257). Beings may be found in various stages and degrees of purification—according to their degree of spiritual discipline—but they are essentially one as Buddha. The final release, however, is possible only by annihilating all views, standpoints and predicaments, in short, through *Sunyatā.* The Mādhyamikas added one more kind to the four kinds of *nirvāna* of the *Yogāchāras*—the state of the Boddhisattva who renounces the Final Release, although "fully entitled to it," and who freely and spontaneously decides to devote himself to the welfare of all beings. The Mādhyamikas call it *apratisthita-nirvāna.*

For the Mādhyamika, *nirvāna* does not involve any change in things, but only a change in our outlook. *Nirvāna* is "what is not abandoned nor acquired; what is not annihilation nor eternality; what is not destroyed nor created." The Mādhyamika *Nirvāna* is quite close to the notion of *mukti* of Advaita Vedānta, although for the Advaitin, *mukti* is "not merely absolute existence, free from suffering, but consciousness *[chit]* and bliss *[ānanda]* as well." For the Mādhyamika it is not so, but "the bare assertion of the Absolute as the implicate of phenomena" and, therefore, indeterminate, although from the religious standpoint, identified with *Tathāgata*—"the principle of mediation between the Absolute that is transcendent to thought *(sunya)* and phenomenal beings" (see Murti, 273–276).

Buddhist Logic

It is interesting to note that in the *Tripitaka* (Three Baskets)—in fact, in the whole of Pali literature—there is not a single treatise on Logic, although there are stray references to logical topics and to a class of people who were called *Tarki* (debators/those who were well-versed in the art of reasoning). It is not known, however, whether these people were Buddhists, Jainas, or Brāhmanas, or a combination of three. They were not logicians in the proper sense of the term, but "sophists who indulged in quibble and casuistry" (Vidyabhusana, 227). The first signs of systematic reasoning are to be found in the works of the four later schools of Buddhism, whose founders—especially those of the Mādhyamika and the Yogāchāra schools—used logical arguments to defend their own standpoints and attacking those of their opponents. Nāgārjuna and Ārya Deva of the Mādhyamika school, and Maitreyanāth, Asanga and Vasubandhu of the Yogāchāra school, took the help of the logical methods of Aksapada (the Nyāya logician and compiler of *Nyāya-Sutra*) and employed these to their own ends.

In the *Mādhyamika-kārikā* Nāgārjuna has occasionally used certain terms of ancient logic, such as *punarukta* (repetition), *siddha-sādhana* (demonstration of what has already been established), and *parihāra* (avoidance). It also contains a criticism of Aksapada's concept of *Pramāna* (evidence). According to Aksapada, just as a lamp illumines itself as well as other objects, so does a *pramāna* establish itself as well as other objects. Nāgārjuna contends that a *pramāna* is not self-established. A lamp cannot illumine itself as there is no darkness in it, and if a lamp could remove darkness without coming in contact with it, it could as well remove the darkness of the entire universe. A *pramāna* cannot be so called if it is totally independent of *prameya* (objects); if, on the other hand, it is dependent on *prameya* (objects), it cannot, having no self-existence, establish the latter. The logical treatise, *Pramāna-vidhvamsana,* which is sometimes attributed to Nāgārjuna, literally signifies "the quelling of *pramāna.*"

Nāgārjuna's *Upāya-kausalya-hrdaya-sāstra* ("the essence of skill in the accomplishment of action"), a work on the art of debate, is supposed to have been written as a kind of answer to the "terminological obscurities" of the Vaisesika system. The book, divided into four chapters, deals with (1) an elucidation of debate, (2) an explanation of the points of defeat, (3) an explanation of the truths, and (4) the farfetched analogy. The first chapter deals with i) an example, ii) a tenet, truth or conclusion, iii) the excellence of speech, iv) the defect of speech, v) the knowledge of inference, vi) the appropriate speech, vii) the fallacy, and viii) the adoption of a fallacious reason. The second chapter, dealing with the "points of defeat," speaks of the following: i) the unintelligible, ii) non-ingenuity, iii) silence, iv) saying too little, v) saying too much, vi) the meaningless, vii) the inappropriate, viii) the incoherent, and ix) harming the proposition. The third chapter deals with the admission of an opinion. The fourth chapter shows the following kinds of farfetched analogy: i) balancing an excess, ii) balancing a deficit, iii) balancing the unquestionable, iv) balancing the nonreason, v) balancing the copresence, vi) balancing the mutual absence, vii) balancing the doubt, and viii) balancing the counter-example.

Similarly, three texts on the art of debate (in Sanskrit and later translated into Chinese) which are no longer extant and another called *Tarka-Sāstra* are attributed to Vasubandhu of the Yogāchāra school. *Tarka-Sāstra* has three chapters, dealing with (1) the five parts of a syllogism *(panchavayava),* (2) the analogous rejoinder *(jāti),* and (3) the points of defeat *(nigraha-sthāna).* A syllogism consisted of five parts: a proposition *(pratijñā),* a reason *(hetu),* an example *(udāharana),* an application *(upanaya),* and a conclusion *(nigamana).* In one of his nonextant texts, however, Vasubandhu is believed to have maintained that a thesis could be proved by two parts only—a proposition and a reason—and that the necessary terms in a syllogistic inference were only three—the minor *(paksha),* the major *(sādhya),* and the middle *(hetu).* Vasubandhu seems to have used the five-part syllogism at the time of a debate and the two-part syllogism on common occasions. The two forms are as follows:

The five-part syllogism:
1. Sound is noneternal.
2. Because it is a product.
3. All products are noneternal, like a pot, which is a product and is noneternal.
4. Sound is an example of a product.
5. Therefore sound is noneternal.

The two-part syllogism:
1. Sound is noneternal.
2. Because it is a product.

Vasubandhu's account of the "analogous rejoinder" *(jāti)* is divided into three kinds. (1) A rejoinder on the basis of reversion *(viparyaya-khandana)* includes a balancing of homogeneity, a balancing of heterogeneity, a balancing of thesis, a balancing of the unquestionable, a balancing of mutual absence, a balancing of nonreason, a balancing of the demonstration, a balancing of the doubt, a balancing of the nondifference, and a balancing of the effect; (2) a rejoinder on the basis of meaninglessness *(nirartha-*

khandana) involves a balancing of the point in dispute, a balancing of the counter-example, and a balancing of the infinite regression; and, finally (3) a contrary rejoinder *(viparita-khandana)* involves a balancing of the nonproduced, a balacing of the eternal, and a balancing of the presumption. *Tarka-Sāstra*'s third and final chapter deals with 22 points of defeat *(nigraha-sthāna).* They are: harming the proposition, shifting the proposition, opposing the proposition, renouncing the proposition, shifting the reason, shifting the topic, the meaningless, the unintelligible, the incoherent, the inappropriate, saying too little, saying too much, repetition, silence, ignorance, noningenuity, evasion, admission of an opinion, overlooking the censurable, censuring the noncensurable, deviating from a tenet, and the semblance of a reason or fallacy.

The texts we have discussed so far were basically philosophical and only incidentally devoted to logic. It was not until the middle of the fifth century A.D. that logic was an independent branch of study for the Buddhists. Dignāga (Dinnāga) was the pioneer of this new school, but his basic texts were criticized and reinterpreted by a group of fine logicians, like Dharmakirti, Dharmapāla, Sankara Svāmin, and Silabhadra. The works of these, together with those of the Jaina logicians, constitute what has been called the Medieval School of Indian Logic. Dignāga's *Pramāna-Samucchaya* and *Nyāya-Pravesa,* and Dharmakirti's *Nyāya-bindu* and *Pramāna-vārtika-kārikā* (a commentary on Dignāga's *Pramāna-Samucchaya)* are four of the major texts of later Buddhist logic. Besides, Dignāga wrote *Pramāna-samucchaya-vrtti* (a commentary on his own basic text), and Dharmottara wrote *Nyāya-bindu-tikā* (a commentary on Dharmakirti's *Nyāya-bindu*). The latter also wrote *Pramāna-parikshā,* involving an examination of the sources of knowledge, *Apoha-nāma-prakarana,* dealing with the determination of a thing by the exclusion of its opposite, and *Para-loka-siddhi,* dealing with the proof of the "other world." The original Sanskrit texts of most of these works are now lost, although their Tibetan versions are still available. We shall here discuss the three major texts: Dignāga's *Pramāna-samucchaya* and *Nyāya-Pravesa,* and Dharmakirti's *Nyāya-bindu.*

Dignāga's *Pramāna-samucchaya,* divided into six chapters, covers the following six topics: (1) Perception *(pratyaksha),* (2) Inference for one's own self *(svarthānumāna),* (3) Inference for the sake of others *(parārthānumāna),* (4) Reason and Example *(hetu-drstānta),* (5) Negation of the opposite *(apoha),* and (6) Analogue *(jāti).* Dignāga avoids a formal definition of perception, and only describes it as that which, "being freed from preconception, is unconnected with name, genus" and other such allied categories. He offers the example of a man who "in twilight" mistakes a rope for a snake and says that the man's knowledge of the snake is a preconception and hence, is not an act of perception. Dignāga concludes that perception is unconnected with the name, for we can perceive a thing without knowing its name. His second example is that of a unique cow, whose peculiarities can be realized only by one who has seen it and therefore defy their description before those who have not seen it and for whom it would remain only a cow possessing the common characteristics associated with the class of cows. Perception, therefore, is unrelated to genus. Of the two means of valid knowledge, perception is *particular* whereas knowledge derived through inference is *general.*

Inference *(anumāna)* is of two kinds, namely, inference for one's own self and inference for the sake of others. In the former kind of inference, knowledge is possible through the object or thing's possession of one of three characteristics as sign or mark (reason or middle term): (1) *effect* of the thing to be inferred (for example, smoke of fire); (2) *identity,* in the sense that the mark may in essence be identical with the thing to be inferred (for example, a pine identical with a tree); and (3) *nonperception* of the mark due to the nonexistence of the thing to be perceived (for example, nonperception of a pot is a mark of the nonexistence of the pot). Inference for the sake of others involves a person's demonstration for others of the conclusion drawn by him through an inference for one's self. Here, the predicate or major term is the object which is desired by one's self to be attributed to the subject or minor term and which is not opposed to perception, inference, or verbal testimony (example: The hill is *fiery*).

The law of the extension of the middle term, which refers to the "local area" of a reason or middle term in relation to its minor and major terms, is stated by Dignāga as follows: (1) the reason or middle term must cover the subject or minor term, (2) the reason or middle term must be present in the homologue of the predicate or major term, and (3) the reason or middle term must be absent from the heterologue of the predicate or major term. According to Dignāga, there are nine reasons or middle terms which are present or absent in the homologues or heterologues wholly or partly; and those which are wholly or partly present in the homologues but wholly absent from the heterologues, are valid, while their opposites are contradictory and the others uncertain. The nine reasons or middle terms, in reference to their homologues and heterologues, are as follows (Vidyabhusana, 284):

	Homologue of the major term *(sapaksha)*	Heterologue of the major term *(vipaksha)*	Nature of the reason
1.	Reason wholly present in the homologue.	Reason wholly present in the heterologue.	Reason uncertain.
2.	Reason wholly absent in the homologue.	Reason wholly absent from the heterologue.	Reason valid.
3.	Reason wholly present in the homologue.	Reason partly present in the heterologue.	Reason uncertain.
4.	Reason wholly absent from the homologue.	Reason wholly present in the heterologue.	Reason contradictory.
5.	Reason wholly absent from the homologue.	Reason wholly absent from the heterologue.	Reason uncertain.
6.	Reason wholly absent from the homologue.	Reason partly present in the heterologue.	Reason contradictory.
7.	Reason partly present in the homologue.	Reason wholly present in the heterologue.	Reason uncertain.

	Homologue of the major term *(sapaksha)*	Heterologue of the major term *(vipaksha)*	Nature of the reason
8.	Reason partly present in the homologue.	Reason wholly absent from the heterologue.	Reason valid.
9.	Reason partly present in the homologue.	Reason partly present in the heterologue.	Reason uncertain.

These nine reasons are illustrated by Dignāga in his *Hetu-chakra* or "The Wheel of Reasons," wherein he assumes the following as reasons or middle terms and major terms. His reasons (or middle terms) are: (1) knowable, (2) a product, (3) noneternal, (4) the produced, (5) the audible, (6) a product of effort, (7) the noneternal, (8) a product of effort, and (9) the tangible. Dignāga's predicates (or major terms) are: (1) the eternal, (2) the noneternal, (3) a product of effort, (4) the eternal, (5) the noneternal, (6) the eternal, (7) a nonproduct of effort, (8) the noneternal, and (9) the eternal. Applying the law of extension of the middle term to the "wheel" of nine reasons, we find that only the second and the eighth reasons are valid while the others are invalid (being either contradictory or uncertain). We may take two cases, the first illustrating the first reason in the wheel and the second illustrating the eighth in the wheel.

1. Illustration of the first reason: Sound is eternal.
   Because it is knowable.
   Like ether and like a pot.

2. Illustration of the eighth reason: This sound is noneternal.
   Because it is a product of effort.
   Like a pot, and unlike lightning and ether.

In the first case, knowability (reason) is wholly present in sound (subject) and in ether (a homologue of eternal the predicate); but being wholly present in a pot as well, which is a heterologue of eternal, knowability becomes *an uncertain reason.* In the second case, a product of effort is in this sound (subject) and in a pot (a homologue of noneternal the predicate), but not in lightning and ether (homologue and heterologue of the predicate). The reason here is thus partly present in the homologue and wholly absent from the heterologue, and hence, is *a valid reason.*

The reason or middle term is of two kinds, namely, affirmative and negative, the former signifying that "the thing signified by it is invariably accompanied by the thing signified by the predicate or major term" (example: "The hill is fiery, because it is smoky," where smoke is an affirmative reason), whereas in case of the latter, "wherever there is absence of the thing signified by the major term, there is also absence of the thing signified by the reason or middle term" (example: "The hill is not smoky, because it is not fiery."). According to Dignāga, it is obligatory on the part of a person who desires to produce before others (as for himself) a definite conclusion that he must *state* the subject, the predicate, and the reason as well as the mutual connection between the last two (predicate and reason). In pointing out the mutual connection, the person should also offer examples. Examples are of two kinds – affirmative or homogeneous, and negative or heterogeneous. Vidyabhusana gives the following illustration of the "stating of examples" *(drstānta)* and it may be seen how the two examples are in fact identical, for they both relate the mutual connection between reason (or middle term) and the predicate (or major term) (Vidyabhusana, 287):

> The hill is fiery.
> Because it is smoky.
> That which is smoky is fiery, as a kitchen (affirmative example).
> But that which is not fiery is not smoky, as a lake (negative example).

In the fifth chapter of *Pramāna-samucchaya,* Dignāga states his doctrine of "the negation of the opposite" or *Apoha,* according to which an object or entity is defined as being the negation of its opposite (example: "A cow is that which is not a not-cow."). It involves a consideration of the mutual relations of substance, quality, action, particularity, generality, and inherence. In the same chapter Dignāga rejects both Comparison and Verbal Testimony (which he calls "Credible Word") as distinct sources of knowledge. When one recognizes a thing through his perception of a similar thing, he is really performing an act of Perception and *not* Comparison. Similarly, when a person is said to speak "a Credible Word" – which implies that either the person or the fact he speaks of is credible – he is only performing an act of Inference (the person as credible) or an act of Perception (the fact as credible). Dignāga also states the law governing the middle term, according to which the middle term (or "mark" or "sign," as he calls it) is present only where the thing to be inferred (major term) or its homologue is present, and it is absent where the thing or its homologue is nonexistent (Example: Smoke is present only where there is fire or any thing homogeneous with it, but absent where there is no fire nor any thing homogeneous with it.)

Dignāga's other major text, *Nyāya-pravesa,* deals extensively with syllogistic reasoning and the possible fallacies. As we have seen already, the whole reasoning process consists of a major term *(sādhya* or *dharma),* a minor term *(paksha* or *dharmin),* a middle term or the reason *(hetu),* and two examples *(drstānta).* The form of the syllogism is as follows:

1. The hill is fiery.
2. Because it has smoke.
3. Whatever is smoky is fiery, like a kitchen, and whatever is not fiery is not smoky, like a lake.

Here hill is the minor term, fiery the major term, smoke the middle term or the reason, kitchen a homogeneous example, and lake a heterogeneous example. A minor term and a major term together constitute a proposition, and a proposition which is offered for proof is a Thesis. There are, however, certain theses which cannot stand the test of proof and are therefore fallacious, such as the following: (1) A thesis that is incompatible with perception (Example: "Sound is inaudible"); (2) A thesis that is incompatible with inference (Example: "A pot is eternal"); (3) A thesis that is partially or wholly incompatible with "the public opinion" (Example: "Leisure is something abominable" – some may agree with this, but many may not);

(4) A thesis that is incompatible with one's own belief (Example: A Vaisesika philosopher saying "Sound is eternal"); (5) A thesis that is incompatible with one's own statement (Example: "I am born of a childless mother"); (6) A thesis that uses an unfamiliar minor term (Example: The Buddhist telling the Sāmkhya philosopher, for whom "Sound" is not a well-known subject: "Sound is perishable"); (7) A thesis using an unfamiliar major term (Example: The Sāmkhya philosopher telling the Buddhist: "The soul is animate"); (8) A thesis using minor and major terms which are both unfamiliar (Example: The Vaisesika philosopher telling the Buddhist: "The soul has feelings which are pleasurable"—the Buddhist is concerned neither with the soul nor with its supposed feelings); and, finally, (9) A thesis that is universally accepted (Example: The thesis "Fire is warm" cannot be offered as proof, as it is accepted by all—a truism).

The Middle term or the reason *(hetu),* according to Dignāga, must possess three characteristics:

1. The whole of the minor term must be connected with the middle term, as in the following example, where "product" (middle term) includes the whole of "sound" (minor term):
   Example: Sound is eternal.
   Because it is a product.
   Like a pot, but unlike ether.
2. All things denoted by the middle term must be homogeneous with those denoted by the major term:
   Example: All products are noneternal, as a pot.
3. None of the things "heterogeneous from the major term" be a thing denoted by the middle term:
   Example: No non-noneternal (i.e., no eternal) thing is a product, as ether.

The three characteristics of the middle term may be represented in the following manner (where "S" is the minor term or subject, "R" is the middle term or reason, and "P" is the major term or predicate):

1. All S is R.
2. All R is P.
3. No R is non-P.

Accordingly, a syllogism may take one of the following forms:

1. All S is all P (conclusion).
   Because All S is all R,
   All R is all P.
2. All S is some P (conclusion).
   Because All S is all R,
   All R is some P.
3. All S is some P (conclusion).
   Because All S is some R,
   All R is all P.
4. All S is some P (conclusion),
   Because All S is some R,
   All R is some P.

The second and third of the three characteristics of the middle term only indicate that the middle term "is universally, invariably, or inseparably connected with the major term," and this connection between the two is called *Vyāpti* (invariable extension/ invariable concomitance/ relative extension)—a logical concept which, as Vidyabhusana writes, was "first discovered by Dignāga" (Vidyabhusana, 292). The connection may be symbolically set forth as follows (middle term = R, and major term = P):

1. All R is all P, *and*
2. All R is some P.

Any violation of one or more of the three characteristics of the middle term leads to what has been called "Fallacies of the Middle Term" or *Hetvābhāsa*. These may be of 14 kinds under three broad categories, namely, the unproved, the uncertain, and the contradictory:

1. When the absence of truth of the middle term is acknowledged by both parties:
   Example: Sound is noneternal.
   Because it is *visible*.
   (*Unproved* fallacy—neither of the parties admits that sound is visible.)
2. When the lack of truth of the middle term is acknowledged by one party only:
   Example: Sound is evolved.
   Because it is a *product*.
   (*Unproved* fallacy—the Mimāmsakas do not admit that sound is a product.)
3. When the truth of the middle term is questioned:
   Example: The hill is fiery.
   Because there is *vapor*.
   (*Unproved* fallacy—vapor may or may not be an effect of fire, and may or may not be connected with it otherwise.)
4. When it is questioned whether the middle term is predicable of the minor term:
   Example: Ether is a substance.
   Because it has qualities.
   (*Unproved* fallacy—it is questioned whether ether has qualities.)
5. When the middle term is too general or common, abiding equally in the major term as well as its opposite:
   Example: Sound is eternal.
   Because it is *knowable*.
   (*Uncertain* fallacy—the "knowable" is too general, and abides in the eternal as well as in the noneternal.)
6. When the middle term is not general or broad enough, abiding neither in the major term nor in its opposite:
   Example: Sound is eternal.
   Because it is *audible*.
   (*Uncertain* fallacy—audibility is not a quality general enough to make sound eternal.)
7. When the middle term abides in *some* of the things homogeneous with, and in *all* things heterogeneous from, the major term:
   Example: Sound is not a product of effort.
   Because it is *noneternal*.
   (*Uncertain* fallacy—the noneternal abides in some of the things

which are not products of effort, such as thunder, and abides in all things which are "not nonproducts of effort".)

8. When the middle term abides in *some* of the things heterogeneous from, and in *all* things homogeneous with, the major term:
   Example: Sound is a product of effort.
   Because it is *noneternal.*
   (*Uncertain* fallacy—the noneternal abides in some of the things which are not products of effort, such as thunder or lightning, and abides in all things which are products of effort.)
9. When the middle term abides in *some* of the things homogeneous with, and in *some* heterogeneous from the major term:
   Example: Sound is eternal.
   Because it is *incorporeal.*
   (*Uncertain* fallacy—incorporeality cannot always be related to eternality, for some incorporeal things are eternal, as ether, but some others are not, such as intelligence or emotion.)
10. When there is "a nonerroneous contradiction," that is, when a thesis and its opposite are *both* supported by what appear to be valid reasons:
    Example: (the Vaisesika speaking to the Mimāmsaka)
    "Sound is noneternal.
    Because it is a product."
    Example: (the Mimāmsaka speaking to the Vaisesika)
    "Sound is eternal.
    Because it is always audible."
    (*Uncertain* fallacy—both the reasonings are tenable, but together they lead to contradictory conclusions.)
11. When the middle term is contradictory to the major term:
    Example: Sound is eternal.
    Because it is a product.
    (*Contradictory* fallacy—a product is inconsistent with eternal.)
12. When the middle term is contradictory to the implied major term:
    Example: The eyes are serviceable to some being.
    Because it is made of particles.
    Like a bed.
    (*Contradictory* fallacy—the major term "serviceable to some being" is ambiguous, for the apparent meaning of "some being" is "the body," but its implied meaning is "the soul," and though things "made of particles" are serviceable to the body, they are not, according to the Sāmkhya, serviceable to the soul, which is without attributes.)
13. When the middle term is inconsistent with the minor term:
    Example: Generality is neither a substance, nor a quality, nor an action.
    Because it depends upon one substance and possesses quality and action.
    (*Contradictory* fallacy—generality does not depend upon one substance, etc.)
14. When the middle term is inconsistent with the implied minor term:
    Example: Objects are stimuli of action.
    Because they are apprehended by the senses.

(*Contradictory* fallacy—"objects" is ambiguous, meaning both things and purposes, and the middle term is inconsistent with the minor term in the second meaning, i.e., "purposes.")

Further, before the time of Dignāga, an example served as "a mere familiar case" cited to help the understanding of the listener. Dignāga converted an example into "a universal proposition," that is, a proposition expressive of the universal, invariable, and inseparable connection between the middle term and the major term, which stand causally or inherently related to each other. An example can be either homogeneous or heterogeneous as in the following two:

1. The hill is fiery.
   Because it has smoke.
   All that has smoke is fiery, like a kitchen (homogeneous example).
2. The hill is fiery.
   Because it has smoke.
   Whatever is not fiery has no smoke, like a lake (heterogeneous example).

Both homogeneous and heterogeneous examples might be fallacious under certain circumstances. We give below illustrations of a few of these fallacies.

A. Fallacies of homogeneous example:
   1. An example which is not homogeneous with the middle term:
      Illustration: Sound is eternal.
      Because it is incorporeal.
      That which is incorporeal is eternal, like the atoms.
      ("Atoms" are not incorporeal, and the fallacy is called Fallacy of the Excluded Middle Term.)
   2. An example which is not homogeneous with the major term:
      Illustration: Sound is eternal.
      Because it is incorporeal.
      That which is incorporeal is eternal, as intelligence.
      ("Intelligence" is not a good example, because it is not eternal, and it is a Fallacy of the Excluded Major Term.)
   3. An example homogeneous neither with the middle term nor the major term:
      Illustration: Sound is eternal.
      Because it is incorporeal.
      That which is incorporeal is eternal, as a pot.
      ("Pot" cannot serve as an example, because it is neither incorporeal nor eternal, and the resulting fallacy is Fallacy of the Excluded Middle and Major Terms.)

B. Fallacies of heterogeneous example:
   1. An example which is not heterogeneous from the opposite of the middle term:
      Illustration: Sound is eternal.
      Because it is incorporeal.
      Whatever is noneternal is not incorporeal, as intelligence.
      ("Intelligence" is noneternal, yet incorporeal, so the middle term "incorporeal" is associated with the heterogeneous example; the fallacy is called Fallacy of the Included Middle Term.)
   2. An example which is not heterogeneous from the opposite of the major term:
      Illustration: Sound is eternal.
      Because it is incorporeal.
      Whatever is noneternal is not incorporeal, as atoms.
      ("Atoms" are not incorporeal and yet they are eternal; the fallacy is called Fallacy of Included Major Term.)
   3. An example which is heterogeneous from neither the opposite of the middle term nor the opposite of the major term:
      Illustration: Sound is eternal.
      Because it is incorporeal.
      Whatever is noneternal is not incorporeal, as a pot.
      (A "pot" is both noneternal and nonincorporeal and thus includes both middle and major terms; the fallacy is called Fallacy of Included Middle and Major Terms.)

The universal proposition, which served as the major premise in the Aristotelian syllogism, was discovered and applied by Dignāga. The discovery was a significant step in the development of the principle of induction in Indian logic. Dignāga's theories were confirmed and extended by his disciple, Dharmakirti, a man with a keen intellect who was well-versed in the Vedas, grammar, the fine arts, and the art of healing (Vidyabhusana, 303). Our concern here, however, is Dharmakirti's criticism of Dignāga's theories. In his *Nyāya-pravesa* Dignāga speaks of the "fallacy of implied contradiction," which is the opposition of the middle term to the implied major term when the latter is ambiguous. Dharmakirti rejects it (in his *Nyāya-bindu*) on the ground that it is included in the broader "fallacy of contradiction," which is the opposition of the middle term to the major term and is accepted by him as well as Dignāga. According to Dharmakirti, "A word, which is the major term of a proposition, can, as such, admit of only one meaning, and if there is ambiguity between the meaning expressed and the meaning implied, the real meaning is to be ascertained from the *context*. If the meaning implied is the real one, there is *a natural contradiction* between the middle term and the major term" (Vidyabhusana, 316; emphasis added).

Dharmakirti also rejects Dignāga's "falacy of non-erroneous contradiction" (under fallacies of *uncertainty*) on the ground that it does not arise in connection with inference and is not based on the scripture. Two conclusions which are contradictory cannot be supported by reasons which are valid. Further, "Two different sets of scripture [which, in this case, relate to Vaibhāsika and Mimāmsaka] too cannot be of any help in the establishment of two contradictory conclusions inasmuch as a scripture cannot override perception and inference, and is authoritative only in the ascertainment of supersensuous objects" (Vidyabhusana, 317). Also, unlike Dignāga, Dharmakirti maintains that "example" cannot be a part of a syllogism, as it is included in the middle term:

Example: The hill is fiery.
Because it is smoky.
Like a kitchen.

The term "smoky" here includes a kitchen, as well as other locales similar to it, and therefore it is "almost unnecessary to cite the example 'kitchen'," although, Dharmakirti concedes, the general expression "all smoky things are fiery" is made more impressive by the particular example of a kitchen.

The Buddhists were able to uphold their logical theories for several centuries against those of the Brāhmanas, and in this they had been encouraged by a host of kings and princes. The Buddhist logician Nāgārjuna lived and worked under the patronage of King Satavāhana; Dignāga received the active support of King Simgha Varman. Gradually, however, there was a revival of Brāhmanism, initially in the South where Buddhism has a stronghold, but later in the North and the East as well. In addition, the Mahomeddan invasions which started around the 11th century A.D., exerted considerable influence on the already declining trend of Buddhism. They were responsible in the destruction of the Buddhist monasteries—the primary centers of intellectual and social activity—and the dispersal of the monks (Smart, 149). Moreover, as Radhakrishnan writes, Buddhism "grew weaker as it spread wider" (Radhakrishnan, *Indian Philosophy,* 605); in fact, later Buddhism soon became a storehouse of superstitions, having accommodated these during its many conquests to neighboring countries and religions. The Buddhist systems of thought were absorbed into the Brāhmanic systems, "smothered in the embrace of Hindu inclusiveness" (Lannoy, 346). As Richard Lannoy writes: "The fate of Buddhism affords us a highly instructive instance of India's efforts to assimilate its own rebellious and intractable elements" (Lannoy, 336).

Works Cited

Chattopadhyaya, Debiprasad. *Indian Philosophy: A Popular Introduction.* New Delhi: People's Publishing House, 1964.

Grimm, George. *The Doctrine of the Buddha: The Religion of Reason and Meditation.* Trans. Bhikku Silacara. Ed. M. Keller-Grimm and Max Hoppe. New Delhi: Motilal Banarsidass, 1982.

Guenther, H.V. *Buddhist Philosophy in Theory and Practice.* Baltimore: Penguin Books, 1972.

Hiriyanna, M. *The Essentials of Indian Philosophy.* 1949, London: George Allen & Unwin; rpt. Bombay: Blackie & Son, 1978.

Kosambi, D.D. *The Culture and Civilisation of Ancient India in Historical Outline.* 1970, London: Routledge & Kegan Paul; rpt. New Delhi: Vikas Publishing House, 1981.

Lannoy, Richard. *The Speaking Tree: A Study of Indian Culture and Society.* London and Oxford: Oxford University Press, 1974.

Murti, T.R.V. *The Central Philosophy of Buddhism: A Study of the Mādhyamika System.* London: George Allen & Unwin, 1980.

Puligandla, R. *Fundamentals of Indian Philosophy.* Nashville, Tennessee and New York: Abingdon Press, 1975.

Radhakrishnan, S. *Indian Philosophy.* Vol. I. (2 vols.). Muirhead Library of Philosophy. London: George Allen & Unwin, and New York: Humanities Press, 1966.

Radhakrishnan, S., and Moore, Charles A. eds. *A Sourcebook in Indian Philosophy.* Princeton: Princeton University Press, 1957.

Ranade, R.D. *Vedānta: The Culmination of Indian Thought.* Bombay: Bharatiya Vidya Bhavan, 1970.

Riepe, Dale. *The Naturalistic Tradition in Indian Thought.* 1961, Seattle: University of Washington Press; rpt. New Delhi: Motilal Banarsidass, 1964.

Smart, Ninian. *The Religious Experience of Mankind.* 1969, New York: Charles Scribner's; rpt. Glasgow: Fontana, 1982.

Stcherbatsky, Theodore. *The Central Conception of Buddhism and the Meaning of the Word "Dharma."* 1923, London: Royal Asiatic Society; rpt. New Delhi: Motilal Banarsidass, 1979.

Takakusu, Junjiro. *The Essentials of Buddhist Philosophy.* Ed. Wing-tsit Chan and Charles A. Moore. 1947, Honolulu: University of Hawaii Press; rpt. New Delhi: Motilal Banarsidass, 1978.

Thapar, Romila. *A History of India.* (2 vols.). Vol. 1. 1966; rpt. Harmondsworth, England: Penguin Books, 1986.

Thittila, Maha Thera U. "The Fundamental Principles of Theravāda Buddhism," in *The Path of the Buddha: Buddhism Interpreted by Buddhists.* Ed. Kenneth W. Morgan. New Delhi: Motilal Banarsidass, 1986.

Verdu, Alfonso. *Early Buddhist Philosophy in the Light of the Four Noble Truths.* New Delhi: Motilal Banarsidass, 1985.

Vidyabhusana, Satish Chandra. *A History of Indian Logic.* 1970; rpt. New Delhi: Motilal Banarsidass, 1978.

Suggested Further Reading

Conze, E. *Buddhist Thought in India.* Ann Arbor: University of Michigan Press, 1967.

Davids, T.W. Rhys. tr. *Buddhist Sutras.* New York: Dover, 1965.

Dutt, Nalinaksha. *Mahāyāna Buddhism*. New Delhi: Motilal Banarsidass, 1978.

Mookerjee, Satkari. *The Buddhist Philosophy of Universal Flux: An Exposition of the Philosophy of Critical Realism as Expounded by the School of Dignāga*. 1935, Calcutta: University of Calcutta Press; rpt. New Delhi: Motilal Banarsidass, 1980.

Rahula, Walpola. *What the Buddha Taught*. New York: Grove Press, 1962.

Stcherbatsky, Theodore. *Buddhist Logic*. 2 vols. New York: Dover Publications, 1963.

________. *The Conception of Buddhist Nirvāna*. With Sanskrit text of *Madhyamaka-karika* 1965, The Hague: Mouton; rpt. New Delhi: Motilal Banarsidass, 1977.

________. *The Soul Theory of the Buddhists*. Delhi and Varanasi: Bharatiya Vidya Prakashan, 1976.

Stryk, Lucien. ed. *World of the Buddha: A Reader from the Three Baskets to Modern Zen*. Garden City, New York: Doubleday, 1969.

Warder, A.K. *Indian Buddhism*. 1970; rev. ed. New Delhi: Motilal Banarsidass, 1980.

5

Vaisesika-Nyāya

Vaisesika and *Nyāya* are two of the six major systems of Indian philosophy of the *Sutra* period, the other four of which are: *Sāmkhya, Yoga, Purva-Mimāmsā,* and *Vedānta,* which is also sometimes called *Uttara-Mimāmsā.* Of these, *Vaisesika* and *Nyāya* share certain common features, and therefore are generally kept together. Similarly, *Sāmkhya* and *Yoga* form one group, while *Purva-Mimāmsā* and *Vedānta* form another. The *Vaisesika* school is best known for its metaphysics or cosmology, while the *Nyāya* school is best known for its interest in logical methods or epistemology. Each of the two schools, however, recognizes the other's conclusions. *Vaisesika* accepts *Nyāya*'s analytical methods and *Nyāya* accepts *Vaisesika*'s atomistic theory regarding the world. As K.M. Sen writes, most of these six schools of *Sutra* philosophy (so called because each was based on a single major text or *Sutra*) "were fully developed after about A.D. 200, though the origin of the systems can be traced to much earlier periods, sometimes as early as 800 B.C." (Sen, 78).

Vaisesika makes a complete analysis of the phenomenal world. It attempts to explain the whole world of phenomena in terms of seven categories or "ultimate reals." Nyāya agrees with Vaisesika in the latter's classification of the world-objects into seven categories and the way it treats each of these categories, but its chief concern is with the ways of knowing these categories. The term "vaisesika" has its origin in the word *visesa,* which in Sanskrit means the "particulars"; thus, *vaisesika* may be said to be a study of particularity. The possibility of a complete knowledge of the particulars is also pointed out by Nyāya. *Nyāya* refers to the study of one or more of the following: *pramāna-sāstra* or epistemology, *tarka-sāstra* or the science of reasoning, and *ānviksiki* or the science of critical inquiry. In both the systems, Reality and its knowledge remain central; it is only in their approach to Reality that they differ from each other. There are a few other points of difference between the two systems. If Vaisesika mentions seven categories, Nyāya has 16 categories. In fact, Nyāya places all the seven Vaisesika categories under *prameya* (knowable), which happens to be the second member in the Nyāya list of categories. The first member of this list is known as *pramāna* or the means of knowing, which determines and justifies Nyāya's predominantly epistemological character. The second point of difference is to be found in their sources of knowledge. Thus, while Nyāya accepts four sources of knowledge, viz. perception, inference, comparison and verbal testimony, Vaisesika mentions only two, viz. perception and inference, where inference subsumes the two other Nyāya categories of comparison and verbal testimony.

Both the systems, however, maintain a perfect balance between their interest in philosophical speculation and their interest in personal salvation. The desire of any individual being to acquire a complete knowledge of the world is as intense as his desire to attain salvation. This is something which is common to all the Indian philosophical systems. Satkari Mookerjee writes: "Perfection in knowledge was believed to culminate in perfection in life, although the conception of perfect life was not uniform or identical" (Mookerjee, 91). A knowledge of the world in its totality serves the purpose of offering a controlled guidance under which the individual, well-protected against the evils and imperfections of life, proceeds towards salvation.

Vaisesika *and* Nyāya Literature

The chief exponent of the Vaisesika school was Kanāda (*c.* 3rd century B.C.), whose *Vaisesika-Sutra* still remains the primary Vaisesika text. In addition to this, there are two other independent works belonging to the later period of the Vaisesika system. They are *Dasapadārthasāstram* of Chandramati and *Padārthadharma Samgraha* of Prasastapāda. Prasastapāda's work is not just a *bhāsya* or commentary on the philosophy propounded in Kanāda's *Vaisesika Sutra* but an extension of it. We have also two other *bhāsyas* or commentaries: Udayana's *Kiranāvali* (10th century A.D.) and Sridhara's *Nyāyakandāli* (10th century A.D.).

The authorship of the original *Nyāya Sutra,* which is the first systematic exposition of the Nyāya philosophy, is attributed to Gautama or Gotama (also known in some quarters as Aksapāda), who lived in the 3rd century (?) B.C. A commentary on *Nyāya Sutra* was written by Vatsāyana around A.D. 400; Uddyotakara's *Nyāya-vārtika,* written during the first half of the 7th century A.D., contains an elaborate refutation of the charges brought against the Nyāya logic by the Buddhist logician, Dinnaga; Vacaspati Misra's *Nyāya-vārtika-tātparyatikā* was written in the 7th century A.D. and Udayana's commentary on it, *Tātparyatikā-parisuddhi,* appeared in the 10th century A.D. along with Jayanta Bhatta's *Nyāya-manjari.* Like Vaisesika, the history of Nyāya may be divided into two phases. The old school of Nyāya ended with and the modern school of Nyāya began with Gangesa, whose *Tattva-chintāmani* builds up a more sophisticated structure of logic than the classical Nyāya school. As Hiriyanna observes, in Gangesa the "logic of the Nyaya attains its final shape" (Hiriyanna, 227).

The Vaisesika *Categories* (padārtha)

The Vaisesika system provides a realistic-rationalistic explanation of the nature of the world of phenomena by means of seven categories or *padārthas.* These seven categories (sometimes also translated as "ultimate reals") are: *Dravya* (substance), *Guna* (quality), *Karma* (action), *Sāmānya* (universal), *Visesa* (particular), *Samavāya* (inherence), and *Abhāva* (nonexistence). We discuss below each of these categories in some detail.

1. ***Dravya* (substance):** The external world, according to Vaisesika, consists of nine ultimate substances or *dravyas*. All the qualities and all actions inhere in and belong to these substances; all the objects of experience are composed of these substances. Unlike the *Lokāyata* school (of which Charvaka was the chief exponent) which was materialistic, Vaisesika is nonmaterialistic, although it includes both material and spiritual substances. A spiritual substance, like all physical and material substances, is a knowable object possessing certain intrinsic qualities. The nine *dravyas* are all eternal and simple. All the compound objects, which are composed of the simple eternal substances and consists of parts, are, therefore, subject to destruction. Substance, then, is found both in its simple, indestructible as well as compound, destructible forms. The nine ultimate substances are earth *(prithivi),* water *(up),* fire *(tejas),* air *(vāyu),* ether *(ākāsa),* time *(kāla),* space *(dik),* self *(ātman),* and mind *(manas).*

i) Material substances: The four material substances are earth, water, air and fire. They do not, however, mean the compound substances that are produced out of them, they rather point to the eternal elements or infinitesimal atoms. A compound element like a jar, for instance, is derived from all the four eternal elements (where earth, water and fire are involved directly while air helps it attain its particular shape). Thus, all the material substances have both a primary existence (in the form of elements or atoms) and a secondary existence (in the form of compound objects). Substance, though generally noticed in its form of compound existence, usually refers to the primary or elementary form. In addition to the four elements or substances already mentioned, there is also the element *ākāsa* (ether), which is found only in its primary existence and does not produce any compound object. It is eternal and infinite and is known only through its quality, sound.

ii) Nonmaterial Substances: The four nonmaterial substances are space, time, self and mind. Space and time, like ether *(ākāsa),* are infinite and do not have an atomic structure. Space cannot be defined directly; it is a presupposition in order to make possible such cognitions like east, west, north, here, there and so on. Similarly, time is responsible for the cognition of the past, the present or the future. Space and time are without parts and hence, cannot be divided.

In the absence of the supposition of a self, Vaisesika would have been merely materialistic in character. Its qualities, like the awareness of a thing or the consciousness of a thing, point to the substance to which they belong. Self, therefore, exists as a spiritual substance, having consciousness as an accidental rather than an essential quality. Apart from consciousness, self has other qualities like desire *(icchā)* and volition *(yatna).* These three qualities or attributes—consciousness, desire and volition—belong to the self, which exists as the subject of such expressions as "I am happy," "I am hungry," "I am sad," or "I am suffering." At this point we must distinguish between the individual self *(ātman)* and the Eternal Self (Ātman, Isvara, or God). The individual selves are many, but the Eternal Self is one and all-pervading. As Theos Bernard writes, "it pervades the body as a whole; therefore, it is infinite in scope, without parts, unproduced, incapable of destruction and, therefore, eternal" (Bernard, 61).

Both Vaisesika and Nyāya advocate the plurality of selves. Each self has a mind *(manas),* which is eternal but atomic in nature. But although it is atomic in nature, it does not produce any compound objects. It is rather the instrument through which the self "knows." The self is assisted by the mind *(manas)* both during external perception and during internal perception, i.e., in the perception of the external objects and in the experience of internal feelings and emotions. To repeat, the five material substances and the four nonmaterial substances together compose the world of objects.

2. ***Guna* (quality):** *Guna* or quality does not exist independently; it inheres in the substance. The Vaisesika concept of *guna* differs from the Sāmkhya concept of *guna;* thus, while in the former case, it is understood in the sense of being an attribute of a substance, in the latter case the *gunas* form the very essence of the causative substance *(Prakrti).* Vaisesika gives equal status to the mental and the physical qualities. It speaks of 24 qualities: i) color, ii) taste, iii) smell, iv) touch, v) sound, vi) number, vii) magnitude, viii) distinctness, ix) conjunction, x) disjunction, xi) nearness, xii) remoteness, xiii) cognition, xiv) pleasure, xv) pain, xvi) desire, xvii) aversion, xviii) effort, xix) heaviness, xx) fluidity, xxi) tendency, xxii) viscidity, xxiii) moral merit, and xxiv) moral demerit (see Puligandla, 153–4).

Out of these 24 qualities, the "smell" of earth, the "color" of fire, the "taste" of water, the "touch" of air and the "sound" of ether are specific qualities (i.e., special marks of particular substances); and qualities like magnitude, distinctness, and effort are common to several substances. Qualities are noneternal and depend so to speak on their substances, but their treatment as a separate and independent category makes obvious the pluralistic attitude of the Vaisesika system, which accepts the distinctness of objects and their possession of special qualities. The classical Vaisesika mentions these 24 *gunas* and the later Vaisesika texts do not show any great variations.

3. ***Karma* (action or movement):** Like quality *(guna),* action is dependant on the substance but is treated as a separate category. Actions belong to the substance and imply the latter's movement. However, movement or action is viewed as the change of place *(parispanda)* rather than as the change of form *(parināma).* It is the dynamic and changing feature of the substance as distinguished from quality, which is its static feature. Vaisesika accepts five kinds of action or movement, namely, *utksepana* or upward movement, *avaksepana* or downward movement, *ākuchana* or contractive movement, *prasārana* or expansive movement, and *gamana* or locomotive movement.

4. ***Sāmānya* (universal or general):** *Sāmānya* or the "universal" is the characteristic or the set of characteristics which is common and essential to

objects belonging to any particular class. The phenomenal world may be analyzed down to the manifold objects as well as to the types, thus implying the formation of a class of objects similar to one another. By virtue of their distinctness objects are identified as "particulars"; by virtue of their similarity they are realized as "universals." Universals are as real as particulars and have objective references in the phenomenal world. They are not just class-concepts but class-essences. For instance, all the individual horses are different from one another in their own particular ways, but it is the presence of the universal—their *horseness*—that distinguishes them from animals like tigers, lions or elephants, thus ultimately referring to the existence of a class called "horse." The universal, then, does not merely include a class-name, since the term "horse" is applicable to all individual horses and yet, the universal *horseness* does not disappear with the disappearance of the individual horses. The universal does not refer to a genus either, consisting of subclasses. It is the sameness that breathes through similar particular objects, both organic and inorganic. "Substance" or *dravya,* for example, refers to all substances and *dravyatva* or "substanceness" is common to all the substances as *guna* (quality) refers to individual qualities and *gunatva* or "qualityness" is common to all qualities. *Dravyatva* and *gunatva* (substanceness and qualityness, respectively) are universals, and among them Being is the highest, for it is common to the largest number of particulars and covers not only the substances but also their quality, actions, and relations. The universal, then, gets manifested or revealed in the particulars. The particulars are produced and destroyed, they appear and disappear, but the universal is not subject to destruction. It is eternal and unanalyzable. While it is manifested, it is difficult to differentiate the exemplified universal from the exemplifying particulars, but this difficulty does not affect the treatment of the two as separate ultimate reals.

5. ***Visesa* (particularity):** *Visesa* or "particularity" does not refer to the particularity or individuality of composite objects; it means the particularity of eternal, indivisible nonmaterial substances or atoms, like self, mind, space and time. These partless ultimate substances have their specific individualities. Particularity means the differentia which forms the very basis of discrimination. Vaisesika admits both qualitative and quantitative pluralism: atoms are both qualitatively and quantitatively unlike each other. Since the school of Vaisesika derives its name from the word *visesa* or "particular," it gives special emphasis to particularity. It sanctions the status of real to all the ultimate substances and their particularities, thus advocating what may be called realistic pluralism.

6. ***Samavāya* (inherence):** *Samavāya* or inherence refers to a kind of relation. It should not be confused with the relation suggested by *samyoga* or conjunction. If one book is placed on the top of another so that the shortest possible distance between them is absent, then the two books are held in such a relation to each other that no change of place and form in either is noticed. In this case, one book can be separated from the other without affecting it in any manner and without affecting in any way the other. We have here a simple instance of conjunction, which is a temporary,

separable, external relation. As against this, inherence or *samavāya* is an eternal, inseparable, internal relation.

We have already known that quality inheres in the substance, that action too inheres in the substance, and that the universal inheres in the particular. Hence, the relation existing between substance and quality, or substance and action, or universal and particular, is one of inherence. Inherence is irreversible, which is to say, the substance cannot inhere in either quality or action, and the particular cannot inhere in the universal. The relation of inherence is not perceivable; it is known through inference from the fact that quality or action cannot be separated from the substance, or the universal from the particular.

7. ***Abhāva* (nonexistence):** This seventh and last of the Vaisesika categories was not introduced by Kanāda, but later it became a logical necessity to postulate nonexistence or *abhāva* as an independent category. The reason behind this is that every kind of knowledge points to an object which is known, and so the knowledge of nonexistence must have an objective reference, i.e., the absence of a thing. We must here distinguish the mere absence of a thing from the knowledge of its absence.

Nonexistence, as advocated by Vaisesika, is of four kinds—namely, *pragabhāva* (prior nonexistence), *dhvamsābhāva* (posterior nonexistence), *anyonābhāva* (mutual nonexistence), and *atyantābhāva* (absolute nonexistence). Prior nonexistence refers to the nonexistence of a thing before its production (e.g., a clay pot is nonexistent before the potter makes it); posterior nonexistence refers to the nonexistence of a thing after it is destroyed; mutual nonexistence refers to the nonexistence of a thing "as something else" (e.g., a pot is nonexistent as a book); and, finally, absolute nonexistence refers to a pseudo-idea (e.g., the bare ground with no pot on it). As it will be seen, prior nonexistence has no beginning, but has an end; posterior nonexistence has no end, but has a beginning; and the last two kinds of nonexistence—the "mutual" and the "absolute"—do not refer to time, have no beginning or end, and hence are eternal.

Unlike the other six Vaisesika categories, nonexistence is relative; and yet, it has been considered an independent and important category. If it had not been introduced and accepted, all material things would have been considered as identical in nature, thus excluding the possible differences among them; in addition, all things would have been treated as existing at all places and all time.

The Vaisesika *Theory of Causation* (Asatkāryavā)

Unlike the Sāmkhya system, Vaisesika and Nyāya refuse to accept the theory of the preexistence of the effect in the cause. According to the two systems, effect is a fresh creation or a new beginning. If, on several occasions, the occurrence of two events are repeated in the same order of succession without any exception, then the two events are related by way of causation. Events occurring in the phenomenal world are known by perception; the connection between them, however, is not perceived but realized intuitively. A cause is that which precedes the effect and is, therefore, the antecedent, but it is a necessary, invariable, and unconditional antecedent.

The Vaisesika and the Nyāya philosophers do not admit the plurality of causes, but they accept three different kinds of cause. The "material cause" *(samavāyi-kārana)* is the one out of which the effect is produced (e.g., clay as the material cause of the pot). The "nonmaterial cause" *(asamavāyi-kārana)* is either a quality or an action. The color of the clay brings about the color of the pot and is, in this regard, the nonmaterial cause of the pot. The conjunction of threads produces the cloth and thus conjunction is a nonmaterial cause of the cloth. The "efficient cause" *(nimitta-kārana)* refers to the efficiency or motivation behind the process of the making of the effect. The potter is the efficient cause of the pot which he makes. This last, the efficient cause, which Karl H. Potter calls the "instrumental cause" (Potter, *Presuppositions,* 112), is of two kinds—"general efficient cause" *(sādhārana-nimitta-kārana)* and "specific efficient cause" *(asādhārana-nimitta-kārana).*

God and the Unseen Power *(Adrsta)* are the best examples of the former. The Vaisesika philosophers believe that God *(Isvara),* assisted by the Unseen Power *(Adrsta),* is the efficient cause of the ordered universe known as the world, which originates from its material cause, the eternal atoms. God or the Unseen Power is thus instrumental in bringing about the world (but not its constituents, the eternal atoms). As different from the general efficient cause, there are also specific efficient causes used for certain specific purposes. Thus the potter, while making a pot, uses his stick to unite the different parts of the pot, where the stick is the instrument used for a particular purpose and is a specific efficient cause.

For the Vaisesika and Nyāya thinkers (and here they are close to John Stewart Mill), cause is the sumtotal of certain relevant and necessary conditions. They call this aggregate or totality of conditions *(kārana-sāmagri).* The necessary conditions can of course be very well differentiated from their accompanying circumstances *(sahakāri).* For instance, although the potter is directly involved in the making of the cause, his stick and the sound or the thickness of the stick are only present on the basis of some sort of indirect involvement: they are not directly involved in the production of the effect.

The Atomic Theory

Vaisesika explains the way in which things are produced in terms of a theory of atoms, according to which the material cause of the whole world of objects consists of the eternal atoms. It is of particular importance to note here, that the *Vaisesika*-definition of the atom *(paramānu)* as "the smallest indivisible part of a thing" came at least 15 centuries before the modern physicists defined it in a similar way, although the details of the

Vaisesika theory of atoms are peculiar to that philosophy and are recognizably different from those of modern physics. The four atoms of earth, water, air and fire, according to Vaisesika, combine in different and several proportions so as to produce the manifold objects of the universe. Ether or *ākāsa* is nonatomic in character and therefore does not actively participate in the process of production. All the atomic combinations, however, are held in ether.

The atoms differ in both quality and quantity. They are described as spherical *(parimandala)* in character. During their *dissolution* (the Vaisesika term to describe their proces of combination), the atoms exhibit complete inaction, and the urge to be active is induced into them by the Unseen Power *(adrsta)*. When this tendency to move is implanted in them, the atoms begin to combine in geometric progression. Two atoms combine to produce a binary molecule or dyad *(dvyānuka);* three dyads combine to make a trinary compound or triad *(trayānuka)*. A dyad is imperceptible, but a triad is perceptible. Four triads combine to make *chaturānaka* and so on to result in grosser molecules. There is, of course, the other view that the atoms have also an inherent tendency to unite, coalesce and combine, and that they do so in twos, threes, and fours, either by the atoms falling into such groups directly or by the successive addition of one atom to each preceding aggregate.

In this context of atomic combinations, the influence of heat cannot be overlooked. While the Nyāya philosophers advocate the theory of the "heating of molecules" *(pitharapāka),* the Vaisesika philosophers advocate the theory of the "heating of atoms" *(pilupāka)*. According to the Vaisesika theory, during their process of combination the atoms are affected by heat particles, and this brings about changes in the atomic quality. The process of the heating of atoms consists in the penetration of heat into the object, which is followed by the disintegration of the object into ultimate atoms, the change in atomic qualities, and finally, the reunion of such qualitatively changed atoms into an object. The process explains the changes occurring in the character of all material objects. The Nyāya philosophers, on the other hand, believe that "no disintegration into atoms is necessary for a change of qualities, but it is the molecules which assume new characters under the influence of heat" (Dasgupta, 327). The heat affects directly the characters of the molecules resulting in their change in quality without affecting the ultimate atoms.

As S.N. Dasgupta elaborates: "Nyāya holds that the heat-corpuscles penetrate into the porous body of the object and thereby produce the change of colour. The object as a whole is not disintegrated into atoms and then reconstituted again, for such a procedure is never experienced by observation" (Dasgupta, 327). This is one of the few points of difference between the two systems which are otherwise so close to each other, although they agree as far as the importance of the heat-particles in effecting change is concerned; both the systems also believe that the production and the destruction of things has its basis in the combination and separation of eternal atoms.

The Nyāya *Categories*

When the heretical, nonvedic systems (Buddhism, Jainism, Materialism) created an environment of faithlessness in eternal, permanent substances, there was a sort of unavoidable necessity to revive the people's faith in the existence of eternal substances like selves *(ātman)* as well as in the existence of a world of phenomena. Buddhist phenomenalism dissolved the external world in the ideas of the mind. The *Nyāya* philosophers (also called *Naiyāyikas)* sought "to restore the traditional substances, the soul within and nature without, but not on the basis of mere authority" (Radhakrishnan, 29–30). *Anviksiki* or the "science of reason" was the result, with its emphasis on a thorough investigation into the modes of knowing and a critical-interpretive inquiry into whatever is supplied to us either by the scriptures or through sensory evidence. Thus Nyāya is the only Indian philosophical system which attaches utmost importance to methods and builds up therewith a well-developed theory of logic. As such, its equivalent cannot be found anywhere except, perhaps, in Buddhism.

Gautama's (the Gautama should not be confused with the other Gautama who later was to become the *Buddha*—"the enlightened one"—and founded *Buddhism*) analysis of the categories displays its all-inclusive nature and takes into account all the possibilities of knowing the truth and the truth alone. His categories are 16 in number and correspond to different stages of a debate. We discuss below each of these categories.

1. ***Pramāna* (ways of knowing):** Nyāya accepts four ways of knowing: perception *(pratyaksa),* inference *(anumāna),* comparison *(upamāna),* and verbal testimony *(sabda).* Perception can be of two kinds—external and internal. The knowledge of the external object, which issues from a contact between the sense organs and the particular object, is known as perceptual knowledge or the knowledge of the same object through perception. In case of internal feelings, like pain and pleasure, the mind directly perceives them and hence, their knowledge is a result of internal perception. Perceptual knowledge must be *determinate* as distinct from indeterminate and doubtful knowledge (e.g., from a distance, a person is not able to distinguish between a snake and a rope and often confuses one for the other); it must be *unnameable,* that is to say, the knowledge of a thing should not have any connection with its name; finally, it should be *nonerratic* (e.g., the perceptual knowledge of water cannot be derived from the perception of a mirage that creates an illusion of water).

Inference has as its basis and antecedent a perceptual knowledge of something (e.g., smoke). There are three kinds of inference. They are i) a priori or *purvavat* inference, involving the knowledge of the effect (e.g., rain) through the cause (e.g., clouds), ii) a posteriori or *sesavat* inference, involving the knowledge of the cause (e.g., past rain) through that of the effect (e.g., flood), and iii) inference on the basis of copresence or *sāmā nyato drsta* (e.g., the color and the extension of a thing are copresent, and hence the knowledge of the color of the thing gives an idea about its extension).

Comparison involves the knowledge of a thing through its resemblance with an already known thing (e.g., Given a description of the points of resemblance between a wild cow and the cow seen in everyday life, a person who has never seen a wild cow would recognize one when he sees one).

Verbal testimony refers to the teachings or sayings of a person known as perfect and trustworthy *(siddhapurusha)*. One develops an awareness of several things by the help of the assertions, injunctions and prohibitions of a person who is trustworthy because he has attained perfection.

2. ***Prameya* (objects of right knowledge):** A person possibly and certainly can have the right knowledge of the soul *(ātman)*, the body *(sarira)*, the senses *(indriya)*, the physical objects *(artha)*, the intellect *(buddhi)*, the mind *(manah)*, the various human activities *(pravrtti)*, the human faults and frailties *(dosa)*, transmigration or rebirth *(pretyabhāva)*, the fruits of action *(phala)*, pain *(dukkha)* and liberation *(apavarga)*. For instance, the *soul* is known through its manifest qualities like desire, vocation, pleasure, pain and cognition, or the *body* is known as that in which gestures (the efforts to get what is desirable and avoid what is painful), the senses, and the sentiments (pleasure, pain and so on) are located.

3. ***Samsaya* (doubt):** According to Nyāya, doubt is not false knowledge, but incomplete knowledge. While false or erroneous knowledge results in a kind of conviction, thus disallowing the mind to seek the truth, doubt induces in the mind an inquisitiveness that urges one to make a proper investigation into the nature of reality. Doubt is a mental state or activity involving conflicting judgments; it points to the incapability of one which is grounded in the absence of certainty (e.g., In the twilight, a person seeing a tall object at a distance is incapable of making a decision as to whether the object perceived is a man or a post). Thus, the act of doubting has certain positive consequences.

4. ***Prayojana* (purpose):** Purpose is the motive which persuades a person to act towards the attainment of something desirable and dissuades him from activities which produce something undesirable. For instance, one has to know the different modes of knowing for the purpose of knowing what is truth.

5. ***Drstānta* (example):** *Drstānta* is an instance of a general truth or principle about which there is no difference of opinion between a common individual and a specialist. Thus the kitchen in which there is both fire and smoke is an instance of the invariable association of smoke and fire.

6. ***Siddhānta* (conclusive assertion):** *Siddhānta* is a theory, a view, or a conclusive assertion. Satis Chandra Vidyabhusana refers to it as "a dogma" or "a tenet" (Vidyabhusana, *A History of Indian Logic*). The *Nyāya-sutra* of Gautama makes a fourfold classification of *siddhānta:* i) *Sarva-tantra* or the assertion common to all schools irrespective of their specific commitments (e.g., All compound objects are composed of the basic elements of earth, water, air, fire and either); ii) *Prati-tantra* or the view peculiar to a particular school and accepted by similar schools but rejected by opposite schools (e.g., The Sāmkhya explanation of the universe in terms of the twin principles of *Purusha* and *Prakrti*); iii) *Adhikarana* or a

hypothetical view of such nature that its acceptance establishes other views (e.g., the hypothetical view that "there is a single soul belonging to a single body," once accepted, would lead to such other acceptable views as "there are many senses" and "each sense has its particular object"); iv) *Abhyupagama* or the view implied by the discussion of associated particulars and thus accepted (e.g., The view that "sound is a substance" follows from the discussion of permanence or impermanence of sound as a substance).

7. ***Avayava* (member or part of *Nyāya* syllogism):** Nyāya syllogism consists of five parts: i) *pratijñā* or the statement of a proposition, ii) *hetu* or the reason in support of the proof of such stated proposition, iii) *udāharana* or example, iv) *upanaya* or application, and v) *nigamana* or conclusion. We shall discuss each of these parts elaborately later in the chapter.

8. ***Tarka* (argument or judgment):** *Tarka* is to argue with a view to ascertaining the character of a certain thing in an indirect way, and the process of reasoning is hypothetical in form. We give below an example:

> If the soul is non-eternal, then it is incapable of enjoying the fruits of its own actions (If p, then q).
> The soul is capable of enjoying the fruits of its own actions ($\sim q$)
> ∴ The soul is eternal (∴ $\sim p$)

[where p stands for "The soul is noneternal" and q stands for "The soul is incapable of enjoying the fruits of its own actions."]

9. ***Nirnaya* (decision):** Doubt and investigation are followed by decision or ascertainment, which is true and certain knowledge attained by the removal of doubt and through the accurate use of the proper methods of knowing. One determines the nature of a thing by the consideration of two opposite views. One initially has a vague awareness of the object, and then starts doubting it, forms alternative and opposite views, applies the rules of reason, finally determining the true nature of the object and hence attaining the right knowledge in it.

10. ***Vāda* (discussion or debate):** *Vāda* or discussion is a systematic argument aiming at proving a proposition. The discussion as a whole finds an explicit statement in the five-member syllogism. An appeal made to reason serves as a means of knowing, and the conclusion is proved to the exclusion of any contradiction.

11. ***Jalpa* (controversy):** *Jalpa* is a kind of discussion which is negative in character and includes quibbling and presenting a false argument like a sophist. The motive behind such discussion is winning the argument and hence is far away from any attempt towards the attainment of truth.

12. ***Vitandā* (cavil):** *Vitandā* is a kind of argument which involves objections raised against half-settled opinions and views. A person using such argument merely embarrasses his opponent without ever trying to establish his own point. However, polemics and cavilling are significant forms of discussion and

> may be used by one in search of Truth in order to protect one's growing knowledge which has not yet matured into a full blossomed conviction. Frequently the student will encounter objectionable personalities who have not attained true knowledge but who are overcome with their

> intellectual attainments . . . These people, not being possessed of a noble character, will violate all the rules of propriety, having no consideration for the beliefs of another [Bernard, 36–37].

It is on such occasions that the learning student may use *vitandā* or cavil "in the same way that nature uses thorns on some plants to safeguard the growth of its fruit" (Bernard, 37).

13. ***Hetvābhāsa* (fallacy):** This refers to a reason which is unfit to offer substantial support to the process of argument and hence, makes the argument fallacious. There are, according to *Nyāya Sutra,* five such fallacies of reason: erratic *(savyabhichāra),* contradictory *(viruddha),* controversial *(prakarana-sama),* unproved or counter-questioned *(sādhyasama),* and mistimed *(kālātita).*

The *erratic* is the fallacy of reason which leads to more than one conclusion and therefore lacks clarity.

Example:	1.	Proposition:	Sound is eternal (to be proved).
		Reason:	Because it is intangible.
	2.	Proposition:	Sound is noneternal (to be proved).
		Reason:	Because it is intangible.

Here two opposite conclusions have been derived from the same reason, ignoring the fact that there is no relationship between intangible and eternal or noneternal.

The *contradictory* is the reason which opposes what is to be established by contradicting views already established.

Example:	Proposition:	A pot is produced.
	Reason:	Because it is eternal.

The reason here contradicts the established view that "That which is eternal is neither produced nor destroyed."

The *controversial* is the reason which only repeats the very question or problem for the solution of which it was employed.

Example:	Proposition:	Sound is noneternal.
	Reason:	Because it is not in possession of the attribute of eternality.

Here the reason does not add anything new to the proposition, which relates to the "eternality of sound," but, to make matters worse, pushes the problem into an unproductive circularity.

The *unproved* or *counter-questioned* is the reason which, instead of proving the proposition, is itself in need of proof.

Example:	Proposition:	Shadow is a substance.
	Reason:	Because it possesses motion.

Since that which possesses quality and motion is a substance, to say that shadow possesses motion amounts to saying that shadow is a substance. Hence it is a counter-questioned reason or "a reason which balances the question" (Vidyabhusana, 64).

The *mistimed* is the reason which is adduced when the time in which it would have held good is already passed.

Example:	Proposition:	Sound is durable.
	Reason:	Because it is manifested by union, as a color.

The color of a jar or pot is manifested when it is in union with a lighted lamp, but it existed before such union and will continue to exist after it. Similarly, the sound of a drum is manifested when the drum comes into contact with the rod with which it is struck. Such sound must be presumed to have existed before the contact or union and to continue to exist after the union has ceased. However, such sound is not manifested at the time the drum comes into contact with the rod, but at a subsequent time when the union has ceased. Hence, the analogy between color and sound is improper and the reason adduced *mistimed.*

14. ***Chala* (quibble):** Quibble or equivocation is the opposition offered to a proposition by the assumption of an alternative meaning. The speaker uses an argument to imply a particular meaning, but his opponent attacks it by suggesting alternative meanings thereby obscuring the speaker's intended meaning. Quibble is of three kinds: quibble in respect of a term *(vāk-chala),* quibble in respect of a genus *(sāmānya-chala),* and quibble in respect of a metaphor *(upchāra-chala).*

The quibble in respect of a term consists of the opponent's deliberate reading of an alternative meaning into a term having a particular meaning for the speaker; it is encouraged by the ambiguity inherent in the term used by the speaker.

Example:	Speaker:	"This boy is *nava-kambala* [possessed of a new blanket]."
	Quibbler:	"This boy is not certainly *nava-kambala* [possessed of nine blankets] for he has only one blanket."

Here the word *nava* (which in Sanskrit means both "new" and "nine") is ambiguous and was used by the speaker in the sense of new, but it has been willfully referred to by the quibbler in the sense of nine.

The quibble in respect of a genus consists in asserting the impossibility of a possible thing, on the ground that it belongs to a certain class which is very wide.

Example:	Speaker:	"This Brāhmana is possessed of learning and conduct."
	Quibbler:	"It is impossible, for how can this person be said to possess learning and conduct merely because he is a Brāhmana? There are little boys who are Brāhmanas, yet not possessed of learning and conduct."

The questioning quibbler knows that possession of learning and conduct was not meant to be an attribute of the whole class of Brāhmanas, but only ascribed to "*this* Brāhmana."

The quibble in respect of a metaphor involves a denial of the proper meaning of a word by taking it literally when it was used metaphorically, and vice versa. Instead of a metaphor, the quibble might involve such other figures of speech as personification, metonymy and synecdoche.

Example:	Speaker:	"The galleries cheered."
	Quibbler:	"The galleries do not cheer, for they are inanimate structures."

Once again, the person objecting is a quibbler, since he knows that what was intended was the persons in the galleries and not the physical structures called galleries.

15. ***Jāti* (Analogue):** *Jāti* refers to a farfetched or inappropriate analogy, which is founded on mere similarity or dissimilarity rather than the invariable association of middle and major terms. It is, therefore, self-destructive and futile.

Example No. 1:	Speaker:	"The soul is inactive because it is all-pervading as ether."
	Opponent:	"If the soul is inactive because it bears a similarity to ether as being all-pervading, why is it not active because it bears similarity to a pot as being a seat of union?"
Example No. 2:	Speaker:	"Sound is noneternal, because, unlike ether, it is a product."
	Opponent:	"If sound is noneternal because, as a product, it is dissimilar to ether, why is it not eternal because, as an object of auditory perception, it is dissimilar to a pot?"

In the two examples cited above, the reason used by the "opponent" is futile because the analogy it bears to that of the "speaker" is inappropriate and far-fetched.

Nyāya mentions 24 kinds of such false analogy. They are: i) *sudharmya-sama* (balancing the homogeneity); ii) *vaidharmya-sama* (balancing of heterogeneity); iii) *utkarsa-sama* (balancing an excess); iv) *apakarsa-sama* (balancing a deficit); v) *varnya-sama* (balancing the questionable); vi) *avarnya-sama* (balancing the unquestionable); vii) *vikalpa-sama* (balancing the alternative); viii) *sādhya-sama* (balancing the question); ix) *prāpti-sama* (balancing the copresence); x) *aprāpti-sama* (balancing the mutual absence); xi) *prasanga-sama* (balancing the infinite regression); xii) *pratidrstānta-sama* (balancing the counter example); xiii) *anutpati-sama* balancing the nonproduced); xiv) *samsaya-sama* (balancing the doubt); xv) *prakarana-sama* (balancing the point at issue); xvi) *ahetu-sama* (balancing the nonreason); xvii) *arthapatti-sama* (balancing the presumption); xviii) *avisesa-sama* (balancing the nondifference); xix) *upapatti-sama* (balancing the demonstration); xx) *upalabdhi-sama* (balancing the perception); xxi) *anupalabdhi-sama* (balancing the nonperception); xxii) *anitya-sama* (balancing the noneternal); xxiii) *nitya-sama* (balancing the eternal); and xxiv) *kārya- sama* (balancing the effect).

16. ***Nigrahasthāna* (a point of defeat):** A point of defeat—also called "a clincher," "an occasion for rebuke," and "an occasion for humiliation"—arises when one either misunderstands or does not understand at all. If a person begins to argue in a fashion which reveals his utter ignorance, or deliberately misunderstands and yet persists in defending himself, the employment of counter-arguments is futile; such a person is unfit to be argued with and it is best to avoid his company.

Nyāya-sastra mentions 22 varieties of points of defeat. They are: i) *pratijñā-hāni* (hurting the proposition); ii) *pratijñāntara* (shifting the proposition); iii) *pratijñā-virodha* (opposing the proposition); iv) *pratijñā-sannyāsa* (renouncing the proposition); v) *hetvantara* (shifting the reason); vi) *arthāntara* (shifting the topic); vii) *nirarthaka* (the meaningless); viii) *avigñātartha* (the unintelligible); ix) *aparthaka* (the incoherent); x) *aprāpta-kāla* (the inopportune); xi) *nyuna* (saying too little); xii) *adhika* (saying too much); xiii) *apratibha* (repetition); xiv) *ananubhāsana* (silence); xv) *ajñāna* (ignornace); xvi) *apratibha* (noningenuity); xvii) *viksepa* (evasion); xviii) *matānujña* (admission of an opinion); xix) *paryanuyojyopeksana* (overlooking the censurable); xx) *niranuyojyanuyoga* (censuring the noncensurable); xxi) *apasiddhānta* (deviating from a tenet); and xxii) *hetvābhāsa* (the semblance of a reason).

Since, within the scope of this book, it is not possible to define and illustrate all the 22 points of defeat, we shall confine ourselves to only the first two of these. Hurting the proposition occurs when one admits in one's own example the character of a counter-example.

Example: Disputant: "Sound is noneternal,
because it is cognizable by sense;
whatever is cognizable by sense is noneternal as a pot;
sound is so (cognizable by sense),
therefore sound is noneternal."

Opponent: "A genus (e.g. 'potness'), which is cognizable by sense,
is found to be eternal: why cannot then the sound which
is also cognizable by sense be eternal?"

Disputant: "Whatever is cognizable by sense is eternal as a pot;

sound is cognizable by sense,
therefore sound is eternal."

By thus admitting in his example (the pot) the character (the eternality) of a counter-example (the genus or type), the disputant hurts his own proposition. Shifting the proposition occurs when a person while opposing a proposition also defends it, by bringing in a new character to his example and counter-example.

Example:	First Speaker:	"Sound is noneternal, because it is cognizable by sense, like a pot."
	Second Speaker:	"Sound is eternal, because it is cognizable by sense, like a genus (or type)."
	First Speaker:	"A genus (or type) and a pot are both cognizable by sense, yet one is all-pervasive and the other is not so: hence the sound which is likened to a pot is non–all pervasive."

The defense thus involves a shifting of proposition. The proposition originally laid down was: "Sound is noneternal." The proposition now being defended is: "Sound is non–all-pervasive" (See Vidyabhusana, 84–90).

Logic and Epistemology

Indian logic has passed through three different stages, each representing a system or discipline: i) Hindu Logic, ii) Buddhist Logic, and iii) Jaina Logic. Apart from these three major systems, other systems of thought have also contributed towards the development of this science, whose history spans over a period of 2,000 years, beginning at the time of *The Mahābhārata* (? 5th century B.C.) and culminating in the system of the Neo-Logicians or *Navya-Nyāya* (10th century A.D. to the present times).

Theory of Meaning and Truth

Nyāya logic (which comes under the broader category of "Hindu Logic") mentions Indeterminate *(nirvikalpa)* and Determinate *(savikalpa)* as the two different stages of the "judgment-being-formed." The Indeterminate stage refers to the mere awareness or sensation, in which activities like naming and categorizing are absent. Later, when a concept is brought to bear upon the sensation, categorization is made, and the object to be known is found in association with a quality, that the indeterminate judgment is transformed into a determinate one or a proposition. A proposition involves three factors – namely, a qualified, a qualifier, and a relation of inherence existing between the two. Thus, the knowledge of the meaning of a judgment involves the knowledge of the meanings of the qualified and the qualifier, and truth is dependent on such knowledge.

True knowledge is known as *pramā,* while the knowledge that is not true is known as *apramā*. A true judgment is also called *pramā; pramatva* or *prāmānya* refers to the common property of any number of true judgments. A true judgment is derived through instruments of true judgment *(pramāna),* which are four in number. We shall briefly discuss the nature and test of truth.

As Karl H. Potter writes, following the 12th century Nyāya philosopher Varadaraja's account in *Tarkikaraksa,* that truth is *anubhava* (consciousness) – "a presentational judgment" – which is *yathārtha* or valid, "as the object actually is" (Potter, 156). That is to say, a true judgment is a valid presentational judgment. This is justified, in the sense that our knowledge is most often in the form of a judgment that involves the two simplest possible existent relations – affirmation and negation. Nyāya classifies judgment into two kinds: presentational judgment (which refers to consciousness or *anubhava*) and representational judgment (which refers to memory). Memory is the representation of past experience and hence, is more often than not, *ayathārtha* or invalid. Invalid knowledge can also be due to doubt *(samsaya),* error *(viparyaya),* and hypothetical reasoning *(tarka).*

The Nyāya theory concerning the validity of knowledge can best be understood by a comparison with the Mimāmsā theory of validity. The Mimāmsakas are of the view that knowledge is self-valid *(svatah-prāmānya),* that knowledge reveals and manifests objects and therefore is a proof of its own truth.

The Nyayāyikas, on the other hand, claim that knowledge reveals both the subject and the object in a specific knowledge-situation. Knowledge is the subjective awareness or apprehension *(upalabddhi)* of the objective existence; but such subjective awareness is incapable of certifying the objective truth. What one actually perceives may not be really so. Chandradhar Sharma writes:

> Knowledge is produced in the soul when it comes into contact with the not-soul. It is an adventitious property of the soul which is generated in it by the object. If the generating conditions are sound, knowledge is valid; if they are defective, knowledge is invalid. A man of sound vision sees a conch white, while a man suffering from jaundice sees it yellow. Correspondence with the object is the nature of truth. If knowledge corresponds to its object, it is valid; if it does not, it is invalid. Valid knowledge corresponds to its object *(yathārtha* and *avisamvādi)* and leads to successful activity *(pravrttisāmarthya).* Invalid knowledge does not correspond to its object *(ayathārtha* and *visamvādi)* and leads to failure and disappointment *(pravrttivisamvāda).* Knowledge intrinsically is only a manifestation of objects. The question of its validity or invalidity is a subsequent question and depends upon its correspondence with its object [Sharma, 192–193].

Thus when knowledge first of all arises, it is neither valid nor invalid, but becomes so at a subsequent time depending on its correspondence or non-correspondence with the object. To quote Sharma again, "Correspondence is the content and successful activity is the test of truth." The Nyāya theory of knowledge is realistic and pragmatic – realistic as regards the nature, and pragmatic as regards the test of *truth*. Nyāya thus disagrees with Mimāmsā but joins hand with Buddhism in establishing its theory that validity of knowledge is extrinsic (not intrinsic or self-evident), and that its ground lies not in itself but elsewhere.

Sources of Knowledge

Nyāya recognizes four sources of valid knowledge: Perception *(pratyaksa)*, Inference *(anumāna)*, Comparison *(upamāna)*, and Verbal Testimony *(sabda)*.

1. **Perception** ***(pratyaksa):*** All the schools of Indian thought have taken perception or *pratyaksa* as a source of valid knowledge. Gautama, the founder of the Nyāya system, defines perception as a direct and immediate cognition that is nonerroneous and produced by sense-object contact. But as we begin to analyze the various kinds of perception, we find that perceptual knowledge does not refer only to the perception of external objects; and, therefore, sense-object contact cannot serve as the common basis of the different kinds of perception. Later Nyāya philosophers brought objections against Gautama's definition of perception. Bhasarvajna, for instance, defines it as the "correct immediate experience" *(samyagaporoksa-anubhava);* Varadarajạ attributes to it the quality of "being pervaded by immediacy and validity"; Viswanatha and Udayana view it as "the direct apprehension which is not caused by any other cognition." Thus perception, while defined as "direct and immediate cognition," has a wider connotation and includes both ordinary and extraordinary perception. It does not involve merely sense-object contact, but the self, the mind, as well as the sense organs in a certain progressive order (self ⟶ mind ⟶ sense organs ⟶ external object ⟶ perceptual knowledge). Perceptual knowledge passes through two different stages: indeterminate *(nirvikalpa)* and determinate *(savikalpa)*. In the initial *nirvikalpa* stage, a formless and nameless percept is presented. Every object has got two aspects, the "this" aspect and the "that" aspect. *Nirvikalpa* or indeterminate perception brings out the "this" aspect of an object. In the later *savikalpa* or determinate stage, a concept is applied to the earlier perception and a detailed knowledge of the "object as having a form, a name, and as belonging to a class" is attained. The complex process of perceptual knowledge as described in Nyāya is close to what Kant calls the "conceptualization of percepts."

Perception is either ordinary *(laukika)* or extraordinary *(alaukika)*. Ordinary perception can be external *(bāhya)* or internal *(mānas)*. External perception involves the senses, which issue out of their respective elements, and we have external perceptual knowledge regarding physical objects. In internal perception, the senses are not employed; rather, the mind directly perceives the internal feeling of pleasure, pain, jealousy or anger.

Both Vaisesika and Nyāya speak of three types of extraordinary *(alaukika)* perception: *sāmānyalaksana*-perception, *jñānalaksana*-perception, and *yogaja*-perception. Extraordinary perception, however, is possible only on the part of a *yogi* who has been able to attain unusual powers; although ordinary individuals, during certain moments, are capable of having the first two *(sāmānyalaksana* and *jñānalaksana)* of the three types of extraordinary perception. There are frequent references to extraordinary perception and intuitive knowledge in all the Nyāya texts, but the most elaborate exposition of the threefold classification is found in *Tattvachintāmani* of Gangesa. *Sāmānyalaksana* is the perception of the universals inhering in the particulars. Thus, the perception of particular cows is an instance of ordinary perception, but to perceive the universal "cowness" in the individual cows is to have *sāmānyalaksana. Jñānalaksana* refers to a complex perception involving two or more senses at a time. For instance, when one says "Ice looks cold," he is using (even if unconsciously) both his sense of sight and his sense of touch. To the question, "How can ice *look* cold?" the Naiyāyika has a simple answer: Ice is perceived in the present, but there is also a recollection of the past experience of its "feeling cold," and hence, the complex synesthetic perception is the result of an association of present perception and memory, of "what is presented" and "what is represented (through memory)."

Yogaja or yogic perception, which is really the intuitive, sense-*less* apprehension of objects present and absent, of events of past, present and future, is confined to the *yogis.* We must note here that the Nyāya theory that "the validity and invalidity of the knowledge must be established with reference to the external world" *(parātah-prāmānya)* cannot be applied to *yogaja* or yogic perception, or even to other two kinds of extraordinary perception. As Ramakant Sinari writes, the different kinds of intuitive knowledge "contain a type of certainty which is hardly explainable externally or logically. In this sense of the self-given certainty, *pramā* [true knowledge] as an attribute of the *alaukika* [extraordinary] perception indicates a kind of metalogical and extraempirical evidence similar to what Descartes has called 'immediate self-evident intuition'" (Sinari, 164). Notwithstanding such an exception, the Nyāya realistic view concerning the world of objects remains unaffected: for the Naiyāyika the phenomenal world exists independent of the knowing mind.

It is interesting to note that Nyāya considers memory as invalid knowledge; as such, perceptual knowledge having memory as an element, becomes erroneous. For instance, a mother whose child died of snakebite, might see a rope but perceive it as a snake. The perceiver here retains a dreadful memory of the snake and combines-confuses the presented sense-data ("rope") with the sense-data represented by memory ("snake" or snake-like features). Such a wrong synthesis of the presented and the represented sense-data results in erroneous knowledge: the snake does exist, but elsewhere and un-presented to the sense of sight. Thus the mother perceives the object ("rope") as some other object ("snake") which exists somewhere else *(anyathā);* reversely, that which exists elsewhere ("snake") is being perceived as existing here and now and, therefore, the judgment "This is a snake" is erroneous. The Nyāya theory explaining this is called *anyathākhyāti*. In the example we have given (and which is one of the most familiar examples often cited in Indian philosophical schools in connection with knowledge and error), the mother confuses the "this" aspect of the object with its "that" aspect and *commits* herself to a false judgment. Hence, the theory of error as conceived in *Nyāya* is also called "the theory of commission."

Much different from this theory of error are the theories of error in the Sāmkhya and the Mimāmsā systems. In Sāmkhya, erroneous knowledge is "incomplete or partial knowledge" and is the result of omission. In Mimāmsā, erroneous perception is explained in terms of one's failure to discriminate between the "this" aspect (mere presence) and the "that" aspect (quality) of a thing. The Nyāya theory differs from the Sāmkhya and the Mimāmsā theories in that the error in Nyāya has "an objective basis and is not a subjective hallucination" (Ranade, 60).

2. **Inference** ***(anumāna):*** Except Chārvaka and his school of materialism, all the systems of Indian thought accept inference as a valid source of right knowledge. While inference *(anumāna)* is the source or means of knowledge, *anumiti* is the knowledge attained through *anumāna* or inference. Perception or *pratyaksa* refers to both the "means of knowing" and "the (perceptual) knowledge itself." Unlike *pratyaksa,* which is immediate cognition, *anumāna* is mediate knowledge, arising *(māna)* after some other cognition *(anu)* has already taken place. Knowledge is first received through perception *(pratyaksa),* or comparison *(upamāna),* or words of sacred authority; and it is only when knowledge is thus received that another knowledge is inferred from it. Inferential knowledge, therefore, is neither direct nor immediate. For instance, on seeing a swollen river, we infer the occurrence of past rain; or, on perceiving that color and fragrance (generally) coexist in a flower, we infer that the knowledge of the color in another flower must be associated with or followed by the knowledge of its fragrance; or, on perceiving the presence of smoke on a hill, we infer the presence of fire on that hill on the strength of our past experience of "the invariable association" *(vyāpti)* of smoke and fire.

Immediate inference does not include "invariable association" or *vyāpti;* hence, Nyāya accepts only the mediate inferences involving *vyāpti.* As D.M. Dutta writes, "The so-called immediate inferences, as not involving the knowledge of any *vyāpti,* altogether fall outside the denotation of anumāna" (Dutta, 204; emphasis added). Nyāya does not, however, offer any reason as to why immediate inferences have been rejected. Certain instances which are considered by the Western logicians as instances of immediate reference, are given the form of mediate inference by Nyāya. We may consider the following:

Example: "Earth is different from the four elements of air, water, fire and ether, because it is earth."

"(Of the four elements) Whatever is not different from these elements is not earth."

Thus *vyāpti* (the invariable association of middle and major terms) serves as the basis of Nyāya sollogism. In the example given above of smoke and fire on the hill, the middle term (smoke) is known as *vyāpya* (pervaded), the major term (fire) is known as *vyāpaka* (pervader), and the relation between the two (smoke in its invariable association with fire) is *vyāpti* (pervasion). *Vyāpti* can be of two kinds—*sama-vyāpti* (equal extension or permeation) and *visama-vyāpti* (unequal extension or permeation). Smoke and fire fed by wet fuel have equal extension, but smoke and fire have unequal extension.

Unlike Buddhism, Nyāya does not take the help of either identity or causality in order to establish a universal proposition (or to ascertain *vyāpti*). *Vyāpti* is not necessarily a cause-effect relation, nor can it be established by means of identity. "If whatever is pine is tree, then whatever is tree should be pine on account of identity," whereas all the trees are not necessarily pines. This hypothetical proposition involves one true proposition (antecedent) and one false proposition (consequent). Identity has an instrumental value in the ascertainment of *vyāpti* only when the inference is from the specific *(simsapā)* to the generic *(vrksa),* but it fails when the inference is from the generic (*vrksa* or tree) to the specific (*simsapā* or pine). *Vyāpti,* as viewed in *Nyāya,* is an invariable concomitance of the *linga* or *hetu* (middle term) and the *sādhya* (major term).

Nyāya inference is of two kinds—*svārtha* (for oneself) and *parārtha* (for others). As long as the inferential argument is on the level of thought, it is for one's own self and hence, there is no need for its verbal expression. But the moment there is the need to convince any other person, the argument has to be verbally expressed, the exposition of which is as follows:

Example:	Proposition *(pratijñā)*:	"This hill is fiery."
	Reason *(hetu)*:	"Because it is smoky."
	Example *(udāharana)*:	"Whatever is smoky is fiery, like the kitchen and unlike the lake."
	Application *(upanaya)*:	"This hill, since it is smoky, is fiery."
	Conclusion *(nigamana)*:	"This hill is fiery."

The five members of the Nyāya argument should not be treated individually and separately, but as parts *(avayava)* of the whole inferential process leading to the inferential knowledge.

We shall here attempt to resolve a minor controversy. The state of being the locus or the minor term (*paksatā:* in the example above, the "hill") has been described by some logicians as "the state in which it is doubtful whether the major term abides in it or not" (Vidyabhusana, 433). However, Gangesa, the author of *Tattva-chintāmani* and leader of the modern school of Nyāya, is of the view that the connection of the major term with the locus or minor term may not necessarily involve a doubt; consequently, Gangesa defines the minor term as "that whose connection with the major term is not known with certainty in consequence of the absence of a desire to know the connection" (See Vidyabhusana, 433). Gangesa mentions that in the proposition, "The hill is full of fire," the connection between the minor term hill and the major term fire was hitherto neither known nor inquired into. One cannot treat the minor term as such merely by proving its connection with the major term if that connection is already known, but he would be justified in treating it as the minor term if there is in him a desire again to establish the connection. The method of investigation to establish the connection involves two examples: i) A homologue, a similar locus, a homogeneous-positive example *(sapaksa),* in which the major term is known with certainty to abide, *e.g.* the hill is full of fire, because it is full of smoke, as a *kitchen,* and ii) A heterologue, a dissimilar locus, a heterogeneous-negative example *(vipaksa),* in which the major term is known not to abide, *e.g.* the hill is full of fire, because it is full of smoke; where there is no fire, there is no smoke, as a *lake.*

3. **Comparison** *(upamāna):* Knowledge attained through comparison is known as *upamiti.* Vaisesika, as discussed earlier in this chapter, accepts only two means of knowledge, namely, perception *(pratyaksa)* and inference *(anumāna)* and does not recognize either "knowledge through comparison" *(upamiti)* or "knowledge through verbal testimony" *(sabda)* as separate kinds of knowledge. In Vaisesika, "knowledge through inference" or *anumiti* includes both "knowledge through comparison" *(upamiti)* and "knowledge through verbal testimony" *(sabda).*

We shall begin with some concrete examples to show how "knowledge through comparison" *(upamiti)* is different from the perceptual *(pratyaksa)* and the inferential *(anumiti)* forms of knowledge. To repeat an example we have given earlier, a villager who owns a cow and is told by a forester how a wild cow *(gavaya)* looks like, would recognize the latter when he finds one in a forest and say to himself, "This animal of the forest resembles my cow in many ways." His knowledge of the animal in the forest (the wild cow) is simply a knowledge attained through comparison. Similarly, a boy who is familiar with a donkey but has never seen a zebra, although he has been given the description of the zebra, would recognize a zebra if he happens to come across one. Such knowledge through comparison involves factors—the recollection of the object perceived in the past (the cow and the donkey), and the perception of the present object (the wild cow and the zebra)—which coalesce through a relation of resemblance. Thus the knowledge of the described unseen objects results in a successful application of the names (or, words) to the respective objects; such knowledge is possible because of certain similarities between the presented data and the description. Accordingly, it may be defined as "the knowledge of the relation between a name and that which can be named," or as "the knowledge of the relation between a *word* and the *thing* referred to." Similarity or comparison serves as the basis of *upamiti.*

Comparison *(upamāna)* is an independent source of right knowledge and as such, cannot be the equivalent of either perception *(pratyaksa)* or inference *(anumāna)* as Vaisesika would have us believe. Perception involves only the presented data to be perceived in the present, and perceptual knowledge is a result of sense-object contact. Comparison, however, is a combination of perception *and* recollection. Similarly, inference (which involves expressions like "I infer") is possible only through *vyāpti* or the invariable concomitance of the middle and the major terms, while comparison is not based on *vyāpti* but on similarity between two objects. Inferential knowledge is the knowledge of the unperceived (fire) as derived from the knowledge of the perceived, but knowledge by comparison is the knowledge of the perceived through the named and described.

The Nyāya view of comparison is slightly different from the views of Mimāmsā and Vedānta. The latter are of the view that when something is like another thing, the other thing must be like that thing; accordingly, the person seeing the wild cow in the forest obtains his knowledge in the form of the judgment, "My cow at home looks like this." From the standpoint of the Nyāya philosopher, on the other hand, such a person obtains the knowledge in the form of the judgment, "This wild cow looks like my cow at home." Although the judgments (in the form in which knowledge is obtained) are different, yet the basis of such judgments remains the same for all the three systems.

4. **Verbal Testimony** *(sabda):* Both the instrument of knowledge and the knowledge that is achieved through such instrument of verbal testimony are called *sabda.* In its sense of the instrument, *sabda* is defined as the statements of trustworthy and reliable persons and our understanding of those statements and their "constituent parts" (Puligandla, 183). Two different views have been offered in regard to the origin of statements that play a significant instrumental role in our acquisition of knowledge. Ancient *Nyāya* logicians, like Vatsāyana and Prasastapāda, have attributed the ancient Hindu scriptures or *vedas* to great seers and sages, while Gangesa and others of the modern school of *Nyāya (Navya-Nyāya)* assert that God alone could be the author of the *vedas.* This difference in opinion led to a distinction between "the statements of seers and sages, or statements of human origin" *(laukika)* and "the statements of divine origin" *(vaidika).* Accordingly, since no human being is perfect, *laukika* testimony is believed to be fallible, while *vaidika* testimony, because of its divine source, is believed to be perfect and infallible.

Irrespective of whether verbal testimony *(sabda)* is human or divine in origin, it is always of two kinds: *drstārtha,* involving statements or assertions regarding objects that are perceivable; and *adrsthārtha,* involving statements about imperceivable objects. Thus, the statements of scientists with regards to electrons, protons, and so on, statements regarding God, and statements regarding virtue, vice, or liberation, belong to the category of *adrstārtha.*

A statement, or a sentence involving an assertion, is a collection of words; and, since a word is a conventional symbol and is used to stand for a definite object or action, a sentence, in order to be meaningful, must be sufficiently qualified so as to be intelligible. According to Nyāya, the qualifications or conditions of a meaningful sentence are: expectancy *(akānksā),* consistency *(yogyata),* contiguity *(sannidhi),* and intention *(tātparya).* Expectancy refers to the interrelatedness of words constituting a sentence. Words stand in need of one another in order to convey a complete meaning; mutual expectancy of words is the basis of any meaningful sentence (*e.g.* "Tell me a story" as against "Story me a tell"). Consistency refers to the compatibility of the words as used in a sentence. For instance, the sentence "Water the plants with fire" is inconsistent because it uses words that contradict each other, and therefore, the sentence is not meaningful. We must here point out that what the Nyāya logicians are concerned with, are simple factual sentences without metaphoric or ironic implications; hence, sentences like "Kill me softly with thy song" or "Kill him with a kiss" do not come under this category. Contiguity or close proximity is an advice against long pauses or other distractions, both conscious and unconscious, in between words in a sentence. If the words "give," "him," "some," "water," are uttered at long intervals it may be impossible to understand what is being said. The last condition is the intention of the speaker. The meaning of a sentence must be understood in association with the speaker's intention. Thus, if a person apprehending danger in the immediate future, tells his friend "Leave this place at once," the latter would have misunderstood the sentence if he thought that the speaker was cruel and without sympathy. Or, if a person taking his food, asks the waiter to bring *saindhava* (which in Sanskrit means both "salt" and "horse"), the waiter (provided he is not inattentive) should not bring a horse.

God in Vaisesika *and* Nyāya

The Vaisesika system is essentially realistic, practical and analytical; it stretches its rational-critical inclinations as far as to include the atomic combinations, which are at the basis of all perceptible objects. The Vaisesika explanation of the universe is scientific and naturalistic, but at the same time it is not mechanical. At the same time as it explains the universe in terms of a theory of essential atoms, it introduces spiritual substances into its catalogue of ultimate substances. The spiritual substance or Self, with its characteristic features of knowing and willing and its association with the performed activities, cannot be adequately explained in the same fashion as the produced physical things. The moral order noticed in the realm of fruit-bearing activities of every individual being, postulates a principle—the principle of *karma*—representing an unseen power, i.e., the unseen power of merit and demerit, of virtues and vices, called *adrsta. Ardsta,* however, is nonintelligent and therefore is supported by God. Both moral and physical order require the intervention of divine agency.

The founder of the Vaisesika system, Kanāda, did not explicitly mention God, but he describes the *Vedas* as containing "His words" and justifies their authority on the ground of their being "His words" *(tadvachanāt amnayasya prāmānyam).* Prasastapada and Udayana, who wrote commentaries on *Vaisesika-sutra* and *Nyāya-sutra* respectively, are known to be theistic. In any case, God in the Vaisesika system is included in the class of self or *ātman;* and to distinguish Him from other individual selves, God is called the Supreme Self or *paramātmā*. In common with all other selves, God shares the qualities of eternality and omnipresence; the only difference between the individual selves and the Supreme Self resides in the latter's association with the quality of "consciousness."

As we have mentioned earlier in the chapter, the presupposition of God is a logical necessity. God happens to be the efficient cause of the world and is responsible for the creation of the world out of the "eternal atoms," the protection of the created world, as well as the destruction of that world in order that it may be created all over again. *Adrsta* or the Unseen Force plays its role in the realm of morality. Both Vaisesika and Nyāya consider *adrsta* as the principle or law of *karma* or human action. The moral laws regulating actions and the fruits thereof, thus bringing about order and harmony in the plant and animal kingdom, are not sufficient to explain the *proper* punishment and reward in a moral life. God helps *adrsta* in such matters as much as His will directs *adrsta* in making the punishments and rewards justifiable and *proper*. But God cannot change the moral laws, which are supposed to be constant: the moral laws, thus, delimit God's "unlimited" power.

In the vedic age, the sages accepted the concept of *Rta,* which is "an indefinable cosmic stuff having its own rule" (Sinari, 36). *Rta* is the principle that regulates and controls the events in the phenomenal world. The Vaisesika-Nyāya concept of *adrsta* is a development on the vedic concept of *Rta*. *Rg Veda* mentions that even the sun and other cosmic beings had to obey *Rta*.

Nyāya proves God's existence by way of inference. The world is an effect or a product which comes into being as a result of a combination of parts best explained by the theory of eternal atoms. Nyāya infers God's existence from the invariable concomitance *(vyāpti)* between the "order and arrangement" and "the existence of a creator." Every case of order and arrangement points to the existence of a creator, *e.g.* a "pot" implying the "potter." Hence, the world, which is an effect and has an order and arrangement, has a creator, i.e. God. It would be appropriate here to say a few words about Udayana's comments on God in his *Kusumānjali*. He prescribes the worship of God as essential for the individual's attainment of emancipation and mentions that even a logical investigation into God's existence would amount to His worship. To the objection brought against God's existence in terms of nonperception, Udayana says that the perceptibility and imperceptibility in regard to ordinary objects are inapplicable to God who is beyond the category of ordinary objects and, therefore, nonperception of God does not disprove His existence.

Bondage and Liberation in Vaisesika-Nyāya

Like all other systems of Indian philosophy, Vaisesika and Nyāya also believe in the liberation of the individual self. Due to ignorance, the self gets associated with body and mind, and the individual is constrained to perform "worldly" activities. If these activities are in confirmity with the vedic injunctions, they produce merit and pleasure; if not, they produce demerit and pain. Both pleasure and pain are the experiencing states of a "bound" self. In order to attain liberation, therefore, the individual self must cease to perform all activities thus avoiding all pleasure and pain. With the cessation of activities, new merits or demerits do not get deposited, and the old ones are gradually destroyed. The self knows its distinction from the not-self and such knowledge helps the self attain liberation. The liberated is a pure substance, devoid of all qualities and free from any association with mind and body, lacking consciousness but maintaining its particularity. As anything eternal maintains its particularity at the expense of every kind of material loss and gain, so the liberated self continues to maintain its particularity *(visesa)* even in its liberated state. Although ancient Vaisesika literature and ancient Nyāya literature do not mention God, later thinkers belonging to those two schools, like Vardhamāna and Udayana, have introduced God as an unavoidable necessity on the path of liberation – as one whose grace quickens the process leading to liberation. Udayana in his *Nyāya-kusumānjali* maintains that "worship of God is essential for salvation." Udayana's "pleadings and advocacy of the necessity and logical possibility of self-surrender and meditation on God are unsurpassable for their devotional ardor, impassioned enthusiasm, and moral fervor. A better and more successful advocacy of theism is difficult to conceive" (Satkari Mookerjee, 123).

Works Cited

Bernard, Theos. *Hindu Philosophy*. 1947; rpt. Delhi: Motilal Banarsidass, 1985.

Dasgupta, S.N. *A History of Indian Philosophy* (5 vols.), vol. 1. Cambridge: Cambridge University Press, 1973.

Datta, D.M. *The Six Ways of Knowing: A Critical Study of Advaita Theory of Knowledge*. 1932; rpt. Calcutta: The University of Calcutta Press, 1972.

Hiriyanna, M. *Outlines of Indian Philosophy*. 1932, London: George Allen & Unwin; rpt. Bombay: Blackie & Son, 1983.

Mookerjee, Satkari. "Nyāya Vaisesika," *The Cultural Heritage of India* (5 vols.), vol. 3, ed. Haridas Bhattacharyya. Calcutta: The Ramakrishna Mission Institute of Culture, 1969.

Potter, Karl H. *Encyclopedia of Indian Philosophies: Indian Metaphysics and Epistemology: The Tradition of Nyāya-Vaisesika up to Gangesa*. Princeton, N.J.: Princeton University Press, and Delhi: Motilal Banarsidass, 1977.

Puligandla, R. *Fundamentals of Indian Philosophy*. Nashville, Tenn.: Abingdon Press, 1975.

Radhakrishnan, S. *Indian Philosophy* (2 vols.), Muirhead Library of Philosophy. London: George Allen & Unwin, and New York: Humanities Press, 1966.

Ranade, R.D. *Vedānta: The Culmination of Indian Thought*. Bombay: Bharatiya Vidya Bhavan, 1970.

Sen, K.M. *Hinduism.* 1961; rpt. Harmondsworth, England: Penguin Books, 1982.
Sharma, Chandradhar. *A Critical Survey of Indian Philosophy.* Delhi: Motilal Banarsidass, 1983.
Sinari, Ramakant A. *The Structure of Indian Thought.* 1970; rpt. New Delhi: Oxford University Press, 1984.
Vidyabhusana, Satis Chandra. *A History of Indian Logic.* 1970; rpt. Delhi: Motilal Banarsidass, 1978.

Suggested Further Reading

Bahadur, K.P. *The Wisdom of Vaisheshika.* New Delhi: Sterling Publishers, 1979.
________. *The Wisdom of Nyaya.* New Delhi: Sterling Publishers, 1979.
Barlingay, S.S. *A Modern Introduction to Indian Logic.* Delhi: National Publishing House, 1976.
Cowell, E.B., and Gough A.E., tr. *Madhavacarya's Sarva-darsana-samgraha.* London: Kegan Paul, Trench, Trubner & Company, 1904.
Guha, D.C. *Navya-Nyāya System of Logic: Basic Theories & Techniques.* Delhi: Motilal Banarsidass, 1979.
Jha, Ganganatha. *The Nyaya Philosophy of Gautama.* Allahbad: Allahbad University Press, n.d.
________. *Gautama's Nyāyasutras, with Vatsāyana's Bhāsya.* Poona, India: The Oriental Book Agency, 1939.
Keith, A.B. *Indian Logic and Atomism: An Exposition of the Nyāya and Vaisesika Systems.* Oxford: Clarendon Press, 1921.
Matilal, B.K. *The Navya-Nyāya Doctrine of Negation.* Cambridge, Mass.: Harvard University Press, 1968.
Sinha, J.N. *Indian Realism.* London: Kegan Paul, 1938.
Sinha, Nandalal, tr. *The Vaisesika Sutras of Kanada, with the Commentary of Samkara Misra, Extracts from the Gloss of Jayanarayana, and the Bhasya of Candrakanta.* The Sacred Books of the Hindus, vol. 6. Allahbad: The Panini Office, 1923.

6

Sāmkhya-Yoga

Although *Sāmkhya* is one of the six major systems in Indian philosophy, its origins are still very much shrouded in mystery. According to one school of scholars, it is an independent system without any discernible roots in any one of the more ancient systems; according to another it had had its first stirrings in the *Upanishads*—that most ancient record of the reflections of the Hindu seers and sages. In the *Upanishads,* questions have been formulated in connection with the nature of Ultimate Truth and Reality and answers carefully offered as attempts to meet the demands of the interrogative minds.

While it is generally believed that almost all the systems of Indian philosophy originate from the upanishadic teachings, it has been now established that at least two principal modes of orthodox philosophy evolved out of the *Upanishads:* the realistic, of which Sāmkhya is the earliest representative, and the idealistic, of which the Vedānta is the foremost representative. Eminent scholars of this century, like S. Radhakrishnan, S.N. Dasgupta and C.D. Sharma are of the view that certain suggestions in some of the major *Upanishads* led to the gradual establishment of the Sāmkhya doctrine. The particular upanishadic texts which, according to these scholars, have served as the background of Sāmkhya philosophy are the *Chāndogya Upanishad,* the *Prasna Upanishad,* the *Kathā Upanishad,* and the *Svetāsvatara Upanishad.* The *Svetāsvatara Upanishad,* for instance, talks about a "single Female of red, white and black colors" who is unoriginated and who produces numerous offsprings resembling herself; by her side lies "one unborn Male out of attachment for her, while another Male, also unoriginated, forsakes her, after having enjoyed her." The passage implies the concepts of *Purusha* and *Prakrti,* the two ultimate principles accepted in the Sāmkhya system. The *Kathā Upanishad* mentions the *purusha* who is "seated in the midst of our self and is no larger than the finger of a man." Several other instances, illustrating the connection between the *Upanishads* and the Sāmkhya, could also be cited.

The earliest Sāmkhya system, on the basis of upanishadic suggestions, accepted "theistic monism"; later on, the system was transformed to that of a combination of "atheistic realism" and "spiritual pluralism." Both the earlier and the later stages of the Sāmkhya system, however, were marked by *realism*. S.N. Dasgupta's remarks with reference to this problem of origin are worth mentioning at this point. According to him, there were two clear lines of thought in the *Upanishads:* one line of thought, by way of considering *Brahman* to be the ultimate principle, resulted in pure monism, while the other line of thought regarded the world as having a reality all its own. Sāmkhya thought, it might be said, was at one time developing on both these lines concurrently. As Dasgupta conclusively states, the Sāmkhya system "unites the doctrine of the permanence of the Upanishads with the doctrine of momentariness of the Buddhists and the doctrine of relativism of the Jains" (p. 212).

Basically speaking, the *Sāmkhya* philosophy is a combination of two subphilosophies: *Sāmkhya* and *Yoga*. Both the subphilosophies are based on the same metaphysical tenets; the difference lies in the fact that while *Sāmkhya* represents the theoretical aspect of the main philosophy, *Yoga* represents its applied aspect. Kapila and Patanjali are, respectively, the chief exponents of the *Sāmkhya* and the *Yoga* schools. The Sāmkhya thought was prevalent before the sixth century B.C., but thereafter went through a gradual process of development and inclusion. During this period of its transition, it had been influenced by two heterodox systems flourishing at that time—those of Jainism and Buddhism.

Sāmkhya and Yoga Literature

Kapila, Asuri, Panchasikha, Isvarakrsna, Vijñāna Bhiksu and Vāchaspati Misra are considered to be the foremost exponents of the Sāmkhya system, although the foundations of the earlier Sāmkhya had been laid by Charaka in the latter half of the first century A.D. Charaka's philosophy is slightly different from the orthodox Sāmkhya system. All the physical and psychical entities, together with *purusha,* are treated with a lot of care in both the "philosophies," but Charaka does not mention *prakrti.* He introduces something called *alinga* (without qualities), which came to be known as *prakrti* at a later stage. Charaka explains the universe in terms of six elements: five elements and *chetanā* or *purusha.*

Kapila's explanation of the nature of the universe carried a theistic undertone, and while his chief disciple, Asuri, made an atheistic interpretation of his master's explanation, Asuri's interpretation was carried further toward a purely rationalistic explanation in the hands of Panchasikha—a development which made Arthur A. MacDonell *(A History of Sanskrit Literature)* acclaim Sāmkhya as the first rationalistic philosophy in the world. Isvarakrsna, who claimed himself as succeeding Panchasikha in the Sāmkhya pantheon, wrote the *Sāmkhya-Kārikā* (A.D. 200), which is considered to be the earliest available text of Sāmkhya since, in the absence of sufficient evidence, it is not possible to attribute the authorship of the two other extant texts—*Sāmkhya-Pravachanasutra* and *Tattvasamāsa*—to Kapila. In the ninth century A.D., Vāchaspati Misra wrote a commentary on Charaka's *Atreyatantra,* known as *Tattvakaumudi;* in the 16th century

A.D., Vijñāna Bhiksu wrote *Pravachanabhāsya,* a commentary on *Sāmkhya Sutras* (believed by some scholars, including C.D. Sharma, to have been written by Kapila). These above-mentioned texts comprehensively present the Sāmkhya thought. In addition to these we have a few more texts, like the commentaries of Gaudapada and Nārāyanatirtha.

Patanjali wrote the *Yoga-Sutra,* which consists of four parts that explain the nature and purpose of "meditation"—the means directed toward ultimate liberation. Vyāsa (A.D. 400) wrote a commentary on the *Yoga-Sutra.* Several commentaries have been written on Vyāsa's commentary itself, like *Tattvavaisāradi* of Vāchaspati Misra, *Yogavarttika* of Vijñana Bhiksu, *Bhojavrtti* of Bhoja, and *Chāyāvyākhyā* of Nagesa.

Theory of Causation

The theory of causation as is known in Indian philosophy, is based on two views: that the effect is pre-existent in the cause prior to its creation, and that the effect does not pre-exist in the cause. Consequently, there have been two main theories of causation: *satkāryavāda* (the doctrine of pre-existence of the effect in the cause) and *asatkāryavāda* (the doctrine of nonexistence of the effect in the cause). Indian Materialism, *Hinayāna* Buddhism, Nyāya and Vaisesika systems advocate *asatkāryavāda.* Effect, for the asatkāryavādins, is a fresh creation, a new beginning. *Kārya* or effect is *asat* or unreal before its coming into being. As opposed to this, the satkāryavādins claim that *kārya* is *sat* or real even before its manifestation, since it exists in the cause in a potential form and is the actualization of whatever is potential in the cause. As Ramakant Sinari writes, "an effect is only an evolved cause, and a cause is only a latent effect" (p. 39). *Satkāryavāda,* again, comprises two different schools of thought. While one school maintains that the effect is only a distorted appearance of the cause, the other believes that the effect is the real transformation of the cause. The Advaita Vedānta philosophy accepts the former view, which is known as *Brahma-vivarta vāda. Brahman* being the only true cause, the world is a distorted appearance of it. The Sāmkhya school supports the latter view—that the effect is a real transformation or *parināma* of the cause. According to it, the whole world, which is viewed as the effect, springs from its material cause or *Prakrti.* Sāmkhya employs this theory of causation (which it calls *Prakrti-Parināma vāda*) to prove the existence of *Prakrti.* Sinari writes: "Isvarakrsna's concept of causality, known as *parināma-vāda,* is meant to account for the whole of creation by postulating something unmanifested or *avyakta* that is ever pregnant with all that we find ourselves experiencing. Thus causality is a transformation in the state or states of *prakrti,* and this transformation, observed or unobserved, constitutes the order of the universe" (p. 39).

A five-fold argument supports the Sāmkhya theory of causation.

1. The nonexistent can never be made an existent object;

2. The product is not different from the material out of which it is produced, e.g., the pot is not different from its material which is clay, the statue is not different from the marble out of which it is made;

3. The product exists in the shape of the material before it comes into being, e.g., the cloth exists in the form of thread, the pot in the form of clay;

4. The efficiency of the cause lies in its necessary potency, which is to say, that which does not have the potentiality to produce can never be regarded as an efficient cause;

5. The effect and the cause are of the same nature.

Sāmkhya accepts two kinds of cause: the material cause or *prakrti,* which is itself uncaused but has within it the tendency to produce, as well as the efficient cause or *purusha,* which neither has been produced nor has a tendency to produce but, like a catalyst, is instrumental in bringing about evolution. Thus Sāmkhya, which believes in evolution rather than antecedentless creation, offers a realistic basis both to the knower and the known, to the subject that knows as well as the object that is known. The object is as much real as the subject; accordingly Sāmkhya presupposes two ultimate principles. It is in this respect that it is dualistic in character. It is, also, a practical system as it envisages the intimate interaction between *purusha* and *prakrti* in order to account for the entire universe.

Purusha

In *Taittiriya Upanishad* it has been mentioned that *Brahman* or the Ultimate Being divided itself into two constituent parts—spirit and matter. Sāmkhya makes "spirit" *(purusha)* the first principle in its system. *Purusha,* in Sāmkhya, is an eternally free, absolutely independent principle, inexplicable and unknowable by the help of ordinary experience. Like the *Brahman* or Absolute of *Advaita-Vedānta, purusha* transcends all experience and is supra-empirical in character, standing as it does outside the limits of the phenomenal world as a mere witness and accepting without hesitation the solitude endowed upon it.

The etymological meaning of Sāmkhya comes close to "counting together." The process of counting implies the existence of several entities and, unsurprisingly, the system explains the whole framework of the universe in terms of 25 categories, all of which (both spiritual and material) can be brought under four major categories:

1. That which is neither produced nor produces;
2. That which is not produced but produces;
3. Those which are produced and do produce; and
4. Those which are produced but do not produce.

Under the first of these four categories there is the postulation of a single principle, i.e., *purusha,* which is neither produced nor produces. To be produced means to have a cause, and *purusha* is the point beyond which the explanation of the world cannot proceed. It is thus uncaused and unproduced. Similarly, it is also unproductive, since producing involves activity whereas *purusha* is completely inactive, having neither "before" nor "after." The absence of before and after eliminates any possible relationship, and noninvolvement in the world-activities qualify it with a sort of aloofness; it remains as pure, nonattributive consciousness.

It has been pointed out earlier that although the products of *prakrti* are perceived, the existence of *prakrti* can be proved only by way of inference from its effects. Such imperceptibility, however, is not unique to *prakrti,* since *purusha* is also imperceptible and its existence is proved by reasoning alone. The following are the reasonings in favor of the existence of *purusha:*

1. *Sanghātaparārthatvāt* (collocation or arrangement to serve others' purpose): The phenomenal world is an arrangement to serve the purpose of a Principle external to it, e.g., the unconscious bed is completely unaware of the person using it even as it is unaware of itself.
2. *Trigunadiviparyayāt* (the logical inference of an entity devoid of attributes): *Prakrti* and its effect, the world of objects, are *sāttvic, rājasic* and *tāmasic* in character, which is to say, they are stained with the influence of the three *gunas* or qualities called *sattva, rajas* and *tamas.* Since the responsibility of proper appreciation and justice cannot be left with either *prakrti* or the world of objects, it is given to an impartial being who is devoid of qualities or *nistrayiguna.*
3. *Adhisthānāt* (seat of all empirical knowledge): The world process is systematic, and there is a unity with reference to the material aspect; but Sāmkhya metaphysics does not overlook epistemology and does not seek a materialistic explanation that discards the many shades of consciousness underlying the world process. The unified and complex material process, in matters of empirical knowledge, requires an underlying unity of consciousness which is the seat or foundation *(Adhisthāna)* of all empirical knowledge.
4. *Bhoktrbhāvāt* (the existence of *purusha* as the enjoyer): Although *prakrti* produces the world, it is not able to enjoy whatever is produced by it. *Purusha* exists as the "enjoyer," the experiencer of pleasure and pain.
5. *Kaivalyārtham-Pravrtteh* (aspiration for liberation): The third of the arguments given above makes *purusha* a necessary principle to make empirical knowledge possible. This argument is from the standpoint of liberation. The individual self, suffering the pain of existence, always has a tendency to escape from this domain of pain so as to attain liberation; but without the aspirant, such aspiration is not possible, and the aspirant or the individual self much exist in order to "aspire for."

Sāmkhya sanctions reality to both noumena and the phenomena, thus differing from monistic Vedānta which makes the phenomenal world only an unreal appearance *(māyā)* and proves the reality of the noumena at the cost of the phenomena, keeping the all-transcending noumena much above the phenomenal world in a fashion that assigns to *purusha* a supreme location. It would be interesting here to note what Ramakanta Sinari says about this: *Purusha* "in all its essence cannot be related to anything except itself. Its presence behind *prakrti* and its products is described as that of the seer *(drastr)* behind the seen *(drsya),* that of the experiencer *(bhoktr)* behind the experienced *(bhogya),* or that of spirit *(sachetana)* behind matter *(achetana).* It is the witnessing or *saksin* awareness—a kind of constantly watching eye—above all that goes on in the realm of *prakrti*" (pp. 174–175).

Apart from the experience of *Purusha* (the transcendental Self),

Sāmkhya advocates the multiplicity of *purushas* (individual selves). The overall cosmology remaining the same, subjective views vary, and this variation in subjective views concerning cosmology is untenable unless there is the supposition of many selves without which the birth and the death of a psycho-physical personality would mean the birth and death of all and the liberation of one self would amount to the liberation of all the selves.

It must be made clear here that the empirical self (ego) is different from the individual self. The empirical self does not adequately explain the extent of inclusiveness of the "world-experience" so that the latter subsumes the changing views of individual selves. The empirical self or ego is a common principle and the ego-oriented qualities are almost similar irrespective of the degree of ignorance and the amount of past impressions carried by different egos or empirical selves. Although one *Purusha* and one *Prakrti* explain the entire world-process without inconvenience, they cannot clearly explain the existences of many selves with their several and various outlooks and experiences. The Sāmkhya analysis of existence and experience, therefore, goes a step further to admit the plurality of selves. The transcendental *Purusha* is known through Sāmkhya metaphysics while the individual selves *(purushas)* are known through Sāmkhya epistemology and ethics.

Prakrti

In Sāmkhya the analysis of experience and existence is as important as the knowledge of the transcendental self. The system makes a naturalistic approach to the phenomenal world and explains the same with reference to a primordial substance called *Prakrti,* which comes under the second of the four major categories mentioned earlier ("That which is not produced but produces"). *Prakrti* is the material principle. It is unintelligent but active, and its activity consists in the unfolding of the world.

When the material atoms combine in a definite proportion to form the different objects of the world, the latter is said to be "created afresh." Such a view of creation is advocated by the Nyāya-Vaisesika sytem. Sāmkhya, on the other hand, believes in *evolution* rather than *creation.* The external world is a product resulting from the process of evolution, which involves the transformation of a thing (which evolves) into a different form of the same thing, all the while its substance remaining the same. In Sāmkhya it is the *Prakrti* which starts evolving into its various evolutes. The world is the effect which lies latent in its material cause, *Prakrti.* The transcendental *Purusha,* remaining outside the world, cannot be its cause and hence, the other ultimate reality *(Prakrti)* is supposed to be the first cause, which nonetheless acts under the influence and supervision of *Purusha.*

Prakrti is a complex substance consisting of three *gunas* or qualities: *sattva, rajas* and *tamas.* The *gunas,* however, are not just constituents; they form the very essence of *Prakrti.* The relation between *Prakrti* and the *gunas* cannot, therefore, be compared with the usual relation between a substance and its attributes or qualities, e.g., a flower and its color, fragrance, etc. The *gunas* are so called because they are the elements of the *only* primordial substance, *Prakrti,* and hence, cannot themselves be treated as substances. This does not, however, mean that they are the different parts of the whole; rather they constitute the very essence of the whole in such a fashion that the whole can be said to be the unity of the three *gunas* held in a state of equilibrium.

The *gunas* are always changing, thus making *Prakrti* ever dynamic in character. The change thus marked in the *gunas* as well as in *Prakrti,* assumes two broad forms: homogeneous and heterogeneous. The homogeneous change does not *produce* any object, as the state of equilibrium remains unaffected by it. The equilibrium is unaffected since the mutually independent *gunas* do not interact; it is merely that *sattva* changes into *sattva, rajas* into *rajas,* and *tamas* into *tamas.* The heterogeneous change implies interaction—*sattva, rajas* and *tamas* interacting with one another in order to produce the world-objects by disturbing the state of equilibrium. The evolutionary process, then, has its origin in the heterogeneous change. During this change the external world sleeps in *Prakrti*—a state known as *Pralaya* (dissolution). Dissolution is followed by evolution and evolution in its turn is followed by dissolution in a continuous, cyclic fashion.

The *gunas* not only constitute *prakrti* but also the world of objects, which is thus composed of *sattva, rajas* and *tamas. Sattva* stands for the tendency to manifest; *rajas* stands for activity; and *tamas* stands for the obstacles on the way to such manifestation. Dale Riepe provides a somewhat different interpretation, according to whom *sattva* is the essence, *rajas* is the energy, and *tamas* is the inertia; accordingly, the primordial stuff at the first level of differentiation is of three kinds—essences, energies, and inertias. The essence strives to assume a form, using energy and in spite of the inertia.

An analysis of the individual experience shows that *sattva* gives pleasure, *rajas* gives pain, while *tamas* is the cause of bewilderment *(moha).* Accordingly, the colors of these three *gunas* are white, red, and black. C.D. Sharma relates the nature of the *gunas* with the eminent Hindi poet Rasalina's description of the eyes of the woman, which are white, red, or dark, and whose sight makes the lover feel at different times or simultaneously "the joy of life, the agony of restlessness and the inertia of death" (Sharma, 155). Similarly, Isvarakrsna refers to *Prakrti* as "the red-white-dark, the unborn mother of all generation." The three *gunas* can never be separated, working as they do together, like the oil, the wick, and the flame of a lamp; and, although their existence cannot be directly perceived, it is proved by reasoning from their effects, i.e., the world-objects. The proof of *Prakrti*'s existence—and thus the proof of the existence of the *gunas*—is grounded in a five-fold argument:

1. *Bhedānām Parimānāt* (from the standpoint of the finitude of objects): The world-objects are all finite. The difficulty in presupposing a finite cause of the world-objects involves the unending process of finding a finite first cause. If the first cause happens to be finite in character, it would always be depenent on something and hence, cannot be independent and complete.

Logically it follows, then, that something finite cannot be the first cause and that the infinite *Prakrti* can only be the first cause of the material world.

2. *Samanvayāt* (on the basis of the common qualities of the world-objects): All the individual objects share at least three common characteristics (derived from the three *gunas*), like the tendency to manifest, the activity or force that will make the manifestation possible, and the obstacle on the way to such manifestation. Thus all objects contain the three gunas, and this common feature points to a common source that contains the three *gunas.*

3. *Kāryatah Pravrttescha* (the tendency in the cause for actualization of what is potent in it): The cause is always potent of something and the potential must find an expression. As a pregnant mother gives birth to her child, or as a poet's mind pregnant with feeling and thought assigns a shape to these in the concrete, palpable form of a poem, so the potent world-cause has the instinct to produce the effect and the constituent *gunas* tend to express themselves in the particular world-objects.

4. *Kāryakāranavibhāgāt* (difference between cause and effect): This argument differs from the first in that the first takes finitude of the objects as its premise and infers the infinite character of the first cause from it. The present argument takes the difference between cause and effect as its point of departure and derives the conclusion that if the effect (i.e, the world) is finite, then the cause *(Prakrti)* must be something other than it, that is, it must be infinite.

5. *Avibhāgāt Vaishvarupyasya* (absence of disorder, pointing to the singleness of the cause): The perfect order and harmony in the world of objects imply that everything is governed by a single principle, just as the different branches of a tree belong to the same tree. As the main trunk of the tree gets divided into several branches, so the single material cause *(Prakrti)* gets divided and subdivided, thus leading to increasing differentiation.

Thus, both *Prakrti* and the *gunas* are known by reasoning of inference and can never be directly perceived. *Prakrti* is imperceptible, eternal, pervasive; in it, force and matter get identified. Theos Bernard sums up the nature of *Prakrti:*

> Prakrti (Cosmic Substance) is the uncaused cause; therefore, it is eternal, indestructible, and all-pervasive. It is formless, limitless, immobile, and immanent. It has position but no magnitude . . . It is inanimate and unintelligent. It is an ultimate and not a derivative principle; it is . . . the seat of all manifestation, the normal cause of the phenomenal world, the potential power of becoming, the instrumental cause of the world, the substance in which all attributes and action inhere. It is not produced, yet it brings everything else into existence; it is the support of all things, yet it is unsupported; it absorbs all things, yet it is not absorbed by anything else [Bernard, 73–74].

Theory of Evolution

Change is the essential feature of *Prakrti.* As it has been said already, the changing phases of *Prakrti* are of two kinds—heterogeneous and homogeneous. The heterogeneous change of the three *gunas* results in the process of evolution, when the *gunas* intensely desire to be expressed in the world-objects; through their combined effort and interaction, the *gunas* let the evolution start. The evolutionary process begins with the activated *rajas,* which then activates *sattva,* together confronting the opposite force of *tamas.* As a result of this, the external world of physical objects and living beings comes into being. All the products of evolution, however, do not have identical characteristics; their differences, often wide and inexplicable in common terms, are due to the combination of the three *gunas* in unequal proportions.

With the changing phases of the *gunas,* the latent cause or *Prakrti* becomes more and more differentiated, more and more determinate. As Brajendranath Seal so lucidly points out, the process of evolution consists in "the development of the differentiated *(vaisamya)* within the undifferentiated *(samyavasthā),* of the determinate *(visesa)* within the indeterminate *(avisesa),* of the coherent *(yutasiddha)* within the incoherent *(ayutasiddha).* The order of succession is neither from parts to whole nor from whole to the parts, but ever from a relatively less differentiated, less determinate, less coherent whole to a relatively more differentiated, more determinate, more coherent whole" (Seal, p. 7).

The reason behind the disturbance of the equilibrium state of *Prakrti* is the interference of the external agent, *Purusha. Purusha* does not directly enter into the realm of *Prakrti;* nor is the contact between the two a conjunction between one physical object and another. The relation between the two is much like the one existing between a magnet and a piece of iron: the influence of *Purusha* acts like a magnet, setting *Prakrti* in motion. The cooperation between *Purusha* and *Prakrti* is similar to the necessary cooperation between a lame person and a blind person—the blind person carrying the lame person on the shoulders and following the directions given by the latter until they reach their assumably common destination. *Prakrti* is blind and *Purusha,* like the lame person, is unable to move; and hence, only their cooperation makes the world-objects possible. It is for the purpose of *Purusha* that the blind unintelligent *Prakrti* moves, allowing the former to enjoy and suffer, to experience and interpret. In the process, *Purusha* becomes increasingly capable of distinguishing between himself and *Prakrti,* thereby spontaneously dissociating himself from the binding chain of *Prakrti. Prakrti,* therefore, functions for the enjoyment and liberation of *Purusha.* Thus, although their association is temporary, it is necessary. The process that originates from this association is purposive or teleological. The way in which the Sāmkhya explanation of the universe is given, is both scientific and mechanical, consisting as we have observed in a combination of *gunas* by definite proportions, but the purpose behind the process makes the Sāmkhya theory of evolution teleological in character. It must, however, be added that the dualistic outlook of Sāmkhya, consisting in its sanctioning of an equal realistic status to that which is material and that which is nonmaterial pure consciousness, sometimes prompts one to call the Sāmkhya evolution semiteleological. In Sāmkhya, the naturalistic approach in explaining the nature of the universe is as much significant and tenable as the attempt made to realize the Self.

Evolutes

The evolutionary process takes place through several stages, starting with the pure intelligence and proceeding to the gross elements. While *Purusha* makes *Prakrti* start the process, the first evolute that comes into existence is known as *Mahat* or the "great principle." *Mahat,* which is cosmic in nature, has a psychological aspect also, known as *buddhi* or intellect. Being an evolute of *Prakrti,* it is material, but it is made of the finest matter and is in possession of such qualities as luminosity and reflectivity—qualities which enable *buddhi* to reflect *Purusha.*

The cosmic nature of *Mahat* produces *Ahamkāra* (ego or self-sense). *Purusha* gets reflected in the luminous intellect or *buddhi,* but because of individual ignorance, the former is erroneously identified with *ahamkāra* or ego. *Ahamkāra* is the principle of self-identity or personal identity and, for all empirical purposes, stands for the experiencer; it brings about awarenesses like "I exist" and "I know." According to the relative predominance of the three *gunas, ahamkāra* is said to have three aspects: *vaikārika* or *sāttvika-ahamkāra,* which contains a high degree of *sattva* and produces the *manas* (mind), the five *jñānendriyas* (sense organs), and the five *karmendriyas* (motor organs); *tāmasika-ahamkāra,* which contains a high degree of *tamas* and produces the five *tanmātras* (subtle elements); and *rājasika-ahamkāra,* involving a predominance of *rajas,* which does not directly produce anything but helps the other two in their function of producing the evolutes. It must be mentioned here that *manas* (mind) is different from *buddhi.* The former is only produced but is unable to produce, while the latter is both produced and is capable of producing. *Manas* (mind) comes in contact with the sense organs, receives the impressions of the world-objects and transforms them into determinate perceptions, and conveys such perceptions to the experiencer or the ego.

Thus, *buddhi, ahamkāra* and *manas* are the three psychological aspects of knowing, willing, and feeling. However, these are not to be understood as three successive stages of the evolutionary process; they occur simultaneously. Theos Bernard writes: "They are the outcome of the unbalance of the three causative constituents; they are universal, and unlimited by time and space, by name and form. Each step is discussed separately only for the purpose of understanding; but as to content of transcendental experience, they are identical" (Bernard, p. 78).

As it has been mentioned already, the five *jñānendriyas* (sense organs) and the five *karmendriyas* (motor organs) are produced by the *sāttvika-*

ahamkāra. The five sense organs are the ones referring to the powers to see *(chaksu),* to hear *(sroto),* to smell *(ghrāna),* to taste *(rasanā),* and to feel *(tvak).* Similarly, the five motor organs relate to the powers of speech *(vāk),* handling *(pāni),* movement *(pāda),* excretion *(pāya),* and procreation *(upasthā).* The ten organs together are known as the *bāhyakaranas* (external organs), while *buddhi, ahamkāra* and *manas* are known as the *antahkaranas* (internal organs). Thus, there are altogether 13 organs, both external and internal.

The powers to see, hear and so on imply the existence of objects that are meant to be experienced. The *tanmātras* or the fine elements derived from the *tāmasika-ahamkāra* are the objects of experience. They are five in number and refer to the essences of *sabda* (sound), *sparsa* (touch), *rupa* (form), *rasa* (flavor), and *gandha* (odor). These fine elements, although simple-seeming individually, combine in different and complex ways to produce the *bhutādi* or the five gross elements. *Sabda-tanmātra* produces *ākāsa* (ether), which has sound as its specific quality. *Sabda-tanmātra* and *sparsa-tanmātra* together produce *marut* (air), with touch as its specific quality. *Sabda* and *sparsa,* with the cooperation of *rupa* (form), produce *teja* (fire), which possesses the quality of color. *Sparsa, sabda,* and *rupa,* in combination with *rasa* (taste) *tanmātra,* produce *ap* (water), which has taste as its specific quality. Finally, all the five *tanmātras* combine to produce *ksiti* (earth) with smell as its specific quality.

Mahat, ahamkāra, and the *tanmātras* come under the category of "that which is both produced and produces," while *manas, jñānendriyas* (sense organs), and *bhutādi* (gross elements) come under the category of that which is "produced, but is incapable of producing." All the evolutes, together with *Purusha* and *Prakrti,* explain the whole process of Samkhya evolution.

Chart showing the principle of Sāmkhya evolution:

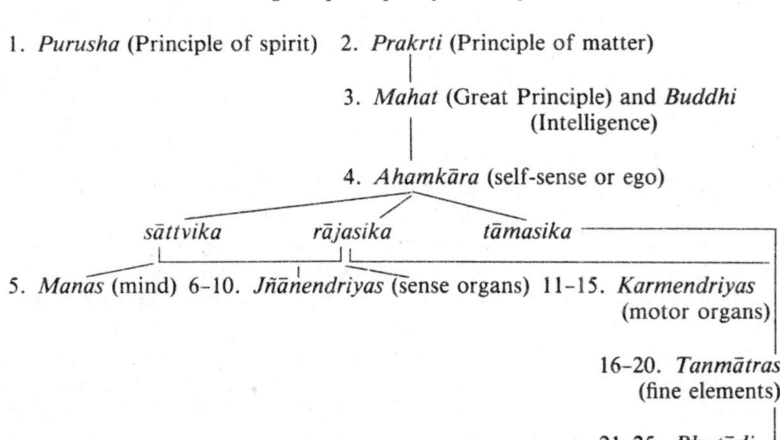

Theory of Knowledge

Sāmkhya sanctions a realistic basis to both the knower and the known. In this system, the function of knowing necessarily implies a) the Pure Self, and b) a mind-body system. The Pure Self *(Purusha),* being outside the known world, cannot be directly the knower; it merely performs the act of mirroring or reflecting. It gets reflected in the fine intellect *(buddhi)* and the latter, containing the reflected *Purusha,* illuminates the object or objects to be known. Knowledge, then, means the illumination of the object through the luminosity of intellect under the influence of the Pure Self.

Not only *buddhi,* but all the three internal organs including *buddhi,* become connective links between the Pure Self and the object. *Manas* (mind) receives the impressions of objects through the sense organs and converts them into determinate percepts through synthesis before carrying the percepts to *buddhi. Buddhi* applies concepts to the percepts, takes the form of the object *(vrtti,* or modification of *buddhi),* and then tries its best to build up, in an indirect way, a contactless relation between the Pure Self and the object, thus completing the knowing process. The Pure Self effects, mirrors, and reflects the modified *buddhi* or *vrtti.* The Pure Self's experience of the illuminated *vrtti,* according to Sāmkhya, is "knowledge."

Sāmkhya accepts three sources of knowledge: perception, inference, and verbal testimony. Perception is the mental apprehension of objects, and perceptual knowledge, like any other form of knowledge, is attained through *vrtti* or modification of *buddhi* or Intellect. It is of two kinds, each of which refers to a phase also: they are indeterminate perception *(nirvikalpaka)* and determinate perception *(savikalpaka),* the former kind being the "immature state" and the latter, the "matured state." When there is an immediate, bare apprehension of an object without any association with either a name or a form, it is indeterminate perception; it involves merely a vague awareness of the object. Later, when a name and a form are assigned to the immediate but vague awareness, the indeterminate perception is converted into a determinate one. Thus, initially, there is just the presentation of the perceivable, which is followed by a much more complex, more determinate state, involving the simultaneous representation and recognition of the former as "such and such."

Sāmkhya texts mention a third kind of perception also, called yogic perception. Such a perception is possible on the part of a yogin alone, who has acquired a certain specific but indefinable power through meditation that allows him to perceive objects in all time and all space. Thus, sense organs (which are an inseparable part of ordinary perception) are unnecessary and irrelevant for the purpose of yogic perception, which includes a lot more than the merely sense-perceived. A yogin believes that at any one moment things are present either in their manifested form or in their unmanifested form. Such a belief is deeply rooted in the Sāmkhya theory of causality, which says that cause and effect are but the latent and actualized states of the same thing. For him, all things are present at all time and in all space. A person possessing yogic power of intuition is capable of perceiving things as they unfold through their different evolutionary phases in the past, the present, and the future.

Inference is another important mode of knowing and source of knowledge. Sāmkhya, as we have seen already, employs inference as the instrument to prove the existence of both *Purusha* and *Prakrti.* As in case of *Prakrti,* whose existence is derived from her effect, i.e., the mimetic world of objects, so in all cases of inference the knowledge of the cause is always derived from our perception of the effect. For instance, the presence of smoke on a hill implies the presence of fire in the same: smoke is *perceived* while the fire is *known* on the ground of their invariable association. Such invariable association is known as *vyāpti* and forms a part of the Sāmkhya syllogistic structure, which explains the entire inferential process in terms of five propositions. Sāmkhya syllogism consists of five members, but it contains only three terms: major, minor, and middle. The form of its inference can be known from the following example: "This hill has smoke, which is invariably associated with fire; therefore, the hill has fire." Also, inference can be both ways—inference of the effect from the antecedent cause *(purvavat)* as well as inference of the cause from the effect *(sesavat).* In addition to these two, there is also analogy *(sāmānyatodrsta),* based on the similarity between two things.

Verbal testimony or authoritative statement *(āptavachana)* is the third source of knowledge. Authoritative statement as conceived in Sāmkhya refers to that statement which has withstood the test of reason. Dale Riepe's account of this is very clear:

> Sāmkhya revelation is authoritative statement. It is authoritative because it squares with the evidence of perception and inference. There is no split between what is known by faith and what is known by reason, or between faith without evidence as opposed to faith with evidence. It is not correct, then, to say that Samkhya's *āptavachana* is superrational or dependent ultimately on external authority or authority of *sruti* [which here means the Vedas] [Riepe, 190].

This is indicative of Sāmkhya's rejection of the approach of the orthodox systems of Indian philosophy in regard to the Vedas, which regarded the Vedas as the supernatural revelation in words or as being written by a single individual.

Sāmkhya adopts the correspondence theory to test the validity of knowledge. Knowledge is said to be valid only when *vrtti* (modification of *buddhi*) accurately corresponds to the objects to be known. Validity, therefore, consists in proper correspondence. In its acceptance of the theory of correspondence, Sāmkhya agrees (as we have known in the previous chapter) with the realistic-naturalistic system of Vaisesika-Nyāya.

It has been known how the three internal organs function in a knowing situation. The sense organs coming into contact with the object, carry their impressions to the mind *(manas)* which, after transforming these to determinate percepts, passes them on to *ahamkāra* (ego or self-sense). *Ahamkāra* makes the impersonal percepts personal and conveys them to *buddhi* (intellect), which then makes out of itself a pattern of modifications corresponding to these personalized percepts. This process of transfers or passings-on may not always make the final correspondence a successful one, and there is every possibility on the part of the experiencing self overlooking certain aspects of the object-to-be-known, resulting in erroneous knowledge. As such, there is no subjective element in the Sāmkhya concept of error: erroneous or invalid knowledge is only incomplete or partial knowledge *(akhyāti)*.

Neither the Self *(Purusha)* nor the intellect *(buddhi)* can independently be the subject in knowing. Knowledge is possible only by a blending of both and a mistaking of the two for a single subject. Thus nondiscrimination *(aviveka)* between the Self and the intellect remains the essential precondition of all individual experiences. Error can be eliminated by a proper discrimination between the two through an act of transcendence; which is to say that valid knowledge is possible only when the Self is capable of seeing itself as different from the intellect. Hiriyanna calls this error "metaphysical" since it has its source in the confusion between the two ontological entities, i.e., Self and intellect. Accordingly, a liberated individual is one who is aware of such discrimination and yet is qualified enough to attain valid knowledge by transcending such discrimination.

Error occurs in two possible cases: i) when there is a single object, and ii) when there are two or more objects. As an instance of the error which comes under the first category, we have the following: One is presented with a shell, but he apprehends it to be silver. Here, the experiencer lacks the complete knowledge of the shell, noticing the points of similarity between the shell and silver but overlooking the points of difference between the two. Valid knowledge is possible only if and when the experiencer can manage to have a complete knowledge of the shell. In the second case, erroneous knowledge is the result of the apprehension of two objects like a transparent crystal and a red rose as that of a red crystal. Once again, there is an absence of a complete knowledge which makes the experiencer mistake two objects for a third; and, once again, the erroneous knowledge is due to the experiencer's overlooking the differences between the two given objects. Hence, in both cases—whether there is one object or two or more objects—error is always due to partial or incomplete knowledge.

We must hasten to add, however, that it is not just misconception or wrong knowledge. While early Sāmkhya literature mentions *akhyāti, Sāmkhya-sutra* mentions the theory of error as *sadāsatkhyāti*—so called because it involves both what is real *(sat)* and what is unreal *(asat)*. Thus the erroneous knowledge of a red crystal involves the knowledge of crystal (which is "real" or *sat*) and that of redness (which is "unreal" or *asat*). Both the Sāmkhya views of error, however, have nondiscrimination as their basis.

Influence on Other Systems

We have seen how, in Sāmkhya, *Purusha,* in cooperation with *Prakrti,* produces the whole universe; and hence, *Purusha* and *Prakrti* together are sufficient to explain the existence and nature of the universe. The inconsistency in Sāmkhya relates to its admission of a plurality of selves *(purushas)*. The single absolute principle of consciousness *(Purusha)* as being the efficient cause, and the several individual selves *(purushas)* as being agents, experiencers and enjoyers, cannot be accepted simultaneously. Sāmkhya makes statements like "There is one Self" and "There are many selves." While it begins with a belief in One Self, it proceeds to—for empirical purposes and in order to justify individual liberation—talk about different selves. A single, indivisible Self cannot explain the diversity of individual experiences, nor justify the possibility of individual liberation. We find the following as a kind of defense of this spiritual plurality in the *Sāmkhya-kārikā* of Isvarakrsna: "Since birth, death, and the instruments of life are allotted severally . . . and since qualities affect variously; multitude of souls (selves) is demonstrated" (trs. T.H. Colebroke, Bombay: Tookaram Tatya, 1887). Puligandla explains the plurality in a clearer way than most other historians: "Sāmkhya defends the plurality of selves from the fact of the existence of men as distinct and unique individuals. The distinctness and uniqueness of men from each other is in turn supported by the undeniable fact of mental and moral differences between them. In short, no two men are . . . identical. Therefore, the Sāmkhya concludes that there must be distinct selves" (Puligandla, 123).

It might be said that the Sāmkhya philosophy, because of these loose ends, almost naturally led to the monism or nondualism *(advaita)* of the Vedānta school of thought, in which the Pure Self becomes the only absolute and ultimate principle and where *Prakrti* is no more an independent principle but only the instrument of the Absolute Self *(Brahman)* in its bringing about the world-order. In the place of the individual self and the empirical ego, there is only a single entity called *jiva,* which is phenomenal in character. The entire world-order, including the *jivas,* is only a distorted appearance of the Ultimate *(Brahman),* and so we have the *Brahma-vivarta-vāda* (the effect as the distorted appearance of the cause) in place of Sāmkhya's *Prakrti-parināma-vāda* (effect as the actual transformation of the cause). It is, therefore, believed that Sāmkhya contained the seeds of the philosophy of Advaita Vedānta.

The System of Yoga

Yoga cannot properly be called a "philosophical system"; it rather defines and describes the path of discipline leading towards the soul's ultimate liberation. While it is true that it is based on the Sāmkhya metaphysics and thus enjoys a fairly strong philosophical foundation, it builds up its own self-complete theory of self-discipline. Yoga as a form of self-discipline is not, however, unique to the system of *Patanjali-Yoga;* it has been accepted by most of the Indian philosophical systems. Jainism and Buddhism, for instance, have their own accepted ways of self-discipline; both Mahāvira, the chief propounder of Jainism, and Buddha, the founder of the religion that takes its name from him, attained enlightenment through a process of rigorous self-discipline. That a proper and sustained training of the body and the mind is essential for the individual aspiring towards the ultimate liberation, cannot be denied, and this remains the chief concern, the central teaching of the Yoga system, which provides us with a complete, systematic exposition of the different steps that would prepare one for the emancipated knowledge.

As it has been mentioned earlier, *Sāmkhya* and *Yoga* are but the theoretical and practical aspects of the same system: *Sāmkhya* is theory, while *Yoga* is practice. The only point of difference between the two lies in Yoga's acceptance of a God. Early Sāmkhya was theistic in character. This initial theism, under the influence of Jainism and early Buddhism, was transformed into the atheism of the classical Sāmkhya. Sāmkhya does not try to disprove God, but it is silent about it. Since the two ultimate principles, *Purusha* and *Prakrti,* are sufficient to explain the universe in a reasonably adequate manner, it did not perhaps feel the need of introducing a third principle. The concept of God as the prime mover, imparting motion to the eternal atoms with a view to creating the world of objects (something which a system like Vaisesika passionately asserts), is implicitly rejected by Sāmkhya, since it does not believe in creation. The process of evolution that it advocates is the natural, spontaneous outcome of the cooperation between *Purusha* and *Prakrti.* Appropriately, it has been called *nirisvara-sāmkhya* (without God), while *Yoga* has been called *sesvara-sāmkhya* (with God). K.M. Sen writes: "The philosophical basis of the *Yoga* is the same as that of the *Sāmkhya,* except that a personal God is introduced into the system. God controls the process of evolution and is, as one might expect, Omniscient and Omnipotent. Periodically He dissolves the cosmos and then initiates the process of evolution again" (Sen, 81).

Both Sāmkhya and Yoga hold that there are many selves *(purushas),* and God or *Isvara* of Yoga is the Supreme Self *(Purushavisesa)*—an embodiment of perfection who does not have an equal even among the liberated selves. Although the existence of *Prakrti* and several *purushas* does not give Him an opportunity to become all-comprehensive, yet, He stands before man as an ideal, manifesting excellence in matters of knowledge and power and exemplifying the possibility of achieving the highest perfection. It was, then, a practical necessity on the part of Patanjali to postulate the Supreme Self as an example for man to inspire him sufficiently to liberate himself from his individual imperfections and limitations so as to attain final liberation *(kaivalya).* Such a man, aspiring towards liberation, is offered every kind of help and assistance to overcome the distracting tendencies latent within him and the obstacles that are brought in his way by his own ignorance *(avidyā).* The invocation of the divine power is made through the utterance of the "central sound" *AUM,* which symbolizes God; its repeated and continuous utterance enables the yogi to proceed towards his anticipated liberation successfully.

As against Sāmkhya metaphysics and epistemology, Yoga uses a single word, *Chitta,* to describe a complex of intellect *(buddhi),* self-sense or ego *(ahamkāra)* and mind *(manas)*. *Chitta,* which is everchanging in character, contains a high degree of *sattva* and, under the influence of the Self *(Purusha)* and through the dual-reflection process (discussed earlier under the Sāmkhya theory of knowledge), makes empirical knowledge possible. It is because of *chitta* that individual life is maintained and preserved; it "performs the life-functions and sense-functions of the body" (Dasgupta, *History,* 262). In addition to these two functions, it also contains the last habitual potency *(samskāra)* and the latent tendencies *(vāsanā)* which deserve to be eliminated in order to make the individual being free from all past impressions. As far as *chitta* (essential mind) is concerned, the Yoga system has been, to a large extent, influenced by different schools of Buddhism.

The *sautāntrika* school of Buddhism, for instance, maintains that the individual consciousness is a sort of continuous knowledge-series, which leaves behind a seed from which a new knowledge-series germinates. The *yogāchāra* school of Buddhism also advocates a similar view. Vyāsa, who was probably the first to comment on Patanjali's *Yoga-sutra,* is believed to have been inspired by such a concept of continuity in knowledge-series enough to incorporate it in his idea of the everchanging *chitta.* Erich Frauwallner, in his *History of Indian Philosophy,* writes:

> The carrier of all psychical occurrences is the psychical organ *(manah* or *chittam).* All psychical states are the qualities *(dharmah)* of this organ. They arise out of impressions *(samskārah)* which cling to the psychical organ and themselves call forth such impressions as later bring forth similar psychic conditions. Every one of these psychical states lasts only for a moment. It appears and again disappears immediately to make place for the next. But all states—not only the present but also the past and the future—are really existent. Only they are found on another level of existence. That is especially important in the case of human passions which in a man, who is affected by them, are present, even if they do not straightway rise to the level of outward expression or operation [Frauwallner, 329].

Thus all the knowledge-processes are a result of impressions *(samskārah* or *vāsanā)* rooted in the *chitta;* and hence, with the effacement of these impressions the *chitta* is purged of them and so ceases to function as an instrument of empirical knowledge. The cleansing of *chitta* of these impressions coincides with its turning inward.

There are five functions of *chitta;* or, there are five mental planes *(chittabhumi).* They are mentioned in the following line from Patanjali's *Yoga-sutra: "ksiptam mudham viksiptam ekāgram niruddham iti chittabhumya"* (Bangali Baba, ed., *Yoga-sutra,* 1). Separately they are: raving *(ksipta),* forgetful *(mudha),* oscillating *(viksipta),* one-pointed *(ekāgra),* and restrained *(niruddha).* According as the three *gunas* predominate, they are five different levels in ascending order: the first in the order is the restless mind *(ksipta)* involving a high degree of *rajas;* the second is *mudha* with a predominance of *tamas* and resulting in ignorance, sleep and lethargy; the third is the distracted mind *(viksipa)* under the dual influence of *sattva* and *rajas;* the fourth is the mind full of concentration *(ekāgra)* and dominated by *sattva;*

and, finally, there is the mind that has been able to completely restrict every possible interference from matter *(niruddha)* or *gunas*. The Yoga system accepts and recommends only the last two of the five stages *(ekāgrachitta* and *niruddhachitta)* for the purpose of achieving individual enlightenment.

Patanjali's *Yogasutra* is divided into four chapters. Its first chapter, titled *Samādhi Pāda,* deals with those spiritual actions without which one cannot control the functioning of the mind. The second chapter, titled *Sādhanā Pāda,* elaborately discusses the means of Practice involving the actions performed for the purpose of removing the gross impurities from the mind. It also contains an analysis of human suffering and its possible elimination. The third chapter, *Vibhuti Pāda,* pertains to the accomplishment of super-normal power through a "Dissolutionary change of the worldly life by means of *samyama* [compound of *dhyāna, dhāranā* and *samādhi,* each discussed later in this chapter]" (Bangali Baba, "Preface" to *Yogasutra*). The final chapter, *Kaivalya Pāda,* deals with emancipation or the individual soul's freedom from material bondage through the realization of the true nature of the Self.

Sufferings and the Removal of Sufferings

Like Buddhism, Yoga regards the world as full of suffering. All experiences are painful. Even those supposedly pleasure-giving experiences are ultimately full of pain, since the experience of pleasure is always associated with the fear of losing it. The quantity of pain is greater than the quantity of pleasure, so that the wise realize it and turn themselves away from the so called pleasures of life. Human sufferings are due to five kinds of affliction or burden *(klesha):* ignorance *(avidyā),* self-sense or egoism *(asmitā),* material attachment *(rāga),* aversion or hatred *(dvesa),* and the complex burden of an irresistible passion for life coupled with an unknown fear of death *(abhinivesha).*

Ignorance *(avidyā)* is the cause of the erroneous knowledge of self in the not-self, of purity in the impure, as, for instance, when a person compares the face of a beautiful woman with the full moon or her eyes with the petals of a blue lotus. Such recognition—which is the basis of establishing relations through metaphorizing—is, however, due to the person's ignorance, which makes him lay unnecessary importance on what is not real or true. Thus, the Yoga system indirectly rejects every kind of metaphoric luxuriance. Similarly, when one confuses the *Purusha* (the power of pure perceptivity) with *chitta* or *buddhi* (the perceiving element), such confusion leads to the production of self-sense or I-consciousness *(asmitā),* which thinks of itself as possessing the material objects. *Rāga* or attachment is *sukhānusayi-rāga* or pleasure-induced attachment. The feeling of pleasure strengthens the tendency in a person to be attached more and more to material objects, when he craves for pleasure through the recollection of a past pleasure associated with particular objects and thus enjoys a false sense of belonging to those objects. Similarly, *dvesa* or aversion is *dukhānusayi dvesah* or pain-induced aversion. A painful experience with specific objects in the past leads to dislike, opposition and resistance when faced with those objects. Finally, there is always the desire for life and the fear of death *(abhinivesa)*. Both the wise and the ignorant have a potential habit of loving life passionately coupled with a constant fear of death.

These five "afflictions" are the burdens which the soul wants to lay off, the hindrances which the soul wants to remove completely. They keep the *chitta* restless, distracted and disintegrated. It is meditation alone that can bring about the cessation of such desires and feelings that dissuade the *chitta* from concentrating on the spirit, realizing thereby the true purpose of human life. In Sāmkhya there are two means of attaining liberation—the path of theoretical and philosophical knowledge, and the path of meditation. The Yoga system, being a development on the Sāmkhya philosophy, utilizes all the philosophical knowledge provided by Sāmkhya in practice and prescribes the path of meditation for the purpose of realizing pure consciousness. All the several modifications of *chitta* are the cause of all experience, which are either apparently painful or pleasant. These modifications of *chitta,* (or *buddhi*) are to be thrown away, the mental operations are to be held totally suspended *(chittavrtti-nirodha),* in order that the *chitta* and its modifications no more become obstacles on the way of direct and immediate apprehension of pure consciousness.

Karma *or Action*

The five afflictions mentioned above give rise to every sort of human activity; and the actions, the fruits of actions, together with the past tendencies and ignorance, bind the self to matter. As there is the need to bring about the cessation of suffering and the elimination of all the past tendencies, so there is also a need to destroy *all* actions, *both* good and bad, of past and future.

The Yoga system describes how *karmas* or actions give rise to one individual life and different individual lives. It has been discussed how the different afflictions produce human activities. To repeat, ignorance creates the wrong impression that the complex of unreal body and mind, subject to destruction, is real; it is the result of a misidentification of not-Self with the Self. This further leads to such conceptions like "my body," "my home," "my family" and so on, with the individual striving intensely to possess the body, the home and so on. All such possessions, which can merely offer the individual unreal and temporary pleasure, only help solidify the will-to-be within him. The series of consequent desires—one desire immediately followed by another—binds him to ultimately meaningless chain of activities, thus keeping him in bondage, enveloped by desires and actions.

Thus the afflictions give rise to actions *(karmas),* but we must hasten to add that a single action is neither the cause of one birth nor the cause of many births, nor many actions produce many births. The actions of the past life leave, as residue, the tendencies to continue in the present, and the actions in the present life determine the life-state, life-time and life-experiences of the future. Thus, the continuous course of actions explains the complete cycle of rebirth. Only the most virtuous actions or the most vicious actions of the present life are immediately followed by reward or punishment. Accordingly, actions *(karmas)* are of two kinds: 1) those which bear fruit in this life *(niyatavipaka),* and 2) those which would bear fruit in other lives *(aniyatavipaka).*

Those actions which are to be fruitful in this life may be those actions of the preceding life or lives

> which being on the point of fruition produced this body, or they may also be those intensive good or bad actions which produce their fruits immediately . . . as distinguished from the fruits of the karmas of other lives enjoyed in this life . . . As regards the karmas accumulated in this life, some of them will be of appointed fruition and produce the life-state of another birth, but those which could not come to the stage of appointed fruition may either be lost through the man's attaining right knowledge or may be awaiting till the coming of such a suitable birth in which they can show themselves, or they may gradually fructify in connection with the fructification of major karmas [Dasgupta, *Yoga Philosophy,* 326–327].

Yoga classifies actions into four kinds, according to their capability to produce pleasure and pain: 1) *Sukla* (white) refers to those actions which produce pleasure as well as the actions of those who are engaged in scholarly activities; 2) *Krsna* (black) refers to vicious or *veda*-prohibited actions that produce pain; 3) *Sukla-krsna* (white-black/ fair-dark) refers to actions which produce both pleasure and pain and involve most of our day-to-day activities; 4) *Asukla-akrsna* (not-white-not-black/ not-fair-not-dark) refers to actions which neither produce pleasure nor produce pain, and thus refers to activities like introspection and self-disciplining—activities that are conducive to yogic aspiration. The actions of a yogi are neither white (since he has renounced the fruits) nor black (since he has withdrawn the sense organs from the external world). The second chapter of Patanjali's *Yogasutra,* titled *Sādhanā Pāda* ("Means of Practice"), makes a clear analysis of the kinds of suffering, the origin of suffering, and the varieties of actions leading to life and its sufferings. The explanations it provides relate to the individual being as existing within the imperfections of the phenomenal world. The individual's awareness of the dissociation of matter and material objects from the spirit *(viveka-jñāna)* alone brings the individual to the center, i.e., the pure and self-luminous consciousness.

Aṣhtānga-Yoga *or "The Eight Limbs of the Yogic Process"*

Yoga is a process of self-disciplining culminating in the state of the knowledge and realization of the Self. Knowing the Self or being conscious of consciousness, amounts to pure consciousness, which necessarily excludes all other perceptual, inferential and authoritative knowledge. This, does not, however, presuppose the annihilation of the body or the mind, although it is preceded by the destruction of desires, habitual tendencies, and actions. One is able to attain such an emancipated state even while continuing and existing in the body. The process of disciplining involves eight steps, known as the eightfold path or *ashtānga yoga.* They are 1) *Yama* or restraint, 2) *Niyama* or observance of principles, 3) *Āsana* or posture, 4) *Prānāyāma* or the control of breath, 5) *Pratyāhāra* or withdrawal of the sense organs, 6) *Dhāranā* or concentration, 7) *Dhyāna* or meditation, and 8) *Samādhi* or spiritual absorption. We give below a description of each of these steps.

Yama ***(restraint):*** From the upanishadic times, it has been successively established that self-knowledge is the only true knowledge; accordingly, all the Indian sages and seers have made quests after the Self, the Ultimate Reality, the Final Truth. *Yoga* system, following upanishadic lines, lays emphasis on self-realization through self-knowledge. All actions, whether virtuous or vicious, keep the individual self in bondage and hence, are to be destroyed. One might be led to believe here that ethical values have been denied their due importance; but, as we begin analyzing the different steps of yogic discipline, we find that the process of disciplining is initiated with the limination of certain immoral potentialities *(yama)* and the conscious cultivation of certain virtues *(niyama).* This strong ethical background prepares the yogi for the hard task of concentration and meditation. *Yama* and *niyama* together constitute the ethical background, and this has been looked upon as a strong stepping-stone to contemplation. The Yoga system makes a fine and subtle differentiation between the prevailing ethical values or standards and the necessity of a background of such values for the purpose of meditative extension.

It is required for an aspirant *(yogi)* to erase the stains of past unethical activities and, further, to restrain himself from indulgence in such activities; in addition, he has to follow certain rules of ethics, like noninjury to other living beings *(ahimsā),* not telling a lie *(satya),* nonstealing *(asteya),* nonindulgence in sexual activities *(brahmacharya),* and nonacceptance of gifts of all kinds *(aparigraha).* These five ethical rules, which should be followed irrespective of caste, place, time and circumstance, are universal in character and together constitute what is called as the "Great Vow" *(Mahāvratam).*

Niyama ***(Observance):*** The impurities having been removed by the avoidance of immoral activities, the aspirant has to develop in a positive way certain moral habits or qualities, like purification *(saucha),* contentment *(samtosa),* penance *(tapas),* study *(svādhyāya),* and devotion to God or *Isvara (Isvara-Pranidhāna).* Purification implies both external and internal purification. A purified, sound body and a pure mind are the most essential necessities. Contentment refers to the state of being satisfied with whatever one already has without the usual desire to have more. Penance involves keeping the body completely still, being absolutely silent, and enduring the opposites like heat and cold, sitting and standing, happiness and sorrow, and so on. Study refers to the study of the ancient scriptures and sacred texts, as well as to the repeated utterance of "AUM"—the central sound or *Pranava.* Devotion to God means one's complete and uninhibited surrender to God, including the surrender of one's fruit-bearing material actions.

The restraints and the observances produce appreciable results. Non-injury or harmlessness results in complete abandonment of enmity; truthfulness yields to the mastery over all actions and the fruits thereof. If one desires to be virtuous, then he finds himself as being so; from nonstealing follows the availability of all good things. Sexual restraint produces a kind of strength unavailable to ordinary men. The individual being becomes physically competent and mentally alert, so that any new entry of evil can be easily detected and successfully resisted. Nonacceptance of gifts over a period of time gives rise to an inquisitiveness concerning self-existence. The cultivation of these restraints make the mind increasingly steady, helping the aspirant toward effectively eliminating negative emotions like fear, jealousy, doubt and anger, and making him turn inward and modify and redefine his position in relation to the outside world.

Similarly, the observances *(niyama)* implant or bring about certain attitudes and qualities, like losing interest in one's own body and in the bodies of others, the attainment of purest happiness (following contentment), the cessation of all impurities (as a result of penance), engaging oneself in the knowledge of enlightened sages and seers (derived from the study of scriptures), and the ability to become successful in spiritual absorption (following one's dedication to God). The *chitta* that turned inward and inquired into the nature of self-existence as a result of *yama* (restraint), gets encouraged, through *niyama* (observance), to proceed in the direction of enlightenment, which is associated with liberation.

Āsana *(posture)*: The actual yoga practice starts at this stage. *Āsana* literally mans the comfortable and steady posture of the body. Keeping the body steady is to be practiced continuously till one reaches such a stage when he does not have to make any conscious effort for such steadiness but can remain *comfortably steady* (that is, without straining himself), keeping the spine, the neck and the head in a straight line. This posture is associated with the "transformation of mind into infinity" (Bangali Baba, 47). This steady body remains unaffected by both heat and cold. There are different kinds of postures, like *Padmāsana* (lotus-posture), *Kaunchanisādana* (curlew-posture), *Dandāsana* (sticklike-posture) and so on. The system of *Yoga* prescribes postures that are useful for the purpose of concentration. The aspirant has to make his body perfectly still, like the trunk of a tree *(sthānu),* thus prepared for the steadiness of the mind. However, Patanjali's *Yogasutra* does not mention anything regarding *mudrā* (the pose of the fingers) and *nyāsa* (the modes of touching the various parts of the body). These were later introduced into the Yoga system by Tāntrism. *Mudrā* is a sort of imitative gesture or a magic symbol, while *nyāsa* refers to the exercise of the whole body, charged with divine energy, with a view to becoming one with God. Perhaps the Patanjali-Yoga system cannot entertain such postures because of its inherent suspicion that any active functioning of the parts of the body might create disturbances and hindrances on the path of smooth spiritual realization.

Prāṇāyāma ***(control of breath):*** After keeping the body steady and keeping the mind associated with the boundlessness of space, the aspirant moves toward the next stage, which is *prāṇāyāma* or control of breath. This consists in the separation of the movement of inspiration and expiration. "That which is outer" is the expiration; "that which is inner" is inspiration; and "that which abides steady," within, is called *Kumbhaka* since, when this takes place, the vital spirits rest motionless like water in a jar *(kumbha).* This threefold regulation of the breath is further particularized by place (the breath must go down as far as 12 inches from the nose), time (for the duration of 36 *mātrās*), and number (so many inspirations and expirations gradually replaced by a definite number and hence increasingly extending over time). By repeating the cycle over and over the mind gradually removes the obstructions (in the form of afflictions), receives the divine light and thereby becomes fit for "acts of attention" (Ballantyne and Sastry Deva, 65–67). No other form of penance, it has been mentioned in the *Yogasutras,* can equal *prāṇāyāma* so far as the removal of obstacles and the consequent power to concentrate are concerned.

Pratyāhāra ***(withdrawal of the senses):*** It consists in the withdrawal of the senses from their respective objects. Since the mind becomes steady through *prāṇāyāma* and gets detached from the objects of the external world, the sense organs too cease to function by abandoning all regard to their respective material objects. Thus, the sense of sight, for instance, does not get attracted toward color. *Pratyāhāra* (withdrawal or restraint) is "as it were the accommodation of the senses to the nature of the mind in the absence of concernment with each one's own object" (Patanjali, *Yogasutras,* Chapter 2, line 54). "When this takes place, the senses simply accommodate themselves to the nature of the mind; for, all the senses are observed to follow obsequiously the mind, as the bees their leader. Hence, when the mind is restrained (from the exercise of its functions), these (senses), are restrained; and their accommodation to the nature thereof (under such circumstances) is what is called 'restraint'" (Ballantyne and Sastry Deva, 67).

Dhāraṇā ***(concentration):*** The above-mentioned five steps—*yama, niyama, āsana, prāṇāyāma,* and *pratyāhāra*—constitute what is called the "external" or practical part of yoga. After passing through these five primary steps, the mind develops the capability to concentrate on any particular object. The three steps that follow these constitute what may be called the "internal" or ultimate part of yoga. They are *dhāraṇā* (concentration or attention), *dhyāna* (meditation or contemplation), and *samādhi* (spiritual absorption).

Dhāraṇā (concentration or attention) involves the fixing of the internal organ *(chitta)* on a place like the central point between eyebrows, or the lotus in the heart or the circle of the navel, by abstracting the internal organ from all other objects. Thus *dhāraṇā* (concentration), "having through 'forebearance,' religious observances, etc., attained to the condition of a seed, and having sprouted by means of the 'postures' and 'regulation of the breath,' and having blossomed by means of 'self-restraint,' will fructify by means of 'attention,' 'contemplation,' and 'meditation'" (Ballantyne and Sastry Deva, 68).

Dhyāna ***(contemplation):*** *Dhyāna* (contemplation) refers to a "course of uniform modification of knowledge at that place where the internal organ is fixed in attention by avoiding the otherwise (not uniform) modification of knowledge" (Ballantyne and Sastry Deva, 69). That is to say, knowledge in the shape of *dhyāna* does not take place unless it has recourse to a certain place and hence, the uniform modification of knowledge at that place where *chitta* (internal organ) is fixed in attention. There is continuous and unbroken flow of the *chitta* towards the place or the object; the *chitta* is completely engrossed in contemplation of the place or the object. Such an unaffected relation between the *chitta* and the place or object contemplated upon, involves the awareness or consciousness of the subject as well as the object.

Such an awareness or knowledge of a yogi is very much different from ordinary knowledge. For empirical purposes, valid knowledge comes through perception, inference and verbal testimony. A yogi's knowledge, as different from ordinary empirical knowledge, does not come through any of the three means. It is a case of direct, nonrational (*not* irrational) cognition – a sort of intuitive apprehension that is clearly distinguishable from intellectual knowledge and is neither perceptual nor conceptual. Since it is so, contemplation of *Isvara* or God (rather than of any other place or object) makes the process of realization more fluent. Since, as we have already seen, God or *Isvara* is the special *purusha,* unaffected by afflictions or any enjoyment that is related to victory or defeat and unconnected with past or future bondage, He remains the most desirable object of contemplation.

Samādhi ***(meditation or spiritual absorption):*** As explained by Bhoja in his commentary on Patanjali's *Yogasutras,* knowledge in the shape of contemplation "always takes place about the following three, i.e., the material substance whether it be animate or inanimate, such as a cow, a jar etc., the term cow, jar etc., and the knowledge itself; but when it takes place only about the material substance and not about the latter two, then, such a knowledge in the shape of contemplation is called Samadhi" (Ballantyne and Sastry Deva, 70). The term *samādhi,* therefore, means that state of knowledge in which the mind, having avoided the obstacles, is well fixed on, or confined to one object only.

There are, broadly, two stages of *samādhi,* depending on the degree of the yogi's concentration. They are *samprajñāta samādhi* (differentiated, conscious spiritual absorption) and *asamprajñāta samādhi* (undifferentiated, super-conscious spiritual absorption). The former, *samprajñāta samādhi,* which involves distinct recognition or consciousness of the object, is found in company with supposition *(vitarka),* clear vision *(vichāra),* joy *(ānanda)* and egotism *(asmitā).* This stage of *samādhi* still contains the residual individuality and is cognitive. But the yogi passes on to a higher stage *(asamprajñāta samādhi),* which is ultra-cognitive and ultra-reflective. It is characterized by "absence of argument" *(nirvichāra),* "complete clearness" *(vaisāradya),* and "perfect inner calmness" *(adhyātmaprasāda).*

It is the absolute state of ecstasy in which the yogi finds rest *(virāma)*. As S. Radhakrishnan writes: "When the feeling of joy passes away and is lost in a higher equanimity, there occurs the state called dharmamegha, in which the isolation of the soul and its complete distinction from matter are realised and karma operates no more" (Radhakrishnan, 359). In this culminating stage in the yogic process, the yogi realizes the "pure consciousness" or *Purusha* as distinct from *Prakrti,* thus attaining liberation or *kaivalya.* We conclude this chapter with S.N. Dasgupta's remarks in this connection: "The purusa having passed beyond the bondage of the gunas shines forth in its pure intelligence. There is no bliss or happiness in this Sāmkhya-Yoga mukti, for all feeling belongs to prakrti. It is thus a state of pure intelligence. What the Sāmkhya tries to achieve through knowledge, Yoga achieves through the perfected discipline of the will and psychological control of the mental states" (Dasgupta, *History,* 273).

Works Cited

Ballantyne, J.R., and Sastry Deva, Govind, tr. *Yogasutras of Patanjali* (with Bhoja's Commentary). 1885; rpt. New Delhi: Pious Book Corporation, 1985.

Bangali Baba, tr. *The Yogasutra of Patanjali with the Commentary of Vyāsa.* Delhi: Motilal Banarasidass, 1982.

Bernard, Theos. *Hindu Philosophy.* 1947; rpt. Delhi: Motilal Banarasidass, 1985.

Colebrooke, T.H., tr. *The Sāmkhya-Kārikā of Isvarakrishna.* Bombay: Tookaram Tatya, 1887.

Dasgupta, S.N. *A History of Indian Philosophy* (5 vols.), vol. I. Cambridge, England: Cambridge University Press, 1973.

________. *Yoga Philosophy in Relation to Other Systems of Indian Thought.* Delhi: Motilal Banarsidass, 1979.

Frauwallner, Erich. *History of Indian Philosophy* (2 vols.), Vol. I. tr. V.M. Bedekar. Delhi: Motilal Banarsidass, 1984.

Hiriyanna, M. *Outlines of Indian Philosophy.* 1932, London: George Allen & Unwin; rpt. Bombay: Blackie & Son, 1983.

MacDonell, Arthur A. *A History of Sanskrit Literature.* New York: Appleton & Co., 1914.

Puligandla, R. *Fundamentals of Indian Philosophy.* Nashville: Abingdon Press, 1975.

Radhakrishnan, S. *Indian Philosophy* (2 vols.), Vol. II. Muirhead Library of Philosophy. London: George Allen & Unwin, and New York: Humanities Press, 1966.

Riepe, Dale. *The Naturalistic Tradition in Indian Thought.* 1961, Seattle: University of Washington Press; rpt. Delhi: Motilal Banarsidass, 1964.

Seal, Brajendranath. *The Positive Sciences of the Ancient Hindus.* London: Longmans, Green & Co., 1915.

Sen, K.M. *Hinduism.* 1961; rpt. Harmondsworth, England: Penguin Books, 1982.

Sharma, Chandradhar. *A Critical Survey of Indian Philosophy.* Delhi: Motilal Banarsidass, 1983.

Sinari, Ramakanta. *The Structure of Indian Thought.* 1970; rpt. New Delhi: Oxford University Press, 1984.

Suggested Further Reading

Bahadur, K.P. *The Wisdom of Sāmkhya.* New Delhi: Sterling Publishers, 1978.

Bhandarkar, R.G. "The Sāmkhya Philosophy." *The Indian Philosophical Review* (January, 1919).

Brena, Stephen F. *Yoga and Medicine: The Merging of Yogic Concepts with Modern Medical Knowledge.* Baltimore: Penguin Books, 1973.

Conger, G.P. "A Naturalistic Approach to Sāmkhya-Yoga." *Philosophy East and West* (October, 1953).

Coster, Geraldine. *Yoga and Western Psychology: A Comparison.* London: Oxford University Pres, 1935.

Dasgupta, S.N. *A Study of Patanjali.* Calcutta: University of Calcutta Press, 1920.

———. *Yoga as Philosophy and Religion.* London: Kegan Paul, and New York: E.P. Dutton, 1924.

Eliade, Mircea. *Patanjali and Yoga,* tr. Charles L. Markmann, New York: Funk & Wagnalls, 1969.

———. *Yoga, Immortality and Freedom.* Princeton: Princeton University Press, 1971.

Garbe, Richard, ed. *Sāmkhya-Pravachana-Bhāsya by Vijñāna Bhiksu.* Harvard Oriental Series, vol. 2. Cambridge, Mass.: Harvard University Press, 1895.

Isherwood, Christopher, and Prabhananda, Swamy, tr. *How to Know God: The Yoga Aphorisms of Patanjali.* New York: Harper & Row, 1953.

Keith, A.B. *The Sāmkhya System.* Oxford: Clarendon Press, 1918.

Roy, S.N. "The Problem of Error." *The Philosophical Quarterly.* Calcutta (April, 1936).

Wood, Ernest. *Great Systems of Yoga.* New York: Philosophical Library, 1954.

Woods, James Haughton, tr. *Yoga System of Patanjali.* Harvard Oriental Series, vol. 17. Cambridge, Mass.: Harvard University Press, 1914.

7

Purva Mimāmsā

Purva Mimāmsā is the first of the two major Indian philosophical systems that are primarily based upon the authority of the Vedas; the other is Uttara Mimāmsā, which is also known as Vedānta. The word Mimāmsā in its literal translation is "revered thought," but its root-word *man* refers to "thinking and investigation." We might therefore say that Mimāmsā relates to "a critical investigation into the Vedas," which incidentally command highest reverence in Hindu tradition. Purva Mimāmsā is so called because it concentrates on the earlier portion of the Veda, particularly the *Brāhmanas* and the *Mantras* (*Purva* = first/earlier), also called *Karma-kānda* (that which is concerned with action); Uttara Mimāmsā is so called because it deals with the later portion of the Veda—that is, the Upanishads—and hence with *Jñāna-kānda* (that which is concerned with knowledge). Consequently, Purva Mimāmsā has also been called Karma Mimāmsā (because it deals with action in the form of rituals and sacrifices) whereas Uttara Mimāmsā (also called Vedānta, since it deals with the end-part of the Veda [*anta* = end]) has been called Brahman Mimāmsā (because it deals with *Brahman* or the knowledge of reality). The two systems are more commonly called Mimāmsā and Vedānta, respectively. Despite controversies and differences, the two systems have always remained together. As C.D. Sharma points out, there has been a long line of teachers before the advent of the great Shamkarāchārya of the Vedānta school, who have regarded Mimāmsā and Vedānta as forming "a single system and who have advocated the combination of action and knowledge, known as *Karma-Jñāna-Samuchchaya-vāda*" (Sharma, 211). According to these teachers, both *Karma* (action) and *Upāsanā* (meditation) are essential in attaining true knowledge. Vedāntins like Rāmānuja and Bhaskarāchārya believed that the two systems together formed one science and that a study of Purva Mimāmsā was a prerequisite for any study of Uttara Mimāmsā or Vedānta; similarly, two other leading Vedāntins, Madhvachārya and Vallabhāchārya, believed that Vedānta was only "a continuation of Mimāmsā" (Sharma, 212).

We have seen how the Vaiseshika-Nyāya philosophy regarded experience from a purely common sense point of view and ignored the possibility that the ultimate conceptions of our common sense experience might be related to an original universal, such as *Prakrti* of the Sāmkhya school. It regarded space, time, soul, and the four elements as substances; and it proceeded to establish how material-things-as-qualities such as taste and color manifest themselves only in connection with the substances, how *karma* and the class notions inhere in substances, although it looked upon each of these as a separate entity. It spoke of knowledge *(jñāna)* as merely a quality belonging to the soul and it viewed causation as only a collocation of conditions. Sāmkhya spoke of a principle which consisted of an infinite number of reals of three different kinds which by their combination produced all substances, qualities and actions, thus refusing to recognize any difference between substances, qualities, and actions. According to it, the reals, which potentially held all possibilities of development, combined and changed in a ceaseless fashion, resulting in the manifestation of material and mental phenomena. The combinations of reals did not produce anything new, but only made manifest a phenomenon which was pre-existent in its causes in another form; so that, what we call knowledge was regarded merely as "a form of subtle illuminating matter-stuff." Sāmkhya conceded, however, that there is a supra-empirical, transcendent entity called "pure consciousness and that by some kind of transcendent reflection or contact this pure consciousness transforms the bare translucent thought-matter into conscious thought or experience of a person" (Dasgupta, 367–368). However, this thesis of a pure consciousness or pure self as distinct from knowledge, fails demonstration in everyday experience and, for this reason, has been strongly criticized by the Nyāya philosophers. Further, since it remained silent about the demonstration of its transcendent *purusha* in ordinary experience, Sāmkhya tried to support its hypothesis of the existence of a transcendent self on the ground of "the need of a permanent entity as a fixed object, to which the passing states of knowledge could cling," and on grounds of moral struggle towards virtue and emancipation. Thus Sāmkhya's admittance of a fixed principle like *purusha* in the face of its first supposition that knowledge is merely a collocation of ever-changing reals, appears to have been only a matter of necessity. As Dasgupta writes: "The self is thus here in some sense an object of inference to fill up the gap left by the inadequate analysis of consciousness *(buddhi)* as being non-intelligent and incessantly changing" (Dasgupta, 368).

Nyāya too had to establish self on the ground "that since knowledge existed it was a quality, and therefore must inhere in some substance"—a hypothesis which is based on the unthinking assumption that substances and attributes are distinct and separate, and that it is natural for the attributes to inhere in the substances. Dasgupta writes about the Nyāya and Sāmkhya standpoints: "None of them could take their stand upon the self-conscious nature of our ordinary thought and draw their conclusions on the strength of the direct evidence of this self-conscious thought" (Dasgupta, 368–369). It was therefore necessary that the importance of the self-revealing thought be brought to bear upon metaphysical constructions, for no metaphysical construction is convincing unless it incorporates the direct and immediate convictions of self-conscious thought. The Mimāmsā system leads us in that direction.

As we have said, Mimāmsā differs from all the four previous systems (Vaiseshika, Nyāya, Sāmkhya, and Yoga) in its emphasis on Vedic authority, on Veda or *sruti* as the eternal source of "revealed truth." But, since such revealed truth comes to us only through the verbal medium, the Mimāmsakas are primarily concerned with the "investigation of the principles according to which the texts enshrining that truth are to be interpreted." It is only when, the Mimāmsakas argue, our reading is aided by reason that the Veda will reveal its true import. Hiriyanna describes the primary aim of Mimāmsā as "getting back from the expression to the idea behind it, the solving of the important problem of the relation of speech and thought" (Hiriyanna, *Outlines,* 298) against the purely secular assumption that language is fully independent of the individual using it. It is thus concerned with the *interpretation* of the Veda, which it holds to be "uncreated" (i.e., not created by God or any such supernatural agency), by a classification of its component parts and treating the rules for the performance of the ceremonies as well as of the rewards which follow from these ceremonies. Consequently, questions of general significance are only incidentally discussed while special prominence is given to the proposition that "the articulate sounds are eternal" and to the related theory that "the connexion of a word with its significance is independent of human agreement, and . . . that the significance of a word is inherent in the word itself, by nature" (Garbe, 16). The Mimāmsā system thus involves a great deal of discussion relating to social or folk psychology and contains a lot of valuable material relating to semantics and grammar. The principles of interpretation formulated by Jaimini in the *Mimāmsā-Sutra* are flexible and general enough to be used while reading texts outside the Vedic canon; in fact, as Hiriyanna observes, these principles have become "widely current and are utilized for arriving at a right interpretation of all old texts, particularly legal treatises *(dharmasāstra)*" (Hiriyanna, *Outlines,* 299).

The Mimāmsā does not confine itself only to a reinterpretation and modification of the Vedic system of rites and rituals, however; it is much more than a mere commentary on the Vedic ritual. Its claim to being a philosophical system *(darsana)* rests in its attempts to provide a philosophical justification for the Vedic views and its own exegetical principles and to replace the orthodox ideal of the attainment of heaven *(svarga)* by the ideal of attaining liberation *(moksha).* It must be pointed out, however, that its philosophical aspect is a later development and is to be found in sources other than the Vedas and Upanishads, although some of its minor tenets are traceable to the philosophic portions of the Veda. Curious as it may seem, a large part of the philosophic principles of the Mimāmsā has been borrowed from the Vaiseshika-Nyāya system. We may trace here the appropriate line of supercessions and replacements. The spirit of the Vedic *Brāhmanas* supersedes the simple nature-worship of the Vedic *Mantras;* similarly, the speculative spirit which underlies the epistemological and metaphysical views of the Mimāmsā supersedes the liturgical principles as stated in the *Brāhmanas* and later systematized in the *Srouta-sutras.* But, as Hiriyanna regretfully points out, "the supersession in neither stage is complete, so that the Mimāmsā as now known is an admixture of the rational and the dogmatic, the natural and the supernatural, and the orthodox and the heterodox" (Hiriyanna, *Outlines,* 300).

Literature

The *Mimāmsā-Sutra* of Jaimini is the earliest work of this school and is a compilation of 2,500 aphorisms. Its date is still very much a matter of controversy, although it is generally believed to have been written sometime around A.D. 200. Though Jaimini is accepted by scholars as the founder of the Mimāmsā system, he did not originate the system, but only systematized and reduced to writing the interpretations that belonged to a fairly long oral tradition. That Jaimini's work is only "a comprehensive and systematic compilation of one school" is evident from his references to other writers preceding him (see Dasgupta, 370). Hiriyanna writes: "The system of thought itself . . . is much older, references to it being found in such early works as the Dharma-sutras and possibly also in the *Mahābhāsya* of Patanjali (150 B.C.)" (Hiriyanna, *Outlines,* 301). The *Mimāmsā-Sutra* sums up the general rules *(nyāyas)* which were in traditional use to distinguish *dharma* (duty/merit/virtue) from *adharma* (demerit/vice), enumerates the different sacrifices and their purposes, and discusses the sources of knowledge and the validity of the Vedas. Divided into 12 chapters and 60 sections, covering nearly 1,000 topics, it is by far the biggest of the philosophical *Sutras.* But it is a difficult text and for the most part unintelligible without the aid of a commentary. Among the earliest commentators on the *Mimāmsā-Sutra* are Bhartrmitra, Bhavadāsa, Hari and Upavarsha, but their texts are no longer extant. The earliest available commentary is Sabarasvāmin's *Sabara-bhāsya,* which still remains the basis of all later Mimāmsā writings.

There are several other commentaries on Jaimini's work. Prabhākara wrote his commentary *Brhati* on Sabarasvāmin's *Bhāsya;* Salinikanātha wrote a commentary on the *Brhati* of Prabhākara, called *Rjuvimalā,* as well as a compendium on the Prabhākara interpretation of Mimāmsā called *Prakarana-panchikā.* It is widely believed in scholarly circles that Prabhākara was a student of Kumārila Bhatta, who is traditionally associated with the Vedāntin Samkara and wrote his own exposition of Sabara's *Bhāsya* in three parts known as *Sloka-vārttika, Tantra-Vārttika,* and *Tuptikā.* Another Mimāmsā scholar, Mandana Misra, was a follower of Kumārila and a commentator of *Tantra-vārttika:* he wrote two important treatises known as *Vidhiviveka* and *Mimāmsānukramani,* but he was converted to Vedānta under the influence of Samkara. There have been several commentators on Kumārila's work, the chief among whom were Parthasārathi Misra (who wrote *Sāstradipikā, Tantra-ratna,* and *Nyāyaratnamālā*), Sucharita Misra (who wrote a commentary on *Sloka-vārttika,* called *Kāsikā*), Somesvara Bhatta (who wrote a commentary on *Tantra-vārttika,* called *Nyāyasudhā*), and Venkata Dikshita (who wrote *Vārttikābharana,* a commentary on *Tuptikā*).

Among other important Mimāmsa works are the following: *Nyāya-mālāvistara* by Mādhava, *Mimāmsābalaprakāsa* and *Subodhini* by Sankara Bhatta, *Nyāyakanikā* by Vāchaspati Misra, *Mimāmsā-paribhāshā* by Krishnayajña, *Mimāmsānyāyaprakāsa* by Anantadeva, and *Bhatta-chintāmani* of Gaga Bhatta. [The reason why we find the use of the world *"nyāya"* so often in these works is that Mimāmsā was originally on a system of maxims or *nyāyas* formulated for a correct exposition of the Vedic texts, i.e, *Mantras* and *Brāhmanas,* which dealt with religious performances (Winternitz, 510)]. The original commentary of Sabara was interpreted in two different ways by Prabhākara and Kumārila, thus bringing into existence two schools of Mimāmsā, although, from the philosopher's standpoint, there does not appear to be any great difference between these two schools.

Theory of Knowledge

The Mimāmsaka theory of the self-validity of knowledge *(svatah-prāmānya),* which forms "the cornerstone on which the whole structure of the Mimāmsā philosophy is based" (Dasgupta, 372), is the natural and inevitable means of establishing the authority of the Veda on "rational grounds" rather than "solely on dogmatic considerations" (Hiriyanna, *Outlines,* 307). The theory refers to the Mimāmsaka's assertion that all knowledge excepting that which is related to or issues from the action of remembering or memory *(smriti)* is valid in itself for the simple reason that it endorses its own truth, depending neither "on any other extraneous condition nor on any other knowledge" (Dasgupta, 372).

This is far from the Nyāya view, which is based on a theory of correspondence, which invariably relates knowledge to an object. For the Nyāya philosopher, when we perceive something as blue, it is the direct result of visual contact and the latter cannot certify the resulting knowledge as true for the simple reason that it is not in touch with the knowledge it has conditioned. Moreover, the Nyāya philosopher argues, knowledge is something mental and hence cannot authenticate the *objective* truth of its representation. According to Nyāya, therefore, the validity (or invalidity) of (perceptual) knowledge can only be ascertained by the *correspondence* of perception with what is met with in practical experience. Nyāya buttresses its argument by offering the example of the illusory knowledge of a mirage, which is ultimately proved to be invalid in the light of the mirage's failure to satisfy our need. "The validity or truth of knowledge is thus the attainment by practical experience of the object and the fulfilment of all our purposes from it . . . just as perception or knowledge represented them to the perceiver. There is thus no self-validity of knowledge . . . but validity is ascertained by *samvāda* or agreement with the objective facts of experience" (Jayanta's *Nyāya-manjari,* cited in Dasgupta, 373).

As Dasgupta sees it, this Nyāya objection is based on the supposition that knowledge is generated by certain objective collocations of conditions, and that such knowledge can only be ascertained in terms of its agreement with objective facts. "But this theory of knowledge," Dasgupta remarks, "is merely an hypothesis; for it can never be experienced that knowledge is the product of any collocations." Knowledge only "photographs" the objective phenomena, but to say that it is generated by these phenomena is to apply the ordinary conceptions of causation to knowledge, which is unwarrantable in the context of the unique character of knowledge itself. Dasgupta defends the Mimāmsā theory of the self-validity of knowledge *(svatah-prāmānya-vāda):*

> There can be no validity in things, for truth applies to knowledge and knowledge alone.... The rise of knowledge is never perceived by us to be dependent on any objective fact, for all objective facts are dependent on it for its revelation or illumination. This is ... the self-validity *(svatah-prāmānya)* of knowledge in its production *(utpatti).* As soon as knowledge is produced, objects are revealed to us; there is no intermediate link [such as collocations of certain conditions, as the Nayiyāikas claim] between the rise of knowledge and the revelation of objects on which knowledge depends for producing its action of revealing or illuminating them.... But in cases of illusory perception other perceptions or cognitions dawn which carry with them the notion that our original knowledge was not valid. Thus though the invalidity of any knowledge may appear to us by later experience, and in accordance with which we reject our former knowledge, yet when the knowledge first revealed itself to us it carried with it the conviction of certainty which goaded us on to work according to its indication.... This is what Mimāmsā means when it says that the validity of knowledge appears immediately with its rise, though its invalidity may be derived from later experience or some other data [Dasgupta, 374–375].

Thus all knowledge except that which originates in memory (since memory is dependent upon an earlier experience whose impressions it carries and therefore cannot be regarded as arising independently by itself) is accepted as valid independently by itself unless and until it is invalidated by yet another experience or by the fact of the knower (or perceiver) having had faulty or defective sense-organs. This brings us to the nature and scope of valid knowledge and the means *(pramānas)* thereof.

Prabhākara defines valid knowledge as apprehension *(anubhuti)* and implies that all apprehension is direct and immediate and therefore intrinsically valid. Kumārila defines valid knowledge as apprehension of an object which is produced by causes that are free from any defect and which is not contradicted by subsequent knowledge. Pārthasārathi defines it as apprehension of an object which has not been previously apprehended, which is not produced by defective causes and therefore truly represents the object, and which is free from contradiction. C.D. Sharma summarizes the four conditions which must be fulfilled in order that any cognition may be called valid: 1) it must not arise from defective causes *(kāranadosha-rahita);* 2) it must be self-consistent, free from contradiction, and it may not be set aside by subsequent knowledge *(bādhakajñāna-rahita);* 3) it must involve the apprehension of a previously unapprehended object *(agrhitagrāhi);* and 4) it must represent the object truly or appropriately *(yathārtha)*. We may thus say that the Mimāmsaka theory of knowledge is realistic; according to the Mimāmsaka "there is no knowledge which does not point to a corresponding object outside it" (Hiriyanna, *Outlines,* 313).

It is interesting to note that both Prabhākara and Kumārila regard knowledge itself as *pramāna* or means of knowledge—a view which is inseparable from the Mimāmsā doctrine of intrinsic validity of knowledge *(Svata-prāmānya-vāda)* as against the Nyāya doctrine of extrinsic validity of knowledge *(Paratah-prāmānya-vāda)*. It is therefore important that any attempt to discuss the several means of knowledge accepted by Mimāmsā does not ignore this basic belief in knowledge-as-*pramāna*. Jaimini admits three *pramānas* or means of knowledge, namely, perception, inference, and verbal testimony. Prabhākara adds two more to the list: they are comparison or analogy *(upamāna),* and implication *(arthāpatti)*. Finally, Kumārila adds nonperception or nonapprehension *(anupalabdhi)*. We discuss each of these six means of knowledge separately.

1. **Perception** ***(pratyaksha):*** Salinikanātha's *Prakarana-panchikā* defines perception or *pratyaksha* as "direct apprehension of the object through sense-contact" *(sākshāt-pratitih)*. The perceptive process takes place in the following temporal order: contact of the object and the sense-organ → the contact of the distinctive characteristics of the object and the sense-organ → the intervention of the mind *(manas)* → the realization by the self. Kumārila explains the initial contact of the sense-organ with the object as "mere relevancy or the capacity to reveal the object, which we infer from its effect" (Kumārila's *Sloka-vārttika* cited by Radhakrishnan, 380). Further, perception relates only to objects that exist or that are perceptible by the senses and thus, by implication, excludes "supersensuous objects." According to Prabhākara, objects that come within the possibility of apprehension may be substances, classes, or qualities.

It may not be out of place here to say a few words about 1) Prabhākara's view as to how the existence of the senses and the mind *(manas)* may be inferred; and 2) the similarities and differences between the Mimāmsaka and the Nyāya theories of the senses. According to Prabhākara, our cognitions of objects do not always occur in the same manner, for these are phenomena which "vary differently at different moments" and are "ephemeral" in character (Dasgupta, 376; Radhakrishnan, 379). The material cause *(samavāyikārana)* of cognitions is the self or soul, since all cognitions take place in the self/soul; but they have also an immaterial cause *(asamavāyikārana),* which makes possible the production of specific cognitions and relates to specific movements or associations. The immaterial cause subsists either in the cause of the material cause, or in the material cause itself; and since the material cause of cognitions is the self/soul and the immaterial cause cannot subsist in the cause of the self (since the self/soul is uncaused), it must therefore subsist in the self/soul itself. Since the immaterial cause necessary for the rise of a cognition must inhere in the self/soul and since what inheres in a substance is a quality, the immaterial cause must be a quality. But qualities are ephemeral and hence cannot arise in the self/soul—.

which is an eternal substance—without the contact of other substances. (It is here that the Mimāmsaka accepts the Nyāya view that the rise of specific qualities in an eternal substance can take place only by contact with some other, but presumably, eternal substances).

Further, since "there is no evidence that the other subsances inhere in still others, they are to be regarded as eternal" (Radhakrishnan, 379). Thus perception, which is a positive mode of cognition, is a specific quality of the self/soul. Such contact-substances are all-pervading, as time and space, or atomic. But the soul is always in contact with time and space and therefore, the eternal soul's uninterrupted contact with all-pervading time and space cannot account for the varied and individualized nature of our cognitions and hence, must refer to some kind of atom "which resides in the body ensouled by the cognizing soul" (Dasgupta, 377). This atom may be called mind or *manas,* and it contains the substratum of the immaterial cause of the cognition of which the self/soul is the material cause. But the mind *(manas)* by itself is devoid of any qualities, such as color and smell, and cannot support the self/soul in cognizing or experiencing these qualities and requires the help of such other organs as may be characterized by these qualities. For the cognition of smell, the mind is in need of an organ of which odor is the characteristic quality; similarly, for the cognition of color, the mind is in need of an organ having color as its characteristic quality. Thus the self/soul cognizes the external world of objects through the contact of these objects with the sense-organs mediated by the mind *(manas).*

In other words, none of these organs is effective without the mind. The relation between the soul and the mind *(manas)* is brought about by merit or demerit, but the soul is not simply passive in its attitude toward the mind of *manas.* In fact, the Mimāmsakas include *manas* among the senses, since it perceives nonmaterial states like pleasure, pain, desire and aversion. They argue that, if we were not dependent on *manas* and the sense-organs, we would have simultaneous cognitions of all things at once.

According to Dasgupta, four necessary contacts have to be admitted in this connection: 1) the contact of the sense-organs with the object, 2) the contact of the sense-organs with the qualities of the object, 3) the contact of the *manas* with the sense-organs, and 4) the contact of the *manas* with the soul. The objects of perception are of three kinds: substances, qualities, and class. The substances are tangible objects of earth, fire, water, and air in large dimensions (Dasgupta, 378), for in their fine atomic states they cannot be perceived. The qualities include color, taste, smell, touch, number, dimension, separateness, conjunction, disjunction, priority, posteriority, pleasure, pain, desire, aversion, and effort. As against Prabhākara, Kumārila was undecided somewhat as to the nature of the senses or of their contact with the objects. Thus, in *Sloka-vārttika* he says that "the sense may be conceived either as certain functions or activities, or as entities having the capacity of revealing things without coming into actual contact with them, or that they might be entities which actually come in contact with their objects" (cited in Dasgupta, 378), but he appears to prefer the last of the three possibilities to the other two.

Let us point out here, that Sāmkhya-Yoga, unlike Nyāya, rejects the possibility of the senses actually going out to meet the objects and holds that there is a special kind of functioning *(vrtti)* which enables the senses to grasp even such distant objects as the sun, the moon, and the stars. In other words, it is the functioning of the senses that reaches out to the objects. But Sāmkhya-Yoga does not further explain the nature of this special kind of functioning *(vrtti)*, thus offering the Mimāmsakas, particularly Pārthasārathi, a chance to declare such functioning as being "almost a different category *(tattvāntara)*" (Dasgupta, 378; notes).

Broadly speaking, the Mimāmsaka accepts the Nyāya theory of the senses except in regard to the auditory sense. According to the Mimāmsaka, spatial proximity and remoteness are perceived not only through vision and touch but also through hearing; which is to say, they are perceived directly. Space is distinguished into locus *(desa)* and direction *(dik)*, both of which are perceived directly as "qualifying adjuncts" *(viseshanas)*. of sounds; the auditory organ comes directly in contact with sound, which is the object. The ear does not go out to the object (sound); instead, the sound is carried to the ear through the air. As Radhakrishnan writes:

> If the ear could apprehend sounds, without coming into direct contact with them, as the Buddhists imagine, then all sounds, far and near, would be simultaneously perceived through the ear, which is not the case. . . The ear does not come into contact with the locus of the sound, but only with the sound which has its locus in the ear-drum. But sounds are always perceived as having the loci in different points of space, and not in the ear-drum. They reach the ear, not as mere sounds, but as coloured by the different directions from which they spring. So, sounds as well as their directions are directly perceived. Even distance is perceived through the ear, since sounds coming from a proximate point are more intense *(tivra)* than those coming from a distance [Radhakrishnan, 380–381].

Thus the Mimāmsaka view accounts for the direct perception of sounds and explains the different degrees of the intensity of sounds.

Both Prabhākara and Kumārila admit two stages in perception, namely, indeterminate *(nirvikalpa)* and determinate *(savikalpa)*. Prabhākara defines perception as direct apprehension; Kumārila defines it as direct knowledge produced by the appropriate contact of the sense-organs with the objects. The indeterminate *(nirvikalpa)* perception of an object is its perception at the first moment of the association of the senses and their objects. Thus, according to Kumārila, the cognition that initially arises is a mere "simple perception" *(ālochanā)* and is nondeterminate "pertaining to the object itself pure and simple, and resembling the cognitions that the new-born infant has of things around himself" (Dasgupta, 378).

In this cognition, neither the genus nor the differentia is *presented* to consciousness, although these are perceived. In other words, although both the genus and the differentia are perceived in the indeterminate stage, these do not manifest themselves to us "only because we do not remember the other things in relation to which, or in contrast to which, the percept has to show its character as genus or differentia" (Dasgupta, 379). Thus, indeterminate perception is due to the object itself; it indicates a stage when we do not yet discriminate between the "qualified and the qualifications and the generic and the specific features" (Radhakrishnan, 381) – something which relates to the stage of determinate *(savikalpa)* perception. Indeterminate perception is the bare awareness of the object; it is nonrelational (Sharma, 219). At the second, determinate stage, the self "by its past impressions brings the present perception in relation to past ones and realizes its character as involving universal and particular" (Dasgupta, 379). Thus, the single element that may be said to distinguish determinate from indeterminate perception is memory or retrospective association. However, as Prabhākara believes, the element of memory or remembrance does not pertain to the object perceived, but to those others with which it is compared, and therefore does not affect the validity of the cognition of the object itself.

We shall here consider some ontological problems which are connected with the doctrine of perception. Both Kumārila and Prabhākara accept the reality of universals and accept them as objects of perception. Kumārila and Pārthasārathi are severely critical of the Buddhist view that "specific individuality alone is real" and universality is only "a product of imagination" (Pārthasārathi, *Sāstradipika,* cited in Radhakrishnan, 383). According to Pārthasārathi, the universal *is* an object of perception, since whenever we perceive an individual object, we also perceive it as belonging to a particular class:

> The act of perception involves both assimilation and discrimination. Perception is inclusive *(anuvrtta)* as well as exclusive *(vyāvrtta).* Inclusion depends on the reality of the universal. The act of inference is also based on it. Nor can the Buddhist contend that the universal is not real, since it is not perceived as different from the individual. For the argument that what is, must be either different or non-different, assumes the universal being *(vastutva).* Nor is it correct to ask whether generality is present in its entirety in each individual or collectively in all, since such a distinction is relevant to individuals, and not to generality, which is partless [Pārthasārathi, *Sāstradipika,* cited in Radhakrishnan, 383; emphasis added].

Both Kumārila and Pārthasārathi also reject the Jaina view of the universal. If universality, as the Jainas contend, is one with similarity, we have to say "This is like a cow" and not "This is a cow." Also, similarity is not possible apart from universality, since things are similar by virtue of their possessing properties in common. According to Kumārila, the universal is not different from the individual, and the relation between the two is one of identity in difference. The universal, which is also called *ākrti* (form), does not mean shape, but identity of character. Kumārila writes: "The class itself is called *ākrti,* which signifies that by which the individual is characterised. It is that which is common to all the individual objects and the means of a collective idea of all these as forming one composite whole" (Kumārila, *Sloka-vārttika,* cited in Radhakrishnan, 383).

Pārthasārathi, however, argues that the universal is not completely different from the individual, for, were it so, we would not be able to perceive the universal in the individual. Thus, in the perception, "This is a cow," we have a cognition of both "this" *(iyambuddhi)* and "that" of the cow *(go-buddhi),* the former kind of cognition having an individual for its object and the latter kind having the universal for its object. The twofold character of perception (the two cognitions having inhered in the same object) points to the nature of the object as both universal and individual, since identity and difference are perceived at one and the same time. The identity and the difference relate to different aspects of one single object.

The followers of Prabhākara offer their objections to this view, however, according to whom, when we perceive the difference between the universal and the individual, we necessarily perceive the two as distinct and, when we perceive the identity between them, we naturally perceive only *one* of them. Radhakrishnan explains the point: "In this case a single object, the universal or the individual, would give rise to two cognitions of both the universal and the individual and their identity. But it is not impossible for the universal to produce a cognition of its identity with the individual any more than for the individual to produce a cognition of its identity with the universal" (Radhakrishnan, 384). Thus is cannot be said that both difference and identity are perceived in a single act of cognition. Pārthasārathi, for whom the cognition of two objects does not necessarily involve the cognition of their difference, contends that the argument of the Prabhākara school is invalid: "When an individual member of a class is perceived for the first time, both the individual and the universal are perceived, but not the difference between them. When another individual belonging to the same class is perceived, it is assimilated to the first individual as belonging to the same class and differentiated from it as being a different individual. The cognition of two objects does not therefore involve the cognition of their difference" (Pārthasārathi, *Sāstradipikā,* cited in Radhakrishnan, 384).

Further, the followers of Prabhākara argue that the universal and the individual cannot be identical, since the former is eternal and common to several individuals while the latter is noneternal and specific. In reply Pārthasārathi says that "a complex or multiform object may be eternal in some respects and non-eternal in others, identical with others in some features and different from them in others" (Pārthasārathi, *Sāstradipikā,* cited in Radhakrishnan, 384). It may be noted here that it was Prabhākara who introduced into Indian philosophy the notion of part and whole (*avayava* = part/ *avayavi* = whole). He believes that the whole is an object of perception and argues that the proof of the true existence of anything must, in the last analysis, rest on our individual consciousness, and that "what is distinctly recognized in consciousness must be admitted to have its existence established" (Dasgupta, 380).

That the gross objects as wholes exist is endorsed by the fact that they are so perceived. We have known that the subtle atoms are the material cause and that their interconnected combination is the immaterial cause. According to Prabhākara, it is the immaterial cause which makes the whole essentially different from the parts of which it is composed, and it is not necessary that all the parts be perceived before the whole is perceived.

Kumārila, however, holds that the whole and the parts are identical, and that the difference between them lies in the separate standpoints from which we look at an object. When we lay stress on the notion of parts, the object appears to be a conglomeration of them, and when we look at it from the point of view of the unity appearing as a whole, the object appears to be a whole of which there are parts. In the larger context of the Mimāmsaka view that when knowledge occurs, the incident, if viewed from the subject's side, seems to be bound with his consciousness, Kumārila's contention regarding the whole and the parts is in order. In this sense there is in every knowing subject an inborn assurance that the knowledge and the sensations are very much his own; by implication, the very act of knowing involves "self-certainty or intuitive indubitability" (see Sinari, 167, 168, for a comparison of the Mimāmsaka theory of the self-validity *[svata-prāmānya]* of knowledge and self-certainty in perceptual knowledge with the Husserlian "noesis-noema unity").

The Mimāmsakas do not support the theory of yogic intuition, by which the *Yogis* (seers) are believed to apprehend objects of the past and the future as well as objects that are imperceptible and distant. If this intuition is sensuous, the Mimāmsaka argues, there can be no cognition of the objects, for the senses cannot come into contact with objects of the past and the future nor objects that are imperceptible and distant. No amount of development in the senses can change the innate nature of the sense-organs. If the yogic intuition apprehends things perceived in the past, it is merely a case of memory; if it apprehends things previously unapprehended, its validity is doubtful. According to the Mimāmsaka, it is the Vedas alone which can give us a knowledge of past, future and distant objects. However, the Mimāmsakas admit mental perception, by which we cognize pleasure, pain, hatred, and the like. They add of course that mental perception is restricted to "non-cognitive activities," since a cognition cannot be "the object of introspection" (Radhakrishnan, 385). Even in dreams, what the cognition renders cognizable is some object of the external world, previously perceived and now revived through the stored impressions.

All knowledge—perceptual, inferential or otherwise—must reveal the knower directly, since all knowledge involves the knower, the object known, and its cognition at the same identical moment. And, since in all knowledge the self is directly perceived, all knowledge may be viewed as perception from the standpoint of the self. The self itself does not have any revealing powers, however, for if it were so, then even in deep sleep one could have knowledge, since even in deep sleep the self is present—a fact which is supported by our remembrance of dreams (*Note:* Kumārila holds that in deep sleep the self is restored to its form of pure consciousness where no dreams are possible.) It is knowledge alone which reveals the self, the knower, and the objects.

"It is generally argued," writes Dasgupta, "against the self-illuminative character of knowledge that all cognitions are of the forms of the objects they are said to reveal; and if they have the same form we may rather say that they have the same identical reality too" (Dasgupta, 383). The Mimāmsakas review these objections in the following way. If the cognition and the cognized were not different from one another, we could not have felt that it is by cognition that we apprehend the cognized objects. The cognition of a person implies the manifestation of a special kind of quality by virtue of which his participation with reference to a specific object is favored or determined, and the object of cognition is that with reference to which the participation of the self has been induced. Cognition has no other character except that of revealing objects in terms of their essential forms. Even the dream cognition takes place with reference to objects that were perceived previously and of which the impressions were stored in the mind and were aroused by the unseen agency *(adrshta)*.

The followers of Prabhākara counter the arguments of those who hold that our cognitions of objects are themselves cognized by some other cognition, by referring to the possibility of a *regressus ad infinitum* and indicating that we do not experience any such double cognition. They argue that if a cognition could be the object of another cognition, it could not be self-valid. The cognition reveals itself to us even as it reveals its objects, which in turn allow us to infer this self-cognizing knowledge. Prabhākara draws a subtle distinction between "perceptuality" *(samvedyatva)* and "being object of knowledge" *(prameyatva)*. A thing can be apprehended by perception alone whereas inference can only indicate the presence of an object without apprehending the object itself. "Inference can only indicate the presence or existence of knowledge but cannot apprehend the cognition itself" (Dasgupta, 384).

Kumarila also agrees with Prabhākara in holding that "perception is never the object of another perception and that it ends in the direct apprehensibility of the object of perception," but adds that "every perception involves a relationship between the perceiver and the perceived, wherein the perceiver behaves as the agent whose activity in grasping the object is known as cognition" (Dasgupta, 384). This is obviously different from the view of Prabhākara, according to whom "in one manifestation of knowledge the knower, the known, and the knowledge, are simultaneously illuminated" (Dasgupta, 384). This is called *triputi-pratyaksha* or "tri-relational perception."

If, as the Mimāmsakas argue, experience by its very nature is valid—if all apprehensions are conclusive and authentic—it is difficult to account for illusory perceptions, on whose evidences the Indian idealists depended vitally. According to them, there were instances which showed that even "waking perceptions were not necessarily perceptions of the objectively real" (Chattopadhyaya, 65). Consequently, the problem of illusion acquired a special importance in Indian philosophy. We have thus five theories of illusion or error, three of which came from the idealists and two from their opponents—a division which is not as neat as it seems, however. The five theories are: 1) *sat-khyāti* (accepted by the Jainas), 2) *ātma-khyāti* (accepted by the Buddhists, especially the Yogāchāra Buddhists), 3) *viparita-khyāti* or *anyathā-khyāti* (accepted by the Vaiseshika, Nyāya, and the Yoga schools, as well as by Kumārila of the Mimāsā school), 4) *a-khyāti* (accepted by the

Mimāmsā school, particularly by Prabhākara and his followers), and 5) *anirvachaniya-khyāti* (associated with the Advaita Vedāntins).

The stock example of illusion in Indian philosophy is the illusory appearance of a piece of broken conch-shell as a piece of silver. While all the schools agree that such an illusion is something which is universally experienced, their differences are with regard to its cause or its psychology. The idealistic Buddhists, for instance, who deny the independent existence of the external world and accept only the forms of knowledge brought about by the accumulated karma of past lives, try to locate the cause of illusory perception (as they do in case of normal perception) in the flow of knowledge alone. They reject external data on the ground that they do not exist and maintain that the flow of knowledge—which creates both the percept and the perceiver and unites them—generates both right perception and illusory perception "on account of the peculiarities of its own collating conditions" (Dasgupta, 385).

According to the Nyāya philosopher, however, this theory is based upon a false hypothesis (that it is the inner knowledge which appears as coming from outside and that the external world as such does not exist) and he argues that if knowledge imposes upon itself the knower and the illusory percept, irrespective of any external condition, then the perception ought to take the form of "I am silver" and not "This is silver." The *viparita-khyāti* or *anyathā-khyāti* theory of Vaiseshika-Nyāya and Yoga schools (and which is also associated with Kumārila's explanation of perceptual error) supposes that the illusion is the result of malobservation, on account of which we do not note the peculiar characteristics of the conch-shell which distinguish it from the silver and yet notice certain other traits which might be common to both (such as the glow, the color, etc.). Kumārila also maintains that "knowledge always points to an object beyond itself" (Hiriyanna, *Outlines,* 315). In the example above, although silver is not directly given, it should not on that account be taken as ideal or utterly nonexistent, for it exists elsewhere and its present idea, being due to the suggestion of a former experience—our memory of it as experienced before—leads us eventually to an objective counterpart.

As Dasgupta writes, "the mere non-distinction is not enough to account for the phenomenon of illusion, for there is a definite positive aspect associated with it" (Dasgupta, 386). Thus, the error in *viparita-* or *anyathā-khyāti* is the result of our wrong synthesis of the presentative and the representative factors *(samsarga-graha);* the error is one of "commission, for it includes as its content more than there is a warrant for in the reality that is presented" (Hiriyanna, *Outlines,* 316). Illusion here is explained as unitary knowledge instead of as two knowledges (the knowledge of the truth and the knowledge of error or of no-knowledge), as a single psychosis (Sharma, 228) and not a composite of two imperfect cognitions. Error thus becomes a unitary cognition, a positive misapprehension (Hiriyanna, *Essentials,* 144: ". . . knowledge partly strays from reality and so far misrepresents it") and therefore one of commission. This misapprehension has its source in some defect in the causes of knowledge and is set aside by a subsequent sublating knowledge, although as long as error is experienced it is valid as a cognition *per se* (Sharma, 228). When error is regarded as misapprehension, it becomes highly suggestive—something which led Prabhākara to expound his own theory of error. Kumārila's admission that knowledge may arise without a corresponding object is not very satisfactory "from the realistic standpoint, for it throws suspicion on the trustworthiness of knowledge as a whole" (Hiriyanna, *Essentials,* 144). Prabhākara's explanation of error "saves knowledge from such suspicion" (Hiriyanna, *Essentials,* 144); it is an explanation in terms of omission *(akhyāti)* and not, as in Kumārila's case, in terms of commission *(anyathā-khyāti)* or substitution *(viparita-khyāti).*

According to Prabhākara, knowledge never involves a reference to anything that is not actually given. We may take the example of a conch-shell seen through a sheet of yellow glass. According to Prabhākara, here we have the perception of the conch in every respect except its true color and the sensation of the *yellowness* of the glass. They are indeed two acts of knowing, but they quickly succeed one another so that we miss the fact that they are two, each of which is valid so far as it goes, for neither the yellowness nor the conch as such is negated even after we discover the error. We merely overlook at first that they are two—a deficiency in our knowledge that is made good later when we discover our mistake.

> Thus the discovery of the so-called error only means a further step in advancing knowledge. It confirms the previous knowledge and does not cancel any part of it as false, so that to talk of "rectification of error" here is a misnomer. In fact, there is no error at all in this view, in its usual sense of a single *unit* of knowledge. In other words, it holds that the mind may fail to apprehend one or more aspects of what is presented, but that it never *mis*apprehends it and that all errors are therefore errors of omission [Hiriyanna, *Essentials,* 144–145].

The two *jñānas* involved in the conch-shell and silver example are not both perceptual: one of the two *jñānas* is the perception of the presented object, but as characterized only by features or a feature which it has in common with some other object, while the other *jñāna* is the recollection of the object which is not presented as a result of perceiving such features. We thus lose sight of the fact of recollection, and hence there is a failure also to notice that there are two *jñānas*—those of perception and memory or recollection. Thus, though the illusory perception is characterized by both apprehension and recollection and, to that extent, is different from the ordinary valid perception—which involves direct apprehension—of actual silver and the sight of the object present is not apprehended, the illusory perception appears at the moment of its production to be as valid as in the case of ordinary valid perception. In other words, the initial or original perception is self-valid at the time of its production—a view which supports the Mimāmsā doctrine of the intrinsic validity of all knowledge *(svata-prāmānya-vāda).*

Thus, two factors are involved in error, one positive and the other negative, the former consisting in the presence of two cognitions which reveal their respective objects only partially, the latter consisting in overlooking the distinction between these two cognitions and their objects. As Sharma points out, both these cognitions may be presentative, or both may be representative, or one may be presentative and the other representative. If both the cognitions are presentative, error is the result of nondiscrimination between perception and perception; if both are representative, error is the result of nondiscrimination between memory and memory; if one is presentative and the other representative, error is the result of nondiscrimination between perception and memory. In all these cases error is due to nondiscrimination, that is, nonapprehension of the distinction between two cognitions and their objects. Let us consider the instance of nondiscrimination—or fusion—between memory and memory such as is involved in cases of doubt. On seeing a tall object from a distance, the perceiver is not sure whether it is a pillar or a post, where both the pillar and the post are only memory images; and, since the perceiver cannot decide in favor of either, there is a confusion between one memory image and another, resulting in doubt.

The same is true about the orthodox rope and snake example, provided of course that *distance* or *blurred vision* is a factor involved. "All these cases involve a fusion of two elements both of which are real and yet in combination lead to error" (Ranade, 60). Thus, in *akhyāti* (nonapprehension), or *alpa-khyāti* (partial-apprehension) as it sometimes has been called, there is an idea of grades of reality. Error thus becomes a grade of reality or partial truth (compare Bradley's view of error). [Very different of course is the example of a perceiver seeing a pillar and a post, confusing one for the other, and, coming near the object, finds it only a tree without branches and leaves or a man standing: the Mimāmsakas, apparently, do not seem to have taken into consideration and explained the error involved in this example.] Chattopadhyaya comments: "As an extreme reaction against the idealistic tendency to count on the evidences of illusion for the purpose of explaining away the evidences of the normal or valid perceptions, the Prabhākara Mimāmsakas wanted to deny the facthood of illusion as such" (Chattopadhyaya, 63–64).

According to Prabhākara, there is no need to verify any knowledge, for all knowledge is true in the sense that nothing of what it reveals is contradicted later; and therefore "to question whether it agrees with reality in any particular instance is . . . to question its very nature" (Hiriyanna, *Essentials,* 145). The supposed error may be partial or incomplete knowledge. Further, human knowledge, in some sense or other, is always incomplete or partial, for it cannot grasp the features of any given object (or situation) in their entirety; on similar grounds, error is partial from a specific standpoint. Hiriyanna writes: "It is *relatively* incomplete and its relative incompleteness is determined by reference to an extrinsic standard." It is judged, for instance, by reference to the fruitfulness of the activity prompted by it; which is to say, that knowledge is true which works, and that which does not is erroneous. Let us consider Hiriyanna's criticism of Prabhākara's view which, according to Hiriyanna, is not the same as that of modern pragmatism, for, unlike the latter, it recognizes the absolute epistemological validity of all knowledge. "In fact," writes Hiriyanna, "Prabhākara's view represents a position which is the very reverse of modern pragmatism for it denies error, in the logical sense, completely. The adoption here of the pragmatic criterion [i.e. in terms of its fruitfulness] is only for the purpose of accounting for the commonly accepted distinction between truth and falsehood" (*Essentials,* 145).

Although Hiriyanna does not forget to praise Prabhākara's theory "for its simplicity as well as for its complete consistency in explaining the logical character of knowledge," he finds it far from convincing. We quote the relevant lines:

> The indirect manner . . . in which it explains the familiar terms "true" and "false" is hardly satisfactory. Further, a purely negative explanation cannot account for error which, as a judgement, presents the two elements in it as synthesized though they may be actually unrelated. There is only a single psychical process, and the resulting knowledge includes a reference to a positive element, viz., the relation between those elements which is not given. Error is therefore misapprehension, and not mere lack of apprehension [*Essentials,* 146].

As it appears, Hiriyanna prefers Kumārila's theory of *viparita-khyāti* to Prabhākara's *akhyāti,* although in his earlier book on Indian philosophy, he had kept himself uncommitted, as is evident in the following objective classification: "Kumārila's attitude towards knowledge is thus primarily detached and scientific; that of Prabhākara, pragmatic" (*Outlines,* 318).

2. **Inference** ***(anumāna):*** The Mimāmsa account of inference as a source or means of valid knowledge generally resembles that of the Vaiseshika-Nyāya; but there are differences also. Sabara (whose commentary *[bhāsya]* on Jaimini's *Mimāmsā-Sutra* is the earliest extant commentary on that basic Mimāmsā text) says, that when a certain fixed or permanent relation has been known to exist between two different things, so that when we perceive any of these things we have an idea of the other, the resulting knowledge is inferential. On the basis of Sabara's definition, Kumārila extends—and makes more inclusive—the scope of inferential cognition, when he tries to show that inference is possible only when we notice that in a large number of cases two things (e.g., smoke and fire) coexist in a third thing (for example, a kitchen) in somewhat independent relation to the exclusion of every other eliminable condition or factor.

It is also imperative that the two things (smoke and fire) coexisting in a third thing (kitchen or hill) should be "so experienced that all cases of the existence of one thing should also be cases involving the existence of the other" (Dasgupta, 387); but the cases of the existence of one of the two things (for example, fire), though including all the cases of the existence of the other (smoke), may have yet a more coextensive sphere where the latter (smoke) may not exist. When once a permanent relation between two things and a third thing which had previously been apprehended in a large number of cases is perceived, they fuse together in the mind into one whole, so that when the existence of one (for example, smoke) in a thing (hill) is perceived, the existence of the thing (hill) with its counterpart (fire) is easily inferred. In all such cases the thing (e.g., fire) which has a sphere extending beyond that in which the other (e.g., smoke) can exist, is called *vyāpaka* or *gamya* whereas the other (smoke) is called *vyāpya* or *gamaka.* It is only by the presence of *vyāpya* or *gamaka* in a thing (e.g., hill) that the other counterpart, the *vyāpaka* or *gamya* (fire) may be inferred. There is thus a necessary or invariable connection between *vyāpaka/gamya* and *vyāpya/gamaka,* although this invariable coexistence (e.g., wherever there is smoke there is fire) cannot be the cause of inference, for it is itself a case of inference.

Inference therefore involves the memory of a permanent relation subsisting between two things (e.g., smoke and fire) in a further relation with a third (e.g., kitchen or hill); but the third is remembered only because the coexisting things must have *a place* where they are found associated. It is by virtue of such a memory that the direct perception of a *spatial* basis (e.g., hill or kitchen) with the *vyāpya* or *gamaka* in it (e.g., smoke) would spontaneously remind us that the same basis (hill or kitchen) must contain the *vyāpaka* or *gamya* also. As Dasgupta writes, every case of inference "proceeds directly from a perception and not from any universal general proposition" (Dasgupta, 388).

According to Kumārila, inference gives us a knowledge of the minor term as associated with the major term (minor = *paksha;* major = *sādhya*) and not of the major alone (that is, it gives us a knowledge of *the fiery hill* and not of fire alone). It thus gives us a distinctly new knowledge, for though it was known that that which contained smoke also contained fire, the case of the "fiery hill" was not anticipated. In the context of this new knowledge of the fiery hill, smoke (middle term or *hetu*) and fire (major term or *sādhya*) are only "the constituent conditions of inference" (Barlingay, 114). Dasgupta notes, following S.C. Vidyabhusana, that it is quite likely that Kumārila was indebted to the Buddhist logician Dignāga for this, since the latter's main contention is that it is not fire, nor the connection between it and the hill, but the fiery hill that is inferred. Novelty, for Kumārila, is an essential condition of knowledge.

It might be asked: "If no inference is possible without a memory of the invariable relation, is not the self-validity of inference threatened on that account, since memory *(smriti)* is not regarded by the Mimāmsakas as self-valid?" Kumārila's answer is that memory is not invalid, but it does not have the status of *pramāna* or "source of knowledge," as it does not by itself produce a new knowledge. Further, as regards the inferential argument, the Mimāmsakas admit the orthodox distinction between inference for oneself *(svārtha-anumāna)* and inference for the sake of others *(parārtha-anumāna).* In the former case the inference need not be verbally expressed, but in the latter case it must be so expressed. According to both Kumārila and Prabhākara, a *parārtha-anumāna* (inference for others) consists of three members only: *pratijñā* (statement of the case), *hetu* (reason), and *(drishtānta* or *udāharana* (example). This is where the Mimāmsā syllogism differs from the Nyāya syllogism, which includes two more members, namely, *upanaya* (application) and *nigamana* (conclusion).

Like Sabara before him, Kumārila divides inference into two kinds: they are 1) *pratyakshatodrishta,* where the invariable relation is between objects that are perceptible or concrete (as in the case of smoke and fire), and 2) *sāmānyatodrishta,* where the invariable relation is observed not between two concrete things but between two general notions, that is, the relation is not apprehended by the senses, but known only in the abstract (as in the case of sun's change of place and its motion, a general notion which is directly perceived like all universals). According to Prabhākara, "the relation must be unfailing, true and permanent, such as that which subsists between the cause and its effect, whole and part, substance and quality, class and individuals. The general principle is not derived from perception, since the latter operates only with regard to things in the present and in contact with sense-organs. It is not due to inference or implication, since these assume it. The general principle is established on the basis of experience" (Radhakrishnan, 386–387).

While Prabhākara admits the need of forming the notion of permanent relation, he refuses to lay any stress on the fact that this permanent relation between two things is viewed in connection with a third thing in which they both subsist. According to him, the notion of the permanent relation of coexistence, identity or causal nexus alone is important, for "in all other associations of time and place the things in which these two (things) subsist together are taken only as adjuncts to qualify the two things" (Dasgupta, 390). It is also necessary, according to him, to recognize the fact that the concomitance of smoke and fire is only *conditional,* that of the fire in smoke is *unconditional* and *absolute.* When the conviction that the concept of the presence of smoke invariably involves the concept of the presence of fire is fixed up in the mind, the inference of fire is made as soon as any smoke is perceived.

3. **Comparison** ***(upamāna):*** Comparison or analogy as a *pramāna* (source of knowledge) is recognized in the Nyāya, but "it is not of much logical significance as conceived there" (Hiriyanna, *Essentials,* 141). Further, the Mimāmsa conception of comparison differs from the Nyāya view. However, the Mimāmsaka, like the Nyāya philosopher, contests the view that comparison or analogy is not an independent source of knowledge and can be categorized, partly or wholly, under one or other of the other sources of knowledge. According to the Nyāya, the one and only object of this *pramāna* is the relation between a word and its meaning learned under certain conditions; it thus refers to the knowledge of "reciprocal similarity" (Hiriyanna, *Outlines,* 319). It is the knowledge of similarity of an hitherto unknown object like a wild cow with a known object like a cow. The only condition here is that the two animals belong to the same species. The knowledge thus takes the following form: "The perceived wild cow is like the remembered cow."

The Mimāmsaka refutes this account of comparison by pointing out that the knowledge between a word and the object denoted by that word is derived by verbal authority (e.g., by the words of the person who states that a wild cow is similar to a cow) and not by comparison; it is known through a recollection of what was earlier learned from the verbal authority of the person, and the knowledge of the wild cow itself is a result of perception rather than comparison. Comparison, according to Mimāmsā, apprehends the similarity of the remembered cow to the perceived wild cow, and the resulting knowledge takes the following form: "The remembered cow is like the perceived wild cow." As Sharma says, "It is the cow as possessing similarity with the wild cow that is known by comparison" (Sharma, 219). Thus the Mimāmsa conception of comparison consists in "cognizing anew in an object, not presented to the senses [the cow is absent at the time of cognition], similarity to an object which is being actually perceived [the wild cow]" (Hiriyanna, *Essentials,* 141).

The Mimāmsā view thus supposes that the similarity in the two cases is "numerically distinct" (Hiriyanna, *Essentials,* 141); it takes for granted that if A is similar to B, the similarity of A to B is not identically the same as the similarity of B to A. Mimāmsā thus conceives similarity as dual. This *pramāna* is not perception, since the cow, in which the similarity with the wild cow is found, is absent at the time of forming this judgment. It is not inference either, since a knowledge of inductive relation or *vyāpti,* which is the basis of inference, is not required to form the judgment. Nor is it mere memory or remembrance, because the similarity in question has not been previously apprehended. Prabhākara and Kumārila differ on this point, however: while Kumārila regards similarity "as only a quality consisting in the fact of more than one object having the same set of qualities," Prabhākara regards it as "a distinct category" (Dasgupta, 391). Hiriyanna points out, however, that though this *pramāna* is different from syllogistic inference, it reduces itself to what modern logic describes as "immediate inference by reciprocal relations" (*Essentials,* 141).

4. **Implication or Presumption** ***(arthāpatti):*** Both Prabhākara and Kumārila admit implication or presumption as an independent means of valid knowledge. Implication/Presumption *(arthāpatti)* is the assumption without which the perception of a thing cannot be explained (see Radhakrishnan, 393). It refers to "postulating something to account for what apparently clashes with experience and therefore in the nature of a hypothesis... rendering explicit what is already implicit in two truths both of which have been properly tested, but which appear mutually incompatible" (Hiriyanna, *Outlines,* 320). It "signifies the discovery of a new fact or the postulation of a new truth, as the result of a contradiction between two other truths that are known to be well established" (Hiriyanna, *Essentials,* 141). "It is the assumption of an unperceived fact in order to reconcile two apparently inconsistent perceived facts" (Sharma, 222).

The Mimāmsaka offers the following example, "trivial in itself but typical" (Hiriyanna, *Essentials,* 141): When we know that a certain person Devadutta is alive and perceive that he is not in his house, we cannot reconcile the two facts of his remaining alive and his not being in the house without presuming his existence somewhere else (somewhere outside his house). This method of cognizing Devadutta's existence outside the house is called *arthāpatti* (presumption or implication). Although the Nyāya philosophers class it under Inference *(anumāna)* on the ground that it is just an instance of "implicative reference" (Ranade, 39) and therefore do not regard it as a distinct *pramāna* (source of knowledge), the Mimāmsakas give it the status of an independent *pramāna*. The latter differ, however, as regards the basis of Presumption or Implication: while Prabhākara locates its basis in the element of doubt *(samsaya)* as to the truth of the two perceived facts (which is removed by presumption, while in inference there is no such doubt), Kumārila believes that the mutual inconsistency of the two perceived facts *is* its basis (which inconsistency is removed by presumption and which is not present in inference). We give below a detailed explanation of their differences.

It is thus seen that Prabhākara and Kumārila disagree on the nature of the psychological analysis of the mind. According to Prabhākara, when we know that Devadutta habitually resides in his house and yet do not find him there, our knowledge that Devadutta is living (earlier acquired by some other means of proof) is made doubtful, and the reason for such doubt is that we do not find Devadutta in his house. Thus, though Devadutta's absence is not the cause of implication, yet it makes doubtful the very existence of Devadutta and thus makes us imagine that he must be somewhere outside. "The perception of the absence of Devadutta through the intermediate link of a doubt passes into the notion of a presumption that he must then remain somewhere else" (Dasgupta, 392). Thus implication becomes the hypothesis without which the doubt cannot be removed. In inference the element of doubt is absent, for it is only when the smoke is perceived to exist beyond the least element of doubt that the inference of fire is possible; but in presumption "the perceived non-existence in the house leads to the presumption of an external existence only when it has thrown the fact of the man's being alive into doubt and uncertainty" (Salinikanātha's *Prakarana-panchikā,* cited in Dasgupta, 392).

Let us review Kumārila's objection to Prabhākara's explanation. According to Kumārila, in the event of the fact that Devadutta is living is made uncertain or debatable by his absence at his house, then such uncertainty could well be removed by the supposition that he is dead, for it does not follow that the uncertainty as to Devadutta's being alive should necessarily be resolved by the supposition that he is outside his house. Dasgupta reframes Kumārila's basic question: "If it was already known that Devadutta was living and his absence from the house creates the doubt, how then can the very fact which created the doubt remove the doubt?" In other words, since doubt can be removed only when its cause is removed, the cause of doubt cannot be the cause of its removal too. The nature of presumption, for Kumārila, is quite different. It is the certainty of Devadutta's being alive (any doubt about it having been removed by previous knowledge) associated with the perception of his absence from the house that leads us to the presumption of his existence outside the house. The opposition is thus between the life of Devadutta and his absence from the house; the two perceived facts are mutually inconsistent. This opposition or inconsistency is removed by the presumption of Devadutta's external residence. Presumption *(arthāpatti)* is thus the result of the contradiction of the present perception with a previously acquired certain knowledge *(arthānupapatti)*.

As regards the thesis of presumption as an independent *pramāna* (as distinguished from inference), both Prabhākara and Kumārila hold that in presumption there is no middle term at all whereas it is the basis of inference. Neither of the two perceived and apparently contradictory facts can separately serve as a middle term, although in their combination they appear to be so. However, this combination already includes the conclusion, while a valid middle term does not include the conclusion; and hence, presumption *(arthāpatti)* is different from inference *(anumāna)*. The Nyāya logicians point out, however, that this *pramāna* can be brought under what modern logicians call disjunctive reasoning and that it is deducible from the disjunctive proposition, "A person who is alive must be *either* in his house or outside it," since no third alternative is possible. This disjunctive reasoning might also be reduced to a categorical syllogistic form:

1. All alive persons who are not in their house are elsewhere.
2. Devadutta is an alive person who is not in his house.
3. Therefore Devadutta is an alive person who is elsewhere.

But Hiriyanna, while conceding that presumption *(arthāpatti)* is disjunctive reasoning, refuses to call it syllogistic (in the ordinary and accepted sense of the term) and defends its independent status on that ground:

> If we reduce it to the syllogistic form, the major premise will be a negative universal referring to things beyond the universe of discourse; and it therefore ceases to be significant.... [U]nlike the Nyāyāyikas, the Mimāmsakas of both the schools reject the negative universal as the major premise in a syllogism. They consider that it can generally be expressed in a positive form. The scope for *arthāpatti* is just where it *cannot be so expressed* [*Outlines,* 321; emphasis added].

Consequently, it is on presumption *(arthāpatti)* that the Mimāmsaka rests his belief in the survival of the self after the body's extinction. The Veda promises appropriate rewards in a future life for ritual deeds in this life; and, since the person who reaps the fruit of a good or bad deed—that is, enjoys the reward or suffers the punishment—cannot, according to the doctrine of *karma,* be other than the one who did it, the self should survive the body.

5. **Verbal or Vedic Testimony *(Sabda-pramāna)*:** Most of the Indian systems of thought have regarded *Sabda* or word as a separate means of proof, although there is a variety of opinion in regard to its value as a philosophical criterion. While the Vaiseshikas do not recognize it at all, the Sāmkhyas recognize it in the hope that the *Upanishads* might be regarded as advocating their philosophy alone. The Naiyāyikas believe in it, but make it subsidiary to God. The Chārvākas and the Buddhists reject it. But the Mimāmsakas exalt it above every other means of knowledge *(pramāna)*, "making it supreme even above God whom they feel no necessity of recognising" (Ranade, 39). For the Mimāmsakas, the validity and authority of the Vedic Word (or, the Vedas) is not derived from the authority of any

trustworthy person or God; it is valid in itself. It was in fact the most important subject for the Mimāmsaka, and Jaimini's *Mimāmsā-Sutra* was written with the sole purpose of laying down rules for the right interpretation of the Vedas.

The very opening sentence of the *Mimāmsā-Sutra* states the basic theme of Mimāmsā and provides a basis for the interpretation of the Vedas: "Next, therefore, comes the enquiry into *dharma*" (Radhakrishnan and Moore, *Sourcebook,* 487; all subsequent citations, unless otherwise indicated, will be to this edition). Thus the aim of Mimāmsā is to ascertain the nature of *dharma* or duty "as conducive to the highest good" (*Mimāmsā-Sutra,* 487). Except *Sabda,* the other *pramānas* are of little or no use in this context, for all of them presuppose the work of perception whereas *dharma* is not a physical existent and therefore unapprehensible through the senses. The *Sutra* says: "*Dharma* [is] not amenable to such means of cognition as sense-perception and the like. . . . [Sense-perception] is not a means of knowing *dharma,* as it apprehends only things existing at the present time. . . . *Dharma* [is] cognisable by means of verbal [Vedic] injunctions" (*Mimāmsā-Sutra,* 487). The Mimāmsakas attempt to prove that every part of the Veda refers to acts of duty (although this attempt of theirs has been criticized in the context of those portions of the Veda which deal with the ultimate problems of the universe and the soul's immortality, that is, portions which do not directly deal with rituals and sacrifices). Hence, their emphasis on the ultimate validity of the Vedic Word.

Verbal cognition, or *Sabda* (verbal testimony) as a source of knowledge, is defined as "the cognition of something not present to the senses, produced by the knowledge of words" (Radhakrishnan, 388), as "the knowledge that we get about things (not within the purview of our perception) from relevant sentences by understanding the meaning of the words of which they are made up" (Dasgupta, 394). These words may be of two kinds: those uttered by ordinary persons and which are valid if we have certain proof that those persons are not untrustworthy, and those which belong to the Vedas and which are valid in themselves. A cognition is invalid if it is contradicted by a subsequent one. But the cognitions produced by Vedic injunctions cannot be set aside at any time or place or under any conditions.

Jaimini writes: "The relation of the word with its denotation is inborn . . . infallible regarding all that is imperceptible; it is a valid means of knowledge, as it is independent, according to Bādarāyana [the author of the basic Vedāntic text, *Braham-Sutra*]." Jaimini's sentence is a fine example of a combination of the sacred or religious aspect (inasmuch as it speaks of the self-valid character of the Vedic Word) and the secular aspect (inasmuch as it cites Bādarāyana to support its thesis, thus indicating the trustworthiness of that author's words) of *sabda.* In his *Bhāsya,* Sabara explains and supports Jaimini's words:

> What we mean by "inborn" *(autapattika)* is "constant." . . . What is meant is that the relation between word and its meaning is *inseparable.*—It becomes the *means of meaning*. . . . Of this "means of knowledge" there is *"infallibility";* i.e., the cognition brought about by

> that means never fails (is never wrong); when a cognition is not found to be wrong, it cannot be said with regard to it that "this is not so," or "the real thing is not as it is represented by this cognition," or "it may be that the idea in the mind of the speaker is different from what is expressed by his words," or "the words used give rise to contradictory ideas, representing the same thing as *existing* and as non-existing."—For these reasons (since cognition brought about by words is not infallible), it is *"a valid means of knowledge, as it is independent."* That is, when a cognition has been brought about by means of words [i.e. the Vedic Word, or the injunctions], there is no need for any other cognition (to corroborate it), or of any other person as having the same cognition [Radhakrishnan and Moore, 487–488).

Thus, Sabara's commentary on Jaimini not only describes the unique nature of the Vedic *sabda,* but carefully distinguishes it from the non-Vedic or ordinary *sabda.*

The Vedas manifest their own validity. In contrast, words used by ordinary people denote things that can be cognized by other means of knowledge, and, if they fail to know them through these other means, then "those who utter them must be of unquestionable authority." Hence, non-Vedic utterances do not possess any "inherent validity" (Pārthasārathi's *Sāstradipika*). Prabhākara goes to the extent of saying that non-Vedic verbal cognition is of the nature of inference, and that the verbal cognition produced by the Vedic Word alone is strictly verbal *(Prakarana-panchikā).* Kumārila, however, maintains that since the utterances of human beings who are trustworthy are valid, their utterances are also to be accepted as sources of verbal cognition.

According to Prabhākara, there is no such thing as "indistinct sound" or *dhvani,* since all sounds are in the form of letters or combination of letters. The single letters cannot yield any meaning and therefore are to be regarded as "elements of auditory perception which serve as a means for understanding the meaning of a word." Dasgupta writes: "The reason of our apprehension of the meaning of any word is to be found in a separate potency existing in the letters by which the denotation of the word may be comprehended" (Dasgupta, 395). There are as many perceptions as there are letters in a word and, on account of the close proximity of the perceptions, we imagine that the perception of the word is one only. The perception of each letter-sound, as soon as it is uttered, leaves behind an impression which combines with the impressions of the successively dying perceptions of single letters which in combination bring about the idea of the whole word which has the potency to denote a meaning. Since the potency of a word depends or originates from the separate potencies of its letters, the letters are the direct cause of verbal cognition.

Thus words have natural denotative powers by which they refer to objects irrespective of *our* understanding of their meanings. The relationship between the word and its meaning is natural and not created by convention (except, as Prabhākara admits, in the case of proper names). Although the hearer might fail to understand this relationship—and therefore the meaning of the word—in the event of his ignorance about the expressive power of the word in question, the word itself is competent to denote that meaning. In other words, words are self-denotative; by implication, therefore, both words and the meanings (or objects) denoted by them are eternal. The words, however, require some manifestive agency by which they are made known to us. The manifestive agency is the effort exerted by the person pronouncing the word. While Nyāya holds that this effort of pronouncing the word is the *cause* that produces the word, Mimāmsā thinks that it only manifests to us the ever-existing word. It is easy to see the bearing of this doctrine on the self-valid character of the Vedic injunctions. In fact, Prabhākara also says that the meanings of words can be known only when they occur in a sentence enjoining some duty. If they are not related to an injunction, but simply remind us of discrete meanings, it is merely a case of remembrance (which, according to Mimāmsā, is not valid cognition). It is on this ground that the Mimāmsakas consider the Vedas as eternal, since the words of which they are composed are eternal (*Note:* For a more detailed treatment of the Mimāmsā treatment of the "word," see the section on Jaimini's *Mimāmsā-Sutra*).

Thus, as far as *sabda-pramāna* (the word as source of knowledge) is concerned, Prabhākara (like Jaimini and Sabara before him) accepts the earliest Indian view of *sabda* as *pramāna,* equating it with the Veda. While the ancient Indians did not ignore the importance of ordinary *sabda* as a means of acquiring knowledge, they thought of it as something primarily related to tradition and ancient belief. As Hiriyanna writes: "The reason for including *sabda* in this sense under *pramānas* will become clear when we remember the vastness of the material of tradition that had accumulated by the time the *pramānas* came to be formally enunciated.... It also indicates the reverence with which the authority of tradition was regarded then" (*Outlines,* 178–179).

According to Kumārila, a verbal statement may refer to an existent something *(siddha)* or to something that is yet to be accomplished *(sādhya),* i.e., to an implied action. For example, "This sentence is grammatically sound," refers to a fact, while the sentence, "Try to write a grammatically correct sentence," refers to a task or duty. While Kumārila admits the two-fold character of the import of propositions (*siddha* or what is existent/a fact, and *sādhya* or what is yet to be done), he restricts it to *sādhya* when speaking of the Veda. Prabhākara, however, refuses to admit that verbal statements, whether Vedic or not, can ever refer merely to *siddha* or existent things and limits their scope to *sādhya,* in keeping with the pragmatic view he takes of all knowledge (Hiriyanna, *Outlines,* 318). All utterance, according to him, should point to an action as its ultimate meaning. Both Prabhākara and Kumārila maintain, however, that it is action which is the final import of the Veda. Its assertive propositions are fully significant only when they are in syntactic combination with an appropriate injunction or prohibition as indicated in the particular context.

6. **Nonperception/Nonapprehension/Negation** ***(anupalabdhi):*** Kumārila admits nonapprehension or *anupalabdhi* as an independent source of knowledge. It is the perception of the nonexistence of a thing. Prabhākara

rejects this as do the Naiyāyikas. Sabara's *Bhāsya* (commentary) on Jaimini's *Mimāmsā-Sutra,* however, mentions it: "*Abhāva,* 'Negation,' 'Non-apprehension,' stands for the non-existence (non-operation) of the (five) means of cognition . . . it is what brings about the cognition that 'it does not exist,' in regard to things not in contact with the senses" (Radhakrishnan and Moore, 488). While the Naiyāyika admits negation as an independent ontological category, he does not believe in nonapprehension as "an independent means of knowledge to know negation" (Sharma, 223). According to the Naiyāyika, negation is known or apprehended either by perception or by inference "according as the correlate *(pratiyogi)* of negation is a subject of perception or of inference": "The same sense-organ which perceives any object perceives its non-existence also" (Sharma, 223). Prabhākara, far from accepting nonapprehension as an independent *pramāna,* refuses to accept negation itself as an independent category.

Kumārila argues that the nonexistence of a thing (e.g., "There is no jar in this room.") cannot be perceived by the senses, for there is nothing with which the senses come into contact while perceiving the nonexistence of something. Those who try to explain this nonperception as a case of inference *(anumāna)*—like the Naiyāyikas—argue that wherever there is the existence of a visible object there is the vision of it by the perceiver and when there is no vision of a visible object (provided all the conditions of apprehension are satisfied), there is no existence of it also. But, as Dasgupta points out, such an inference presupposes *the perception of want of vision and want of existence.* But, Dasgupta asks, how these nonperceptions are to be accounted, that is, how can the perception of want of existence or want of vision be comprehended? It is for this reason that we have to admit a separate mode of *pramāna.* In the jar example, for instance, we perceive the vacant space and immediately think of the absent jar. Thus nonapprehension is a means of knowledge or *pramāna* "with reference to the object negated" (Radhakrishnan, 394). According to Kumārila, *abhāva* (literally, lack of or absence) is a positive object of knowledge; what we call emptiness is the locus unoccupied by any object (Kumārila's *Sloka-vārttika*). Thus the word *anupalabdhi* means "absence of apprehension" or the absence of knowledge as derived through any of the five foregoing *pramānas.* We may look at Hiriyanna's explanation: "[A]s knowledge got through any of the *pramānas* points to the existence *(bhāva)* of objects, the absence of such knowledge indicates, other conditions remaining the same, their non-existence *(abhāva).* Only it should be remembered that the absence, to serve as the index of non-existence, must be aided by the mental presentation of the relevant object" (*Outlines,* 321–322; emphasis added).

All things exist in places either in a positive *(sadrupa)* or in a negative *(asadrupa)* relation; in the former case they come within the scope of the senses, but in the latter case the perception of the negative existence can only be had by "a separate mode of the movement of the mind," namely, *anupalabdhi* or nonapprehension. Prabhākara, however, does not accept it as a separate *pramāna,* since, according to him, the cognition of nonexistence is inferred from "the non-perception of something that would have been perceived if it were present" (Radhakrishnan, 394); in other words, the nonperception of a visible object in a place is only "the perception of the empty space" (Dasgupta, 398). Dasgupta, who appears to be on Kumārila's side, systematically refutes Prabhākara's basic notion of the empty space and defends the notion of negation or the negatively qualified nature of the empty space. We quote him at some length:

> If it is necessary that for the perception of the non-existence of the jug there should be absolutely empty space before us, then if the place space is occupied by a stone we ought not to perceive the non-existence of the jug, inasmuch as the place is not absolutely empty. If empty space is defined as that which is not associated with the jug, then the category of negation is practically admitted as a separate entity. If the perception of empty space is defined as the perception of space at the moment which we associated with a want of knowledge about the jug, then also want of knowledge as a separate entity has to be accepted ... Whatever attempt may be made to explain the notion of negation by any positive conception, it will at best be an attempt to shift negation from the objective field to knowledge ... to substitute for the place of the external absence of a thing an associated want of knowledge about the thing (in spite of its being a visible object) and this naturally ends in failure, for negation as a separate category has to be admitted either in the field of knowledge or in the external world [Dasgupta, 398].

Further, the perception of the ground cannot by itself generate the notion of the nonexistence of the jug, since even where there is a jug our perception does not *exclude* the ground on which the jug exists. The clause, "only the ground is perceived," would be meaningless unless the things whose presence is excluded were not indicated as negative conditions qualifying the perception of the ground; this would imply that we had already the notion of negation in us, which appeared to us of itself in a manner unaccountable by other means of proof. Hence, the necessity of a means of knowledge by which the absence or lack of a sensible object – the negation of a thing – can be grasped. This special means of knowledge or *pramāna* is *anupalabdhi* or nonapprehension.

The Word (Sabda): *A Survey of* Mimāmsā-Sutra

Jaimini, the author of *Mimāmsā-Sutra,* accepts the Word or *Sabda* alone as the only means of knowledge, for, according to him, all the other means of knowledge are not infallible when it comes to dealing with the invisible effects of ritual. To support his position, Jaimini offers five propositions: 1) Every Word or *Sabda* has an inherent power to convey its meaning which is eternal; 2) The knowledge derived from the Word is called instruction or teaching *(Upadesa);* 3) The Word alone is the infallible guide in the realm of the invisible; 4) In the opinion of Bādarāyana, the word is authoritative; and 5) The Word does not depend upon any other for its meaning, being in itself self-sufficient. Before we proceed further, it should be pointed out that when Jaimini speaks of the Word, he means the Vedic Word only.

Jaimini refutes several objections raised against the eternal character of the Word:

(1) Jaimini's fictive objector contends that the Word, being a product of verbal utterance, cannot be eternal. "Word is a product (non-eternal), because it is seen to follow (after effort)." Sabara explains the objection *(purvapaksha)* in the *bhāsya* which follows it: ". . . finding that there is an invariable concomitance (between the appearance of the word and human effort, the word appearing only when there is human effort) we infer that the word 'is produced' by the effort" (See Radhakrishnan and Moore, *Sourcebook,* 488, 489; all subsequent citations to Jaimini's *Sutra* and Sabara's accompanying *Bhāsya* [commentary] are to this edition). Jaimini asserts that only its pronunciation or oralization is the product of effort, the Word itself must have existed already, otherwise it could not have been pronounced or oralized. Sabara writes: "The word is *manifested* (not *produced*) by human effort; that is to say, if, before being pronounced, the word was not manifest, it becomes manifested by the effort (of pronouncing). Thus . . . the fact of word being "seen after effort" is equally compatible with both views [i.e., the view that the word is self-existent and eternal, and the view that it is "visually" manifested in speech]" (*Sourcebook,* 489).

(2) The objector contends that the Word does not persist, that it disappears soon after it is pronounced, and hence it is not eternal. Jaimini points out that it is the sound alone which disappears; the Word still remains "as does the drum after the sound is produced." Jaimini writes: "What happens (When the word ceases to be heard) is that there is no perception of the extant word on account of the non-reaching of the object (by the manifesting agency)" (*Sourcebook,* 489).

(3) The objector contends that since the term "to make" is used in connection with the Word, it cannot be eternal. Jaimini explains that the verb "make" has reference only to the sound which manifests the Word, which existed previously and the pronunciation or oralization only made it audible. Jaimini writes: "The term ['to make'] refers to the using [of the word in utterance]." Sabara comments: "If it is beyond doubt that word is eternal, then the meaning of these expressions would be 'make *use* of the word'" (*Sourcebook,* 489).

(4) The objector contends, that since the Word is heard simultaneously by several people standing at an equal distance, there must be more than one sound, and therefore the Word is not eternal. Jaimini writes: ". . . because there is simultaneity (of the perception of the word) in diverse places." He answers the doubt thus: "The simultaneity is as in the case of the sun." Sabara comments: "Look at the sun. . . . Being only one he is seen as if occupying several places" (*Sourcebook,* 489). There is only one sound (although it is heard by many) even as there is only one sun (although it is seen by many).

(5) The objector contends the Word undergoes forms and modifications" *(Mimāmsā-Sutra)*. Sabara explains the objector's contention: "Whatever is liable to modification must be non-eternal." Jaimini answers that changes of letters are not modifications of the Word, but new words; the

original Word still exists. "It is a different letter not a modification" (Jaimini, *Mimāmsā-Sutra, Sourcebook,* 489).

(6) The objector argues, when several people utter a sound, there is an increase in volume, and hence it is not eternal. Jaimini's text reads: "Further, there is an augmentation for the word (sound), due to the multiplicity of its producers (speakers)." Sabara explains the objection: "If the word were only *manifested* (and not *produced,* by the utterance), then the sound heard would always be the same, whether it were uttered by many or fewer persons. From this we conclude that some portion of the word is *produced* by each of the speakers." Jaimini answers that the Word never increases (in volume); it is only the sound which manifests the Word which increases. To quote Jaimini: "The 'augmentation' spoken of is the augmentation of the noise (not of the word)" (*Sourcebook,* 489, 490).

After having countered each of his fictive objector's argument against the eternality of the Word, Jaimini makes the following conclusive statement: "In fact (the word) must be eternal; as (its) utterance is for the purpose of another." That is, as Sabara explains, "for the purpose of making known the meaning to 'another.' If the word ceased to exist as soon as uttered, then no one could speak of (make known) anything to others; and in that case the word could not be uttered for the purpose of another." Jaimini writes of several other possible objections, one of which is of special importance. One might contend, the word may be the product of air, which, through certain conjunctions and disjunctions, becomes the word. To this Jaimini's answer is that "there is no idea of the connection (of the word, with any material cause)." Sabara explains Jaimini's defense:

> It cannot be so [the word being the product of air]; if the word were the product of air, then it could only be air in a particular shape. As a matter of fact, however, we do not recognise any particle of air in the consitution of the word.... If the word were a product of air, then we could perceive it with our tactile organ (as we perceive air); and yet we do not feel by touch any air-particles in the word. Hence word cannot be a product of air. Therefore it must be eternal [*Sourcebook,* 490].

Further, the word is not "dependent," in the sense "we do not perceive any material cause, on the destruction whereof the word itself would be regarded as ceasing to exist" (Sabara's *Bhaāsya,* in *Sourcebook,* 490). Having established the eternal character of the Word *(Sabda),* Jaimini proceeds to show how the words in the Vedic sentences have a meaning just as they have in ordinary, non-Vedic language. He then proceeds to defend the authorlessness of the Veda.

The Mimāmsakas regard the Vedas as self-revealed *(apurusheya).* If they had been written by any person(s)—like the *Rāmāyana,* which was written by Vālmiki, and the *Mahābhārata,* which was written by Vyāsa—their authors would have been remembered by us. The Vedic teachers and disciples have maintained a continuous chain of the study of the Vedas from time immemorial, but none of them ever heard of an author of the Vedas. As Jaimini writes, "there is an unbroken continuity of the [Vedic] text." Sabara explains Jaimini's cryptic clause: "We must not think that someone has connected the Vedic words with their meanings in order to give currency to the Vedic rites and ceremonies. This relation is self-evident. Had there been any man who connected the Vedic words with their meanings and introduced the Vedic rites, then at the time of performing such rites the performer must have remembered the author. This remembrance of the connection between the author and the user of the text is absolutely essential to the fulfillment of the aim and object of such performance.

For instance, Panini [the well-known Indian grammarian] coined the word *vrddhi* for certain vowel modifications. If we remember him when we hear this word, then only we know that the word *vrddhi* denotes such and such, and can use it according to the method invented by him and obtain the appropriate result. But when we do not remember the word as a definition of his, we do not ascribe to it any such meaning, nor use it according to his rules, nor get the result thus obtainable.... It follows therefore that unless a sect becomes extinct we always remember the author and user of the technical terms current in the usages of that sect. This is the general rule. "It is now clear that had the Vedas been created by any man and the rites depending on them been first performed by him, then we should always have remembered the author.... We do not know of any author or originator of the Vedic rites and ceremonies; yet we have been performing them continually from the beginning. Hence it cannot be established by any direct proof that someone conceived the relationship between the Vedic words and their meaning and introduced the Vedic rites of his own free will, and thus was the creator of the Vedas" (Sabara's *Bhāsya,* cited in Tarkabhushan, 152–153).

Kumārila explains Sabara's passage thus: "The study of the Vedas has always been dependent on previous study; for this study is carried on through words, as the present system of Vedic study will show" (Kumārila's *Sloka-vārttika,* cited in Tarkabhushan, 153). The Mimāmsaka rejected the Naiyāyika's view of the divine origin of the Veda as declared in the scriptures. The Naiyāyika quoted the following line from the *Bhagvad-Gitā* in support of his view: "Then the Vedas came out of His mouth. Thus in the beginning of each cycle [it is believed that each such cycle coincides with *one* of Brahmā's days, a mundane period of 2,160,000,000 years: see the chapter on "Hindu Gods and Goddesses] different Vedas are composed."/ "I have composed the Vedānta and I am the knower of the Vedas." The Mimāmsaka argument against this view is well summarized by Radhakrishnan: "God, who is incorporeal, has no organs of speech, and cannot therefore utter the words of the Veda. If it is said that he assumes a human form for the purpose of revelation, then he will be the subject to all the limitations of material existence, and his utterance will not carry any authority" (Radhakrishnan, 392).

It is contended that the Vedas are human compositions, since the names of their authors – the *rishis* or seers – are prefixed to them. The Mimāmsaka answers that the *rishis* only made a special study of them in order that they may teach them to others; they only apprehend the truths and transmit them. Jaimini writes: "The name [of any *rishi* or other appended to the

Vedic texts] is due to [their] expounding [of the relevant texts]." Sabara chooses the example of the prefix "Kathaka" in explaining Jaimini's words: "No such presumption (of the author) is justifiable; as people might call a text by the name of one who is not the author at all; it is possible that all that Katha and other persons (whose names are applied to certain Vedic texts) have done is such superior *expounding* of the text as has not been done by any one else; and there are people who call texts by the names of such exceptional expounders" (*Sourcebook,* 491).

Mimāmsā Ritualism

Hiriyanna writes about the "admixture of the rational with the dogmatic" which characterizes both the theoretical and practical teachings of the Mimāmsā (*Outlines,* 326). We have noticed this in the Mimāmsaka's defense of the self-validity of the Veda and, to support this defense, his enthusiastic attempt to establish the self-validity of all knowledge. Dasgupta explains the Mimāmsaka's ultimate purpose behind all this: "This would secure for the Veda the advantage that as soon as its orders or injunctions were communicated to us they would appear to us as valid knowledge, and there being nothing to contradict them later on there would be nothing in the world which could render the Vedic injunctions invalid" (Dasgupta, 403–404). True to his end, the Mimāmsaka accepted the other means of cognition *(pramānas)* only to vindicate the fact of their inability to show to us how *dharma* (duty) could be acquired, for it was not "an existing thing" which could be perceived by those other means of knowledge, but a thing which could only be produced and acquired by acting according to the Vedic injunctions.

The Mimāmsaka also knew that it was imperative to have a knowledge of the other means of cognition, for without them it would be difficult to "discuss and verify the meanings of debatable Vedic sentences." The Mimāmsaka also rejected the generally-accepted Hindu doctrine of creation and dissolution; its acknowledgement would have endangered the eternality of the Vedas. He did not hesitate to dispense with God. In other words, the Mimāmsaka laid all emphasis on the Veda to the exclusion of everything else, including divinity. So far as common or ordinary morality is concerned, the Mimāmsā adopts a point of view which is severely secular and empirical and explains virtue as a conscious or semi-conscious adjustment of conduct to interest; it judges conduct by a utilitarian standard. However, it refuses such morality the highest place in a man's life and speaks of another sphere of activity whose significance is extra-empirical. True spirituality consists in fixing one's attention on *dharma* or such acts of duty as lead to success in the life beyond. However, the Mimāmsā does not keep the two kinds of morality separate; the two kinds of morality do not involve any shifting of the attention from the present life to the one that is yet to come. For, ceremonial life does not exclude common morality; it is, on the other hand, founded in it. The Mimāmsaka regards ethical purity as a precondition as well as a necessary accompaniment of religious or spiritual life (see Hiriyanna, *Outlines,* 326–327). As the Mimāmsaka says, citing Bādarāyana, "The Vedas cleanse not the unrighteous."

Dharma, however, yields its result mediately and not directly. Hiriyanna finds the reason for this in the fact that ceremonial acts signified by *dharma,* being necessarily "transient, can have no direct causal connection with their result." It is therefore assumed that the acts give rise to some unseen effect or transcendental potency (which Prabhākara calls *apurva* = "never before"). Similar effects, but of an undesirable kind, are produced in the case of *adharma* or those acts which are prohibited, like injury to living beings. These invisible effects, which "mediate between good and bad acts and their respective results of pleasure and pain," abide in the self until they bear fruit, whereafter they cease to exist. This transcendental or unseen potency *(apurva)* may thus be regarded "either as the imperceptible antecedent of the fruit, or as the after-state of the act"; it is the metaphysical link between work and its result. The concept of *apurva* presupposes the Mimāmsakas' refusal to trace the results of actions to God's will, since, according to them, "a uniform cause cannot account for the variety of effects" (see Hiriyanna, *Essentials,* 146–147, and Radhakrishnan, 421).

As Sinari remarks, with the notion of *apurva* the Mimāmsā

> ventured the assumption of a reality, an order which, unlike *adrishta* [the Unseen Force or Power], could be cognized as being different for different persons suiting the nature of their deeds. While, as with the Naiyāyikas and the Vaiseshikas, God could be looked upon as the *modus operandi* of *adrishta,* His existence becomes superfluous in relation to the individually working *apurva* . . . [which] becomes a transcendental potency, a self-contained tribunal, reigning over all conative consciousness and creating the aftermath of their actions [Sinari, 50].

Perhaps Ninian Smart has this in mind when he speaks of the conservatism and paradoxicality of the Mimāmsā doctrines. While their conservatism consists in their emphasis on the complexities of Vedic ritual, their paradoxicality is due to their novel way of treating the Vedic texts. The Vedic hymns were interpreted as injunctions about ritual, but the statements they make about the gods were regarded as secondary in importance; that is, ritual was regarded as efficacious in itself. "Thus Mimāmsā illustrates how a sacrificial religion can become totally detached from the gods to whom the sacrifices were originally addressed" (Smart, 165). However, it would have been easy for the Mimāmsaka to counter Smart's charge of paradoxicality. When the authoritativeness of the Vedas, for instance, is criticized on the ground that they contain references to names, the Mimāmsaka points out that the hymns deal with the eternal phenomena of nature and as such the names occurring in them have universal applicability and do not have any historical or theistic reference. Thus "Visvāmitra" ("world-friend") means the all-friendly and not any theistic or historical character.

To return to our main line of discussion, while Prabhākara conceives *apurva* as the result of sacrificial and such other ceremonial acts, abiding in the self—"a subjective feature to be distinguished from the objective act leading to it" (Hiriyanna, *Outlines,* 327)—Kumārila considers these forms of activity as themselves *dharma* and *adharma,* the former representing those acts which are obligatory and the latter standing for those acts which are prohibited. It is to know the difference between what is prescribed and what is prohibited that we have seek the aid of the Veda. Though there is nothing "transcendental about the acts themselves described as *dharma* and *adharma,* the fact of their being the means of a supernatural good is not humanly ascertainable"; they are known through "revelation and revelation alone" (Hiriyanna, *Outlines,* 328). However, the Veda cannot—and does not—generate the desire to perform any particular kind of act; its purpose is only to "communicate to a man a knowledge, otherwise attainable, of certain means to certain ends" (Hiriyanna, *Essentials,* 147). Prabhākara, on the other hand, contends that to appeal to a desirable result in order to make *dharma* acceptable, is to "divorce it from all that it stands for," and he therefore affirms that the ideal of *dharma* should be pursued for its own sake. Hiriyanna comments: "Here we have the true imperative of obligation *(niyoga);* and it is this 'ought,' and not the ceremonial act that is meant by *dharma.* That is to say, *dharma* is an intrinsic value in this school [the school of the Prabhākaras] and not merely an instrumental one—a good in itself, and not what leads to it as in the other [the school of the Kumārilas, or the Bhatta school as it is generally called—from Kumārila's surname 'Bhatta']" (*Essentials,* 148).

Both the schools of Mimāmsā assume the individual's freedom to choose or not to choose any particular form of activity, however, for otherwise the individual cannot be held responsible for his acts. There are several kinds of act *(karma)* mentioned in the Veda: to gain salvation, one has to observe *nitya-karmas* and *naimittika-karmas* (daily and occasional acts), and these are obligatory; to gain special ends, one may perform *kāmya-karmas* (optional acts), but he may not if he does not care for these ends; and, finally, there are the *nishiddha-karmas* (forbidden acts), whose avoidance saves one from the punishments of hell. Of these, only the first three are positive acts, while the last, *nishiddha,* refers only to the negative *avoidance* of certain acts. Further, of the three positive acts, only the daily or regular and the occasional acts *(nitya-karmas* and *naimittika-karmas)* are given the status of injunctions by Prabhākara, whereas Kumārila considers all the three kinds as injuctive.

As we said earlier, the Mimāmsā refers basically to an interpretation of the Vedic texts and to the evolution of a methodology for such interpretation. For this purpose, the contents of the Vedas are classified under five broad divisions. They are: 1) *Vidhi* (injunctions), 2) *Mantra* (hymns), 3) *Nāmadheya* (names), 4) *Nishedha* (prohibitions), and 5) *Arthavāda* (explanatory passages). These are further divided as follows (see Bernard, 106–112):

1. *Vidhi,* which is a precept or order and is obligatory, is of four kinds: *Utpatti-vidhi, Viniyoga-vidhi, Prayoga-vidhi,* and *Adhikāra-vidhi.* We consider each of these separately.
    - i) *Utpatti-vidhi* refers to a command involving a particular object, thereby creating a desire for that object.

ii) *Viniyoga-vidhi* lays down and explains the details of a sacrifice. The Vedic texts speak of six accompaniments for the interpretation of the sacrificial procedure, as well as of two kinds of actions relating to any sacrifice. The "six accompaniments" are: *Sruti* (or, the primary sense of a word or collection of words, which is independent of any other word or collection of words for its meaning); *Linga* (or, the secondary sense of a word inferred from another word or collection of words); *Vākya* (or, the meaning of a word or collection of words as indicated by the sentence in which it is used); *Prakarana* (or, the meaning of a clause or sentence in the context in which it appears); *Sthāna* (or, the meaning in relation to the word-order or location in the text); and *Samākhyā* (or, the necessity to split compound words up into their component parts in order to ascertain the meaning of the former).

The "two kinds of actions" enjoined by *Viniyoga-vidhi* are: Principal, or that which produces the transcendental fruit *(apurva),* the invisible result to mature in another life; and, Subordinate, or that which leads up to the completion of the "principal" action. The "subordinate" actions *(Anga)* are of two kinds: *Siddharupa,* which refers to an accomplished thing, consisting of class, material number, and the like, and having a visible effect; and, *Kriyā-rupa* or the action in itself. *Kriyārupa* is further divided into *Pradhāna-karma* or the primary action, and *Guna-karma* or secondary action, each of which is subdivided into *Sannipatyopakāraka* (actions enjoined with respect to the substance and produce visible and invisible results), and *Ārādupakāraka* (actions which are enjoined with any reference to any substance or divinity, and which are the essence of sacrifice and lead directly to the ultimate result).

iii) *Prayoga-vidhi* lays down the order of performance of the subsidiary or minor parts. The order or succession *(krama)* is of six kinds: *Sruti-krama* or the order determined by a text; *Artha-krama* or the order determined by the object; *Pātha-krama* or when the order of the execution of things is governed by their order in the text; *Sthāna-krama* or the transposition of a thing from its proper place because of sequential change; *Mukhya-krama* or the sequence of the subsidiaries of the subordinate parts according to the order in the principle; and, *Pravritti-krama* or the order of a procedure which, once begun, will apply to others as well.

iv) *Adhikāra-vidhi* refers to an injunction which assigns certain rights to the person following it.

2. *Mantra* is a text which helps one to remember—and hence, to follow—the procedure of a sacrifice and is in the form of hymns. It is of three kinds: *Apurva,* or when a text lays down a new injunction for the attainment of an object which cannot be known by any other means; *Niyama* or a restrictive rule as to one particular mode of doing a thing which the text lays down when the same thing could be done in alternative ways; and, *Parisamkhyā* or an implied prohibition laid down by a text.
3. *Nāmadheya* is a proper noun which is used in defining the matter enjoined by it, such as a conventional name given to a particular sacrifice, the description of which is given elsewhere in a separate treatise.
4. *Nishedha* or prohibition is the opposite of *Vidhi.* It is a negative precept which prevents a person from doing a thing which is harmful to him. It is of two kinds: *Paryudāsa,* or a negative precept that applies only to a person who is undertaking to perform a sacrifice; and, *Pratishedha,* or a negative precept of general applicability.
5. *Arthavāda* are passages in praise or blame of a *Vidhi* or *Nishedha,* and hence, are explanatory in character. *Arthavāda* includes the following three: *Gunavāda* or a statement made by the text that is contradictory to the existing state of affairs and means of proof; *Anuvāda* or a statement made by the text which is in keeping with the existing state of facts; and, *Bhutārthavāda* or a statement made by the text which is neither against the existing state of facts nor in conformity with it, i.e., a neutral statement.

As we have seen, the Mimāmsaka school gives an elaborate analysis of the origin of the religious motive or the impulse to pious conduct and a minute consideration of the effects—both immediate and mediate—of the *Vidhis* or the Vedic injunctions. These *vidhis,* properly interpreted and understood, are the main source of *dharma* or duty. It should be remembered that anything found in the Vedas which cannot be connected with the *vidhis* or injunctive orders as forming part of them is to be regarded as "untrustworthy or at best inexpressive" (Dasgupta, 405). It is in this context that we have to view Jaimini's answers to the nine objections raised against the Vedic *mantras.* We give below a few of them (for a fuller account, see Bernard, 109–111).

1. *Objection:* Vedic *mantras* do not convey any meaning because they stand in need of other passages to explain or support them.
   Answer: All Vedic words have a significance just as these words do in ordinary language.
2. *Objection:* Vedic *mantras* are useless because they depend upon a complicated system of grammar.
   Answer: Vedic sentences have a subject, a predicate and an object, and these are governed by the same rules of grammar as non-Vedic sentences.

3. *Objection:* Vedic *mantras* are useless because they have many self-contradictory passages.
   Answer: These so-called "self-contradictory passages" are descriptive of subordinate qualities.
4. *Objection:* Vedic *mantras* are useless because there are many *mantras* whose meaning cannot be known.
   Answer: Every *mantra* has a meaning, whose ignorance is due to our indolence and our careless reading of the *mantras.*
5. *Objection:* Vedic *mantras* are useless because they describe what does not exist, viz., "It has four horns, three feet, two heads, seven hands; the bull, being tied threefold, cries: 'The great god entered amongst the mortals'."
   Answer: Such descriptions are only figurative. In the example, the sacrifice is compared with a bull by reason of its producing the desired effect; it has four horns in the form of four kinds of priests; its three feet are the three libations (performed three times a day); the sacrificer and his wife are the two heads; the seven hands are the seven desires *(chhandas).* Being tied up by the three Vedas, viz, the *Rig-Veda, Yajur-Veda,* and *Sāma-Veda,* it resounds with the chanting by the priests: this great god in the form of the sacrifice is amidst the mortals.
6. *Objection:* Vedic *mantras* are useless because they are addressed to inanimate objects as if they possessed life.
   Answer: Such address is only to extol the sacrifice and induce the adherent to practice it.

The Mimāmsakas recognize two kinds of energy in injunctions, namely, verbal and actual. Verbal energy is "the special function which conduces to a man's impulse," inhering in an inspirer like the preceptor; it is a wish or an intention taking the quasi-imperative form, "Let him be induced to do it," and therefore is expressed as "an incitement, inducement, or mandate." In the context of the authorless and impersonal origin of the Vedas, the injunction cannot be the intention of any identifiable person and hence is construed as "an operation conducive to a person's inclination which resides in the imperative in the Vedic text" (Tarkabhushan, 161). It is manifested in an attitude such as indicated by the sentence: "I am urged by the Vedic imperative." It is also called *bhāvanā* since it "conduces to the production or being *(bhāvanā)* of the human impulse, and, as inhering in the Vedic words, it is called verbal." Thus, the verbal energy is "a peculiar transcendental function which lodges in the imperative in an injunction sentence" (Tarkabhushan, 161). Some Mimāmsakas, like Mandana Misra, hold that verbal energy *(sābdi-bhāvanā)* is a special property which resides in the intended import of the verb and is of the nature of a means or instrument of the desired result. This interpretation, however, is not accepted by all.

Actual energy refers to the operation pertaining to the performer of sacrifices and tending to the production of the result. The feature which is common to both the kinds of energy is a special function of incitement "which conduces to the effecting of that which is to be" and which is signified by the predicative portion. Propositions like "shall sacrifice," "shall donate," and "shall offer oblation," imply the result, the operation leading to it, and the exertion necessary for the purpose. Of these, the result and the relevant operation are connoted by the verb, while the effort is signified by the predicative mood. Some Mimāmsakas (like Somesvara) hold that it denotes the special effort itself. This special effort—the actual energy—which produces the result directly, through the "sense of the verb," is considered by several Mimāmsakas as the major part of the significance of predication. The conclusion of the Mimāmsakas is that "this exertion or operation causes performance of the sacrifice, and through that the invisible potency *[apurva]*, and through that the result" (Tarkabhushan, 162).

To avoid the possibility of negligence or inattention in ritualistic work, the Mimāmsakas give more importance to ordained acts—the sacrifices *(yajña)*, the offering of oblations in the consecrated fire *(homa)*, and charity *(dāna)*—than to the deities to whom the sacrifices and oblations are offered. Tarkabhushan writes: "The deities occupy a secondary place in this system; nay, it even denies their existence as something separate from the *mantras*" (Tarkabhushan, 162). Dasgupta writes "Mimāmsā does not admit the existence of any God as the creator and destroyer of the universe" (Dasgupta, 402). Sinari calls Kumārila's *Sloka-vārttika* "his notably atheistic treatise," in which the latter "argues against the very necessity of the idea of God for the apportioning of *dharma* or merit and *adharma* or demerit to the deserving ones" (Sinari, 48). Ninian Smart writes of how the Mimāmsā, "uniquely among schools of Indian philosophy," denied belief in the "pulsating" universe: "It did not teach a theory of alternating periods of destruction and re-creation in the everlasting history of the cosmos, since this theory would imply that the Veda itself would be destroyed from time to time. The school, then, is of some interest in the history of mankind's religious experience, since it expresses in the clearest and starkest form the effect of basing everything on the ritual dimension of religion" (Smart, 165).

Radhakrishnan refers to Shastri's attempt to reconcile the Mimāmsā and the Vedānta views of God in the book *Introduction to Purva Mimamsa.* Shastri argues that while Jaimini repudiates the idea of God as the distributor of rewards, he does not deny the existence of God as the creator of the world. While the other systems hold that God is the creator of the world *as well as* the apportioner of the fruits, Jaimini contends against the latter view. Jaimini felt that if God had the sole responsibility for the inequalities of the world, he could not be free from the charge of partiality and cruelty, and for this reason traced the varying fortunes of individuals to their past conduct. For Shastri, the explanation is not convincing, for things should first exist before they could produce happiness or misery. If, on the other hand, *apurva* (the transcendental potency) is the apportioner of all happiness and misery, then it must also be the creator of things. If God is necessary for creation, then *apurva* must be simply "the principle of *karma* which God takes into account in the creation of the world." Therefore, "directly or indirectly, God becomes the creator as well as the apportioner of the fruits" (Shastri, cited in Radhakrishnan, 427; emphasis added).

Radhakrishnan writes of how the later Mimāmsakas slowly smuggled in God to fill the theistic lacuna in the Purva Mimāmsa. These later Mimāmsakas felt the truth of the criticism that "the unconscious principle of *apurva* cannot achieve the harmonious results attributed to it" and therefore introduced the divine principle. But, as Radhakrishnan remarks, "this superintending Lord need not be regarded as bound by the law of karma, for no one is bound by his own nature. The law of karma [only] expresses the constancy of God." Thus, when Kumārila says that both *karma* (work/action) and *upāsanā* (worship/meditation) are necessary for effecting liberation, he is implicitly positing God and paving the way for Advaitā Vedānta (*Advaita* = non-dual). His view of the self "as potential consciousness, his emphasis that action is not an end in itself but only a means to obtain liberation, his acceptance of the view that knowledge of the self born of true meditative act is the immediate cause of liberation, and his implicit theism—all go to make him a veritable link between Prabhākara and Shankara, between the Purva and the Uttara Mimāmsās" (Sharma, 327). Later Mimāmsakas, like Apadeva and Laugakshi Bhāskara, maintain that only when the sacrifice is performed in honor of the supreme Lord, it will lead to the highest good or, in Kumārila's words, "blissful liberation." Other later exponents of the system (like Khandadeva and Gaga Bhatta) are of the opinion that Purva Mimāmsa has nothing new to add to what has been so extensively discussed (i.e., about God and salvation) in the Uttara Mimāmsa or Vedānta. Hence, according to them, there is no reason to conclude that Jaimini, Sabara, and Kumārila did not believe in the existence of God or salvation.

Metaphysics

The Mimāmsaka has been called a pluralistic realist, who believes in the reality of the external world and of the individual souls. There are innumerable elemental atoms as well as eternal and infinite substances; similarly, there are as many individual souls as there are living bodies, as well as the bodiless, liberated souls. And, as we have already seen, the Mimāmsā believes in the law of *karma,* in the Unseen Power (which it calls *apurva*), in heaven and hell, in liberation, and in the ultimate authority of the eternal Veda. Prabhākara speaks of seven categories: substance *(dravya),* quality *(guna),* action *(karma),* generality *(sāmānya),* inherence *(paratantratā),* force *(shakti),* and similarity *(sādrishya).* Of these, the first five are similar to the Vaiseshika categories (though inherence here is called *paratantratā* and not, as in Vaiseshika, *samavāya*) while the last two are added. Prabhākara thus rejects the category of negation. Kumārila rejects particularity and inherence (equating the former with the quality of distinctness and the latter with identity-in-difference or *tādātmya* or *bhedābheda*) and recognizes four positive categories—substance, action, quality and generality—as well as the fifth category of negation which, according to him, is of four kinds—prior, posterior, mutual and absolute. Kumārila rejects force and similarity as independent categories and brings them under the single category of substance. Further, he accepts the nine substances of the Vaiseshika (earth, water, fire, air, space, time, ether, mind and soul) and adds two more, namely, darkness and sound (which two are of course rejected by Prabhākara). Thus, the Mimāmsā categories and substances are more or less the same as those in the Vaiseshika-Nyāya.

The Mimāmsaka's acceptance of the existence of soul was necessarily linked to his emphasis on sacrificial activity, for without it, as Dasgupta asks, "who would perform the Vedic commandments, and what would be the meaning of those Vedic texts which speak of men as performing sacrifices and going to Heaven thereby?" Both Prabhākara and Kumārila admit the soul as something entirely distinct from the body, the senses, the mind, and the understanding; and they regard it as an eternal *(nitya),* infinite *(vyā-paka),* omnipresent *(sarvagata),* ubiquitous *(vibhu)* substance which is the substratum *(āshraya)* of consciousness and which is the real knower *(jñātā),* enjoyer *(bhoktā)* and agent *(kartā).* The body is merely the vehicle of enjoyment *(bhogāyatana),* the senses the instruments of enjoyment (bhogasādhana), and the internal feelings and external things the objects of enjoyment *(bhogyavishaya).* Dasgupta answers the objection that is sometimes raised as to the soul as an agent: "If the soul is omnipresent, how can it be an agent or mover?" For the Mimāmsaka, Dasgupta argues, movement does not mean "atomic motion," but the "energy which moves the atoms" and which is possessed by the omnipresent soul: the soul causes the movement of the body by imparting its energy to the latter (Dasgupta, 400).

The Mimāmsakas do not regard consciousness as the essence of the self. Prabhākara agrees with the Vaiseshika-Nyāya when he views the self as essentially unconscious and regards consciousness as "only an accidental quality which may or may not be possessed by the soul-substance" (Sharma, 234). According to him, cognitions, feelings and volitions are the properties of the self and arise due to merit and demerit, so that in its liberated state – a result of the exhaustion of merit and demerit – the self remains as "a pure substance divested of all its qualities including consciousness and bliss" (Sharma, 234). Kumārila, however, views consciousness as a modal change *(parināma)* in the self, as a process of the self by which the self cognizes the objects. Like the Jainas, Kumārila regards the self as both changing and changeless: as substance, it is changeless, but as modes, it changes and becomes diverse, which is to say, while the modes appear and disappear, the substance remains permanent. Also, Kumārila differs from Prabhākara and the Vaiseshika-Nyāya in maintaining that the self is "conscious-unconscious" *(jadabodhātmaka* or *chidāchidrupa)* and *not* wholly unconscious. As substance, the self is unconcious; but as modes, the self, characterized by the potential consciousness, is eminently conscious. Although Kumārila, like Prabhākara and the Vaiseshika-Nyāya, believes that in liberation *(moksha)* the self remains a "pure substance divested of all qualities and modes including consciousness and bliss," he adds that the self still continues to be characterized by potential consciousness.

How the self is cognized? Prabhākara and Kumārila have different answers to this question. Prabhākara, who advocates *triputi-pratyaksha-*

vāda – the theory of simultaneous revelation of the knower, the known, and the knowledge – holds that the self as knower is never known apart from the object known, nor is the object ever known without the knower "entering into the cognition as a necessary factor." Both the self as the knower-subject and the object known "shine forth in the self-luminous knowledge" in *triputi-pratyaksha.* Thus it is not the soul but knowledge which is self-luminous and reveals both the self and the object in a single operation. As Dasgupta writes: "Cognition is not soul, but the soul is manifested in cognition as its substratum, and appears in it as the cognitive element 'I' which is inseparable from all cognitions" (Dasgupta, 400). There can be no "direct knowledge of a permanent identical self," which is only known "indirectly from the fact of the recognition of permanent objects of thought"; that is, there is nothing like self-consciousness "apart from object-consciousness" (Radhakrishnan, 410). It follows, therefore, that in deep sleep, when no object is cognized, the self also is not cognized. Thus, while Prabhākara believes, like the Nyāya philosopher, that the self is essentially unconscious, he maintains, unlike the Nyāya philosopher, that knowledge is self-luminous.

Kumārila however thinks that the soul *(ātman)* which is distinct from the body cognizes itself by a mental perception *(mānasa-pratyaksha),* and the knowledge of its own nature "shines forth in consciousness as the 'I'." The soul, according to Kumārila, is consciousness as well as the basis of cognition, which is a product of the soul. The self does not reveal itself as the knower but as "an object of a separate intuitive process of the mind" (Dasgupta, 401). Like the Nyāya philosopher and unlike Prabhākara, Kumārila regards self-consciousness as "a later and a higher state of consciousness"; however, unlike the Nyāya philosopher, for whom both consciousness and self are directly revealed through introspection, Kumārila believes that consciousness is only inferred through the cognizedness of the object, though the self is directly revealed as the object of self-consciousness through the notion of "I." Consciousness is not self-luminous and thus cannot reveal either itself or the subject; it can reveal only the object. Consciousness is "a dynamic mode of the self" and its result is seen only in the object which is revealed by it. Hence, the self is known as the object of the I-notion, for the self is of the nature of the "I" and is apprehended "by itself and by nothing else" (Sharma, 235). Pārthasārathi, who seems to support Kumārila's view, says that self-consciousness marks "a higher degree of conscious life than the mere consciousness of the object" *(Sāstradipikā).* "There is a distinction," writes Radhakrishnan, "between direct or primary experience as the apprehension of the object and reflective or secondary experience as the return of the mind on itself" (Radhakrishnan, 412).

As C.D. Sharma remarks, both Prabhākara and Kumārila struggle for the correct view of the self and miss it. Though Prabhākara is right in maintaining that knowledge is self-revealing and that the self as the subject-knower is necessarily involved in every knowledge-situation but can never be known as an object, he is wrong in "confusing pure knowledge with momentary cognitions and in regarding the self as the unconscious substance and consciousness as its accidental quality." Likewise, Kumārila is right in maintaining that consciousness is not an accidental quality of the self and that the latter is only implicitly revealed in all knowledge and that self-consciousness is "higher" than consciousness, but he is wrong in regarding consciousness as only a dynamic mode of the self, in confusing the self with the ego, in denying the self-luminosity of knowledge and making it a thing only to be inferred, in treating the self as the object of the I-notion, and in regarding it as merely the potency of knowledge. Under the influence of the Vaiseshika-Nyāya, according to Sharma, both Prabhākara and Kumārila fail to treat the self as the real subject and stick to the erroneous view that it is essentially a substance. We have to wait for the Vedāntin to restore the self to its status of the transcendental knower, which, as the ultimate subject, is "identical with eternal and foundational consciousness" (see Sharma, 235–236). We turn to Radhakrishnan for an overall criticism of the Purva Mimāmsā as a school of philosophy:

> As a philosophical view of the universe it is strikingly incomplete. It did not concern itself with the problems of ultimate reality and its relation to the world of souls and matter. Its ethics was purely mechanical and its religion unsound.... There is little in such a religion to touch the heart and make it glow. No wonder a reaction occurred in favour of a monotheism ... which gave man a supreme God on whom he could depend and to whom he could surrender himself in sorrow and suffering [Radhakrishnan, 428–429].

Works Cited

Bernard, Theos. *Hindu Philosophy*. 1947; rpt. New Delhi: Motilal Banarsidass, 1985.

Chattopadhyaya, Debiprasad. *Indian Philosophy: A Popular Introduction*. New Delhi: People's Publishing House, 1964.

Dasgupta, S.N. *A History of Indian Philosophy*. (5 vols). Vol. I. Cambridge: Cambridge University Press, 1973.

Garbe, Richard. *The Philosophy of Ancient India*. Chicago: The Open Court Publishing Co., 1899.

Hiriyanna, M. *The Essentials of Indian Philosophy*. 1949, London: George Allen & Unwin; rpt. Bombay: Blackie & Son, 1978.

________. *Outlines of Indian Philosophy*. 1932, London: George Allen & Unwin; rpt. Bombay: Blackie & Son, 1983.

Radhakrishnan, S. *Indian Philosophy*. (2 vols). Vol. II. Muirhead Library of Philosophy. London: George Allen & Unwin, and New York: Humanities Press, 1966.

Radhakrishnan, S., and Moore, Charles A. eds. *A Sourcebook in Indian Philosophy*. Princeton: Princeton University Press, 1957.

Ranade, R.D. *Vedanta: The Culmination of Indian Thought*. Bombay: Bharatiya Vidya Bhavan, 1970.

Sharma, C.D. *A Critical Survey of Indian Philosophy*. New Delhi: Motilal Banarsidass, 1983.

Sinari, Ramakant A. *The Structure of Indian Thought*. 1970; rpt. New Delhi: Oxford University Press, 1984.

Smart, Ninian. *The Religious Experience of Mankind.* 1969, New York: Charles Scribner's; rpt. Glasgow and London: Fontana/Collins, 1982.
Tarkabhushan, Pramathanath. "Purva-Mimāmsā," *The Cultural Heritage of India.* (5 vols). Vol. III. ed. Haridas Bhattacharyya. Calcutta: The Ramakrishna Mission Institute of Culture, 1969.
Winternitz, M. *History of Indian Literature.* trns. Subhadra Jha. (3 vols). Vol. III. New Delhi: Motilal Banarsidass, 1985.

Suggested Further Reading

Edgerton, Franklin. trans. *The Mimāmsā Nyāya Prakāsa of Apadeva: A Treatise on the Mimāmsā System by Apadeva.* New Haven: Yale University Press, 1929.
Jha, Ganganath. *Prabhākara School of Purva Mimāmsā.* Benaras: Benaras Hindu University, 1918.
________. *Purva Mimāmsā in Its Sources: With a Critical Bibliography by Umesha Mishra.* Benaras: Benaras Hindu University, 1942.
________. trans. *Sloka-vārttika.* Calcutta: The Asiatic Society of Bengal, 1907.
________. trans. *The Purva Mimāmsā Sutras of Jaimini.* Sacred Books of the Hindus. Vol. X. Allahabad: The Panini Office, 1916.
Keith, A.B. *The Karma Mimāmsā.* London: Oxford University Press, and Calcutta: Association Press, 1921.
Sandal, Pandit Mohan Lal. trans. *The Mimāmsā Sutras of Jaimini.* Sacred Books of the Hindus. Vol. 27. Allahabad: The Panini Office, 1923.
Shastri, Pasupatinath. *Introduction to the Purva Mimāmsā.* Calcutta: A.N. Bhattacharya, 1923.
Sirkar, Kisarilala. *The Mimāmsā Rules of Interpretation: As Applied to Hindu Law.* Calcutta: University of Calcutta Press, 1909.
Thadani, N.V. *The Mimāmsā: The Sect of the Sacred Doctrines of the Hindus.* Delhi: The Bharati Research Institute, 1952.

8

Vedānta (Uttara-Mimāmsā)

Vedānta has long been considered "the most influential of the philosophical systems" (Sen, 82). Radhakrishnan indicates the reason for the close attention it obviously deserves: "In one or other of its forms the Vedānta determines the world view of the Hindu thinkers of the present time" (Radhakrishnan, 431). The Vedānta philosophy is "closely bound up with the religion of India" (Radhakrishnan and Moore, *Sourcebook,* 506). As we have seen (see the preceding chapter), the term "Vedānta" literally means "the end of the Veda," or the philosophical views set forth in the closing portions of the Vedas, which of course are the Upanishads. The Upanishadic views constitute the final aim, the ultimate import, or the essence of the Vedas. All the schools of Vedānta are thus based upon the Upanishads. To put it differently, Vedānta is the culmination of the philosophy of the Upanishads. The Upanishads, however, are far from giving us a systematic, consistent and definite philosophy; they are "but a series of glances at truth from various points of view" (Radhakrishnan, 431). It is this indefiniteness and diffuseness in the teaching of the Upanishads which ultimately gave rise to the philosophy of Vedānta, which is a systematic exposition of Upanishadic teachings. Although the term "Vedānta" occurs in the Upanishads (where it means no more than "the final portion of the Vedas"), Vedānta as we understand it today includes not merely the teaching of the Upanishads or even some of the earlier portions of the Veda, but also those of the *Bhagvadgitā* (commonly known as *Gitā*) and the *Vishnu Purāna,* both of which supplement and extend the original Upanishadic doctrine.

The first to undertake this work of systematizing the varied and scattered philosophical doctrines as found in the several Upanishadic texts was Bādarāyana (? 500–200 B.C.), whose celebrated *Vedānta-Sutra* remains, along with the *Upanishads* and the *Bhagvadgitā,* the basic text of the Vedanta philosophy. The three together form what has been known as the *"prasthāna-traya"* or the "triple-foundation" of Vedānta.

Bādarāyana's *Vedānta-Sutra* has come to be known under various names: as *Brahma-Sutra* (since it deals with the doctrine of *Brahman*), as *Uttara-mimāmsā-Sutra* (since it deals with the later portion of the Vedas, in contrast to Jaimini's *Purva-mimāmsā-Sutra,* which deals with the earlier portion of the Vedas and thus forms the basis of the Mimāmsā philosophy), and as *Sāririka-Sutra* (since it is concerned primarily with the embodiment of the unconditioned Self [*Sarira* = body/ *Sāririka* = relating to the body]). The 555 sutras in Bādarāyana's text are unusually cryptic half-sentences, which are difficult to understand without an extended commentary. Its chief commentators are Samkara, Rāmānuja, and Madhva, who are also its principal interpreters. It is but natural that, while providing their explanatory commentaries, they should have *interpreted* the original *sutras* to fit into their individual philosophical standpoints and, accordingly, we have three major schools of Vedānta: the *Advaita Vedānta* (the School of Nondualism), whose chief exponent was Samkara; the *Visishtādvaita Vedānta* (the School of Qualified Nondualism), whose chief figure was Rāmānuja; and the *Dvaita Vedānta* (the School of Dualism), whose foremost exponent was Madhva. Besides these three main schools, there are several minor Vedānta schools also. Before we proceed to treat each of these schools in detail, it is important to pause for a while and look at Bādarāyana's text.

The *Vedānta-Sutra* is in four chapters, each of which is divided into four quarters or sections *(padas)*. Its ambiguous nature is obvious from its opening line, which reads: "*Athato Brahman-jijñāsa*" ("Now therefore the inquiry into *Brahman*"). The several commentators on the *Vedānta-Sutra* interpret the word *atha* (in *athato*) differently. For Samkara, for instance, *atha* refers to the acquisition of the "four *sādhanās* or prerequisites" which are indispensable for an understanding of the text. Rāmānuja is of the view that *atha* implies an antecedent inquiry into the nature of action or *karma*. For Madhva, *atha* indicates the beginning of the subject; for Vallabha, the word is used to signify the "auspicious." The interpretations indicate, above all else, the inevitable relationship between *jñāna* (knowledge/realization) and *karma* (action), between *Karma-* or *Purva-Mimāmsā* and *Jñāna-* or *Uttara-Mimāmsā* (or Vedānta).

Rāmānuja thinks that *karma* or action has an instrumental value in the inquiry into *Brahman* insofar as it generates knowledge. Samkara too recognizes the instrumental relevance of *karma,* but he considers that "it is not an invariable rule that the inquiry into *karma* should precede the inquiry into *Brahman* in the present life, as it suffices if *karma* has been performed in previous births" (Sastri, 187). He therefore holds that those who have taken to *sannyāsa* (the fourth and last of the stages of an ideal life for the Hindu, the others being *brahmacharya* or the period of discipline and education, *gārhasthya* or the life of the householder and active worker, and *vānaprasthya* or the period when one loosens the material links) or the life of a hermit immediately after *brahmacharya* stage are fully competent to inquire into *Brahman* even before any inquiry into *karma.*

It is rather unfortunate that the *Vedānta-Sutra,* which is supposed to be a systematic presentation of the philosophical implications of the Upanishads, should have been so ambiguous in its phrasing. Radhakrishnan finds the reason for such ambiguity elsewhere—in the commentators' own enthusiastic, often far-fetched and unwarranted, interpretation of what is really quite simple. In their eager attempts to see things in the light of their own preconceived opinions, they have overlooked the literal and the obvious sense of the words. As Radhakrishnan writes, "The *Sutra* is one of those rare books where each, in accordance with his merits, finds his reward" (Radhakrishnan, 432). The *Vedānta-Sutra* is thus a paradise for critical and philosophical interpretation. There are other reasons for its being so.

Bādarāyana's work is "not so much systematic philosophy as theological interpretation" (Radhakrishnan, 431). Paul Deussen writes: "The work of Bādarāyana stands to the Upanishads in the same relation as the Christian Dogmatics to the New Testament; it investigates their teaching about God, the world, the soul in its conditions of wandering and of deliverance, removes apparent contradictions in the doctrines, binds them systematically together, and is especially concerned to defend them against the attacks of opponents" (quoted in Radhakrishnan, 431). The *sutras* refuse to be pinned down by any particular interpretation. All the interpreters agree, however, that the subject of inquiry as stated in the opening *sutra* is the knowledge of *Brahman* or the Ultimate/Supreme Reality.

The first chapter of the *Sutra* deals with the theory of *Brahman* as the Supreme Reality. The aim of Bādarāyana in this chapter is *samanvaya* or a reconciliation of the different Vedic statements on this subject, especially those Upanishadic passages which are controversial. He offers an account of the nature of *Brahman,* its relation to the world and to the individual soul; he also refutes the Sāmkhya doctrine of *Prakriti* as the sole cause and replaces it by the theory of *Jiva* or the unconditioned Self as the sole cause.

The second chapter, called *avirodha,* devotes itself to the task of defending the views stated in the first chapter against actual and possible objections. It carefully refutes the objections from systems such as Sāmkhya, Vaiseshika, and Buddhism. It also takes into account the question as to whether the phenomenal world evolves out of and is reabsorbed into the *Brahman* or whether it is merely an appearance of it. Besides, it contains discussions about the nature of the individual self/soul, its attributes, its relation to *Brahman,* the body and actions peculiar to the body. In Samkara's view, the individual self/soul *(Jiva)* is coeternal with *Brahman* or the Supreme Reality, whereas in Rāmānuja's view, it is an *effect* of *Brahman* existing in a modified form. The chapter also takes into account other considerations, like whether intelligence is an attribute of the individual self, whether the latter is of a very minute size and so on.

The third chapter deals with *sādhanā* or the ways and means of attaining the knowledge of the *Brahman (Brahma-vidyā).* All the Vedānta schools accept the nature of the *Jiva* in regard to death and rebirth as stated in this chapter, i.e., the *Jiva*'s passing out of the body at the time of death and its return at the time of rebirth. This chapter also deals with the self in the dreaming state; it states that all the associations of the self in dream are due to illusion or *māyā.* The fourth section *(pada)* of this chapter enumerates the qualifying attributes necessary for the practice of meditation leading to liberation or *moksha.* The different Vedāntic schools, however, propose separate ways and means toward such liberation or release. While Vallabha envisages a path which combines action *(karma)* and knowledge *(jñāna),* Rāmānuja maintains that action is subservient to knowledge.

The fourth chapter of the *Sutra* deals with *phala* or "fruits" of the knowledge of *Brahman.* The fruits are viewed differently by different schools, but all in the context of the state of the soul/self along the two paths of the gods and fathers following its departure after death as well as in the context of the nature of the release from which there is no return. The commentators agree on another point: although infinite knowledge and power are attributes of the liberated soul, creation, control and dissolution are activities which issue from God alone.

To return to the idea of *prasthāna-traya* or the triple canon of Vedānta, the Upanishads constitute the revealed texts of *Sruti-prasthāna,* since they mark the culmination of the Veda which is *Sruti* (the heard/the revealed). The Gita is offered a status which is almost equal to that of the Upanishads, but since it forms a part of the *Mahābhārata* which is a *Smriti* (the remembered, that is, a text *based on* the Veda), it is called *Smriti-prasthāna.* The third of the canonical texts, the *Vedānta-Sutra* or *Brahma-Sutra,* is regarded as *Nyāya-prasthāna,* for it sets forth the Vedāntic teachings in a logical order *(nyāya* = logic).

Bādarāyana speaks of two sources of knowledge, *sruti* and *smriti,* and he calls them, respectively, perception *(pratyaksham)* and inference *(anumānam),* for, according to him *sruti* is revealed truth and therefore self-evident whereas *smriti* is dependent on *sruti.* Further, Bādarāyana distinguishes "the thinkable" (which includes the elements, the mind, and the ego) from "the unthinkable," which is *Brahman* itself and can be realized with the help of the *sāstras* or scriptures alone. For Bādarāyana, "any reasoning which is not in conformity with the Veda is useless" (Radhakrishnan, 436), for purely secular reasoning aimed at a description or confirmation of the *Brahman* is an impossibility. "Reasoning, therefore, is subordinate to intuitional knowledge, which can be obtained by devotion and meditation" (Radhakrishnan citing the *Sutra,* 436). However, as far as the exact relation between the changeless *(avikari)* and eternal *(nityam) Brahman* and the ever-changing and impermanent World is concerned, Bādarāyana simply asserts that the former develops itself into the phenomenal world and remains transcendent: "(*Brahman* is the material cause) because of action related to Itself by way of change of form."/ "And because *Brahman* is declared to be the source *(yoni)*" (*Brahma-Sutra-Bhāsya of Sankarāchārya,* trans. Swami Gambhirananda, 295).

To the question, "How can such an impermanent effect (the World) issue from a changeless cause (the *Brahman*)?", Bādarāyana does not provide an answer. He is equally silent regarding several other doubts and objections. As Radhakrishnan writes: "The *Sutra* . . . reflects the indecision and vagueness characteristic of the Upanishads, whose teachings it attempts to set forth, and harbours within it many seeds of doubt and discussion" (Radhakrishnan, 444). The many schools of Vedānta, each different from the others, are a pointer to the incomplete and limited nature of the *Sutra* itself.

Schools of Vedānta

1. Advaita Vedānta

Gaudap̄da

S.N. Dasgupta believes that some of the earliest commentators on the *Vedānta-Sutra* were Vaishnavites who held "some form of modified dualism, that their interpretations differed from Samkara's and that these dualistic interpretations were "probably more faithful to the *sutras* than the interpretations of Sankara" (Dasgupta, I, 420, 421; emphasis added). According to Dasgupta, Bādarāyana "was probably more a theist than an absolutist like his commentator Sankara" (Dasgupta, I, 422). And, although Samkara is generally regarded as the greatest exponent of *advaita* (absolutism or nondualism), it was Gaudapāda who seems to have been responsible in reviving the monistic principles of the Upanishads and formulating them in a cogent manner. As Samkara himself admits, the absolutist creed was recovered from the Vedas by Gaudapāda. The latter's commentary on the *Māndukya Upanishad,* entitled *Māndukya-kārikā,* is the earliest systematic treatment of the Upanishadic thesis that "*Brahman* alone is real and all else is appearance or *māyā.*"

It is interesting to note that Gaudapāda, a teacher of Samkara's teacher Govinda and an avid student of Mahāyāna Buddhism, did not make any reference to any other writer of the monistic school. Dasgupta finds sufficient evidence in *Māndukya-kārikā* to prove that Gaudapāda was "possibly himself a Buddhist, and considered that the teachings of the Upanishads tallied with those of Buddha" (Dasgupta, I, 423). Radhakrishnan, however, appears to be less sure regarding Gaudapāda's Buddhist connection, when he writes about the philosopher's acceptance of Buddhist doctrines only when "they were not in conflict with his own Advaita": "To the Buddhists he appealed on the ground that his view did not depend on any theological text or revelation. To the orthodox Hindu he said that it had the sanction of authority also" (Radhakrishnan, 453).

Gaudapāda's *Māndukya-kārikā* is divided into four chapters. The first chapter, called "Āgama" (scripture), explains the *Māndukya-Upanishad;* the second, called "Vaitathya" (unreality), explains and confirms the phenomenal nature of the world; the third, called "Advaita" (unity), establishes the theory of the Absolute; and, the fourth and last, called "Alātasānti" (fire-extinction), is an extended reaffirmation of the sole reality of the all-pervasive, unembodied Spirit *(Ātman)* and the contingent character of our ordinary experience. In his last chapter, Gaudapāda uses the following simile, which is frequently used by the Mādhyamika Buddhists, to explain the pluralistic character of the phenomenal world: "As a stick burning at one end, when waved round, quickly produces an illusion of a circle of fire *(alātachakra),* so is it with the multiplicity of the world" (trans. Radhakrishnan, 453). Thus, the last three chapters of the *Kārikā* are "the constructive parts of Gaudapāda's text" without any explicit connection with the Upanishadic text of which they are supposed to be elucidative commentaries (Dasgupta, I, 424).

Gaudapāda's primary argument is against the theory of the origination and transformation of anything in the mimetic world, for that theory presupposes that "whatever is, was not there before it came into existence." Consequently, for Gaudapāda, "all the conceivable distinctions, such as those between mind and matter, the knower and the known, the nonexistent and the existent, the beginning and the end . . . are illusory" (Sinari, 105, 106). Gaudapāda's basic doctrine is that of Non-origination or No-origination *(ajātivāda);* it asserts that origination *(utpada)* is inconceivable. C.D. Sharma points out the two sides of this theory, a negative side and a positive side: "Negatively, it means that the world, being only an appearance, is in fact never created. Positively, it means that the Absolute, being self-existent, is never created" (Sharma, 242). Thus, from the negative standpoint, "the entire domain of spatiotemporal beings and psychic impressions is a massive panorama of illusions," an inevitable result of our "naive regard to contingency and practical utility" (Sinari, 106). From the positive standpoint, the Absolute is a self-luminous transcendental principle which might be temporarily shrouded by the "dread-like smoky veil" of our individual and short-term "imaginations and fantastic designs" (Sinari, 106).

Gaudapāda's greatest contribution to Advaita philosophy is his doctrine of *Asparshayoga* or Pure Knowledge. The doctrine could be traced to at least three Upanishadic texts—the *Brihadāranyaka,* the *Chhāndogya,* and the *Māndukya.* Gaudapā identifies the Unborn and Non-dual Absolute with the *Ātman/ Brahman/ Amātra/ Turiya/ Advaita* and argues that it can only be directly realized by Pure Knowledge or *Asparshayoga* (also called *Vaishāradya* and *Amanibhāva*). In the first chapter of his *Kārikā,* Gaudapāda attempts to characterize the Absolute: it is unseen, unrelationable, ungraspable, indefinable, unthinkable, unspeakable, the quiscent, the good, and the one. However the Absolute manifests itself in three forms, although in reality it absorbs and transcends all the three forms. Its symbol is "AUM" (also called *Pranava*), both in its pure as well as its relative aspects. But there is no distinction between the symbol and the symbolized: "AUM" or *Pranava* itself is the Absolute. The Absolute or *Brahman* is identical with the shining Self or the self-luminous Consciousness. It is called *Vaisvānara* or *Vishva* (All) when it has the consciousness of outside or the physical and, in the universal or macrocosmic sphere, is paralleled by *Virāt* or Cosmic Manifestation; it corresponds to the waking state and is symbolized by the "A" of *AUM.* It is called *Taijasya* (Luminous) when it has the consciousness of inside or the mental and, in the macrocosmic sphere, is paralleled by *Hiranyagarbha* or the Universal Mind; it corresponds to the dream state and is represented by the "U" of *AUM.* It is called *Prajñā* (Intelligent) when it is concentrated consciousness or consciousness of one's intellectual condition and, in the macrocosmic sphere, is paralleled by *Isvara* or First Cause or God; it corresponds to the state of deep sleep and is symbolized by the "M" of *AUM*. To repeat, the three levels or expressions of consciousness or manifestations of the self are: the self or consciousness as the wakeful perceiver of phenomenal occurrences, the self or consciousness as the experiencer in the dream state, and the self or consciousness as the experiencer in deep sleep *(sushupti)*. Thus, the *Vishva-ātmā* enjoys the gross; the *Taijasa-ātmā* enjoys the subtle; the *Prajñā-ātmā* enjoys the bliss *(ānanda)*. *Turiya* is often referred to as the fourth state of the self, whereas it is not a state at all, being identical with existence itself; it is *Turiya* that "appears as having the three states." It is the Transcendental that "runs through all the states and forms the basis of the sense of self-identity felt with regard to the changing states" (Swami Tyagisananda, 29, 31). Although for convenience it is called the fourth state, it is really the Whole, being the *Brahman-Ātman* (the Inmost Self—the Ultimate Reality); it is the Soundless aspect *(amātra)* of *AUM*, the silence of the Infinite.

As pure and self-luminous Consciousness, *Turiya* is all-seeing, all-pervading, changeless, non-dual, and capable of removing all sufferings. And, as C.D. Sharma points out, though duality is absent in both *Prajñā* and *Turiya*, yet the former is connected with deep sleep where the seed of ignorance is present, while the latter knows no sleep. Sharma writes:

> *Vishva* and *Taijasa* are connected with dream or false knowledge *(anyathāgrahana* or *vikshepa)* and with sleep or absence of knowledge *(agrahana* or *āvarana* or *laya)*; *Prajñā* is connected with sleep. In *Turiya* there is neither sleep nor dream. In dream we know otherwise; in sleep we do not know the truth.... When the negative absence of knowledge which is sleep, and the positive wrong knowledge which is dream and waking, are transcended, the Fourth, the Goal is reached.... When the individual self *(jiva)*, slumbering in beginningless Ignorance, is awakened, then the Unborn, the Dreamless, the Sleepless, the Non-dual Absolute *(ātman)* is realized. It moves nowhere; there is no going to or coming from it. It is the Lord immanent in the universe abiding in the hearts of all [Sharma, 248–249; emphasis added].

In the second chapter of his *Kārikā*, Gaudapāda discusses the unreality of the world of duality. For Gaudapāda, the criterion of reality is not mere coherence, or correspondence, or even practical efficiency, but absolute, eternal, unchanging existence, uncontradicted and uncontradictable by anything else at any time. For Gaudapāda, as for all Advaitins, *Satya* (truth) and *Nitya* (permanence) are convertible terms; that is, that which is not *nitya* cannot be *satya*. From this standpoint, the reality of the world is only "relative" *(vyavahārika-satyatva)* whereas the reality of the *Turiya* is "absolute" *(pāramārthika-satyatva)*.

Gaudapāda proceeds to demonstrate this difference by showing how waking experience is similar to dream: as in dream, so in the waking state, what we really cognize are ideas only. The feeling that the object experienced is external to oneself and is common to both the states. Even in dreams, so long as the dream lasts, the subject feels the consciousness of the external objects exactly as they are felt by "dream people with whom he feels himself as communing in that state," for otherwise we cannot have dream-relations with others. To say that dream-objects last for a shorter duration than the objects of the waking state is to confuse the standards of dream-time with those of waking-time. If we were to judge one from the standpoint of the other, then each would be seen to be unreal. Gaudapāda applies his argument not only to time but to space and causation as well. The dream-space and causal relations within the dream should not be expected to agree with the waking standards; similarly, waking-space and its related causality need not agree with dream standards. Each is independent of the other; and, if dream is contradicted by waking phenomena, the latter is equally contradicted by dream phenomena. The saner view, according to Gaudapāda, is to admit the similarity between the two states.

To the objection that, unlike dream-objects, which do not appear with any regularity and consistency every time one goes to sleep, the objects of the waking state appear with a certain regularity and consistency every time we wake up from sleep, Gaudapāda replies that even this regularity/consistency is something which is perceived only in the waking state. Hence, to say that water in dream does not quench one's thirst is wrong, the dream-water quenches dream-thirst as much as waking-water quenches waking-thirst. It is hard to locate any real difference between dream-experience and waking-experience. It is imagination which is at the root of world-phenomena; it subserves both the individual souls and their separate experiences, subjective as well as objective, dream-based as well as waking-based. It is the *Ātman* that is variously imagined as elements, gods, time, space, mind, virtue, vice and so on; it is the one, non-dual *Ātman* that appears as the variegated world of subjects and objects. Thus, from the standpoint of the highest realization, there is neither death nor birth, neither bondage nor release, neither any seeker after liberation nor the liberated, all of which are only relative terms which hold good only in the relative world of ignorance. A realized man is free from all imaginations, uncommitted to Vedic injunctions and rituals, deriving bliss only from the non-dual *Ātman* which is "one with everything including himself" (Swami Tyagisananda, 36).

In the third chapter of his *Kārikā,* we find Gaudapāda's well-known analogy of *ākāsa* or space to establish how the Absolute or *Ātman* manifests Itself ("Himself," according to Gaudapāda) as the world phenomena without undergoing any change. As the *ghatākāsa* (the space in a jar) is not different from *mahākāsa* (Unrestricted Space), so the individual *Jiva* is not really different from the absolute *Ātman.* When the jars *(ghatas)* are destroyed, their spaces merge into the Unrestricted Space; similarly, when Ignorance is destroyed by Right Knowledge, the *jivas* merge into the *Ātman.* Just as nothing new has come out of *mahākāsa* when we cognize the *ghatākāsa,* so nothing new is produced when we cognize various different individual *jivas;* and, as with creation, so with preservation, dissolution and related changes that *appear* to take place in the *Ātman.* Every change is only imaginary. Again, as one *ghatākāsa* is not affected by the smoke or dirt in another *ghatākāsa,* so one *jiva*'s conditions of happiness or misery need not necessarily affect another.

Just as any difference in the spaces in jars in terms of form, function and name does not indicate a difference in Unrestricted Space, the differences among *jivas* in terms of form, function and name do not refer to any real difference in the *Ātman*. Again, just as the *ghatākāsa* is neither a transformation nor a modification nor a part of *mahākāsa*, a *jiva* is neither a transformation nor a modification nor a part of the *Ātman*. All things that appear as compounded are but *svapna* (dream) and *māyā* (illusion); duality is a distinction imposed upon the One *(advaita)* by *māyā*. Ultimately, however, there are "no grades of reality, no degrees of truth." As C.D. Sharma writes: "The same immanent Absolute is reflected in all pairs of objects related by sweet Reciprocity *(madhuvidyā)*, in microcosm as well as in macrocosm, just as the same space is immanent in the outside world as well as inside the stomach" (Sharma, 249; emphasis added). Gaudapāda carries his attack on the creationist theories of God into his fourth and final chapter – theories which the dualistic theists are obliged to hold because of their doctrine of the reality of the world.

Gaudapāda's ideas have not, however, gone without criticism. Radhakrishnan writes of the possible attack from an imagined, compound critic on the ground that a theory has "nothing better to say than that an unreal soul is trying to escape from an unreal bondage in an unreal world to accomplish an unreal supreme good, may itself be an unreality." As Radhakrishnan proceeds to remark: "The greatest condemnation of such a theory is that we are obliged to occupy ourselves with objects, the existence and value of which we are continually denying in theory. The fact of the world may be mysterious and inexplicable. It only shows that there is something else which includes and transcends the world; but it does not imply that the world is a dream" (Radhakrishnan, 463). Radhakrishnan locates the reason for Gaudapāda's exaggerated metaphysics in the Vijñānavāda and Mādhyamika schools of Buddhism.

Although both Bādarāyana and Samkara emphasize the difference between the dream impressions and waking ones and maintain that the latter are not independent of external objects, Gaudapāda treats the two kinds as if they were similar. While Samkara is anxious to free his system from the subjectivism peculiar to Vijñānavāda, Gaudapāda welcomes it; in fact, he goes beyond the Vijñānavādins when he declares that even the experiencing subject is as unreal as the experienced object, thus coming perilously near the nihilist position. Like the Buddhist Nāgārjuna, he denies the validity of causation and the possibility of change. Gaudapāda might be said to have founded his absolutistic philosophy on the basis supplied by the teachings of Nāgārjuna, using almost the same terminology and method of argument as Nāgārjuna's. Winternitz writes of how Gaudapāda's *māyā-vāda* and the Mahāyāna Buddhist's *sunya-vāda* are in agreement not only in the denial of reality of the world, but in their common rhetorical pictures of the illusoriness of the world of phenomena (Winternitz, 521–522).

We close this section on Gaudapāda with Radhakrishnan's words: "The *Kārikā* of Gaudapāda is an attempt to combine in one whole the negative logic of the Mādhyamikas with the positive idealism of the Upanishads. In Gaudapāda the negative tendency is more prominent than the positive. In Samkara we have a more balanced outlook" (Radhakrishnan, 465).

Samkara

It has often been said that Samkara is the most misunderstood of all Indian thinkers—a remark which implicitly refers to the fact that his philosophy "tolerates no human weakness and requires its followers to sever connection with all that is dear to the heart" (S. Bhattacharya, 237). Heinrich Zimmer writes of Samkara's Vedānta as representing "the final period of Vedic, Brāhmanical development," in which, "though the language of Indian orthodox philosophy is still that of the nondual, paradoxical, Āryan-Brāhman tradition, the mood, the ideals, and point of view have become those of the world-renouncing sounders of the call to retreat. The earlier, buoyant, exultant, world-affirmative inflation of the Vedic and Upanishadic ages has disappeared and a monkish, cold asceticism dominates the field" (Zimmer, 413–414). The much-misunderstood Advaitism of Samkara is thus chiefly due to his radical interpretation of well-preserved, orthodox doctrines of the Hindus. As Radhakrishnan writes, his is "a system of great speculative daring and logical subtlety."

George Thibaut, who was the first to translate Samkara's commentary on Bādarāyana's *Vedānta-Sutra* into English, writes of the philosopher's "boldness, depth and subtlety of speculation." Radhakrishnan comments further on the strictly rationalistic character of Samkara's philosophy: "Its austere intellectualism, its remorseless logic, which marches on indifferent to the hopes and beliefs of man, its relative freedom from theological obsessions, make it a great example of a purely philosophical scheme" (Radhakrishnan, 445). Hiriyanna calls him a great reformer and sees him as one who entered fully into the practical struggles of the age in which he lived and yet succeeded in making a contribution of enduring value to the history of human culture (*Essentials,* 154). "His philosophy stands forth complete, needing neither a before nor an after. It has a self-justifying wholeness characteristic of works of art. It expounds its own presuppositions, is ruled by its own end, and holds all its elements in a stable, reasoned equipoise. . . . A master of the strictest logic, he is also master of a noble and animated poetry which belongs to another order" (Radhakrishnan, 446, 447).

Literature

The most important texts of the Advaita school are Samkara's commentaries on the following: the eleven principal Upanishads (the *Chāndogya,* the *Brihadāranyaka,* the *Taittiriya,* the *Aitareya,* the *Svetāsvatara,* the *Kena,* the *Kathā,* the *Isa,* the *Prasna,* the *Mundaka,* and the *Māndukya*), the *Bhagvadgitā,* and the *Vedānta Sutra.* In writing these commentaries, Samkara was carrying on the work of his teacher Gaudapāda. As Dasgupta notes, there is ample evidence in his commentary on the *Brahma-Sutra (Vedānta-Sutra)* that he was contesting "some other rival interpretations of a dualistic tendency which held that the Upanishads partly favoured the Sāmkhya cosmology of the existence of *prakrti.* That these were actual textual interpretations of the *Brahma-Sutras* is proved by the fact that Samkara in some places tries to show that these textual constructions were faulty" (Dasgupta, I, 432, 433). At one place in his commentary, Samkara offers the reason for his annotating Bādarāyana's text: it is to refute all those who were opposed to the doctrine of seeing everything as the unity of the self *(ātmaikatva).* Samkara, it appears, did not consider himself a philosopher, for he throughout contended that ultimate validity does not belong to reason but to the scriptures. Samkara's two other books, *Upadesasahasri* and *Vivekachudāmani,* define his general philosophical position; his many religious hymns in *Dakshinamurti Stotra, Ānandalahari* and *Saundaryalahari,* reflect his intense faith in life.

In addition to these, he is said to have written several treatises on Advaitic metaphysics and epistemology, such as *Ātmabodha, Āptavajrasuchi, Dasasloki* and *Aparoksānubhuti.* It should, however, be realized that Advaita Vedānta literature did not come to an end with Samkara; several later Advaitins have written books and monographs, defending their master's position. The chief among these are Suresvara's *Vārttikas* and *Naishkarmyasiddhi,* Vāchaspati Misra's *Bhāmati,* Padmapāda's *Panchapādikā,* Ānandagiri's *Nyāyanirnaya,* Appayadikshita's *Siddhāntalesa,* Vidyāranya's *Panchadasi* and *Jivanmukti-viveka,* Sri Harsha's *Khandanakhandakhādya,* Chitsukha's *Tattvadipika,* Madhusudana's *Advaitasiddhi,* Rāmāchārya's *Tarangini,* Brahmānanda's *Guruchandrika,* Dharmarāja's *Vedāntaparibhāshā,* Vijñānabhikshu's *Vijñānāmrita,* Govindananda's *Ratnaprabhā,* and Sadānanda's *Vedāntasāra.* Besides, we have several commentaries on the original texts: Amalānanda's *Kalpataru* is a commentary on Vāchaspati's *Bhāmati,* while Appayadikshita wrote a commentary on *Kalpataru,* entitled *Kalpataruparimala;* Rāmāchārya wrote a critical commentary on Madhusudana's *Advaitasiddhi,* called *Tarangini.* Most of these texts and commentaries were written between the 12th and 16th centuries. More recently, we have had Sri Aurobindo, whose philosophy (as reflected in his books and recorded speeches) was basically Advaitic, although (as we shall see in the following chapter) he was to offer the original Advaita philosophy a much more radically mystic and intuitive turn than it had hitherto known.

Metaphysics

Before we discuss Samkara's important philosophical concepts, we would like to make a quick survey of his philosophy, as well as offer a summary of his criticism of the metaphysical views of other schools of thought. Samkara started with the thesis that "all experience starts and moves in an error which identifies the self with the body, the senses, or the objects of the senses," that all cognitive acts presuppose this illusory identification, for without it the pure self can never behave as "a phenomenal knower or perceiver, and without such a perceiver there would be no cognitive act." Samkara does not, however, try to prove the existence of the pure self as distinct from everything else; he just takes the Upanishadic view of it for granted in the light of the revealed nature of the Upanishads. He does not try to prove that the world is an appearance or illusion *(māyā),* but merely refers to it as something which necessarily and inevitably follows from the fact of the ultimately real nature of the self alone. Thus, the ultimate reality is *Ātman* or *Brahman,* which is Pure Consciousness *(jñāna-svarupa)* or Consciousness of the Pure Self *(svaruta-jñāna).* It is devoid of all attributes *(nirguna)* and all categories of intellect *(nirvishesha),* and therefore is something which cannot be (as the Mimāmsakas held) meditated upon or worshipped.

According to Samkara, the Upanishads revealed the highest truth as *Brahman* and "one reached absolute wisdom and emancipation when the truth dawned on him that the Brahman or self was the ultimate reality" (Dasgupta, I, 435, 436). When associated with its potency, *māyā, Brahman* appears as the qualified *Brahman (saguna-* or *savishesha-* or *apara-Brahman)* or *Ishvara* (Lord), who is the creator, preserver and annihilator of this world, which is His appearance. As Samkara writes in his *bhāsya* on Bādarāyana's *Brahma Sutra:* "That omniscient and omnipotent source must be *Brahman* from which occurs the birth, continuance, and dissolution of this universe that is manifested through name and form, that is associated with diverse agents and experiences, that provides the support for actions and results, having well-regulated space, time, and causation, and that defies all thoughts about the real nature of its creation" (trans. Swami Gambhirananda, 14).

The *Jiva* or individual self is essentially the same as *Brahman* and is therefore self-luminous, unlimited, and free. Its limitedness and all its consequent effects are due to certain conditions *(upādhis),* which, again, appear through nescience *(avidyā)* and as such are unreal. Thus, an elimination of the "conditions" *(upādhis)* amounts to an elimination of the apparently dual nature of the *Jiva.* As Surendranath Bhattacharya writes, "To be Brahman is not the extinction of the individual, rather it is the expansion of one's individuality into the infinitude of Brahman" (244). The *Jiva* is thus always *Brahman;* during bondage, this truth is screened by the aforementioned *upādhis,* while in the state of freedom, the *Jiva* shines forth as *Brahman,* as what it always is. *Brahman* only *appears* as the world through *avidyā* or *māyā* (ignorance or illusion); it has only a phenomenal reality, but no reality of its own. Brahmanhood is realized by the knowledge of the absolute identity of the *Jiva* and *Brahman,* a fact which is revealed by the Upanishadic dictum *"Tat tvam asi"* ("That thou art").

According to Samkara, liberation *(moksha)* is nothing but the realization of this identity. It should be pointed out, however, that although Samkara does not admit kinds of truth, yet for the sake of *convenience,* he speaks of three kinds of truth: *paramārthika* truth, attributable to *Brahman* alone; *vyavahārika* truth, attributable to the objective world; and *pratibhāsika* truth, attributable to the illusions of an individual so long as the former last. No wonder, Samkara emphasizes that, from the phenomenal point of view, the world is quite real. Following the same logic, Samkara says that i) from the point of view of *Brahman,* the question of the existence or non-existence of *māyā* is of no value *(tuccha);* ii) from the standpoint of strict logic, *māyā* is inexplicable *(anirvachaniyia),* for it fails to explain any relationship between *Brahman* and the objective world; iii) from the standpoint of common experience, *māyā is the very life of the world and, to that extent, is real (vāstava).*

Although Samkara agrees with Sāmkhya in maintaining that the design or harmony in the universe presupposes an eternal and unlimited single cause, he rejects the Sāmkhya view that this cause is the unintelligent *Prakrti,* which, according to Samkara, is too poor and powerless to be such a cause. Further, *Prakrti* and *Purusha* can never be related, for the former is unconscious and the latter indifferent and Sāmkhya does not speak of a third principle which can relate the two independent and eternal entities, one of which is the subject while the other is the object. It must therefore recognize "a higher conscious principle which transcends and yet gives meaning to and preserves at a lower level, the subject-object duality" (Sharma, 255). It is only the ever-conscious *Brahman* associated with its potency, *Māyā,* which can be the cause. Samkara replaces Sāmkhya's *Prakrti* by *Māyā,* its *Prakrti-parināma-vāda* by his own *Brahma-vivarta-vāda,* its *Purusha* by his *jiva,* its *sat-kārya-vāda* by *sat-kārana-vāda,* its negative *kaivalya* by his positively blissful *moksha.* While Samkara maintains that the effect must pre-exist in the cause, he refuses to distinguish the two, for the cause alone is real and the effect is only its appearance. This view is known as *vivarta-vāda.* Samkara agrees with the Buddhist Sunyavādins and Vijñānavādins in maintaining, against Sāmkhya, that if the effect really pre-existed in the cause, then it is already an accomplished fact and as such its production is a mere repetition.

Samkara also criticizes the *Paramānu-kārana-vāda* as well as the categories of Vaiseshika-Nyāya. We may recall that, according to Nyāya, the four substances (earth, water, fire and air) in their subtle form as causes are atomic and eternal, and that *ākāsa* (space), though itself not atomic, binds the atoms together. The Vaiseshika atoms are both quantitatively and qualitatively different, are by their very nature at rest, and are distinct from souls. God assisted by the Unseen Power *(adrshta)* generates motion in these atoms, which then combine to produce the gross objects of the world. According to Vaiseshika, the cause must transmit its qualities to the effect (e.g., white threads produce white cloth and black threads produce black cloth). It is therefore the atoms, and not the conscious *Brahman,* which are the cause of the unconscious world.

Samkara, in refuting this theory, asks, "Are the atoms essentially active or inactive, or both, or neither?" If they are active, then creation would be permanent; if not, there would be no creation; if both active and inactive, the conception would be self-contradictory; if neither, then their activity must be caused by an outside agency which may be either seen or unseen; if seen, then it could not exist prior to creation, and if unseen, then by virtue of its association with the atoms, creation would be permanent, but if such association is denied, creation is an impossibility. Thus, there can be no creation from atoms alone and so the theory that the atoms are the cause is unjustifiable (Samkara's *bhāsya* on *Vedānta-Sutra,* Chapter 2).

Samkara also rejects the six Vaiseshika categories which, according to him, are nothing but mere assumption. He also rejects the Vaiseshika view that God is only the efficient cause and the ruler of primordial Matter and Souls; for, if He is the former, then He will be justifiably charged of being actuated by partiality, hatred, attachment and such other qualities which are peculiar to common man and, if He were the latter, then He could not rule Matter and Souls without being connected with them and there can be no such connection. In the latter case, according to Samkara, it cannot be conjunction, for God, Matter and Souls are regarded as infinite and without parts; it cannot be inherence either, for it is impossible to decide as to which is the abode and which the abidee. This difficulty does arise in Samkara's case, for he (like other Advaitins) maintains the identity of the cause and the effect. Further, if Matter and Souls are infinite, God could not possibly have any control over them and thus cease to be omniscient and omnipotent. The infinite, according to Samkara, can be only one and one only.

Samkara's criticism of Buddhism begins with his attack on the Sarvāstivada Buddhist's theory of two aggregates—external and internal. The Sarvāstivādins (who are of course divided into the Vaibhāshikas and Sauntāntrikas) maintain that external reality is either element *(bhuta)* or elemental *(bhautika)* and that internal reality is either mind *(chitta)* or mental *(chaitta)*. According to Samkara, the unintelligent and momentary external atoms and the momentary internal *skandhas* are incapable of forming any systematic whole, since the Buddhists do not admit any intelligent principle which might unite them. The Buddhists hold that existence arises from non-existence. Samkara replies that an entity can never arise from a nonentity, for if existence were to arise out of non-existence, "all the effects would be imbued with non-existence"—something which goes against experience. As for the Buddhist theory of Dependent Origination, the antecedent link in the causal sequence, according to Samkara, cannot even be regarded as the efficient cause of the subsequent link, for as the Buddhist theory would have us believe, the preceding link ceases to exist as soon as the subsequent link arises.

The Buddhist argument that the antecedent moment in its fully developed form becomes the cause of the subsequent moment is untenable, because the assertion that a fully developed moment is causally efficient necessarily presupposes its connection with the subsequent moment and thus repudiates the theory of universal momentariness. Samkara also proves the impossibility of the other Buddhist argument that the mere existence of the preceding moment is its causal efficiency; according to Samkara, no effect can arise without absorbing the nature of the cause, and to admit this amounts to admitting the permanence of the cause and thereby rejecting the theory of momentariness. Similarly, Samkara rejects the Yogāchāra Buddhist's theory that the self is no more than a series of impermanent mental states, for on the basis of this theory, it is difficult to account for the facts of memory and recognition. The Buddhist Sunyavādins, who declare that there is no permanent self, have also been criticized by Samkara, for whom the existence of the self is beyond any doubt. "Even if we declare the whole world to be a mere void, this void presupposes a cogniser of itself" (Radhakrishnan, 478).

According to Samkara, it is impossible for us to know or understand the self through analysis and logic, since such analysis is only "a part of the flux belonging to the region of not-self"; the self or *Ātman* is "prior to the stream of consciousness, prior to truth and falsehood, prior to reality and illusion, good and evil." And yet, it is impossible to ignore the self, for there is "no consciounsess or experience possible apart from it" (Radhakrishnan, 476). From the standpoint of logic, it is a postulate and thus has to be taken for granted. In his *bhāsya* Samkara writes:

> Neither from that part of the Veda which enjoins works nor from reasoning, anybody apprehends that self which, different from the agent that is the object of self-consciousness, merely witnesses it; which is permanent in all (transitory) beings; uniform; one; eternally unchanging; the Self of everything. Hence it can neither be denied nor be represented as the mere compliment of injunctions; for of that very person who might deny it it is the Self. And as it is the Self of all, it can neither be striven after nor avoided [Radhakrishnan and Moore, 512].

Suresvara's *Vārttikas* reinforce Samkara's view: "The very existence of understanding and its functions presupposes an intelligence known as the self, which is different from them, which is self-established, and which they subserve" (cited in Radhakrishnan, 476). The truly real is thus the being-in-itself-for-itself, so that any affirmation of the reality of the eternal and permanent self or *Ātman* amounts to an affirmation of the reality of the eternal *Brahman: "Ātman cha Brahman" (Ātman* is *Brahman).* As an answer to the conflicting opinions as to the nature of the self *(Ātman),* Samkara says that "we get the notion of the *Ātman* if we divest it of all that surrounds it, discriminate it from the bodily frame with which it is encompassed, strip it of all contents of experience" (cited in Radhakrishnan, 480). Radhakrishnan, defending Samkara's position, says that to our minds, steeped in logic, it may appear that "we have reduced it to a bare potentiality of thought, if not mere nothing, but it is better to regard it this way than as a whole of parts or a thing with qualities or a substance with attributes. It is undifferentiated consciousness alone *(nirviseshachinmātram)* which is unaffected even when the body is reduced to ashes and the mind perishes" (Radhakrishnan, 480).

Ātman is the fundamental, ultimate, pure consciousness, which is self-luminous and which absorbs and transcends the subject-object duality, the supreme principle in which there is no differentiation of knower, knowledge and known; it is the essence of absolute knowledge, so that "He who knows

Brahman (which is the same as *Ātman*) becomes *Brahman*." C.D. Sharma writes: "Ultimately there is no distinction between the true knower and pure knowledge" (Sharma, 284). Samkara cites an analogy from the *Brihadā ranyaka Upanishad* to explain the nature of the Self or *Ātman* as pure consciousness: "As a lump of salt is without interior or exterior, entire, and purely saline in taste, even so is the Self without interior or exterior, entire, and pure Intelligence alone." Samkara has his own analogy to re-establish the Upanishadic truth: "As the sun shines when there is nothing for it to shine on, so the *Ātman* has consciousness even in the absence of an object." It is Pure Consciousness which is also Pure Existence and Pure Bliss, and so is *Brahman*. Existence and Consciousness are one. *Ātman* cannot be existence without consciousness or intelligence, it cannot be consciousness or intelligence without existence. It is also of the nature of bliss or *ānanda*, which is freedom from all suffering. *Ātman* has nothing to acquire and nothing to discard; it is without activity, since activity by its very nature is noneternal. In his *bhāsya* Samkara remarks: "The self cannot be the abode of any action, since an action cannot exist without modifying that in which it abides" (cited in Radhakrishnan, 483). Every mode of activity, which presupposes the self-sense, also assumes a subject-object duality.

According to Samkara, however, the subject *(vishayin)* can never be the object *(vishaya)*; the "I" can never be anything other than the "I." As such, when one says "I have known myself," what he has actually known is not the self but something other than the self; that is, whatever becomes an object of knowledge becomes, for that very reason, something other than the self. The body, the mind *(manas)*, intellect *(buddhi)*, and the ego *(ahamkāra)* are variable objects of knowledge and therefore are not the *Ātman*. Although the subject-knower can never be the object-known, it is a habit of human nature—"a necessity of thought"—to transfer the essential qualities of one to the other and thus identify the two. The true "I" is unknown and unknowable. This is not a message of Vedāntic despair, however, for although the *Ātman* can never become the object, it ever remains the subject, unaffected by mental stimulus or bodily changes. Human bondage merely refers to our usual indentification of the *Ātman* with the *anātman* (nonself); it lasts so long as one fails to realize the pure and unaffected *Ātman* and disappears with this realization. We quote the relevant lines from the *Mundaka Upanishad:* "All knots of the heart are cut asunder, all doubts are dissolved, and all *karmas* are ended, when the highest *Brahman* is realized as one's self."

It must once again be made clear that Samkara's self is *not* the individual knowing subject. If Samkara, as Radhakrishnan says, tried to establish the reality of the individual knowing subject "in abstraction from or as oppoed to the not-self, he would get a plurality of finite countless selves or an abstract universal self" (Radhakrishnan, 484). The *Ātman* of Samkara, however, is neither the individual self nor "a collection of such selves." Although the world apart from the individual selves has no reality, it has also "no other truth to show than this self," for all other events are but passing appearances. Radhakrishnan writes:

> It is because Samkara finds the essence of personality in its distinction from other existences that he contends that the *Ātman* which has no other existences independent of it is not a person. It is true, however, that the empirical self is the only reality from the logical point of view and the pure self but a shadow. But when we rise to intuition, where the subject and the object coincide, we realise the truth of the ultimate consciousness. It is the absolute vision that is its own visibility [Radhakrishnan, 484–485].

For Dasgupta, the one thing which distinguishes consciousness from everything else is "the fact of its self-revelation." He distinguishes the "so-called momentary flashing of consciousness"—which only refers to the objects revealed *by* it as reflected *through* it from time to time—from consciousness itself, which is "steady and unchangeable" and whose immediacy is proved by the fact that it is always "self-manifested and self-revealed" (Dasgupta, II, 63). Consciousness or Self *(Ātman)* is thus "incapable of particularisation," for it is as much in one as in another. "We live *because* we share the universal life; we think *because* we share the universal thought. Our experience is *possible because* of the universal *Ātman* in us" (Radhakrishnan, 485; emphasis added).

The real self, which is identical with "the pure manifesting unity of all consciousness," is not the same as the *jiva* or individual soul, which passes through the several and various worldly experiences. The aim of Vedānta is to lead us from an analysis of the individual human soul to the reality of the absolute self, although such passage does not ever ignore the fact that the human soul/self is essentially one with the absolute self. The empirical human self, which is the agent of all activity and the object of self-consciousness, is not the pure self. Samkara carefully distinguishes the self that is implied in all experience *(jiva)* from the self which is "an observed fact of introspection" *(Ātman),* the metaphysical subject or the "I" from the psychological subject or the "me" (Radhakrishnan, 595). The *jiva* is thus the *Ātman* "limited or individuated by the object"; it is the *Ātman* in association with a total absence of understanding or ignorance *(ajñāna);* its sense of individuality is caused by mere logical knowledge *(avidyā);* its distinctive characteristic is its connection with understanding *(buddhi),* "which endures as long as the state of *samsāra* [mundane existence] is not terminated by perfect knowledge," which is of course the knowledge the *jiva–Ātman* identity. The soul's connection with understanding is said to continue beyond death and can be broken only by the attainment of freedom or liberation *(moksha),* which is coeval with "perfect knowledge." This connection is potential during deep sleep and death; it is actual on waking and rebirth. Unless we assume such a potential continuance, it would be impossible for us to explain the law of causality, since nothing can arise without an existing cause (Radhakrishnan, 596).

The *jiva* or the individual human soul is the *Ātman* clothed in the *upādhis* or limiting adjuncts. The *jiva* is the ruler of the body and the senses and is connected with the fruits of actions; and, since its essence is *Ātman,* it is all-pervading *(vibhu)* and not atomic *(anu),* for, if it were the latter, it could not experience the sensations extending over the whole body. Samkara speaks of three different states of the soul. In its waking state, when the whole perceptual mechanism is active, we apprehend objects by means of the senses and the mind *(manas).* In its dream state, when the senses are completely dormant and the mind alone is active, it cognizes objects in terms of the impressions left on the senses by the waking condition. In the state of deep sleep, when the senses and the mind are at rest, the soul is "dissolved in its own self and regains its true nature." However, even in deep sleep, as at death, the nucleus of individuality is active and intact; even in deep sleep the adjunct *(upādhi)* which limits the *jiva* to mundane existence, is potentially present. Radhakrishnan asks a pertinent question: "If, in deep sleep as in liberation, there is an entire absence of special cognition, how and in what does the sleeping person retain the seed of *avidyā* on account of which waking takes place?" (Radhakrishnan, 600).

Samkara, however, makes a distinction between the soul's temporary union with *Brahman* in deep sleep and its permanent absorption in *Brahman* in *moksha* or liberation. In the case of deep sleep, according to Samkara, the limiting adjunct *(upādhi)* exists, "so that when it starts up into being, the *jiva* must start up into existence"; in the state of *moksha,* "the seeds of *avidyā* are all burnt up" (Samkara's *bhāsyas* on *Brahma-Sutra* and Gaudapāda's *Kārikā,* cited in Radhakrishnan, 600). The differences amongst souls are explainable in terms of the limiting adjuncts or *upādhis,* and as such they do not involve any confusion of actions and their fruits. In his *Brahma-Sutra-bhāsya* Samkara offers the following comparison by way of elucidation: "As when one reflected image of the sun trembles, another reflected image does not on that account tremble also, so when one soul is connected with actions and results of actions, another soul is not on that account connected likewise. There is therefore no confusion of actions and results" (cited in Radhakrishnan, 601). This need not, however, be taken as a contradiction of the fact that the *jivas* are only empirically many but intrinsically one, for "each is alike the supreme reality" (Hiriyanna, *Outlines,* 364).

We may now turn to a discussion of the Advaita concept of *Brahman* or the Ultimate Reality or Supreme Spirit. To understand this, however, we must refer to Samkara's conception of the world/universe. According to Samkara, the world is the effect of something which is absolutely real, eternally conscious and infinite. The diversity of the universe is an impossibility without a cause which is absolutely perfect and self-sufficient. This uncaused or self-caused cause is *Brahman,* which expresses itself through an infinite number of things and patterns, all of which are merely appearances that have some practical or empirical truth but lack any metaphysical status. All these appearances, however, depend upon and are implicitly related to the *Brahman,* which is both their material cause *(upādāna-kārana)* and their efficient cause *(nimitta-kārana).* Thus, while Samkara accepts the Buddhist view of the ever-changing nature of all things, he envisages a suprasensible, transcendent reality which is not within the world of change. Samkara regards all diversity as being an illusion *(mithyā)*—something which urges us to look beyond its finite limits, to escape from one's own finitude, and thus to admit an absolute reality. Samkara's conception of the real *(sat)* is that of the eternal and causeless *Brahman;* his conception of the unreal *(asat)* is that of absolute nothing.

The world, for all its variety and beauty, does not belong to either of the two categories. It is not real, since it is anything but eternal; it is not unreal either, for it is clearly experienced by us in a manner no nonentity can be experienced, and because it is empirically efficient and serviceable. In Advaitic terms, it is something other than the real and the unreal *(sadāsad-vilakshana)*—an illusory appearance which is psychologically tenable but which cannot be logically established and must, therefore, be described and explained in terms of some higher reality. Unlike theological philosophers, however, Samkara refuses to accept this higher reality as a theological entity with definite attributes. For him, *Brahman* as the absolute reality is present to every individual as the ultimate fact of life; it is the basis and end of all "integral experience" *(anubhava),* the means as well as the proof of the highest religious insight. It is its own proof, although the necessity of its logical proof points to the inability of the mind to rest in the relative, its refusal to account for experience except in terms of an absolute.

Samkara's basic assumption in regard to nondualism is a restatement of the position of Gaudapāda, his spiritual grandfather: *Brahman* and the world "would not be seen as the cause and effect respectively had man been at once gifted with a supernatural and unalloyed insight to perceive transcendence qua transcendence" (Sinari, 109). His well-known argument that *Brahman appears* as the world because of ignorance *(avidyā),* must be understood to mean, as Sinari writes, that "it is the element of naiveté, the unenlightened common sense, that derives consciousness from grasping the exact structure of the Real, i.e., the foundation of the worldly" (Sinari, 109).

From the ontological point of view, *Brahman* is not the cause of anything, although Samkara's attempt to justify the dependence of the spatio-temporal reality on *Brahman* urges him to offer a theory of causality. For Samkara, the causal nature is universal *(sāmānya* or *svabhāva),* whereas the effect is a particular condition *(visesha* or *avasthā).* He writes in his commentary on the *Brihadāranyaka Upanishad:* "There are in the world many *sāmānyas* with their *viseshas*—both conscious and unconscious. All these *sāmānyas* in their graduated series are included and comprehended in one great *sāmānya,* i.e. in *Brahman*'s nature as a mass of intelligence" (quoted in Radhakrishnan, 534). Thus, to understand the nature of this universal-real is to know all the particulars involved in it; and therefore, to say that *Brahman* is the only reality is to distinguish it from the phenomenal, the temporal, the spatial and the sensible. As Dharmarāja says in *Vedānta-paribhāshā,* although *Brahman* is what is assumed as foundational, it is in no sense substantial: it is everywhere and all things imply and depend on it, but it cannot be located anywhere, and since it is not a thing and cannot therefore have spatial relationship with anything else, it is also nowhere. As is evident in our preceding half-line, paradox is the only means of describing its otherwise inexplicable and mysterious nature.

In his commentary on the *Bhagvadgitā* Samkara indicates the necessarily denotative character of every description of a thing: "Every word employed to denote a thing denotes that thing as associated with a certain *genus,* or act, or quality, or mode of relation." Thus every piece of denotation is based on certain empirical distinctions. *Brahman,* however, has nothing similar to it, nothing different from it, is not associated with any genus, possesses no qualities, does not act, and has no internal variety. "As it is opposed to all empirical existence, it is given to us as the negative of everything that is positively known. . . . It is the 'wholly other,' but not non-being. Though the words used are negative, what is meant is intensely positive. A negation is only an affirmation of absence. . . . We can at best say what *Brahman* is not, and not what it is" (Radhakrishnan, 535–536).

The famous Upanishadic formula *"neti neti"* ("not this, not this") does not merely refer to a simple process of elimination, it drives home the fact that whatever has the potentiality of being presented as an object/thing is ultimately unreal and that its obvious negation presupposes the Absolute, the Ultimate-Real; it recognizes the positive *Brahman* as something which transcends the glaring oppositions of empirical experience. The *Brahman,* however, is not eternal in the sense of its persistence through time like the motionless being of Parmenides, the "mindless, unmoving fixture" that Plato derides in his *Sophist;* it is eternal in the sense of "absolute timelessness and incorruptibility," in the sense that its perfect completeness is unrelated to time (see Radhakrishnan, 537).

Brahman, for Samkara, is the transempirical origin and destination of all phenomena. It is *sat-chit-ānanda* (real-consciousness-bliss): it is real *(sat)* in the sense that it is not unreal *(asat),* it is consciousness or intelligence *(chit)* in the sense that it is not unconsciousness or nonintelligence *(achit),* and it is bliss *(ānanda)* in the sense that it is not of the nature of pain *(duhkha-svarupa).* Samkara's realization that *Brahman* symbolizes *sat-chit-ānanda* compels him, as Sinari observes, to resort to an intellectual explanation of how *Brahman* becomes the world. Sinari writes:

> That is why the relation construed by him between the worldly and the other-worldly, or the immanent and the transcendental, has so much in common with the monistic metaphysics in the West – a metaphysics rooted in the basic intellectual need to know how the phenomenal world issues from Being. Sankara sees, as Hegel, F.H. Bradley, Kierkegaard, Josiah Royce and Karl Jaspers have seen, that the philosophical imperative preeminently figures in the form of a logical demand to justify the universe in relation to the beyond [Sinari, 110].

Sinari goes on to explore the status and implications of the *Brahman*-World connection in Samkara in the context of Bradley's twin concept of appearance-reality. Samkara could not possibly be unaware of the logical implication "that if *Brahman* is not subject to causal determination, then the world, for whose being *Brahman* forms the ground *(adhishtāna),* also ought to remain free from causality" – something which our experience does not support. For Sinari, therefore, the prime endeavor of Samkara's philosophy is to establish the compatibility of the noncausal *Brahman* with the causal order of the universe. The success of Samkara in this endeavor relates to his regarding (as does Bradley) our mimetic experience as having no status behond the confines of our ignorant or naive selves: "Being inseparable from our bondage-oriented life, the world responds to our natural dispositions, and makes us incur punishment on ourselves according to the deeds done by us. For Samkara, the appearance of the world has a moral significance. It is as if the result of our being alienated from the Absolute" (Sinari, 111). Radhakrishnan writes: "For Samkara, as for Bradley, the weakness of logic is in its assumption of the distinction between the knower and the known. All duality is mental" (Radhakrishnan, 526).

Nondualism remains the basis of Samkara's statement, *"Ātman* is *Brahman,"* as well as of its secular parallel, "The purely subjective *is* the purely objective." "*Brahman* seems to be mere abstract being, even as *Ātman* seems to be mere abstract subjectivity to the eyes of intellect. When we strip the Absolute of all its veils, we find that it is being refined away . . . The differenceless *Brahman* which we reach by an everlasting No . . . is likely to be confused with an indeterminate blank, an uncomfortable night of nothing" (Radhakrishnan, 537–538). Samkara silences such doubts as the foregoing passage describes.

In his commentary on the *Chāndogya Upanishad* he says: "*Brahman,* free from space, attributes, motion, fruition and difference, being in the highest sense and without a second, seems to the flow of mind no more than non-being." In his interpretations of the principal Upanishads, Samkara offers a reconciliation of the negative and the positive descriptions of *Brahman.* Integral knowledge *(vidyā)* gives the highest positive conceptual account of *Brahman* by calling it *sat-chit-ānanda* (being-consciousness-bliss) which in itself is self-sufficient; ignorance *(avidyā)* or lower knowledge assigns attributes which are relational, and which refer to the creatorship and rulership of the universe and serve the purposes of worship. When the negative form of *"neti neti"* ("not this, not this") relating to an exact metaphysics fails to convince us, we are inclined, "in the interests of our religious needs, to lay a different emphasis" (Radhakrishnan, 541).

The Unconditioned Consciousness then becomes a "conditioned *Ishvara* or God"—a creation of the finite intellect, which is explained and supported by human logic. *Ishvara* is "the personal aspect of the impersonal *Brahman*" (Sharma, 280), the *apara* or lower *Brahman* as contrasted with the *Para Brahman* or the Higher/Unconditioned *Brahman.* The following lines from Samkara's *Brahma-Sutra-Bhāsya* make this rather painful distinction from the Advaitin's standpoint: "The Superior *Brahman* is spoken of where It is indicated by such terms as 'not gross' through a negation of all the distinctions of names, forms, etc. called up by nescience. That very *Brahman* becomes the inferior *Brahman* where It is thought as possessed of some distinct name, form, etc. for the sake of meditation, as in such words as 'Identified with the mind, having *prāna* (i.e. the subtle body) as his body, and effulgence as his form'." To the objection that, in this context, the texts about nonduality are compromised, Samkara says:

> Not so . . . The results accruing from that meditation on the qualified *Brahman,* mentioned in the relevant contexts and consisting in the

> divine powers over the world and so on ... however, are confined within the transmigratory state itself on account of the continuance of ignorance. Since the result is associated with some particular space, any travelling for Its attainment involves no contradiction. Even though the Self is omnipresent ... [the qualified Self or *Brahman*] is presented merely as an apparent, alternative view by way of helping the (student's) development of the power of intellect [Swami Gambhirananda, 892].

The qualified *Brahman* is thus related to the beginning student's initiation into *Advaita* or nonduality, to his relative inability to realize the unqualified Self through temporal human endeavor, to his natural ability to know the *Brahman* only in terms of metaphoric superimpositions. *Ishvara* is the Supreme Consciounsness or *Brahman* brought under "the spell of a personal role, and as such is a manifestation of the finest, highest, most subtle and sublime aspect or level of ignorance and self-delusion" (Zimmer, 424); this God, who is the creator, maintainer and dissolver, is the all-embracing aspect of *māyā* (cosmic illusion) in its evolution and pervading of the cosmos. Some Vedantins draw a distinction between *māyā* (the cosmic illusion and the potency of the *Brahman*) and *avidyā* (individual ignorance), both of which come under the broad category of *ajñāna* (absence of knowledge). *Māyā* is that aspect of *ajñāna* by which the finest attributes are projected, whereas *avidyā* is that aspect by which impure qualities are projected: in the *māyā*-aspect the functions are more of a creative and generative kind *(vikshepa),* whereas in the *avidyā*-aspect, characteristics of veiling *(āvarana)* are more prominent.

Dasgupta writes: "The relation of the *chit* or pure intelligence, the highest self, with *māyā* and *avidyā* ... [respectively explain] the phenomenal *Ishvara* and the phenomenal *jiva* or individual" (Dasgupta, I, 475; emphasis added). *Ishvara* is thus the determinate *Brahman* (*saguna-Brahman,* as against indeterminate or *nirguna-Brahman,* which is the Ultimate-Real) regarded as "the supreme personality." For Heinrich Zimmer, the meaning of all this is that, when the pure metaphysical essence or *Brahman*—beyond all attributes and personal masks—sinks into the state in which, under a personal mask, "it fancies itself to be the Universal God, then the clarity of pure spiritual being is clouded, and this cloud is self-delusion on a cosmic scale"; it is "universal consciousness, forgetful of the true state and nature of Brahman."

Zimmer writes: "it imagines itself to be possessed of a divine personality: this is the crucial mystery of creation. The highest Lord, under this illusion, acquires the consciousness of being the highest Lord; fancies and feels himself to be endowed with omniscience, omnipotence, universal sovereignty, and all the other similar supreme virtues" (Zimmer, 425). The possession of these attributes, however, is itself "but a reflex of delusion": "Impersonal, anonymous, inactive-*Brahman* remains untouched, beyond these popular veiling clouds, the supreme eclipse. Only apparently is the universal substance implicated in this highest personal figure, which has been born, as a magnificent superego, out of a sublime state of godly consciousness-in-ignorance" (Zimmer, 425). Notwithstanding certain terminological inexactitudes (e.g., the identification of *Brahman* with "the universal *substance*"), Zimmer's is a lucid account of the nature of *Ishvara* in Advaita Vedānta.

We have already spoken of the importance of *Ishvara* for the uninitiated student, who arrives at a point in the process of his yogic evolution where he becomes identified with this personal creator of the world illusion and feels that he is one with the Supreme Lord, partaking of the latter's virtues of omniscience and omnipotence – all in all a critical phase in his spiritual career, since he must subsequently realize that this inflation is only a subtle form of self-delusion and that he must therefore go beyond it so he may realize the transpersonal essence of his actual Self. The otherwise attractive personality of the highest godhead or *Ishvara* will then dissolve "as the last, most tenuous and tenacious, cosmic illusion" (Zimmer, 426). However, as we have said, for the common man and for the aspiring yogi, *Ishvara* is the center of devotional exercises of self-surrender. By making *Ishvara* the center of one's daily activities, one is able to transcend one's individual ego; it is a step towards the conquest of the "I-Thou" dualism, towards a preliminary realization that all creatures, everywhere and at all times, are only *Ishvara*'s continuously changing manifestations. *Ishvara* is the highest appearance we have, the most subtle phenomenal being, the most magnificent and flattering appearance in the general panorama of erroneous self-deceptions, "a majestic, lordly face painted on the sublime blank of *Brahman*" (Zimmer, 427).

Critics who believe that *Ishvara* in Advaita is unreal and irrelevant, however, have missed not only the significance of *Ishvara,* but also the true significance of *Māyā*. *Ishvara* becomes unreal only for him who has realized his oneness with *Brahman* by transcending speech and mind. For the ordinary human being, *Ishvara* is all in all inasmuch as finite thought can never grasp *Brahman*. "And therefore," writes C.D. Sharma, "all talks about *Brahman* are really talks about *Ishvara*. Even the words 'unconditioned *Brahman*' refer really to 'conditioned *Ishvara*,' for the moment we speak of *Brahman,* He ceases to be *Brahman* and becomes *Ishvara*" (Sharma, 280). *Ishvara* cannot be said to be taken in by his own illusion, in which case He would have been a contradiction of everything advaitic; He is only seemingly involved in *māyā,* and that too in the purest, most refined and serene aspect of *māyā*. As Zimmer so insightfully elaborates this point:

> When the Lord seems to be enacting his cosmic role, he is not implicated in the net of illusion he creates; the pantomime of the divine part does not fool the actor. Therefore, if "God" is to be conceived of as unfolding, maintaining, and pervading the universe, and directing the mental propensities of finite beings through his universal, all-controlling power, it must be understood that He is performing a sort of play [what the Upanishads call *"līlā"*] for which there is no spectator – like a child. "God" is the lonely cosmic dancer whose gestures are all beings and all the worlds. These stream forth without end from his tireless, unremitting flow of cosmic energy as he executes the rhythmic, endlessly repetitious gestures. Siva, the dancing god, is not enthralled; and that is the principal distinction between the Lord *(Ishvara)* and the life-

monads *(Jiva)* that are dancing also in this universal play [Zimmer, 427–428].

Ishvara is "qualified *Brahman.*" Having said that, we ought to distinguish *Ishvara* from *Jiva* or individual soul. The *Jiva* (as stated earlier) is the agent and enjoyer, the experiencer of pleasure and pain, the acquirer of merit and demerit; *Ishvara* remains untouched by all this and is even indifferent to all this. The *Mundaka Upanishad* offers the analogy of "one bird" *(Jiva)* eating and enjoying the sweet fruit while "the other" *(Ishvara)* merely looks on. One is the enjoyer, the other is the ever-observant ruler. In the last analysis, however, there is little difference between *Jiva* and *Ishvara.* Radhakrishnan writes: "If *Ishvara* is *Brahman,* if the *jiva* is also metaphysically one with *Brahman,* and if the two are subject to limitations, the difference between God and the individual seems to be minimised" (Radhakrishnan, 608). From the metaphysical standpoint, both *Jiva* and *Ishvara* are *Brahman,* but on the phenomenal level—from the religious standpoint—their relation is in terms of master and servant. *Ishvara* the Master knows his oneness with *Brahman* and therefore enjoys eternal bliss, whereas *Jiva* the servant is ignorant of his higher, divine origin and is therefore subject to the self-deceptive trials and tribulations of a mundane existence.

Later Advaitins have suggested other modes of relation between *Jiva* and *Ishvara,* but these suggestions have very little value for the philosopher. As a conclusion to this part of our discussion, we may repeat something already said, since it is ultimately related to Advaitic ethics and the related concept of liberation *(moksha):* As long as the *Jiva* views *Brahman* as *samsāra,* God, Soul and Nature arise simultaneously, but when the *Jiva* realizes his own essence, which is of course *Brahman,* God, Soul and Nature vanish simultaneously (Sharma, 282). Ultimately, both samsaric bondage *and* liberation are phenomenal, for *Jiva* is really nondifferent from *Brahman;* the statement that *"Jiva* becomes *Brahman"* is only a verbally convenient way of indicating the purely nondual nature of *Brahman-Ātman.*

C.D. Sharma writes of the reckless use of several terms by Vedantins as very nearly synonymous: *Māyā, Avidyā, Ajñāna, Adhyāsa, Anirvachaniya, Vivarta, Bhrānti, Bhrama, Nāma-rupa.* There are two schools among later Advaitins divided on the question whether *Māyā* and *Avidyā* are the same or different. Samkara treats the two terms as synonymous but distinguishes between the two aspects of *Māyā/Avidyā,* which are called *vikshepa* and *āvarana,* the former being the positive aspect of projection and the latter the negative aspect of concealment. Those Advaitins who view *Māyā* and *Avidyā* as different, say that *Māyā* is something *positive,* though absolutely dependent on and inseparable from *Brahman,* which provides a medium for the reflection of *Brahman* and for the projection of this world, being an essentially indistinguishable power or potency *(shakti)* of *Brahman,* while *Advidyā* is something entirely *negative,* being sheer ignorance or absence of knowledge of Reality. Further, *Māyā,* "the cosmic power of projection," conditions *Ishvara,* who remains unaffected by *Avidyā,* the individual ignorance which conditions the *Jiva. Brahman* reflected in *Māyā* is *Ishvara,* whereas *Brahman* reflected in *Avidyā* is *Jiva.* Radhakrishnan makes the following distinction: "When we look at the problem from the objective side, we speak of *māyā,* and when from the subjective side, we speak of *avidyā*" (Radhakrishnan, 587; emphasis added). Also, *Māyā,* since it is directly associated with the pure spirituality of *Brahman,* has a preponderance of *sattva* (purest clarity), while *Avidyā* is made of all the three *gunas* or generative essences—sattva, rajas (passionate activity) and *tamas* (dull and dark inertia). Broadly speaking, however, the two schools of Advaita agree that, even as *Brahman* and *Ātman* are one, so are *Māyā* and *Avidyā* (also called *Mulavidyā* and *Tulāvidyā* respectively).

Every discussion of *māyā* and *avidyā* presupposes an understanding of the *Brahman* and the world. According to Samkara, *Brahman* and the world are nondifferent, and hence there cannot be any question as to their relation. The empirical world has its basis in *Brahman. Brahman,* however, is both "is and is not identical with the world": "It is, because the world is not apart from *Brahman;* it is not, because *Brahman* is not subject to the mutations of the world" (Radhakrishnan, 566). Samkara asserts that it is impossible—even as it is irrelevant—to explain the relation of *Brahman* and the world through logical categories. Samkara's assertion is based upon his distinction between the scientific principle of causality *(kāryakāranatva)* and the philosophical principle of nondifference *(ananyatva).* In his *bhāsya* on *Māndukya Upanishad* he writes: "The real is never known to have any relation with the unreal." For him, the relation of the world to *Brahman* is indefinable *(anirvachaniya).*

This has its parallel in the well-known and much abused analogy of the rope and the snake, which involves our mistaking the former for the latter: it is impossible to explain the relation of *Brahman* and the world even as it is so in case of the rope and the snake. The snake *is* there; the snake is *not* there. Samkara, however, makes it clear, that although the world "hangs on *Brahman,*" it does not affect the *Brahman;* he speaks of that kind of causality where the cause, without undergoing any change, produces the effect *(vivartopādāna)* as contrasted with the more common kind of causality where the cause is itself transformed in producing the effect *(parināmopādāna). Brahman* is that of which the *vivarta* ("turning point" or "perversion") is the world of time and space. Radhakrishnan writes: "*Vivarta* signifies the appearance of the absolute *Brahman* as the relative world of space and time.... The world of multiplicity is an aspect which reality takes for us, though not for itself" (Radhakrishnan, 570).

Samkara's many illustrations involving optical illusion—of the rope and the snake, of the shell and the silver, of the desert and the mirage—are essentially indicative of this "one-sided dependence of the effect on the cause and the maintenance of the integrity of the cause." The spatio-temporal world resides in *Brahman* even as the illusion of a snake resides in the rope. "In the case of transformation, the cause and the effect belong to the same order of reality, while in that of appearance the effect is of a different order of being from the cause" (Dharmarāja's *Vedāntaparibhāshā,* cited in Radhakrishnan, 570). Though phenomena are not identical with the cause, they can never be defined except in terms of the cause.

Māyā is not only the absence of knowledge, but positive wrong knowledge; it is not only nonapprehension, but misapprehension. It finitizes the Infinite and makes the perfect and unlimited *Ātman* or *Brahman* appear as limited *jivas;* it produces the false notions of plurality and difference. Radhakrishnan brings together the different implications of the term *Māyā* as used in Advaita Vedanta: 1) That the world is not self-explanatory shows its phenomenal character, which is signified by the term *Māyā*. 2) The problem of the relation between *Brahman* and the world has meaning for those who admit the pure being of *Brahman* from the intuitive standpoint and demand an explanation of its relation to the world; but it is impossible to articulate the relation of the ultimate reality to the world of plurality, since the two are heterogeneous, and thus every attempt at such an explanation is self-defeating. This incomprehensibility is signified by the term *Māyā*. 3) If *Brahman* is to be viewed as the cause of the world, it is only in the sense that the latter rests on the former, which remains unaffected by its effect. The world which rests on *Brahman* is called *Māyā*. 4) The principle which accounts for the appearance of *Brahman*-as-the-world is called *Māyā*. 5) The perfect personality, *Ishvara,* who is the result of our misplaced attention to the empirical world on the basis of the dialectic of logic, has power of self-expression. This power or energy is called *Māyā* (see Radhakrishnan, 573–574).

Sinari points out how, as a metaphysical conception, *Māyā* can be "an effective foundation for humanism," with its remarkable power of "suggesting to an entire community the virtue of sympathy and compassion towards all": "Since life is basically an illusory spectacle where the victor and the vanquished, the gifted and the miserable, the high and the low are all children of the same eternal sport *(lilā, kridā)* of *Brahman,* it could be argued that the sole objective one may live to realize is the emancipation of all." However, as Sinari observes, people have literally adhered to the *Māyā* hypothesis, with the result that "even obnoxious things have been explained away as shadowy and therefore not deserving any concern from man":

> Coupled with the deterministic theory of *karma,* it has sometimes left Indian masses inactive, fatalistic, chronically oblivious of the solid circumstances of life, and to unpreparedly aspire after the otherworldly bliss at the cruel cost of indispensable material necessities. And much more strangely than its original expounders might have visualized, it has taught some to justify their behaviour, however, antisocial or selfish, under the pretext of world's nonbeing [Sinari, 135–136].

When Gaudapāda and Samkara describe the phenomenal world as illusion *(adhyāsa),* indescribable *(anirvachaniya),* ignorance *(ajñāna),* transformation *(vivarta),* names-and-forms *(nāma-rupa),* or *māyā,* they are only reasserting the ancient Upanishadic thesis that the world is an appearance but *not* an absolute unreality, thus liberalizing what Sinari calls "the strong version of the *maya* hypothesis"—that is, the theory of absolute emptiness or *Sunya-vāda*—and conceding some degree of existence to the world (for a comparative discussion of Advaitic *Māyā* and the finite world-consciousness of 20th century phenomenologists, see Sinari, 147–152).

The concept of *Māyā* is intimately and invariably related with that of *Avidyā,* which is related to the individual human intellect and to which can be traced the entire world of experience. In his Introduction to his *Brahma-Sutra-Bhāsya,* Samkara speaks of the superimposition of the non–Self on the Self, which is "considered by the learned to be *avidyā,* nescience." Samkara elaborates the point:

> And the ascertainment of the nature of the real entity by separating the superimposed thing from it is called *vidyā* (illumination). This being so [i.e. superimposition being a product of nescience], whenever there is a superimposition of one thing on another, the locus is not affected in any way either by the merits or demerits of the thing superimposed. All forms of worldly and Vedic behaviour that are connected with valid means of knowledge and objects of knowledge start by taking for granted this mutual superimposition of the Self and non–Self, known as nescience; and so do all the scriptures dealing with injunction, prohibition, or emancipation [trans. Swami Gambhirananda, 3–4].

Thus, *avidyā* has its seat in the human intellect, more specifically in our cognitive mechanism. It is "the fall from intuition, the mental deformity of the finite self that disintegrates the divine" into innumerable forms, each of which is supported by logic; it is the twist of the mind which forces the latter to view things only through the texture of space-time-cause. As Radhakrishnan points out, it is not conscious dissimulation—for, that would involve a capacity to differentiate—but the unconscious tendency of the finite mind to confuse the transcendental with the empirical, the very kernel of our being with illusory phenomenal entities. As is evident in the quotation from Samkara's Introduction to *Brahma-Sutra,* it is on the basis of *avidyā* that he implicitly rejects the Mimāmsaka's undue and ill-placed emphasis on action *(karma).*

Avidyā is either absence of knowledge or doubtful or erroneous knowledge. Samkara, however, declares *avidyā* to be inexplicable. "The question is meaningless in Samkara's metaphysics," writes Radhakrishnan, for we cannot make "a transcendent use of an empirical category" (Radhakrishnan, 577). In his commentary on *Gitā,* Samkara offers the view that if we can understand the relation of *Ātman* to *avidyā,* we must be beyond the two. Further, if *avidyā* were a property of the *Ātman,* the latter could never get rid of it, but the *Ātman* "does not take in or part with anything whatsoever" (Radhakrishnan, 577). *Avidyā* cannot belong to any "finite being, whether he be God or man, since the latter must first be created in order that his *avidyā* may be possible"; which means that his creation cannot be due to his or anyone else's *avidyā.* Radhakrishnan writes: "The individualisation of *Brahman,* the rise of finite spirits, cannot be due to the *avidyā* characteristic of finite life. It is an occurrence due to divine activity. But how *avidyā* and *Brahman* can coexist is just the problem for which we do not have any solution" (Radhakrishnan, 577). In his commentary on the *Brihadāranyaka Upanishad* Samkara writes: "We admit that *Brahman* is not the product of *avidyā* or is itself deluded, but we do not admit that there is another deluded conscious being (besides *Brahman*) which could be the producer of the ignorance."

Ethics and Liberation

According to Samkara, of all items of the universe, the human individual alone is the ethical subject, for he alone knows his two-way connection—with the infinite as well as the finite. It is because the infinite *Brahman* is "revealed to a larger extent in human beings that they are entitled to ethical and logical activity" (Radhakrishnan, 612, 613). Samkara holds that man's state of bondage and suffering—the state of inmost strain—is due not to any original sin but to *avidyā* or original and beginningless ignorance. Thus the realization of the *Brahman*—the identity of *Ātman* and *Brahman*—is the end of all activities and the object of all striving. This end or goal is directly deducible from the Advaitic explanation of the character of the individual self, which, according to the system, is *Brahman* itself, and its apparent distinction from it is entirely due to the illusory adjuncts *(upādhi)* with which it identifies itself.

It is for this reason that the knowledge of reality in Advaita is called liberating knowledge. The only thing that can give us permanent satisfaction is the experience of *Brahman (brahmānubhava)*—an experience which is equivalent to the supreme state of unqualified joy and peace and marks the perfection of individual development. It denotes our journey beyond the mocking semblances of finite satisfactions. In his commentary on *Mundaka Upanishad* Samkara writes: "The individual sinks down in sin and grief so long as he believes that his body is the *Ātman*, but when he realises he is one with the self of all things, his grief ceases." It is not for the individual to manipulate reality to fit into any ideal state of mind; he has only to recognize it. As Radhakrishnan writes: "Philosophy with Samkara is not the production of what *ought to be,* but is the apprehension of what *is*" (Radhakrishnan, 614).

Krishnachandra Bhattacharyya writes in a similar vein:

> The individual self has not only to correct for himself his subjective illusion of individuality, not only to wait for the cosmic illusion of individuality to be corrected, but also to contemplate all correction to be itself illusory. He has to contemplate *moksha* [liberation or emancipation] not as something to be reached or effected or remanifested, not even as an eternal predicament of the self, but as the self itself or the *svarupa* [essential form] of *Brahman.* The self or the absolute is not a thing having freedom but freedom itself [K. Bhattacharyya, 249].

The liberated man, the one "released even while living" *(jivan-mukta),* represents the supreme ideal of the divine man on earth and is comparable to the various ideals for man that have served to shape the raw materials of life in other cultures: "the Hebrew patriarch, the Greek athlete-philosopher, the Roman stoic-soldier, the knight of the chivalrous Middle Ages, the eighteenth-century gentleman, the objective man of science, the monk, the warrior, the king, or the Confucian scholar-sage" (Zimmer, 441). From this standpoint, all ethical goods, although bound up with the world of distinctions, are a valuable means to the most desirable end, which is *brahmānubhava.*

This does not, however, mean that there is no need to undergo any practical discipline. In common with the other Indian systems, Advaita discipline consists of two parts, the first of which is meant for pursuing detachment *(vairāgya)* and the second, for acquiring knowledge *(jñāna)* of the ultimate reality through direct experience (and not merely through theoretical reasoning or reflection). *Vairāgya* signifies adherence to duty in the manner taught in the *Gitā* with a view to perfecting character and in a spirit of absolute disinterestedness. Duty begins with the fulfillment of the daily obligations of life and the demands of household piety: these produce a frame of mind conducive to realization, make the ordinary individual duly qualified to study Vedanta *(sādhana).*

The qualifications necessary for the study of Vedānta are the following two: 1) The person having studied all the Vedas with the right accessories (e.g. grammar, lexicon, etc.) is in full possession of the knowledge of the Vedas; 2) He must have performed only the obligatory duties (*nitya-karma,* such as daily prayer) as prescribed in the Veda and must have avoided all end-oriented actions (*kāmya-karmas,* such as the performance of sacrifices for going to Heaven) and all prohibited actions (*nishiddha-karmas,* such as murder), so that his mind is purged of all good and bad actions. In his *Ātmabodha* Samkara writes: "Though the *Ātman* is at all times and in all things, it does not shine in all things. It shines only through understanding, just as reflection appears only in polished surfaces." Samkara attaches great importance to philosophical wisdom, which is attainable only through a practice of virtue.

Advaita admits four virtues: 1) The knowledge of what is eternal and what is transient; 2) Disinclination to the pleasures of this life as well as of the life after death; 3) Extreme distaste for all enjoyments, and anxiety for attaining the means of right knowledge; 4) A strict control over the senses so that the senses are restrained from everything except that which aids the attainment of right knowledge and the ultimate salvation. The next part of the discipline is threefold: formal study *(sravana),* reflection *(manana),* and meditation *(dhyāna). Sravana* signifies the study and discussion of the *sāstras* (the Upanishads and the *Gitā*) with the active assistance of a proper preceptor *(guru),* that is, one who has realized the truth he teaches, which is the sole reality of *Brahman.* It thus signifies that the ultimate philosophic truth is to be learned through a study of the revealed texts; it also emphasizes the need for training under a competent teacher in order that the study may be fruitful. *Manana* refers to that stage when, as a result of formal study of the relevant texts, the disciple comes to know the fundamental identity of the individual and the absolute. Having discovered the final truth through *sravana* (formal study), the disciple must remove all doubts *(asambhāvanā)* as to the rightness of that truth. Hence the stage of reflection, when the disciple convinces himself of the correctness of advaitic teaching with the help of examples from ordinary life. "It is intended to transform what has been received on trust into one's own true conviction and brings out well the place assigned to reason in the Advaita" (Hiriyanna, *Outlines,* 380).

This recognition of the value of analytical reasoning or reflection is something unique in a doctrine whose ultimate emphasis is on mystic experience. But, as Hiriyanna points out, the arguments based on commonplace examples are only analogical for, while they are drawn from the realm of everyday experience, *Brahman* by hypothesis transcends them: "They can thus only give support to, or indicate the probability of, Vedantic truth, and cannot demonstrate it independently of revelation" (Hiriyanna, *Essentials,* 172).

Dhyāna (also called *Nididhyāsana*) refers to that stage of transformation of the mediate knowledge of ultimate reality acquired by the study of the Upanishads and by subsequent reflection into direct experience. Although *manana* (reflection) ensures intellectual conviction, there may be obstacles in the way of self-realization – "an unconscious reassertion of old habits of thought *(viparita-bhāvanā)* incompatible with what has since been learnt" (Hiriyanna, *Outlines,* 380). *Dhyāna* or *Nididhyāsana* (meditation) is meant to overcome precisely this kind of obstacle. It is meditation upon the identity between the individual Self and *Brahman;* it is a focusing on a long-enduring inner vision, a fervent concentration beyond the sphere of argument and intellectual reflection. It should be carried on till the desired intuitive knowledge is attained and the *Ātman-Brahman* identity becomes immediate *(aporaksha)* in the verbally translated form of "I am *Brahman*" *("Aham Brahma asmi");* this ultimate point in this stage is *jivan-mukti* or "freedom-in-this-life." The person who has reached this stage is a *jivan-mukta* or a "free-while-living-man" and may continue to be associated with his "several physical accompaniments."

As Hiriyanna describes this state: "He is in life and yet lifted out of it. He will necessarily continue to work and help others, but the service he renders will be the natural expression of his felt conviction regarding the oneness of all . . . the constraint of obligation is replaced in that stage by the spontaneity of love" (*Essentials,* 173–174). The *jivan-mukta* does not grow indifferent to the world, but only duty *as such* ceases to be significant to him. His stage is one of "transcendent wakefulness" (Zimmer, 433). When a *jivan-mukta* casts off his physical body at death, he becomes freed in the absolute sense of the term *(videha-mukta* or "free-without-the-body").

It is widely believed that Samkara's Advaita, though a masterpiece of intellect, cannot inspire religious piety, that his Absolute cannot generate a passionate love and kindle adoration in the soul. However, the worship of God is not a deliberate alliance with falsehood, since God is the only form in which the finite mind can picture the Absolute. "The conception of a personal God is the fusion of the highest logical truth with the deepest religious conviction" (Radhakrishnan, 649). He is an object of genuine worship and not "a non-ethical deity indifferent to man's needs and fears"; He possesses the qualities of power and justice, righteousness and mercy; He is regarded as creator, sustainer and judge of the universe and is omnipresent, omnipotent and omniscient; He is perfectly holy and morally beautiful. For Samkara, religion is not a doctrine or ceremony but life itself; it starts with the soul's sense of the infinite and comes to its fruition with the soul's becoming the infinite through a process of spontaneous and intuitive absorption.

Religious worship is broadly of two kinds: first, the worship of a personal God *(saguna-Brahman)* and second, that of symbols *(pratika)* when the worshipper looks upon God as external to him. But a personal God has meaning only for the immediate and practical religious consciousness and not for the highest insight; He has meaning only for the finite individual blinded by the empirical veils of ignorance in the same manner that bondage and redemption have a meaning for one whose consciousness is tarnished by his lower nature. Radhakrishnan states Samkara's argument:

> If a personal God exclusive of the individual were the highest, then mystic experiences would become unintelligible, and we should have to remain content with a finite God. God is no God if he is not the All; if he be the All, then religious experience is not the highest. If God's nature is perfect, it cannot be so, so long as man's imperfect nature stands over against it; if it is not perfect, then it is not the nature of God [Radhakrishnan, 650–651].

There is thus a fundamental contradiction in the religious experience, pointing to its imperfect nature and indicating that it belongs to the province of individual ignorance *(avidyā)*. This does not, however, lead Samkara to reject the Vedic deities, whom he regards as personifications of natural forces that act as presiding agents of different life functions but remain unaffected by the experiences of the individual soul. This is established by the fact that at death, these deities do not accompany the life organs but simply withdraw their assisting power. Samkara questions the immortality of the deities who, having been created by the Supreme like everything else, are involved in *samsāra* (mundane existence) and subject to transitoriness. This view, according to Samkara, does not affect the eternal character of the Vedas, for the Vedic deities do not represent individuals but general notions. The word "Indra," for example, does not refer to any specific deity but to a certain place *(sthāna-visesha)* in the complex hierarchy of beings, and thus, whoever occupies that place is "Indra."

To the objection that their individuality is neither real (since the deities are not *seen* at sacrifices) not possible (since an individual cannot be at more than one place at one time so as to receive the sacrificial offerings), Samkara replies that the gods are not seen because they have the power to make themselves invisible and that they can multiply their bodies a thousandfold as the yogins do. While Samkara's spiritual faith does not include ritual and shrines, he had sufficient historical sense to recommend them to those who were in need of them. In matters of both religion and philosophy Samkara combined a clear-eyed realism with an unflinching loyalty to the ideal and emphasized the religion of truth rooted in spiritual inwardness. By laying stress on the *personal* character of religious experience, Samkara "broadened and spiritualised Hinduism" (Radhakrishnan, 654). As an explicit religion, Advaitism insists on the conservation of one's spiritual individuality or *svadharma,* while implicitly as philosophy, it recognizes the *svadharma* of everyone else as absolutely sacred. Again, as an explicit philosophy, it takes every individual self as the Supreme Self or Reality, and as an implicit religion, it denies the world of commonality and retires into the solitude of subjectivity.

Theory of Knowledge

Although Samkara refers to only three sources of knowledge, namely, perception, inference and scriptural testimony, later Advaitins have added three more—comparison, implication and negation or noncognition. Broadly speaking, the Advaita theory of knowledge is not very much different from that of Mimāmsā. As we have seen already, in the Indian systems the factors constituting and connected with knowledge *(jñāna* or *pramā)* are usually analyzed into the subject *(jñatr* or *pramātr),* the object *(jñeya* or *prameya),* and the means of knowledge *(pramāna).* However, consciousness is not always regarded as the product of any relation between the subject and the object. While the Sāmkhya, the Vedā and the Jaina schools view the self as possessed of intrinsic consciousness, so that knowledge is no more than the relation of the object to an already existing consciousness of the self, the Vaiseshika-Nyāya and the Mimāmsā schools maintain that knowledge is a product of the relation of a previously unconscious self to some object in a particular way.

The Buddhists regard consciousness and knowledge as fleeting products of several conditions. Both Sāmkhya-Yoga and Vedānta make a distinction, however, between consciousness-in-itself *(svarupa-chaitanya)* and consciousness of objects *(vrtti-chaitanya).* According to Sāmkhya-Yoga, the self as the knower is real and is different from the object(s) of knowledge; so that, unless the object produces through the senses and the mind some image of itself in the intellect *(buddhi),* there cannot be any knowledge. But Advaita regards the distinction between the knower and the known as a matter of convenience and, in the ultimate analysis, untenable, and hence, unlike Sāmkhya-Yoga, it does not admit the reality of even the role of the self as knower: the knower and the known are but "the two apparent aspects of one basic reality, the real Self or *Brahman*" (Dutta, 549). The Advaitin does not therefore consider knowledge as an external relation, although, in order to explain knowledge in terms of the dualistic beliefs of the ordinary individual, he adopts to a limited extent the Sāmkhya theory of knowledge—that the object in contact with the external sense or directly present to the internal sense *(antahkarana)* causes a modification *(vrtti)* of the internal sense. The modification *(vrtti)* only serves to remove the illusory distinction between the knower and the known.

As we have seen, all the Indian systems admit perception *(pratyaksha)* as the basic source of knowledge. The Advaitins speak of the potential omniscience of every individual. The self is really one with the absolute *Brahman,* and what limits its knowledge is its ignorance of its true nature; when ignorance is removed, what remains is the self-shining consciousness, the *Brahman.* Immediacy is primarily the nature of this basic consciousness and only secondarily is involved with sense perception. Every such perception has its basis in a removal of the ignorance that divides the knower from the known. "Perception is therefore a momentary restoration of the lost identity between the two and the flashing forth of the basic consciousness which underlies all—the knower, the known, and the entire mechanism of knowledge" (Dutta, 552). Thus, the appearance or perception of an object is the self-shining of the pure consciousness *(chit)* through a modified state *(vrtti)* of a form resembling an object of knowledge.

Similarly, inference *(anumāna),* according to Vedānta, is related to our notion of concomitance *(vyāpti-jñāna)* between two things in terms of specific past impressions *(samskāra).* The notion of concomitance being altogether subjective, the Vedāntist does not emphasize the necessity of perceiving such concomitance in a large number of cases. As Dasgupta writes, "Vedānta is not anxious to establish any material validity for the inference, but only subjective and formal validity" (Dasgupta, I, 473). Although the Advaita Vedāntist admits the Nyāya distinction between the inference for one's own sake *(svārtha-anumāna)* and inference for the sake of others *(parārtha-anumāna),* in the latter case it advocates only three members (instead of the five of Nyāya), namely, proposition or *pratijñā* ("The hill is fiery"), reason or *hetu* ("Because it has smoke"), and example or *dristānta* ("As in the kitchen"). The Advaita school admits scriptural testimony *(sabda)* as a valid source of knowledge, although it defends the authority of the Vedas on grounds other than those of the Nyāya and the Mimāmsā philosophers. According to Advaita, the archetypal forms are not eternal in the sense in which *Brahman* is eternal, since they are all the products of ignorance or *avidyā.* The origination of the world from the word *(sabda)* does not, according to Advaita, mean that the word constitutes the material cause of the world as *Brahman* does (see Radhakrishnan, 496). Creation is only the actualization of the "everlasting words, whose essence is the power of denotation in connection with their eternal significations" (Samkara's *Brahma-Sutra-Bhāsya,* quoted in Radhakrishnan, 496).

As far as comparison *(upamāna)* as a source of knowledge is concerned, both the Mimāmsā and Advaita schools think that this knowledge can be said to be obtained in part by verbal testimony and in part by inference *(sabda* and *anumāna)* and need not therefore be admitted as an independent source of knowledge. Both Mimāmsā and Advaita schools admit implication or presumption *(arthāpatti)* as an independent source of knowledge, however, even as they accept nonapprehension or noncognition *(anupalabdhi)* as one. There is very little difference in their views regarding these two sources of knowledge (see the relevant section in the chapter on "Mimāmsā").

For Samkara, anything that does not bring forth the true nature of things *(vastu-svarupam)* is *avidyā,* for it is only relational and contingent and, to that extent, imperfect. Empirical knowledge revels in the distinctions of knower, knowledge and the known whereas the real is free from such distinctions and hence is beyond the possibility of being treated as an object of knowledge. "While the process of knowledge is nothing more than a manifestation of the ultimate reality, it is impossible to catch the real in a process of self-consciousness" (Radhakrishnan, 502). Samkara thus emphasizes the inadequacy of discursive thinking in apprehending the real. Samkara's view does not, however, reject ordinary and scientific knowledge, for so long as we do not reach "a higher plane attainable only by higher intelligences, our conclusions are quite valid, except that they remain on the same plane as their premises." Unfortunately, however, all our attempts to know the real are demonstrative of something other than the real and are carried out in terms of characteristic functions of the real, which is absolute and nonrelational.

Samkara's theory of error relates to our attributing to the real that which it is not (nonreal), our superimposition of a world of duality and plurality on the nondual and unique identity of the individual self and *Brahman*. Samkara's word for this is *adhyāsa,* which is defined as "the appearance of a thing where it is not." According to Samkara, all knowledge of finite things is in a sense the negation of pure being, since it involves the superimposition which brings into view a multitude of beings, interests and conflicting opposites whereas there is only one indivisible Reality. All the sources of knowledge, therefore, are valid only till that time when the absolute truth is attained and hence, have relative value for the finite understanding. "All determinate knowledge is a self-abnegation, involving, as it does, a modalisation of the ultimate consciousness into the subject, mode and object" (Radhakrishnan, 509). Later Advaitins, however, have offered a different theory of error and have evolved this theory from their interpretation of illusory perception.

In every such case of illusory or erroneous perception, there is an undeniable positive appearance directly present to the mind, and it is "a misrepresentation of experience to explain it either as the vividly revived memory-idea of something perceived in the past or to explain it negatively as a lack of discrimination between the perceived and the reproduced" (Dutta, "Indian Epistemology," 561). The illusory snake (in our erroneous perception of a rope in semidarkness) is as objectively present to consciousness as a real snake, although it is momentary and contradicted by subsequent experience. It cannot therefore be described as perfectly real (for it is contradicted subsequently), nor can it be described as absolutely unreal (for it appears to consciousness). The illusory object should be recognized as indescribable. The later Advaitins' theory of error is therefore known as the theory of the appearance of the indefinable or indescribable *(anirvachaniya-khyāti-vāda).* The illusory object is the vanishing creation of ignorance *(avidyā),* which is responsible for all errors.

To counter such possible errors, Samkara admits the reality of an intuitional consciousness *(anubhava)* which supersedes the distinctions of subject and object – the state of consciousness which is the result of the individual's casting off of all finite conditions, including his intelligence. It is related to moments of selfless contemplation and purely aesthetic enjoyment, a kinship which shows that *anubhava* "is not the immediacy of an uninterpreted sensation, where the existence and the content of what is apprehended are not separated. . . . *Anubhava* and *adhyāsa,* intuition and intellect, point to a fissure between the infinite reality and the finite mind" (Radhakrishnan, 513). But, as Samkara says, while *anubhava* is open to all, it is attainable only by a few. This should not of course mean that Samkara agrees with the view that it is only to the chosen ones that the Real reveals itself. Reality—objective, ever-present—is waiting to be seized by those few who are anxious to seize it.

2. Visishtādvaita Vedānta

The Visishtādvaita school came as a reaction to the Advaitism of Samkara. Its foremost exponent is Rāmānuja (11th century); its striking feature is its attempt to combine personal theism with the philosophy of the Absolute. Not surprisingly, therefore, it has been treated as an instance of qualified nondualism. The harmonious combination of absolutism with personal theism is not something new and can be traced back to the *Bhagavadgitā,* the *Mahābhārata,* and the *Purānas,* especially the *Vishnu Purāna* and the *Bhāgavata Purāna.*

The earliest attempts to bring together theism and the philosophy of the Absolute are evident in parts of Vedic literature itself (Hiriyanna, *Outlines,* 382). Later attempts to combine the two took three main lines, namely, Vaishnavism, Shaivism and Shāktism, according as the Personal God was identified with Vishnu, Shiva, or Shakti. Among the Vaishnavas, there are four main sects: Shri-sampradāya (Vishishtādvaita) of Rāmānuja, Brahma-sampradāya (Dvaita) of Madhva, Rudra-sampradāya (Shuddhādvaita) of Vallabha and Vishnusvāmi, and Sanaka-sampradāya (Dvaitādvaita) of Nimbārka.

The Vaishnavas, the Shaivas and the Shāktas have their different sacred texts, called *Āgamas,* which are treated with the same respect as the Vedas. The *Āgamas* are generally divided into four parts: *Jñāna* (or Knowledge), *Yoga* (or Concentration), *Kriyā* (or acts related to the founding of temples and installing idols therein), and *Charya* (or the methods of worship). The *Āgamas* of Vaishnavism are called *Pancharātra,* those of Shaivism are called the *Shaiva Āgama,* while those of Shāktism are called the *Tantra.* While all the Viashnava schools recognize the sacred authority of the *Pancharātra* (also called *Pancharātra-Samhitā*), for Rāmānuja's Shri-sampradāya (also called Shrivaishnava-sampradāya) it is the most sacred text. There have been at least three interpretations as to the title *Pancharātra* (*Pancha* = five, *rātra* = night): first, because it deals with five philosophical topics; second, because it incorporates the essence of the four Vedas and the Sāmkhya-Yoga; and third, because it is believed to have been taught by Nārāyana (Vishnu) to his five disciples over five nights.

As we have said, Rāmānuja's theistic-absolutism or qualified nondualism came as a reaction to Samkara's Absolutism. Radhakrishnan identifies the reason for this: "The Absolute of Samkara, rigid, motionless, and totally lacking in initiative or influence, cannot call forth our worship.... [T]he Absolute remains indifferent to the fear and love of its worshippers, and for all those who regard the goal of religion as the goal of philosophy—to know God is to know the real—Samkara's view seems to be a finished example of learned error" (Radhakrishnan, 659).

For Rāmānuja, Samkara's view seemed to satisfy neither the natural instincts nor the trained intelligence. Samkara's theories of world-appearance and God as a bloodless Absolute could not satisfy man's genuine religious aspiration. To counter Samkara's barren and abstract Absolute, Rāmānuja provided an interpretation of Vedānta that at once preserved the identity of and difference between *Ātman* and *Brahman,* between man and God. For Ṣamkara's *jñāna* (knowledge), Rāmānuja offered *bhakti* (devotion); for Samkara's *jñāna-mārga,* Rāmānuja had his *bhakti-mārga;* for Samkara's intellectualism he had a substitute in devotionalism. Rāmānuja's devotionalist message consisted in an unrestrained love for God, which, as he said, is sure to liberate man from his mundane suffering and worldly bondage. Accordingly, he concentrates his attention on the world, the worldly souls, and God, all of which are equally real. However, God is both real and independent, while the reality of the souls is wholly dependent on that of God. He insists on a spiritual principal at the basis of the world, so that for him the world is not an illusion; he believes in the continued individual existence of the liberated souls. But Rāmānuja also says, that although the world of unconscious matter and the individual souls have a real existence of their own, they owe their existence to *Brahman.*

Brahman is eternally perfect, matter and the individual souls have their imperfections—matter is inanimate and unconscious, the individual souls are subject to ignorance and suffering prior to their release. Yet God, the souls, and the world form a unity, since matter and souls have existence only as the body of *Brahman,* for *Brahman* is the self and the controlling power of the body, which includes the world and the worldly souls. These have no existence apart from *Brahman* and yet are different from *Brahman.* Rāmānuja's theory, therefore, is nondualism *(advaita)* with a difference or qualification *(visesha),* which is its admittance of plurality: the supreme spirit subsists in a plurality of forms as souls and matter. Hence, it is called *Visishtādvaita* or "qualified nondualism."

On the ethical side, we have already noted the reaction against the ritualism of the Mimāmsakas also. As Radhakrishnan notes, the sacrificial cult had always to contend with "the devotional worship of the Supreme through symbols": "In the sacrificial religion of the Vedas, the priest who officiates is more important than the deity. But the dative case offers no solace to the aching heart" (Radhakrishnan, 661).

To add to this, Kumārila, the Brāhmin Mimāmsaka, in his enthusiastic attempt to restore order to a society that had gone chaotic by the disintegration of Buddhism through a revival of the Brāhmanical cult, made the already existing gulf between the upper classes and the lower ones wider. The people at large, who could not participate in sacrificial occasions, were left to their devotional cults. The reaction against the partial nature of sacrificial participation that Mimāmsā encouraged, led to the development of the three theistic religions of Vaishnavism, Saivism, and Shāktism. These were catholic religions and were quite liberal and inclusive as far as distinctions of caste, race or social and economic status were concerned. Further, though Samkara was against any interpretation of *jñāna* in terms of theoretical learning, there was a tendency among his followers to make religion more an affair of the head than of the heart or will – something that was soon replaced by "intelligent devotion" or *bhakti*. Notwithstanding doctrinal differences, all the four Vaishnava schools *(sampradāyas)* agreed in rejecting the conception of *māyā,* in regarding God as personal, and the soul "as possessed of inalienable individuality, finding its true being not in an absorption in the Supreme but in fellowship with him" (Radhakrishnan, 662).

Rāmānuja's philosophy is not mere speculative thought, nor his religion mere faith in dogmas; for him a true philosophy of religion avoids the two extremes of belief in the omnipotence of reason and blind faith in scriptural authority. Faith in what the scriptures reveal needs verification through intuition, which in turn should conform to the rational demands of certainty and universality. The role of reason is to mediate between faith and intuition and make the truths of revelation realizable and those of intuition intelligible. In his Visishtādvaitic exposition of the nature of Reality, Rāmānuja harmonizes the claims of revelation, intuition, and reason. Rāmānuja's genius for synthesis – his inclusive attitude towards things both theological and secular – is evident in his acceptance, on equal terms and with equal respect, of the Vedas, the *Pancharātra,* the intensely devotional hymns of the Ālvārs (Vaishnava poet-saints of South India), and the highly eclectic *Purānas.* All of these were equally authoritative for Rāmānuja. His Vedāntic liberality "consists mainly in the harmony it effects between revelation and realization, and the invitation it extends to humanity to experience the beatitude of *Brahman*" (Srinivasachari, 301). Radhakrishnan compares Samkara and Rāmānuja, the two great exponents of the Vedānta: "Their minds were driven to the same problems, their texts were practically the same, their methods were based on the same presumptions, and yet their results show striking differences. . . . Rāmānuja trusts firmly to the religious instinct, and sets forth a deeply religious view which reveals God to man through creation, through the theophanies, through the prophets, through the incarnations" (Radhakrishnan, 666–667). Rāmānuja's God was no longer the abstract pure being of Brāhmanism, but "a being full of love and forgiveness, and although the relationship was posed in philosophical terms it was essentially a personal relationship based on Love. The emphasis on the individual in this relationship carried almost a protestant flavour. Rāmānuja was an effective bridge between the devotional cult and Hindu theology, attempting as he did to weave together what appeared to be two divergent strands" (Thapar, 217). But although his basic ideas became increasingly popular with the masses, his emphasis on God's forgiveness led to a schism in his school: while the Northern group of Visishtādvaitins maintained that man must strive for this forgiveness and eventual salvation, the Southern group was of the view that God himself selects those that are to be saved. Despite this schism, Rāmānuja's liberal ideas were to affect deeply the contemporary theological and scholarly thought and practice. Romila Thapar writes:

> Although the temple was not opened to the *shudras* [the lower castes], the deities and rituals of a vast number of subsidiary cults crept into the temple. This was an inevitable process if the temple was to retain its vitality as the centre of social and religious life . . . This in turn led to some physical changes in the temple. Subsidiary shrines had to be accommodated, pavilions built for the recitation of sacred literature before large audiences, and images of the saints in addition to the gods had to be housed within the temple precincts [Thapar, 218].

By founding "a theological basis for spiritual love, Rāmānuja went far towards providing caste society with a universal ethic" (Lannoy, 208).

Literature

We have already mentioned the sacred texts of the Hindus in which Rāmānuja found his initial inspiration. He was also influenced to a great degree by the hymns of the Ālvār saints as well as the *Āchāryas* (theologians) who succeeded the Ālvārs. The chief among the Vaishnavite teachers of Vedānta who preceded Rāmānuja are Nāthamuni and Yamunāchārya. Nāthamuni, who was a disciple of the last of the Ālvār saints and arranged some 4,000 Ālvār hymns, is believed to have written *Nyāyatattva* and *Yogarahasya*. Yamunācharya, who struggled hard to assign to the Vaishnava *Āgamas* the status of the Vedas, wrote *Āgamaprāmānya, Mahāpurushanirnaya, Siddhi-trayam, Gitārtha-samgraha, Chatussloki* and *Stotra-ratna*. Rāmānuja's own works attempt to synthesize the thought of the Upanishads, the *Gitā* and the *Brahma-Sutra*—the Sanskrit *Prasthāna-traya*—and the faith and belief of the Vaishnava saints as contained, especially, in the Ālvārs' Tamil *Prabandham*. His commentary on Bādarāyana's *Brahma-Sutra*, called *Sri-bhāsya* (literally, "*the* Commentary," or "the masterly commentary"), is considered to be "one of the most important works of thought that India has produced" (Rudolph Otto, quoted in Winternitz, 532) and, rather exaggeratedly, as "one of the most important productions of world-literature" (M. Walleser, quoted in Winternitz, 333). His other works include a commentary on the *Gitā, Vedārtha-samgraha, Vedānta-sāra, Vedānta-dipa, Gadya-traya,* and *Bhagavad-ārādhanā-krama*. Sudarsana Suri's *Sruta-prakāsika* (13th or 14th century) is the principal commentary on Rāmānuja's *Sri-bhāsya*.

Sometime in the 13th century the differences between the Tengalais (the Southern School) and the Vadagalais (the Northern School) became prominent. The Tengalais regarded the Tamil *Prabandham* alone as truly canonical, whereas the Vadagalais accepted both the Sanskrit and the Tamil Vaishnava texts as canonical literature. Lokāchārya was the chief exponent of the Tengalai school and wrote as many as 18 works, together called

Rahasyas ("secrets" or "mysteries"), the most important of which are *Artha-panchaka* and *Tattva-traya.*

Venkatanātha (also known as Vedānta Desika), who was the founder of the Vadagalai school, wrote several works of philosophical and religious value. These include *Paramatabhanga* and *Rahasyatraya-sāra;* a commentary on Rāmānuja's *Sri-bhāsya* called *Tattva-tikā,* and a commentary on Rāmānuja's commentary on the *Gitā* called *Tātparya-chandrikā; Sesvara Mimāmsā,* in which he treats the "Purva" and the "Uttara" Mimāmsās as parts of one whole and offers the thesis that *karma* is incapable of producing its fruit independent of divine intervention; *Nyāya-parisuddhi,* a comprehensive logical work of the Visishtādvaita school, as well as a work supplementary to it, called *Nyāya-siddhānjñana; Tattva-muktā-kālāpa,* and a commentary on it called *Sarvārtha-siddhi;* and, among others, a polemical attack on Advaita called *Sata-dusani.* Apart from these, there are innumerable independent texts and commentaries, some of which we shall refer to in the course of our discussion.

Theory of Knowledge

Rāmānuja recognizes only three sources of knowledge—perception, inference and verbal or scriptural testimony. He admits the distinction between indeterminate and determinate perception *(nirvikalpa-pratyaksha* and *savikalpa-pratyaksha),* though unlike the Nyāya philosophers, he maintains that both involve a complex content. For him, indeterminate *(nirvikalpa)* perception is neither the bare apprehension of an absolutely undifferentiated object, nor the apprehension of a qualified object and its discrete qualifications. It is not the former, since discrimination is the basis of all knowledge and it is impossible to apprehend objects devoid of all elements of distinction.

All knowledge involves the apprehension of an object qualified by some special attribute, for, even in determinate *(savikalpa)* perception, only those specific characteristics which were apprehended in indeterminate perception are recognized and remembered. The difference between the two is that while in indeterminate perception an object or individual is apprehended along with its class character and yet the class character as such is not recognized as such, there is determinate perception when the object (or individual) is apprehended a second or third time and we recognize its generic character as common to the whole class.

Thus, Rāmānuja accepts recognition or remembrance *(smrti)* as valid knowledge and gives it a special place. He distinguishes it from determinate perception by pointing out that though both involve a revival of past impressions, yet in determine perception (unlike in recognition) the object is not necessarily the same as the one perceived in the past. Rāmānuja's treatment of inference is nearly similar to that of the Vaiseshika-Nyāya. For him, inference is knowledge derived from a general principle. While a single instance is sufficient to suggest the general principle, several instances help us in removing residual doubts. In his *Sarvārtha-siddhi* Venkatanātha says that by means of indirect proof *(tarka)* and by the use of both positive and negative instances, it is possible to eliminate the nonessentials and establish the general principle. The Visishtādvaita school does not recognize comparison as an independent source of knowledge, since it is only an instance of either remembrance or inference. Likewise, it brings both implication *(arthāpatti)* and subsumption *(sambhava)* under inference.

In addition to inference both Rāmānuja and Venkatanātha accept the authority of scripture or scriptural testimony *(sabda-pramāna)*. Rāmānuja puts the *Pancharātra* side by side with the Veda; further, he assigns equal importance to the earlier and the later portions of the Veda, i.e. that which relates to ritual and that which relates to *Brahman*. For him, the *karma-kānda* (the portion relating to duty or action) and the *jñāna-kānda* (the portion relating to the knowledge of the highest reality) of the Veda supplement each other; while the former teaches the modes of worshipping God, the latter describes the nature of God. It is in this that he differs from Samkara and other Advaitins, who subordinate *karma-kānda* to *jñāna-kānda* and maintain that the former is desirable only in the context of the self's purification and is thus negative in its import. Rāmānuja's synthetic theory is therefore called *karma-jñāna-samuchchaya* (*samuchchaya* = harmonious combination). Rāmānuja differs also from the Mimāmsaka in maintaining that the assertive propositions of the Veda are as important as the injunctive and that the various duties are to be performed only to secure God's Grace and not to find for oneself a place in the heaven *(svarga)*.

The highest reality, according to Rāmānuja, is known through the *sāstras* only, and no experience-based generalization can prove or disprove the reality of *Brahman*. Scripture is the only source of knowledge regarding "supersensuous matters, though reason may be employed in support of scripture." In his *Siddhi-traya* Yamunāchārya remarks: "All this teaching may carry weight with believers; we are not credulous, and so we require logic to convince us" (cited in Radhakrishnan, 674). But, at the same time, Rāmānuja admits, that thought alone is not sufficient to make us know the reality of *Brahman;* he adds that even the Vedas give us this knowledge only indirectly. What is required of us is something more than just an understanding of scriptural language. In *Sri-bhāsya* Rāmānuja refers to intuitive apprehension and remarks that intuition of reality, "which is not the logical knowledge of it, is possible only in mediation bearing the character of devotion" (cited in Radhakrishnan, 674).

All knowledge involves discrimination and it is not possible to know an undifferentiated object; knowledge "is always in and through difference" (Sharma, 343). Rāmānuja agrees with the Nyāya and Mimāmsā philosophers in maintaining that all knowledge relates to a corresponding object "existing really and outside of it." In Rāmānuja's view all knowledge—as resulting from perception, inference, and scriptural-intuitive testimony—is valid and is an affirmation of reality. But while all knowledge is of the real, knowledge is not of the whole of reality. Our knowledge is generally partial and imperfect. But while both true and erroneous knowledge are incomplete, only true knowledge recognizes the features that are necessary and useful for the end in view. The mirage is an error, not because the element of water is absent in it, but because the water in it does not satisfy our need. Thus the true is what represents the real *(yathārtha)* and what is practically useful *(vyavahārānuguna)*.

This is related to Rāmānuja's view that a thing may be a substance as well as an attribute. Thus light is an attribute in relation to its source (i.e. the lamp), but it is a substance in relation to its rays. The whole world, "as an adjective of God, is an attribute in relation to Him," though it contains many substances. Similarly, knowledge is both a substance *and* an attribute; it is a substance because it possesses the qualities of contraction and expansion; it is an attribute because it belongs to a subject, whether that subject is a self or God Himself.

Rāmānuja's famous theory of *dharma-bhuta-jñāna* or consciousness as an attribute (as distinct from substantive consciousness) avoids the defects inherent in the two extremes of realism and idealism. Although realism insists on the reality of the external world and of external relations and thus saves knowledge from the perils of subjectivism, it creates a gulf between thought and things; similarly, if idealism defines reality as a mental or spiritual construction and thus saves knowledge from the perils of materialism, its results are likely to be purely subjective and impressionistic. Rāmānuja's theory of *dharma-bhuta-jñāna* emphasizes the reality of the subject-object *(chit-achit)* relation. Both the subject *(chit)* and the object *(achit)* are amenable to logical thinking, but their existence is not independent. Their relation, however, is eternal, and the *Brahman* expresses itself in their intimate relationship. Both sentient and nonsentient beings *(chit* and *achit)* are expressive of the Absolute and belong to it. Knowledge always belongs to the self and exists for it and hence is called *dharma-bhuta-jñāna* or attributive knowledge. But it is also substantive inasmuch as it constitutes the essence of the selves and of God.

Rāmānuja here agrees with Jainism, with this difference, that he regards the self as atomic and as a part of God and that he insists on the presence of the objects as essential for the function of knowledge. Even in dreams, God creates objects for the enjoyment or suffering of the dreaming individual in accordance with his *karma,* although the resulting knowledge is dim and vague. As Rāmānuja remarks in his *Sri-bhāsya,* God,

> while producing the entire world as an object of fruition for the individual souls, in agreement with their respective good and evil deserts, creates certain things of such a nature as to become common objects of consciousness, while certain other things are created in such a way as to be perceived only by particular persons and to persist for a limited time only. It is this distinction of things that are objects of general consciousness and those that are not so which makes the difference between what is called "things sublating" and "things sublated" [quoted in Radhakrishnan, 676].

As Radhakrishnan points out, it is therefore a mistake to think that certain cognitions have false things for their objects while others have true ones. In liberation, however, all *karmas* (both good and evil) cease and so knowledge becomes all-pervasive, thus generating in the liberated soul the quality of God's omniscience. Radhakrishnan writes: "Thought reaches the full apprehension of God as self-conscious intelligence" (Radhakrishnan, 678).

Dharma-bhuta-jñāna or attributive knowledge is "a vital link between *chit* and *achit Ishvara* and nature, self and God." Although it is restricted by kārmic imperfections, it has the potentiality to break the bonds of finiteness and thus expand into the infinite, bringing about thereby an immediate intuition of God. "Finite consciousness has thus really an infinite possibility" (Srinivasachari, 302): it can perceive matter *(achit)* as it is in its entirety, recognize the self as the center and source of consciousness, and realize the Absolute as the all-self which is the ultimate subject of all knowledge. Every judgment thus ultimately refers to the whole of Reality or *Brahman*. To this end, therefore, even the negation of certain attributes in *Brahman* has a positive import, and the well-known negative definition of *Brahman* as *"neti, neti"* ("not this, not this") refers only to the impossibility of an adequate description of *Brahman* in terms of finite categories and does not imply any denial of finite things. "It negates the finiteness of the Infinite and not the finite itself" (Srinivasachari, 302).

All knowledge, according to Rāmānuja, is self-valid. His theory of *Sat-khyāti* or *Yathārtha-khyāti* means that in knowledge "it is the existent real alone which is cognized." The object, appearing in false perception, is not illusory but real, for, according to the doctrine of quintuplication *(panchi-karana)*, all objects of the finite world are compound substances, containing the five elements (fire, water, etc.) in varying proportions. Thus when a conch-shell is mistaken for silver, silver is actually (though partially) presented to consciousness, since some particles of silver are actually present in the shell. "Likeness in certain respects is the indication of a partial identity of substance" (Radhakrishnan, 675). We perceive water in the mirage just because water exists in connection with light and earth particles.

The theory does sound unscientific, but it shows Rāmānuja's assertion that knowledge is intrinsically valid, that it is always of the real. This view is closely related to Rāmānuja's view that plurality is not unreal. In his commentary on *Brahma-Sutra* Rāmānuja attacks the tenability of the assertion that all difference presented in our cognition is unreal because such difference does not persist. He calls this view altogether erroneous and it is the result of our failure to distinguish between "persistence and non-persistence, on the one hand, and the relation between what sublates and what is sublated, on the other hand":

> When two cognitions are mutually contradictory ... there is non-persistence of what is sublated. But jars, pieces of cloth and the like, do not contradict one another, since they are separate in place and time. If on the other hand the non-existence of a thing is cognised at the same time and at the same place where and when its existence is cognised, we have a mutual contradiction of two cognitions, and then the stronger one sublates the other cognition which thus comes to an end.... In the case of the snake-rope [this refers to the mistaking

> of the rope for a snake and is used to illustrate the one-sided dependence of the world on *Brahman:* just as the existence of the rope does not depend on the appearance of the snake although the appearance of the snake is dependent on the existence of the rope, so the world is dependent on *Brahman* although *Brahman* is not dependent on the world], there arises a cognition of non-existence in connexion with the given place and time; hence there is contradiction, one judgement sublates the other and the sublated cognition comes to an end. But the circumstance of something which is seen at one time and in one place not persisting at another time and in another place is not observed to be invariably accompanied by falsehood, and hence mere non-persistence of this kind does not constitute a reason for unreality [trans. George Thibaut, in Radhakrishnan and Moore, 545–546].

The quotation establishes, though indirectly, Rāmānuja's belief in "an immanent necessity operating in the nature of knowledge"—a necessity which enables the indeterminate cognition to pass over into the determinate. Our cognitive judgments always and implicitly attempt to relate the subjects to the larger whole and have a reference to the ideal of perfect knowledge that the self attains in liberation (Radhakrishnan, 676–677). Error is therefore only partial knowledge, and there is no logical distinction between knowledge and error. As Radhakrishnan writes: "The world for knowledge is an orderly whole, the detailed development or expression of a single principle. God and the world are equally real, and each must be real through the other . . . Reality is an individual of which the elements are the lesser individuals" (Radhakrishnan, 678). According to Meghanādari, one of the earliest members of the Rāmānuja school, "validity means the manifestation of any form of content not awaiting the confirmation by other means of knowledge, and such a conviction of validity is manifested along with cognition itself" (cited in Dasgupta, III, 250). That is to say, all cognitions are associated with a general conviction of their validity.

Metaphysics

From our discussion of Rāmānuja's theory of knowledge it is easy to arrive at three important conclusions as regards his metaphysics. First, all knowledge involves distinctions of some kind and therefore, pure identity is as unreal as pure difference. It follows from this that there is no undifferentiated pure consciousness and as such *Brahman* cannot be an indeterminate and differenceless being. As the incarnation of all perfection and goodness, *Brahman* is God. He is not a formless identity but an Individual who is always qualified by matter and souls, which together are His body. Next, the self is distinct from knowledge: although it is an eternal self-conscious subject, it is at the same time a self-luminous substance possessing attributive knowledge *(dharma-bhuta-jñāna).* All the individual souls, which are atomic in nature, are real spiritual substances inasmuch as they are pervaded by God and form His body; their liberation therefore does not mean any merging with God, it only means their serving God through their realization that they are only His body. Finally, knowledge does not merely belong to a subject, but points to an object which exists "really" and outside of it. All objects are real, including God, souls and knowledge, which are presented to the consciousness as objects—God and souls as spiritual objects *(chetanā)*, and knowledge as nonmaterial object *(ajada)*. It is easy to see how all the three conclusions are opposed to the Advaitic position of Samkara.

Like Samkara's before him, Rāmānuja's metaphysics had had its basis in the Upanishads and, again like Samkara, he had to contend with the vagueness of Upanishadic teaching, particularly in reference to the relation of *Brahman* to the individual soul on the one hand and to the physical world on the other. Although "statements about their identity are many and prominent, those distinguishing them are not altogether wanting" (Hiriyanna, *Essentials*, 152). The first problem for any philosopher who is attempting to evolve a systematic interpretation of the Upanishads, therefore, is to harmonize and reconcile these two, apparently contradictory, sets of statements. Rāmānuja's method is unique in this respect.

As shown by common usage, we often identify things that are distinct. We say, "The rose *is* red." (Note: We may in this case say, "The rose *has* redness," but such optional usage is not tenable in the case of all distinct entities. We may point out, in this connection, that Rāmānuja criticizes the *bhedābheda* identity *and* difference view as strongly as Samkara does.) That is, we take the help of mere linguistic usage to identify the rose, which is a substance, with redness, which is a quality or attribute. Likewise, we say "I *am* a man," thus identifying the all-surviving soul with the mortal human form in which it appears. Such usage, Rāmānuja points out, is not found in the case of all distinct things. We can *not*, for example, say that "The man is the coat." We are forced to say, once again following a specific tradition of linguistic usage, that "The man *has* a coat on him," indicating the distinction between the man and his coat. There are two forms of usage.

Contrasting these two forms of usage, Rāmānuja concludes that the relation in the first two cases ("The rose *is* red"/"I *am* a man") is different from and more intimate than that in the third (the man and his coat), which is only a case of mere conjunction. This relation of intimacy is called *aprthak-siddhi* ("inseparability") and connotes that one of the two related entities is dependent upon the other inasmuch as it cannot exist without the other also existing, and that it cannot be rightly known without the other also being known at the same time. Such an intimate relation is found to exist between a substance and its attribute(s), and between body and soul—that is, between two substances of which one is always and necessarily spiritual. According to Rāmānuja, the relation between *Brahman* and the soul or the world is of the second kind: the individual human being and the physical universe are the body of which the soul is *Brahman* or God. It is impossible to think of the individual soul and the world apart from God. According to Rāmānuja, the essential Upanishadic teaching is that, while God, the individual soul, and the physical world are all different and equally eternal, they are at the same time inseparable.

It is this inseparable unity of matter, souls, and God which is the *Brahman* or Absolute of Rāmānuja. The Absolute is an organic unity in which, as in a living organism, one element predominates and controls the rest; it is an identity which is qualified by difference. Rāmānuja's *Visishtādvaita* is nondualism qualified by difference. The Absolute is a concrete whole *(visishta)* which includes interrelated and interdependent subordinate elements called *visheshanas* as well as the controlling spirit, called *visheshya*. As the immanent and controlling spirit, God is the Supreme Real who holds together in unity both matter and individual souls.

Rāmānuja recognizes three factors *(tattva-traya)* as ultimate and real: these are matter *(achit)*, souls *(chit)*, and God *(Ishvara)*. As we have said, though all three are equally real and ultimate, matter and souls – substances in themselves – are only the attributes of God and are entirely dependent on Him. In explaining the relation between substance and attribute, Rāmānuja rejects the Vaiseshika-Nyāya relation of inherence *(samavāya)*, on the ground that such relation is external and thus involves infinite regress. His relation of "inseparability" *(aprthak-siddhi)* is "an inner, inseparable, vital and organic" one (Sharma, 347). God is qualified by matter and souls; reversely, matter and souls form God's body and are inseparable from and absolutely dependent on Him. True to his theory of inseparability, Rāmānuja defines a body as "that which is controlled, supported and utilized for its purpose by a soul" (*Sri-bhāsya*, cited in Sharma, 347). Matter and souls (which are attributes of God) are the "controlled" *(niyamya)*, the "supported" *(dhārya)*, the "parts" *(amsha)*, and the "accessory means" *(shesha)*, while God is their "substance" *(prakari)*, the "controller" *(niyanta)*, the "support" *(ādhāra)*, the "whole" *(amshi)*, and the "principal end" *(sheshi)*. While matter and souls are external *with* but not external *to* God, God is free from all external differences, both homogeneous and heterogeneous, since there is nothing either similar or dissimilar which is external to Him. God possesses "internal differences" *(svagata-bheda)*, however, for His body is made of real and diverse elements like matter and souls.

Rāmānuja finds justification for his doctrine of the Absolute as a Triune Unity in several Upanishadic passages. The *Svetāshvatara Upanishad* says: "There are three ultimate existences – the eternal and all-knowing and all-powerful God, the eternal powerless soul and the eternal matter, and these three constitute the Absolute." Again: "This alone need be known and there is nothing else to be known – that there are three entities, the enjoyer, the enjoyed and the mover, which constitute the Absolute. One who knows these three knows the *Brahman*." The *Taittiriya Upanishad* says: "All beings arise from, live in and return to the *Brahman*." It describes God as "the soul of Nature and also the soul of souls," as the One who is both immanent and transcendent. The *Brihadāranyaka Upanishad* describes him as the thread-like principle which binds together all the worlds and all the souls, as the immanent inner controller *(antaryāmi)* of all. He is in matter and yet is different from it; and just as the spokes are bound together with the wheel, so all the elements and all the souls are bound together within this Soul *(Ātman)*. "They are real; He is their reality. They are true; He is their truth. Hence he is called the Truest of the true" (quoted in Sharma, 347-348).

Rāmānuja's theory of knowledge suggests that the real cannot be a bare identity. It is a determinate whole, which maintains its identity in and through the differences. We have seen that, according to Rāmānuja, the nature and existence of this determinate whole or God can be known only through scriptural testimony and not through inference. One of Rāmānuja's chief followers, Venkatanātha, points out the inadequate nature of the Sāmkhya theory that the world-creation is due to the movement of *prakrti,* set in operation through its contiguity with the *purushas.* Venkatanātha cites the Upanishadic assertion that just as the spider weaves its net, so does God create the world. In his *Sarvārtha-siddhi* Venkatanātha also refers to the further scriptural assertion that God entered into both *prakrti* and the *purushas* at the time of creation and generated the necessary creative movement in them. Venkatanātha also rejects the Yoga view of God—that He is only an emancipated being who adopts some pure body. The world-creation could not be the result of any cooperative activity of the emancipated souls, for it is both against scriptural testimony and normal possibility: there cannot be such an agreement of wish among the infinite number of emancipated beings so as to result in the creation of the world by "unobstructed co-operation" (Dasgupta, III, 296).

Venkatanātha argues, that on the strength of scriptural testimony, it has to be admitted that God has engaged Himself in world-creation, "either for the good of the created beings or through His own playful pleasurable activity," which of course is not to be taken as something negative—a way of avoiding ennui or languor—but an activity or "movement which produces pleasure of itself" (*Sarvārtha-Siddhi,* cited in Dasgupta, III, 296).

> While Ramanuja is clear that there exists an absolute self, he is equally clear that every finite reality is an expression of this self. To make reciprocal interaction among a plurality of existents possible, the constituent elements of the world-whole must have a common bond of unity and interdependence, which must be a spiritual principle. Not only logic, but religious experience, demands a conservation of the finite and an admission of the infinite as a personal being [Radhakrishnan, 682].

The possibility of personal communion with God points to a fellowship with a divine personality. Thus, Rāmānuja's God is none other than Samkara's *Saguna-Brahman.* He is the Infinite who causes finitude and absorbs it.

Rāmānuja rejects Samkara's *Nirguna-Brahman* (the One without attributes) as something which is beyond all modes of worship. "The *nirguna Brahman* which stares at us with frozen eyes regardless of our selfless devotion and silent suffering, is not the god of religious insight." Samkara's interpretation of *Brahman* as something utterly undifferentiated, leads him to a "void, which he tries to conceal by a futile play of concepts." His *Nirguna-Brahman* is "a blank, suggesting to us the famous mare of Orlando, which had every perfection except the one small defect of being dead" (Radhakrishnan, 682-683). For Rāmānuja, God *is* the Absolute—the *Brahman* who is a qualified unity. We quote the relevant parts from Rāmānuja's *bhāsya* on *Brahma-Sutra:*

> [W]e maintain that also the text "True, knowledge, infinite is *Brahman,*" does not prove a substance devoid of all difference . . . Now whether we take the several terms, "true," "knowledge," "infinite," in their primary sense, i.e., as denoting qualities, or as denoting modes of being opposed to whatever is contrary to those qualities, in either case we must needs admit a plurality of causes for the application of those several terms to one thing. . . . What the phrase "without a second" really aims at intimating is that *Brahman* possesses manifold powers, and this it does by denying the existence of another ruling principle different from *Brahman*. . . . If it were meant absolutely to deny all duality, it would deny also the eternity and other attributes of *Brahman* [Radhakrishnan and Moore, 548].

According to Rāmānuja, *Brahman* possesses internal difference and is a concrete synthetic whole, with matter and souls as his "moments" *(chidāchid-visishta);* the Absolute is the ultimate unity-in-and-through-trinity (Sharma, 348). Rāmānuja's God is the perfect personality (as against the imperfect personalities that the individuals are) and contains all experience within himself, including those differences that are necessary for personality. *Brahman* is the Absolute Truth without a second and It wills the many and differentiates Itself into the manifold of sentient and nonsentient beings. It is the all-inclusive unity that imparts substantiality to all beings and thus sustains their existence and value. Though It is the ground of all changes, It is changeless-in-Itself. While *Prakrti* or matter *(achit)* undergoes modifications, and while the intelligence of individual souls is subject to expansions and contractions on account of their *karma* (action or deeds), *Brahman* is entirely free from all these. *Brahman* is not only "the real of reals" *(satyasya satyam);* It is also intelligent and conscious *(jnāna).* It is the Self underlying all, the ultimate subject of experience, abiding within all beings without being touched by their imperfection.

The idea that *Brahman* is the cause of all things does not imply that creation is an act having a beginning in time, but that the universe of the sentient and nonsentient is an eternal cyclic process of dissolution *(pralaya)* and creation *(srshti).* In dissolution, the world remains latent as a real possibility; in creation it is only actualized. During the state of dissolution *(pralaya), Brahman* remains as the cause with subtle matter and unembodied souls as His body; during the state of creation *(srshti),* the subtle matter becomes gross and the unembodied souls (except the liberated ones) become embodied according to their *karma.* The latent, causal-state *(kāranāvasthā)* of *Brahman* thus becomes the actual, effect-state *(kāryāvasthā).* The whole process is the self-expression of the Absolute: God reveals Himself in creation. There is also an ethical side to it. The cosmic process is to provide an opportunity for the finite selves to realize their divine character; the world of nature serves as an environment for the soul's liberation. God is immanent, but He is also transcendent. He is the perfect personality, untouched by the evils, errors and imperfections of the world. Rāmānuja's idea of God combines the immanent *Brahman* of the Upanishads with the transcendent *Ishvara* of the *Pancharātra*. Srinivasachari writes:

> The goodness of God as the creator of creatures functions through the moral freedom of man, and hence there is really no contradiction between the infinite might of God and the moral freedom of man. *Ishvara* is not an absentee God who makes the world and lets it go. Nor is He identical with the created universe.... While being immanent in the universe, God also transcends it. The idea of immanence guarantees the intimacy of union between God and the finite self; and the concept of transcendence justifies the absolute infinity and perfection of the Godhead and inspires religion, reverence, and humility [Srinivasachari, 306].

Or, as Radhakrishnan writes: "The ideal world is inherent in God" (Radhakrishnan, 686). It is through God that the inherently legal conception of *karma* (which implies the rigorous mode of reward and punishment in accordance with the law of retributive justice) is transformed into the ethical idea of redemption through divine grace and love *(kripā)*. The apparent contradiction between retribution and redemption, between *karma* and *kripā,* is removed by Rāmānuja's aesthetic conception of God as "the Beautiful." *Brahman* is infinitely beautiful, and the physical universe is "the expression of the creative urge and spontaneity of the divine will to be beautiful." "The Lord of splendour takes delight in sporting with the finite self with a view to transmuting it into its own nature" (Srinivasachari, 307, 308). Metaphysically, God is the all-inclusive reality; ethically, he is the perfect personality; aesthetically, he is the Beautiful One.

The Vaishnava theology—which forms the background and the basis of Rāmānuja's theism—is a compound of the Vedas, the *Pancharātra-Āgamas,* the *Purānas* and the Tamil *Prabandham*. The Vedas speak of the Absolute-in-itself; the *Pancharātra-Āgamas* offer the theory of manifestations *(Vyuhas);* the *Purānas* describe the incarnated Absolute *(Avatārs)* and their worship; the Tamil *Prabandham* are intensely devotional songs addressed to the deistist images of South India. The "highest mode" *(para)* is identified with Nārāyana, whose citadel is Vaikuntha and who is said to exist in a body made of pure *sattva* (*shuddha sattva* = essential purity and goodness). His qualities are "eternal, infinite, numberless, unlimited, undefiled and matchless." "He is knowledge to the ignorant, power to the powerless, mercy to the guilty, grace to the afflicted, parental affection to the impure and helpless, perennial attachment to those who fear separation, nearness to those who pine for Him, and kindness to all" (*Tattva-traya,* cited in Sharma, 349).

Although God is complete in Himself, he is said to exist in five different modes, images, incarnations or manifestations, thus making possible personal relations with His devotees, although His "perfect personality is not exhausted in its cosmical aspects" by such relations. As Nārāyana, the Lord is seated on the serpent *Sesha* in Vaikuntha and is supported by His consort Lakshmi, who, as the symbol of the Lord's creative potency, becomes, in later Vaishnavism, the divine mother of the universe. "While *Ishvara* symbolises justice, Lakshmi stands for mercy, and the two are united in the godhead" (Radhakrishnan, 689). As the power of Vishnu or Nārāyana, Lakshmi subsumes the two essential principles of *kriyā* (the principle of regulation and control) and *bhuti* (the principle of becoming or change), which together enable Vishnu to become the efficient as well as the material cause of the universe.

As we said, the Supreme expresses itself in five different manifestations or forms *(Vyuhas)*. As the immanent soul of the universe and inner ruler of all, He is Antaryāmi (first *Vyuha*). As the transcendent personal Lord, He is Nārāyana or Vasudeva (second *Vyuha*). In His revealed form, He has four manifestations (third *Vyuha*). His manifestation as the Lord is called Vāsudeva (not to be confused with the other Vasudeva, who is the highest mode or *Para*). As the ruler of the cognitive aspects of the individual souls *(buddhi-sattva* or *jiva-sattva)* and as the annihilator of this universe, He is called Samkarshana. As the ruler of the volitional aspect of individual souls *(ahamkāra-tattva)* and as the preserver of this universe, He is called Aniruddha. As the ruler of the emotional aspect of the individual souls *(mana-tattva)* and as the creator of this universe, He is called Pradyumna. These four are the partial or incomplete manifestations of the Supreme Lord *(Para)* or Vasudeva.

While the Supreme Lord possesses all the six perfections—knowledge, energy, strength, lordship, vigor and brilliance—the other *vyuhas* possess only two of these and, to that extent, are incomplete. When God assumes a human or animal form and settles for a while on the earth, He is called *Vibhāva* or *Avatāra* (incarnations). The *Vibhāva-rupas* or *Avatāras* are the incarnations of Vishnu (fourth *Vyuha*). Such incarnation is of two kinds—"primary incarnation" *(mukhya-vibhāva)* when, like Krishna, the Lord Himself descends on the earth, and "secondary incarnations" *(gauna-vibhāva)*, when the Lord takes the form of inspired souls, like Shiva or Buddha. In his Introduction to the commentary on the *Gitā*, Rāmānuja says that the infinitely merciful God "assumed various forms without putting away his own essential godlike nature, and time after time incarnated himself . . . descending not only with the purpose of relieving the burden of the earth, but also to be accessible to men, even such as we are, so revealing himself to the world as to be visible to the sight of all, and doing such other marvelous deeds as to ravish the hearts and eyes of all beings, high and low" (Rāmānuja's *Gitā-bhāsya*, quoted in Radhakrishnan, 689). Thus, Rāmānuja's God is not Samkara's impassive absolute, looking down upon us from an unreachable distance, but one who is within every human being "like a flash of lightning in the heart of a blue cloud" (Rāmānuja, *Vedārtha-samgraha*, cited in Radhakrishnan, 690).

Rāmānuja qualifies God's absoluteness by admitting the existence of free spirits within the scope of the former's universality. These spirits are free inasmuch as they draw their existence from God and yet possess "such spontaneity and choice that they deserve to be called persons." Radhakrishnan writes: "Rāmānuja wages a vigorous and telling polemic against those who regard persons as vain variations of the self-same absolute"

(Radhakrishnan, 690). The individual soul, though an attribute or mode *(prakāra)* of God and forms part of His body, is yet a spiritual substance in itself—real, eternal, unique, self-conscious and intelligent, partless, unchanging, atomic and imperceptible. It is beyond creation and destruction. In the state of creation, it is embodied as a consequence of its *karmas* (deeds or actions); in the state of dissolution, it remains in its essential form, although this form is tinged with *karmas* that urge it into yet another cycle of creation and mundane existence. Thus, the relation of the soul and *karma* is beginningless, though in its liberated state, it enjoys its essential purity untouched by karmic matter, and hence, defies every possibility of another mundane embodiment. This implies that all through its births and deaths—on the mundane, empirical plane—the soul retains its identity and essential nature. The soul, in this respect, is different from its body, sense-organs, mind *(manas),* vital breath, and cognition *(buddhi).* There are numberless individual souls, which are essentially alike. At each destruction of the world, the particular forms of the souls are destroyed, but the souls themselves are indestructible.

As C.D. Sharma writes, Rāmānuja advocates "qualitative monism and quantitative pluralism of souls" (Sharma, 350). According to Rāmānuja, birth or death refers only to the souls' association with or dissociation from bodies, resulting in the contradiction or expansion or intelligence. In dissolution or destruction of the world *(pralaya),* however, the souls become one with a "subtle stuff which does not admit of differentiation by name and form" (Radhakrishnan, 692). In his commentary on *Brahma/Vedānta-Sutra,* Rāmānuja says:

> The individual self is a part of the highest Self; as the light issuing from a luminous thing such as fire or the sun is a part of that body; or as the generic characteristics of a cow or horse, and the white or black colour of things so coloured, are attributes and hence parts of the things in which those attributes inhere; or as the body is a part of an embodied being. For by a part we understand that which constitutes one place *(desa)* of some thing, and hence a distinguishing attribute *(viseshana)* is a part of the thing distinguished by that attribute. Hence those analysing a thing of that kind discriminate between the distinguishing element or part of it, and the distinguished element or part. Now, although the distinguishing attribute and the thing distinguished thereby stand to each other in the relation of part and whole, yet we observe them to differ in essential character [Radhakrishnan and Moore, 555].

Since *Brahman* is indivisible, the individual self *(jiva)* is not "a part cut out of the whole," but a qualified form or an attributive mode of *Brahman.*

Rāmānuja regards the individual souls/selves as effects of *Brahman,* for they have no existence apart from *Brahman,* although they are not produced effects, as ether and the like. The indwelling of the supreme spirit does not, however, affect the soul's inherently autonomous nature; and yet, the mere will of the soul is not sufficient enough for action. Though Rāmānuja speaks of the autonomy of the soul in determining its own future, he also presupposes God's active cooperation in the soul's effort to transcend its bound nature, for God alone is the supreme moral personality, unattached to matter and *karma*. God is "the sovereign lord" *(seshi);* the soul is his loyal subject.

This relation of lord and liege does not, however, affect the characteristic essence of the soul, which is "self-consciousness" *(ahambuddhi)* or "self-distinction," for otherwise it would be impossible on the part of the soul to attain liberation. The soul is the knowing subject as well as an active agent. Acts belong to the soul and it undergoes the consequences of these acts. But so long as the souls are bound to bodies, their acts result in bodily consequences, but in their liberated state, unattached to bodies, they realize their wishes by their "mere will" *(samkalpad eva).* Rāmānuja insists on both individual freedom and divine sovereignty. God has offered freedom to the individual to act as he likes, to work for good or evil, but, once again, according to the laws of *karma,* which are expressive of God's nature. Countering doubts as regards the relation in which the laws of *karma* stand to God, Radhakrishnan writes:

> If the law of *karma* is independent of God, then God's absoluteness is compromised. The critic who declares that we cannot save the independence of God without sacrificing the doctrine of *karma* has not the right conception of the Hindu idea of God. The law of *karma* expresses the will of God. The order of *karma* is set up by God, who is the ruler of *karma (karmādhyākshah).* Since the law is dependent on God's nature, God himself may be regarded as rewarding the righteous and punishing the wicked.... [I]t is sometimes said that, though God can suspend the law of *karma,* still he does not will to do so. Pledged to execute the moral law which is the eternal expression of his righteous will, he permits evil which he might otherwise arrest. The inner ruler has regard in all cases to the volitional effort which prompt a man's action. He does not care to upset his own laws and interfere with the world-scheme [Radhakrishnan, 694–695].

Thus, notwithstanding his immanence, God is not intrusive. The soul, though atomic in size, is infinite in knowledge and is capable of recognizing the kārmic obstructions and avoiding them, restoring thereby its *dharma-bhuta-jñāna* (the God-given "attributive knowledge") to its original pristine status.

Rāmānuja describes three classes of souls *(jivas):* the eternal and ever-free *(nitya-mukta),* who were never subjected to *karma* and *prakrti* (mundane action and matter) and who always live in Vaikuntha, enjoying divine bliss and in constant service of the Lord; the released or liberated *(mukta),* who were bound but who attain freedom through their good action, wisdom and devotion; and the bound *(baddha),* who are still going through the samsaric cycles of birth and death because of their ignorance and selfishness. (There are some Visishtādvaitins, like Venkatanātha, who believe that there is a fourth class of *jivas*—those who are irretrievably bound to the wheel of mundane existence *[nitya-baddha]*). The souls wandering in *samsāra (baddha)* are further divided into four classes: superhuman or celestial, human, animal, and immobile or stationary. While all souls are alike—neither merely human nor heavenly and not caste-bound – their differences are on account of the bodies with which they are associated. The samsaric souls are grouped into those desirous of mere mundane pleasures and those desirous of release or deliverance. It is impossible, according to Rāmānuja, to explain the soul's subjection to *karma,* however, for the cosmic process is beginningless *(anādi).*

We spoke of three factors which Rāmānuja considers as ultimate and real *(tattva-traya)* – God, souls, and unconscious matter. Unconscious matter *(achit)* is of three kinds: ordinary matter *(Prakrti),* time *(kāla),* and pure matter *(nitya-vibhuti). Prakrti* or ordinary matter is the basis of *samsāra.* It is an object of enjoyment and suffers change. It has all the three qualities *(gunas)* of *sattva, rajas* and *tamas* and is therefore called "compound matter" *(Mishra-sattva).* It forms the body of God and is much more dependent on him than the souls who enjoy free will. It is the starting point of the process of world-evolution and hence, is "uncreated" *(aja),* though it undergoes formal change.

It is important here to distinguish the Sāmkhya conception of *Prakrti* from that of Visishtādvaita. While in Sāmkhya, *sattva, rajas* and *tamas* are the constitutive elements of *Prakrti,* in Visishtādvaita (especially in Rāmānuja), they are merely the qualities of *Prakrti.* While in Sāmkhya, *Prakrti* is infinite, in Visishtādvaita it is controlled by "pure matter" or *nitya-vibhuti,* which is made up of pure *sattva* and is therefore called *Shuddha-sattva.* In Visishtādvaita, *Prakrti* is caused and controlled by God and is inseparable from him. "Pure matter" *(Nitya-vibhuti* or *Shiddha-sattva)* is made up of pure *sattva.* It is the stuff of which is made the ideal world, the body of God, and the liberated souls. Radhakrishnan describes the character of pure matter and its inevitable connection with ordinary matter or *Prakrti:* "It is the stuff of the body of God in his condition of *nityavibhuti.* It does not conceal the nature within. God reveals himself as a cosmic force through his *lilāvibhuti* [creative sport] with the aid of *prakrti,* and in his transcendent existence through his *nityavibhuti* with the aid of *suddhatattva*" (Radhakrishnan, 697).

Time *(kāla),* the third of the three kinds of matter, is an unconscious substance and is given a separate, independent status. It is the form of all existence and is devoid of any of the three *gunas* or qualities *(Tattva-shunya* or *Sattva-shunya).* All the three unconscious substances, which together form matter, work in accordance with the will of God. Neither good nor bad in themselves, they bring pleasure or pain to the individuals according to their *karma.* In other words, every individual is intrinsically *capable* of controlling the actions of these substances.

For Rāmānuja, creation is absolutely real. The world and the souls are neither created nor destroyed. He believes in the Sāmkhya theory of *sat-kārya-vāda,* according to which every effect pre-exists in its material cause and is therefore only an externalization of what was already existing in an implicit form. Rāmānuja believes in the *parināma-vāda* form of *sat-kārya-vāda,* according to which the effect is only a transformation *(parināma)* of the material cause. Thus, the entire universe of matter and souls is a real –

and not just apparent—transformation or modification of *Brahman (Brahma-parināma-vāda);* and yet, though matter and souls are the modes of God, they enjoy "the kind of individual existence which is theirs from all eternity, and cannot be entirely resolved into Brahman" (Radhakrishnan, 697-698). They exist in two different conditions which periodically alternate.

The first is a subtle condition when they remain undifferentiated, when matter is unevolved *(avyakta)* and intelligence is contracted *(samkuchita):* it is the condition of dissolution or *pralaya* when *Brahman* is in "a causal condition" *(kāranāvasthā).* But when, following the will of God, creation takes place, the subtle matter *(Prakrti)* evolves into gross elements and the immaterial souls take the form of gross bodies with consequent expansion *(vikāsa)* of their intelligence. In this condition of creative manifestation, *Brahman* is in "the effect condition" *(kāryāvasthā).* Creation and dissolution are thus only relative and refer to different conditions of *Brahman;* accordingly, souls and matter have a causal existence and an effect existence. Creation is God's way of enabling the souls to reap the fruits of their past deeds *(karma).* In the language of C.D. Sharma, the law of *karma* "necessitates creation," and to that extent, "God's creative act is not independent or absolute" (Sharma, 358; Radhakrishnan, 698). And yet, for God, the creation of the world is said to be mere sport or *lilā*—a metaphor which, as Radhakrishnan sees, implies "the disinterestedness, freedom and joy underlying the act of creation." The entire process of creation is a drama in which God throughout remains the overall supervisor.

It is difficult, however, to reconcile the idea of *Brahman* as having an absolutely nonconditioned existence with the view of the changing states of his attributes, i.e., souls and matter. Rāmānuja concedes that God is, in a certain specific sense, also subject to change:

> The ruling element of the world, i.e., the Lord, finally, who has the sentient and non-sentient beings for his modes, undergoes a change in so far as he is, at alternating periods, embodied in all those beings in their alternating states [that is, subtle and gross states]. The two modes, and he to whom the modes belong, thus undergo a common change in so far as in the case of all of them the causal condition passes over into a different condition [i.e., the effect condition] [Rāmānuja's *bhāsya* on *Vedānta-Sutra,* in Radhakrishnan and Moore, 554-555].

Rāmānuja contends that, as the true relation between soul and body is beyond the scope of logic, so the relation between God's "transcendent delight which is perfect and incapable of variation and that derived from the changes of his body i.e., the modifications of his attributes is not intelligibly stated" (Radhakrishnan, 700-701). Rāmānuja goes on to counter Advaitins' assertion of the unity of the Absolute and condemnation of multiplicity by saying that the relevent Upanishadic passages deny only "the *independent existence* of the world of plurality outside *Brahman*" and *not* that world's *reality.* He strongly attacks Samkara's doctrine of *Māyā* or *Avidyā* and the phenomenality of the world. Rāmānuja levels seven important charges against the theory of *Māyā* or *Avidyā.* They are as follows:

1) His first charge relates to the locus or support *(āshraya)* of *Māyā*. It could not, he argues, reside in *Brahman,* for if it did then it would affect the nondual character of *Brahman.* Again, since *Brahman* is said to be pure self-luminous Knowledge or Consciousness and *Avidyā* is ignorance, it is unlikely that the latter can exist in the former. *Avidyā* cannot exist in the individual self either, since the individuality of the self is said to be the creation of *Avidyā;* the cause *(Avidyā)* could not reside in its effect (the individual self). Hence, *Avidyā* is a "logical myth," "an illusory concept," "a figment of the Advaitin's imagination."

2) Rāmānuja's second charge relates to the concealing of *Brahman* by *Avidyā.* If *Brahman* is self-luminous Knowledge which validates its own purity and essence, it is absurd to talk of its concealment or extinction *(tirodhāna)* by *Avidyā* or ignorance.

3) Rāmānuja's third objection relates to the exact nature *(svarupa)* of *Avidyā,* to whether it is positive or negative or both or neither. *Avidyā* cannot be positive since it means absence of knowledge; to accept it as positive is to accept self-contradiction, for it is destroyed or removed by knowledge and nothing which is positive can be destroyed. *Avidyā* cannot be negative either, for if it were so it could not, as Advaitins say, project the world-illusion on *Brahman.* In other words, the nature of *Avidyā* cannot be logically ascertained.

4) Rāmānuja's fourth charge relates to what the Advaitins call the "indefinability" or "indescribability" *(anirvachaniyatva)* of *Avidyā.* Rāmānuja finds this illogical, since it involves self-contradiction. The Advaitin qualifies his view by equating such indescribability with being neither real nor unreal, which, for Rāmānuja, is no more than a game of words, for reality and unreality are both exhaustive and exclusive and together they remove all possibilities of predication. All our cognitions relate to either entities or nonentities and hence, to accept a third alternative, is to flout the traditional canons of logic.

5) Rāmānuja's next charge relates to the means of knowledge *(pramāna)* by which *Avidyā* is cognized. Neither perception nor inference establishes it; further, the scriptures speak of *Māyā* as that power possessed by God by which he has created this wonderful world and as such has nothing to do with *Avidyā.*

6) Rāmānuja's next charge relates to the removal or cessation *(nivartana)* of *Avidyā.* According to the Advaitin, *Avidyā* is removed through a knowledge of the unqualified attributeless *Brahman.* Such knowledge is impossible, however, for knowledge presupposes discrimination and distinction, which the purely abstract *Brahman* is supposed to defy. In the absence of such knolwedge, it is impossible to remove *Avidyā.*

7) Rāmānuja's final charge is a natural corollary of his previous one. It relates to the abolition *(nivrtti)* of *Avidyā.* The Advaitin claims that *Avidyā* is positive, a concrete reality; as such, its abolition cannot be brought about by abstract knowledge. "A thing which positively exists cannot be removed from existence by knowledge" (Sharma, 360). *Avidyā* or ignorance of the soul is overcome only when the *karmas* are destroyed, since

it is the *karmas* which keep the soul in bondage. The *karmas* are destroyed through the merciful intervention of the Lord in answer to the soul's devotion *(bhakti)* and *not* by means of knowledge as claimed by the Advaitin.

The charges of Rāmānuja against *Māyā* or *Avidyā* have not been uncritically accepted by later scholars, however. We shall here concentrate on their evaluation by C.D. Sharma, according to whom Rāmānuja's charges are based on a misunderstanding of the two terms, *Avidyā* and *Māyā*. According to Sharma, it is called "indescribable either as real or as unreal" simply because of the genuine difficulty of our finite intellect to reach Reality, but Rāmānuja uses it in the senses of something real and demands a locus and a *pramāna* for it. *Brahman* is the seat of *Avidyā,* but its nonreal nature may not necessarily affect the monistic, nondual *Brahman*. The rope is not really affected if it is mistaken for a snake. It may be said that the individual self and *Avidyā* go on determining each other in a beginningless cycle. "Rāmānuja himself, when he fails to explain the cause of bondage of the pure soul, falls back upon the notion that the relation of *Karma* and ignorance with the soul is beginningless" (Sharma, 360–361). Further, *Avidyā* does not really conceal *Brahman* even as a cloud does not really conceal the sun. *Avidyā* is called positive only to emphasize the fact that it is not *merely* negative. In fact, it is neither positive nor negative, and the Advaitin himself admits its self-contradictory character—something which can be realized only by those who rise above it. As long as error or illusion lasts it is *quite real,* though not in the absolute sense in which Rāmānuja interprets it. *Avidyā* is neither absolutely real nor absolutely unreal. "These two terms are not contradictories and hence the Laws of Contradiction and Excluded Middle are not overthrown. The Law of Contradiction is fully maintained since all that which can be contradicted is said to be false. The Law of Excluded Middle is not overthrown since 'absolutely real' and 'absolutely unreal' are not exhaustive" (Sharma, 361).

Rāmānuja is not the only Visishtādvaitin who criticized Samkara. In his *Sata-dusani* Venkatanātha, one of the chief followers of Rāmānuja and the founder of the Vadagalais school (Northern School), is believed to have attacked Samkara's Advaita on a hundred grounds (*Sata-dusani* = "hundred refutations"), although the work itself contains only 66 refutations, 61 of which have philosophical value while the last five are only of "doctrinal and sectarian interest" (Dasgupta, III, 305). Most of these refutations are a repetition of Rāmānuja's charges on a more extended scale and the interested reader will find a fine summary of these in S.N. Dasgupta's *A History of Indian Philosophy* (Vol. III, pp. 306–346).

Ethics and Liberation

"The *jivas* in *samsāra,*" writes Radhakrishnan, "with their souls shrouded in bodies, are like islanders who live unconscious of the sea. They believe that they are not so much modes of God as products of nature" (Radhakrishnan, 703). *Avidyā* is that power of illusion which makes us believe that both souls and matter are independent of *Brahman*. Rāmānuja does grant to the individuals free will and views each individual as a different person. But each individual is "an other to God," although most often he fails to recognize this fact and degrades himself by his association with matter. God, however, helps the soul to realize the truth by the machinery of *karma*, which "inflicts punishments on the soul, thus reminding it of its sinful efforts." As Radhakrishnan writes, "In Rāmānuja's philosophy great emphasis is placed on the conviction of sin and man's responsibility for it" (Radhakrishnan, 703). True to his theistic convictions, Rāmānuja recommends devotion *(bhakti)*, self-surrender *(prapatti)* and grace *(prasāda)* as the means to the attainment of eternal bliss. In other words, he does not accept mere meditation or concentrated contemplation *(dhyāna* and *nididhyāsana)* as a means to salvation; neither does he accept knowledge *(jñāna)* and action *(karma)* as the only means to salvation, although he does not fully reject them. His major emphasis, however, is devotion or *bhakti*. For Rāmānuja, *jñāna* and *karma* are means to *bhakti*.

Although the term *bhakti* has been used variously, sometimes vaguely, in Indian philosophy and religion, and has referred to everything "from the lowest form of worship to the highest life of realisation" (Radhakrishnan, 704), Rāmānuja is quite clear about its character. For him, *bhakti* is the individual's "reaching out towards a fuller knowledge of God quietly and meditatively." Not every individual is sufficiently equipped for such reaching out, and hence, Rāmānuja recommends an elaborate preparation for *bhakti*, which includes *viveka* or discrimination of food, *vimoha* or freedom from all else except the thought of God, *abhyāsa* or ceaseless thinking of God, *kriyā* or doing good to others, *kalyāna* or wishing well to others, *satyam* or truthfulness, *ārjavam* or integrity, *dayā* or compassion, *ahimsā* or nonviolence, *dāna* or charity, and *anavasāda* or cheerfulness and hope. In his *bhāsya* on the Gitā, Rāmānuja points out that *bhakti* is not mere emotionalism, but a conscious and continuous effort at training one's will and intellect so that these may make one *capable* of knowing God and obeying his will. *Bhakti* finds its culmination in an intuitive realization of God and his redemptive love.

As Radhakrishnan writes, *bhakti* and *moksha* (salvation/liberation) "are organically related, so that at every stage of *bhakti* we are perfecting ourselves." "*Bhakti* is salvation in becoming, and is regarded as superior to the other methods, since it is its own reward" (Radhakrishnan, 705). *Bhakti* is distinguished into "formal" *(vaidhi)* and "supreme" *(mukhya)*. The formal or ordinary *bhakti* consists in prayers, ceremonial rituals and image-worship, which are a means to the realization of the supreme or highest *bhakti* which is pure *jñāna* or the immediate intuitive knowledge of God. Although prayers, ceremonies and image-worship help the soul towards the realization of the supreme *bhakti*, they cannot "by themselves save the soul," for ultimately, nothing else except the worship of the Supreme can serve as the object of meditation. In this connection, Rāmānuja quotes one of his teachers: "From *Brahmā* [one of the gods of the Hindu trinity, as distinguished from *Brahman*, which is the Supreme Reality] to a tuft of grass all things that live in the world are subject to *samsāra* due to *karma,* therefore they cannot be helpful as objects of meditation, since they are all in ignorance and subject to *samsāra*" (quoted in Radhakrishnan, 705).

The act of *bhakti* entails an attitude of complete self-surrender *(prapatti)* or resignation to God. In his *bhāsya* on the *Gitā,* Rāmānuja speaks of five factors as a means to *prapatti:* acquisition of qualities that would help make one a proper offering to God; avoidance of conduct not acceptable to God; a complete faith in God's power to protect; an intense appeal for such protection; and a feeling of one's smallness. While the path of *bhakti* involves *jñāna* and *karma* (in the sense of a knowledge of the scriptures and performance of duties in the form of sacrifices), and therefore is confined to the three upper classes, *prapatti* is open to all including the *Shudras* (the lowest caste). There is, however, a difference of opinion between the Rāmā-nuja schools as regards the nature and scope of *prapatti.* According to the Southern Tengalais school, *prapatti* is the sole means to salvation; for the Northern Vadagalais school, it is only *one* of the many ways of reaching the goal. While the Southern school believes that nothing depends on man's effort since the grace of God selects the individuals to be liberated and that "the soul is seized by God in one supreme act, which need not be repeated," the Northern school believes that conscious effort on the part of the individual is an essential factor in salvation and that the soul must continuously offer itself to God.

In the *Bhāgavata Purāna,* which influenced to a considerable degree Rāmānuja's philosophy and religion, *bhakti* is "a surging emotion which thrills the whole frame, chokes speech, and leads to a trance" (Radhakrishnan, 706). The opening of the religious sense in a man is believed to coincide with a certain tendency to extravagant enthusiasm and material wastefulness. The intensity of *bhakti* is accompanied by "physiological symptoms like sleeplessness, suspension of physical activities, and bodily deterioration. Mentally there is a gradual wasting way in desperation, resulting in spiritual inanity and blankness. The Lord of love is likewise seized by soul-hunger; and scorning His heavenly aloofness and infinite glory, He invades the mystic's soul and longs for union with him. In the ecstasy of the unitive experience that follows, the agonies of the dark night of the soul are forgotten, and its separative existence is swallowed up in the ocean of bliss that is *Brahman*" (Srinivasachari, 310–311). The *Bhāgavata* God has something intimately human about him.

Rāmānuja, however, does not go this far and seems to stop where the *Bhāgavata* declares that the soul who remains ever distinct from the God he worships is happier than one who becomes absorbed in God. The unitive experience that the *Bhāgavata* suggests along with the possibility of an alternation between the bliss of union and the anguish of separation (since it is unlikely that such ecstatic experience could be permanent) were to remain the basis of the philosophy of later Vaishnavite Vedāntins, like Sri Chaitanya and Rāmakrishna. For Rāmānuja, salvation *(moksha)* is not the disappearance of the self or its total absorption in God but its "release from the limiting barriers." "The released soul attains the nature of God, though not identity with him" (Radhakrishnan, 710). It realizes itself as the body of *Brahman* and dwells in direct and continuous communion with God and like the latter, enjoys infinite consciousness and infinite bliss. It retains its individuality, however, for egoity and *not* individuality is the cause of bondage and, without such retention of individuality, the enjoyment of bliss in communion with God is not possible. The state of release means a restoration of the natural qualities of intelligence and bliss through a transcendence of the law of *karma* and mundane existence. It refers to the replacement of the "imperfect *prakrtic* body of the *jiva*" by "a perfect one" and *not* to any "disembodied state" (Hiriyanna, *Outlines,* 412). Thus, unlike in the world of mundane existence *(samsāra),* where distinctions have a meaning, in the state of release—where the souls are all of the same kind—there are no distinctions. The samsaric distinctions are due to the souls' unfortunate connection with matter, which the souls must get rid of in order to attain the nature of *Brahman* and manifest their intrinsic nature. In other words, the released state implies only a recovery of the soul's true nature and not its development into any "new character" (Radhakrishnan, 710).

One important point needs to be mentioned here. Though the liberated soul, in its perfection, becomes essentially similar to the Supreme, it is still atomic and finite, a mode qualifying the Supreme, whereas the latter is all-pervading and infinite. Though the soul may yet enter into different bodies and thus experience the variety of God's creation, it does not share with Him his immanent power of controlling the universe nor his transcendent power of creating and destroying that universe. It has no power over "the creative movements of the world, which belong exclusively to *Brahman*" (Radhakrishnan, 710).

C.D. Sharma is of the opinion that Rāmānuja "has failed to express the relation between the universe and God." Although Rāmānuja speaks of matter, souls and God as the three realities which together make up the Absolute, he identifies the Absolute with one of his three realities, namely, God. Further, although he assigns reality to matter and souls, he makes them the attributes or modes of God. He "abolishes the distinction between attributes and modes," and though he explicitly maintains the distinction between attributes and substance, "he implicitly undermines this distinction." For, according to him, the distinction between substance and attribute is only relative: a thing can be both a substance and an attribute. Though matter and souls are substances in themselves, yet in relation to God they are only his attributes. He seems to ignore the essentially independent existential character of a substance by implying that a thing may be dependent and yet be a substance. C.D. Sharma asks: "If matter and souls are absolutely dependent on God, how can they be as real as God?" Radhakrishnan writes:

> The finite centres of experience seem to be resolved, in Rāmānuja's system, into movements in the life of God. If the Absolute is a perfect personality including all selves and the world, it is difficult to know how the finite selves, with their respective consciousnesses, unique meanings and values, are sustained.... Rāmānuja's

> *Brahman* is not only a supreme self, but an eternal society of eternal selves. How can God both include and exclude the individual in the same ultimate sense? [Radhakrishnan, 714].

Rāmānuja appears to hang somewhere between maintaining the relative character of souls and matter and abolishing Absolutism, between Upanishadic Absolutism and Vaishnavite recognition of ultimate distinctions.

> When he emphasises the monistic character of his system, he makes out that the supreme reality has the unity of self-consciousness, and matter and souls are but moments in the being of that supreme spirit. When he is anxious to preserve the independence of the individual, he argues that the individual souls are all centres of consciousness, knowing subjects possessing self-consciousness, though their selfhood is derived from God [Radhakrishnan, 714].

Rāmānuja's inconsistency becomes more obvious in his simultaneous identification of the soul with the individual *jiva,* the "I"-consciousness, the finite subject of all empirical knowledge as well as with the self-luminous and self-conscious subject which preserves its identity through the cycles of birth and death and is essentially changeless. If the soul is essentially changeless, then the body and all its various experiential associations are not fundamental to it. Which would mean that it is the transcendental Self, the pure subject, the supreme background of all empirical knowledge and as such, can never become the *object* of experience and cannot be called finite and individual. C.D. Sharma asks: "How can then it be identified with the empirical 'I'? . . . How can it be a real agent and a real enjoyer? How can its plurality be proclaimed?" (Sharma, 369).

The same criticism is extended to Rāmānuja's claim that the soul of God is the efficient cause and his body the material cause. If, as Radhakrishnan argues, the finite is equated with matter and thought, "such opposed factors cannot belong to the same reality." Rāmānuja, in his enthusiasm to offer a more humane alternative to Samkara's ill-accessible Absolute, combines the unity of the whole and the distinction of the attributes into one Absolute—an organic whole whose parts exist in and through "a supreme principle which embodies itself in them":

> Rāmanuja intends to give us a more satisfying unity which is neither an identity nor an aggregate of parts, but comprehends all differences and relations. One may well ask whether such an absolute experience is not an arbitrary fancy incapable of verification. . . . If the Absolute is supposed to be a transcendent changeless substance, it is a problem how such an Absolute, which has no history ["beginningless"] includes the time process and the evolution of the world. Unless Rāmānuja is willing to explain away the immutable perfection of the Absolute, and substitute for it a perpetually changing process, a sort of progressing perfection, he cannot give us any satisfactory explanation of the relation of the soul of the Absolute to its body [Radhakrishnan, 716].

In the absence of any explanation on Rāmānuja's part in this regard, it is easy to presume that God's body is an accident to his soul even as the individual's to his. "Verily, then," writes Sharma, "Rāmānuja's Absolute is Shankara's *Brahman* bound to the world, while Shankara's Absolute is Rāmānuja's *Ishvara* liberated from this world" (Sharma, 370).

While Radhakrishnan admits that Samkara and Rāmānuja are "the two great thinkers of the Vedānta," he cautiously points out that "the best qualities of each were the defects of the other." He writes:

> Samkara's apparently arid logic made his system unattractive religiously; Rāmānuja's beautiful stories of the other world, which he narrates with the confidence of one who had personally assisted at the origination of the world, carry no conviction. Samkara's devastating dialectic, which traces all—God, man and the world—to one ultimate consciousness, produces not a little curling of the lips in the followers of Rāmānuja. Samkara's followers outdo the master, and bring his doctrine perilously near atheistic mentalism. The followers of Rāmānuja move with as much Olympian assurance through the chambers of the Divine Mind as Milton through the halls of heaven [Radhakrishnan, 720].

Having said this, Radhakrishnan proceeds to defend Rāmānuja's religious genius. In Rāmānuja, religious need was as strong as the philosophic spirit, and he tried his best to bring together the demands of the religious feeling and the claims of logical thinking. Much more remarkable than Rāmānuja's failure to give us a systematic and self-contained philosophy of religion, is "the deep earnestness and hard logic with which he conceived the problem" and attempted to reconcile "the apparently conflicting claims of religion and philosophy": "A thin intellect with no depth of soul may be blind to the wonders of God's ways, and may have offered us a seemingly simple solution. Not so Rāmānuja, who gives us the best type of monotheism conceivable, inset with touches of immanentism" (Radhakrishnan, 720, 721).

3. Dvaita Vedānta

Dvaita Vedānta (*Dvaita* = dualistic) is associated with the name Madhvāchārya, commonly known as Madhva. His dualistic philosophy came as a reaction to Samkara's Advaitism and it has several points in common with the philosophy of Rāmānuja. Madhva, also known as Ānandatirtha and Purnaprajña, is regarded by his followers as an incarnation of Vāyu, the son of Vishnu. He is the champion of unqualified dualism and he advocates the five great distinctions of God and the individual soul, God and matter, the individual soul and matter, soul and soul, and matter and matter. Madhva's philosophy, being a defense of dualism and pluralism, shows a bias for *difference*. It resembles Rāmānuja's Visishtādvaita in being theistic and in identifying the supreme God with Vishnu (or Nārāyana), but it is more explicitly pluralistic. Madhva says: "Diverse and of diverse attributes are all things of the universe." For him, not only individual souls but also material objects are different from each other. His doctrine is also realistic inasmuch as it accepts the existence of objects quite apart from our knowledge of them.

There is little authentic information regarding Madhva's life and whatever is known about him has been through legendary and semi-mythical biographies of his, called *Madhva-vijaya* and *Mani-manjari*, both of which were written by Nārāyana Bhatta, who is believed to be the son of one of Madhva's disciples. Madhva was born in A.D. 1197 in the South Indian city of Rajatapitha (the modern Kalyānapura), near Udipi, which was not far from Sringeri, where there was the celebrated *matha* ("monastery") of Samkara. Even today, Udipi remains the chief center of Madhvism in South India (Dasgupta, IV, 52). Madhva was a disciple of Achyuta-preksha and initially studied the views of Samkara under him, although he soon developed his own system of thought and was successful in converting his master to his own doctrines. According to S.N. Dasgupta, Madhva wrote as many as 37 works, which include his commentary on *Brahma-Sutra* called *Madhva-bhāsya, Gitā-bhāsya, Anuvyākhyāna, Bhāgavata-tātparya-nirnaya, Mahābhārata-tātparya-nirnaya, Vishnu-tattva-nirnaya, Tattvod-dyota, Tattva-viveka, Tattva-samkhyāna, Tantra-sāra-samgraha,* and commentaries on at least nine principal Upanishads. Besides these important works, he also wrote a commentary on the first 40 hymns of the *Rig-Veda*. Among the important works of Madhva's followers are: Jayatirtha's *Tattva-prakāshika,* a commentary of *Madhva-bhāsya* and *Nyāya-sudha,* a gloss on Madhva's *Anuvyākhyāna;* Vyāsatirtha's *Tātparya-chandrikā,* a commentary of Jayatirtha's *Tattva-prakāshika, Nyāyāmrita* and *Tarka-tāndava;* Rāmāchārya's *Tarangini,* a commentary on Jayatirtha's *Nyāyām-rita;* and Purnānanda's *Tattva-muktāvali,* an independent treatise containing a vigorous attack on Samkara's Advaitavāda.

Theory of Knowledge

Madhva defines *pramāna* (source of valid knowledge) as "that which makes an object of knowledge cognizable as it is in itself." There are thus two functions in a *pramāna:* to render an entity an object of knowledge, and to make it cognizable. So far as the first of these two functions is concerned, all *pramānas* perform it directly, but in case of the second of the two functions, there is the distinction between the two kinds of *pramānas*—*kevala* (intuitive) and *anu* (sense-contact), the former performing it directly *(sakshāt)* and the latter performing it indirectly *(asakshāt)*. The two functions also distinguish a *pramāna* from the *pramata* ("subject") and the *prameya* ("object"), since "neither the subject nor the object can be called the instrumental causes of knowledge" (Dasgupta, IV, 160–161). According to Madhva (whose views are later elaborated by Jayatirtha), our knowledge does not in any way modify an object of knowledge. Truth, which is the exact agreement of knowledge with its object, belongs to knowledge alone; the instruments of knowledge are true only insofar as they produce true knowledge. But the instruments are also true in the sense they too are directed towards the object even as knowledge of it is and, so far as they are directed towards the *right* object of which we have *right* knowledge, the extent of their activity is in agreement with the extent of the object of knowledge.

There are two kinds of *pramāna: pramāna* as true knowledge *(kevala-pramāna),* and *pramāna* as the instrument or *sādhana* of true knowledge *(anu-pramāna).* The value of Madhva's definition of *pramāna* as "agreement with objects of knowledge" is implicit in the fact that it includes memory *(smrti)* of "previous valid experience" as valid, "whereas most of the other systems of Indian philosophy are disposed so to form their definition as purposely to exclude the right of memory to be counted as *pramāna*" (Dasgupta, IV, 162).

There are three cases of *anu-pramāna — pratyaksha* (perception), *anumāna* (inference), and *āgama* (verbal testimony). According to Madhva, these three *pramānas* are comprehensive enough to include "all other so-called *parmānas,*" such as postulation or presumption *(arthāpatti),* comparison *(upamāna),* and noncognition *(anupalabdhi). Pratyaksha* or perception implies "defectless sense-organ" and includes seven such sense-organs: *sākshin* (identified with self), *manas* (mind), and the five outward sense-organs (eye, ear, nose, tongue and skin). The outward or surface sense-organs operate when they are in contact with their objects on the one hand and with *manas* on the other, the latter being an active entity in continuous contact with the knowing self. Their operations characterize the waking state. *Manas,* an internal organ and the proximate cause of memory *(smrti),* works through the impressions *(samskāras)* deposited in it as the result of the previous experiences of the knower. Thus the knowledge caused by surface or external sense-organs in association with memory consists of the modifications of *manas.*

In the dream-state, however, *manas* functions independently of external sense-organs on the basis of stored impressions *(samskāras).* These instances of knowledge are called *vrtti-jñāna* and "are owned by the knower as *mine* in its witnessing capacity" (Raghavendrachar, 322). This witnessing capacity or principle is called *sākshin.* It is as enduring as the knower and is active in deep sleep as well. "It apprehends the knower as 'I' and pleasure, pain, etc. as what occur to 'I.' This apprehension forms the background of all cases of knowledge — *sākshin* and *vrtti*" (Raghavendrachar, 322).

Ānumāna or inference is "defectless proof giving rise to the knowledge of something relevant to it" and it is based on the knowledge of *vyāpti* (invariable or unconditioned concomitance) between the proof and the proved *and* the fact that the proof is in a suitable position to give the knowledge of the proved. The basis for the determination of such invariable concomitance *(vyāpti)* may be perception *(pratyaksha),* inference *(anumāna)* or verbal/scriptural testimony *(āgama).* In his *Tarka-tāndava* Vyāsatirtha insists that *vyāpti* really refers to a contradiction of experience leading to inadmissible assumption or implication *(anupapatti).* He says: "When anything experienced in a particular space-time relation must be invalid except on the assumption of some other thing, in some other space-time relation, it must be admitted that such a particular relation subsisting between the two is a relation of concomitance *(vyāpti),* leading to the inference of the latter through the former" (*Tarka-tāndava,* cited in Dasgupta, IV, 184).

Vyāsatirtha further says that when we are satisfied that there are no vitiating conditions, there arises the notion of invariable concomitance, but while the ascertainment of the *absence* of vitiating conditions is required in most cases of doubt as to their possible existence, it should not be insisted upon as indispensable in all cases, for then "this ascertainment of absence of vitiating conditions being dependent on determination of concomitance and that on previous ascertainment of absence of vitiating conditions, there would be infinite regress" (*Tarka-tāndava,* cited in Dasgupta, IV, 199). Madhva's third *pramāna, āgama,* is faultless verbal testimony.

Whenever Madhva refers to verbal testimony, he generally means the testimony of the Vedas, which he regards (like the Mimāmsakas and other Vedāntins) as having by themselves independent force of knowledge, for they are uncreated *(apaurusheya)* and eternal *(nitya).* The view that the Vedas are uncreated is set (as we have elsewhere indicated) against the Nyāya view that they were created by God or *Ishvara.* Vyāsatirtha regards God as the great teacher *(mahopadhyāya)* of the Vedas, being the first to utter or teach them. God always remembers the Vedas, so that there is no possibility of the Vedic order of words being destroyed. "Ordinarily the claim of facts to validity is prior to that of the words which express them, and the latter depends on the former; but in the case of the Vedas the words and passages have a validity which is prior to facts and independent of them. The Madhva view thus combines the Nyāya and Mimāmsā views of the Vedas without agreeing with either" (Dasgupta, IV, 203). Madhva, however, admits two cases of *āgama* or testimony—*apaurusheya* or Vedic testimony, and *paurusheya* or ordinary verbal testimony. Unlike *apaurusheya, paurusheya* is that which admits of change in the verbal order, although it becomes the source of valid knowledge only when it is consistent with the Vedas. As regards *apaurusheya,* it is necessarily the source of the knowledge of *Brahman* when it is recognized as uncreated and impersonal.

So far we have concerned ourselves with *anu-pramāna* or *pramāna* as the instrument of true knowledge. Madhva spoke of another kind of pramāna, *kevala-pramāna,* which is that by which we cognize objects by direct and immediate intuition. The Madhva school recognizes four kinds of such direct intuition: God's intuition, the intuition of His consort Lakshmi, the intuition of yogins or sages, and the intuition of ordinary persons. God's intuition is always correct, independent, beginningless and eternal, absolutely clear and includes everything. Lakshmi's intuition is dependent on God and inferior in clearness to God's knowledge, although it is equally correct, beginningless and eternal, and has for its object "everything except the entire extent of God Himself" (Dasgupta, IV, 181).

The intuiton of sages refers to the special kind of knowledge attained by *yoga,* and it is of three kinds, the first of which is of those "straight sages" *(rju-yogins)* who deserve Brahmahood. "Excepting that this kind knows Ishvara and Lakshmi only partially, it knows everything; this knowledge increases with the increase of *yoga,* until *mukti* is attained." These Yogins know of God more than any other individual souls can do. The second in order of importance is the knowledge of Gods, which is inferior in scope to the knowledge of Yogins. Next comes the knowledge of ordinary persons, who have been further divided into three classes—those that deserve liberation, those that suffer rebirth, and those who are in a still lower state of existence. We must of course distinguish *pramāna* as intuition *(kevala)* from means of instruments of such intuition or *anu-pramāna*. There are three cases of *kevala-pramāna* corresponding to the three cases of *anu-pramāna* according as such means are perceptual, inferential or scriptural.

Madhva believes in the doctrine of self-validity of knowledge which, according to him and his followers, means the consideration of any knowledge as valid by the intuitive agent *(sākshi)* which experiences that knowledge unhindered by any defects or obstruction. The *sākshi* is "an intelligent and conscious perceiver which can intuitively perceive space and distance, and when the distance is such as to create a suspicion that its defect may have affected the nature of perception, the intelligent intuitive agent suspends its judgment for fear of error, and we have then what is called doubt" (Dasgupta, IV, 168). Vyāsa Yati, a follower of Madhva, however, is of the opinion that *sākshi* is capable of comprehending both the knowledge and its validity and despite obstructions it retains this capability, although it may not exercise it. In the event of an illusion of validity, the *sākshi* remains inactive while the internal organ/mind *(manas)*, being affected by its passions of attachment, makes a misperception, resulting in illusory perception. The true operation of *sākshi* is possible only when there is no obstruction through which its activity may be affected by the illusory perceptions of *manas*.

"Thus," writes Dasgupta, "though there may be doubts and illusions, yet it is impossible that the *sākshi*, experiencing knowledge, should not at the same time observe its validity also, in all its normal operations when there are no defects; otherwise there would be no certainty anywhere" (Dasgupta, IV, 168). The disturbing influence affects the "natural power" *(sahaja sakti)* of the *sākshi*, leading to the creation of doubts and illusory perceptions by the *manas*, but in the absence of such disturbing influence, the *sākshi* comprehends knowledge *as well as* its validity. Vyāsatirtha is of the view that in the absence of faults and doubts the subjective realization of an objective fact carries validity with it, that the validity of knowledge arises from the datum of knowledge *(jñāna-sāmagri)* itself. Sense-contact is useful only when there are doubts or obstructions in the production of knowledge, but "it does not by itself produce validity of knowledge" (Vyāsatirtha, *Tarka-tāndava*, cited in Dasgupta, IV, 172). The absence of defects itself cannot be the cause of the validity of knowledge, for it is only a negative factor and is a necessary but not "the constitutive element of the positive realization of self-validity, which proceeds immediately and directly from the datum of knowledge"; we might still have time knowledge despite the presence of defects.

The followers of Madhva, especially Vyāsatirtha and Vādirāja, hold the theory of *paratah-aprāmānya*, which means that all instances of invalid knowledge are due to sources (such as defects and obstructions other than the datum of knowledge, although in most cases of perception under normal conditions we have right knowledge. In his *Yukti-mallikā* Vādirājā says that if in every step of knowledge there were doubt regarding its validity, there would be an infinite regress *(anāvasthā)* and thus we could never feel the validity of any knowledge. Vyāsatirtha points out that it is our realization of the validity of knowledge which leads us to action, and therefore the determination of the validity of knowledge by subsequent tests from without (as in Nyāya) would only result in an infinite regress and thus inaction.

For Madhva and his followers, illusion consists in the knowing of an object in a manner different from what it is, while its contradiction consists in the knowing of the illusory form as false through the rise of right knowledge *(samyak-jñāna)*. In illusory knowledge one entity appears as another, "that which is non-existent appears as existent, and that which is existent appears as non-existent" (Jayatirtha, *Nyāya-sudhā,* cited in Dasgupta, IV, 173). The defects which affect the senses and thus produce illusions, not only obstruct but cause a false representation of the object; they are responsible for *nonobservation* as well as *malobservation*. According to Jayatirtha, even a nonexistent entity can be an object of knowledge; nonexistent entities may not produce the knowledge, but they certainly determine it by virtue of their existing as an idea or concept. However, it should not be insisted that, since there can be knowledge without an object, no knowledge is trustworthy, for as a rule knowledge is self-valid. The self-conscious witness or *sākshi* "perceives and certifies to itself the validity of the mental states without the mediation of any other process or agent" (Jayatirtha, *Nyāya-sudhā,* cited in Dasgupta, IV, 174).

The *sākshi* thus remains in the foreground of all discussions of cognition and is the basis of Madhva's dualistic philosophy, which offers the individual as much independence as it does to *Ishvara*. For the dualists, the notion of the unreality of the world means that there is something real which we mistake for something else, but it does not mean that there is nothing at all. "To speak of knowledge, independent of a knowing subject or a known object, is meaningless. Knowing subjects and known objects must exist. The world is not an unreality. If we do not admit distinctions of things, we cannot account for distinctions of ideas. Our knowledge tells us that differences exist. We cannot regard them as merely conventional, for convention does not produce distinctions" (Radhakrishnan, 740–741).

According to the Madhva school, all explanations of *avidyā* or ignorance (which is said to be beginningless by the Advaitins) presuppose space and time, which cannot be explained away as mere products of *avidyā*. Space and time, according to the dualists, are real wholes having parts, for otherwise we cannot have distinctions of "here and there, now and then." "We are presented with parts of space, for it is incorrect to hold that everything presented to us occupies all space, unlimited and indivisible. We are conscious only of limited bodies occupying portions of space and resisting one another. We perceive parts of space and time, and so they must be regarded as existing" (Radhakrishnan, 741). According to Madhva, they are objects of perception to the self-conscious, witnessing self or *sākshi*.

The distinctionist philosophy of the Madhva school becomes obvious in Vyāsatirtha and Srinivāsa's defense of pluralism *(bheda)* on the basis of the difference between God and the individual *(jiva)* in perceptual terms. In his *Bhedojjivana* Vyāsatirtha says that the difference between God and the individual "is perceived on our side by us and on God's side by Him," that "we know we are different from Him, and He knows that He is different, from us," for "even though we may not perceive God, we may perceive our difference in relation to Him; the perception of difference does not necessarily mean that that from which the difference is perceived should also be perceived; thus even without perceiving a ghost one can say that he knows that a pillar is not a ghost" (cited in Dasgupta, IV, 178). Vyāsatirtha uses inference in support of his argument that the individuals are different from *Brahman:* the individual *jivas* are objects of pain and suffering, which the *Brahman* is not.

Further, since the individuals and the *Brahman* are "permanent eternal entities, their mutual difference from each other is also eternal and real." The opponents of the Madhva school argue that the suffering soul is strictly limited in character and is different from the pure consciousness, which is the individual, and, since such suffering lasts only as long as there is limitation, the difference ultimately vanishes along with the vanishing of the limitation and cannot therefore be real. The followers of Madhva do not, however, consider such limited individuals to be false and, consequently, do not consider the difference depending on their nature to be false.

The individuals and God cannot be identical, for there is an eternal and real difference between the nature of the two in the form of suffering and its absence. The individual souls are only instances of the class-concept of "soulhood," which again is a subconcept of substance. Though the souls do not possess qualities of substances (such as color, smell or shape), they do possess numerical qualities associated with substances—something which differentiates the Madhva view from the Samkara view of self as pure shining consciousness. The self as a class-concept implies similarity between different selves which are only single instances or constituents of the class-concept; it also implies difference among selves "insomuch as each particular self is a separate individual numerically different from all other selves and also from God." The Samkarites suppose that there is no intrinsic difference among the selves and that the apparent difference is caused by the limitations of "the immediately influencing entity, the minds or *antahkaranas,* which is reflected in the selves and produces a seeming difference in the nature of the selves, though no such difference really exists." According to Vyāsatirtha, on the other hand, it is the differences of the selves that really distinguish the minds and bodies associated with them. "It is because of the intrinsic difference that exists between the two individual selves that their bodies and minds are distinguished from each other" (Dasgupta, IV, 179).

Metaphysics

In his *Tattva-samkhyāna* Madhva speaks of reality *(tattva)* as of two broad kinds, independent *(svatantra)* and dependent *(asvatantra),* although elsewhere (in his *Bhāsya*) he speaks of four categories *(padārtha),* namely, God, *prakrti,* soul and matter. God *(Ishvara)* is the only independent reality. The dependent reality is of two kinds, positive *(bhāva)* and negative *(abhāva)*. There are two varieties of the positive—conscious *(chetana),* to which belong the souls *(jivas),* and unconscious *(achetana),* to which belong entities like matter and time. Unconscious existence is either eternal (like the Vedas), eternal-noneternal (like *prakrti,* time and space), or noneternal (like the products of *prakrti*).

S.N. Dasgupta attempts a more comprehensive classification, however. According to his reading of the texts of Madhva school, the philosophy of Madhva admits ten categories: substance *(dravya),* quality *(guna),* action *(karma),* class-character *(samānya* or *jāti),* particularity *(visesha),* qualified *(visishta),* whole *(amsi),* power *(sakti),* similarity *(sadrsya)* and negation *(abhāva)*. Substance or *dravya* is described as the material cause *(upādāna-kārana)* with reference to evolutionary changes *(parināma)* and manifestation *(abhivyakti)* or to both. The world is subject to evolutionary changes, but God and souls can only be manifested and do not undergo any evolutionary change. Ignorance *(avidyā)* may be said to undergo evolutionary changes and to be the object of manifestation as well.

According to Dasgupta, Madhva school admits of 20 substances: the highest self/the supreme person or God *(paramātmān),* Lakshmi, souls, unmanifested vacuity *(avyakrtākāsa), prakrti,* the three *gunas, mahat* (intellect), *ahamkāra* (ego-sense), *manas* (mind), the external senses *(indriya),* the elements *(bhuta),* the element-potentials *(mātrā),* ignorance *(avidyā),* speech-sounds *(varna),* darkness *(andhakāra),* root-impressions or tendencies *(vāsanā),* time *(kāla)* and reflection *(pratibimba)*. The qualities of Madhva include all the 24 Vaiseshika qualities as well as mental qualities, such as self-control *(sama),* mercy *(kripā),* endurance *(titikshā),* strength *(bala),* fear *(bhaya),* shame *(lajjā),* sagacity *(gāmbhirya),* beauty *(saundarya),* heroism *(saurya),* and liberality *(audarya)*. Actions *(karma)* lead one, directly or indirectly, to merit *(punya)* or demerit *(pāpa),* and there is no action which is morally indifferent. Actions are divided into three classes, namely, those enjoined by the sacred texts *(vihita-karma),* those prohibited by them *(nishiddha-karma),* and those not contemplated by them or indifferent *(udāsina)*. Actions of creation, sustenance and destruction in God are "eternal in Him and form His essence" *(svarupa-bhutah)*. The contradictory actions of creation and destruction abide in God, but while one is in the actual form, the other is in the potential form. Actions in noneternal things are noneternal and are directly perceived by the senses.

Next, while Vaiseshika-Nyāya considers class-character or universals *(sāmānya* or *jāti)* as one and immutable, the Madhva school views them as eternal in eternal substances *only* (e.g. "souls" or *jivas*). In noneternal substances they are considered to be "destructible and limited specifically to the individuals where they occur" (Dasgupta, IV, 151). It should be pointed out that in the Madhva school, the relation of similarity between two or three individuals is viewed as existing uniformly between the number of individuals so related, but not completely in any one of them. "When two or three terms which are said to be similar exist, the relation or similarity is like a dyadic or triadic relation subsisting between the terms in mutual dependence; the relation of similarity existing between a number of terms is therefore not one, but many, according as the relation is noted from the point of view of one or the other of the terms. The similarity of *A* to *B* is different from the similarity of *B* to *A,* and so forth" (Dasgupta, IV, 152).

As regards the doctrine of specific particulars *(visesha),* the Madhva school holds that every substance is made up of an infinite number of particulars associated with each and every quality that it might possess; also, there are specific particulars corresponding as the basis to each one of the qualities. According to the Madhva school, therefore, the acceptance of specific particulars becomes necessary only in those cases where the unity and difference of two entities (such as the substance and the qualities) cannot otherwise be satisfactorily explained, so that the doctrine of *viseshas* introduces "some supposed particulars, or parts, to which the association of the quality could be referred, without referring to the whole substance for such association" (Dasgupta, IV, 153).

The Madhva school rejects the Vaiseshika-Nyāya category of *samavāya* or the relation of inherence (the view that since the appearance of the cause in the effect and of the qualities in the substance is of the nature of a relation which is not one of "contact" or *samyoga,* it must be one of inherence or *samavāya*). "If without any such series of relations a relation of inherence can be related in the manner of a quality and a substance, then that sort of relatedness or qualifiedness *(visishta)* may serve all the purposes of *samavāya*" (Dasgupta, IV, 154). The Madhva school therefore accepts related or qualified as a category distinct and separate from the categories of quality *(guna)* and substance *(dravya)* as well as the relation between the two. Similarly, the whole *(amsi)* is not either the relations or parts or both, but a separate category by itself.

The category of power *(sakti)* exists in four differeent forms: i) as mysterious power *(achintya-sakti),* as in God; ii) causal power *(kārana-* or *sahaja-sakti),* which exists in things and by virtue of which they are capable of producing all sorts of changes; iii) a power brought about by "a new operation in a thing" *(adheya-sakti),* as in an idol through the ritual operations of the installation ceremony; and iv) the "significant" power of words *(pada-sakti).* Similarly, negation *(abhāva)* is of three kinds: i) the negation prior to a production *(prag-abhava);* ii) the negation following destruction *(dhvamsābhāva);* and iii) negation as otherness *(anyonābhāva),* such as the negation of the jug in the pot and of the pot in the jug (this is equivalent to what is called "differences," which are considered to be the essence of all things, although Jayatirtha in his *Nyāya-sudhā,* asserts that differences in both eternal and noneternal things are always eternal—a view supported by Padmanābhatirtha in his *Anuvyākhyāna*). As we have said earlier, according to Madhva school (with the exception of Jayatirtha and Padmanābhatirtha), when things are destroyed, their differences are also destroyed, with the following exceptions: the difference between God and souls, between single souls, between single inanimate objects, between these objects and God, and between these objects and the souls. These specific differences are eternal, for as it is generally held by the school, the differences in eternal things are eternal. Next comes the category of unmanifested space *(avyakrta ākāso dig-rupah),* which is different from *ākāsa* as element *(bhutākāsa)* and is limited. The unmanifested space is eternal and remains absolutely unaffected in creation and destruction.

The Madhva system accepts *prakrti* as the "material cause of the material world." While Time is directly produced by it, all else is produced through the series of changes which it undergoes through the categories of *mahat, ahamkāra,* the *indriyas,* the *bhutas* and so on. It is considered as a substance *(dravya)* and recognized as *māyā,* "a consort of God," though impure, material and evolving *(dosha-yukta, jada* and *parināmini)* and under God's full control. It may therefore be regarded almost as God's will or strength. As far as the world is concerned, *prakrti* is the cause of all bondage. It is the source of the subtle bodies of all living beings *(linga-sarira)* as well as of the three *gunas* of *sattva, rajas* and *tamas.* Ignorance *(avidyā)* is a negative substance which, by God's will, covers our natural intelligence (Jayatirtha in his *Nyāya-sudhā*). However, there is no common *avidyā* which uniformly appears in different individuals, but differs from individual to individual. "As such," writes Dasgupta, "it seems to denote our individual ignorance and not a generalized entity such as is found in most of the Indian systems; thus each person has a specific *(pratisviki) avidyā* of his own" (Dasgupta, IV, 159).

For Madhvites, Time *(kāla)* is coexistent with all-pervading or unmanifested space *(avyakrta-ākāsa)* and is produced directly from *prakrti* stuff "having a more primeval existence than any of the derived kinds"; it is self-existent and, like space, is the vehicle *(ādhāra)* of everything else; it is also the common cause of all produced objects. Like Time, darkness *(andhakāra)* is also a separate substance and is not mere negation of light. Similarly, reflection *(pratibimba)* is a separate substance and denotes the character of the individual souls *(jivas).* The souls are reflections of God, for they cannot have any existence apart from His existence and cannot behave in ways independent of God's will and, being conscious entities possessing will and feeling, are essentially similar to Him. However, they are not destructible like ordinary mirror-reflections, but are eternal.

Like Rāmānuja, Madhva believes in God or *Paramātmān,* souls and matter (or the world) as the three entities which are real and eternal, but speaks of souls and matter as subordinate to God and entirely dependent on him. God (or *Brahman,* for Madhva seems to speak of the two as one) is the only independent reality, "the fullness of infinite qualities," "the author of creation, maintenance, destruction, control, knowledge, bondage, salvation, and hiding." He is omniscient, and "all words in their most pervading and primary sense refer to Him" (Dasgupta, IV, 155). However, his nature is not indefinable (as the Advaitins maintain), for it can be known through a careful study of the Vedas and, on such occasions when he is said to be indefinable, all that is meant is that "a complete knowledge of him is difficult to acquire," for he "cannot be described, reasoned out, and known (entirely as such and such)." Madhva in his commentary on *Brahma-Sutra* quotes from the *Garuda Purāna:* "For want of thorough comprehension, *Brahman* though declared by the whole body of scripture and capable of being known and inferred by reasoning, is said to be beyond the reach of words, reasoning and knowledge" (see Radhakrishnan and Moore, 556). God is transcendent, but he is also immanent as the inner ruler *(antaryāmi)* of all souls. He is a perfect personality and is identified with Vishnu, creating and dissolving the world repeatedly. He manifests himself in various forms *(vyuhas),* periodically appears in incarnations *(avatārs),* and is "mystically present in the sacred images." His consort is Lakshmi, who too is capable of assuming various forms, but without a material body, and is coeternal with him and all-pervading, an ever-present witness to his glory. Unlike those gods and goddesses who attain release *(mukti)* after many existences, Lakshmi is eternally redeemed and ever-liberated *(nityamukta).* She is the personification of God's creative power and is identified with *prakrti,* though God is "greater than she in point of subtlety and in the extent of qualities" (Radhakrishnan and Moore, 569).

God is the efficient and not the material cause of the universe, and as such, does not create the souls and matter "from nothing or reduce them to nothing": "An unintelligent world cannot be produced by a supreme intelligence. God's activity is the result of his overflowing perfection" (Radhakrishnan, 743). Though everything exists because and for him and functions for him, he has nothing to gain through them, he being intrinsically perfect. "The multifarious activity of the universe is but a revelation of this perfection; and the entire creation is meant only to afford an opportunity to all for self-realization through proper discipline" (Hiriyanna, *Essentials,* 192). Although God is guided in his soul-related actions – condemning some and redeeming others – by the *karma* of the individuals, he is not dependent on *karma* (we must here distinguish between *karma* as individual deeds or actions and *karma* as the law of cause and effect bringing about the fruits of such action). In his commentary of *Brahma-Sutra* Madhva writes: "Though the Supreme Being and *karma* (action) are both the cause of fruit, *karma* does not guide the Supreme Being; on the other hand it is the Supreme Being that guides and rules (our) action" (Radhakrishnan and Moore, 567).

The individual souls are infinite in number and atomic in size, but each is different from others according to its past *karma,* and each is imperfect in its own way, although the imperfections of all the souls is on account of its ignorance and suffering. Madhva regards the distinction between *Brahman* and the individual soul *(jiva)* as real, and holds that "it is wrong to think that the *jiva* and *Brahman* are non-different in release and different in *samsāra,* since two different things cannot at any time become non-different" (Radhakrishnan, 743).

Though totally dependent on *Brahman,* the souls are not (unlike matter) absolutely different from *Brahman,* for they have certain features common with *Brahman,* like sentience and bliss. Though God is their inner controller, the souls are real and active agents and as such, have certain responsibilities to bear. Though they are atomic in size, they pervade their bodies on account of their quality of intelligence. The soul is by nature conscious and blissful, though it is subject to pain and suffering on account of its connection with material bodies, and so long as it is not freed from its material impurities, it is subject to cycles of transformation. Though the souls are eternal, they are spoken of as being born with reference to their embodied connection: "Though the self is eternal, still it is possible to speak of him as being born, with reference to the (embodied) condition (to which he is subjected)" (Madhva's commentary on *Brahma-Sutra,* in Radhakrishnan and Moore, 564). The released soul, in its blissful restoration, is very much similar to God.

It is on this principle of similarity that Madhva explains Upanishadic statements like *"Aham Brahma asmi"* ("I am *Brahman*") and *"Tat tvam asi"* ("That thou art"), which do not imply "identity of essence as in Advaita, but mere resemblance" (Hiriyanna, *Essentials,* 192). He also refers to the separateness as declared in such Upanishadic statements as "The eternal of the eternal, the intelligent of the intelligent" and "Two birds which are inseparable friends." Madhva attempts to remove any possibility of contradiction by quoting from *Kaushitaki Upanishad:* "The Supreme Lord is absolutely separate from the whole class of selves; for He is inconceivable, exalted far above the selves, most high, perfect in excellence and He is eternally blessed, while from that Lord this self has to seek release from bondage" (see Radhakrishnan and Moore, 565). Further, no two *jivas* are identical, each having its own worth and place in the scheme of things. They are separate from God as well as from one another, but they are dependent on God, who "impels them to action according to their previous conduct," who "confers knowledge (on the devoted self) for his righteousness, and absolves him from sin and leads him to eternal bliss" (Radhakrishnan, 744; Radhakrishnan and Moore, 567).

The souls are of three kinds: i) those who are eternally free *(nitya-mukta),* like Lakshmi; ii) those who have freed themselves from mundane existence, the recurrent round of birth and death *(mukta),* such as gods and men, sages and ancestors or fathers *(pitr);* and iii) those who are still bound *(baddha).* According to Radhakrishnan, the last class includes both those souls who are "eligible for release" *(mukti-yogya)* and those others who are "not eligible for it." The ineligible souls are either those intended for "hell or the blinding darkness" *(tamoyogya)* or those who are "bound to the circuit of *samsāra* for all time" *(nitya-samsārinah).* "While some are preordained for salvation by their inherent aptitude, others are destined for hell, while a third class keeps revolving on the wheels of *samsāra* from eternity to eternity, now enjoying, now suffering, in endless alternation" (Radhakrishnan, 744).

The threefold classification is based on the three *gunas* of *sattva, rajas* and *tamas.* The *sattva*-dominated souls go to heaven, the *rajas*-dominated revolves in the samsaric cycle, while the *tamas*-dominated go to hell. Slightly different from the orthodox classification of souls is Dasgupta's: i) those who are "fit for emancipation" *(mukti-yogya),* like gods such as Brahmā and Vāyu, or sages like Nārada, or kings like Ambārisa, or advanced men;

these advanced souls think of God as being, bliss, knowledge and *ātman;* ii) those souls that are subject to transmigration and suffer the pleasures of Heaven and the sufferings of Earth and Hell; and iii) those souls who remain in the form of demons, ghosts or the like (Dasgupta, IV, 155-156). Each of these souls is different from every other soul, and even in emancipation the souls differ from one another in respect of their merits, qualifications and desires. In the Madhva school, a more or less fixed gradation dependent on distinctions *(tāratamya)* of souls is worked out on an elaborate scale which, however, has very little value for the student of philosophy.

As stated earlier, everything in the world of nature originates from *prakrti* or the primary matter and, in course of time, returns to it. *Prakrti,* which appears to be homogeneous but is really composed of different principles in a subtle state, develops into the perceptible universe through the workings of God and the souls. *Prakrti* passes through 24 transitional products of creation before it is completely manifested. God is instrumental in molding empirical forms out of *prakrti* (which is thus the material cause of the universe) and himself exists in it in various forms. *Avidyā* (ignornace) is one of *prakrti*'s forms and is of two kinds: that kind of ignorance which obscures the latent spiritual powers of the soul *(jivācchā-dika),* and that kind which conceals the Supreme from the soul's view *(paramācchādika).* According to Madhva, these two forms of *avidyā* are "positive principles formed out of the substance of *prakrti*" (Radhakrishnan, 745).

Madhva rejects all earlier attempts to reduce the world of matter and souls to a mere illusion or an emanation of God and offers a philosophy of absolute dualism. Although he appears to agree with Rāmānuja on several points, he rejects the latter's qualified absolutism. According to Rāmānuja, differences have no separate and independent existence and belong to identity which they qualify; for Madhva, differences constitute the unique nature of things and are not mere qualifications of identity. Madhva rejects the relation of inseparability *(aprthak-siddhi)* and the distinction between substance and nonsubstance *(dravya* and *adravya),* and he explains the relation of identity and difference in terms of unique particulars *(visesha)* in the attributes of a substance, which he considers as absolutely real. Consequently, Madhva does not regard the world of matter and souls as the body of God: matter and souls are different from each other as well as from God. Although the individual soul is dependent on God, "since it is unable to exist without the energising support of the universal spirit, even as the tree cannot live and thrive without its sap" (Radhakrishnan, 745), it does not qualify God.

Both matter and souls have "substantive existence themselves" (Sharma, 374); they depend on God as their immanent ruler, but are absolutely different from Him and thus do not form His body. Further, whereas Rāmānuja advocates qualitative monism and quantitative pluralism of the souls (he believes that all souls are essentially alike), Madhva advocates both qualitative and quantitative pluralism of souls. While Rāmānuja regards God as both the efficient *and* the material cause of the universe, Madhva (who does not make any distinction between the body and soul of God) regards God as only the efficient cause of the universe inasmuch as He activates those subtle elements in *prakrti* (which is the material cause of the universe) in His creative desire to give them a material form. Rāmānuja makes the liberated soul similar to God in all respects except in regard to the latter's power to create, preserve and dissolve the universe and as regards His power as the inner ruler of that universe. Madhva, however, asserts the difference of the liberated soul from God. Sinari writes: "In the same vein in which Rāmānuja preached the course of liberation, and equated the liberated with one in the form *(prakāra)* of God, Madhva propagated his concept of *mukti* or absolute freedom as a state of abode in God *(sālokya),* as closeness to God *(sāmipya),* as accomplishing God's form *(sārupya)* and as entry into God's body *(sāyujya)*" (Sinari, 200).

Even this fourfold bliss enjoyed by the redeemed or liberated soul is not inclusive enough to constitute anything like the full bliss of God. If the liberated soul, according to Rāmānuja, enjoys "the full bliss of the realization of *Brahman* which is homogeneous, ubiquitous and supreme, according to Madhva even the most qualified soul which is entitled to *sāyujya* form of liberation can share only partial bliss of *Brahman* and cannot become similar to *Brahman (Brahma-prakāra)* in the strict sense of the term" (Madhva's commentary on *Gitā,* cited in Sharma, 374; emphasis added). Finally, Madhva believes in the doctrine of eternal damnation for some souls (the third class of beings in S.N. Dasgupta's threefold category, demons, ghosts and the like), Rāmānuja rejects it. In fact, as Sharma points out, the doctrine of eternal damnation is peculiar to Madhva-Vedānta and Jainism alone.

Ethics and Liberation

According to Madhva, any description of *Brahman* as "attributeless" *(nirguna)* or "of auspicious qualities" *(kalyānaguna)* has only empirical import, for It is transcendent *(alaukika)* and as such, It is ever doubted. It is therefore the object of continuous inquiry *(jijñāsā).* Such inquiry, however, is not empirical, but *Brahma-jijñāsā. Brahman* is independent and everything else is derived from It; It is the source *(bimba)* of all that is created or derived (*pratibimba* = reflection). The created or derived – the reflection – is not an illusion, for it is the work of *Brahman,* which is the principle behind all. To understand the world as *pratibimba* is to understand its principle, which is *Brahman.* The world is the expression of the fullness of *Brahman; Brahman* is "bliss itself" *(ānandamaya).* To know this truth is to attain bliss *(ānanda),* which is *Brahman.* "It is knowledge that produces the feeling of absolute dependence on God and love for him" (Radhakrishnan, 747).

Having established that reality is *Brahman,* and *jijñāsā* is the only approach to it, Madhva rejects *karma* (action/duty) as a discipline, since "it arises from superimposing doership on the individual self," which is a nondoer *(parātantra).* He also rejects *bhakti* (devotion) in the usual sense as well as *dhyāna* (meditation) that is independent of *jijñāsā*. They attract the individual self when it is beset with preconceptions. *Jijñāsā* occurs only to him who is free from all preconceptions. Madhva calls this freedom *vairāgya* and it consists in one's realization that things of the world (Lakshmi including), are nonenduring *(anitya)* and essenceless *(asāra)*. The result of *vairāgya* is total devotion to Vishnu. *Jijñāsā* occurs only to one who has this disposition, although to have this disposition or *jijñāsā* is not the individual's own making. When an individual is seen to have *jijñāsā*, it is an indication that he is having the grace *(prasāda)* of Vishnu. *Jijñāsā* is thus the process of *Brahman*'s creative will; it is "the process of all aspects of *ānanda*" (Raghavendrachar, 331). The process of *jijñāsā* is coextensive with the realization of one's self as "nondoer" *(parātantra)*, which is also the attainment of salvation or liberation *(mukti)*. In his *Tattva-viveka* Madhva writes: "Surely *he* finds release from *samsāra* who understands that all this limited existence is ever under the control of Hari [identified with Vishnu]" (quoted in Radhakrishnan, 747).

One attains a true knowledge of onself as *parātantra* ("nondoer") by a study of the scriptures, although such knowledge is mediate and becomes immediate only when final liberation is achieved through God's grace *(prasāda)*. "A knowledge of God, as the author of the universe and the lord of all, is thus more essential than self-knowledge for release" (Hiriyanna, *Essentials*, 198). Although this too is achieved through the scriptures, it has to be transformed into "direct experience, chiefly through steadfast meditation."

At this point, something we have said already warrants repetition, and we quote Hiriyanna:

> The ideal is the attainment by the selves of bliss, appropriate in each case to its intrinsic worth, so that the distinction of one self from another, though both become free, persists even in *moksha*. The bliss of the self in this state and . . . its knowledge also are finite as compared with the bliss and knowledge of God which are infinite; but even such bliss and knowledge are not completely realized in mundane life, as after liberation. A vessel may be big or small or even a small one . . . may or may not be full of water. Similar is the difference between the states of transmigration and release in the case of selves [*Essentials*, 198].

Although a knowledge of God is essential to release, it is not the final means of reaching it. The ultimate means is the unbroken love of God or *bhakti*, which is the result of a realization of his greatness and goodness and which brings in its wake God's grace. In his *Vishnu-tattva-nirnaya* Madhva calls this grace the crowning cause of salvation. As Hiriyanna writes: "Herein is seen best the theistic character of the doctrine, and the source of its popular appeal" (*Essentials*, 198).

We may now turn to Radhakrishnan's criticism of Madhva's philosophy. "The fact of knowledge," writes Radhakrishnan, "leads to an organic conception of the world, but does not justify the division of the world into God, souls and objects externally related to one another. Nor can we understand the relation of the so-called essence or the individual soul to the universal principles operating in it" (Radhakrishnan, 749–750). Although Madhva's view that the beginning of the world-process is the result of the desire of the divine self is quite acceptable, it is difficult to conceive of God as the supreme perfection in the light of His desire and feeling of a want. Madhva has not sufficiently explained the nature of the dependence of the world on God: "If God were really independent, then there must not be anything to limit him from without. A dualism makes the independence of God impossible. Madhva conceives the infinite in an abstract manner, and is therefore not able to see any unity between it and the finite." It is difficult to see *Brahman* as coeternal with the world, for a coeternal relation would make the supreme spirit bound to objects other than itself.

> We cannot say that it is the nature of the supreme spirit to stand related to individual souls, since the former does not contain the reason of the latter's existence. It is difficult to believe that the essence of God involves a relation to objects whose existence it does not necessitate. It is equally difficult to hold that the relation is a non-essential or accidental one, for an eternal accident, which subjects unborn spirits to itself and binds down the Supreme also, cannot be a mere accident [Radhakrishnan, 750].

Radhakrishnan is also critical of Madhva's theory of "election," which is against the normal tenets of ethics. He writes:

> The predestinarian scheme of thought puts an excessive strain on the other parts of Madhva's theology. The moral character of God is much compromised and the qualities of divine justice and divine love are emptied of all meaning and value. Individual effort loses its point, since whether one believes oneself to be the elect or the non-elect, one is bound to lapse into indifferentism and apathy.... [T]his theory will overwhelm us in despair and raise the question: Is not God playing a practical joke on us, when he implants in us a desire for heaven while making us unfit for it? Unless we are in a position to believe in the spiritual possibilities of every one who bears the human form divine, we cannot have a really useful ethics [Radhakrishnan, 750–751].

Radhakrishnan refers to those passages where Madhva speaks of the individual soul as of the form of knowledge and bliss but not conscious of its nature and of God as of the nature of knowledge and bliss and eternally conscious of His nature. For Radhakrishnan, the distinction between God and man, "however great, is not one of kind." "The essence of each soul may perhaps represent its degree of obscuration, but it is difficult to prove that there are eternal essences persisting in souls even when they are released. In all this we are simply transferring the distinctions of experience to the kingdom of God" (Radhakrishnan, 751).

4. Three Other Schools of Vedānta

In this section we propose to discuss, briefly, the high points of three other Vedāntic schools, all of which were influenced (like Visishtādvaita and Dvaita schools) by the prevalent Vaishnava faith. They are: the school of Nimbārka, the school of Vallabha, and the school of Sri Chaitanya. Nimbārka, who (along with Samkara, Rāmānuja, Madhva and Vallabha) was one of the five principal commentators on Bādarāyana's basic Vedantic text, *Brahma-Sutra,* flourished in the 11th century A.D. His commentary, called *Vedānta-pārijāta-saurabha,* and his ten-stanza work on *Dasa-sloki,* are the chief sources of his theory of *Dvaitādvaita* (dualistic nondualism), also called *Bhedā-bheda* (difference-cum-nondifference). His philosophy is largely indebted to the Visishta-vada of Rāmānuja, who preceded him. Like Rāmānuja, Nimbārka admits the three realities of God, souls and matter, and makes souls and matter dependent on God. The individual soul *(jiva)* is of the nature of knowledge *(jñānasvarupa),* but it is also the possessor—the substratum—of knowledge, just as the sun is light as well as its source. The relation of the soul to its attribute is that of the qualified to that of "the qualification" *(dharmi-dharma-bhāva).* It is one of difference as well as nondifference "Between the qualification and the qualified there is no absolute identity, but only the non-perception of the difference" (Radhakrishnan, 752). For Nimbārka, *Brahman,* souls and matter are equally real and coeternal entities.

The inanimate is of three kinds: i) *Aprakrta* (what is not derived from the primordial *prakrti*), which is "immutable super-matter" (Sharma, 376) of which the divine body is made and which is akin to *Shuddha-sattva* or *Nitya-vibhuti* of Rāmānuja; ii) *Prakrta,* which is derived from *prakrti* with its three *gunas* of *sattva, rajas* and *tamas;* and iii) *Kāla,* or time. These three categories are also eternal like the individual souls.

Nimbārka refutes the predicateless character of *Brahman.* God as the highest *Brahman* is, by His very nature, the abode of good and auspicious qualities and is identified with the mythological Krishna, whose consort is Radha. The universe is a manifestation *(parināma)* of what is contained subtly in the nature of God and hence, cannot be dismissed as a mere illusion. Souls and matter are parts of God in the sense that they are His powers. God is both the efficient and the material cause of the universe. He is the efficient cause, for as the lord of *Karma* and the inner ruler of the souls, "he brings about the union of the individual souls with their respective *karmas* and their results and the proper instruments for experiencing them" (Radhakrishnan, 753). He is the material cause, since creation is only a manifestation of his powers of *chit* (sentient) and *achit* (nonsentient) in their subtly transformed forms.

The relation of the three principles of God, matter/world and the individual soul is not one of absolute identity or nondistinction, nor one of absolute distinction. If the supreme spirit were absolutely distinct from the individual souls and the world, it could not be omnipresent. Further, the scriptures have both monistic and dualistic texts and hence, to accept any *one* of the views as right would amount to ignoring the scriptures. Nimbārka brings himself to a position of compromise by saying that both difference and nondifference are real, that *Brahman* is at once different from and identical with the world of spirits and matter—"not by any imposition or supposition, but as the specific peculiarity [*svābhāvika* or natural] of its spiritual nature" (Dasgupta, III, 406). "Just as the spider spins out of its own self its web and yet remains independent of it, so the *Brahman* also has split itself into the numberless spirits and matter but remains in its fullness and purity" (Dasgupta, III, 406).

The difference signifies distinct and dependent existence *(parātantra-sattvabhāva),* while nondifference signifies the impossibility of independent existence *(svatantra-sattvabhāva).* Nimbārka interprets the Upanishadic text, *"Tat tvam asi"* ("That thou art"), in the light of his doctrine of difference-nondifference/identity-and-difference: *tat* refers to the eternal all-pervading *Brahman; tvam* refers to the dependent individual soul; and *asi* refers to the relation of difference-cum-nondifference between them. The souls and matter are both distinct and nondistinct from the *Brahman,* like the rays of the Sun from the Sun itself or like the coils of a rope from the rope itself. We should not regard the distincts as "mutually exclusive and absolutely cut off from each other": "Difference and identity are both equally real, and what is different is also identical" (Radhakrishnan, 754).

Nimbārka discards the theory that the conscious and the unconscious world, together with *Brahman,* form a composite personality, which is the material cause of the world. According to him, the *sakti* does not in any manner affect *Brahman*'s integrity. Nimbārka's *sakti* is Ramanuja's body of *Brahman.* God is all-powerful and is able to create the world by his mere will. In his commentary on *Brahma-Sutra* Nimbārka speaks of each soul as "a ray of *Brahman* individualized." As Radhakrishnan writes: "The theory attempts to avoid the affirmation of an absolute identity, where attributes are confused and distinctions abolished, and, at the same time, tries to escape from mere pluralism, which would impair the omnipresence of *Brahman* and limit his nature and sovereignty" (Radhakrishnan, 755). In their state of bondage, however, the individuals naturally and inevitably forget their aspects of unity with God and feel themselves independent in all their actions and experiences.

The ultimate ideal, therefore, is to realize the relation with God, to "abnegate all actions, desires and motives, and to feel oneself as a constituent of Him" and abide in Him "as a part of his energy." Vedānta distinguishes three kinds of *karma: Sanchita-karma,* which are the seeds of destiny already stored as a result of former acts and which have not yet begun to germinate, but which, left alone, "would generate in time a set of latent dispositions, which should yield a biography"; *Āgāmi-karma,* which are the seeds that would normally collect and be stored "if one were to continue in the path of ignorance basic to the present biography," that is, "the destiny not yet contracted"; and *Prārabdha-karma,* which are the seeds collected and stored in the past that have actually begun to grow, that is, the *karma* bearing fruit in the shape of present events—"the incidents and elements of our present biography, as well as the traits and dispositions of the personality producing and enduring them" (Zimmer, 441, 442).

With the realization of the true nature of God and one's relation with Him, all three kinds of *karma* are immediately destroyed. Dasgupta writes:

> The realization of *Brahman* consists in the unflinching meditation on the nature of God and the participation in Him as His constituent which is the same thing as the establishment of a continuous devotional relationship with Him. This is independent of the ontological fusion and return in Him which may happen as a result of the complete destruction of the fructifying deeds *(prārabdha-karma)* through their experiences in the life of the saint *(vidyā-yoni-sarira)* or in other lives that may follow [Dasgupta, III, 415].

After exhausting his fructifying deeds, a saint is said to leave his gross body through the nerve in his subtle body called *sushumna* and, passing beyond the material regions *(prakrta-mandala),* reaches the transitional region between the material regions and the abode of Vishnu, whereupon he leaves aside his subtle body in the supreme being and is absorbed into the transcendent essence of God. "Such emancipated beings, however, are never sent down by God for carrying on an earthly existence. Though the emancipated beings become one with God, they have no control over the affairs of the world, which are managed entirely by God himself" (Dasgupta, III, 415).

While Rāmānuja emphasizes *bhakti* as a distant relation of "awe and reverence" *(aisvarya-pradhāna-bhakti),* Nimbārka speaks of *bhakti* as a close and continuous relation of love and friendship *(mādhurya-pradhāna-bhakti).* "Although religion begins in awe and reverence, it ends in love and most intimate fellowship. In this sense, Nimbārka has given us the last word, the inner core, the real essence of religion" (Chaudhuri, 345). Both Rāmānuja and Nimbārka regard difference and nondifference as necessary, and both treat animate and inanimate existences as attributes of *Brahman,* but while Rāmānuja lays relatively more emphasis on the principle of identity, Nimbārka treats both identity and difference as "separately and equally real" (Sharma, 377). Nimbārka rejects Rāmānuja's view that the individual souls and the world are attributes *(prakāras* or *viseshanas)* of *Brahman* or God and its related emphasis on the nonduality of the supreme being. According to Nimbārka, "the presence of a body does not necessarily imply the possession of attributes; for an attribute has for its object the distinction of the thing which possesses it from others which do not possess it. If *chit* [sentient, individual souls] and *achit* [insentient, material world] are the attributes of *Brahman,* then, what is that reality from which *Brahman* is distinguished by the possession of these marks?" (Radhakrishnan, 756).

Finally, as we have hinted at elsewhere, Nimbārka rejects the distinction between the body and the soul of God and the view that matter and souls constitute God's body, for if it were so, God could not be beyond all the pains, defects and imperfections of the world: "One portion of God cannot be reserved for change and imperfection and the other for eternity and perfection" (Sharma, 377). For Nimbārka, therefore, matter and souls are the parts and powers of God. Nimbārka's philosophy, as Roma Chaudhuri writes, "Strikes a happy balance between the rigid intellectualism of Advaitism and the effusive emotionalism of later dualistic schools" (Chaudhuri, 345).

Vallabhāchārya, commonly known as Vallabha, was a Telugu

Brahmin who was born in A.D. 1473 (S.N. Dasgupta: A.D. 1481) in a family with leanings toward Vedic rituals and the worship of "Gopālakrishna" ("the cowherd Krishna"). His philosophy, which is said to have been an extension of the views of the 13th century Vedāntin Vishnusvāmin, is known as *Shuddhādvaita* or "Pure Non-dualism undefiled by *Māyā,*" and according to which the whole world is real and is subtly *Brahman.* Since he emphasizes "divine grace" *(pushti)* as the all-powerful means of enjoying the highest bliss, the religious aspect of his system is also known as *Pushti-mārga* or "the Path of Divine Grace." Vallabha is believed to have written 84 books, which include his commentary on *Brahman-Sutra* called *Anubhāsya,* his commentary on the *Bhāgavata-Purāna* called *Subodhini,* as well as such other significant works as *Siddhhānta-muktāvali, Siddhānta-rahasya, Tattvārthadipa* (or *Tattvadipa*) and *Vedastutikārikā.*

The highest entity is *Brahman,* who is *Sat* (Existence), *Chit* (Knowledge), *Ānanda* (Bliss) and *Rasa* (Sentiment); the *Brahman* is also *Purna Purushottama* ("Perfect and the Best of Beings") and is therefore *personal* in nature. He is identified with Srikrishna or Gopālakrishna. He is endowed with several divine qualities, of which wisdom *(jñāna)* and action *(kriya)* are the most significant. According to Vallabha, the Upanishadic reference to *Brahman* as "attributeless" only means He is devoid of material or worldly qualities. He is both the agent *(kartr)* and the enjoyer *(bhoktr),* and He has created the universe out of Himself for his divine sport *(lilā).* He is the material as well as the efficient or instrumental cause of the universe. He is the abode of good qualities as well as those qualities which are seemingly contradictory in nature; and, though He does not need to have a body, he appears in various forms to please his devotees. When He is associated with action *(kriya)* alone, He is *jaña-rupa* and can be propitiated by ritual deeds *(karmas),* as stated in the Vedic *Brāhmanas;* when He is associated with wisdom *(jñāna)* alone, He is *Parābrahman* (the highest *Brahman*) and can be attained through knowledge *(jñāna),* as stated in the Upanishads.

God's worldly manifestation is neither an error nor an illusion. The universe is not an "appearance" or *Vivarta,* for it is a real manifestation; it is not a "transformation" or *Parināma,* for it does not involve any change on the part of God. It is "a natural emanation from God which does not involve any notion of change" (Sharma, 378) and is therefore called *avikrta-parināma* or "unchanged transformation." The divine quality of bliss *(ānanda)* is suppressed in human and animal souls, while "in matter consciousness is also suppressed" (Radhakrishnan, 757).

Notwithstanding this, the entire universe is unconditionally pervaded by *Brahman.* It represents the material *(ādhibhautika)* form of *Brahman.* From God's nature as Existence *(sat)* issue life-breath *(prāna),* the senses and bodies, and all the rest which act as elements of bondage for the souls; from His nature as Knowledge *(chit)* issue the atomic souls, which are the subjects of bondage; and from His nature as Bliss *(ānanda)* spring forth the "presiding deities" *(antaryāmins)* of the souls and which are as many in number as the souls. However, beyond all *antaryāmins* is God as the one supreme *Antaryāmin,* the inner ruler of the universe.

In the world of matter it is only the *sat* or the aspect of Existence which is manifested, while the aspects of Knowledge and Bliss *(chit* and *ānanda)* remain obscured; in the individual souls, it is the aspects of *sat* and *chit* (Existence and Knowledge) which are manifested, while the aspect of Bliss *(ānanda)* remains obscured; it is only in the *antaryāmins* (presiding deities of the souls) that all the three aspects of *sat, chit* and *ānanda* (Existence, Knowledge and Bliss) are combinedly manifested. According to Vallabha, all the three forms of matter, souls and presiding deities *(jagat, jivas* and *antaryāmins)* are essentially identical with God, and the latter "runs through all the three forms which are non-different from Him." In his own commentary on *Tattvadipa* Vallabha says that there is "no difference either homogeneous or heterogeneous or internal in God" (cited in Sharma, 379).

Vallabha regards the world as the real manifestation of *Brahman* and, consequently, regards it as the effect of *Brahman.* Creation and destruction of the world relate only to the manifestation and nonmanifestation of *Brahman.* In the state of creation, *Brahman* is apprehended as a product, while in destruction the world "returns to its original form, and ceases to be an object of perception." The world *(jagat)* cannot be regarded as an illusory appearance, for it is as eternal and real as *Brahman,* who is both its creator and destroyer. The world is the effect of *Brahman*'s innate desire for self-expression. For Vallabha, *māyā* is the power through which *Ishvara* brings about the evolution and the dissolution of the world; as such, the world of *māyā* is not unreal. *Māyā* is different from *avidyā* (ignorance), which is responsible for "the obscuration of the unity of things and the production of the consciousness of difference" (Radhakrishnan, 759).

There is a difference, however, between the manifold world *(jagat)* and the cycle of births and deaths *(samsāra),* the former being the real manifestation of God while the latter is a product of ignorance-induced imagination of the soul. "The soul is right in regarding the world as real, but is wrong when it ascribes to it plurality" (Radhakrishnan, 759). The world is true, though the experience of it by individual souls may be false. Radhakrishnan distinguishes three kinds of souls insofar as their experience of the world is concerned:

> To those who have attained to the truth, the world appears as *Brahman.* To those who have learnt the truth from the scriptures, it appears as both *Brahman* and *māyā, i.e.* something other than *Brahman,* though they know that the former is real and the latter not. The ignorant make no distinction between the reality of *Brahman* and the unreality of the plural appearances which set themselves forth as objective and independent [Radhakrishnan, 759].

According to Vallabha, it is the same *Brahman* who is present in all His fullness in all material objects and in the individual souls, but only manifests some qualities "in their preponderating manner in the different forms." Consequently, multiplicity does not involve any change; it only refers to the *Brahman*'s "universal and unconditional pervasion" (Dasgupta, IV, 330).

For Rāmānuja, the soul, though different from God, is essentially one with God insofar as it forms His body; for Madhva, the soul, though a dependent part of God, is fundamentally different from Him; for Nimbārka, the soul, though identical with God as the latter's power, is different from God in its limitedness and dependence. For Vallabha, however, "the soul as a part of God is identical with Him and appears as different on account of the *limited manifestation* of some divine aspects and *obscuration* of others" (Sharma, 379; emphasis added). The *Brahman* is thus represented as manifesting Himself in His partial aspects. Vallabha admits Time or *kāla* as a separate category, involving activity and nature *(karma-svabhāvam);* it represents the *Brahman*'s power of action or *kriyā-sakti.* Consequently, the determination of the creation or dissolution through time or *kāla* amounts to a subtle limitation of *Brahman*'s power of action. By His will *Brahman* conceives His selves as different from Him and through these different forms He manifests Himself; the diverse aspects or characters of *Brahman—sat, chit* and *ānanda*—manifesting Himself in diverse forms appear to do so in diverse ways, each differing from the others. Hence, even though *Brahman* is identical with knowledge and bliss, He appears as the possessor of these. The power of God consists in manifesting His nature "as pure being, as action and as producing confusion in His nature as pure intelligence." This confusion, which manifests itself as experiential ignorance, is a part of the *māyā* which creates the world and which is God's instrument in His manifestation as the world.

Dasgupta explains it and distinguishes it from *avidyā:*

> This *māyā* thus appears as a secondary cause beyond the original cause, and may sometimes modify it and thereby act as a cause of God's will. It must, however, be understood that *māyā* thus conceived cannot be regarded as the original cause; it serves in the first instance to give full play to the original desire of God to become many; in the second place it serves to create the diversity of the grades of existence as superior and inferior. It is in relation to such manifestation of God's knowledge and action that god may be regarded as the possessor of knowledge and action. The aspect of *māyā* as creating confusion is regarded as *avidyā*. This confused apperception is also of the nature of understanding such as we possess it; through this confused understanding there comes a desire for association with the nature of bliss conceived as having a separate existence and through it come the various efforts constituting the life in the living. It is by virtue of this living that the individual is called *jiva* [Dasgupta, IV, 331].

This explains the diversity of character in different individuals, which is due to the will of God. It, however, brings into question the difference between good and bad *karmas,* for such a distinction is futile and purposeless in the light of God's all-important will. To this Vallabha replies that God, having endowed the individual with diverse powers for his own self-enjoyment, "holds within His mind such a scheme of actions and their fruits that whoever will do such actions will be given such fruits" (Dasgupta, IV, 367). It should be known that God does all this for His own self-enjoyment in diverse ways. As Vitthala, son of Vallabha, writes in his *Vidvān-mandana,* "the law of *karma* is dependent on God and is dominated by Him." Vallabha, however, is of the opinion that God, having explained the goodness and badness of actions in the scriptures, does not interfere in a particular individual's following a specific course of actions. But although, he concedes, the *jiva*'s will is the cause of his *karma* and is determined by his past *karma,* God's will—acting through all this—is the ultimate dispenser.

It is at this point that Vallabha's important distinction between *maryādā-mārga* and *pushti-mārga* finds its relevance. *Maryādā-mārga* is "satisfied that in the original dispensation certain *karmas* should be associated with certain fruits, and leaves the individual to act as he pleases; but the *pushti-mārga* makes the playful activity of God the cause of the individual's efforts and also of the law of *karma*" (Vitthala in his *Vidvān-mandana,* cited in Dasgupta, IV, 368). [For an elaborate discussion of the two *mārgas,* the reader is advised to refer to G.H. Bhatt's "The School of Vallabha," in *The Cultural Heritage of India,* III, 353–355.]

Thus the individual soul, bound as he is by *māyā,* cannot attain *moksha* except through God's grace. *Bhakti* is the only means of salvation. Vallabha's concept of *bhakti,* which is defined as a firm, overwhelming and all-surpassing affection for God with a full sense of His greatness, is different from Vedic *bhakti,* which is mere devotion and is attained by individual effort in terms of *karma* (action/duty), *jñāna* and *upāsanā* (prayer). For Vallabha, though *bhakti* is the *sādhanā* or means while *moksha* (salvation/emancipation) is the goal, yet "it is the *sādhanā* stage that is the best." In his *Tattvadipa* Vallabha says: "Those who enter into the bliss of *Brahman* have the experience of that bliss in their selves; but those devotees who do not enter into this state nor into the state of *jivan-mukti,* but enjoy God with all their senses and the *antahkarana* (internal organ), are better than the *jivan-muktas,* though they may be ordinary householders" (cited in Dasgupta, IV, 347). If, according to the Vedic *Maryādā-mārga, bhakti* is attainable through individual effort, for Vallabha, who was a follower of the *Pushti* school, it is attained without any effort on the part of the individual and only by the grace of God. For Vallabha, therefore, the highest goal is not personal emancipation or *mukti,* but rather "eternal service of Krishna and participation in his sports in the celestial Brindavana" (Radhakrishnan, 760). Not surprisingly, he interprets *"Tat tvam asi"* ("That thou art") as literally true, as against Rāmānuja and Nimbārka, who interpreted it figuratively. "When the souls attain bliss, and the inanimate world both consciousness and bliss, the difference between *Brahman* and these will lapse" (Radhakrishnan, 760).

In his *Sevāphala-vivrti* Vallabha speaks of the individual's attainment, through *bhakti,* of a superior power of experiencing the nature of God, of his experience of continual contact with God, and of a body qualified for the service of God. Purushottama, one of Vallabha's disciples, writes in his *Bhakti-vardhini-vivrti* that, it is only when the affection for God grows into a "passion" *(vyāsanā)* that one attains one's end easily, and whereafter the *bhakta*'s role is one of "passive reception of an otherworldly trance, to seek a sanctuary within a region of consciousness that seems to flow from something pervading universally and indeterminately, to immerse himself in a well of grace" (Sinari, 201).

Sri Chaitanya (1485–1533), who was the last of the Vaishnava Vedāntin to succeed Nimbārka and Vallabha, was also one of "the most revered saints to have shrouded himself with abundance of this grace" (Sinari, 201). It was Chaitanya who was responsible in reviving the *Bhakti* cult into "a powerful religious movement" (Sen, 94), as well as in producing devotional poems and songs that brought the Vedāntic God closer to the ordinary mass of people. His intense devotionalism and longing for a union with Krishna—whom he identified with *Brahman*—manifested themselves in his rapturous, body-negating singing about God's pastimes *(lilās)*, resulting (as it is believed) in bouts of tearful fainting. The streak of anti-intellectualism which marked Rāmānuja's Vedāntism, becomes more obvious in Chaitanya, the essence of whose teaching lay in "the humbleness of the grasses, the fortitude of the trees, self-abasement for the sake of fellow men, and constant remembrance of God's name" (quoted in Lannoy, 209).

Chaitanya's school is known as *Achintya-bhedābheda* ("indescribable identity-in-difference"), although Chaitanya himself did not write any work treating his philosophy. All that we know of his philosophy is from the works of his followers and later admirers, the most important of which are Krishnadāsa Kavirāja's *Chaitanya-charitāmrta,* Vrindāvanadāsa's *Chaitanya-bhāgavata,* Rupa Gosvāmi's *Ujjvala-nilamani* and *Bhakti-rasāmrta-sindhu,* Jiva Gosvāmin's commentaries on Rupa Gosvāmin's two works and his own *Shat-sandarbha,* and Baladeva Vidyābhushana's commentary on *Brahma-sutra* called *Govinda-bhāsya,* with its well-known introduction known as *Siddhānta-ratna.* The views of Achintya-bhedābheda school (also known as the Bengal School, since Sri Chaitanya was born in Bengal) differs from the monistic school of Samkara in its mode of interpretation of the Upanishadic texts. While the Samkara school based its conclusions in terms of indirect and derivative textual meanings *(lakshana* or *gauni vrtti),* the Bengal school asserts that the Upanishads are self-authoritative and that their true spirit can only be revealed in terms of direct or primary and denotative textual meanings *(mukhya vrtti).* The secondary and derivative interpretation of the Upanishads are only inferential and therefore not consistent with the self-authoritativeness of the Upanishads.

According to *Chaitanya Charitāmrta,* Chaintanya believed that *Brahman* could never be indeterminate *(nirvisesha),* and that any attempt to prove the indeterminateness of *Brahman* would only establish His determinate nature as well as the fact of His possessing all possible powers. These powers are threefold: the *Vishnu-sakti,* the *kshetrajña-sakti,* and the *avidyā-sakti. Vishnu-sakti,* in its transcendent incorporation, holds together the three other powers of *hilādini* (bliss), *saudhini* (being) and *samvit* (consciousness), nearly corresponding to *sat, chit* and *ānanda* (although not in that order). The two other *saktis*—the *kshetrajña-sakti* or *jiva-sakti* (the power of God as souls of individuals) and the *avidyā-sakti* (the power by which God creates the world-appearances)—exist outside the transcendent sphere of God.

Thus, *kshetrajña-* or *jiva-sakti* (also called *tatastha-sakti*) is the power by which God manifests Himself in the form of souls, while *avidyā-sakti* (also called *māyā-sakti* and *bāhiranga-sakti*) is the power through which He manifests Himself as the material world. The *saktis* or "powers" are inseparably and eternally associated with *Brahman* and hence, the latter is "eternally qualified" *(savisesha* and *saguna). Brahman* has endless, supernatural attributes *(gunas),* all of which is derived from His *Vishnu-sakti* (also called *Svarupa-sakti*). Thus, *Brahman* is full of nonphenomenal attributes, but is devoid of all phenomenal attributes, and it is from this point of view that the Upanishads describe *Brahman* as *nirguna* or "devoid of attributes or qualities." *Brahman* is therefore both *saguna* (full of qualities) and *nirguna* (devoid of qualities).

The individual soul *(jiva)* and *Brahman* are "nondifferent" *(abhinna)* inasmuch as both are consciousness *(chit),* but they are also "different" *(bhinna)* inasmuch as their attributes are distinctly different. While *Brahman* is "all-pervading consciousness" *(vibhu-chit),* the individual soul is "the smallest imaginable portion of consciousness" *(anu-chit).* The individual soul is a part *(amsa)* of *Brahman* and, therefore, the relation between them is one of simultaneous "difference" *(bheda)* and "nondifference" *(abheda).* The relation, however, is hard to describe or conceive *(achintya).* Hence, Chaitanya's doctrine is known as "the theory of indescribable difference-cum-nondifference" or *achintya-bhedābheda.*

For Chaitanya, *bhakti* is the sole means of liberation. *Bhakti* is of two kinds, namely, *vidhi-bhakti,* which is according to the Vedas and the Sāshtras, and *ruchi-bhakti,* or intense personal affection resulting in ecstatic self-surrender. In his *Bhakti-rasāmrta-sindhu* Rupa Gosvāmi observes that *bhakti* consists in "attaching oneself to Krishna for His satisfaction alone, without being in any way influenced by the desire for philosophic knowledge, *karma* or disinclination from worldly things *(vairāgya),* and without being associated with any desire for one's own interests" (cited in Dasgupta, IV, 391). *Ruchi-bhakti,* which is the end, consists in the intense spiritual love for God like that of the beautiful young damsels *(gopis)* sporting around Krishna and who are believed to be His *saktis;* it culminates in the love of Krishna's beloved, Rādhā. Such love is a manifestation of the power of God in its aspect of *hilādini* (bliss), and since such power forms a constituent of the individual soul, God's attraction of individual souls towards Him is an undeniable fact. This may remain uninspired and inactive for a while, but, on account of its innateness in every individual soul, is bound to wake under encouraging conditions. Liberation thus consists in the eternal enjoyment of this blissful love for Krishna in His own abode.

Chaitanya's concept of *bhakti*—ecstatic, bordering on the pathological, and embracing as it did all the possibilities of male-female relationship, like absence, estrangement, "a dark night of the soul in despair," and the final rapturous reunion—marks the culmination of Vedānta in its highly personalized, theistic-mystical aspect. Dasgupta writes about how "without the life of Chaitanya our storehouse of pathological religious experience would have been wanting in one of the most fruitful harvests of pure emotionalism in religion" (Dasgupta, IV, 389). Chaitanya's life was his message. His own mystic faith and love for Krishna, the ever-loving God, strengthened the devotional movements and has remained, even to this day, a source of guidance to the realm of transcendental peace. Geoffrey Parrinder writes:

> In the Western world we have become accustomed to the sight of yellow-robed young men and women singing and playing musical instruments, selling books and chanting 'Hare Krishna'. Since many of their converts seem to be young American men and women it is a significant indication of the appeal of theistic and emotional religion today, and a change from the more intellectualist and often agnostic attraction of philosophical Vedānta and Buddhism some years ago [Parrinder, 103].

Parrinder's words could well be true of a considerable portion of contemporary Hindu population in India: its religious orientation is primarily mystical.

Works Cited

Bhatt, Govindlal Hargovind. "The School of Vallabha," *The Cultural Heritage of India.* (5 vols). Vol. III. ed. Haridas Bhattacharyya. Calcutta: The Ramakrishna Mission Institute of Culture, 1969.

Bhattacharyya, Krishnachandra. "The Advaita and Its Spiritual Significance," *The Cultural Heritage of India.* Vol. III.

Bhattacharyya, Surendranath. "The Philosophy of Sankara," *The Cultural Heritage of India.* Vol. III.

Chaudhuri, Roma. "The Nimbārka School of Vedanta," *The Cultural Heritage of India.* Vol. III.

Dasgupta, S.N. *A History of Indian Philosophy.* (5 vols). Vols. I, II, III, IV. Cambridge: Cambridge University Press, 1973.

Dutta, Dhirendra Mohan. "Indian Epistemology," *The Cultural Heritage of India.* Vol. III.

Hiriyanna, M. *The Essentials of Indian Philosophy.* 1949, London: George Allen & Unwin; rpt. Bombay: Blackie & Son, 1978.

————. *Outlines of Indian Philosophy.* 1932, London: George Allen & Unwin; rpt. Bombay: Blackie & Son, 1983.

Lannoy, Richard. *The Speaking Tree: A Study of Indian Culture and Society.* London: Oxford University Press, 1974.

Parrinder, Geoffrey. *Mysticism in the World's Religions.* New York: Oxford University Press, 1976.

Radhakrishnan, S. *Indian Philosophy.* (2 vols). Vol. II. Muirhead Library of Philosophy. London: George Allen & Unwin, and New York: Humanities Press, 1966.

————, and Moore, Charles A. eds. *A Sourcebook in Indian Philosophy.* Princeton: Princeton University Press, 1957.

Raghavendrachar, H.N. "Madhva's Brahma-Mimāmsā," *The Cultural Heritage of India.* Vol. III.

Sastri, Anantakrishna. "Brahma-Mimāmsā," *The Cultural Heritage of India.* Vol. III.

Sen, K.M. *Hinduism.* 1961; rpt. Harmondsworth: Penguin Books, 1982.

Sharma, C.D. *A Critical Survey of Indian Philosophy.* New Delhi: Motilal Banarsidass, 1983.

Sinari, Ramakant A. *The Structure of Indian Thought.* 1970, Springfield, Illinois: Charles C. Thomas; rpt. New Delhi: Oxford University Press, 1984.
Srinivasachari, P.N. "The Visishtādvaita of Rāmānuja," *The Cultural Heritage of India.* Vol. III.
Swami Gambhirananda. trans. *Brahma-Sutra-Bhāsya of Sri Sankarāchārya.* Calcutta: Advaita Ashram, 1977.
Swami Tyagisananda. "Philosophy of the Bhāgavata," *The Cultural Heritage of India.* Vol. III.
Thapar, Romila. *A History of India.* (2 vols). Vol. 1. 1966; rpt. Harmondsworth: Penguin Books, 1986.
Winternitz, Maurice. *History of Indian Literature.* (3 vols). Vol. III. New Delhi: Motilal Banarsidass, 1985.
Zimmer, Heinrich. *Philosophies of India.* ed. Joseph Campbell. London: Routledge & Kegan Paul, 1953.

Suggested Further Reading

Bhattacharyya, Kokileswar. *An Introduction to Advaita Philosophy.* Calcutta: University of Calcutta Press, 1924.
Dasgupta, S.N. *Indian Idealism.* Cambridge: Cambridge University Press, 1933.
Dutta, D.M. *The Six Ways of Knowing: A Critical Study of the Advaita Theory of Knowledge.* 1932, London: George Allen & Unwin; rpt. Calcutta: University of Calcutta Press, 1960.
Deussen, Paul. *The System of the Vedanta, According to Bādarāyana's Brahmasutras and Sankara's Commentary.* Trans. Charles Johnston. Honolulu: East-West Center Press, 1973.
Deutsch, Eliot. *Advaita Vedānta: A Philosophical Reconstruction.* Honolulu: East-West Center Press, 1969.
Raghavendrachar, H.N. *Dvaita Philosophy and Its Place in the Vedānta.* Mysore, India: University of Mysore Press, 1941.
Rao, P. Nagaraja. *Epistemology of Dvaita Vedānta.* Wheaton, Illinois: The Theosophical Publishing House, 1972.
Sengupta, Anima. *A Critical Study of Rāmānuja.* Banaras: Chowkhamba, 1967.
Shastri, Prabhu Dutt. *The Doctrine of Māyā.* London: Luzac & Company, 1911.
Srinivasachari, P.N. *The Philosophy of Bhedābheda.* Madras: The Adyar Library, 1950.
________. *The Philosophy of Visishtādvaita.* Madras: The Adyar Library, 1943.
Urquhart, William Spence. *The Vedānta and Modern Thought.* The Religious Quest of India Series. London: Oxford University Press, 1928.

9

Hindu Gods and Goddesses

This book began with the *Vedas,* the *Upanishads,* and the *Gitā;* and, with this chapter on the Hindu gods and goddesses, the circle we started drawing with that set of three early Hindu philosophical-religious texts, is now complete. For, it is in the *Vedas* that we find the earliest statements regarding God and His nature; or, to be more precise, the gods and their natures. We have seen how the early polytheism of the *Vedas* developed into henotheism—each god elevated in turn to the position of the supreme Deity—which, in due course, developed into monotheism, thus paving the way for monism. This development holds true as far as Hindu philosophy is concerned, but even today the galaxy of Hindu gods and goddesses remains complex and colorful despite protests from monistic philosophers like Samkara and rationalistic reformers like Raja Rammohan Roy, who could see the weaknesses of some of the Hindu doctrines and sought to remove them either by appealing to the purer speculations of the Hindus themselves or by pointing out the inconsistencies of their religious lives.

In Hinduism, there has always been "room for the old gods if they retained their usefulness and for new gods if they carried gifts in their hands." Since an understanding of the ultimate nature of reality was always regarded by the Indians as beyond the grasp of man's mind, Indian thinkers never found a sufficient basis for "intolerance of the multitude of popular gods," for there was always this possibility: "The lowliest worshipper of the lowliest god might glimpse some ray of light from the truth which no one, not even the philosopher, could completely know" (Haydon, 90). The Hindu gods and goddesses have therefore survived in the mellow atmosphere of universal tolerance. H.A. Rose refers to the "marvellous catholicity and elasticity" of Hinduism, which in the first place is "essentially a cosmogony, rather than a code of ethics" (Rose, 1). It is this flexibility to meet new situations that has saved the Hindu religion from degenerating into a tribal custom or a mere social habit.

It is interesting to read E.W. Hopkins' remarks about the locus of adoration in his book, *Origin and Evolution of Religion:* "Man has worshipped everything on earth, including himself . . . He has worshipped everything he could think of beneath the earth . . . Finally, he has worshipped everything between earth and heaven and everything in the heavens above ... though only in part has he worshipped the spirits of all these objects" (quoted in Bhattacharyya, 155). That Hopkins' remarks are not an exaggeration is proved by a reference to the Vedic religion, where the boundaries of worship go far beyond the special gods ruling the different departments of nature (such as *Dyaus,* sky; *Agni,* fire; *Surya,* Sun; and *Vāta* or *Vāyu,* wind) to include even the indistinguishable aspects and functions of the same divinity (such as *Surya, Mitra, Vishnu,* all representing different functions of the Sun), abstract agent gods (such as *Dhātr* and *Visvakarmā*) and abstract goddesses (like *Sraddhā,* faith; *Aramati,* devotion; and *Anumati,* favor). In Vedic religion we find even the deification of objects associated with the sacred ritual, such as the fee paid to the priest *(Dakshinā),* the press-stone *(Grāvan),* water *(Āpas),* clarified butter *(Ghrita),* and the sacrificial post *(Yupa).* The earliest forms of Hindu worship were indeed all-inclusive—a fact which is indicated by the coexistence of the gods of the conquering Aryans and those of the highly cultured Indus Valley people who were to conquer them. "The environment determines the object on which faith fastens itself; a change in the environment would not kill faith but would simply alter the character of the object" (Bhattacharyya, 156).

The Vedic religion, which, like all ancient religions, possessed a generous measure of polytheism, allotted the many aspects of Nature and the manifestation of natural power to a multiplicity of gods, each supreme in his own sphere. All the Aryan gods were beneficent nature powers whose personality was yet in a "state of gristle—vague, shadowy figures not fully personified, with physical associations too oppressively prominent to allow a thorough anthropomorphism or effective moralisation" (Bhattacharyya, 165). Such were *Dyaush-pita,* the Sky-father with *Prithivi-mātā,* the Earth-mother, *Vāyu* the Wind-spirit, *Parjanya* the Rain-god, *Surya* the Sun-god, *Savitā* one of the many other spirits of the sky, and *Ushas* the Dawn-goddess; such were *Soma* the sacred beverage, *Sarasvati* the sacred stream, *Maruts* the thunder-storm, and above all *Agni* the Fire-god. Maurice Bloomfield calls them "transparent gods"; they were "half-humanised, mostly resisting imagery and lending themselves to further speculative treatment with advancing thought" (Macdonell, 17). About *Agni* (fire) Bloomfield writes: "In the hieratic (in distinction from the popular) hymns of the *Rg-Veda* there will be few cases in which *Agni* is not more or less directly connected with the sacrifice. And it is well now to take this simple article, the sacrifice fire, and let it unfold its own story step by step. How it turns in the hands of these priestly poets into a person gifted with the thinly disguised qualities of fire; into a messenger mediating between men and gods; into an archpriest typical of holy rites; and finally into a god" (Bloomfield, 157).

The chances of complete and clear personification were, however, considerably minimized by the Aryans' tendency to create mythological synonyms—gods belonging to the same department of nature but possessing special physical basis, distinguishing characteristic and theophanic moment. Harvey De Witt Griswold writes: "The Sun has many distinguishing aspects and function. It is a bright orb *(Surya),* a light-giving friendly power of nature *(Mitra),* a great stimulator of life and activity *(Savitar),* a nourisher and protector of cattle, shepherding them and finding them when lost *(Pushan),* wide-striding from earth through mid-air to zenith, 'he of the three steps' *(Vishnu),* and the one who at dawn shines in every direction *(Vivasant)*" (Griswold, 83–84). [*Note:* Griswold offers an alternative view regarding this, however, that each special Sun-god was, in origin, the creation of a particular Vedic tribe, all of which were finally brought together in the Rg-Vedic pantheon as "parallel forms" of the Sun-god (see Griswold, 270). For a discussion of a similar worship of the Sun in a multiplicity of forms in Egyptian religion, see Bhattacharyya, 167.]

In a similar fashion, the functions of the god of lightning and of the god of storm are differentiated. This process of differentiation certainly multiplied the gods of nature, but it prevented their personification. As Bhattacharyya remarks, their connection with the three physical realms (earth, air/water, and heaven) was so persistent that both the *Rg-Veda* and the *Atharva-Veda* divided the entire pantheon of Vedic deities into three groups—celestial, atmospheric and terrestrial—although deities belonging to more than one region are also mentioned in later classifications (see Macdonell, 19).

But, as Macdonell points out, deified forces of nature were not the only gods that the Vedic Aryans worshipped. We find traces of animism and fetichism in their worship of inanimate objects like hills, rivers, forests, plants, implements and weapons. And, although totemism has not yet been established in relation to the Vedas, there are evidences of the praise or invocation of some animals that were associated with particular gods or served as symbols and thus attained a semi-divine status. In his book *Mohenjo Dāro and the Indus Civilisation,* Sir John Marshall writes about the religion of the Indus people being the linear progenitor of Hinduism and indicates the importance of totemic symbols to that early religion: "We must guard against assuming that all the animals which served as charms or talismans at Mahenjo Daro were necessarily objects of cult. Nevertheless, it is safe . . . to infer that the images of composite animals with human faces were intended for worship" (quoted in Bhattacharyya, 170).

The cow, for instance, had become a sacred animal and thus inviolable. By the time of the *Samhitās* and *Brāhmanas* the boar and the tortoise had become identified with the Creator *Prajāpati*—"an identification that was to have far-reaching consequences in the history of Vaishnavism at a later time when they came to be regarded as incarnations of Vishnu" (Bhattacharyya, 170). There were also "the tutelary deities of the household and the field," spirits of the air, departed ancestors, ancient priests, seers and heroes, the wives of the gods (some of whom—like *Indrāni, Varunāni* and *Agnāyi*—were without much independent status, but many others—like *Ushas, Sarasvati, Vāc, Prithvi* and *Rākā*—were sufficiently independent to be separately worshipped), and the demons and malevolent spirits.

All of these gods, directly or indirectly, were partakers in an elaborate system of sacrifice conducted by a highly trained priesthood. Since the proper uttering of the *mantras* was essential for the success of a sacrificial rite, a presiding deity of "holy speech" *(Vāc)* became necessary, even inevitable.

At the time of the *Brāhmanas* this presiding deity of holy speech was identified with the sacred stream, *Sarasvati,* on whose banks sacrifices were performed. There was yet another important personification—that of the "Lord of Prayer" *(Brihaspati),* who is supposed to favor the man offering prayer and destroying the hater of prayer. These two personifications—of the holy speech and of the Lord of the Prayer—were to have significant influence on the later history of Hinduism. The first of the two developed into the pantheistic Absolute *(Brahman)* and through it into *Brahmā,* the first god of the Hindu Trinity, while the second developed into the God of theism and later into *Vishnu,* the second god of the Trinity.

Eustace Haydon remarks on the process of deitic transformation and the consequent loss of power on the part of humanized, personal gods: "In the properly performed ritual was an energy, an effective work, *karma,* which controlled the order of the world. The ritual word of power was *Brahman.* This force which controlled the gods and spanned time and space was like an immanent cosmic energy, a fundamental reality, the soul of all existence. In the presence of this super-personal power, *Brahman,* the colorful, pesonal gods were little more important than men" (Haydon, 96). If Haydon visualizes the medley of gods in the larger philosophical perspective of the Absolute/Supreme *(Brahman),* Bhattacharyya locates a common basis for a plurality of humanized gods in the gods themselves, in their sharing qualities and attributes which were similar in nature: "A sacrificial religion which was often pragmatically interested in the gods as helpers in war and givers of plenty in peace had little incentive to look beyond the power, the grace and the bounteousness of the gods approached for favour. This will explain why most of the gods, personal or abstract, were invested with many similar attributes by the poets and worshippers" (Bhattacharyya, 174). Thus, in the *Atharva-veda* the gods hardly differ from one another and all are demon-killers. Again, the fact that tutelary deities were few and most of the gods were cosmic and nationally or tribally worshipped, favored "development of speculation about their nature and a sublimation of their functions" (Bhattacharyya, 174–175).

There was of course a serious threat to the status of these Vedic gods, which came from the increasing importance of the sacrificial technique. "The power of the ritual was so magnified that it tended to reduce the gods to puppets pulled by priestly strings" (Haydon, 95–96). A more serious threat however came from the tendency toward speculation. There was even an ancient tradition which considered the gods to have been originally mortal and to have acquired immortality by the grace of *Agni* or by drinking *Soma* [a beverage prepared by fermenting the juice of a climbing plant and ritually filtered] or by practicing continence and austerity (Macdonell, 17)—"a tradition which was exploited not only in the interest of later Absolutism [there was in fact a point where *Soma* itself was raised to the status of the Supreme Being and worshipped as such] but also for sceptical and agnostic purposes" (Bhattacharyya, 175).

At a later period, when man was considered the most important of the elements and self-knowledge came to be regarded as synonymous with salvation, the gods became superfluous for spiritual blessing. In the *Upanishads* the gods retained only a shadowy kind of existence, having been deprived of their boon-giving capacity. In Buddhism and Jainism they were shown as being themselves in need of the saving knowledge and as approaching enlightened souls for spiritual illumination (see Deussen, *Upanishads,* 173, and Winterneitz, I, 201). There was a reaffirmation of the mortality of the gods and an assertion of their heavens as transitory in character—"good enough as temporary places of reward for the ritualistically virtuous but non-existent to the spiritually wise": "So far as reality was concerned, there was not much to choose between god and man, heaven and earth, for ultimately all were transient manifestations of a single impersonal spiritual principle, namely, *Brahman*" (Bhattacharyya, 178). Along with the growing emphasis on self-knowledge there was also the emphasis on pantheism, the latter being a result of the intensely animistic status assigned to practically every kind of thing. The entire universe, as one of the theories propounded, was derived out of a primeval *Purusha* "sacrificed by the gods": "Whatever is, is *Purusha*—both what has been and what shall be" (Macdonell, 16). [*Note:* The celebrated Rgvedic hymn, "Purusha Sukta," has generally been interpreted in a pantheistic sense by Western scholars. But, as Haridas Bhattacharyya writes, "the verses are not unequivocal in meaning. Thus the *Purusha* is said to extend ten *āngulas* (fingers) beyond the earth *(bhumi);* and though in one place the immortals are said to constitute three-fourths of him, yet in the later portion of the hymn *Indra, Agni* and *Vāyu* are said to be derived out of the one-fourth part that created the things of the earth. This permits the interpretation that even if All is God, God is not All, for He is something more. The question of the freedom of the finite spirit which in its ethical aspect is relatively independent of God does not arise in the context of the hymn, which is essentially a cosmogonic speculation" (Bhattacharyya, 178).]

Similarly, the goddess *Aditi* is identified "not only with all the gods, but with men, all that has been and shall be born, air and heaven." Two other divinities, both with the suffix *pati* (a suffix which Western scholars have regarded as a sign of later speculative development), also helped pantheistic speculation. These were *Brāhmanas-pati,* found in the *Upanishads,* and *Prajā-pati,* found in the Vedic *Brāhmanas.* In the *Rg-Veda, Prajāpati* is described as embracing all things; in the *Satapatha Brāhmana* he is regarded as all and everything. Similarly, *Brāhmanaspati,* who appropriated the deeds and powers of all the gods, gradually supplanted the worship of the nature-gods as the ritual power of Prayer *(Brahman)* rose in popularity until he "effected a transition from the semi-personal god of the *Vedas* to the impersonal Absolute of the *Upanishads*" (Bhattacharyya, 179). The *Rg-Veda* had raised the question about the "wood" and the "tree" out of which the heaven and the earth had been fashioned by *Visvakarman* (world-fashioner) and the *Visvadevah* (All-gods) and the place at which *Visvakarman* effected the process of creation. The reply to the question came from the *Taittiriya Brāhmana:* "*Brahmā* was the wood, *Brahmā* was the tree out of which they created the heaven and the earth. Wise ones, with my mind I declare unto you, he *[Visvakarman]* took his stand on *Brahmā* when he made fast the world." Taking the hint from this passage, the *Upanishads* made *Brahmā (Brahman)* the impalpable, all-pervasive spiritual essence (we may refer back here to the two metaphors of the *Nyagrodha* (fig) seed – which does not reveal the form of the future tree – and of the salt dissolved in water, which becomes all-pervasive in the container, discussed in the introductory chapter of this book) of the entire creation.

Combined with the other Vedic idea of the Ultimate Principle of existence possessing, like some gods, the mysterious Power *(Māyā)* of manifesting Itself in innumerable forms, it cleared the way for the nondualism of Advaita Vedānta. In the system of Yoga too God was "retained for cosmic functions, but so far as individual salvation was concerned, He was regarded as only *one* of the many means for the attainment of *samādhi* (the last and eighth limb of the eight-step yoga and refers to the mind's absorption in the object of contemplation) which is essential for the individual's self-realization. The inscrutable nature of the Absolute, which could be only negatively described "as possessing none of the attributes of worldly objects" *(neti neti),* promoted mystic contemplation rather than sacrificial worship. The supercession of religion by philosophy was a gradual and quiet affair. "An Absolute that could never be defined, which gathered all souls, divine and human, into the enfolding unity of its own being, made theological controversy meaningless.... Rivalries between lesser gods could always be overcome by remembering that devotion to one was really devotion to the other, since all were one in *Brahman*.... All pointed beyond themselves to the eternal, unknown One" (Haydon, 102).

The king of the gods, *Indra* and *Varuna,* and the divine priests of the gods *(Agni, Mitra, Brihaspati),* no longer received their due of prayer and sacrifice. Instead of directing the mind to these "symbolic guardians and the models of the natural and the social orders, supporting them and keeping them effective through a continuous sequence of rites and meditations, men were turning all of their attention inward, striving to attain and hold themselves in a state of unmitigated Self-awareness through sheer thinking, systematic self-analysis, breath control, and the stern psychological disciplines of yoga" (Zimmer, 8). The antecedents of this "radical introjection," as Zimmer finds, were there, quite ironically, in the *Vedas* themselves and were to be more extensively treated in the *Upanishads.*

The Vedic sacrifice involved (as we have already said) both material objects and magical-ritual chants *(mantras).* As Winternitz points out, when we reach the period of the *Brāhmanas* (a class of prose composition appended to the Vedic hymns in the centuries immediately following the age of theological/liturgical analysis and which contained long, elaborate discussions of the elements and connotations of the Vedic sacrifice: see "Introduction"), we find the cessation of the practice of composing new hymns – something which invested the ancient texts with "an inviolable sanctity and a mystic significance" to such an extent that these texts were believed to exercise a *coercive* force on the gods. "If the formalities of a religious ceremony have been faithfully fulfilled, its attendant fruits are bound to follow – not because the gods would be pleased to bestow them but because they cannot prevent their arrival" (Bhattacharyya, 182–3). The attempt to justify such a belief resulted in the formulation of a philosophy that showed that *mantras* have a force of their own and theory of sound known as *Sphota-vāda.*

As we have seen, the Mimāmsa philosophy, which laid all its emphasis on the rules of Vedic interpretation, carried the belief to an extreme by showing that the hymns were in a way more powerful than the gods they were addressed to, and that a flawless performance of the Vedic rites was capable of producing a "meritorious result" *(apurva/adrshta)* which was bound to bring, sooner or later, a favorable destiny *(bhāgya).* There was yet another threat to the importance of the gods – it came from the increased emphasis on the "self-sufficiency of the moral law," the theory that *Karman* (deeds or actions, or the accumulated whole of deeds/actions) produced its fruit without reference to divine favor or disfavor. The Mimāmsa system, which often thought of godhead in the singular as the locus of worship but left very little of the divine capacity to this God, led to the theory that "His only function was to bring about a dissolution of the world at the end of each cycle of existence in order to give a temporary respite to souls suffering from continuous rebirths, without being able to mitigate . . . their merited doom. . . . In extreme speculation even this little initiative of God was taken away and *Karman* was supposed to operate directly without the co-operating activity of God" (Bhattacharyya, 184–5). Thus, an inexorable fate *(adrshta)* above the gods steadily replaced a God of grace.

The Sāmkhya system took a more radical position: it disbelieved in the potency or effectiveness of religious rites, in the possibility of *proving* the existence of God, and therefore, of fixing one's attention on Him as a means to the mystic contemplation *(Samādhi)* that effects the release of the soul *(Purusha)* from its association with body/matter *(Prakrti),* and in the ultimate absorption of the personal finite in the impersonal Absolute. "It appears, therefore, that the majority verdict of Indian philosophers went against a belief in God as understood in the Semitic religions, namely, a unitary and ethical personality ruling the universe by moral law but capable of forgiving and willing to forgive the penitent sinner out of His abundant grace" (Bhattacharyya, 185–6). What prevented "godlessness in the bad sense of the term," however, was the Indian's spiritual and ethical approach as against the narrowly religious. The philosophical-speculative mind, which started with a host of major and minor gods, refused to be monotheistic and was feeling satisfied by referring either to the impersonal Absolute *(Brahman)* or the impersonal Moral Order *(Rta).* Soon, however, a renewed interest in devotional religion manifested itself when the various *Purānas* (popular versions of Vedic teaching composed in the post–Vedic times, which were mainly concerned with *Vishṅu* and *Siva* but drew freely on the Vedic gods and demons, "who were re-mythologized in new legendary settings, often at the expense of chronistic probability" [Strutley, 236]: see "Glossary") were composed, resulting in "a curious intermixture of absolutistic, magico-ethical and theistic speculations" (Bhattacharyya, 186).

At this time the Supreme God and the impersonal Absolute were either identified or placed equally. The *Purānas* portrayed the demons as capable of forcing any boon from the unwilling hands of the gods through proper worship; similarly, sages *(rishis)* were shown to have been tempted with the help of heavenly dancers *(apsarās)* so that they could not dethrone, through their austerities, the "existing authorities of heaven who had won their posts by similar efforts in the past." The attainment of these heavenly positions did not require any grace or aid of god; further, the gods ruled for only one cosmic age "to be replaced in the succeeding age by a fresh set." Thus the mortality of the gods, declared originally in the *Rg-Veda,* was re-established.

Even while philosophic speculation was about to attain its climax by claiming that even the gods needed self-knowledge in order to be saved and that an individual, finite soul attaining heaven might be regarded as being on its way to salvation—its heavenly residence being only an intermediate stage—religious speculation was getting more serious, refusing to reduce the gods to mere transient manifestations of an impersonal Absolute or helpless wheels of a moral machine. Its task, as Bhattacharyya observes, was "much more formidable, for the Vedic gods hardly formed a pantheon with well-defined duties and and relations" (Bhattacharyya, 187).

While it is true that the large number of gods, spirits, and demons mentioned in the Vedic hymns is "an indication of the richness of the mythological dimension of the Aryans' religion" (Smart, 87), it is also true that there was no well-recognized head of the Vedic pantheon as was Zeus in the Greek religion or Jupiter in the Roman religion. Although *Dyaus Pitar* (Father Sky) as the god of heaven along with *Prithvi Mātar* (Mother Earth) had generally been regarded as the parents of all the gods *(devas), Dyaus* does not appear to have been more than "a colourless head of the divine clan in India." Imperfectly personified, *Dyaus* and *Prithvi* are not always regarded as being "ancient born," for they are themselves spoken of as being begotten or created. Besides, as Macdonell's research has shown, the paternity of the gods does not belong to them alone, for other parents are ascribed to the gods collectively or individually in several places (see Macdonell, 14); further, "being too nearly related to the gods of nature, they are not usually regarded as being also the parents of men and other creatures though that relation is not entirely absent" (Bhattacharyya, 188). Thus, *Dyaus* could not satisfy the Aryan's need for a divine unity, and we hardly find any reference to *Dyaus* in later speculations. However, the idea that the gods were related familially—by birth—persisted, and despite conflicting accounts of their origin, they were conceived to form "something analogous to a human tribe or clan (and even to be divided into castes) and to be actuated by a common clan-spirit or group-mind" (Bhattacharyya, 188).

They were often invoked in a group and represented collectively, so that we find in the later Vedic literature and the *Brāhmanas* a comprehensive reference to all the earthly gods by the term *Vasus* (with *Agni* or Fire-god as their leader), and to the heavenly gods by the term *Ādityas* (with *Varuna* as their leader). The highest group comprehending all the gods received the appellation of *Visvadevāh* (All-gods)—a group of gods that are sometimes distinguished from the *Vasus* and the *Ādityas* in the *Rg-Veda.* But while "the idea of a confederacy of the gods materially helped the growth of monotheism" through extolling a particular god as the greatest and highest, "inadequate personification and ill-defined functions" obscured the deitic boundaries, thus making it difficult to keep separate the deities whose principal functions had either a joint or an identical effect. For instance, *Parjanya, Varuna, Indra, Dyaus, Rudra* and the *Maruts* were all involved in the work of rain-giving; *Rudra, Varuna, Soma,* the *Asvins* and the *Maruts* were together treated as physician gods; and, *Brihaspati,* the *Maruts* and the *Angirasas* were all regarded as gods of song (see Griswold, 104, for other instances).

In course of time, while sharing certain functions, the gods began to appropriate each others' attributes. Thus *Agni* (Fire-god) and *Indra* (the god of lightning), who initially appeared as a dual divinity were later regarded as identical, for both fire and lightning served the common function of illumination. The "loose association of functions and attributes with the gods made it possible to invest at least the major gods with all powers incidental to supreme divinity; and when in this way their distinctiveness was lost, the different deities came to be regarded as different forms of one and the same ultimate principle" (Bhattacharyya, 189). It implied the Vedic Aryan's search for the idea of unity—something which he also sought to convey by depicting the mutual dependence of the deities. But the idea of a unitary godhead was more easily reached than an agreed name, for, as it appears, there were champions of different deities. There is a hymn in the *Rg-Veda* which shows that the different gods were essentially nothing but *Agni;* and there are other passages which advance similar claims for *Varuna, Surya* and *Indra.* The use of terms like "the One," "the One unborn," and "the One unknown," indicates the tendency towards adopting an indefinite god as the ultimate unity, towards monism rather than just monotheism.

A world which is characterized by order and harmony implies a certain all-inclusive law and points to the existence of a single being that manifests itself in *acts of creation,* one who not merely exercises the power that has brought the world into being but also the will and intelligence to modulate its working. Such a conscious fashioner of the world, for the Vedic Indian, was *Prajāpati,* the supreme Lord of all beings. The acceptance of *Prajāpati* as a separate deity does not, therefore, represent a process of conscious generalization, but "a necessary stage of development of the mind, able to imagine a deity as the repository of the highest moral and physical power" (Dasgupta, I, 19).

In the idealized worship of *Varuna/Agni/Indra,* we had the nearest approach to monotheism; in *Prajāpati* we find a total displacement of a polytheistic anthropomorphism by a spiritual monotheism (see Radhakrishnan, 90–91). Soon, *Prajāpati* replaced the pre-Vedic *Tvashtar* (the divine craftsman), as well as the Vedic deities *Dhatar* (supporter), *Vidhātar* (disposer) and *Visvakarman* (all-creator), who were "personifications of the architectonic and controlling activities of the Creator" (Macdonell, 116).

Prajāpati was *not* a nature-god, and hence it was easy to invest him with supreme wisdom as well as qualities which are plainly ethical, although his original or principal function as the god of offspring and of creation in general was always remembered; so that, in due time he came to be identified with *Brahmā,* the first person of the Hindu Trinity, who is supposed to be the creator of the world and who also absorbed the intellectual function of *Prajāpati* to become the revealer of the *Vedas.*

In later Hinduism, we find the legends current about *Prajāpati* being transferred to *Brahmā.* As *Prajāpati* was born from an egg in the primeval waters in order to turn chaos into cosmos, so *Brahmā* was born in the same way and for the same purpose. As *Prajāpati* assumed the form of a tortoise in order to create progeny and blessed the boar that raised the earth, so *Brahmā,* at the time of the deluge, assumed the form of fish and as a boar raised up the earth from the savage waters—an act which earned him the name *Nārāyana* ("he who moves on the waters"), which afterwards became the distinguishing title of *Vishnu.* Thus, having been associated with "the sacrificial god" *Prajāpati* of the *Brāhmanas,* as well as with the "philosophical unity *Brahman*" of the *Upanishads, Brahmā* stood a good chance of being raised to "the supremest position" (Carpenter, 10, 170). [*Note:* The *Upanishads* recognized a *Saguna* (with attributes) and a *Nirguna* (without attributes) *Brahman* but did not give the *Saguna-Brahman* or *Isvara* the name of *Brahmā,* although, on the popular side, *Brahmā* developed into the concrete male god *with* attributes. In the two epics, *Rāmāyana* and *Mahābhārata, Brahmā* is shown as occupying the throne of the Universe, and is addressed as the grand sire, the guardian, and the refuge of gods and men, although, even in these epics, his original glory is perceptibly diminished before the rising splendor of *Vishnu* and *Siva,* while in the *Purānas* he is completely superceded by these two deities or merged into the one or the other, his name being retained in the *Trimurti* (the three persons, i.e. *Brahmā, Vishnu,* and *Siva* or *Mahesvara*) "as a relic of his former greatness" (see Phillips, 51-52)].

Several things, however, went against *Brahmā*'s supremacy. For instance, popular enthusiasm was absent for a God who "made no appeal to the emotional life of man and remained mostly a god of the sacrificial class." Though he remained the advisor of the gods in difficult situations, he retired from the active government of the world after peopling it with diverse creatures, including the gods" (Bhattacharyya, 192). His titles "are amplified more for grandiloquence than for added meaning" (Hopkins, *Epic Mythology,* 192), while he himself passed back into the universal world-power out of which he emerged, the neuter *Brahman* (Absolute). Further, although he has been called *ātmabhu/svayambhu* (self-existent/self-born), he carried with him the Vedic tradition of the waters being the source of everything and of a primeval "golden egg or germ" (he is also equated with *Hiranyagarbha,* the "germ of gold") out of which all things arose, so that, in later times—in the *Rāmāyana,* particularly—he was represented as being born in the lotus issuing out of the navel of the primeval *Purusha* resting on the waters *(Vishnu,* or *Nārāyana)* who curtly orders *Brahmā* to attend to his creative business (thus the independent *Brahmā* is transformed into an agent of *Vishnu*). The view that *Brahmā* was the "original god" *(Ādideva)* was to be totally set aside in the *Mahābhārata* in favor of *Vishnu* or *Siva,* "with one exception," which "indeed implies that the god is 'lotus-born' and so comes under the head of Vishnu's general superiority" (Hopkins, *Epic Mythology,* 192).

There was yet another thing which went against *Brahmā*'s possibility of being raised to the supremest position. The creation of the world by him was not consistently nonsexual and "an obscure Vedic text concerning the incest of a father with his daughter and the birth of *Vastoshpati* out of that incest was foisted on him in his character as *Prajāpati* and he was represented as begetting *Manu,* the progenitor of the human race, on his own mind-born daughter *Satarupa*" (for which *Siva* cursed him and as a consequence of which he lost one of his five heads, and was afterwards to be known as *Chaturmukha* or the "four-faced one"): "The rational and moral instincts of the race rejected a god who was neither causally first nor ethically ideal" (Bhattacharyya, 193). When the idea of *Brahmā, Vishnu* and *Siva/ Mahesvara* as the Trinity was more or less well established, "possibly there disappeared also the religious motive [issuing from the old idea of ascetic fervor as the cause of creation] for worshipping Brahma" (Bhattacharyya, 193).

As Hopkins writes: "*Brahmā* comes into the group as a matter of form, because it was impossible for the sectarian worshipper to deny the old orthodox Creator, who had been chief of the pantheon, the old Father of gods and men, since the end of the Vedic age" (*Origin and Evolution of Religion,* quoted in Bhattacharyya, 193). By the sixth century A.D. the small group which regarded him as the Supreme God died out, so that there are only a few places in India today where his name is explicitly invoked in religious services, the most important of which is the temple at Pushkar in the Rajasthan state. In his well-researched book, *Epic Mythology,* however, Hopkins shows *Brahmā* (he is called *Brahman* throughout that book, thus nearly equated with the Universal One/Absolute or *Brahman*) as possessing the additional powers related to preservation and destruction/annihilation. "The usual view that *Brahman* having created remains inactive, is true only in part," for he appoints in the beginning the functions of his "children," the gods. Thus he hands over to *Indra* the kingship of the gods and "entrusts to him the combat with demons."

But he himself is no idle observer, for he continues to create (he is said to be creating death); makes the sun rise day by day, keeps daily guard over individuals as well as over the course of nature; provides food "in general, but in particular provides wives and husbands"; determines sex of the new creature and imparts to it folly or cleverness; creates laws and awards punishment; curses bad demons for the good of the world (for instance, in the *Rāmāyana* he curses *Rāvana*'s brother and his own grandchild, *Kumbhakarna,* to sleep half the year, because the demon "harries gods and men"), awards immortality to good demons (in the *Rāmāyana,* he gives immortality to *Vibhishana*), refuses immortality to the sinful worshipping demons; allows the demons to grasp the shadow, not the substance; fashions the strong heart of the warrior and gives him the necessary weapons to defend himself; arbitrates between the quarrelling breaths. But, aside from these, *Brahmā* has other activities—those that are inextricably linked with his being a god of asceticism.

As Hopkins writes, his "activity and impartiality lead to the fundamental weakness of his character," for, as the god of asceticism and father of gods and demons, he allows the latter to practice asceticism in order to win his favor; and because he is an impartial father, he grants boons, such as invulnerability and immortality, to either god or demon indifferently. As the demons always take advantage of his weakness, he is "ever engaged in preserving the world from the result of his own folly" (it is folly and *not* ignorance, for he is prescient).

In fact, the whole drama of *Rāmāyana* is based on the terrible folly of *Brahmā* in giving the demon-villain *Rāvana* his supreme power over the three worlds of heaven, earth and hell. But he is also shown as having taken a vow that sinners must be slain and waits the issue calmly, confident that virtue will win, though his lack of initiative in slaying leads eventually to his dishonor: "One does not honor very much the gods that do not kill." But he is not altogether disregarded: "In his honor is performed a celebration, *mahotsava,* like that of *Siva,* at the autumn harvest festival, in which wrestling and gladiatorial games are performed, perhaps at the time of the new moon, when seers visit the god in *Brahmaloka* [the abode of *Brahmā*], as if the Father God were still a god delighting in destruction" (Hopkins, *Epic Mythology,* 195–6).

Brahmā created Death in order that the world might be preserved, but he is also known as the god "whose anger burned the world," and this anger "seems to be ever in the mind of the unsectarian worshipper." However, the world-destruction caused by his falling asleep is but a phase of eternal life. "How long it lasts is doubtful, as the epic authorities cannot agree even on so vital a point as this." John Dowson writes:

> When *Brahmā* has created the world it remains unaltered for one of his days, a period of 2,160,000,000 years. The world and all that is therein is then consumed by fire, but the sages, gods, and elements survive. When he awakes he again restores creation, and this process is repeated until his existence of a hundred years is brought to a close . . . When this period is ended he himself expires, and he and all the gods and sages, and the whole universe are resolved into their constituent elements [Dowson, 56].

He is called *chaturmukha* and *chaturānana* ("the four-faced" and "the four-directional one"), but not in the literal sense of having four faces or heads (although he is represented as such); he is omniscient, seeing in all directions. He is *sarvajñya* or "all-knowing," and as such he is *chaturveda* or "embracing four forms or divisions of *Veda*"; he is *amitadhih* or "of unmeasured wisdom," more particularly *bhuta-bhavya-bhavisyavid* or "one who knows the past, the present, and the future." As the true god, he is god of troth, and thus, any oath taken in front of *Brahmā* is to be fulfilled. "It is only surprising in epics infected by later views to find so much that still recalls the glory that was *Brahman*'s before the rise of unorthodox sects" (see Hopkins, *Epic Mythology,* 192-8).

Brahmā, as we saw, represents power and glory, but the human mind does not always seek power as such in God. If that were the case—if power had been the essential qualification of godhead—*Agni,* who consumed everything, or *Indra,* whose power was so often extolled in the *Vedas,* or *Soma,* who invigorated men and even made the gods immortal, would have attained the foremost position in Hindu religion. But although the Vedic seers frequently approached these gods, "the future belonged to gods of a very different type—gods that did not engage the hand or employ the head so much as attracted the heart of man" (Bhattacharyya, 194). The Upanishadic identification of *Ātman* or the self with *Brahman* or the Ultimate Reality in terms of a pursuit of self-knowledge to the exclusion of everything else, was soon challenged and the Vedic relation of man and God, with its accompanying rites and rituals, was restored with "a deep spiritual significance and ethical meaning."

The ground for this process of restoration was being prepared by the Vedic hymns themselves, in which gods were distinguished from other kinds of beings by their possession of "the qualities of power, sovereignty, wisdom, beneficence and beauty" (Griswold, 109), acting in unison and answering as a group to the sacrifices and prayers of men. They were believed to possess perfect understanding among themselves in regard to their proper functions and to act harmoniously together for the benefit of the dutiful worshipper. Thus, the gods are related to *Rta* or the Eternal Cosmic Order existing in the physical and the moral world.

Griswold remarks: "All the gods are alike in either determining, or expressing or guarding some aspect of *rta* . . . Through the great conception of *Rta* the multiplicity of nature is reduced to a unity and the multiplicity of the gods (corresponding to the multiplicity of nature) is seen to reflect to a single will, because all are 'labourers together' in maintaining a single all-comprehensive cosmic order" (Griswold, 108). Thus, gradually, the unity that the intellect sought, came to be identified with the divine power that makes for righteousness and moral concord. It would, however, be wrong to say that the ethical character of the gods was a late achievement of Vedic speculation, for, as Hopkins observes, what really took place was that the ethical quality, which was initially associated with a particular god or a group of gods, became "the common property of all the gods through identification or association with the ethical divinity" (see Hopkins, *Ethics of India,* 13).

But this could happen only when anthropomorphism had "sufficiently covered up the physical origin of most of the Vedic gods," thus making easier the transference of the ethical qualities of *Varuna* (one of the earliest of the Vedic gods, identified with the all-encompassing sky, but steadily transformed and idealized so as to become the supreme ruler of the physical and moral world and the custodian of *rta,* the "most moral god of the *Vedas*" [Radhakrishnan, 77]) and the *Ādityas* (the sons of *Aditi,* the Vedic goddess of unlimited space, who collectively represent the whole range of phenomenal manifestation and of whom *Varuna* is one) to these deities. During the course of this transference, however (and, as felt by several scholars, unfortunately), the ethical *Varuna* quietly disappeared from the forefront. Further, as the personification of the constancy and regularity that characterize physical and moral order, *Varuna* had failed to gather round him "any considerable myth of having bestowed gifts on worshippers," so that later generations "did not see the utility or logic of approaching him with frequent rites on the principle of reciprocal service" (Bhattacharyya, 197).

Notwithstanding the fact that these causes conspired to diminish the original importance of the supremely ethical *Varuna,* there was no substantial lowering of the moral standard of the community. In fact, as Haridas Bhattacharyya writes, the Vedic *Varuna* did not "really die," but "rose phoenix-like out of his own ashes in more attractive divine colours" (Bhattacharyya, 197–8; see also Macdonell, 24). The *Rg-Veda* describes him as a noble lord, a king and a universal monarch, possessed of mysterious powers that urge the whole world to obey his laws. In the *Atharva-Veda* he is said to look on all deeds from his "heavenly mansion of a thousand doors and seat of a thousand columns," to behold the truth and falsehood of human beings, to be an invisible witness of man's acts, thoughts and intentions: "Whatever thing two sitting down together talk about, *Varuna* as a third knows." The entire sphere of brightness is his realm; the sun and the stars are his spying agents, who keep a watch upon the conduct of men and report it to him. He is the "terrible hater of the false" and "an all-sufficient protector" (Haydon, 60) against oppressors, tyrants, liars, evil-minded enemies, the human companions of demons and the forces of darkness.

But he has a benign aspect as well. He supports his own creation through timely gifts—rain for the fields, glorious strength in bodies, increase of herds and families, adequate nourishment, honor in assemblies, victory in battles, and a life-span of a hundred autumns. He understands human failings and is liberal about penitent sinners; he is merciful and gracious and a failed person can be restored to his favor by "moral seriousness in trying to discover his 'hidden faults', by a spiritual confession, by longing to be justified in the sight of Varuna, by prayer for the remission of penalty, by oblations and sacrifices and hymns of praise" (Griswold, 129). There is in fact no hymn to *Varuna*—and to his *Āditya*-brothers—in which "the prayer for forgiveness of guilt does not occur, as in the hymns to other deities the prayer for worldly goods" (Macdonell, 27). Identical to the Greek Ouranos and the Ahura Mazda of the Avesta, his character is that of "the divine ruler in a monotheistic belief of an exalted type" (Macdonell, 3).

As S. Radhakrishnan points out, the theism of the Vaishnavas and the Bhagavatas, "with its emphasis on *bhakti* [devotion], is to be traced to the Vedic worship of *Varuna,* with its consciousness of sin and trust in divine forgiveness" (Radhakrishnan, 78). In spite of *Varuna*'s grandeur, the "future allegiance of Hinduism belonged to other gods":

> Simultaneously with the Aryanisation of the land, there went on an imperceptible absorption of indigenous culture and this led to a shifting of emphasis to such Vedic gods as could be easily assimilated to objects of worship.... The Vedic gods, again, were gods of the whole tribe, although it is not improbable that this or that god was occasionally preferred as being the best and the highest. But as the area of Aryan culture extended, local considerations must have dictated the ranking of different gods with the effect that, after the period of the Upanishads, sectarianism began to rear its head and to look upon this or that god as the supreme entity and the source of all things. A change in the popular idea regarding the proper method of approaching god, howsoever caused, was also responsible for the development of theism [Bhattacharyya, 200].

As loving devotion was displacing intellectual contemplation as the proper means to gain divine favor, so the impersonal *Brahman* was being replaced by the personal gods of later Hinduism. Thus two gods were singled out for popular devotion, namely, *Vishnu* and *Siva.* They were savior-gods and, along with *Sakti* (the Mother Goddess), fused together Vedic and local, aboriginal beliefs. *Ganesa,* "probably the god of a local cult" (Bhattacharyya, 200), also attracted a following and was duly incorporated in the cults of *Siva* and *Sakti.* At the same time, many of the Vedic gods were either excluded from the new pantheon or affiliated to the new divinities, even while conservatives were struggling to restore the older deities to their original status of glory and trying to bring order into the growing family of celestial beings. In fact, the Vedic solar worship did manage to survive in a residual form through the several centuries by the side of *Vaishnavism* (the cult of *Vishnu*) and *Savisim* (the cult of *Siva*). However, during the past several centuries, the worship of *Vishnu, Siva* and *Sakti,* has remained the most important feature of Hinduism, their cults constituting the expresion in three forms of what recently has been called "the polymorphous monotheism" (Nirad C. Chaudhuri, 237) of the Hindus and mark the most important development in Hinduism "in its transition from the prehistoric to the historic age."

Vishnu, Nārāyana, Bhagavat, Hari and *Krishna* are often used as synonymous names of the supreme lord. *Vishnu* is of course an important god of the *Rg-Veda,* who is the twelfth son of *Aditi* and *Kāsyapa* and thus the youngest of the *ādityas.* He is said to make three strides in the sky, probably referring to the three stages of the sun's progress in the morning, at midday and at evening. The *Rg-Veda* also describes him as a great fighter and an ally of *Indra* (although later Purānic literature speak of the opposition between *Indra* and *Krishna,* the latter an *avatāra* of *Vishnu*). He has two earthly steps and another higher step which is known only to himself. One of his names in the *Rg-Veda* is *Sipivishta,* which has been explained as surrounded with the early rays. This indicates that *Vishnu* was regarded as the sun, or at least was assigned the qualities of the sun.

In the *Satapatha-Brāhmana, Taittiriya-samhitā* and in the *Atharva-Veda* he is referred to as the chief of the gods, whose place is the zenith, the highest place of the sun; his is a superior place transcending everything. The

Satapatha-Brāhmana speaks of the concept of *Vishnu* as sacrifice—something that was to make him extremely popular in later times: In the struggle between the demons *(asuras)* and the gods *(devas)*, the latter were losing and the former were about to distribute the world among themselves, when the gods decided to make *Vishnu* their sacrificial leader whereupon the demons agreed to give only so much ground as would be occupiea by *Vishnu* when he lay down (*Vishnu* being a dwarf). The gods thereafter approached *Vishnu* with various *mantras* and as a result got back the whole world. The *Satapatha-Brāhmana* also refers to Kurukshetra as the place of the sacrificial performances of the gods, and since *Vishnu* was superior to all the other gods in asceticism, faith, industry and love, he is spoken of as himself the sacrifice. Hence, Haridas Bhattacharyya sees in the later raising of *Vishnu* to the supreme position "an attempt to combine the power of *Indra*, the sacrificial and creative aspects of *Brāhmanaspati* and *Brahmā*, and the moral government of the world associated hitherto with Varuna" (Bhattacharyya, 202).

The post-Vedic Indian, disillusioned with the Vedic sacrificial cruelty and fanciful rites and with the unresponsive speculative unity of *Brahman*, longed for a simplified rite and a god capable of responding to the needs of the heart. The unity of godhead was nearly achieved in the Vedic age; monotheism had given way to absolutistic monism in the Upanishadic age. "All that was needed was to fix up the name and attributes of the unitary God and to define the proper attitude of worship towards him." Thus *Vishnu*, with his sacrificial association and his attitude of willing helpfulness to man, was found most suitable for the purpose. He was the moral governor of the world, periodically descending onto the earth to set matters right, "not because of any sacrificial compulsion but out of his own free will and grace" (Bhattacharyya, 203).

It is at this point that he was identified with *Purusha-Nārāyana*, who, as an archetypal personification of solar or cosmic energy and of creative power, had become the symbol of spiritual enlightenment in the *Rg Veda*, and as the Vedic *Purusha* had allowed himself to be sacrificed in order that the universe might come into being [*Note:* The name *Nārāyana* is derived from *"narāh"* (the primeval waters, the source of all life) and *"ayana"* (the abode of the creator who moves upon the waters and periodically renews the universe, a belief common to other ancient river-civilizations, the most well-known being that which is expressed in the Genesis: "And darkness was upon the face of the deep; and the spirit of God moved upon the face of the waters."). "Of the several Indian creation theories, held regionally or advanced by independent priestly schools, that relating to the role of *Nārāyana*, and to the action of the sun upon the waters is possibly a more rational explanation of the appearance of life than some others, and also suggests the natural relationship between the Vedic solar *Vishnu* and the *Vishnu* of the *Purānas*." This is indicated when the world dissolves into its undifferentiated state at the end of every *yuga* or age, when *Vishnu* rests on the cosmic serpent *Sesha*, floating on the primeval waters, before he recreates the world when the next *yuga* is due (see Stutley, 205)]. *Vishnu*'s self-sacrificial character – to take even an actual human form if it was necessary – became the basis of the theory of incarnation *(avatāra),* while his fluent willingness to reciprocate the love which his spiritually awakened devotees bestow on him, was the basis of the theory of devotion *(bhakti).*

Added to these two aspects of *Vishnu* was the ethical character of the supreme God by the usual Indian supposition that *Nārāyana* was born as a son of *Dharma* or Righteousness [*Note: Dharma* is also believed to be an ancient sage, sometimes classed among the *Prajāpatis,* who married 13 of the daughters of *Daksha* (a son of *Brahmā* and, like *Dharma,* is considered to be one of the *Prajāpatis*) and had a numerous progeny, though all his children – including *Nārāyana* – are "manifestly allegorical, being personifications of intelligences and virtues and religious rites, and being therefore appropriately wedded to the probable authors of the Hindu code of religion and morals, or the equally allegorical representation of that code, *Dharma,* moral and religious duty" (H.H. Wilson, *Essays and Lectures on the Religion of the Hindus,* quoted in Dowson, 88–89)].

The cult of Vaishnavism, however, was a result of several other, sometimes extremely esoteric, modes of worship and thought, whereas its rise to fame and popularity had something to do with the Brāhmanic reaction against the "godlessness" in Buddhism. Literary and archaelogical sources mention a *Bhagavata,* a *Vasudeva* (who claimed a sect of followers), and a *Krishna* (the son of *Vasudeva* and *Devaki*), but what "clans, tribes or peoples worshipped the supreme God in these different names can only be a matter of conjecture now," although the traditional association of *Krishna* with the cowherds and the worship of *Vasudeva-Krishna* by the Satvata section of the Yadava people "lends colour to the supposition that possibly these gods were worshipped by people who were neither scripturally or intellectually incapable of, or traditionally averse to, performing Vedic rites and understood the deep Upanishadic philosophy." It is also probable that, being outside the Vedic pantheon and originally having no association with *Vishnu,* these new gods "could not be worshipped in the Vedic way and consequently the simple worship practised by their original adherents passed over into the Brahmanic cult" (Bhattacharyya, 205; see also Charles Eliot, *Hinduism and Buddhism,* II, 156, and Maurice Phillips, *Evolution of Hinduism,* 58–61).

This refers to the time of Buddha and Buddhism, which appealed to the masses and had broken the power and destroyed the gods of the Brāhmins, who "felt it necessary in self-defence to take advantage of the godward tendency of the human mind to furnish the people with more popular deities than those of the ancient creed." The Brāhmins accomplished this by amalgamating the Vedic *Vishnu* with the chief animals and fetishes worshipped by the tribals "dwelling on the fringes of the Aryan settlements in the north-west" as well as the chief heroes revered by the Aryans (in much the same way as the Brāhmins accomplished this, in the case of Saivism, by identifying the Vedic *Rudra* with the demons, the *linga*-fetish and some animals worshipped by the tribal people), thus establishing the cult of Vaishnavism. They even absorbed Buddha into the *Vishnu* cult by making "the arch-heretic" an incarnation of *Vishnu* so as to silence the multitudes who were hostile to the new cult of *Vishnu* but adored Buddha as a god, "notwithstanding his [Buddha's] denial of God" (Phillips, 61).

In the *Mahābhārata* we are told that *Dharma*'s son, *Nārāyana,* had three brothers—*Nara* (a previous incarnation of the Pāndava hero, Arjuna), *Hari* (or Vishnu), and *Krishna* who, being regarded as the son of Vasudeva and Devaki, was also called *Vasudeva.* Earlier to this, in the *Taittiriya Āranyaka,* we find a mention of *Nārāyana, Vāsudeva* and *Vishnu* as "three phases of the same god." A philosophy of emanation *(Vyuhas)* was assigned to the relationships of *Vāsudeva,* with the deification of his brother *Balarāma,* son *Pradyumna* and grandson *Aniruddha,* each with a different divine function; but sometimes the whole group was considered as "a hierarchy of beings emanating from *Nārāyana,*" as in the intensely Vaishnavite school of the 16th century mystic, Chaitanya. Through his union with *Vāsudeva,* the Yādava (also referred to as "Yadu") hero, *Krishna,* had risen above "the limitations and trammellings of local nature deities while retaining the memory of his exploits which endeared him to the folk." The union of the Vedic *Vishnu* with *Krishna-Vāsudeva* "gathered into one divine figure a heavenly god of light, enriched by the Aryan heritage, a popular god of grace and beneficence, and a deified human hero, revered for efficient service in time of need. The lowly folk-god had become a supreme, cosmic deity worthy of complete loyalty and devotion" (Haydon, 106).

In *Vishnu-Nārāyana-Krishna* the Indians had found a self-sufficient unitary divinity, creating and controlling the physical and the moral universe and holding spiritual and moral relations with man. Joseph Carpenter writes:

> *Vishnu* is no mere metaphysical entity transcending the Three Strands [the three *gunas* of *sattva, rajas* and *tamas*], an abstract magnitude, an intellectual identification of Cause and Effect, a ritual harmony of sacrificer, priest, offering and deity. He is God with a character, Source of all Morality, Revealer of Truth.... True, he is the destroyer of sin as well as of grief and pain; but he has no personal anger against the wicked; he forgives all injuries, he is inclined to show favour to all, he purifies the sinner and protects the pious, and he has come on earth a hundred times. Such a Deity needed no slaughtered animals on his altar ... and the path to union of spirit with him lay through lowly surrender of all desire for personal reward of right action, and that meditation of the Eternal which freed the soul from bonds of sense and time [Carpenter, 242-3].

Such an idea of *Vishnu* as All-god and man's relation with him opened new avenues of Upanishadic interpretation for the philosophers, who challenged the earlier absolutistic interpretation of Samkara and gave the "whole system a theistic turn" (Bhattacharyya, 209). Hopkins writes:

> The most surprising and historically important fact in the various lauds of *Vishnu* as All-god is that he is nowhere called by the sancrosanct formula of the Vedānta. He is wise, knowing, blest, true, joy, etc., but he is not even said to be possessed of *chit,* still less is he designated as being *sacchidānanda* in the phrase of the later *Upanishads* and

Vedānta, though he is the supreme philosophical principle [*Epic Mythology,* 208].

The post-Samkara schools of Vedānta—those of Rāmānuja, Nimbārka, Madhva, Vallabhāchārya, and Chaitanya—agreed that the universe was not "a regrettable necessity whose existence was to be deplored, nor was it to be thought away as an illusion," that both God and his devotee were real and that the relation between them could only be described in terms of divine love and personal devotion. Such a creed, based as it was on love alone, contained within itself the possibility of "a serious emotional imbalance when sensuous elements effected an entrance into the constitution of devotion":

> The disinterested love of God got mixed up with illegal human love that brings no return except social obloquy, and a secondary growth of unsavoury myths round the personality of Krishna tended to undo, in minds prone to confusing symbols with facts, the good achieved by emphasising the emotional needs of man.... An association with the lower *Sakti* cult—partly due to Vedic tradition of female deities, partly due to the identification of *Sakti* with the Vedāntic *Māyā* and partly due to the psychological necessity of postulating an eternal object of Divine love—transformed the spontaneous sportiveness of God in creating the world and the longing of the finite for the infinite into the guilty amours of a cowherd *Krishna* and the wanton abandon of the youthful girls of Brindāvana [Bhattacharyya, 209-210].

As Bhattacharyya points out, the danger came from "an altered conception of the nature and necessity of divine incarnation," for while the *Vedas* had mentioned about deified men, of gods making their descent to the seat of sacrificial grass, of the several forms which *Indra* could assume through the occult powers, mainly because of a need of meeting a definite situation ("...the god descends expressly to save the world" [Hopkins, *Epic Mythology,* 210]), the "later idea of a god beginning his life on earth with infancy and ending it with death like ordinary human beings necessitated the filling in of the details of temporal life with miraculous deeds and heroic exploits." Such a need was strengthened by the popular belief in the incarnate Deity's exclusive possession of superhuman vigor, which of course included the possession of sexual virility. "Still," writes Bhattachāryya, "it is only candid to admit that the influence of this debased conception of God on the unconscious mind might be considerable, and that in certain deformed cults Krishnaism did exercise a baneful influence just as a literal imitation of the union of the two generative principles of *Siva* and *Sakti* produced orgiastic rites in 'left-handed' Sāktaism" (Bhattacharyya, 212).

The *Krishna* of the *Bhagavad-gitā,* however, is a worthy object of adoration and worship and in fact, is spoken of appropriating "all worship paid to other gods." The *Gitā,* which recognized class-division but ignored it as far as spiritual matters were concerned, taught the importance of ordained duties without expectation of reward of any kind (see Chapter 1 of this book) and set up "the toiling Lord as the great exampler of disinterested service" (Bhattacharyya, 213).

In *Krishna* the champions of Vaishnavism had found a Divine Deliverer who was "merciful rather than stern, anxious to save His creatures rather than solicitous of their oblations and offerings," thus making allowance for individual immortality and a blessed personal existence in close proximity to God as a reward of virtuous and devotional life. With a personal god who was supposed to have walked the earth and not just a mythical or symbolic entity, Vaishnavism soon developed into a definite religious community with its own organization. The communal spirit was in all likelihood intensified by its rivalry with Saivism, Jainism, and Buddhism; and "that spirit is not dead even today," although there have been attempts to bring the two cults together through the device of a composite divinity, called *Hari-Hara* (half *Vishnu* and half *Siva*), or the idea of the divine Trinity, called *Trimurti* (a combination of *Brahmā, Vishnu* and *Siva*), or even through an identification of *Siva* with *Vishnu* by making one a form of the other and assigning the function of each to the other—all of which goes to prove "the complementary character of the major deities" (see Bhattacharyya, 215–6).

The same is also true of the many incarnations of *Vishnu,* of whom *Krishna* is the most important as well as the best known. Although, initially, in order to make *Vishnu* acceptable to the aborigines, the leaders of the Brāhmanical reaction (i.e., against Vaishnavism, which found its basis in the *Kshatriya* sect, both *Krishna* and *Rāma* being Kshatriyas) not only fused him with the principal animals worshipped by them, but associated him very closely with others that were worshipped by certain tribes, such as the serpent, the vulture, the monkey and the bear, thus eventually producing some 39 incarnations of *Vishnu;* these were to be reduced to a small group of 10 incarnations *(dasavatāras).* The composition of the group varies, but one that is often referred to comprises, (1) the Fish *(Matsya avatāra),* (2) the Tortoise *(Kurma avatāra),* (3) the Boar *(Varāha avatāra),* (4) the Man-lion *(Narasimha avatāra),* (5) the Dwarf *(Vāmana avatāra),* (6) *Parashurāma avatāra,* (7) *Rāma avatāra,* (8) *Balarāma avatāra,* (9) *Buddha avatāra,* and (10) *Kalki avatāra.* Much of what we know about these incarnations is to be found in *Harivamsa,* a work written in the Purānic style and forming an appendix to the *Mahābhārata.* We examine below these incarnations in some detail.

The Earth, "burdened with creatures, incapable of dying in the perfect *(Krita)* age, appeals to *Vishnu,* who becomes a 'unicorn boar' and with his tusk or horn raises her a hundred leagues, which distance she had sunk into *Patala* [the underworld]. This causes excitement among the gods, till *Brahman [Brahmā]* explains that the boar is the eternal spirit *Vishnu*" (Hopkins, *Epic Mythology,* 210). In order to understand this cryptic quotation from Hopkins' book, one must recall the basic cycle of Hindu cosmology—"the day of *Brahmā*" *(kalpa)*—which is further divided into other units including four *yugas* (ages) that are "similar to the Hellenistic four ages and, like them, manifest a steady decline from supreme virtue" (Mitchell, 13). We have mentioned how, at the beginning of each *kalpa* or "day of *Brahmā,*" *Brahmā* rises again from his cosmic sleep out of a lotus growing from *Vishnu*'s navel. After that took place at the start of the present *kalpa, Vishnu* turned himself into a boar *(varāha),* descended to the bottom of the ocean and rescued the Earth which had been abducted and hidden there by a demon by bringing it to the surface and making it "ready to support life by modelling the mountains and shaping the continents." It is "a creation myth, perhaps belonging to non-Hindu mythology, that has been incorporated into the *Vishnu* legend in the form of an *avatāra*" (Mitchell, 13).

The story is found in *Vishnu-Purāna,* but there are also other stories in the ancient quasi-Purānic texts that associate *Vishnu* with a boar, one of which highlights *Vishnu*'s capacity to adopt the form of his enemies. As A.G. Mitchell notes, there are two main groups of *varāha-avatāra* images—those entirely in animal form and those having a boar's head on a human body. With the increasing need for a more satisfying relationship between the worshipper and the worshipped and the consequent need for devotion towards a personal god, there grew a desire for images which would make the deity "more easily approachable." "Their introduction was almost certainly a slow, uneven process and it is likely that images were at first only made of minor deities in the pantheon" (Mitchell, vi). It is of significance that one of the earliest references to images meant solely for worship—that by the famous grammarian Panini, who belonged to the fifth century B.C. (?) and wrote a treatise called *Ashtādhyāyi*—is of tree-spirits *(yakshas)* and snake-gods *(nāgas)*. The *Matsya* and similar *avatāras* of *Vishnu* must have had origin in the early worship of these popular "images." During the course of his development, *Vishnu* thus acquired the characteristics of a number of folk deities who were absorbed into Vaishnavism in the form of *Vishnu*'s incarnations. [*Note:* "Students of Indian iconography will be aware that, in spite of authoritative descriptions of deities given in the sacred texts, many exceptions can be found which account for the variety of representations of the same deity particularly those made for the less sophisticated worshippers" (Mithcell, 9)].

The 10 incarnations of *Vishnu* partly correspond to his particular aspects in his role as creator, since they represent the forms that he takes at the beginning of each *kalpa* or "day of *Brahmā*" in order to appear in the world as its savior. The obvious associations between fish *(matsya)* and water, linking them with the primeval waters of creation in Indian mythology and with some mythic traditions of universal deluge, emphasize this aspect of *Vishnu* as creator. The earliest mention of the fish-incarnation *(matysa-avatāra)* occurs in the *Satapatha Brāhmana* in connection with the Hindu legend of the deluge and the saving of the best of mankind and everything precious from the Flood [*Note:* Both the Hebrew and Indian versions regard the Flood as a consequence of man's decadence, and both stem from the Sumerian Deluge story recorded in a tablet dated c. 1750 B.C. (see Stutley, 186–7)].

In the *Mahābhārata* the fish-incarnation reappears, but it is in the *Matsya-Purāna* that it receives its most embellished and complex treatment. Here the object of the incarnation is to save *Vaivasvata,* the seventh *Manu* and the progenitor of the human race, from destruction by a deluge [*Note:* In the *Rg-Veda* the term *Manu,* which is derived from the root *man,* "to think," is an archetypal description of "Man," who was the first to offer an oblation to the gods; also, it refers to the Aryan man as distinct from, and superior to, the non–Aryan *dasyu* (those with dark skins, ugly features, who were the natives of northwestern India and who, according to the Vedic priests, were "riteless," "followers of strange ordinances," and "revilers of gods"—something which has been negated by the excavations in the Indus Valley, which suggest a civilization of a high level). From the mythical standpoint, however, the name *Manu* belongs to the 14 progenitors of mankind and rulers of the earth, each of whom rules for a period called *manvantara* or *manu-antara,* "the age of Manu," which is believed to be a period of no less than 4,320,000 earthly years. The first of these Manus was *Svayam-bhuva,* who sprang from *Svayam-bhu,* "the self-existent" identified with *Brahmā,* who divided himself into two persons, male and female. The *Manu* myth gradually expanded, culminating in his appearance as *Vaivasvata,* the seventh *Manu* (the *Manu* of the present age, also called *Manu-Satyavrata*) of the cosmic evolutionary theory. Thus, *Manu* may be called the First Man, an equivalent of the Hebrew Noah.]

One day, while *Manu* was bathing, a tiny fish came into his hands and begged him to remove it from the sea where no small fish was ever safe. *Manu* carefully guarded it until it grew so rapidly in size that nothing but the great sea could contain it. *Manu* soon recognized it as *Vishnu*'s incarnation and worshipped it. The fish-god told *Manu* of the impending Deluge and asked him to prepare for it. When the Deluge finally came, the fish-god duly appeared and Manu bound his ship to the most stupendous horn on the fish using the body of the serpent *Vāsuki* as a rope. He embarked on the ship with all the sages *(rishis),* carrying with him the seeds of all existing things. The ship weathered the great storm and carried *Manu* to safety, thus ensuring the repeopling of the world by the virtuous descendants of *Manu* and his sage-companions. The story is further elaborated in the *Bhāgavata-Purāna* by the addition of a fight between *Matsya* and the demon *Hayagriva* ("horse-headed") who had stolen the Vedas while *Brahmā* was asleep (*Brahmā* is believed to be the "guardian of the *Vedas*"). *Vishnu* took on a horse-headed form to kill *Hayagriva* and retrieve the *Vedas* in the same way that he took on a boar's head while fighting out a boar demon.

Like the *Matsya* and *Varāha avatāras,* the *Kurma-avatāra* (the tortoise-incarnation) is also associated with the theme of Universal Deluge/ Destruction. In the *Satapatha Brāhmana,* in which the origin of the *Kurma-avatāra* is to be found, it is said that *Prajāpati,* "having assumed the form of a tortoise, created offspring. That which he created he made *(akarot);* hence the word *Kurma*" (quoted in Dowson, 35). There, the tortoise *(kurma)* figures in one of the early cosmogonic theories, which equates the cosmos to an egg which *Prajāpati* the creator broke open, squeezing the outer shell, and the fluid that came out of it became the tortoise, with its lower shell representing the earth, the curved upper shell the vaulted sky, and its body the atmosphere. The tortoise thus denotes the three worlds of earth, atmosphere and sky; it is also identified with the life-sap, the vital element in the creative process, and hence is associated with the creator *Prajāpati* (see Stutley, 157). It is not surprising that the figure of a tortoise should often be found "in the central place of the [Hindu] temple" (S.A. Dange, *Legends in the Mahabharata,* quoted in Stutley, 157). Also, in the *Mārkandeya Purāna, Bharata* (India) is represented as resting on a giant, east-facing tortoise, around which the constellations and countries are arranged in nine divisions. In the later and more developed version of the *kurma* incarnation, *Vishnu* appears in the form of a tortoise in the *Satya-yuga* (the "perfect," first age) to retrieve the precious things lost in the deluge. He placed himself at the bottom of the "sea of milk" *(kshira-sāgara)* in the form of a tortoise and made his back the base of the mountain Mandara.

Later, when the gods and the demons set out to obtain ambrosia *(amrita)* by using the mountain as a churning rod which they rotated by twisting the great serpent *Vāsuki/Ananta/Shesha* round it and pulling it in the two opposite ways, thus churning the entire sea of milk, they recovered the desired objects. Along with ambrosia *(amrita)* 13 other objects came onto the surface. These were: (1) *Dhanvantari,* the divine physician who carried the pot which contained *Amrita;* (2) *Lakshmi,* goddess of fortune and beauty, and *Vishnu*'s consort; (3) *Surā,* the goddess of wine; (4) *Chandra,* the moon; (5) *Apsarāses/Apsarās* (sing. *Apsarās/Apsarā*), the seductive celestial nymphs; (6) *Kaustubha,* the precious gem adorning *Vishnu*'s body; (7) *Uchchaihshravās,* the divine horse, swift as thought; (8) *Pārijata,* the wish-granting celestial tree; (9) *Surabhi,* the cow that grants all desires, the "cow of plenty"; (10) *Airāvata,* the wonderful, four-tusked celestial elephant, who became *Indra*'s mount *(vāhana);* (11) *Sankha/Panchajanya,* the conch-shell of victory; (12) *Dhanu,* the invincible bow; and (13) *Visha/Halāhala,* the terrible poison which nearly neutralized the power of *amrita* (ambrosia) and for a moment enveloped the universe, before *Siva* held it in his throat (an act which is associated with one of his 1,000 names, *Nilakantha* or the "Blue-throated") and then swallowed it to save all mankind. This quasi-creation-myth "envisages all parts of the cosmos, from the largest to the smallest unit, as belonging to a cyclical process in which creation and destruction, birth and death, follow each other in eternal rotation" (Mitchell, 12); it establishes *Vishnu* as the very pivot of the creative process.

The last of the first four *avatāras* which are supposed to have appeared in the *Satya-yuga* ("the first age of the world"), is the Man-lion or *Narasimha-avatāra* of *Vishnu*—"the upper part of the body being a lion, the lower, a man" *(Agni-Purāna)*—is the form he assumed to free the world from the demonic tyranny of *Hiranyakasipu* who, by the favor of *Brahmā,* had become invulnerable, and could not be slain either by man or beast, inside or outside his palace, by day or night. Responding to the prayer of *Hiranyakasipu*'s *Vishnu*-loving son *Prahlāda* (it is said that the demon-king was so incensed at *Prahlāda*'s worship of *Vishnu,* that he challenged the god's omnipotence and omnipresence and demanded to know if *Vishnu* was present in a certain stone-pillar in the hall which he tried to demolish, when *Vishnu* came out of the pillar and tore the demon-king to pieces), "approached the palace at dusk and hid in a pillar at the entrance" out of which he could spring forth at the right time. *Narasimha* is the "embodiment of valour as a divine attribute, and hence is especially suitable for worship by rulers and warriors" (Stutley, 205). He is also said to embody the verses of the *Yajur-veda,* especially those from which spring strength and courage; in the *Agni-Purāna* he is shown as being invoked to protect his worshippers from the evil incantations of enemies. As Jan Gonda has shown, the *Narasimha* myth has been transformed a number of times. In the *Bhagavad-gitā,* for instance, *Prahlāda* is a manifestation of *Krishna*'s power, which was personified and "became the principal character of the myth of *Vishnu*'s man-lion *avatāra,* to which he originally did not belong" (Jan Gonda, *Vishnuism and Sivaism: A Comparison,* quoted in Stutley, 205). Notwithstanding the several textual/canonical transformations and a host of uncanonical man-lion cults, the main emphasis of the incarnation has remained the same throughout its sculpture-history: fierceness, bravery and independence. If in the first four incarnations *Vishnu* appears either as an animal, or a half-animal half-human creature, the *avatāras* which belong to the following *yugas*—that is, *treta, dvāpara,* and *kali*—are all in human form.

The Dwarf-incarnation *(Vāmana-avatāra),* the fifth of the 10 *avatāras* found in the orthodox list (some schools of thinkers have stretched the number to 39!), like the first four incarnations, also concerns creation. The Purānic *Vāmana* myth, which describes the three steps of the dwarf incarnation and is the Vaishnava counterpart of the Rg-vedic myth of the "three strides" of the solar *Vishnu,* relates to *Bāli,* the great-grandson of *Hiranyakasipu,* who was, in contrast to his great-grandfather, so virtuous and just a ruler that his growing reputation began to overshadow that of *Indra* who sought *Vishnu*'s help in order to regain his supremacy. *Vishnu* wanted to satisfy *Indra,* but he could not use any harsh method against so virtuous a person like *Bāli.* He therefore took the form of a dwarf ["*Vishnu* was born as a diminutive son of *Kasyapa* and *Aditi*" (Dowson, 37; see also Hopkins, *Epic Mythology,* 211]) and asked *Bāli* to give him a piece of land three paces wide "on which he could sit and meditate" (Mitchell, 15)—a request which the generous *Bāli* unhesitatingly granted. Thereafter the dwarf-*Vishnu* took three strides, the first two of which covered heaven and earth, thus depriving *Bāli* of his entire kingdom, while the third landed on the king's head, forcing him down to the underworld, of which *Bāli* was made the ruler; it was a reward offered in recognition of *Bāli*'s magnanimity. The *Vāmana-avatāra* of *Vishnu* is worshipped under the name *Trivikrama,* "the god who took three steps," the number three indicating the god's universal character, since he incorporates within himself the upper regions, the earth, and the waters. Further, these three strides, when ritually resorted to by the sacrificer, are believed to annihilate evil *(Taittiriya Samhitā).*

The five incarnations so far discussed are purely mythological; the next three incarnations *(Parashurāma, Rāma,* and *Balarāma)* emphasize the "heroic element" (Dowson, 37) and perhaps reflect—at least in the *Parashurāma* incarnation—"struggles for economic and political power which took place at an early stage in Indian history" (Mitchell, 16), that is, things that are more worldly than superhuman. *Parashurāma* ("Rama with the battle-axe" *[parashu]*) was a *Brāhmana* and the son of the sage *Jamadagni* and *Renuka.* A brilliant archer, he was a worshipper of *Siva,* who gave him several gifts and weapons, the most magnificent of which was the axe. According to another source, *Vishnu* became his *Parashurāma* incarnation to re-establish the social order which had been disrupted by arrogant *kshatriyas* (the regal caste) attempting to usurp the spiritual and social leadership traditionally claimed by *brāhmanas.* It is said that he could achieve this after 21 attempts, but he was defeated by the other *Rāma,* the son of *Dasaratha* in the epic *Rāmāyana* and the seventh *avatāra* of *Vishnu.* He thus appears in the *Mahābhārata,* the *Rāmāyana,* and the *Purānas,* but always in a completely human form even while keeping his status as a deity. Vaishnava legends refer to him as *Rāmā-Bhārgava* (since he was a member of the priestly family of Bhārgavas which claimed descent from the great sage *Bhrigu*) and as *Rāmā-Jamadagni* (since he was the son of *Jamadagni*), names which serve to distinguish him from *Rāma,* the seventh *avatāra* of Vishnu, who was born as *Rāmachandra* ("the moon-like/gentle *Rāma*) to Dasaratha, king of Kosala and of the Solar race.

He too, like *Parashurāma,* was born in the *Treta*-age, for the purpose of slaying the demon-king *Rāvana* of Lanka. Mitchell writes, "From a comparatively minor incarnation . . . the story of *Rama* has entered deeply into Indian life as a deity, a subject for literature, and an example of moral excellence. As one of the chief protagonists in Indian epic poetry he has passed into the mythologies of countires other than India whose cultures have been influenced by it or its regional variations" (Mitchell, 17). His many qualities, as well as those of his wife *Sita* (who was held captive by *Rāvana*—an event which becomes the basis of the epic *Rāmāyana*), are described in the *Mahābhārata* and, at greater length in the *Rāmāyana.*

The eighth *avatāra* of *Vishnu* is *Balarāma,* who was *Krishna*'s elder brother, although several sources refer to *Krishna* himself as the eighth incarnation. We must here bear in mind that *Krishna* was not just an *avatāra* of *Vishnu,* but his "full manifestation," "a full divinity" (Dowson, 40); he is the "god without end, unborn" (Hopkins, *Epic Mythology,* 213). The *Mahābhārata,* however, places both *Balarāma* and *Krishna* as equals. According to another view, *Balarāma* was an incarnation of the great serpent *Sesha* (on which *Vishnu* is said to relax in a reclining posture), and when he died the serpent is said to have issued from his mouth; this has led to the production of images of *Balarāma* as a snake-man *(Nāga).* Since, according to one Purānic source, *Balarāma* and *Krishna* were sons of *Vishnu*—formed from a white hair and a black hair respectively from *Vishnu*'s head—they are sometimes regarded as joint incarnations, while some sects hold that "*Krishna* is a full incarnation and substitute *Balarāma* for *Rāma* in seventh place [i.e. as the seventh avatāra, thus leaving the eighth place for *Krishna*]" (Mitchell, 25). Both brothers seem to have been "the most human of the human incarnations, neither of whom had the aspect of saintliness usually associated with *Rāma,* and both of whom exhibited normal human weaknesses even when participating in super-human exploits. Once, intoxicated, *Balarāma* commanded the river-goddess *Yamunā* to come near him so he could bathe, and when the river did not respond, he dragged it with his ploughshare behind him wherever he went until the river-goddess cried for mercy and was released only when she promised that the country would be "well-watered." The *Bhāgavata-Purāna* and *Harivamsa* repeat this story from *Vishnu-Purāna,* which "probably alludes to the construction of canals from the Jumna." *Balarāma* is thus identified with an agrarian deity, a culture-hero associated with irrigation and viticulture, as well as with agriculture, "but factual and mythical elements are so intermingled that it is impossible to distinguish them" (Stutley, 38, 37). With the increasing popularity of the *Krishna* cult during the Middle Ages, *Balarāma*'s importance steadily waned until, today, it is difficult to find a temple dedicated to him alone.

The ninth *avatāra, Buddha,* is very much a historical figure (see chapter on "Buddhism") and was adopted by the Brāhmins as their own. He is said to have come to the earth "to encourage demons and wicked men to despise the Vedas, reject caste, and deny the existence of the gods, and thus to effect their own destruction" (Dowson, 38). *Kalki* is the *avatāra* of *Vishnu* yet to arrive and is believed to appear at the end of our present age, *Kali-yuga,* as a hero mounted on a white horse, bearing a drawn sword blazing like a comet, or as a giant with a white horse's head, or as a *Brāhmana* on a white horse, or simply as a white horse, for the final destruction of the evil and the wicked, the renovation of creation, and the restoration of *dharma* or the law of right and justice. Maurice Phillips writes: "This conception originated naturally in the hopelessness of sin-suffering humanity to save itself without the intervention of the deity. The form . . . is also natural to the Hindu mind; for a *Brāhman* is the highest Hindu type of a man, and the horse was an animal highly prized in ancient times; the horse-sacrifice being considered the most efficacious" (Phillips, 63).

The *Kalki-avatāra* represents the Indian's hopes and aspirations, secure from the whims of possible religious fanatics and the elaborate, often excessively formalized, interpretations of philosophers; it envisions a sort of Apocalypse with a difference, which difference is indeed essentially Hindu and which belongs to Hinduism's grand cosmic scheme of things, including as it does the quiet and necessary restoration of order and harmony following a righteous deity's self-fulfilling, annihilatory strides over disorder, chaos and darkness.

As it should be clear from the above discussion of the *avatāras,* the career of *Vishnu* through his several incarnatory forms is an example of the "way in which the changing demands of religious life in India brought about changes in the status of the deities or the qualities they represented" (Mitchell, 6). Whereas *Vishnu* manifested himself through *avatāras, Siva* is represented by different aspects of his own powers. The mythical metamorphoses of *Siva* (in the *Linga-Purāna* he is described as the Lord of all Being, the Divine Cause, who expresses himself through his *vibhāvas* and *vyuhas*) were devised, as Margaret and James Stutley conjecture, to counterbalance those of *Vishnu.*

Hinduism was divided into two main groups, one focusing its attention on *Vishnu* (and are called Vaishnavites) and the other on *Siva* (called Saivites). The division – resulting eventually in the two cults of *Vaishnavism* and *Saivism* – is not "entirely clear cut" and "a tendency towards the fragmentation and assimilation of dogma has never ceased." "Broadly speaking," writes A.G. Mitchell, "in contrast to *Vishnu*'s reputation as a benevolent creator god, *Shiva* represents destruction, austerity and the more malignant forces of life." Mitchell is quick to concede, however, that his distinction is "an oversimplification and should be seen in the context of creation and destruction being a continuous part of the life cycle" (Mitchell, 31).

Though the origins of Saivism are rather shadowy, it is quite clear that the Saivism of history is a blend of two lines of development – the pre-Aryan and the Aryan/Vedic. Its influence, as recent archeological research has established, extends not only over the whole of India, from Kashmir to the deep South (there is in fact a school of "Kashmir or Northern Saivism," and a second major school of "Southern or Lingāyat Saivism"), but at one time extended to Greater India and the Archipelago, as well as beyond the Himalayas to Central Asia.

In order to explain its enormous influence on the people, we must turn to popular Hindu worship, in which offerings are made to Law/Morality *(Dharma)*, Knowledge *(Jñāna)*, Spiritual and Material Power *(Aisvarya)*, and Detachment *(Vairāgya)* – virtues whose essence is believed to be represented by *Varuna, Brahmā, Vishnu* and *Siva* respectively. *Siva* is thus "the ideal *Yogin* and, in his aspect of a meditative god, is the patron deity of *Sannyasins*." He lives away from urban points, in the inhospitable mountains, holding the Ganges *(Gangā)* in his formalized knot of matted locks, with a mountain-maid as his wife; for armband, girdle and sacred thread he has snakes; for his loincloth, the skin of a tiger; for his vehicle, the bull (*Note:* As John Marshall has shown in his book, *Mahenjo-Daro and the Indus Civilisation,* the Mahenjo-Daro excavations prove, among several other *Siva*-related things [viz., representations of fertility goddesses, phallic symbols, and figures in yogic posture, which signify an austere god, associated with fertility, and point to the *Siva* of later history], that the bull was the object of an extensive cult among the pre-Aryans from whom probably *Siva* has been borrowed [see Bhattacharyya, 219]); and for his eartops the extremely poisonous *dhatura* flower. Consequently, much more than the urbane cult of *Vishnu, Saivism* has exhibited "a close alliance with *yoga* and thaumaturgy, and a constant tendency to run into the extremes of ascetic fervour": "It is not a single cult, but a federation of allied cults, whose practices range from the serenest form of personal life in the faith to the most repulsive excesses that alienate one's sympathy for the cult" (Sastri, 63).

But *Siva* is conceived, also, as a dweller of the plains, though even here he is pictured as living in cremation grounds and cemeteries, wearing a garland of bare skulls and besmeared with ashes. He is said to have burnt *Kāmadeva* (the God of Love) to ashes for disturbing his meditation, but he is also believed to be quick in his forgiveness and is noted for his ready bestowal of boons. Freely accessible to all persons in all conditions, pleased with simple offerings, and not in need of elaborate rituals with a Brāhmin as an officiating priest, *Siva* remains the "most democratic of the gods." While his terrible *(rudra, bhairava, ghora)* form is associated with the commitment of crime, his benign *(siva, dakshina, aghora)* form is associated with his bestowing of blessings and boons. He is the ordainer of death and disease, but he is also the great healer, being himself the "conqueror of death" *(Mrityunjaya).*

The intensely personal nature of *Siva*'s relation with his devotees is described in the *Svetāsvatara Upanishad,* a treatise resembling the *Bhagavad-gitā,* inasmuch as it expounds the supremacy of *Siva* according to the theistic strain of thought developed in the *Upanishads* just as the *Gitā* expounds the supremacy of *Vishnu* according to broad philosophical principles developed in the *Mahābhārata.* That particular Upanishadic text describes *Siva* as a "god who has no parts, who does not suffer change, who is all peace, who has no defects and is unpolluted, the bridge for crossing over to immortality"; as one who is all-pervading, "the internal soul of all beings, the witness of all, the life-giver, absolute and without qualities," the "God of all gods, potent for good and evil"; as one who can be known or realized only by the loving faith of a pure heart *(bhāva),* and whose knowledge is synonymous with the attainment of eternal peace. *Siva* is thus identified with the eternal Absolute and regarded as "the origin as well as the ultimate refuge of finite souls" (Bhattacharyya, 220).

Let us at this point turn to the antecedents of *Siva.* Eustace Haydon writes: "He had his birth in the ancient, native culture long before the coming of the Aryans" (Haydon, 107). If the excavations at Mahenjo-Daro, Harappa and other places are trustworthy, "the cult of *Siva* (both figured and phallic) is not an Aryan monopoly or even an Aryan discovery" (Marshall, *Mahenjo-dāro,* cited in Bhattacharyya, 221); in fact, the initial attitude of the Aryans towards the phallic symbol or *linga* (there were other prototypes of *Siva* in pre–Aryan Indus valley civilization, like the *yoni* or the female generative organ which was almost always seen in combination with the *linga* or phallus, the yoga attitude, the three faces, and the lordship over animals or *pasupati*) was definitely hostile, for in the *Rg-Veda Indra* is invoked to prevent "those whose god is the phallus" *(sisnadevas)* from disturbing their sacrificial rites, although there is evidence that the Aryans "were slowly accepting this mode of worship" (see Bhandarkar, 115f), by reckoning with "the ancient gods as dangerous enemies": "They despised their phallic rites but held them in awed respect as dealers in death and destruction" (Haydon, 107).

In course of time, the spread of the Aryan settlements eastward brought them into a friendlier relationship with the natives, some of whose divine figures were absorbed into the Aryan pantheon under the name *Rudra-Siva,* a name which indicates the blending of the Vedic *Rudra* with non–Aryan deities, "especially with the *linga* fetish" (Phillips, 79). Thus, *Siva* is not a god in the Vedas, although the word "Siva" (which literally means "auspicious") frequently occurs in the *Rg-Veda* as an important qualifier, "a propitiatory epithet" applied to the Vedic storm-god *Rudra* who, to the Vedic

Indian, represented "the uncultivated, unconquered and greatly feared Nature 'experienced as a divinity'" (Jan Gonda, *Vishnuism and Saivism: A Comparison,* cited in Stutley, 279) and united within himself the dangerous and the beneficent aspects of the fertility process. In the *Rg-Veda* he is referred to as the

> lord of songs, the lord of sacrifices, who heals remedies, is brilliant as the sun, the best and most bountiful of gods, who grants prosperity and welfare to horses and sheep, men, women, and cows; the lord of nourishment, who drives away diseases, dispenses remedies, and removes sin; but, on the other hand he is the wielder of the thunderbolt, the bearer of bow and arrows, and mounted on his chariot is terrible as a wild beast, destructive and fierce.

It is therefore natural that he should be addressed with placatory epithets, such as *siva,* which means auspicious, propitious, benign, and gracious, in the hope of averting his destructive manifestations (just as the Hebrew deity Yahweh or the Greek Zeus Melichios have been referred to, rather euphemistically, as "rain-giver" or "kindly" [see Hastings, *A Dictionary of the Bible,* and Farnell, *The Cults of the Greek States*]). In the *Yajur-Veda* there is a long prayer called *"Satarudriya,"* which is addressed to him and appeals to him under a variety of laudatory epithets; but in the *Atharva-Veda,* in which he is still "the protector of cattle," his character is fierce, "dark, black, destroying, terrible"—the angry god who is implored to look elsewhere and "not assail mankind with consumption, poison, or celestial fire." Though the Vedic and sub-Vedic texts (except the *Svatāsvatara Upanishads*) indicate *Rudra*'s ambiguous character—as being both benevolent and malevolent—his malevolent aspect gradually prevailed. He and his companions (most often the *bhutas* or ghosts) are said to receive the bloody entrails of the sacrificial victim and therefore are treated on the same level as demons. "He was even regarded as the patron of robbers and pilferers and as being similar to them in nature. No wonder, therefore, that in the *Brāhmanas* and the *Sutras Rudra* should be isolated from the other gods, who are generally beneficent in character and disposition" (Bhattacharyya, 223).

In the *Satapatha Brāhmana* it is stated of him that when the gods attained heaven, *Rudra* remained behind. The process of the raising of the epithet *siva* attached to *Rudra* to the status of a noun, however, is visible in the *Yajur-Veda* where we read: "Thou *[Rudra]* art *Siva* by name." *Rudra* was an amalgamated form of several pre-Aryan deities—patrons of the working class, the "outcasts beyond the Aryan pale"—who were known by many names: *Sarva,* the swift archer and launcher of thunderbolts; *Bhava,* the lord of land, air, and sky, the overseer of everything on earth; *Ugra,* the fierce ruler of the "four quarters of the lower world"; and *Mahādeva,* the "great god." In the *Atharva-Veda,* these lords—their names, titles, and functions—are shown as one with *Rudra.* "In the approved Indian manner, out of the many deities arose one divine figure with many names, but best known as *Siva,* the auspicious," so that only centuries later, *Rudra-Siva* appears "adorned with the highest attributes, perfectly at home among the Aryan gods": "In him the age-old religion of India, with its roots deep in the soil, asserted its rights to equal sovereignty with the Aryan *Brahmā* and the Aryanized *Vishnu*" (Haydon, 109). The memory of his fierce past still clung to *Siva,* however, and the later literature "depicts in no uncertain manner the anti-Vedic propensities of the followers of *Siva*" (Bhattacharyya, 223-4).

The gradual progression of *Siva* towards supremacy was also a consequence of "an intermediate identification" with Vedic deities like *Agni* (we should know that in the *Rg-Veda* the word *Rudra* itself is used for *Agni*), *Vāyu, Parjanya, Prajāpati, Indra* and *Āditya (Surya),* some of whose attributes were transferred to him. Thus *Rudra-Siva* had a benign character (acquired from the Vedic deities) as well as a terrible, even repulsive character (inherited from the non-Aryan divinity), the latter of the two identifications leading "not only to easy unconventional worship but probably introduced the originally condemned phallic cult into the Aryan religion" (Bhattacharyya, 225).

We may at this point pause a while to consider the rather controversial, orthodox interpretation of the *linga* (also called, by its association with *Siva,* the *siva-linga*) as a phallic symbol and the consequent scholarly declaration of a "phallic cult" as existing in the post-Vedic/post-Aryan times. Haridas Bhattacharyya writes:

> We may admit ... that just as the guilty love of *Krishna,* when dwelt upon in excess of religious need, may lead to corrupt thoughts, so also an immoderate pre-occupation with the sexual symbol of *Siva* may lead to orgiastic rites, especially when complicated by extreme *Sākta* tendencies [*Sākta:* from *Sakti* or "divine energy," personified as female and dynamic as distinct from its male or passive aspect, the two aspects being equated, in the Samkhya system, with *Prakrti* and *Purusha* respectively. *Sāktism,* which figures prominently in Saivism, is, apart from its association with such female deities as *Durgā* and *Kāli* (who are considered to be *Siva*'s consorts in their destructive energised forms), was also associated with certain extremely "secret and esoteric doctrines and practices."].... But sex-symbols have a less activating effect on imagination and action in a country where climatic conditions enforce a semi-nudity on its male inhabitants during the hot months and where traditions of austerity and detachment have made even the complete nudity of the ascetic followers of some religious sects [viz., the Jaina monks of the Digambara sect] not a matter of shame.

While it is quite likely that the *linga* may have been originally just a symbol of *Siva* even as the *sālagrāma* is of *Vishnu* [*Sālagrāma:* a stone of fossilized shells of an extinct species of mollusks found in the Ganduki river in the western part of India and is held sacred and worshipped by the Vaishnavites, because its spirals are supposed to be pervaded by *Vishnu*'s presence, thereby showing his power to assume any shape. These stones are of various colors, nine of which represent the principal *avatāras* of *Vishnu.*] and not associated with vegetation myths or esoteric obscenity nor meant to be "the earliest *representation* of *Siva,*" its worship, once started, could not exclude a confusion in the popular mind between this and the cult of the phallus and the invention of legends to support the cult.

The earliest references like the *Mahābhārata* and the *Vāyu-Purāna* ascribe the origin of the *linga* to *Siva*

> discarding his organ of generation and becoming a *yogin,* when other gods had been found to undertake the task of creation. The shedding of the *linga* was thus symbolic of abstention from creative activity and its worship, therefore, an adoration of sexual restraint.... It is almost certain also that in the earliest Brahmanic literature the *linga* (the male genital) was not associated with a *yoni* (the female genital) and that the *linga* became a procreation symbol later when *yoni* was added [Bhattacharyya, 226].

This changed conception of the sexual symbol was reflected in iconographic representation also, and thus we have *Ardha-nāri-svara* images, in which the left side of the body is a representation of *Siva* while the right side is a representation of his spouse *Pārvati.* The consorts of the Vedic gods were only shadowy figures, but the increasing association of *Siva* with *Sakti* indicates that "equality of the female with the male was a trait of the people from whom the *Siva-Sakti* cult was derived or, if two independent cults fused into one, their gods, male in one case and female in another, had already been developed too much on monotheistic lines into supreme deities to be subordinated to each other in the new synthetic creed":

> Just as in the worship of the Trinity, when not complicated by sectarian bias, no godhead is really subordinate to the other two, so also in the composite *Siva-Sakti* cult an attempt was made to recognise both the gods as complementary to each other and neither as subordinate to the other. It is not unlikely that a polyandrous social organisation and an extensive Mother-cult provided the soil for the equality of the female principle with the male and that both the Vedantic Maya and the Samkhya *Prakrti* were pressed unconsciously or consciously into the service of the *Siva-Sakti* cult [Bhattacharyya, 226–7].

In the hermaphroditic combination of *Ardhanārisvara* the feminine half is considered more "violent, impulsive and creative" than the male half, and only when the male-female distinction is transcended and the impersonal *Brahman* realized can liberation occur. To quote Joseph Campbell, the *Ardhanāri* guides the mind "beyond the objective experience in a symbolic realm where duality is left behind" (Campbell, 152).

To return to our discussion of the *linga,* in the context of the interpretation of *linga* as "that which is destroyed or which is ultimately dissolved" (*Note:* Just as "death" and the "God of death" are both denoted by the term *mrityu,* so "destruction" and the "God of destruction" are both denoted by the term *linga.*) it is possible to speculate that the destructive aspect of the Vedic *Rudra,* which eventually made *Siva* the third person of the Trinity, would receive the epithet "linga," and then, by the "principle of symbolisation or visual representation," the latter would take the form of the other, more common, meaning of *linga,* namely, sexual organ.

Again, as Haridas Bhattacharyya remarks, it is not improbable that "by a similar process of transference the epithet *sthanu,* which means immobile existence, was transferred to the immobile ascetic god rooted at one spot like a post or a bare tree-trunk," which of course is the other meaning of *sthānu;* so that, it is possible to relate this aspect of immobility to the general rule that a *Siva-linga,* once fixed, "should on no account be removed" (Avalon, *The Great Liberation: Mahānirvana Tantra,* 93). The tree-analogy is evident in the *Vāyu-Purāna,* in which *Vishnu* is shown as digging into the ground as a boar to locate the root and *Brahmā* as flying in his swan-mount to discover the top of the *Linga.* In the *Linga-Purāna,* the origin of the *linga* is ascribed to *Siva* becoming a "pillar of fire" (with all its connotations of shapelessness and substancelessness) whose top and bottom could not be seen by *Brahmā* and *Vishnu.* Thus, a certain belief in shapelessness seems to have been at the basis of *linga*-worship—a belief which ultimately resulted in "using a shapeless stone as the proper symbol of one whom philosophy had described as formless by nature": "The Saiva *linga* and the Vaishnava *sālagrāma* are both shapeless stones, and it is not very unlikely that the so-called Svayambhu linga, or pebble rounded and shaped by the forces of nature, was the original form under which *Siva* was worshipped" (Bhattacharyya, 228–9). The sylvan, colorful origin of the *linga* as claimed by some religious historians, has not prevented the eventual representation of *Siva* in terms of a "supra-ethical and supra-personal dynamic evolution" (Heimann, 66) nor his identification (as *Mahādeva*) with the all-obliterating unity of the impersonal *Brahman.*

It is interesting to read Arthur Barth's conclusive comments on the *linga*-controversy:

> Of all the representations of the deity which India has imagined, these *(lingas)* are perhaps the least offensive to look at. Anyhow, they are the least materialistic; and if the common people make fetishes of them, it is nevertheless true that the choice of these symbols by themselves to the exclusion of every other image was, on the part of certain founders of sects . . . a sort of protest against idolatry [Barth, 262].

As K.A. Nilakanta Sastri thinks, this indeed is the ground for the Purānic exaltation of *linga*-worship over *archa*- or image-worship, "the former leading to release, and the latter only to some variety of prosperity" (Sastri, 68n). Thus *Siva* the personal god, symbolized in the nonpersonal *linga,* was raised to the realm of philosophic abstractions. The *Svetāsvatara Upanishad* describes *Siva,* "the lord of all creatures" *(Pasupati),* as "the one God concealed in all beings, all-pervading, the internal soul of all beings, presiding over all actions, the support of all beings, the witness of all, the life-giver, absolute and without qualities." And yet, *Siva,* like *Vishnu,* has "eluded the invitation to philosophic devitalization" and has continued to serve, again like his peer *Vishnu,* as a real, personal god for the common man (see Haydon, 110).

Both *Siva* and *Vishnu* have been seen as "remarkably efficient as popular gods," demanding no difficult intellectual effort, no austere and ascetic discipline; and, though different in origin, development and character, they have been "shaped by cultural influences to serve a single end" and have been "co-workers in the cause of man's salvation"—a fact which is suggested by the following words of *Vishnu* in the *Mahābhārata:* "He who worships thee, worships me. There is no difference between us two." But even while the two gods have served a common purpose as saviors, each sinking his personal distinctiveness in the qualityless, eternal *Brahman,* they have always been different in *character* and thus have produced different sets of followers, namely, the Saivites and the Vaishnavites. Of the two sects, the Saivites seem to form a more compact group, for the simple reason that even while *Siva,* "in his many moods, is a picturesque figure" (Haydon, 111) and even while there are differences in the philosophies of the various Saivite sects, the god worshipped has remained one; the eight forms of *Siva—Sarva, Bhava, Rudra, Ugra, Asani, Pasupati, Mahādeva,* and *Isāna*—have no separate biographies, and his five faces—*Isāna* or *Sadāsiva, Vāmadeva, Aghora, Tatpurusha* and *Sadyojāta* on the top, north, south, east and west sides respectively—signify "the single deity's power of superintendence in all directions" (Bhattacharyya, 231). [*Note:* Sir Charles Eliot, in his three-volume work, *Hinduism and Buddhism: An Historical Sketch,* writes of instances of *Siva* having more and less than five faces. Arthur Avalon, in his *Principles of Tantra* (Introduction to Vol. I), writes of specific functions as ascribed to the conventionally accepted five faces. According to one school of thought, the four Vedas issued out of the four mouths, while the *Tantra* (see "Glossary") of the higher tradition issued out of the central mouth; according to a second school of thought, the 28 *Tantras* of the higher tradition sprang from the upward current and issued from the five mouths while the *Tantra* of the lower tradition was produced by the downward current, below the navel."]

There are two clearly different schools of interpretation as regards the superiority of either of the two deities over the other. Eustace Haydon, for instance, writes: "As a god within reach of the common man, *Vishnu* had an advantage over *Siva.* Devotion to *Vishnu* did not need to span the chasm between god and man for he was incarnated in several human forms. *Siva* had no incarnations" (Haydon, 119). Haridas Bhattacharyya presents the opposite viewpoint:

> *Siva* has no *avatāras* as *Vishnu* has; hence it is easier to think of him as eternal.... We might even go so far as to assert that he *[Siva]* has been more democratically conceived than other gods: he has been given a permanent earthly residence in Mount Kailasa ... [But] *Brahmā* and *Vishnu,* even when resting in the ocean of milk—the one on the navel-lotus of the other, are farther away from the land of mortals and they are more often thought of as residing in heaven than on earth.... [Further], Vaishnavism claims allegiance on behalf of a god who periodically becomes man to share men's sorrows and bring succour to them in distress. Saivism, on the other hand, calls upon men to worship a god who is easily accessible but who does not at any time forsake his divinity and subject himself to human infirmities [Bhattacharyya, 231].

It is admitted, however, that in the characteristically Indian atmosphere of intellectual tolerance, "the presence of no single god dominates the centuries" (Haydon, 119) and, at least in the southern parts of India, both Saivism and Vaishnavism grew in their influence in the later centuries by their conflict with the heterodox schools of Buddhism and Jainism.

Moreover, both Saivism and Vaishnavism were against the old Vedic religion of sacrifice, which had failed to satisfy the deeply spiritual longing of the human heart and denied forgiveness to the erring soul except as it might through elaborate ritualistic ceremonies involving an enormous amount of expenditure. Both sects therefore laid down *bhakti* or loving devotion as the essential condition of religious life and slackened the authority of the *Vedas* by admitting non-Vedic authority as embodied in sectarian literature. It is of importance to note that the two sects not only made provision for "a less formal mode of worship but [also granted the *Sudras* or the lower castes] . . . a right to use this sacred literature in lieu of the *Vedas,* which they could not read, and to worship God without the help of the *Brāhmana [Brāhmin]* priest." The regionally-induced ugly features of *Siva* were forgotten or ignored to "satisfy the need of an ideal, and the hymns offered to *Siva,* as to *Vishnu,* are the purest expressions of monotheistic devotion" (Bhattacharyya, 232–3).

As a personal God, *Siva,* with the impressionistic interplay of vivid highlights and contrasting shadows so characteristic of him, was regarded not only as *Mahākāla,* who destroys all creation, but also as the creator and preserver of the world; as *Sankara* or *Siva* ("the auspicious") who is the reproductive power perpetually restoring that which has been dissolved; as the ideal ascetic *(Mahāyogi* or *Digambara* or *Dhurjati)* who sets an example of self-restraint; as the moral governor who punishes sin and rewards virtue; as *Isvara* or the supreme and gracious Lord (or *Mahādeva* or the great god), who forgives the repentant sinner and offers him fresh opportunities of a new spiritual life, thereby showing him the path to salvation. "The secret of the success of sectarianism in India," writes Haridas Bhattacharyya, "lies in the fact that in India Philosophy and Religion are far more intimately associated than anywhere else and the theory of the savant becomes the common belief of the popular mind within a short time" (Bhattacharyya, 233).

As we have said earlier, the Upanishads and the Vedānta system, by establishing the sole reality of *Brahman,* have led the common man to identify every supreme god—*Brahmā, Vishnu* and *Siva*—with the Vedāntic Absolute and to recognize the other gods as "merely different forms of this supreme god, if not his creatures and attendants." All the many gods are realized to be ultimately one in essence, "sharing among themselves the different aspects, attributes and functions of one supreme deity" (Bhattacharyya, 233). Bhattacharyya warns against the dangers involved in any strictly historical treatment of a god, for it may not adequately reflect, and may even totally misinterpret, the spiritual evolution of man's ideas about that god. We quote Bhattacharyya at some length:

> It is not difficult to point out in a religion, ennobled or degraded by the imagination of the inhabitants of a vast continent teeming with a heterogenous population with different grades of culture, the shady past of a god or a mixture of light and shade in his character. What is more difficult is to understand and appreciate how the tribal memory manages to forget most of the unsavoury tales about a god in the same way as the individual mind represses its own unpleasant memories. If

> the idea of a moral god ennobles human ideals, so do advancing moral ideals raise the standard of divinity; and this is what has actually occurred in India as elsewhere [Bhattacharyya, 234].

Bhattacharyya admits the possibility on the part of a weak mind to find an imitator from a bad divine example as well as the other possibility of a bad prophetic example resulting in something harmful, but he finds such cases rare and unlikely to occur "when the developing ethical sense of society eliminates the ugly features of a god" (Bhattacharyya, 234). Utlimately, therefore, it is a society's or an individual's "will to believe" which determines the nature of devotion and practice.

The five gods *(pancha-devatā)* who have a following in India today are *Vishnu, Siva, Sakti, Ganesa,* and *Surya,* although *Ganesa* and *Surya* (Sun-god) have steadily declined in their theological importance, notwithstanding references to the existence at one time of as many as six classes of devotees of each of these two gods (see Bhandarkar, 149, 152).

Of the five deities, *Surya,* though one of the five chief Vedic deities (the others being *Agni, Soma, Indra,* and *Vāyu*), could not be personified to any very great extent (except as the Sun) and did not gather around himself many myths. [*Note:* The Sun however is represented anthropomorphically or by symbols, such as the wheel *(chakra)* or by the opened lotus *(padma),* to denote its creative function. Elsewhere it is described as a celestial bird or a beautiful white horse accompanying the goddess of dawn or *Ushas* (Stutley, 291).] It is therefore not surprising that he has remained mostly as a Vedic god to whom the Brāhmins offer their daily twilight and midday oblations. The continuance of his worship and the longevity of his cult "must be due to the fact that the solar worship comes nearest to the veneration for the glowing *Agni* (and *Surya* is a form of *Agni*) which was such a prominent feature of the Vedic religion and that it alone represents whatever has been left of the Vedic religion, the cult of all the other gods having developed non-Vedic features or worship." The Solar cult is a survival of Vedic worship. "It is probable that while *Vishnu* appropriated the personal aspect of godhead and its relation to man, its impersonal element and its function of supporting the physical world were assigned to *Surya*" (Bhattacharyya, 235).

The qualities, powers and functions of *Surya*—sometimes identified with *Āditya* (he has been called the *Āditya par excellence,* thus differentiated from other *Ādityas,* all of whom are associated with light but generally referred to as only as aspects of *Surya*) and the other solar deity, *Savitr,* who is said to be not only the bright sun of the day, but also the invisible sun of the night, and is described as having a lofty moral side—are mostly reminiscent of those assigned to him in the 10 or so hymns in the *Rg-Veda,* some hymns in the *Atharva-Veda,* as well as some metaphorical references in the *Upanishads* (particularly the *Chhāndogya,* the *Prasna,* and the *Maitri Upanishads*). He is the great source of light, warmth and health; he surveys the whole world, sees beyond the sky, the earth and the primordial waters, "looking down on men, protector of all that travel or stay, beholding right and wrong among men," setting the example of regularity and beneficence to human conduct, his vivifying light falling on saints and sinners alike; he quickens the intellect, and it is from him that man derives his visionary faculties; he is believed to have revealed the *Yajur-Veda;* he possesses healing powers and thus is the preserver of life; as light he represents immortality, which man may attain following his ascent from the "dark valley of death" (i.e., a metaphoric equivalent of the world/earth).

The *Satapatha Brāhmana* declares *Surya* as representing both death *and* life, and as the intermediary between darkness and light. As *Savitr* he is "the celestial door to immortality" *(Chhāndogya Upanishad),* for the sun is the center of creation, the "point where the manifested and unmanifested worlds unite." As the sun consists of fire which forever consumes itself, in the *Prasna Upanishad* it is identified with the Cosmic Sacrifice—the Cosmic Being who rises as life and fire. As *Pushan,* yet another solar god with whom *Surya* is sometimes identified, he is the pastorally-oriented guardian of cattle and nourisher of all beings; as *Vishnu* he is the supporter of all the worlds; as *Aryaman* (again, one of the *Ādityas* like *Surya* himself—a fact which suggests the nature and extent of god-god identification or absorption), he is the wise ruler who forgives sins, regulates the performance of rituals, and guides his worshippers along safe and easy paths. As usually has happened, however, the multiplicity of forms in which the Sun was worshipped in the Vedic age was gradually discarded (with the exception of *Vishnu*) in favor of a unitary Solar deity who was raised, in sectarian worship, to the status of a supreme god (see Macdonell, *Vedic Mythology,* 29f; Farquhar, 151f).

The lack of vigor of the Solar cult has been ascribed to the fact that "a deification of the visible luminary is difficult except in primitive times and such a cult could thrive only as a survival of ancient belief, modified and allegorised to suit the monotheistic and moral needs of an advanced religious community" (Bhattacharyya, 236). The cult in due course was incorporated into the more inclusive cult of the Trinity, within which the morning-sun, the noon-sun and the evening-sun came to represent *Brahmā, Vishnu* and *Siva* respectively.

Our second example of the working of the spiritual sense is the cult of *Ganesa. Ganesa* is the "Lord of the *Ganas* or troops of inferior deities, especially those attendant upon *Siva*" (Dowson, 106). These "inferior deities," the *Maruts* (the Storm-gods who were originally associated as friends or allies of *Indra, Agni,* and *Vāyu* in the *Atharva-Veda,* but who, in the *Vishnu-Purāna,* are described as the sons of *Rudra/Siva*), were mostly demonic in character, and it is easy to conclude at this point that their Lord, *Ganesa,* could not have possessed an attractive character. In fact the *Mahābhārata* mentions these malevolent demons, who are called by different names *(Vināyakas, Ganesvaras,* and *Ganapatis)* and were originally many in number, "being identified with the lords of malevolent spirits who were present everywhere." Later, however, their number was fixed at four (sometimes six), and it was believed that "possession by them was . . . to work sure evil, which could be prevented only by exorcising them by appropriate ceremonies" (Bhattacharyya, 237; see Bhandarkar, 147).

The mysterious religious need of men in later times reduced these spirits to a unity and raised a single *Ganapati* or *Vināyaka* to supreme godhead. The wild, elephant-headed deity of an earlier time was transformed into an ideal of wisdom and beneficence. Even today *Ganesa* is invoked at the beginning of every non–Vedic religious worship as a preliminary rite. Such invocation is also supposed to have the effect of sending away the hindering demons or "demon-removing" *(bhuta-apasārana).* His figure, which shows the body of a short fat man of a yellow color with a protuberant belly, four hands (holding a shell, a discus, a club, and a water-lily), and a single-tusk head of an elephant, adorns every business house, as he is supposed to bring success in all undertakings. In the *Purānas* he is the son of *Siva* and *Pārvati,* but the accounts of his parentage vary. In one *Pārvati* created him from the scurf of her body; in another he is described as having been conjured out of a piece of cloth by *Siva* to give a son to *Pārvati.* There is also a variety of legends, narrated at length in the *Brahma-Vaivartta-Purāna,* accounting for his elephant-head with a single tusk *(ekadanta).* His obesity is said to contain the whole universe, his trunk is bent to remove obstacles, and his four arms represent the four categories into which things can be divided. His companion animal or mount *(vāhana),* the bandicoot, illustrates "the different ways in which obstacles can be removed to reach religious ends": the elephant tramples down everything on its path, but the bandicoot "can creep through small holes and cracks to achieve the same goal" (Mitchell, 37).

Despite his animistic origin and his originally malignant nature, *Ganesa*'s later developments serve to show "how the religious mind can transform almost intractable materials into lovable figures" (Bhattacharyya, 238), how it can change a malevolent spirit into the genial protector of households and the personification of commonsense. Regarding the development of the cult of *Ganesa* despite the barriers of brāhmanic conservatism, Margaret and James Stutley write: "It may seem strange that such a cult should have emerged when speculation about the nature of the self and the universe had passed from the mythical to the philosophic, when theriomorphism had come to be generally regarded as part of ancient folklore, but these two levels are, as they have always been, characteristic of Indian religious belief" (Stutley, 92). Today *Ganesa* is one of the most popular of folk deities.

The same process of transformation is evident in the *Sakti* cult, "although there the original form is not so definitely anti-divine." While the Aryan aspect of the *Sakti* cult lay emphasis on the creative side, the non–Aryan aspect is "probably more concerned with the destructive side" of the "divine power" *(Sakti). Sakti* is the "root idea of Hindu goddess" (Phillips, 98) – the "divine power or energy" that is personified as female and dynamic as distinct from its male or passive aspect. The concept of Sakti is generally lacking in the *Rg-Veda,* however, although the ancient text regards the power of the gods as not inherent, but derived from a separate source called *Sachi,* very often personified as *Indra*'s consort. Besides, there are several references to the association of "nature power" with female energies in the hymns of the *Artharva-Veda.*

It should be remembered however that in the *Vedas* the goddesses do not occupy important positions and almost always derive their greatness from association with their respective husband-gods: "It was the genius of the ancient Aryans to look upon *male* deities *only* as exercising divine functions. They neither admitted goddesses to supreme authority nor allowed to the wives of the gods an equal share in Government" (Phillips, 97). Thus the Aryan prototypes of *Sakti* are the colorless wives of the Vedic gods, who in later times were assigned the function of "energising their lethargic husbands" and using them as the "instruments of their creative activity" (Bhattacharyya, 238; see also Keith, I, 218).

But there are, also, *Aditi,* the mother-goddess who created the universe and is a personification of infinite space; *Māyā,* whose association with *Brahman* alone results in creation; and *Prakrti,* who is the cause of the drama of creation of this varied world to which *Purusha* (the male principle) is only a silent spectator. By and large however, the mother-cult is Tauranian rather than Aryan in its origin. The Tauranians regard female deities as Supreme, exercising all the great functions of the Vedic/Aryan gods: "The ancient Babylonians worshipped Dakina, the goddess of the earth, as reverently as they worshipped Ea, the lord of the deep. Every Babylonian city had its titular goddess who was worshipped as its founder and guardian. The same practice is in vogue among the aboriginal inhabitants of India" (Phillips, 98).

Haridas Bhattacharyya's words seem to echo the same feeling: "Possibly the mother-cult came from people worshipping female spirits of dark intentions who were propitiated by suitable offerings" (Bhattacharyya, 239). Thus, corresponding to the malevolent *ganas* (associated with *Ganesa*) are "female furies" associated with *Devi,* "the great goddess" and the *Sakti* or female energy of *Siva,* and without whom the supreme god is powerless. As *Siva*'s "female energy" and consort, *Sakti* appears in innumerable forms, some mild and genial, the others extremely fierce, but all of which have become a part of Saivism. As Arthur Barth observes, though the personification of *Sakti* is not peculiar to Saivism (having had a long history of worship independent of *Siva*), it is in Saivism that the *Sākta* ideas have found a fertile ground for the expansion as well as for their "most monstrous developments" (see Barth, 199–200). In her milder form, *Sakti* is *Umā* ("light"), *Gauri* ("brilliant/yellow"), *Pārvati* ("the mountaineer"), *Haimavati* ("daughter of Himavat [the Himālaya mountains]"), *Jagan-mātā* ("the mother of the world"), and *Bhavāni* (the female counterpart of *Bhava,* which is one of the many names of *Siva,* and in translation, means "the giver of existence"). In her terrible form, *Sakti* is *Durgā* ("the inaccessible"), *Kāli* and *Shyāmā* ("the dark/black"), *Chandi* ("the fierce"), *Bhairavi* ("the terrible"), and *Mahāmāyā* ("the great illusion"). It is in her dark and forbidding character that she has received the homage of her worshippers—a proper consort of the terrible *Rudra.* Before she was drawn into the company of *Siva, Durgā* was a virgin goddess of the Vindhya mountains, famous for her chastity, but delighting in wine, flesh, and animal sacrifices (Haydon, 112).

As an image meant for worship, however, *Durgā* is "a beautiful yellow woman, riding on a tiger in a fierce and menacing attitude" (Dowson, 86); she has eight arms, and she holds on the left trident, sword, snake and bell, and on the right, drum, shield, cup and water-pot; she is sometimes seated in *sukhāsana* ("joyous and relaxed") posture on a double lotus throne and wears a garland of skulls (Mitchell, 46). The other form of *Durgā, Mahishamardini* ("the destroyer of *Mahisha,* a demon who took the form of a buffalo"), is one of the earliest variations, and it is in this form (in which she has 12 or more arms, each carrying a weapon of an important god) that she is worshipped in an annual rite. As *Kāli* or *Kālikā* she is represented with a black skin, a hideous and terrible countenance, dripping with blood, encircled with snakes, hung round with skulls and human heads. Her insatiable blood-thirst has been symbolized by the *Chhinna-mastā* image, in which she is shown as a headless female figure holding the severed head in her hand and sending up a fountain of blood into her own mouth, symbolizing "the lust of life culminating in death" (Haydon, 112).

The bloody rituals and the wild orgies associated with *Sakti/Devi* worship are mostly Tāntric in origin and, except in the aboriginal modes of worship, are nearly always deliberately exaggerated, thus terrifying the humble believer and persuading him to participate readily in the expenditure that the rites involve. Arthur Barth's view of these rites is commonsensical and sympathetic: "There is something else than licentiousness in these aberrations. The books which prescribe these practices are . . . filled with lofty speculative and moral reflections, nay, even with ascetic theories; here, as well as elsewhere, there is a profession of horror at sin, and a religiosity full of scruples; it is with pious feelings, the thoughts absorbedly engaged in prayer, that the believer is to participate in these mysteries, and it would be too profane them, to resort to them for the gratifications of sense" (Barth, 205). The mysterious and wonderful character of these rites and of the worship of *Sakti* in general is very much related, once again, to the origin and the nature of religious devotion.

The "unerring human instinct," which finds in the mother the source of creation and preservation, also longs for protection, which involves, though indirectly, the mother's "capacity to destroy" every hindrance to such protective functioning. "The cruel and destructive aspect of *Sakti* served to show that if due occasion should arise, she would not be found wanting even in that capacity either: probably there was an element of over-compensation in the process and the terrifying colours were painted more thick than necessary" (Bhattacharyya, 240). From an essentially human standpoint, there was the need of a female deity—a kind of Heavenly Mother—before whom the individual could lay open his soul more fully than before a male deity—a kind of stern Heavenly Father—and with "surer chance of forgiveness." In Vaishnavism, where the goddess *Lakshmi* (*Vishnu*'s consort) is a loving and devoted wife, "she is prayed to for interceding on behalf of the sinner and securing the relenting grace of her husabnd" (B.N. Seal, *Comparative Studies in Vaishnavism and Christianity,* cited in Bhattacharyya, 240).

But, as A.B. Keith remarks, *Sakti* or *Devi* is "a far more independent deity" and she herself absolves the sinner from his guilt "out of motherly affection" (Keith, I, 218). Philosophically speaking, *Sakti* or "energy" and *Saktimat* or "the being in possession of the energy" are inseparable, and hence we cannot separate *Siva* from *Sakti,* for the former cannot act without the latter. Theologians and religious thinkers have moved beyond this stage and have seen *Sakti* as the support of the entire universe; they have viewed *Brahmā, Vishnu* and *Siva* as only "forms assumed or created by *Sakti* to fulfil different cosmic functions," which is mythically exemplified by the three supreme gods as the "children of *Sakti* who then chooses *Siva* as her spouse, presumably because destruction is a more palpable expression of energy than creation and preservation" (Bhattacharyya, 241).

Thus *Sakti* is ultimately identified with the formless Absolute *(Brahman)* of Vedānta. In fact, there are several passages in the *Tantras* (particularly, the *Mahānirvāna Tantra*) and in the *Sākta* canonical texts that read like excerpts from a Vedantic treatise. We must not forget *Sakti*'s Absolutistic antecedents in *Kena Upanishad,* where *Umā* is the revealer of the nature of Brahman and is frequently identified with *Sarasvati,* the personified Vedic lore, who, as the river-goddess is also the *Sakti* of *Brahmā.* In due time *Sakti* became the revealer of *Nigama* or the body of spiritual truths which she communicated to *Siva* for the benefit of the entire creation in the present age *(Kali-Yuga).* The *Tantras* (the Tantric texts) asserted the power of *mantras* or hymnic chants and prescribed *yantras* or specific diagrams that represented the exact forms in which the different deities received their offerings. The *mantras* and the *yantras,* in proper combination, formed a mystic divine body helping in the Tāntric initiation which qualified one for eventual salvation. The Purānic mythology of the gods was being strengthened by the Tāntric rituals.

In course of time the Sākta cult moved beyond its original Saiva limits by acknowledging the wives of the other gods as *Saktis* of these gods and by prescribing modes of ritualistic worship for all the deities, both male and female. While it is true that the Sākta cult provided for congregational worship of "a questionable type" in the *Sri-chakra* or *Sri-yantra* ("the blissful circle")—which, according to Haridas Bhattacharyya, is "practically the only other congregational worship outside Vaishnavism"—it raised the status and dignity of women, since it implicitly asserted their being the earthly analogues of the Heavenly Mother or the Supreme Goddess, by positively supporting the marriage of widows and decrying the practice of *Sati* or immolation of women on the funeral pyres of their dead husbands (these reformistic objectives of the Sākta cult were to be given further impetus by the 19th century Arya Samajists like Raja Ram Mohan Roy, Devendra Nath Tagore and Keshab Chandra Sen, who had grown up under the transforming influence of Muslim and Christian monotheism). Further, the cult redefined the "hero" or *vira*—as one who has complete control over his senses, is truthful and ever engaged in worship and has sacrificed lust and related passions—in a language which recall passages from the *Upanishads.*

In fact, as Bhattacharyya claims, the aim of the entire Tāntric discipline is to sublimate the lower instincts and to raise the soul from sex *(Mulādhāra)* to salvation *(Sahasrāra)* after transcending the intermediate obstacles, commonly known as *chakras* or "centers" (*Note:* They are six in number: *Mulādhāra, Svādhishthāna, Manipura, Anāhata, Visuddha* and *Ājñā*. These *chakras,* which often have been identified with the plexuses, must be pierced one after another before *Jiva* is united with *Parama-Siva,* the latter being the spiritual or *sāttvika* meaning of *Maithuna* or coition, iconographically represented by the paired *(mithuna)* figures of *Siva-Pā rvati, Vishnu-Lakshmi,* or *Gandharvas-Apsarāses* and regarded as auspicious, being symbols of creation.)

As always, however, "the danger has come from using equivocal language in spiritual matters, for the ordinary mind, failing to make out the symbolism, has fixed upon the letter of the text and thereby excused itself into indulgences, superstitions and magical practices" (Bhattacharyya, 243–4). These exaggerations notwithstanding, the rites of contemporary India exhibit the profound influence of the Tāntric view of the godhood of the individual; indeed, as Heinrich Zimmer remarks, "they have been for centuries more Tantric than Vedic" (Zimmer, 602).

As we have seen during our discussions of the different forms of faith, the Indo-Aryan mind "gradually outgrew its Vedic polytheism with unaided effort only to transcend theism altogether and land in a speculative monism which, while degrading the status of the gods, increased enormously the prestige of the wise man." The popular mind gradually reconciled itself to the loss of most of the Vedic rituals, but was reluctant to abandon his gods, with the result that monotheism in one form or other has always been existent. Even the Vedānta system, admittedly nontheistic, was to make compromises on the theological front by providing the reality of God for devotional purposes.

At the same time, however, increased acquaintance with simpler forms of worship has led not only to an increased emphasis on devotion but also to the near-dissolution of caste distinctions. We sum up the chapter by yet another quotation from Haridas Bhattacharyya's excellent book, *The Foundations of Living Faiths:*

> In its search after an ideal godhead the growing ethical sense moralised the character of one or other of the ancient gods and laid emphasis not only on the unitary character of God but also on His holiness, His abhorrence of sin and His ready forgiveness of sins confessed and abandoned. While the danger of lapsing into an unethical religion, owing to the persistence of early literary traditions and the equivocal language of devotion, could not be entirely overcome, a sense of propriety limited its extension to society at large in the past and has not practically overcome it altogether [Bhattacharyya, 244–5].

It is not surprising, therefore, to see the contemporary Indian thinkers still seeking for "a spiritual anchorage beyond the naturalistic world" (Haydon. 124).

Works Cited

Avalon, Arthur. *The Principles of Tantra.* (2 vols). London, 1916; rpt. Madras: Ganesh & Co., 1952.

________. *The Great Liberation (Mahanirvāna Tantra).* Text and translation. Madras: Ganesh & Co., 1953.

Barth, Arthur. *Religions of India.* Trans. J. Wood. London: Kegan Paul, Trench, Trubner & Co., 1921.

Bhandarkar, R.G. *Vaishnavism, Saivism and Minor Religious Systems.* Strassburg: Trubner & Co., 1913.

Bhattacharyya, Haridas. *The Foundations of Living Faiths: An Introduction to Comparative Religion.* Stephanos Nirmalendu Ghosh Lectures. (2 vols). Vol. I. Calcutta: Calcutta University Press, 1938.

Bloomfield, Maurice. *The Religion of the Veda, the Ancient Religion of India.* New York & London: G.B. Putnam & Sons, 1908.

Campbell, Joseph. *The Hero with a Thousand Faces.* New York: Pantheon Books, 1949.

Carpenter, Joseph Estlin. *Theism in Medieval India.* London: William & Norgate, 1921; rpt. London: Constable & Co., 1926.

Chaudhuri, Nirad C. *Hinduism: A Religion to Live By.* London: Chatto & Windus, 1979.

Dange, S.A. *Legends in the Mahabharata.* New Delhi: Motilal Banarsidass, 1969.

Deussen, Paul. *The Philosophy of the Upanishads.* Trans. A.S. Geden. The Religion and Philosophy of India Series. Edinburgh & New York: T. & T. Clark, 1908; rpt. New York: Dover Publications, Inc., 1966.

Dowson, John. *A Classical Dictionary of Hindu Mythology and Religion: Geography, History, and Literature.* Trubner's Oriental Series. London: Kegan Paul, Trench, Trubner & Co., 1928.

Eliot, Charles Norton Edgecumbe. *Hinduism and Buddhism: An Historical Sketch.* (3 vols). London: Edward Arnold & Co., 1921; rpt. London: Routledge & Kegan Paul, 1954.

Farnell, Lewis Richard. *The Cults of the Greek States.* (5 vols). Oxford, Oxford University Press, 1896–1909.

Farquhar, John Nicol. *An Outline of the Religious Literature of India.* London: Oxford University Press, 1920.

Griswold, Hervey De Witt. *The Religion of the RgVeda.* London: Oxford University Press, and New York: Humphrey Milford, 1923.

Hastings, James (ed.). *A Dictionary of the Bible.* (5 vols). Edinburgh: T. & T. Clark, 1906.

Haydon, A. Eustace. *Biography of the Gods.* New York: Frederick Ungar Publishing Co., 1967.

Heimann, Betty. *Facets of Indian Thought.* London: George Allen & Unwin, and New York: Schocken Books, 1964.

Hopkins, Edward Washburn. *Epic Mythology.* Strassburg: Trubner & Co., 1915; rpt. New Delhi: Motilal Banarsidass, 1974.

________. *Ethics of India.* New Haven: Yale University Press, 1924.

Keith, Arthur Barriedale. *The Religion and Philosophy of the Veda and Upanishads.* (2 vols., being Vols. 31 and 32 of the Harvard Oriental Series). 1925; rpt. Cambridge, Mass.: Harvard University Press, 1970.

Macdonell, A.A. *Vedic Mythology.* Strassburg: Trubner & Co., 1897.

Marshall, John. *Mohenjo-Daro and the Indus Civilisation*. (3 vols). London: Oxford University Press, 1931.
Mitchell, A.G. *Hindu Gods and Goddesses*. The Victoria and Albert Museum Monographs Series. London: Her Majesty's Stationery Office, 1982.
Phillips, Maurice. *The Evolution of Hinduism*. 1903; rpt. New Delhi: Asian Publication Services, 1987.
Radhakrishnan, S. *Indian Philosophy*. (2 vols). Vol. I. Muirhead Library of Philosophy. London: George Allen & Unwin, and New York: Humanities Press, 1966.
Rose, H.A. *Hindu Gods and Goddesses*. ed. S.P. Gulati. New Delhi: Amar Prakashan, 1986.
Sastri, K.A. Nilakanta. "An Historical Sketch of Saivism," in *The Cultural Heritage of India*. (5 vols). Vol. IV. ed. Haridas Bhattacharyya. Calcutta: The Ramakrishna Mission Institute of Culture, 1969.
Smart, Ninian. *The Religious Experience of Mankind*. New York: Charles Scribner's, 1969; rpt. Glasgow: Collins, 1982.
Stutley, Margaret and James. *A Dictionary of Hinduism: Its Mythology, Folklore and Development: 1500 B.C.-A.D. 1500*. London: Routledge & Kegan Paul, and New York: Harper & Row, 1977; rpt. New Delhi: Heritage Publishers, 1986.
Wilson, H.H. *Essays and Lectures on the Religion of the Hindus*. (2 vols). ed. R. Rost. London: Trubner & Co., 1861.
Winterneitz, Maurice. *A History of Indian Literature*. (3 vols). Trans. S. Ketkar, H. Kohn, and S. Jha. Calcutta: Calcutta University Press, 1927, 1933, 1959.
Zimmer, Heinrich. *Philosophies of India*. ed. Joseph Campbell. London: Routledge & Kegan Paul, 1952; rpt. Princeton University Press, 1969.

Suggested Further Reading

Aiyangar, S.K. *Early History of Vaishnavism in South India*. London: Oxford University Press, 1920.
Bhattacharji, S. *The Indian Theogony*. Cambridge: Cambridge University Press, 1970.
Bhattacharyya, Haridas (ed.) *The Cultural Heritage of India*. (5 vols). Vol. IV The Religions. Calcutta: The Ramakrishna Mission Institute of Culture.
Bergaigne, Abel. *Vedic Religion*. Trans. V.G. Paranjape. New Delhi: Motilal Banarsidass, 1978.
Buck, C.H. *Faiths, Fairs, and Festivals of India*. Calcutta: Thacker Spink & Co., 1917.
Campbell, Joseph. *The Masks of God: Oriental Mythology*. London: Martin Secker and Warburg, and New York: Viking Press, 1962.
Coomaraswamy, Ananda K. *The Dance of Shiva*. London: Simpkin Marshall, 1924; rpt. New York: The Noonday Press, 1957.
________. *Hinduism and Buddhism*. New York: The Philosophical Library, 1943.
Daniélou, Alain. *Hindu Polytheism*. London: Routledge & Kegan Paul, and New York: Pantheon Books, 1964.
Dubois, J.A. *Hindu Manners, Customs, and Ceremonies*. Oxford, Clarendon Press, 1906.

Gonda, Jan. *Change and Continuity in Indian Religion.* The Hague: Mouton, 1965.

Kramrisch, Stella. *The Hindu Temple.* Photos by Raymond Burnier. (2 vols), Calcutta: Calcutta University Press, 1946.

Kumar, Sehdev. *The Lotus in the Stone: An Allegory for Explorations in Dreams & Consciousness.* Concord, Canada: Alpha & Omega Books, and New Delhi: Motilal Banarsidass, 1984.

Morgan, Kenneth W. (ed.). *The Religion of the Hindus.* New York: Roland Press, 1953.

Parrinder, Geoffrey. *Avatar and Incarnation.* London: Faber and Faber, 1970.

________. *Worship in the World's Religion.* London: Faber and Faber, 1961.

Radhakrishnan, S. *East and West in Religion.* London: George Allen & Unwin, 1933.

Rawson, P. *The Art of Tantra.* London: Thames and Hudson, 1973.

Renou, Louis. *Religions of Ancient India.* Trans. Sheila M. Fynn. London: The Athlone Press, 1953.

Singer, Milton B. (ed.). *Krishna: Myths, Rites and Attitudes.* Honolulu: East-West Center Press, 1965.

Sivapadasundaram, S. *The Saiva School of Hinduism.* London: George Allen & Unwin, 1934.

Woodroffe, John (Arthur Avalon). *Shakti and Shākta.* Madras: Ganesh & Co., 1920.

Zaehner, R.C. *Mysticism, Sacred and Profane.* London: Oxford University Press, 1957.

Zimmer, Heinrich. *Myths and Symbols in Indian Art and Civilization.* ed. Joseph Campbell. New York: Pantheon Books, 1946.

Glossary of Major Terms

ābhāsa: (in Vedānta) the immanent aspect of the Ultimate Principle *(Brahman),* of which the manifest world is said to be an appearance or *ābhāsa;* (in Nyāya) fallacious reasoning.

abhāva: nonexistence, absence, negation, being a means of correct knowledge *(pramāna):* the deduction of the existence of one or two opposite things from the nonexistence of the other.

abheda: nondualism, monism.

***Abhidharma* (Pali: *Abhidhamma*):** "superior *dharma.*" It refers to a collection of Buddhist treatises belonging to the "Three Baskets" *(Tripitaka;* Pali: *Tipitaka)* of the Pali canonical literature.

āchāra: conduct, behavior, observance, discipline; custom; an established rule of conduct.

āchārya: "one who knows or teaches the *āchāra*"; "great teacher"; spiritual guide; a title affixed to name of such teachers.

achit: "without consciousness"; (in Vedānta) matter.

ādhāra: support.

adharma: moral demerit; (in Jainism) a substance which makes rest possible.

ādheya: the supported.

adhyāsa: superimposition (see chapter on Vedānta).

ādhibhautika: proceeding from extrinsic causes, such as other men, birds, beasts, or inanimate objects; (in Sāmkhya) one of the three causes of misery, the other two being *ādhyātmika* and *ādhidaivika.*

ādhidaivika: proceeding from supernatural causes, such as influences of the atmosphere or planets; (in Sāmkhya) one of the three causes of misery, the other two being *ādhyātmika* and *ādhibhautika.*

ādhyātmika: proceeding from intrinsic causes, such as disorders of the body and mind; (in Sāmkhya) one of the three causes of misery, the other two being *ādhibhautika* and *ādhidaivika.*

adrshta: "unseen, invisible, unknown"; that which is beyond the reach of observation or consciousness, such as the merit attaching to a man's conduct in one state of existence and the corresponding reward or punishment with which he is visited in another; potential worth resulting from past conduct; latent effect; the Unseen Power (see ***karma***).

Advaita: "non-dualism" or monism, a school of Vedānta whose chief advocate was Samkara.

āgama: "that which has come down"; scriptural authority; another name for *tantra*.

Agni: the Vedic god of fire.

ahamkāra: (from the personal pronoun *aham,* "I") the "*aham-* or I-maker"; (in Sāmkhya) the individuating principle, responsible for the limitations, division and variety in the manifest world; (in Yoga) the ego, a self-conscious principle.

ajiva: the inanimate, the "non-*jiva*" or "non-soul."

ākāsa: ether or space as an element; (in Vaiseshika-Nyāya) the fifth Eternal Reality and the substratum of sound; (in Sāmkhya) the first Sense-particular or *mahābhuta* of the five *mahābhutas* or "great elements" (see under ***mahābhutas***).

alaukika: supernatural, extraordinary.

anādi: beginningless.

ānanda: bliss; (in Vedānta) one of the three attributes of the Ultimate Principle or *Brahman,* the other two being *sat* and *chit.*

anavasthā: infinite regress.

anekānta-vāda: (in Jainism) the doctrine of the multifaceted character of reality.

anitya: impermanent.

antah-karana: the internal organ; Mind in the collective sense, including intelligence *(buddhi, mahat),* ego-sense *(ahamkāra),* and mind *(manas).*

anu: the fine, the indivisible, the atomic; (in Vaiseshika) a positional reality that has no length, breadth, or thickness.

anumāna: inference, a means of correct knowledge *(pramāna).*

anupalabdhi: noncognition; (in Advaita Vedānta) one of the six means of correct knowledge.

aparāvidyā: empirical, relative knowledge (see ***parāvidya***).

aparoksha: immediate, direct, without mediation of the senses.

āpas: water as an element; (in Vaiseshika) the second Eternal Reality or *dravya;* (in Sāmkhya) the fourth Sense-particular or *mahābhuta,* the principle of liquidity.

apurva: (in Purva-Mimāmsā) the mysterious result of action which comes to fruition in another life.

Āranyakas: "forest treatises," so called because they were composed by forest-dwelling Brāhmanical sages; the portion of the Vedas primarily concerned with rites and rituals; in tone and content they mark a transition to the Upanishads.

***Arhat* (Pali: *Arhant*):** the perfected saint, one who has attained the Buddhist enlightenment.

artha: "aim, purpose"; "means of life, wealth"; (in Nyāya) an object of right knowledge or *prameya;* (in Yoga) the intuitive knowledge of reality; one of the four goals of human life or *purushārthas,* the other three being *dharma, kāma,* and *moksha.*

arthāpatti: presumption; (Advaita Vedānta) one of the six means of correct knowledge, defined as the deduction of one thing from the declaration of another thing; (in Nyāya) this is included in inference or *anumāna*.

āsana: (in Yoga) discipline of the body consisting of steady and comfortable postures; one stage in the eight-stage or *ashtānga-yoga*.

asat: "non-being"; (in Vedānta) the passive condition of the transcendental aspect of the Ultimate Principle or *Brahman;* its opposite is *sat* (see ***sat***).

asatkārya-vāda: the theory that effect does not pre-exist in the cause; its opposite is *satkārya-vāda* (see ***satkārya-vāda***).

ashtānga-yoga: (in Yoga) the eight-limbed (*ashta* = eight, *anga* = limb) or eight-stage yoga as described by Patanjali in his *Yoga-sutras*.

ashtāngika-mārga: (in Buddhism) the Fourth Noble Truth or the "Eightfold Path" taught by Buddha as a means of overcoming suffering.

Ātman: the soul, the inmost Self which is eternal, nameless, and formless; the principle of life and sensation; the individual in the abstract; (in Nyāya) an object of right knowledge or *prameya;* (in Vaiseshika) the eighth Eternal Reality or Substance *(dravya)*.

avayava: members of a syllogism; (in Nyāya) one of the 16 categories.

avidyā: ignorance, particularly in the spiritual sense; (in Vedānta) it is caused by the operation of the cosmic *Māyā* (see ***māyā***).

avyakta: another name for *prakrti* or "unmanifest matter."

bhava: existence.

bhāva: being, nature, reality, true condition.

Bhāva-chakra: (in Buddhism) the wheel of existence or becoming (another name for *Pratityasamutpāda*).

bhāvanā: conception, imagination, apprehension, supposition, fancy, thought, meditation; (in Nyāya) that cause of memory which arises from direct perception, demonstration, or argument.

bhedābheda: "different, yet not different"; identity-in-difference (*bheda* = dualism/difference, *abheda* = non-dualism/non-difference); (in Vedānta) the basis of the school of Rāmānuja.

***Bodhisattva* (Pali: *Bodhisatta*):** (in Buddhism) one who aspires to *bodhi* or enlightenment, a potential Buddha; it is the Mahāyāna ideal as contrasted with the Hinayāna ideal of *Arhat* (Pali: *Arhant*).

Brahmā: one of the gods of the Hindu Trinity, along with Vishnu and Siva.

Brahman: "evolution," "development," "growth," "expansion"; (in Vedānta) the eternal, nameless, formless Ultimate Principle or Reality of which the world of phenomena is a manifestation; the Absolute, the Eternal, the Self-existent, the Universal Spirit, which is not an object of worship, but rather of mediation and knowledge, and whose three attributes are being *(sat)*, consciousness *(chit)*, and bliss *(ānanda)*, and hence called *sacchidānanda*.

Brāhmana (Brāhmin): the person belonging to the highest caste; the highest caste.

Brāhmanas: the portion of the Vedas dealing with rites, ceremonies, duties, and conduct; they include the Āranyakas and Upanishads.

buddhi: intellect or intelligence *(mahat);* (in Nyāya) an object of right knowledge or *prameya* and is described as the faculty of forming and retaining conceptual notions, the faculty of the mind which discerns, judges, comprehends and understands the meaning of right knowledge.

chala: equivocation; (in Nyāya) one of the 16 categories and defined as opposition offered to a proposition by means of word-play *(vāchas),* generalizations *(sāmānyas),* and metaphors *(upachārās);* an unfair reply by which one attempts to contradict or refute the opponent's statement by taking it in a sense other than the one intended.

chitta: mind.

darsana: view, doctrine, or philosophical system (from *dars* = to see); vision of truth or reality.

dhāranā: concentration; (in Yoga) a stage in *ashtānga-yoga.*

dharma: (from *dhar* = to hold, support, maintain, preserve); used in the metaphysical sense, it refers to those universal laws of Nature that support the Universe and maintain all things; when applied to the individual, it refers to that code of conduct that sustains the soul and produces virtue and morality, thus leading to the overall development of man; (in Jainism) an extended substance which makes motion possible.

Dharma-chakra: wheel of law, wheel of existence, wheel of becoming (another name for *Pratityasamutpāda*).

dhyāna: meditation, contemplation (a stage in *ashtānga-yoga*).

dik: direction, Space; (in Vaiseshika) the seventh Eternal Reality or *dravya* and refers to that force which keeps all discrete things in their respective positions in relation to each other as they appear in space or ether *(ākāsa).*

doshas: defects, flaws, weaknesses; (in Nyāya) an object of right knowledge or *prameya* and defined as the cause of all action.

dravya: substance (*dravyatva* = substantiality or state of being a substance).

drshtānta: illustration or example; an accepted fact illustrating a general rule; (in Nyāya) a familiar instance, one of the 16 categories and defined as that thing about which an ordinary person and a scholar have the same opinion; the third and last member of the Nyāya syllogism.

duhkhah: pain, suffering; (in Nyāya) an object of right knowledge or *prameya* and defined as a hindrance in the soul's progress.

Dvaita: "dualism"; (in Vedānta) a school of Vedānta which denies that the Ultimate Principle/Reality or *Brahman* is the cause of the world and assigns the soul an independent existence of its own with only *an association* with *Brahman.*

Dvaitādvaita: "dualism-and-non-dualism"; a school of Vedānta.

guna: "quality"; (in Sāmkhya) the cosmic constituent; one of the three constituents of the cosmic substance or *Prakrti,* viz. *sattva, rajas,* and *tamas.*

hetu: reason, cause; (in Nyāya) the second member or the middle term of the five-membered syllogism and defined as the vehicle of inference or *anumāna* used to prove the proposition.

hetvāvhāsa: fallacies, such as the erratic, the contradictory, the equal to the question, the unproved, and the mistimed; fallacy of inference; (in Nyāya) one of the 16 categories.

Hinayāna: one of the two major schools of Buddhism; also known as Theravāda Buddhism.

Indra: the Vedic god of the atmosphere and sky.

indriyas: sense-organs/sense-powers; they are divided into two groups—*jñānendriyas* or five abstract sense-powers of recognition (the power to hear, the power to feel, the power to see, the power to taste, and the power to smell), and *karmendriyas* or five abstract working-sense-powers (the powers to express, to procreate, to excrete, to grasp, and to move); (in Nyāya) an object of right knowledge or *prameya*.

Isvara (Ishvara): God, supreme deity; creator, sustainer, and annihilator of the universe (see ***Saguna-Brahman***).

jalpa: controversy, polemics; an unproductive wrangling in which each party is solely concerned with winning an argument; (in Nyāya) one of the 16 categories and described as a defense or attack of a proposition by means of *chala* or equivocation, *jāti* or futility, *nigrahasthāna* or disagreement in principle, for the purpose of winning an argument rather than establishing the truth or gaining further knowledge.

jāti: class as determined by birth; universal as distinct from particular; (in Nyāya) one of the 16 categories and described as offering objections based on false analogy without consideration of the universal connection *(vyāpti)* between the middle term and the major term (see ***jalpa***).

jijñāsa: inquiry; (in Nyāya) first member of the five-membered syllogism.

jiva: animate substance, the principle of life, the individual soul; (in Sāmkhya) the individual soul as distinguished from the Universal soul or *Purusha*.

jñāna: knowledge, particularly spiritual knowledge derived from meditation on the Ultimate Reality/Spirit.

jñāna-kānda: that part of the Vedas which relates to the knowledge of Ultimate Reality or *Brahman* (refers to the Upanishads).

jñāna-lakshana: (in Nyāya) a certain kind of extraordinary perception, in which different sense-perceptions are so intimately related as to make one feel they are parts of a single perception, as when one says, "I smell the wind through the leaves" (it is close to what literary theorists call "synaesthetic").

jñānendriyas: see ***indriyas.***

kaivalya: absolute freedom, perfect happiness; (in Sāmkhya) the final liberation or *moksha*.

kāla: Time; (in Vaiseshika) the sixth Eternal Reality or Substance *(dravya)*.

kāma: wish, desire, pleasure, passion, love; one of the four *purushārthas* (see ***purushārtha***), or goals of life, along with *artha, dharma,* and *moksha*.

karma: action, effect or fruit of action; (in Vaiseshika) the third Predicable or *Padārtha;* the principle of causality, commonly known as the Law of Cause (action) and Effect (of action).

karma-kānda: that part of the Vedas which relates to ceremonial acts and sacrificial rites; it includes the *Samhitās, Brāhmanas,* and *Āranyakas.*
karmendriyas: see ***indriyas.***
kartr: doer, agent (as against *bhoktr* or "enjoyer").
kevala-jñāna: (in Jainism) perfect, all-inclusive knowledge.
laukika: ordinary, secular (as distinct from scriptural and as opposed to *alaukika* or supernatural/extraordinary).
lilā: the cosmic playfulness of the Ultimate Spirit or *Brahman.*
linga: the phallic symbol of Siva; (in Nyāya) the invariable sign that proves the existence of anything; (in Mimāmsā) the secondary meaning of a word inferred from another word or a collection of words.
Mādhyamika: a school of Buddhism which believes in the doctrine of the "Middle Path."
mahābhutas: "the great elements"; (in Sāmkhya) the Sense-particulars, viz., space or ether *(ākāsa),* air *(vāyu),* fire *(tejas),* water *(āpas),* and earth *(prthvi);* their existence is dependent upon the subtle elements or *tanmātras.*
mahat: intellect or *buddhi;* (in Sāmkhya) the Cosmic Intelligence, the first evolute or product of the Cosmic Substance or *Prakrti.*
Mahāyāna: one of the two major schools of Buddhism, the other being *Hinayāna.*
manana: discriminative understanding, reflection; the second stage of self-culture.
manas: mind; all the mental powers, such as intellect, intelligence, perception, understanding, will, and conscience; (in Nyāya) an object of right knowledge or *prameya;* (in Vaiseshika) the ninth Eternal Reality or Substance *(dravya)* and refers to the internal organ of perception and cognition through which thoughts enter or objects affect the individual Soul or *Ātman;* (in Yoga) the attentive and discriminating individual mind.
māyā: "delusion"; cosmic illusion; the power by which the formless Ultimate Reality or *Brahman* manifests itself as the world of phenomena; the principle which accounts for the apparent conditioning of the unconditioned Absolute; (in Advaita Vedānta) the phenomenal world, which is neither real nor unreal but only an appearance.
moksha: absolute freedom from worldly bonds, emancipation, liberation; one of the four *purushārthas,* the other three being *artha, dharma,* and *kāma.*
mukta: "liberated," "released"; one who is emancipated from mundane existence; one who has attained *moksha.*
nāma-rupa: "name-form"; it refers to the world of phenomena.
naya: (in Jainism) partial knowledge.
nigamana: "conclusion," "summing-up"; (in Nyāya) the last member of the five-membered syllogism and defined as that which shows the coming together of the four means of right knowledge *(pramāna)* toward the same object or proposition.
nigrahasthāna: disagreement in principle; (in Nyāya) one of the 16 cate-

gories and is said to arise when one misunderstands; it is the basis on which an argument is conceded to have been lost and therefore stopped.

Nirguna-Brahman: *Brahman* without attributes; *Brahman* as Ultimate Reality transcending all names and forms *(nāma-rupa),* all perceptions and conceptions.

nirnaya: ascertainment, removal; reliable knowledge obtained by any of the accepted means of knowledge or *pramānas;* (in Nyāya) one of the 16 categories and defined as the removal of doubts by a consideration of two opposite views.

nirvāna: "blowing out of the flame of life"; (in Buddhism) the near-equivalent of *moksha* and *kaivalya;* it refers to the state of final emancipation from matter, ignorance and delusion (which are the cause of suffering or *duhkhah*); the state of Buddhistic enlightenment.

nirvikalpa: indeterminate.

nitya-mukta: one who is eternally free.

niyama (niyamya): regulation, self-culture; (in Yoga) refers to total purification attained through the study and practice of inner control; (in Purva-Mimāmsā) the restrictive rule, when the text indicates *one* mode of doing something that could be done in several ways.

pada: a step, mark, sign, place, position.

pāda: the foot, a stanzaic measure; (in Sāmkhya) the power to move, one of the five abstract working-senses or *karmendriyas* (see ***indriyas***).

padārtha: the meaning of a word, object of experience, category, the knowable; (in Vaiseshika) that which may be predicated or affirmed of existing things.

paksha: part; (in Nyāya) the minor term of the Nyāya syllogism.

parā-vidyā: higher knowledge, the knowledge of *Brahman* and *Ātman.*

paramānu: "atom," the smallest divisible part of matter; (in Vaiseshika) the essentials of all things, the first four Eternal Realities or Substances *(dravyas),* viz. Earth, Water, Fire, and Air.

parārtha: for others; (in Nyāya) inference for others (as distinct from oneself).

parināma-vāda: the theory that an effect brings about a real transformation of the cause, or an effect *is* a real transformation of the cause, as opposed to *vaivarta-vāda,* or the theory that when an effect is produced, there is only an apparent but no real transformation of the cause into the effect.

paroksha: mediate (as opposed to *aparoksha* or immediate).

paryāya: accidental or modal quality of a substance.

pradhāna: first cause, primary matter, fundamental substance; (in Nyāya) another name for *Prakrti.*

prajñā: direct, intuitive insight into Ultimate Reality or *Brahman.*

prajñā-pāramitā: perfect wisdom.

prakarana: (in Mimāmsā) when the meaning of a clause or sentence depends upon the relevant context.

Prakrti: Primal Nature, Cosmic Substance/Matter; (in Sāmkhya) the second principle (as distinct from the first Principle, *Purusha*) postulated by the system, the primary source of all things, the uncaused cause of phenomenal existence; it is eternal, all-pervasive, indestructible, formless, limitless, immobile; it consists of the three constituents *(gunas)* of *sattva, rajas,* and *tamas;* (in Vedānta) identified with *Māyā*.

pramā: valid knowledge.

pramāna: means or criterion of valid knowledge.

prameya: an object of right knowledge; one of the 16 categories accepted by the Nyāya system.

prāna: vital air, life-breath; its seat is the heart.

prānāyāma: control and regulation of breath (one of the stages or "limbs" of *ashtānga-yoga*).

prapatti: total surrender to God.

pratijñā: hypothesis, proposition; (in Nyāya) the first member of the five-membered syllogism and defined as the enunciation of the object of knowledge to be proved as laid down in the *Sāstras,* that is, by verbal testimony *(sabda)*.

Pratityasamutpāda: (in Buddhism) the Doctrine of Dependent Origination.

pratyāhāra: withdrawal of the senses or *indriyas* from external objects; one of the stages or "limbs" of *ashtānga-yoga.*

pratyaksha: direct, immediate (as opposed to mediate or *paroksha*); refers to the perceptual means of right knowledge or *pramāna.*

prayojana: purpose; (in Nyāya) one of the 16 categories; the fourth member of the five-membered syllogism introduced by later logicians to establish the object to be examined, and defined as that which determines whether the object is something to be sought, avoided, or ignored.

pudgala: material substratum of personality.

Purāna(s): (from *pura* = formerly, of old); it refers to the sacred treatises that followed the epic poems; these are legendary in character and are said to have (according to the ancient Sanskrit lexicographer, Amara Sinhā) five distinguishing topics *(pancha-lakshana):* the creation of the universe, its destruction and re-creation, the geneology of the gods and patriarchs, the reigns and periods of the Manus (see chapter on "Hindu Gods and Goddesses), and the history of the Solar and Lunar races of kings; these topics are treated from ethical, philosophical, theological, and scientific viewpoints; purānic literature comprises two broad groups—the primary or major *(Mahā-purānas),* and the secondary or minor *(Upa-purānas),* each group consisting of 18 texts.

Purusha: Cosmic Spirit or Spiritual Substance; (in Sāmkhya) the first principle (as distinct from the second priniciple, *Prakrti*) postulated by the Sāmkhya system and it accounts for the subjective aspect of nature; the ultimate principle that regulates, guides, and directs the process of cosmic evolution; the efficient cause of the universe; it is without attribute and activity, formless, pure, eternal, indestructible; elsewhere refers to the self, chiefly in its spiritual aspect.

purushārthas: the four goals of human life: *artha, dharma, kāma, moksha.*

purvapaksha: the first objection to an assertion in any discussion; the antithesis.

rajas: energy, activity; (in Sāmkhya) the active principle of existence, one of the three constituents of the Cosmic Substance or *Prakrti;* (in Yoga) the quality of egoism.

Rta: the Cosmic Law or Order, the Universal Principle of Righteousness.

sabda: "sound," verbal testimony; as the latter a means of correct knowledge *(pramāna)* and is defined as the instructive statement of a "reliable person"; it thus refers to the Vedas, also, for they are believed to be *apurusheya* (not to have been composed by any individual or group of individuals); the Vedic Word, which is claimed to be eternal, beginningless; (in Sāmkhya) the subtle element *(tanmātra)* of sound.

sadāyatana: the six organs of knowledge (the five sense-organs *and* the mind).

sādhya: (in Nyāya) the major term of the Nyāya syllogism.

Saguna-Brahman: *Brahman* with attributes, qualified *Brahman; Brahman* conceived as having *nāma-rupa* or name-and-form (as distinct from *Nirguna-Brahman*); same as *Isvara.*

sākshin: *Ātman,* or the conscious self.

samādhi: "putting together"; the last and eighth stage or "limb" of *ashtānga-yoga,* in which the mind is completely absorbed in the object of contemplation; a condition of profound and unqualified blissfulness and indicates emancipation *(moksha).*

sāmānya: general, universal, common; (in Nyāya) generalization, which is one of the three forms of equivocation or *chala;* (in Vaiseshika) generality, the fourth Predicable or *padārtha.*

samavāya: combination, concomitance; the Nyāya-Vaiseshika category of inference.

Samhitās: collection; that portion of the Vedas which contains the hymns.

samsāra: "flowing about"; mundane existence, empirical reality; the recurrent passage of the soul through the cycles of births and deaths.

Samsāra-chakra: "the wheel of existence and becoming" (another name for *Pratityasamutpāda*).

samsaya: doubt, state of uncertainty/anxiety; (in Nyāya) one of the 16 categories and defined as a conflicting judgment about the exact character of an object.

samskāra: mental impression, memory; the effects of action *(karma);* kārmic impressions.

samvrti: empirical standpoint (as opposed to the higher spiritual standpoint).

samyama: self-control; (in Yoga) *dhāranā, dhyāna,* and *samādhi* taken as a whole.

samyoga: combination, union, absorption; the Nyāya-Vaiseshika category of conjunction.

saptabhanginaya: (in Jainism) the scheme of sevenfold standpoint.

sat: being, good; (in Vedānta) the active condition of the transcendental aspect of the Ultimate Reality or *Brahman.*

satkārya-vāda: the doctrine that effect pre-exists in cause, a distinguishing feature of the Sāmkhya metaphysics (compare *asatkārya-vāda*).

sattva: being, existence, reality, essence; (in Sāmkhya) one of the three constituents of the Cosmic Substance or *Prakrti;* signified by pure and calm illumination; (in Yoga) the quality of purity and/or goodness.

savikalpa: determinate.

siddhānta: view, doctrine, conclusion; (in Nyāya) an established opinion; one of the 16 categories and defined as a dogma resting on the authority of a hypothesis or implication.

skandhas: the constituents of individual personality.

Sruti: revealed knowledge, the Vedas; (in Mimāmsā) the primary sense of a word or group of words independent of any other word or group of words.

sthāna: location; (in Mimāmsā) when the meaning is dependent upon the location of a word or a word-order.

sthula-sarira: the gross body, which is perishable (as opposed to *linga-* or *sukshma-sarira,* which is the subtle body, the imperishable and invisible vehicle of the soul).

***Sutra-Pitaka* (Pali: *Sutta-Pitaka*):** (in Buddhism) the second of the "Three Baskets" *(Tripitaka).*

svabhāva: one's innate disposition.

svadharma: one's own duty.

svarupa: one's essential nature or character.

syad: relative to some standpoint; invariably used as a prefix.

syād-vāda: (in Jainism) the theory that all judgments are relative.

tamas: darkness; (in Sāmkhya) one of the three constituents or *gunas* of the Cosmic Substance or *Prakrti* and signified by inertia/inaction; it obstructs the other two *gunas,* namely *sattva* and *rajas;* (in Yoga) the quality of ignorance.

tanhā: craving.

tanmātra: "thatness"; the subtle elements (as distinct from gross elements), viz. the essence of sound *(sabda),* touch *(sparsa),* odor *(gandha),* flavor *(rasa),* and form *(rupa);* the subtle form of actual matter and perceived mediately through the gross objects.

Tantra: that body of *sāstra* or scripture which is said to have been revealed by Siva as *the sāstra* of the present age *(kali-yuga);* it is presented in the form of a dialogue between Siva and his consort Pārvati, in which Siva's answers are called *Āgama* and Pārvati's are called *Nigama;* the *Tantras* (the Tantric texts) give prominence to the female energy of Siva, whose active nature is personified in the person of *Sakti,* his consort in one of several forms.

tapas: penance.

tarka: confutation; a hypothetical argument by which one offers an indirect justification for a proposition by showing that its contradiction leads to absurdity; (in Nyāya) one of the 16 categories and is defined as a hypothesis for the sake of knowing the truth in respect of an unknown object by eliminating all contrary suppositions.

tattva: truth, reality, essence, principle.

tejas: Fire as an element; (in Vaiseshika) the third Eternal Reality or *dravya;* (in Sāmkhya) the third Sense-Particular or *mahābhuta,* representing the principles of luminosity and expansion.

***Tripitaka* (Pali: *Tipitaka*):** "the Three Baskets" (the Buddhist Pali canon).

trshnā: "thirst"; craving (in this sense same as *tanhā*).

udāharana: example, illustration; (in Nyāya) the third of the five-member syllogism which illustrates, with the help of an example, the invariable connection between *pratijñā* and *hetu.*

upādhi: limiting adjunct.

upamāna: comparison; (in Vedānta) one of the six means of correct knowledge or *pramāna* and described as knowledge of a thing in terms of its similarity to another thing already well known.

upanaya: application; (in Nyāya) the fourth member of the five-member Nyāya syllogism and described as the application of a universal proposition to the case in hand.

vāc: a word; (in Nyāya) one of the three forms of equivocation or *chala;* (in Sāmkhya) one of the five abstract working-senses or *karmendriyas* and represents the power to express.

vāda: theory, view doctrine; (in Nyāya) one of the 16 categories and described as the testing of any proposition by applying every principle of logic with a view to arriving at the truth of the proposition.

vāk: same as ***vāc.***

vāyu: Air as an element; (in Vaiseshika) the fourth Eternal Reality or *dravya;* (in Sāmkhya) the second Sense-Particular or *mahābhuta,* representing the principles of motion and impact; *Vāyu* is the Vedic god of air.

vedanā: sense-experience.

videhamukti: freedom from both gross *(sthula)* and subtle *(linga/sukshma)* bodies *(sariras);* absolute and unqualified freedom.

vijñāna: consciousness.

Vinaya-Pitaka: the first of the "Three Baskets" *(Tripitaka)* of the Buddhist Pali canon and deals with matters of discipline (*vinaya* = discipline).

visesha: particularity, individual characteristic or special property that distinguishes a thing from all other things; (in Vaiseshika) the fourth predicable or *padārtha;* it is in terms of *viseshas* or individual properties that the *paramānus* (the first four Eternal Realities, being Earth, Water, Fire and Air) are distinguished from one another.

vitandā: cavil; any argument in which one is interested in refuting the opponent's position without any desire to establish one's own position.

vivarta-vāda: the theory that every effect only brings about an apparent change and that there is no real transformation of the cause into the effect (as opposed to *parināma-vāda*); (in Vedānta) the phenomenal world, or the world of apparent change, is a mere illusion *(māyā).*

viveka-jñāna: discriminative knowledge, true knowledge; right discrimination between the eternal and the noneternal, the real and the unreal; (in Vedānta) one of the four qualifications prescribed by Samkara for a student of philosophy: *viveka* (right discrimination), *vairāgya* (dispassion), *shatsampad* (right conduct), and *mumukshutva* (right desire).

vrtti: mode of life, course of action, especially relating to moral conduct; mode of being, mental state.

vyakta: manifest matter; (in Sāmkhya) a product of *prakrti.*

vyāpti: the state of being pervasive; (in Nyāya) the logical basis of inference or *anumāna,* being the relation of the invariable connection between the middle term *(hetu)* and the major term *(sādhya).*

vyavahārika: empirical or common standpoint.

yama: (in Yoga) the first stage or "limb" of *ashtānga-yoga* and refers to the cultivation of the qualities of moral restraint, truthfulness, self-control, forbearance; *Yama* is the Vedic god of death.

yogaja: (in Nyāya) a kind of extraordinary perception; an intuitive or yogic perception of spatiotemporality.

Index